JESUS CH[illegible] AND HIS GOSPEL

BOARD OF EDITORS

JESUS CHRIST AND HIS GOSPEL

SELECTIONS FROM THE

ENCYCLOPEDIA OF MORMONISM

EDITED BY

DANIEL H. LUDLOW

DESERET BOOK COMPANY
SALT LAKE CITY, UTAH

This collection of articles from the *Encyclopedia of Mormonism* is published by Deseret Book Company under license from Macmillan Publishing Company.

Library of Congress Catalog Card Number: 94-68130

ISBN 0-87579-922-1

Printed in the United States of America

10 9 8 7 6 5 4 3 2 1

CONTENTS

LIST OF ARTICLES

LIST OF CONTRIBUTORS

Lisa Ramsey Adams
Attorney, Salt Lake City
Eternal Progression

Dan W. Andersen
Brigham Young University
Immortality

Wilson K. Andersen
Brigham Young University
Spirit Body

Howard M. Bahr
Brigham Young University
Individuality

Arthur A. Bailey
Church Educational System, Ephraim, UT
Elect of God

Lowell Bangerter
University of Wyoming
Children: Blessing of Children

Grant E. Barton
Church Missionary Training Center, Provo, UT
Last Days

Arthur R. Bassett
Brigham Young University
Endless and Eternal

Alexander L. Baugh
Church Educational System, Columbia, SC
First Estate
Second Estate

Elouise M. Bell
Brigham Young University
Holiness

James P. Bell
Brigham Young University
Mortality
Purpose of Earth Life: LDS Perspective

Reed A. Benson
Brigham Young University
Pride

Sue Bergin
Writer, Editor, Santa Monica, CA
Life and Death, Spiritual

H. George Bickerstaff
Bookcraft Publishing Co., Salt Lake City
Gifts of the Spirit

Susan Easton Black
Brigham Young University
Celestial Kingdom
Terrestrial Kingdom

Mae Blanch
Brigham Young University
Prayer

V. Ben Bloxham
Brigham Young University
Law of Adoption

David E. Bohn
Brigham Young University
Freedom

Walter D. Bowen
Brigham Young University
Spirit World

M. Gerald Bradford
University of California at Irvine
Doctrine: Meaning, Source, and History of Doctrine

William S. Bradshaw
Brigham Young University
Baptism of Fire and of the Holy Ghost
Remission of Sins

F. Neil Brady
San Diego State University
Unity

Edward J. Brandt
Church Correlation Dept., Salt Lake City
Ahman

Douglas E. Brinley
Brigham Young University
Faith in Jesus Christ

Cheryl Brown
Brigham Young University
Obedience

Gayle Oblad Brown
Writer, Arabic Translator, Orem, UT
Premortal Life

S. Kent Brown
Brigham Young University
Gethsemane

Victor L. Brown, Jr.
Church Welfare Services, Citrus Heights, CA
Men, Roles of

Gary L. Browning
Brigham Young University
Blasphemy
Thankfulness

Glade L. Burgon
Church Educational System, Bountiful, UT
God the Father: Names and Titles

Alma P. Burton
Church Educational System, Provo, UT
Doctrine: Distinctive Teachings
Endowment
Salvation

H. David Burton
Church Presiding Bishopric's Office, Salt Lake City
Baptism for the Dead: LDS Practice

Lysle R. Cahoon
Former Church Temple President, Chicago, IL
Holy of Holies

Douglas L. Callister
Attorney, Glendale, CA
Resurrection

Tad R. Callister
Attorney, Glendale, CA
Jesus Christ: Resurrection of Jesus Christ

Elaine Anderson Cannon
Author, St. George, UT
Mother in Heaven

K. Codell Carter
Brigham Young University
Godhood

Dong Sull Choi
Brigham Young University
Confession of Sins

Bryce J. Christensen
Rockford Institute Center on the Family in America, Rockford, IL
Chastity, Law of

Christine Quinn Christensen
Writer, Belmont, MA
Blessing on Food

John R. Christiansen
Brigham Young University
Fear of God

Helen Lance Christianson
Writer, Provo, UT
Birth

Alice T. Clark
University of North Dakota
Humility

Bruce B. Clark
Brigham Young University
Blessings

D. Cecil Clark
Brigham Young University
New and Everlasting Covenant

Dix S. Coons
Rhode Island College, Warwick, RI
Commandments

Ralph L. Cottrell, Jr.
Church Educational System, Ogden, UT
Born in the Covenant

Stephen R. Covey
Stephen R. Covey Associates, Provo, UT
Discipleship

Rulon G. Craven
General Authority, Salt Lake City
Confirmation

Larry E. Dahl
Brigham Young University
Degrees of Glory
Doctrine: Meaning, Source, and History of Doctrine

Paul E. Dahl
Church Educational System, La Mesa, CA
Godhead

Colin B. Douglas
Church Curriculum Dept., Salt Lake City
Justification

Roy W. Doxey
Church Correlation Dept., Salt Lake City
Calling and Election

C. Kent Dunford
Church Educational System, Belmont, MA
Laying on of Hands
Light of Christ

Kay P. Edwards
Brigham Young University
Opposition

Richard M. Eyre
Author, Salt Lake City
Joy

Gladys Clark Farmer
Brigham Young University
Chastening

Dean B. Farnsworth
Brigham Young University
Fulness of the Gospel

James E. Faulconer
Brigham Young University
Foreknowledge of God

Mary Finlayson
Author, Woodside, CA
Elijah, Spirit of

Dennis D. Flake
Church Educational System, Fresno, CA
Buffetings of Satan

Joel A. Flake
Church Educational System, Morgantown, WV
Gospel of Abraham
Jesus Christ: Latter-day Appearances of Jesus Christ

Lawrence R. Flake
Church Educational System, Bozeman, MT
Holy Spirit of Promise

Christie H. Frandsen
Author, La Canada, CA
Trials

Russell M. Frandsen
Attorney, La Canada, CA
Antichrists

Elma W. Fugal
Genealogist, Lindon, UT
Salvation for the Dead

Addie Fuhriman
University of Utah
Charity

David B. Galbraith
Brigham Young University: Jerusalem Center for Near Eastern Studies
Messiah: Messiah

Marvin K. Gardner
Ensign, Salt Lake City
Righteousness

John Gee
Master's student, University of California at Berkeley
Jesus Christ: Forty-Day Ministry and Other Post-Resurrection Appearances of Jesus Christ

Jerry C. Giles
Church Educational System, Fairfield, MT
Angels: Archangels
Jesus Christ: Firstborn in the Spirit

L. Kay Gillespie
Weber State University, Ogden, UT
Death and Dying

Michaelene P. Grassli
General President, Church Primary, Salt Lake City
Children: Roles of Children

Bruce C. Hafen
Brigham Young University
Grace
Justice and Mercy

Marie Kartchner Hafen
Brigham Young University
First Principles of the Gospel

Gerald Hansen, Jr.
Ricks College, Rexburg, ID
Jesus Christ: Only Begotten in the Flesh

James R. Harris, Sr.
Brigham Young University
Jesus Christ in the Scriptures: Jesus Christ in the Pearl of Great Price

Leon R. Hartshorn
Brigham Young University
Discernment, Gift of

Carl S. Hawkins
Brigham Young University
Baptism
Law: Divine and Eternal Law

Carol Lee Hawkins
Brigham Young University
Perfection

John P. Hawkins
Brigham Young University
Ceremonies

Dawn M. Hills
Surgeon, Pasadena, CA
Fasting

Celia Hokanson
Writer, Provo, UT
Contention

Jeffrey R. Holland
General Authority, Salt Lake City
Atonement of Jesus Christ

Richard Neitzel Holzapfel
Church Educational System, Irvine, CA
Damnation

N. Gaylon Hopkins
Church Educational System, Logan, UT
Heirs: Joint-Heirs with Christ

Sherwin W. Howard
Weber State University, Ogden, UT
Cursings

A. James Hudson
Church Educational System, Boise, ID
Elias, Spirit of

Paul Nolan Hyde
Church Educational System, Simi Valley, CA
Intelligences

Dean Jarman
Church Educational System, Salt Lake City
Judgment

Jay E. Jensen
Church Curriculum Dept., Salt Lake City
Spirit

Clark V. Johnson
Brigham Young University
Jesus Christ in the Scriptures: Jesus Christ in the Doctrine and Covenants

Hollis R. Johnson
Indiana University
Worlds

Eleanor Knowles
Deseret Book Co., Salt Lake City
Doctrine: Treatises on Doctrine

Dennis L. Largey
Brigham Young University
God the Father: Work and Glory of God

Courtney J. Lassetter
Businessman, Phoenix, AZ
Dispensations of the Gospel

June Leifson
Brigham Young University
Afterlife

Gerald N. Lund
Church Educational System, Salt Lake City
Jesus Christ: Second Coming of Jesus Christ
Plan of Salvation, Plan of Redemption

John L. Lund
Church Educational System, Fountain Valley, CA
Council in Heaven

James K. Lyon
University of California, San Diego
Hope
Repentance

John M. Madsen
Brigham Young University
Enduring to the End

Evelyn T. Marshall
General Board of the Relief Society, Salt Lake City
Garments

Robert J. Matthews
Brigham Young University
Fall of Adam
Jesus Christ in the Scriptures: Jesus Christ in the Bible

James B. Mayfield
University of Utah
Covenant Israel, Latter-day

Joseph Fielding McConkie
Brigham Young University
Holy Ghost

Oscar W. McConkie
Attorney, Salt Lake City
Angels: Angels
Angels: Guardian Angels

Daniel B. McKinlay
Writer, Provo, UT
Amen

Byron R. Merrill
Brigham Young University
Condescension of God
Original Sin

Harold L. Miller, Jr.
Brigham Young University
Light and Darkness

Robert L. Millet
Brigham Young University
Jesus Christ: Overview
Jesus Christ, Fatherhood and Sonship of

Merrill C. Oaks
Physician, Provo, UT
Jesus Christ: Crucifixion of Jesus Christ

D. Kelly Ogden
Brigham Young University
Messiah: Messianic Concept and Hope

C. Eric Ott
Church Missionary Training Center, Provo, UT
Sanctification

Leaun G. Otten
Brigham Young University
Immortality and Eternal Life

George W. Pace
Brigham Young University
Kingdom of God: In Heaven
Kingdom of God: On Earth

Dennis J. Packard
Brigham Young University
Intelligence

Rand H. Packer
Church Educational System, Provo, UT
Dispensation of the Fulness of Times

Spencer J. Palmer
Brigham Young University
Reincarnation

Douglas H. Parker
Brigham Young University
Law: Divine and Eternal Law

Catherine Corman Parry
Brigham Young University
Eternal Life

Robert J. Parsons
Brigham Young University
Spirit Prison

David L. Paulsen
Brigham Young University
Doctrine: Harmonization of Paradox
Evil
Omnipotence of God; Omnipresence of God; Omniscience of God
Temptation

Vivian Paulsen
Friend Magazine, Salt Lake City
Love

Daniel C. Peterson
Brigham Young University
Jesus Christ: Ministry of Jesus Christ
Purpose of Earth Life: Comparative Perspective

Ed J. Pinegar
Church Educational System, Provo, UT
Born of God

Max L. Pinegar
Nu Skin International, Provo, UT
Preaching the Gospel

Paul B. Pixton
Brigham Young University
Communion
Millennium

Louise Plummer
Brigham Young University
Spirit of Prophecy

Margaret McConkie Pope
Brigham Young University
Exaltation

Bruce Douglas Porter
International Broadcasting, Springfield, VA
Gift of the Holy Ghost

Bruce H. Porter
Church Educational System, San Marcos, CA
Altar

Dennis Rasmussen
Brigham Young University
Testimony of Jesus Christ

Ellis T. Rasmussen
Brigham Young University
Abrahamic Covenant

Lenet Hadley Read
Author, San Francisco, CA
Jesus Christ, Types and Shadows of

Noel B. Reynolds
Brigham Young University
Gospel of Jesus Christ: The Gospel in LDS Teaching
Gospel of Jesus Christ: Etymological Considerations for "Gospel"

Shirley S. Ricks
Writer, Provo, UT
Eternal Lives, Eternal Increase

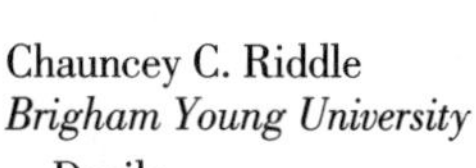

Chauncey C. Riddle
Brigham Young University
Devils
Revelation

Stephen E. Robinson
Brigham Young University
Doctrine: LDS Compared with Other Christian Doctrines
God the Father: Overview
Jesus Christ, Names and Titles of

Kent E. Robson
Utah State University, Logan, UT
Time and Eternity

Richard M. Romney
New Era Magazine, Salt Lake City
Spiritual Death

Calvin P. Rudd
Church Educational System, Salt Lake City
Children: Salvation of Children

J. Philip Schaelling
Church Educational System, Austin, TX
Jesus Christ: Baptism of Jesus Christ
Jesus Christ, Sources for Words of

David R. Seely
Brigham Young University
Jehovah, Jesus Christ

Thomas E. Sherry
Oregon State University
Jesus Christ, Second Comforter

Andrew C. Skinner
Ricks College, Rexburg, ID
Jesus Christ: Birth of Jesus Christ

Timothy W. Slover
Brigham Young University
Brotherhood

Huston Smith
Graduate Theological Union, Berkeley, CA
Purpose of Earth Life: Comparative Perspective

Kay H. Smith
Brigham Young University
Conversion

Lowell M. Snow
Attorney, Salt Lake City
Blood Atonement

John L. Sorenson
Brigham Young University
Origin of Man

Krister Stendahl
Harvard Divinity School
Baptism for the Dead: Ancient Sources

Joseph Grant Stevenson
Brigham Young University
Heirs: Heirs of God

Gloria Jean Thomas
University of North Dakota
Sacrifice

M. Catherine Thomas
Brigham Young University
Hell
Paradise

Brent L. Top
Brigham Young University
Foreordination

Rodney Turner
Brigham Young University
Burnings, Everlasting
God the Father: Glory of God

Wouter Van Beek
Utrecht University, Netherlands
Covenants

Kent M. Van De Graaff
Brigham Young University
Physical Body

Adrian P. Van Mondfrans
Brigham Young University
Teaching the Gospel

Gary Lee Walker
Brigham Young University
Jesus Christ: Prophecies About Jesus Christ

Steven C. Walker
Brigham Young University
Mankind

Arthur Wallace
University of California at Los Angeles
Heaven

C. Terry Warner
Brigham Young University
Accountability
Agency
Truth

Paul R. Warner
Church Educational System, Orem, UT
Jesus Christ, Taking the Name of, Upon Oneself

Clark D. Webb
Brigham Young University
Mysteries of God

John S. Welch
Attorney, Los Angeles
Law: Overview

John W. Welch
Brigham Young University
Jesus Christ in the Scriptures: Jesus Christ in the Book of Mormon

David J. Whittaker
Brigham Young University
Articles of Faith

Clyde J. Williams
Brigham Young University
Telestial Kingdom

Richard N. Williams
Brigham Young University
Knowledge
Soul

Jerry A. Wilson
Church Educational System, Logan, UT
Baptismal Covenant
Baptismal Prayer
Holy Spirit

Johann A. Wondra
Vienna Theatre, Vienna, Austria
Worship

Donald N. Wright
Brigham Young University
Judgment Day, Final

David H. Yarn, Jr.
Brigham Young University
God

PREFACE

This preface appears in volume 1 of the Encyclopedia of Mormonism. *Its spirit applies to all the volumes containing selections from the* Encyclopedia.

According to a standard definition, an encyclopedia is to "treat comprehensively all the various branches of knowledge" pertaining to a particular subject. The subject of this *Encyclopedia* is The Church of Jesus Christ of Latter-day Saints, widely known as the Mormon church. This is the first major encyclopedia published about the Mormons. It presents the work of hundreds of Latter-day Saint (LDS) lay scholars and others from throughout the world and provides a comprehensive reporting of Mormon history, scripture, doctrines, life, and knowledge, intended for both the non-Mormon and the LDS reader. Readers will find an article on almost any topic conceivably related to the general topic of Mormonism, and yet no article is exhaustive because of space limitations. Most articles include bibliographic references; cross-references to other articles in the *Encyclopedia* are indicated by small capital letters.

When Macmillan Publishing Company asked authorities at Brigham Young University whether they would be interested in developing an encyclopedia about The Church of Jesus Christ of Latter-day Saints, President Jeffrey R. Holland took the query to his Board of Trustees. They instructed him to proceed. Working closely with Church authorities and Macmillan, President Holland chose an editor in chief and a board of editors. Discussion of possible titles concluded that the work should be called the *Encyclopedia of Mormonism* since that is the term by which the Church is most widely known, though unofficially.

The contract called for a work of one million words in about 1,500 articles in four volumes including pictures, maps, charts, appendices, indices, and a glossary. It soon became apparent that references to what the Church calls the standard works—the Bible, the Book of Mormon, the Doctrine and Covenants, and the Pearl of Great Price—would be so frequent that readers who did not have ready access to those works would be at a serious disadvantage in using the *Encyclopedia.* A fifth volume was decided upon to include all the LDS standard works except the Bible, which is readily available everywhere.

The Church does not have a paid clergy or a battery of theologians to write the articles. It functions with a lay ministry, and all members are encouraged to become scholars of the gospel. Over 730 men and women were asked to write articles on topics assigned because of previous interest and study.

Six major articles unfold the history of the Church: (1) the background and founding period in New York; (2) the Ohio, Missouri, and Illinois period ending with the martyrdom of Joseph Smith; (3) the exodus west and the early pioneer period under Brigham Young; (4) the late pioneer Utah period ending at the turn of the century and statehood; (5) a transitional period during the early twentieth century; and (6) the post-World War II period of international growth. The history of the Church has been dramatic and moving, considering its brief span of just over 160 years. Compared to Catholicism, Judaism, ancient Far East religions, and many Protestant churches, the Church has a very short history. Nearly 250 articles explain the doctrines of the Church, with special emphasis on basic principles and ordinances of the gospel of Jesus Christ. Twenty-four articles are clustered under the title "Jesus Christ," and another sixteen include his name in the title or relate directly to his divine mission and atonement.

Over 150 articles relate the details on such topics as the First Vision, Zion's Camp, Handcart Companies, Plural Marriage, the Salt Lake Temple, Temple Square, and the Church throughout the world. Biographies cover men and women contemporary in the life of Joseph Smith, Presidents of the Church, and auxiliary founders and past presidents. The only biography of a person living at the time of publication is on the present prophet and President of the Church, Ezra Taft Benson.

And finally, there are over a hundred articles primarily concerned with how Latter-day Saints relate to their families, the

Church, and to society in general. It is said there is a "Mormon Culture," and several articles explore Mormon lifestyle, folklore, folk art, artists, literature, and other facets that distinguish Latter-day Saints.

It may be that the growth of the Church in the last decades has mandated the encyclopedic account that is presented here. Yet, even as the most recent programs were set down and the latest figures listed, there is an acute awareness that the basic tenet of the Church is that its canon is open-ended. The contemporary President of the Church is sustained as a "prophet, seer, and revelator." While this makes some theological discussion moot, the basic beliefs of the Latter-day Saints, summarized in the Articles of Faith (see Glossary) do not change.

In several areas, the Church shares beliefs held by other Christians, and a number of scholars from other faiths were asked to present articles. However, the most distinctive tenets of the Church—those regarding the premortal and postmortal life, living prophets who receive continuous and current revelation from God, sacred ordinances for deceased ancestors, moral and health codes that provide increasingly well-documented benefits, and the potential within man for progression into an infinite future—are all treated primarily by writers selected from among Latter-day Saints.

Lest the role of the *Encyclopedia* be given more weight than it deserves, the editors make it clear that those who have written and edited have only tried to explain their understanding of Church history, doctrines, and procedures; their statements and opinions remain their own. The *Encyclopedia of Mormonism* is a joint product of Brigham Young University and Macmillan Publishing Company, and the contents do not necessarily represent the official position of The Church of Jesus Christ of Latter-day Saints. In no sense does the *Encyclopedia* have the force and authority of scripture.

ACKNOWLEDGMENTS*

The support and assistance of many persons and groups are necessary to produce a work as extensive as an encyclopedia. Special thanks are extended to the executives of Macmillan Publishing Company who introduced the idea of the the *Encyclopedia of Mormonism* to Brigham Young University. Charles E. Smith made initial contacts on the project, while Philip Friedman, President and Publisher of Macmillan Reference Division, and Elly Dickason, Editor in Chief of Macmillan Reference Division, have followed through on the multitudinous details, demonstrating skill and patience in working with us in the preparation of this five-volume work.

The editors also wish to thank the General Authorities of the Church for designating Brigham Young University as the contractural Author of the *Encyclopedia.* Two members of the Board of Trustees of the university, who are also members of the Quorum of the Twelve Apostles, were appointed by the First Presidency to serve as advisers to the project: Elder Neal A. Maxwell and Elder Dallin H. Oaks. Other General Authorities who accepted special assignments related to the project include four members of the Quorum of Seventy: Elders Dean L. Larsen, Carlos E. Asay, Marlin K. Jensen, and Jeffrey R. Holland.

Special support also came from the Administration of BYU. Jeffrey R. Holland, president of BYU at the time the project was initiated, was instrumental in appointing the Board of Editors and in developing early guidelines. Rex E. Lee, current president of BYU, has continued this support.

* The major parts of the acknowledgments appear in volume 1 of the *Encyclopedia of Mormonism.* The statement has been modified here by (1) deleting credits to individuals and institutions providing illustrations and photographs for the *Encyclopedia* and (2) adding the names of those giving special assistance to the preparation of this particular publication.

The efforts of the Board of Editors and the Project Coordinator, whose names are listed at the front of each volume, have shaped and fashioned every aspect of the project. We offer special thanks to them, and to companions and family members for graciously supporting our efforts over many months. Others who shared in final editing include Bruce B. Clark, Soren F. Cox, Marshall R. Craig, and Ellis T. Rasmussen.

Many others have provided assistance in specialized areas, including Mark and Angela Ashurst-McGee, Mary Lynn Bahr, Larry E. Dahl, Robert O. Davis, Michelle Eckersley, Gary R. Gillespie, Lisa Bolin Hawkins, Devan Jensen, Lisa Johnson, Jack M. Lyon, McRay Magleby, Daniel B. McKinlay, Robert J. Matthews, Frank O. May, Charlotte McDermott, Robert L. Millet, Don E. Norton, Monte S. Nyman, Patricia J. Parkinson, Bruce A. Patrick, Charlotte A. Pollard, Larry C. Porter, Merle Romer, Amy Rossiter, Evelyn E. Schiess, Judith Skousen, William W. Slaughter, J. Grant Stevenson, Charles D. Tate, Jr., Jay M. Todd, and John Sutton Welch. Special thanks also to Ronald Millett and Sheri Dew at Deseret Book Company for their help with this volume.

Finally, we express appreciation to the 738 authors who contributed their knowledge and insights. The hopes of all who were involved with this project will be realized if the *Encyclopedia* assists readers to come to a greater understanding and appreciation of the history, scriptures, doctrines, practices, and procedures of The Church of Jesus Christ of Latter-day Saints.

TOPICAL OUTLINE

The topical outline is designed to help the reader discover all the articles in this volume related to a particular subject. The title of every article in this volume is listed in the topical outline at least once.

The volume *Jesus Christ and His Gospel* contains the major articles from the *Encyclopedia of Mormonism* concerned with the essential teachings of the gospel of Jesus Christ associated with God's plan of progression and eternal life for his children.

A. The nature and characteristics of God and the other members of the Godhead.

1. *God the Father:* Ahman; Condescension of God; Endless and Eternal; Fear of God; Foreknowledge of God; God; God the Father*; Godhead; Godhood; Heaven; Holiness; Omnipotence of God, Omnipresence of God, Omniscience of God; Worship.

2. *Jesus Christ the Son:* Atonement of Jesus Christ; Faith in Jesus Christ; Godhead; Gospel of Jesus Christ; Heirs*; Holy Spirit of Promise; Jehovah, Jesus Christ; Jesus Christ*; Jesus Christ, Fatherhood and Sonship; Jesus Christ in the Scriptures*; Jesus Christ, Names and Titles of; Jesus Christ, Second Comforter; Jesus Christ, Sources for Words of; Jesus Christ, Taking the Name of, Upon Oneself; Jesus Christ, Types and Shadows of; Light of Christ; Messiah*; Second Coming of Jesus Christ; Testimony of Jesus Christ.

3. *The Holy Ghost (or Holy Spirit):* Godhead; Holy Ghost; Holy Spirit; Holy Spirit of Promise.

* Indicates additional related articles are clustered under that entry title.

B. The pre-earthly existence of mankind.

1. *The pre-earthly spiritual existence as sons and daughters of our Heavenly Father:* Born of God; Brotherhood; Council in Heaven; First Estate; Intelligences; Kingdom of God*; Mother in Heaven; Origin of Man; Paradise; Pre-existence, Pre-earthly Existence; Premortal Life; Spirit; Spirit Body.

2. *The Grand Council in Heaven:* Accountability; Agency; Atonement of Jesus Christ; Celestial Kingdom; Council in Heaven; Devils; Doctrine*; Fall of Adam; First Estate; Foreknowledge of God; Foreordination; Jehovah; Light and Darkness; Life and Death, Spiritual; Millennium; Mortality; Obedience; Perfection; Physical Body; Plan of Salvation, Plan of Redemption; Purpose of Earth Life*; Resurrection; Revelation; Sacrifice; Salvation; Second Estate; Soul; Telestial Kingdom; Terrestrial Kingdom.

3. *The devil and other evil spirits:* Antichrists; Buffetings of Satan; Burnings, Everlasting; Contention; Council in Heaven; Cursings; Damnation; Devils; Evil; Hell; Opposition; Pride; Spirit Prison; Spiritual Death; Temptation.

C. Purposes of a mortal, physical, earthly existence.

1. *The importance of a physical body:* Birth; Mankind; Men, Roles of; Mortality; Physical Body; Purpose of Earth Life*; Trials; Worlds.

2. *The spirit and the physical body constitute the soul of man:* Intelligence; Mankind; Physical Body; Resurrection; Second Estate; Soul; Spirit; Spirit Body; Spirit World.

D. The birth, life, ministry, and atonement of Jesus Christ.

1. *Persons and events associated with the birth of Jesus Christ:* Birth; Condescension of God; God; God the Father*; Heirs*; Holy Ghost; Jesus Christ*; Jesus Christ in the Scriptures*.

2. *The life and ministry of Jesus Christ:* Gospel of Jesus Christ; Jesus Christ*; Jesus Christ in the Scriptures*; Jesus Christ, Names and Titles of; Jesus Christ, Second Comforter; Jesus Christ, Sources for Words of; Jesus Christ, Types and Shadows of; Kingdom of God*; Messiah*; Preaching the Gospel.

3. *The atonement of Jesus Christ, including his becoming the Savior and Redeemer of all mankind:* Atonement of Jesus Christ; Blood Atonement; Charity; Death and Dying; Gethsemane; Grace; Jesus Christ*; Jesus Christ in the Scriptures*; Original Sin; Resurrection; Second Coming of Jesus Christ.

E. **Basic principles and ordinances of the gospel of Jesus Christ.**

1. *Faith in the Lord Jesus Christ:* Faith in Jesus Christ; Hope; Jesus Christ*.

2. *Repentance:* Remission of Sins; Repentance.

3. *Baptism by immersion for the remission of sins:* Baptism; Baptism for the Dead*; Baptism of Fire and of the Holy Ghost; Baptismal Covenant; Baptismal Prayer; Gift of the Holy Ghost; Gifts of the Spirit.

4. *Receiving the gift of the Holy Ghost by the laying on of hands:* Born of God; Confirmation; Discernment, Gift of; Gift of the Holy Ghost; Holy Ghost; Laying on of Hands.

5. *Other topics associated with the gospel of Jesus Christ:* Afterlife; Altar; Amen; Angels*; Articles of Faith; Atonement of Jesus Christ; Blasphemy; Blessing on Food; Chastening; Commandments; Communion; Confession of Sins; Conversion; Covenants; Elect of God; Endless and Eternal; Endowment; Enduring to the End; Fasting; First Principles of the Gospel; Foreordination; Freedom; Fulness of the Gospel; Gospel of Jesus Christ; Grace; Holy of Holies; Humility; Individuality; Jehovah, Jesus Christ; Jesus Christ*; Jesus Christ in the Scriptures*; Jesus Christ, Second Comforter; Judgment; Judgment

Day, Final; Justice and Mercy; Justification; Kingdom of God*; Knowledge; Law*; Light of Christ; Love; Messiah; Millennium; New and Everlasting Covenant; Paradise; Plan of Salvation, Plan of Redemption; Prayer; Preaching the Gospel; Purpose of Earth Life; Reincarnation; Revelation; Righteousness; Sacrifice; Sanctification; Teaching the Gospel; Testimony Bearing; Thankfulness; Truth; Unity; Works.

F. **Other principles and ordinances pertaining to exaltation and eternal life.**

1. *Blessing and naming children:* Blessing; Born in the Covenant; Children*.

2. *Confirmation as a member of the Church:* Confirmation; Covenant Israel, Latter-day; Discipleship; Gift of the Holy Ghost; Holy Ghost; Holy Spirit; Law of Adoption; Laying on of Hands; Spirit of Prophecy; Testimony; Testimony of Jesus Christ.

3. *The Holy Endowment:* Endowment; Garments; Salvation for the Dead.

4. *Marriage of husband and wife, and the sealing of children to parents:* Ceremonies; Chastity, Law of; Eternal Life; Eternal Lives, Eternal Increase; New and Everlasting Covenant; Time and Eternity.

5. *Other topics associated with exaltation and eternal life and with the eternal nature of the family:* Abrahamic Covenant; Brotherhood; Calling and Election; Celestial Kingdom; Degrees of Glory; Dispensation of the Fulness of Times; Dispensation of the Gospel; Elias, Spirit of; Elijah, Spirit of; Eternal Progression; Exaltation; Godhood; Gospel of Abraham; Heaven; Heirs*; Immortality; Immortality and Eternal Life; Joy; Judgment Day, Final; Justification; Last Days; Mysteries of God; Obedience; Plan of Salvation, Plan of Redemption; Purpose of Earth Life*; Resurrection; Salvation; Sanctification.

KEY TO ABBREVIATIONS

AF	Talmage, James E. *Articles of Faith.* Salt Lake City, 1890. (All references are to pagination in printings before 1960.)
CHC	*Comprehensive History of the Church,* 6 vols., ed. B. H. Roberts. Salt Lake City, 1930.
CR	*Conference Reports.* Salt Lake City, 1898–.
CWHN	*Collected Works of Hugh Nibley,* ed. S. Ricks, J. Welch, et al. Salt Lake City, 1985–.
Dialogue	*Dialogue: A Journal of Mormon Thought,* 1965–.
DS	Smith, Joseph Fielding. *Doctrines of Salvation,* 3 vols. Salt Lake City, 1954–56.
ER	*Encyclopedia of Religion,* 16 vols., ed. M. Eliade. New York, 1987.
F.A.R.M.S.	Foundation for Ancient Research and Mormon Studies. Provo, Utah.
HC	*History of the Church,* 7 vols., ed. B. H. Roberts. Salt Lake City, 1st ed., 1902; 2nd ed., 1950. (All references are to pagination in the 2nd edition.)
HDC	Historical Department of the Church, Salt Lake City.
IE	*Improvement Era,* 1897–1970.
JC	Talmage, James E. *Jesus the Christ.* Salt Lake City, 1915.
JD	*Journal of Discourses,* 26 vols., ed. J. Watt. Liverpool, 1854–86.
JST	*Joseph Smith Translation of the Bible.*
MD	McConkie, Bruce R. *Mormon Doctrine,* 2nd ed. Salt Lake City, 1966.
MFP	*Messages of the First Presidency,* 6 vols., ed. J. Clark. Salt Lake City, 1965–75.
PJS	*Papers of Joseph Smith,* ed. D. Jessee. Salt Lake City, 1989.
PWJS	*The Personal Writings of Joseph Smith,* ed. D. Jessee. Salt Lake City, 1984.
T&S	*Times and Seasons,* 1839–46.
TPJS	*Teachings of the Prophet Joseph Smith,* comp. Joseph Fielding Smith. Salt Lake City, 1938.
WJS	*Words of Joseph Smith,* ed. A. Ehat and L. Cook. Provo, Utah, 1980.

A

ABRAHAMIC COVENANT

The divine archetypal covenant, of which Abraham's covenant is an example, is the everlasting covenant of the GOSPEL OF JESUS CHRIST. By accepting the gospel, humankind can be redeemed from the doom of death and the blight of sin to enjoy ETERNAL LIFE with God.

Abraham's mission was not new; it was like the mission of Adam, Enoch, and Noah. The same divine power—or priesthood—that gave them authority to promulgate the covenant of divine redemption for God's children in their time was renewed with Abraham and his seed; it was explicitly to be perpetuated by him and his literal and spiritual heirs for all time (Gen. 12:1–3; Abr. 1:18–19; 2:6, 9–11).

ABRAHAM'S IMPLEMENTATION OF THE COVENANT MISSION From the records of his forefathers, Abraham learned of the true and living God and the saving priesthood powers. Although his immediate ancestors had fallen away from the gospel, he desired and received that true priesthood from Melchizedek, with its powers and responsibilities (Abr. 1:1–7, 18, 19, 31; D&C 84:14; Alma 13:14–19; Gen. 14:18–20).

The idolatrous Chaldeans had rejected Abraham and placed him to be sacrificed on an altar (Abr. 1:5–12); but the Lord rescued him and directed him to leave his home in Ur for a new land of promise (Gen. 11:27–32; 12:1–3; Abr. 1:1, 17; 2:1–5). Abraham took other family members with him to a place they named Haran, where he won additional converts to the way of the Lord. With them he departed to undertake his ministry in the land promised to him and to all his descendants who would hearken to the voice of the Lord (Abr. 2:6, 14–20; Gen. 12:4–8).

Abraham and his company settled first in the Bethel area, built an altar, and proclaimed the name of the Lord—a procedure he perpetuated in the homes he established thereafter (Gen. 12:8; 13:4, 18). Near Bethel, the covenant promises and responsibilities were renewed, and circumcision was made the token of the covenant, to remind all bearers to keep themselves pure and free from sin (Gen. 17). Abraham became a man of good repute (Gen. 14:13, 18–20; 23:1–16) and was trusted by God, who commended him, saying, "I know him, that he will command his children and his household after him, and they shall keep the way of the Lord, to do justice and judgment" (Gen. 18:19). The ultimate test and a revelation of the meaning of the redemptive covenant came to him in the divine requirement that, in anticipation of the sacrifice of the Savior, he be willing to sacrifice his own birthright son. He passed the test, his son was saved, and he learned how all may be saved by the divine Redeemer (Gen. 22:1–18; John 8:56; Jacob 4:5; Gal. 3:8).

PERPETUATION OF THE MISSION BY ABRAHAM'S HEIRS Abraham's lineal and spiritual successors learned to keep the covenant by the things they suffered. Their efforts sometimes prospered and their neighbors were impressed (Gen. 17:1–7; 26:1–5, 24–28; 28:13–22; 30:25–27; 32:24–29; 35:1–15; 39:1–6, 21–23; 40:8; 41:9–16, 37–42).

A patriarchal blessing given by Abraham's grandson Jacob (Israel) to his twelve sons indicated future covenant roles for his descendants, particularly those through Judah and Joseph (Gen. 49:10, 22–26).

In addition to Jacob's progeny, Abraham had descendants through Ishmael, the son of Hagar—Sarah's handmaiden. Of Ishmael's family, "twelve princes" are named who established "towns" and "nations" (Gen. 25:12–16). Six sons by Abraham's wife Keturah are also named among his families: Zimran, Jokshan, Medan, Midian, Ishbak, and Shuah (Gen. 25:2). To all these, he promised gifts before his death (Gen. 25:1–7), including spiritual gifts. One descendant, Jethro (or Reuel), priest of Midian, provided Moses with a wife, ordained him to the priesthood, and advised him in organizing, governing, and judging Israel (Ex. 2:16–22; 18:12–27; D&C 84:6–16). Scores of descendants of Esau, with their tribal leaders and kings, are also named (Gen. 36).

Today, millions claim Abraham as their father. All may have his covenant privileges if they will but do the works of Abraham. The Lord never told Abraham that he alone would be blessed by the covenant or that it would bless only his birthright seed; the charge was that in him and his seed all families of all nations should be blessed. All who accept the covenant of the divine Redeemer become Abraham's seed spiritually and receive the same blessings as his biological descendants (Gen. 12:1–3; Abr. 2:8–11; Gal. 3:7–9, 26–29; cf. John 8:33, 37, 39; Rom. 9:6–8).

THE ABRAHAMIC HERITAGE THROUGH MOSES AND THE PROPHETS The mission of Moses was to deliver the children of Israel from the bondage of slavery and death in Egypt and return them to the promised land. They were to enter the land only after the iniquity of the prior inhabitants had become so excessive that they were no longer worthy to retain it (1 Ne. 17:35; Gen. 15:13–16; 17:7–9; JST Gen. 17:4–7; Ex. 4:22–23; 6:1–8). Through Moses, the Lord gave the Israelites laws, ordinances, statutes, and commandments to help them remember their duties to God and to make them a kingdom of priests, a holy people, and a peculiar treasure as God's exemplary servants (Ex. 19:1–6, 20ff; Deut. 4:1–6; Mosiah 13:27–30).

Israel did well in living according to the covenant in the last days of Moses and in the time of his successor, Joshua; but in the days of the judges and beyond, the Israelites lapsed into the ways of neighboring nations instead of following the moral and religious laws of the true God (Judg. 2:7–13; 17:6; 21:25). Because cycles of apostasy were repeated throughout Israel's history, the Israelites were periodically castigated by the prophets for their sins and called to repentance (e.g., Isa. 1:1–4; Hosea 4:1–6; Amos 3; Micah 3; Jer. 2; Ezek. 2).

Two themes dominate the messages of the Old Testament prophets: (1) the promised Redeemer would come, and though he would suffer rejection by many, he would establish the promised way of salvation for all; (2) in the last days the covenant of Abraham would be reestablished (Isa. 2:2–5, 11; 7:14–16; 9:1–7; 52:13–15, 53; Jer. 23:5–8; Ezek. 37:11–28; Dan. 9:21–27; Micah 5:2–5; Zech. 9:9–11; 11:10–13; 13:6; 14:4–9).

FULFILLMENT AND PERPETUATION The Redeemer did come, and the laws and prophecies prepared the faithful to receive him (Gal. 3:16–24, 25–29; Acts 2:47; 5:14; 1 Cor. 15:6). He accomplished his mission of personal teaching and sacrifice on earth and then commissioned the new Christian heirs of the covenant to make it known unto all the world (Matt. 24:14; 28:19–20; Mark 16:15–16). However, over a period of centuries, the priesthood power to administer the proper ordinances of the covenant and some vital facets of doctrine were lost. All these have now been restored in the latter-day dispensation of the gospel (D&C 110:11–16) and are again available to all families and nations of the earth.

BIBLIOGRAPHY

Brandt, Edward J. "The Covenants and Blessings of Abraham." *Ensign* 3 (Feb. 1973):42–43.

Kimball, Spencer W. *Abraham: An Example to Fathers.* Salt Lake City, 1977.

Nyman, Monte S. "Abraham, the Father of the Faithful." *Sperry Lecture Series.* Provo, Utah, 1975.

Topical Guide, "Abrahamic Covenant"; and Dictionary, "Abraham, Covenant of." In LDS Edition of the King James Version of the Bible. Salt Lake City, 1979.

ELLIS T. RASMUSSEN

ACCOUNTABILITY

In LDS doctrine, to be "accountable" means that one must answer to God for one's conduct. Answering for the deeds done in mortality is not simply an administrative requirement but an aspect of human nature itself: to be a child of God is to possess AGENCY, which is both the power to choose between OBEDIENCE and rebellion and the accountability for how that power is used.

The scriptures teach that accountability is not limited to public behavior; everyone will be asked to answer for all they do and say and even for what they think (Matt. 12:36; Alma 12:12–14), and for the use they make of every resource and opportunity God gives them (*TPJS*, pp. 68, 227). Joseph Smith taught that strict accounting is represented in the New Testament parable of the talents (Matt. 25:14–30): the master commits a certain sum in talents (an ancient currency) to each of three servants and later calls for an accounting. Two of the three use and double the resources entrusted to them, while the third, out of fear, buries his portion and thereby steals the increase that rightfully belongs to the master: "Where the five talents were bestowed, ten will be required; and he that has made no improvement will be cast out as an unprofitable servant" (*TPJS*, p. 68).

Only those capable of committing sin and of repenting are accountable (D&C 20:71). Children younger than eight and the mentally impaired are not. Satan has no power to tempt little children or other unaccountable individuals (D&C 29:46–50).

While individuals are usually accountable for their own sins, leaders may also be accountable for the sins of their people if they do not "teach them the word of God with all diligence" (Ezek. 3:17–21; Jacob 1:19). Parents may have to answer for the wrongdoing of their children if they do not teach them the gospel (2 Ne. 4:5–6; D&C 68:25; Moses 7:37).

It is sometimes claimed that people cannot help doing some of the things that God calls sin, such as acts of homosexuality and substance abuse. Regarding such conduct, however, Church leaders teach that "we are to control [feelings and impulses], meaning we are to direct them according to the moral law" (Packer, 1990, p. 85). "One's parents may have failed," wrote President Spencer W. Kimball, "our own backgrounds may have been frustrating, but . . . we have within ourselves the power to rise above our circumstances, to change our lives. Man can change human nature" (p. 176).

BIBLIOGRAPHY

Brown, Victor L. "Agency and Accountability." *Ensign* 15 (May 1985):14–17.

Kimball, Spencer W. *Faith Precedes the Miracle.* Salt Lake City, 1972.

Packer, Boyd K. "Atonement, Agency, Accountability." *Ensign* 18 (May 1988): 69–72.

———. "Covenants." *Ensign* 20 (Nov. 1990):85.

C. TERRY WARNER

AFTERLIFE

[*Other articles related to this topic are:* Degrees of Glory; Heaven; Hell; Immortality and Eternal Life; Paradise; Plan of Salvation, Plan of Redemption; Salvation; Spirit Prison.]

Latter-day Saints believe that life continues after the death of the mortal body and that death is but a separation of the PHYSICAL BODY and the SPIRIT. The spirits of all individuals, "whether they be good or evil, are taken home to that God who gave them life" (Alma 40:11). President Brigham Young said that the transition from death into the SPIRIT WORLD is "from a state of sorrow, grief, mourning, woe, misery, pain, anguish and disappointment into a state of existence, where I can enjoy life to the fullest extent; . . . my spirit is set free; . . . I go, I come, I do this, I do that; . . . I am full of life, full of vigor, and I enjoy the presence of my heavenly Father" (*JD* 17:142). The desire, personality, and disposition that individuals develop, shape, and mold in this life will continue into the afterlife.

If individuals are evil in their hearts, their spirits will enter the spirit world intent upon doing evil; if individuals are good and strive to do the things of God, that disposition will also continue, only to a greater degree—learning, increasing, growing in grace and in knowledge of truth (see Brigham Young, *JD* 7:333). Amulek explained that the "same spirit which doth possess your bodies at the time that ye go out of this life, that same spirit will have power to possess your body in that eternal world" (Alma 34:34).

Life did not begin at mortal birth, nor will it end at mortal death. God's gift to all individuals is everlasting life. Every person will die physically; every person will receive a literal RESURRECTION of the body and never die again.

JUNE LEIFSON

AGENCY

"Agency" refers both to the capacity of beings "to act for themselves" (2 Ne. 2:26) and their ACCOUNTABILITY for those actions. Exercising agency is a spiritual matter (D&C 29:35); it consists in either receiving the enlightenment and COMMANDMENTS that come from God or resisting and rejecting them by yielding to the devil's temptations (D&C 93:31). Without awareness of alternatives an individual could not choose, and that is why being tempted by evil is as essential to agency as being enticed by the Spirit of God (D&C 29:39). Furthermore, no one is forced either to act virtuously or to sin. "The devil could not compel mankind to do evil; all was voluntary. . . . God would not exert any compulsory means, and the devil could not" (*TPJS*, p. 187).

Agency is an essential ingredient of being human, "inherent in the spirit of man" (McKay, p. 366) both in the premortal spirit existence (D&C 29:36) and in MORTALITY. No being can possess sensibility, rationality, and a capacity for happiness without it (2 Ne. 2:11–13, 23; D&C 93:30). Moreover, it is the specific gift by which God made his children in his image and empowered them to grow to become like him through their own progression of choices (L. Snow, *JD* 20:367). It was because Satan "sought to destroy the agency of man" (Moses 4:3) that the war was fought in heaven before earth life (cf. Rev. 12:7). What was then, and is now, at stake in the battle to preserve agency is nothing less than the possibility of both the continued existence and the divine destiny of every human being. This principle helps explain the Church's strong position against political systems and addictive practices that inhibit the free exercise of agency.

Agency is such that men and women not only *can* choose obedience or rebellion but *must* (B. Young, *JD* 13:282). They cannot avoid being both free and responsible for their choices. Individuals capable of acting for themselves cannot remain on neutral ground, abstaining from both receiving and rejecting light from God. To be an agent means both being able to choose and having to choose either "liberty and eternal life, through the great Mediator" or "captivity and death, according to the captivity and power of the devil" (2 Ne. 2:27–29; 10:23). A being who is "an agent unto himself" is continually committing to be either an agent and servant of God or an agent and servant of Satan. If this consequence of choosing could be overridden or ignored, men and women would not determine their own destiny by their choices and agency would be void.

The captivity resulting from sin is also called "the bondage of sin" (D&C 84:49–51). Sin sets up dispositions in the sinner that empower Satan to control the sinner's thoughts and behavior by means of temptation. As this happens, the individual still possesses agency in name, but his capacity to exercise it is abridged. In this sense, to misuse one's agency is to lose that agency: "Evil, when listened to, begins to rule and overrule the spirit [that] God has placed within man" (B. Young, *JD* 6:332). Conversely, using agency to receive and obey the influence of the spirit of Christ liberates one from this bondage. Thus, though agency, in the sense of the capacity to choose life or death, is a kind of freedom, it differs in quality from the liberty that is inherent in obedience to Christ. Jesus said, "If the Son therefore shall make you free, ye shall be free indeed" (John 8:36). When King Benjamin's people in the Book of Mormon received a REMISSION OF SINS and were spiritually born again, they attested that their affections and desires had been so changed that they had "no more disposition to do evil, but to do good continually" (Mosiah 5:2). Obedience expands agency, and the alternative to obedience is bondage.

Thus, in the LDS concept of agency, obedience and agency are not antithetical. On the one hand, Church leaders consistently stand against all coercion of conscience ("We are not disposed, had we the power, to deprive anyone of exercising . . . free independence of mind" [*TPJS*, p. 49]) and counsel Church members to depend first of all on themselves for decisions about the application of gospel principles. On the other hand, obedience—willing and energetic submission to the will of God even at personal sacrifice—is a central gospel tenet. Far from contradicting freedom, obedience is its highest expression. "But in rendering . . . strict obedience, are we made slaves? No, it is the only way on the face of the earth for you and me to become free. . . . The man who yields strict obedience to the requirements of Heaven, acts upon the volition of his own will and exercises his freedom" (B. Young, *JD* 18:246).

Church leaders consistently call agency a gift of God. Sin abridges the agency of sinners to the point that unless some power releases them from this bondage, they will be "lost and fallen" (Mosiah 16:4). That power is Christ's atonement, which overcomes the effects of sin, not arbitrarily, but on condition of wholehearted REPENTANCE. "Because . . . they are redeemed from the fall they have become free forever . . . to act for themselves" (2 Ne. 2:26). Thus, human agency was purchased with the price of Christ's suffering. This means that to those who blame God for allowing human suffering, Latter-day Saints can respond that suffering is less important than the gift of agency, upon which everything else depends, and that none of us has paid a greater price for this gift than Christ.

BIBLIOGRAPHY
Madsen, Truman G. *Eternal Man*, pp. 63–70. Salt Lake City, 1966.
McKay, David O. *IE* 53 (May 1950):366.
Packer, Boyd K. "Atonement, Agency, Accountability." *Ensign* 18 (May 1988):69–72.
Romney, Marion G. "Decisions and Free Agency." *IE* 71 (Dec. 1968):73–76.
Stapley, Delbert L. "Using Our Free Agency." *Ensign* 5 (May 1975):21–23.

C. TERRY WARNER

AHMAN

Ahman is twice mentioned as one of the names of God in the Doctrine and Covenants. In each instance, Jesus Christ is called Son Ahman, suggesting Son God and son of Ahman (D&C 78:20; 95:17). Orson Pratt, an apostle, suggested that this was one of the names of God in the pure language (*JD* 2:342; cf. Zeph. 3:9).

Ahman is also an element of the place-name Adam-ondi-Ahman, Missouri, where the Lord visited Adam and "administered comfort" to him and where Adam prophesied concerning "whatsoever should befall his posterity unto the latest generation" (D&C 107:53–57; cf. D&C 78:15–16). Adam lived in the region of Adam-ondi-Ahman (D&C 117:8), and prophecy anticipates a future visit of Adam at this place (D&C 116:1; cf. Dan. 7:13).

BIBLIOGRAPHY
Pratt, Orson. "The Holy Spirit and the Godhead." *JD* 2:334–47.

EDWARD J. BRANDT

ALTAR

A focal point of religious worship throughout the ages, and in most cultures, has been the altar—a natural or man-made elevation used for prayer, sacrifice, and related purposes. Sacrifice on the altar was a basic rite. The characteristic worship practice in Old Testament times was sacrificial in nature, and consequently the altar became one of the most important ritual objects described in that book of scripture.

Sacred and symbolic meaning is ascribed to the altar. The stipulations of the "law of the altar" (Ex. 20:24–26) suggest that its construction is associated with the creation of the world and God's COVENANTS with humankind. As the waters of creation receded, dry land appeared and was known as the primordial mound (first hill). Here, according to legend, the gods stood in order to complete the Creation. Because of divine presence, this spot became sacred or holy ground, a point of contact between this world and the heavenly world. The altar was built that people might kneel by it to communicate and make covenants with their God. The altar in Ezekiel 43:15 is named "the mountain of God" (Hebrew term, *hahar'el*), and becomes the symbolic embodiment of the Creation, the primordial mound, and the presence of God.

At an altar Adam learned the meaning of sacrifice (Moses 5:5–8). Following the Flood, the patriarch Noah immediately built an altar and offered his sacrifices to the Most High. When Abraham received the promise and covenant of an inheritance for his posterity, he marked this sacred event with an altar (Gen. 12:6–7). On Mount Moriah the young Isaac was bound upon the sacrificial table or altar in preparation for his father's supreme offering and demonstration of obedience (Gen. 22:9–14). Tradition says the place of this consecrated altar became the locus of the temple in Jerusalem.

The temple complex in Jerusalem had four different altars. In an ascending order of sacral primacy, they were as follows: First, the Altar of Sacrifice, often called the altar of burnt offering or the table of the Lord (Mal. 1:7, 12; 1 Cor. 10:21), was placed outside of the temple itself in the Court of Israel and was more public than the others. Sacrifices for the sins of Israel were offered here, anticipating fulfillment in the sacrifice of Jesus Christ (Heb. 9:25–26; Alma 34:9–10, 14–16). Second, the Altar of Incense stood in the "holy place" before the veil inside the temple proper. John describes the smoke of this altar as the "prayers of all saints upon the golden altar which was before the throne" (Rev. 8:3–4). Third, within the same area of the temple stood the Table of Shewbread, upon which rested twelve loaves of bread, frankincense, and a drink offering. And fourth, the ark of the covenant rested in the HOLY OF HOLIES, the most inner, sacred area within the temple. The ark was to Israel the portable throne or Mercy Seat and symbolized the presence of the Lord. It was here that the high priest, once a year on the Day of

Atonement (Heb. 9:7; Lev. 16:1–17), made covenants with the Lord for all Israel, as though he represented all at the altar.

In LDS temples, altars of a different sort play a major role. Kneeling by them, Latter-day Saints participate in covenant-making ceremonies. They make these covenants, as was done anciently, in the symbolic presence of God at the altar (Ps. 43:4; cf. Ps. 118:27). Thus, while kneeling at an altar in a temple, a man and woman make covenants with God and each other in a marriage ceremony that is to be binding both in MORTALITY and in the eternal world. Here, if parents were not previously married in a temple, they and their children may be sealed together for time and eternity by the power and authority of the priesthood. Likewise, these ordinances may be performed by proxies at an altar within the temple on behalf of people identified in genealogical records as having died without these privileges.

As the ancients came to the altar to communicate and commune with God, so also do members of the Church, in a temple setting, surround the altar in a prayer circle and in supplication. United in heart and mind, the Saints petition God for his blessings upon mankind, his Church, and those who have special needs.

In a more public sacrament meeting, the Altar of Sacrifice is symbolized by the "sacrament table." On this table are emblems of the sacrifice of Jesus Christ, the bread and the water respectively representing the body and blood of the Savior (Luke 22:19–20). Each week individuals may partake of the sacrament and renew their covenants.

Today members of the Church make sacred covenants with God and consecrate their lives and all that they have been blessed with as they "come unto Christ" and lay all things symbolically upon the altar as a sacrifice. To them a sacred altar is a tangible symbol of the presence of God, before whom they kneel with "a broken heart and contrite spirit" (2 Ne. 2:7; 3 Ne. 11:20).

BIBLIOGRAPHY

Eliade, Mircea. *Patterns in Comparative Religion.* New York, 1974.

Talmage, James E. *The House of the Lord.* Salt Lake City, 1971.

Packer, Boyd K. *The Holy Temple.* Salt Lake City, 1980.

BRUCE H. PORTER

AMEN

Among Latter-day Saints the saying of an audible "amen" is the seal and witness of all forms of worship and of priesthood ordinances. The Hebrew word, meaning "truly," is transliterated into Greek in the New Testament, and thence to the English Bible. It is found many times in the Book of Mormon. The Hebrew infinitive conveys the notions "to confirm, support, uphold, be faithful, firm." In antiquity the expression carried the weight of an oath. By saying "amen" the people solemnly pledged faithfulness and assented to curses upon themselves if found guilty (Deut. 27:14–26). And by saying "amen" the people also sealed their praises of God (1 Chr. 16:36; Ps. 106:48; Rom. 11:36; 1 Pet. 4:11). Nehemiah records a dramatic instance: "And Ezra blessed the Lord. . . . And all the people answered, Amen, Amen, with lifting up their hands: and they bowed their heads, and worshipped the Lord with their faces to the ground" (Neh. 8:6).

By saying "amen," Latter-day Saints officially sustain what is said in formal and private prayer, as also in the words of sermons, official admonition, and testimony (see D&C 88:135). In the sacrament service, by repeating "amen" at the end of prayers on the bread and on the water, they covenant to always remember Christ, "that they may have his Spirit to be with them" (D&C 20:77–79). At temple dedications in solemn assembly they stand with uplifted hands and shout "Hosanna to God and the Lamb," followed by a threefold "amen."

BIBLIOGRAPHY

Welch, John W. "Amen." *BYU Religious Studies Center Newsletter* 3 (Sep. 1988):3–4.

DANIEL B. MCKINLAY

ANGELS

[*This entry consists of three articles:*

Angels
Archangels
Guardian Angels

The first article discusses the nature of angels as pertaining to their ministry to people on the earth, showing that different classes perform different types of service. The second article examines a hierarchy among angels, and identifies Michael as an archangel. The last article explores the concept of guardian angels, and examines what the scriptures and the Brethren have said. It proposes the Holy Spirit as a type of guardian angel.]

ANGELS

Latter-day Saints accept the reality of angels as messengers for the Lord. Angels are mentioned in the Old and New Testaments, the Book of Mormon, the Doctrine and Covenants, and the Pearl of Great Price and are prominent in the early history of The Church of Jesus Christ of Latter-day Saints. Angels are of various types and perform a variety of functions to implement the work of the Lord on the earth.

The skepticism of the modern age has tended to diminish belief in angels. However, Jesus Christ frequently spoke of angels, both literally and figuratively. When Jesus' disciples asked him to "declare unto us the parable of the tares of the field," he responded, "He that soweth the good seed is the Son of Man; the field is the world . . . and the reapers are the angels" (Matt. 13:36–39). Angels are actual beings participating in many incidents related in scripture (e.g., Luke 1:13, 19; 2:25; John 20:12, etc.). They exist as a part of the "whole family in heaven" (Eph. 3:15). All people, including angels, are the offspring of God.

In form angels are like human beings. They do not, of course, have the wings many artists symbolically show (*TPJS*, p. 162). Concerning the two angels who visited Lot's home in Sodom, the local residents inquired, "Where are the *men* which came in to thee this night?" (Gen. 19:1, 5, emphasis added). Daniel described the angel Gabriel as having "the appearance of a man" (Dan. 8:15). At the sepulcher of the risen Savior "the angel of the Lord descended from heaven" (Matt. 28:2) as "a young man . . . clothed in a long white garment" (Mark 16:5). A quite detailed description of an angel was given by Joseph Smith in recording the visit of the angel Moroni (JS—H 1:30–33, 43).

The angels who visit this earth are persons who have been assigned as messengers to this earth: "There are no angels who minister to this earth but those who do belong or have belonged to it" (D&C 130:5).

There are several types and kinds of beings, in various stages of progression, whom the Lord has used as angels in varying circumstances. One kind is a spirit child of the Eternal Father who has not yet been born on the earth but is intended for earthly mortality. Such is probably the type of angel who appeared to Adam (Moses 5:6–8).

In the early days of the mortal world, many righteous persons were taken from the earth, or translated. Enoch and his people (Moses 7:18–21, 31, 63, 69; Heb. 11:5), Moses (Alma 45:19), and Elijah (2 Kgs. 2:11–12) were all translated. The Prophet Joseph Smith taught that translated beings "are designed for future missions" (*TPJS,* p. 191), and hence can be angelic ministrants.

Another kind of angel may be an individual who completed his mortal existence but whose labors continue in the SPIRIT WORLD while he awaits the RESURRECTION of the body. Such are referred to as "the spirits of just men made perfect" (Heb. 12:22–23; D&C 76:69; *TPJS,* p. 325). "Are they not all ministering spirits, sent forth to minister for them who shall be heirs of salvation?" (Heb. 1:13–14).

Since the resurrection of Jesus Christ, some angels have been "resurrected personages, having bodies of flesh and bones" (D&C 129:1). The Prophet Joseph Smith indicated that resurrected angels have advanced further in light and glory than spirits (*TPJS,* p. 325). Such are the beings who have been instrumental in the restoration of the gospel in the DISPENSATION OF THE FULNESS OF TIMES. It was of this type of angel that John wrote, "And I saw another angel fly in the midst of heaven, having the everlasting gospel to preach unto them that dwell on the earth, and to every nation, and kindred, and tongue, and people" (Rev. 14:6). Elias, Moses, Elijah, Moroni, John the Baptist, Peter, and James are examples of resurrected angels who ministered to the Prophet Joseph Smith.

Pursuant to John's prophecy in Revelation 14:6, the fulness of the gospel, in word and power, has been restored to the earth through the ministration of angels. The angel Moroni, a resurrected being, revealed the record of the Book of Mormon which contains the fulness of the gospel of Jesus Christ (D&C 20:8–11). Later he who was called John the Baptist in the New Testament, now also a resurrected being, came as an angel and restored the Aaronic Priesthood to

Joseph Smith and Oliver Cowdery on May 15, 1829 (D&C 13; JS—H 1:68–72). Likewise, Peter, James, and John, as angelic embodied messengers from God, restored the Melchizedek Priesthood (D&C 27:12–13). Moses, Elias, and Elijah each appeared as angels and committed once again the "keys of the gathering of Israel," the "dispensation of the gospel of Abraham" (including celestial or patriarchal marriage), and the keys of the sealing powers to "turn the hearts of the fathers to the children, and the children to the fathers" (D&C 110:11–16).

Other "divers angels" have come to deliver keys, power, priesthood, and glory (D&C 128:18–21); to teach (2 Ne. 10:3; Mosiah 3:2–3; Rev. 1:1), guide, and inspire (Rev. 5:11); and to make the gospel operative in the lives of men and women. However, the work of the angels of the restoration is not complete, and the scriptures indicate that there will yet be other angelic administrations before "the hour of [God's] judgment is come" (D&C 88:103–104; 133:36).

Angelic messengers bring knowledge, priesthood, comfort, and assurances from God to mortals. However, when priesthood or keys are to be conveyed, the ministering angel possesses a body of flesh and bones, either from resurrection or translation. Spirits can convey information, but they cannot confer priesthood upon mortal beings, because spirits do not lay hands on mortals (cf. D&C 129).

The Lord himself may also at times be called an angel, since the term means "messenger." He is the "messenger of salvation" (D&C 93:8), and the "messenger of the covenant" (Mal. 3:1), and is the "Angel which redeemed me" of whom Jacob spoke in Genesis 48:15–16.

Some of the Father's spirit children "kept not their first estate" (Jude 1:6; D&C 29:36–38; Rev. 12:3–9), and, as Peter explained, "God spared not the angels that sinned, but cast them down to hell" (2 Pet. 2:4). These are angels to the devil. Thus, Satan and those who chose to follow him are sometimes referred to as angels (2 Cor. 11:14–15; 2 Ne. 2:17; *see also* FIRST ESTATE).

A different usage of the term "angel" is applied to those who, because they have not obeyed the principles of the new and everlasting covenant of marriage, do not qualify for EXALTATION but remain separately and singly as ministering angels without exaltation in their saved condition for all eternity (D&C 132:16–17).

BIBLIOGRAPHY
McConkie, Bruce R. *Mormon Doctrine.* Salt Lake City, 1966.
McConkie, Oscar W. *Angels.* Salt Lake City, 1975.
Pratt, Parley P. "Angels and Spirits." In *Key to the Science of Theology,* 10th ed., pp. 112–19. Salt Lake City, 1973.

OSCAR W. MCCONKIE

ARCHANGELS

Traditionally, angels have been viewed as guardians of persons or places, and bearers of God's tidings. The prefix "arch" intensifies this meaning to denote one who rules or is outstanding, principal, or preeminent. Several biblical texts give prominence to four, six, or seven angels (Ezek. 9:2; Rev. 8:2). Dionysius, a sixth-century Christian theologian, purports the existence of nine angelic orders called choirs, one of which is called "archangels." Milton's *Paradise Lost* has the archangels Raphael and Michael appear to and instruct Adam concerning the fall of the angels, the Creation, and the history of the world. Dante also refers to archangels in *The Divine Comedy.*

In the literature of The Church of Jesus Christ of Latter-day Saints, an archangel is a chief angel, holding a position of priesthood authority in the heavenly hierarchy. Michael (Adam) is the only one precisely so designated in scripture (D&C 29:26; 88:112; 107:54; 128:21; 1 Thes. 4:16; Jude 1:9), although others (Gabriel, who is also Noah; Raphael, Raguel, etc.) are mentioned in scriptural, apocryphal, and pseudepigraphic works. Teachings of Latter-day Saint prophets indicate that a priesthood organization exists among the heavenly hosts (*TPJS,* pp. 157, 208). However, discussion of specific positions or functions in the celestial hierarchy beyond the scriptures cited above is conjectural.

JERRY C. GILES

GUARDIAN ANGELS

One of the functions of angels is to warn and protect mortals. The Lord whispered to David, "There shall no evil befall thee, neither shall any plague come nigh thy dwelling. For he shall give his angels charge over thee, to keep thee in all thy ways. They shall bear thee up in their hands, lest thou dash thy foot against a stone" (Ps. 91:10–12). The angel of the Lord's presence saved Israel (Isa. 63:9).

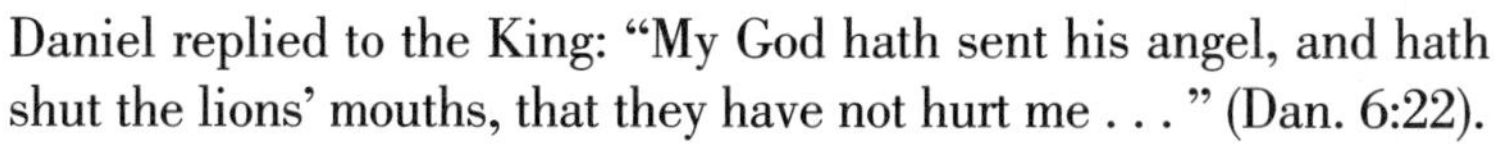

Daniel replied to the King: "My God hath sent his angel, and hath shut the lions' mouths, that they have not hurt me . . . " (Dan. 6:22).

This well-known guardian function of angels has given rise to an assumption on the part of some that all persons, or at least the righteous, have individual angels assigned to them throughout life as guardians. There is no scriptural justification for this tradition, although it has been entertained sometimes among Latter-day Saints and others (*TPJS*, p. 368).

Latter-day Saints believe that every person born into the world is accorded protecting care and direction by God, provided in part by the LIGHT OF CHRIST (D&C 84:44–48; Moro. 7:12–19). Those who have the GIFT OF THE HOLY GHOST may be warned, guarded, or shielded through the spirit of revelation (D&C 8:2–4). The term "guardian angel" may best be viewed as a figure of speech that has to do with God's protecting care and direction or, in special instances, with an angel dispatched to earth in fulfillment of God's purposes.

OSCAR W. MCCONKIE

ANTICHRISTS

Antichrists are those who deny the divinity of Jesus Christ or essential parts of his gospel and actively oppose the followers of Christ or seek to destroy their faith.

The epistles of John explicitly condemn as antichrists those with a lying spirit who deny that Jesus is the Christ and deny the physical resurrection. Antichrists are to be notably active in the last days (1 Jn. 2:18, 22; 4:3; 2 Jn. 1:7).

The Book of Mormon profiles many subtle and sophisticated aspects of antichrist characters, though the text explicitly refers to only one of them as antichrist.

Sherem (c. 540 B.C.) rejected the prophetic Christian teachings of the Nephite prophets, arguing that belief in the coming Christ perverted the law of Moses. He employed several archetypical arguments and methods, claiming that no one could know of things to come, including the coming of Christ. When confronted, Sherem asserted that if there were a Christ he would not deny him, but he knew "there is no Christ, neither has been, nor ever will be," thus contradicting his own argument that no one could "tell of things to come." Demanding a sign of divine power, Sherem was stricken by God, and then confessed that he had been deceived by the devil in denying the Christ (Jacob 7:1–23).

Nehor (c. 91 B.C.), a practitioner of priestcraft, preached and established a church to obtain riches and worldly honor and to satisfy his pride. He taught that God had created everyone, had redeemed everyone, and that people need not "fear and tremble" because everyone would be saved. Furthermore, he said priests should be supported by the people. Nehor attacked and killed a defender of the true doctrine of Christ, and was tried before $Alma_2$ and executed (Alma 1:2–16). He was not executed for being an antichrist, but for having enforced his beliefs "by the sword."

Korihor (c. 74 B.C.) was an extremist, rejecting all religious teachings, even to the point of not posturing either as a defender of traditions or as a reformer of corrupted religious practices. He was labeled "Anti-Christ" because he taught that there was no need for a Christ and that none would come. He described the religious teachings of the church as foolish traditions designed to subject the people to corrupt and lazy priests. In a dramatic confrontation with the Nephite chief judge, and with the prophet $Alma_2$, Korihor claimed that one cannot know anything that cannot be seen, making knowledge or prophecy of future events impossible. He ridiculed all talk of visions, dreams, and the mysteries of God. He called belief in sin, the atonement of Christ, and the remission of sins a derangement of the mind caused by foolish religious traditions. He denied the existence of God and, after demanding a sign as proof of his existence, was struck dumb. After Alma accused him of possessing a lying spirit, Korihor confessed that he had been deceived by Satan, had taught words and doctrines pleasing to the carnal mind, and had even begun to believe them himself (Alma 30:6–60).

BIBLIOGRAPHY

Riddle, Chauncey C. "Korihor: The Arguments of Apostasy." *Ensign* 7 (Sept. 1977):18–21.

RUSSELL M. FRANDSEN

ARTICLES OF FAITH

In 1842, in response to a specific request from John Wentworth (editor of the *Chicago Democrat*), Joseph Smith sent a succinct overview of his own religious experiences and the history of the Church over which he presided. At the end of the historical sketch, he appended a list summarizing the "faith of the Latter-day Saints." Later titled "Articles of Faith," these thirteen items were first published in the Nauvoo *Times and Seasons* in March 1842 and were later included in the 1851 British Mission pamphlet *The Pearl of Great Price,* compiled by Elder Franklin D. Richards. That pamphlet was revised in 1878 and again in 1880. In 1880, a general conference of the Church voted to add the Pearl of Great Price to the standard works of the Church, thus including the thirteen articles. The Articles of Faith do not constitute a summation of all LDS beliefs, and they are not a creed in the traditional Christian sense, but they do provide a useful authoritative summary of fundamental LDS scriptures and beliefs.

The articles begin with an affirmative declaration that the GODHEAD is composed of three personages: the Father, his Son Jesus Christ, and the Holy Ghost (cf. Acts 7:55–56; 2 Cor. 13:14; 2 Ne. 31:21; JS—H 1:17).

The second item focuses attention on the beginning of mortal history and affirms that human beings have moral AGENCY and therefore accountability for their own acts: "Men will be punished for their own sins, and not for Adam's transgression" (cf. Deut. 24:16; 2 Ne. 2:27).

The third article directs attention to the centrality of the Atonement of Christ and how mankind benefits in relationship to it: "Through the Atonement of Christ, all mankind may be saved, by obedience to the laws and ordinances of the Gospel" (Mosiah 3:7–12; D&C 138:4).

The fourth article spells out the foundational principles and ordinances: faith in Jesus Christ, repentance, baptism by immersion for the remission of sins, and the laying on of hands for the GIFT OF THE HOLY GHOST (cf. Acts 8:14–19; Heb. 6:1–2; 3 Ne. 11:32–37).

The next two articles address issues of authority and organization: A man must be called of God, confirmed by divine inspiration and by the laying on of hands by those in authority, in order to preach the gospel and administer its ordinances (cf. 1 Tim. 4:14; D&C 42:11); further, the Church is essentially "the same organization that existed in the Primitive Church, namely, apostles, prophets, pastors, teachers, evangelists, and so forth" (cf. Eph. 4:11).

The seventh item affirms the LDS belief in the GIFTS OF THE SPIRIT, specifically naming several: the gift of tongues, prophecy, revelation, visions, healing, and the interpretation of tongues (cf. 1 Cor. 12:10; D&C 46:10–26).

The place of sacred scripture is addressed in the eighth article: Latter-day Saints "believe the Bible to be the word of God as far as it is translated correctly"; they also "believe the Book of Mormon to be the word of God" (cf. Ezek. 37:16; John 10:16; 2 Tim. 3:16).

The ninth article states that the restored gospel is not bound up in a closed set of books, but rather declares the principle of continuing REVELATION, and therefore an open canon. Latter-day Saints affirm belief in all past and present revelation, and they look forward to many future revelations (cf. Amos 3:7; D&C 76:7).

Article ten summarizes four great events of the last days: the literal gathering of Israel and the restoration of the Ten Tribes; the building of Zion, the New Jerusalem, in the Western Hemisphere; Christ's personal reign on earth; and the eventual renewal of the earth itself, when it will receive its paradisiacal glory, the state of purity it had before the Fall of Adam (see 3 Ne. 21–22).

The eleventh article declares the LDS belief in freedom of worship and of conscience for both themselves and all others. It states: "We claim the privilege of worshipping Almighty God according to the dictates of our own conscience, and allow all men the same privilege, let them worship how, where, or what they may." And the twelfth article states the political stance of the Latter-day Saints as law-abiding citizens (D&C 134).

The final declaration provides a broad perspective for life and an invitation to the LDS approach to life: "We believe in being honest, true, chaste, benevolent, virtuous, and in doing good to all men; indeed, we may say that we follow the admonition of Paul—We believe all things, we hope all things, we have endured many things, and hope to be able to endure all things. If there is anything virtuous, lovely, or of good report or praiseworthy, we seek after these things" (cf. 1 Cor. 13:7; Philip. 4:8).

The Wentworth Letter was not the first attempt to summarize basic LDS beliefs. Earlier lists, some of which may have influenced the Wentworth listing, had appeared prior to 1842. As early as June 1829, Joseph Smith and Oliver Cowdery were committing to paper the "Articles and Covenants" of the soon-to-be-organized Church. Later known as Doctrine and Covenants Section 20, this text enumerates a number of basic beliefs, including the existence of God; the creation and fall of man; the centrality of Jesus Christ; the fundamental ordinances of the gospel, including baptism; and the basic duties of members (20:17–36). This document, the first accepted by a Church conference vote, was not an exhaustive listing of all beliefs but rather a basic charter for the infant organization, rooted in the Bible and the Book of Mormon.

In the first issue of the *LDS Messenger and Advocate* (Oct. 1834), published in Kirtland, Ohio, Oliver Cowdery enumerated eight "principles," all of which had their parallel in section 20.

Other early lists that summarized the leading principles of Latter-day Saint beliefs prior to the Wentworth Letter include one prepared by Joseph Young for publication by John Hayward in *The Religious Creeds and Statistics of Every Christian Denomination in the United States* (Boston, 1836, pp. 139–40). In five paragraphs, he outlined the doctrines of (1) the Godhead and atonement of Jesus Christ; (2) the first principles and ordinances of the gospel performed by apostolic authority as in the ancient Church of Christ; (3) the gathering of lost Israel and the restoration of spiritual gifts to her; (4) the Second Coming of Christ; and (5) the resurrection and judgment of all mankind.

Another list of eighteen "principles and doctrines" was included by Parley P. Pratt in the introduction to his *Late Persecution of the Church of Jesus Christ of Latter-day Saints* (New York, 1840, pp. iii–xiii). For example, "The first principle of Theology as held by this Church, is Faith in God the eternal Father, and in his Son Jesus Christ, who verily was crucified for the sins of the world . . . and in the Holy Ghost who bears record of them" (pp. iii–iv). Many phrases in Pratt's list are similar to those in the Wentworth Letter.

Orson Pratt offers an expansive and eloquent "sketch of the faith and doctrine" of the Church in his *Interesting Account of Several Remarkable Visions* (Edinburgh, 1840, pp. 24–31). The order in which it presents its themes in nineteen paragraphs (many of which begin, "We believe that . . .") is nearly identical to that of the thirteen points of the Wentworth Letter. Orson Pratt's explanations include biblical references and personal testimony of the truth and divine origins of these teachings.

Orson Hyde published in German a history of the Church that included a chapter of sixteen articles (actually essays) on such topics as the Godhead, the use of scripture, faith, repentance, baptism, confirmation, sacrament of bread and wine, confession of sins and Church discipline, children, revelations, lay priesthood, baptism for the dead, prayer, holidays, washing of the feet, and patriarchal blessings (*A Cry from the Wilderness* [Frankfurt, 1842]).

Even after the Wentworth Letter was published in March 1842, many other lists of LDS beliefs continued to appear for the next generation. In April 1849, James H. Flanigan included a list of fourteen statements in a pamphlet published in England, and this list was quoted and sometimes modified in various publications throughout the nineteenth century. For example, it was quoted in Charles MacKay's popular book *The Mormons; or the Latter-day Saints* (London, 1851, pp. 46–47). This list follows the Wentworth Letter almost verbatim, adding such points as "the Lord's supper" to Article 4; including "wisdom, charity, [and] brotherly love" among the gifts of the spirit in Article 7; and inserting a fourteenth article regarding the literal resurrection of the body. Other lists (usually composed by missionaries) were published in various parts of the world throughout this era.

The canonization of the Wentworth Letter as part of the Pearl of Great Price in 1880 reflected and assured its undisputed priority. And when James E. Talmage was asked by the First Presidency in 1891 to prepare a work on theology for use as a textbook in Church schools, it was to these Articles of Faith that he turned for the outline of his volume. First published in 1899 and still in use today, Talmage's *Articles of Faith* greatly elaborate on the themes of Joseph Smith's Wentworth list. In twenty-four chapters, Talmage provides extensive commentary and scriptural references regarding each of the concepts mentioned in the thirteen articles, plus sections on the sacrament of the Lord's Supper and resurrection (as in Flanigan's listing), and finally a section on practical religion (benevolence, tithes

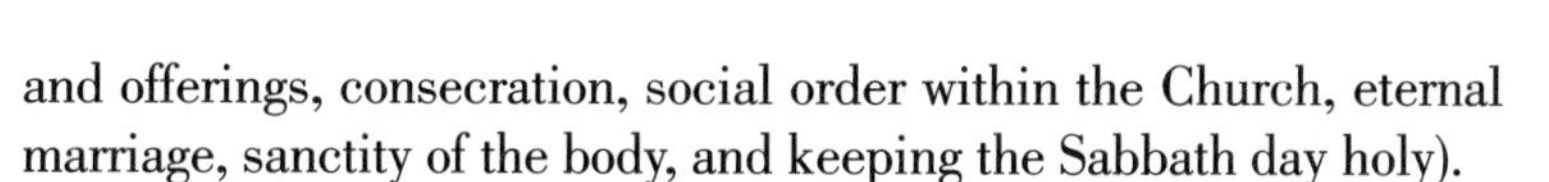

and offerings, consecration, social order within the Church, eternal marriage, sanctity of the body, and keeping the Sabbath day holy).

As early as the 1850s, LDS missionaries printed broadsides that contained the Articles of Faith. In time, these missionary placards were reduced to wallet size and are still used by missionaries throughout the world. In the primary classes of the Church, children memorize the Articles of Faith as a requirement for graduation at age twelve, and adults have also been encouraged to learn and use them for personal study and in missionary work.

Although not a formal creed, the Articles of Faith are a marvelously abridged summary (less than 400 words) of the basic beliefs of The Church of Jesus Christ of Latter-day Saints. While there have been many variations published since Joseph Smith's day, a central core of beliefs stated in all these articles comes from the earliest years of the Restoration—a fact that testifies both to its internal consistency and its constancy.

BIBLIOGRAPHY

Lyon, T. Edgar. "Origin and Purpose of the Articles of Faith." *Instructor* 87 (Aug.–Oct. 1952):230–31, 264–65, 275, 298–99, 319.

McConkie, Bruce R. *A New Witness for the Articles of Faith.* Salt Lake City, 1985.

Sondrup, Steven P. "On Confessing Faith: Thoughts on the Language of the Articles of Faith." In *Literature of Belief,* ed. N. Lambert, pp. 197–215. Provo, Utah, 1981.

Talmage, James E. *AF.* Salt Lake City, 1899.

Welch, John W. "[Joseph Smith and Paul:] Co-Authors of the Articles of Faith?" *Instructor* 114 (Nov. 1969):422–26.

Whittaker, David J. "The 'Articles of Faith' in Early Mormon Literature and Thought." In *New Views of Mormon History, A Collection of Essays in Honor of Leonard J. Arrington,* ed. D. Bitton and M. Beecher, pp. 63–92. Salt Lake City, 1987.

DAVID J. WHITTAKER

ATONEMENT OF JESUS CHRIST

The atonement of Jesus Christ is the foreordained but voluntary act of the Only Begotten Son of God. He offered his life, including his innocent body, blood, and spiritual anguish as a redeeming ransom (1) for the effect of the fall of Adam upon all mankind and (2) for the personal sins of all who repent, from Adam to the end of the world. Latter-day Saints believe this is the central fact, the crucial foundation, the chief doctrine, and the greatest expression of divine love in the PLAN OF SALVATION. The Prophet Joseph Smith declared that all "things which pertain to our religion are only appendages" to the atonement of Christ (*TPJS*, p. 121).

The literal meaning of the word "atonement" is self-evident: at-one-ment, the act of unifying or bringing together what has been separated and estranged. The atonement of Jesus Christ was indispensable because of the separating transgression, or fall, of Adam, which brought death into the world when Adam and Eve partook of the fruit of the tree of knowledge of good and evil (Gen. 2:9; 3:1–24). Latter-day Saints readily acknowledge both the physical and the SPIRITUAL DEATH that Adam and Eve brought upon themselves and all of their posterity, physical death bringing the temporary separation of the spirit from the body, and spiritual death bringing the estrangement of both the spirit and the body from God. But they also believe that the Fall was part of a divine, foreordained plan without which mortal children would not have been born to Adam and Eve. Had not these first parents freely chosen to leave the Garden of Eden via their transgression, there would have been on this earth no human family to experience opposition and growth, moral AGENCY and choice, and the joy of RESURRECTION, redemption, and ETERNAL LIFE (2 Ne. 2:23; Moses 5:11).

The need for a future atonement was explained in a premortal COUNCIL IN HEAVEN at which the spirits of the entire human family were in attendance and over which GOD THE FATHER presided. The two principal associates of God in that council were the premortal Jesus (also known as Jehovah; *see* JEHOVAH, JESUS CHRIST) and the premortal Adam (also known as Michael). It was in this premortal setting that Christ voluntarily entered into a covenant with the Father, agreeing to enhance the moral agency of humankind even as he atoned for their sins, and he returned to the Father all honor and glory for such selflessness. This preordained role of Christ as mediator explains why the book of Revelation describes Christ as "the Lamb slain from the foundation of the world" (Rev. 13:8) and why Old Testament prophets, priests, and kings, including Moses (Deut. 18:15, 17–19), Job (19:25–27), the Psalmist (Ps. 2, 22), Zechariah (9:9; 12:10; 13:6), Isaiah (7:14; 9:6–7; 53), and Micah (5:2), could speak of the Messiah and his divine role many centuries before his physical birth. A Book of Mormon prophet wrote, "I say unto you that none of the prophets have written, nor prophesied, save they have spoken concerning this Christ" (Jacob 4:4; 7:11). To the brother of Jared who lived some two thousand years before the Redeemer's birth, the premortal Christ declared, "Behold, I am he who was prepared from the foundation of the world to redeem my people" (Ether 3:14). Such scriptural foreshadowings are reflected in the conversation Christ had with two of his disciples on the road to Emmaus: "Beginning at Moses and all the prophets, he expounded unto them in all the scriptures the things concerning himself" (Luke 24:27; cf. also 24:44).

For Latter-day Saints, it is crucially important to see the agreed-upon and understood fall of man only in the context of the equally agreed-upon and understood redemption of man—redemption provided through the atonement of Jesus Christ. Thus, one of the most important and oft-quoted lines of Latter-day Saint scripture says, "Adam fell that men might be; and men are, that they might have joy. And the Messiah cometh in the fulness of time, that he may redeem the children of men from the fall" (2 Ne. 2:25–26).

LDS scripture teaches that the mission of Christ as Redeemer and the commandment to offer animal sacrifice as an anticipatory reminder and symbol of that divine atonement to come were first taught to Adam and Eve soon after they had been expelled from the Garden of Eden (Moses 5:4–8). The atonement of Christ was taught to the parents of the family of man with the intent that they and their posterity would observe the sacrificial ordinances down through their generations, remembering as they did so the mission and mercy of Christ who was to come. Latter-day Saints emphatically teach that the extent of this atonement is universal, opening the way for the redemption of all mankind—non-Christians as well as Christians, the godless as well as the god-fearing, the untaught infant as well as the fully converted and knowledgeable adult. "It is expedient that there should be a great and last sacrifice," said Amulek in the Book of Mormon, "an infinite and eternal sacrifice. . . . There can be nothing which is short of an infinite atonement which will suffice for the sins of the world" (Alma 34:10, 12).

This infinite atonement of Christ—and of Christ only—was possible because (1) he was the only sinless man ever to live on this earth and therefore was not subject to the spiritual death that comes as a result of sin; (2) he was the Only Begotten of the Father and therefore possessed the attributes of Godhood, which gave him power over physical death (see 2 Ne. 9:5–9; Alma 34:9–12); and (3) he was the only one sufficiently humble and willing in the premortal council to be foreordained there to that service (*JC,* pp. 21–62).

The universal, infinite, and unconditional aspects of the atonement of Jesus Christ are several. They include his ransom for Adam's original transgression so that no member of the human family is held responsible for that sin (A of F 2; *see* ORIGINAL SIN). Another universal gift is the resurrection from the dead of every man, woman, and child who lives, has ever lived, or ever will live, on the earth. Thus, the Atonement is not only universal in the sense that it saves the entire human family from physical death, but it is also infinite in the sense that its impact and efficacy in making redemption possible for all reach back in one direction to the beginning of time and forward in the other direction throughout all eternity. In short, the Atonement has universal, infinite, and unconditional consequences for all mankind throughout the duration of all eternity.

Emphasizing these unconditional gifts arising out of Christ's atoning sacrifice, Latter-day Saints believe that other aspects of Christ's gift are conditional upon obedience and diligence in keeping God's commandments. For example, while members of the human family are freely and universally given a reprieve from Adam's sin through no effort or action of their own, they are not freely and universally given a reprieve of their own sins unless they pledge faith in Christ, repent of those sins, are baptized in his name, receive the GIFT OF THE HOLY GHOST and confirmation into Christ's church, and press forward with a brightness of hope and faithful endurance for the remainder of life's journey. Of this personal challenge, Christ said, "For behold, I, God, have suffered these things for all, that they might not suffer if they would repent; but if they would not repent they must suffer even as I; which suffering caused myself, even God, the greatest of all, to tremble because of pain, and to bleed at every pore, and to suffer both body and spirit—and would that I might not drink the bitter cup, and shrink" (D&C 19:16–18).

Furthermore, although the breaking of the bonds of mortal death by the resurrection of the body is a free and universal gift from

Christ, a product of his victory over death and the grave, the kind or nature of the body (or "degree of glory" of the body), as well as the time of one's resurrection, is affected very directly by the extent of one's faithfulness in this life (*see* DEGREES OF GLORY). The apostle Paul made clear, for example, that those most fully committed to Christ will "rise first" in the resurrection (1 Thes. 4:16). Paul also speaks of different orders of resurrected bodies (1 Cor. 15:40). The bodies of the highest orders or degrees of glory in the Resurrection are promised to those who faithfully adhere to the principles and ordinances of the gospel of Jesus Christ; they will not only enjoy IMMORTALITY (a universal gift to everyone) but also ETERNAL LIVES in the celestial kingdom of glory (D&C 88:4; 132:24; *see also* RESURRECTION).

Latter-day Saints stress that neither the unconditional nor the conditional blessings of the Atonement would be available to mankind except through the grace and goodness of Christ. Obviously the unconditional blessings of the Atonement are unearned, but the conditional ones are also not fully merited. By living faithfully and keeping the commandments of God, one can receive additional privileges; but they are still given freely, not fully earned. They are always and ever a product of God's grace. Latter-day Saint scripture is emphatic in its declaration that "there is no flesh that can dwell in the presence of God, save it be through the merits, and mercy, and grace of the Holy Messiah" (2 Ne. 2:8).

The Church is also emphatic about the salvation of little children, the mentally impaired, those who lived without ever hearing the gospel of Jesus Christ, and so forth: these are redeemed by the universal power of the atonement of Christ and will have the opportunity to receive the fulness of the gospel in the SPIRIT WORLD (*see* SALVATION FOR THE DEAD).

To meet the demands of the Atonement, the sinless Christ went first into the Garden of GETHSEMANE, there to bear the spiritual agony of soul only he could bear. He "began to be sorrowful and very heavy," saying to his three chief disciples, "My soul is exceeding sorrowful, unto death" (Mark 14:34). Leaving them to keep watch, he went further into the garden, where he would suffer "the pains of all men, yea, the pains of every living creature, both men, women, and children, who belong to the family of Adam" (2 Ne. 9:21). There he "struggled and groaned under a burden such as no other being who has lived on earth might even conceive as possible" (*JC,* p. 613).

Christ's atonement satisfied the demands of justice and thereby ransomed and redeemed the souls of all men, women, and children "that his bowels may be filled with mercy, according to the flesh, that he may know according to the flesh how to succor his people according to their infirmities" (Alma 7:12). Thus, Latter-day Saints teach that Christ "descended below all things"—including every kind of sickness, infirmity, and dark despair experienced by every mortal being—in order that he might "comprehend all things, that he might be in all and through all things, the light of truth" (D&C 88:6). This spiritual anguish of plumbing the depths of human suffering and sorrow was experienced primarily in the Garden of Gethsemane. It was there that he was "in an agony" and "prayed more earnestly." It was there that his sweat was "as it were great drops of blood falling down to the ground" (Luke 22:44) for he bled "at every pore" (D&C 19:18). It was there that he began the final march to Calvary.

The majesty and triumph of the Atonement reached its zenith when, after unspeakable abuse at the hands of the Roman soldiers and others, Christ appealed from the cross, "Father, forgive them; for they know not what they do" (Luke 23:34). Forgiveness was the key to the meaning of all the suffering he had come to endure.

Such an utterly lonely and excruciating mission is piercingly expressed in that near-final and most agonizing cry of all, "Eli, Eli, lama sabachthani? that is to say, My God, my God, why hast thou forsaken me?" (Matt. 27:46). In the depths of that anguish, even nature itself convulsed, "and there was a darkness over all the earth. . . . The sun was darkened. . . . And, behold, the veil of the temple was rent in twain from the top to the bottom; and the earth did quake, and the rocks rent" (Luke 23:43–45; Matt. 27:51–52). Finally, even the seemingly unbearable had been borne and Jesus said, "It is finished" (John 19:30), and then, saying "Father, into thy hands I commend my spirit," he "gave up the ghost" (Luke 23:46). Latter-day Saints believe that every tongue will someday, somewhere confess as did a Roman centurion at the Crucifixion, "Truly this was the Son of God" (Matt. 27:54).

"The Savior thus becomes master of the situation—the debt is paid, the redemption made, the covenant fulfilled, justice satisfied, the will of God done, and all power is now given into the hands of the Son of God—the power of the resurrection, the power of the redemption, the power of salvation. . . . He becomes the author of eternal life and exaltation. He is the Redeemer, the Resurrector, the Savior of man and the world" (Taylor, p. 171). Furthermore, his atonement extends to all life—beasts, fish, fowl, and the earth itself.

To the thoughtful woman and man, it is "a matter of surpassing wonder" (*AF,* p. 77) that the voluntary and merciful sacrifice of a single being could satisfy the infinite and eternal demands of justice, atone for every human transgression and misdeed, and thereby sweep all mankind into the encompassing arms of his merciful embrace. A President and prophet of the LDS Church writing on this subject said:

> In some mysterious, incomprehensible way, Jesus assumed the responsibility which naturally would have devolved upon Adam; but which could only be accomplished through the mediation of Himself, and by taking upon Himself their sorrows, assuming their responsibilities, and bearing their transgressions or sins. In a manner to us incomprehensible and inexplicable, He bore the weight of the sins of the whole world, not only of Adam, but of his posterity; and in doing that opened the kingdom of heaven, not only to all believers and all who obeyed the law of God, but to more than one-half of the human family who die before they come to years of maturity as well as to the heathen, who having died without law, will, through His mediation, be resurrected without law, and be judged without law, and thus participate . . . in the blessings of His atonement [Taylor, pp. 148–49].

Latter-day Saints sing a favorite hymn, written by Charles H. Gabriel, that expresses their deepest feelings regarding this greatest of all gifts:

> I stand all amazed at the love Jesus offers me,
> Confused at the grace that so fully he proffers me.
> I tremble to know that for me he was crucified,
> That for me, a sinner, he suffered, He bled and died.
> Oh, it is wonderful that he should care for me
> Enough to die for me!
> Oh, it is wonderful, wonderful to me! [*Hymns,* No. 193].

BIBLIOGRAPHY
McConkie, Bruce R. *The Promised Messiah.* Salt Lake City, 1978.
Nibley, Hugh W. "The Atonement of Jesus Christ," *Ensign* 20 (July 1990):18–23; (Aug. 1990):30–34; (Sept. 1990):22–26; (Oct. 1990):26–31.
Taylor, John. *The Mediation and Atonement.* Salt Lake City, 1882.

JEFFREY R. HOLLAND

B

BAPTISM

The fourth ARTICLE OF FAITH of The Church of Jesus Christ of Latter-day Saints declares that "baptism by immersion for the remission of sins" is one of the "first principles and ordinances of the Gospel." Latter-day Saints believe, as do many Christians, that baptism is an essential initiatory ordinance for all persons who are joining the Church, as it admits them to Christ's church on earth (John 3:3–5; D&C 20:37, 68–74). It is a primary step in the process, which includes faith, repentance, BAPTISM OF FIRE AND OF THE HOLY GHOST, and enduring to the end, whereby members may receive remission of their sins and gain access to the CELESTIAL KINGDOM and ETERNAL LIFE (e.g., Mark 16:15–16; 2 Ne. 31:13–21; D&C 22:1–4; 84:64, 74; *MD*, pp. 69–72).

Latter-day Saint baptisms are performed for converts who have been properly instructed, and are at least eight years of age (the age of accountability). Baptism must be performed by one who has proper priesthood authority. The major features of the ordinance include the raising of the right hand, the reciting of the prescribed BAPTISMAL PRAYER by the one performing the baptism, and the complete immersion of the candidate (3 Ne. 11:23–26; D&C 20:71–74; 68:27). Baptism symbolizes the covenant by which people promise to come into the fold of God, to take upon themselves the name of Christ, to stand as a witness for God, to keep his commandments, and to bear one another's burdens, manifesting a determination to serve him to the end, and to prepare to receive the spirit of Christ for the remission of sins. The Lord, as his part of the covenant, is to pour out his spirit upon them, redeem them from their sins, raise them in the first resurrection, and give them eternal life (Mosiah 18:7–10; D&C 20:37).

The rich symbolism of the ordinance invites candidates and observers to reflect on its meanings. Burial in the water and arising out of the water symbolize the candidate's faith in the death, burial, and resurrection of Jesus Christ, as well as the future resurrection of all people. It also represents the candidate's new birth to a life in Christ, being BORN OF GOD, thus born again of the water and of the spirit (Rom. 6:3–6; Mosiah 18:13–14; Moses 6:59–60; D&C 128:12–13).

Latter-day Saint scriptures indicate that the history of this ordinance predates the ministry of John the Baptist. Beginning with Adam (Moses 6:64–66), baptism by immersion in water was introduced as standard practice, and has been observed in all subsequent dispensations of the gospel when priesthood authority was on the earth (D&C 20:25–27; 84:27–28). For variants of such precedents, Latter-day Saints trace the baptismal initiations in many pre-Christian religions (see Meslin, 1987). As recorded in the Book of Mormon, Lehi and $Nephi_1$ foresaw the baptism of Jesus Christ in vision and taught their people to follow his righteous example (1 Ne. 10:7–10; 11:27; 2 Ne. 31:4–9). Moreover, before the time of Jesus Christ, $Alma_1$ initiated converts into the church of God by baptism as a sign of their covenant (Mosiah 18:8–17; Alma 4:4–5).

According to the account of his appearance to the Nephites, Jesus taught the necessity of faith, repentance, baptism, and the GIFT OF THE HOLY GHOST, and he authorized twelve disciples to baptize (3 Ne. 11:18–41; 19:11–13; 26:17–21). The Book of Mormon provides adequate instructions for baptism and proper words for the baptismal prayer (3 Ne. 11:23–28; Moro. 6:1–4; cf. D&C 20:73).

In addition to relying on information in the Book of Mormon, Latter-day Saints follow the New Testament teachings on baptism. Jesus taught that baptism is necessary for salvation. He told Nicodemus, "Except a man be born of water and of the Spirit, he cannot enter into the kingdom of God" (John 3:1–5). He required baptism of those who professed to become his disciples (John 4:1–2). His farewell commission to his apostles was that they should go to all nations, teaching and baptizing (Matt. 28:19), and he declared, "He that believeth *and is baptized* shall be saved; but he that believeth not shall be damned" (Mark 16:16; emphasis added). Paul, after his miraculous vision on the road to Damascus, was taught the gospel by Ananias who told him to "arise, and be baptized, and wash away thy sins" (Acts 22:16). To the penitent multitude on the day of Pentecost, Peter proclaimed, "Repent, and be baptized every one of you in the name of Jesus Christ for the remission of sins" (Acts 2:38).

Latter-day Saints do not accept baptismal practices and teachings that arose among some Christian groups in the centuries after the death of the apostles, including infant baptism, baptism by means other than immersion, and the idea that baptism is not necessary for salvation. The Nephite prophet Mormon denounced the practice of infant baptism, which had apparently crept in among his people, and declared that anyone who supposed that little children need baptism would deny the mercies of Christ, setting at naught the value of his atonement and the power of his redemption (Moro. 8:4–20).

The authority to baptize was restored by John the Baptist to Joseph Smith and Oliver Cowdery on May 15, 1829 (JS—H 1:68–72). From the early days of the restored Church, missionaries have been sent to "declare repentance and faith on the Savior, and remission of sins by baptism" (D&C 19:31; 55:2; 84:27, 74). "He that believeth and is baptized shall be saved, and he that believeth not, and is not baptized, shall be damned" (D&C 112:29). This is the central teaching of the GOSPEL OF JESUS CHRIST (3 Ne. 11:31–40).

Consequently, persons coming into The Church of Jesus Christ of Latter-day Saints at age eight or older are required to submit to baptism, even though they may have been previously baptized in other churches (D&C 22). Likewise, excommunicants undergo baptism again once they have qualified for readmission into the Church.

The form of the ordinance is prescribed in latter-day revelation, which makes clear that the baptism must be performed by a person who has priesthood authority and that it requires completely immersing the penitent candidate below the water and then bringing the person out of the water (3 Ne. 11:25–26; D&C 20:72–74). Baptism is followed by the LAYING ON OF HANDS for the gift of the Holy Ghost.

Contemporary Church practice provides for the candidate to be interviewed and approved by an authorized priesthood official (usually the bishop or other officer presiding over the congregation or a mission official), who determines whether the applicant meets the qualifying conditions of repentance, faith in the Lord Jesus Christ, and an understanding of and willingness to obey the laws and ordinances of the gospel. It is also necessary that an official record of each baptism be kept by the Church.

Baptism may be performed in the font provided in many meetinghouses or in any body of water that is suitable for the sacred occasion and deep enough for complete immersion. The candidate and the person performing the ordinance will be dressed in plain and modest white clothing. The ceremony is unpretentious, typically attended by the candidate's family, close friends, and interested members of the congregation. A speaker or two may offer a few words of instruction and joyous welcome to the candidate.

The earlier practice of rebaptism to manifest repentance and recommitment, or for a restoration of health in time of sickness, is no longer practiced in the Church.

Belief that baptism is necessary for the salvation of all persons who reach the age of accountability (D&C 84:64, 74) does not condemn persons who have died without the opportunity to hear the true gospel of Jesus Christ or to receive baptism from proper priesthood authority. Latter-day Saints believe that proxy BAPTISM FOR THE DEAD should be performed vicariously (1 Cor. 15:29; D&C 124:28–35, 127–128), and that it becomes effective if the deceased beneficiary accepts the gospel while in the spirit world awaiting resurrection (see 1 Pet. 3:18–20; 4:6; cf. D&C 45:54). This vicarious work for the benefit of previous generations, binding the hearts of the children to their fathers (Mal. 4:5–6), is one of the sacred ordinances performed in Latter-day Saint temples (D&C 128:12–13).

BIBLIOGRAPHY

Meslin, Michel. "Baptism." In *Encyclopedia of Religion*, Mircea Eliade, ed. Vol. 2, pp. 59–63. New York, 1987.

Smith, Joseph Fielding. *Doctrines of Salvation*, Vol. 2, pp. 323–37. Salt Lake City, 1955.

Talmage, James E. *AF*, pp. 109–42. Salt Lake City, 1984.

CARL S. HAWKINS

BAPTISMAL COVENANT

When a person enters into a Latter-day Saint baptism, he or she makes a covenant with God. Baptism is a "sign . . . that we will do the will of God, and there is no other way beneath the heavens whereby God hath ordained for man to come to Him to be saved" (*TPJS*, p. 198).

Candidates promise to "come into the fold of God, and to be called his people, . . . to bear one another's burdens, . . . to mourn with those that mourn, and . . . to stand as witnesses of God . . . even until death" (Mosiah 18:8–9). A person must enter this covenant with the proper attitudes of HUMILITY, REPENTANCE, and determination to keep the Lord's commandments, and serve God to the end (2 Ne. 31:6–17; Moro. 6:2–4; D&C 20:37). In turn, God promises remission of sins, redemption, and cleansing by the Holy Ghost (Acts 22:16; 3 Ne. 30:2). This covenant is made in the name of the Father, the Son, and the Holy Ghost.

The baptized can renew this covenant at each sacrament meeting by partaking of the sacrament. This continual willingness to remember Christ and to keep his commandments brings the Lord's promise of his Spirit and produces the "fruits" (Gal. 5:22) and "gifts" (D&C 46) that lead to ETERNAL LIFE.

BIBLIOGRAPHY

Tripp, Robert M. *Oaths, Covenants and Promises*, pp. 11–19. Salt Lake City, 1973.

JERRY A. WILSON

BAPTISMAL PRAYER

The wording of the baptismal prayer used in The Church of Jesus Christ of Latter-day Saints is prescribed in the earliest compilation of instructions for Church operations (D&C 20). When an individual is baptized, the person with the proper priesthood authority goes down into the water with the candidate, raises his right arm to the square, calls the individual by the full legal name, and says, "Having been commissioned of Jesus Christ, I baptize you in the name of the Father, and of the Son, and of the Holy Ghost. Amen," and then immerses the candidate (D&C 20:73). A version of the prayer that differs only slightly from this was given by Jesus Christ to the Nephites and is recorded in the Book of Mormon (3 Ne. 11:25).

Earlier in the Book of Mormon there is a somewhat different account of the baptismal prayer that was spoken. When Alma$_1$ in the second century B.C. established the Church among the Nephites, he prayed: "O Lord, pour out thy Spirit upon thy servant, that he may do this work with holiness of heart" (Mosiah 18:12). The baptismal prayer that followed emphasized the COVENANT represented in BAPTISM and the need for a subsequent baptism of the Spirit: "I baptize thee, having authority from the Almighty God, as a testimony that ye have entered into a covenant to serve him until you are dead as to the mortal body; and may the Spirit of the Lord be poured out upon you; and may he grant unto you eternal life, through the redemption of Christ, whom he has prepared from the foundation of the world" (Mosiah 18:13; *see* BAPTISM OF FIRE AND OF THE HOLY GHOST).

BIBLIOGRAPHY

It is informative to compare LDS practice and scriptural accounts with the Christian tradition as reported in E. C. Whitaker, *Documents of the Baptismal Liturgy*, London, 1970.

JERRY A. WILSON

BAPTISM FOR THE DEAD

[*This entry consists of two articles:*

LDS Practice
Ancient Sources

The first article traces the development of the LDS doctrine of baptizing for the dead. In the second article, the dean of the Harvard School of Theology discusses the practice in ancient times.]

LDS PRACTICE

Baptism for the dead is the proxy performance of the ordinance of baptism for one deceased. Joseph Smith taught, "If we can baptize a man in the name of the Father [and] of the Son and of the Holy Ghost for the remission of sins it is just as much our privilege to act as an agent and be baptized for the remission of sins for and in behalf of our dead kindred who have not heard the gospel or fulness of it" (Kenney, p. 165).

The first public affirmation of the ordinance of baptism for the dead in the Church was Joseph Smith's funeral sermon for Seymour Brunson in Nauvoo in August 1840. Addressing a widow who had lost a son who had not been baptized, he called the principle "glad tidings of great joy," in contrast to the prevailing tradition that all unbaptized are damned. The first baptisms for the dead in modern times were done in the Mississippi River near Nauvoo.

Revelations clarifying the doctrine and practice have been given from time to time:

1. This was a New Testament practice (1 Cor. 15:29; cf. D&C 128; *see* BAPTISM FOR THE DEAD: ANCIENT SOURCES).
2. The ministry of Christ in the SPIRIT WORLD was for the benefit of those who had died without hearing the gospel or the fulness of it (1 Pet. 4:6; *see* SALVATION FOR THE DEAD).
3. Such baptisms are to be performed in temple fonts dedicated to the purpose (*TPJS*, p. 308; cf. D&C 124:29–35). In November 1841 the font in the unfinished Nauvoo Temple was so dedicated.
4. The language of the BAPTISMAL PRAYER is the same as for the living, with the addition of "for and in behalf of" the deceased.
5. Witnesses are to be present for proxy baptisms and a record is to be kept in Church archives (D&C 128:3, 8).
6. Women are to be baptized for women and men for men.
7. Not only baptism but CONFIRMATION and the higher temple ordinances may also be performed by proxy (*TPJS*, pp. 362–63).
8. The law of AGENCY is inviolate in this world and the world to come. Thus, those served by proxy have the right to accept or reject the ordinances.

In the early years of the Church, proxy baptisms were performed only for direct blood ancestors, usually no more than four generations back. Today, Latter-day Saints are baptized not only for their own forebears but also for other persons, unrelated to them, identified through the name extraction program. The practice reflects the yearning of children for their parents and of parents for their children, and charitable feelings for others as well, that they receive the fulness of the blessings of the gospel of Jesus Christ. In LDS perspective, whatever else one may do to mourn, give honorable burial to, cherish, or memorialize the dead, this divinely authorized ordinance of baptism is a demonstration of love and has eternal implications.

BIBLIOGRAPHY

Kenney, Scott G., ed. *Wilford Woodruff's Journal*, Vol. 2. Midvale, Utah, 1983.

Widtsoe, John A. "Fundamentals of Temple Doctrine." *Utah Genealogical and Historical Magazine* 13 (July 1922):129–35.

H. DAVID BURTON

ANCIENT SOURCES

In his first epistle to the Corinthians Paul wrote: "Otherwise, what shall they do who are being baptized for the dead? If the dead are not raised at all, why are they being baptized for them" (Conzelmann, *1 Corinthians* 15:29).

This verse is part of Paul's argumentation against those who denied a future resurrection (cf. 2 Tim. 2:18, Justin, Dial. 80). He refers to a practice of vicarious baptism, a practice for which we have no other evidence in the Pauline or other New Testament or early Christian writings. Interpreters have puzzled over the fact that Paul seems to accept this practice. At least he does not see fit to condemn it as heretical, but Paul clearly refers to a distinct group within the Church, a group that he accuses of inconsistency between ritual and doctrine.

A practice of vicarious baptism for the dead (for example among the Marcionites, A.D. 150) was known and seen as heretical by the ancient commentators. Thus they interpreted Paul's words in 1 Corinthians 15:29 so as not to lend support to such practices or to any theology implicit in it. Through the ages their interpretations have persisted and multiplied (B. M. Foschini reports and evaluates forty distinct explanations of this verse). Most of the Greek fathers understood "the dead" to refer to one's own body; others have interpreted the verse as referring to pagans seeking baptism "for the sake of joining" lost Christian relatives. Still others have suggested different sentence structures: "Otherwise what will they achieve who are being baptized? Something merely for their dead bodies?"

Once the theological pressures from later possible developments of practice and doctrine are felt less constricting, the text seems to speak plainly enough about a practice within the Church of vicarious baptism for the dead. This is the view of most contemporary critical exegetes. Such a practice can be understood in partial analogy with Paul's reference to how the pagan spouses and joint children in mixed marriages are sanctified and cleansed by the Christian partners (1 Cor. 7:14). Reference has often been made to 2 Maccabees 12:39–46, where Judas Maccabeaus, "taking account of the resurrection," makes atonement for his dead comrades. (This was the very passage which Dr. Eck used in favor of purgatory in his 1519 Leipzig debate with Martin Luther. So it became part of the reason why Protestant Bibles excluded the Apocrypha or relegated them to an Appendix.)

To this could be added that the next link in Paul's argument for a future resurrection is his own exposure to martyrdom (1 Cor. 15:30–32), a martyrdom that Paul certainly thinks of as having a vicarious effect (Phil. 2:17, Rom. 15:16, cf. Col. 1:24).

Such a connection may be conscious or unconscious. In either case it makes it quite reasonable that Paul's remark refers to a practice of a vicarious baptism for the dead.

BIBLIOGRAPHY

Conzelmann, H. *1 Corinthians.* Hermeneia Series. Philadelphia, 1975.

Foschini, B. "Those Who Are Baptized for the Dead; 1 Cor. 15:29." *Catholic Biblical Quarterly* 12 (1950):260–76, 378–88; 13 (1951):46–78, 172–98, 276–85.

KRISTER STENDAHL

BAPTISM OF FIRE AND OF THE HOLY GHOST

Baptism of fire and of the Holy Ghost refers to the experience of an individual who receives the ordinance of the LAYING ON OF HANDS for the GIFT OF THE HOLY GHOST. It is the second in a two-part sequence following baptism by immersion in water through which a repentant person committed to Christ and his gospel is BORN OF GOD or born again. As Jesus explained to Nicodemus, "Except a man be born of water and of the Spirit, he cannot enter into the kingdom of God" (John 3:5). Commenting on this passage, Joseph Smith remarked, "Baptism by water is but half a baptism, and is good for nothing without . . . the baptism of the Holy Ghost" (*TPJS,* p. 314). The baptism of fire, ministered by the Holy Ghost, is manifested through a set of personal sensations, impressions, and insights that constitute a spiritual witness from deity that one has received a remission of sins (2 Ne. 31:17). The baptism of fire inaugurates the transmission of spiritual gifts to the faithful to assist them throughout life in remaining true to their baptismal COVENANT (1 Cor. 12; Moro. 10:8–23; D&C 46:10–33).

The doctrine of the two baptisms was taught by John the Baptist: "I indeed baptize you with water, . . . but he that cometh after me . . . shall baptize you with the Holy Ghost, and with fire" (Matt. 3:11). At Christ's baptism the Holy Ghost was manifested in the sign of a dove (Luke 3:22), and he appeared to the disciples on the day of Pentecost as cloven tongues of fire (Acts 2:3; see JESUS CHRIST). The ordinance of conferring the Holy Ghost initiated early Christian converts into the Church (Acts 8:12–17; 3 Ne. 18; Moro. 2–3; 6), and is a practice (often referred to as CONFIRMATION) restored to the latter-day Church and administered by the Melchizedek Priesthood (D&C 20:38–41).

As symbols for baptism, both water (used for washing) and fire (used in the smelting of metals, hence a "refiner's fire," Mal. 3:2–3) represent agents that cleanse and purify, the former externally, the latter internally, leading to SANCTIFICATION (Alma 13:12; Moro. 6:4). In addition, fire suggests warmth and light, realized in tangible sensations such as a burning in the bosom and an awareness of enlightenment accompanying the reception of the divine spirit (D&C 9:8; 88:49).

For Latter-day Saints, baptism by fire and the Holy Ghost is a real phenomenon in literal fulfillment of God's covenant to those who repent and are baptized (2 Ne. 31:10–21). Through this experience a person may realize the promises Jesus made with regard to how the Holy Ghost would function as a Comforter, a witness of the ATONEMENT, a teacher, and a guide to truth (John 14:16, 26; 15:26).

BIBLIOGRAPHY

Cannon, Elaine, and Ed J. Pinegar. *The Mighty Change.* Salt Lake City, 1978.

WILLIAM S. BRADSHAW

BIRTH

The Church of Jesus Christ of Latter-day Saints teaches that every person experiences a series of "births." All were born as spirit children of God in a PREMORTAL LIFE. Second, these individual spirit children received a mortal, physical body when they were born on earth. Third, those who accept and live the GOSPEL OF JESUS CHRIST go through a process of being born again in a spiritual sense (*see* BORN OF GOD). Although these births are real, they do not in any way constitute any type of REINCARNATION.

Men and women become conscious of their divine origin and birthright when they recognize their relationship with the Supreme Being, address him as Father, and become aware that in scripture God addresses mankind as his children (1 Jn. 3:1–2; Matt. 6:9).

In the COUNCIL IN HEAVEN, God the Father offered his spirit children the opportunity to progress toward becoming like he is by leaving his presence and being born on earth in a mortal, physical body and learning to live by faith (Abr. 3:22–28). Mortal birth is the event by which one's SPIRIT BODY is temporarily joined with a mortal tabernacle begotten by earthly parents. The exact time when the premortal spirit enters the unborn physical tabernacle is not specified in divine revelation. Through the FALL OF ADAM, and birth into mortality, mankind becomes subject to two deaths: the physical or temporal death, which is a death of the body, and the spiritual death, which is being shut out of God's presence (*see* LIFE AND DEATH, SPIRITUAL; PLAN OF SALVATION, PLAN OF REDEMPTION).

Through the ATONEMENT of Jesus Christ all people are given opportunity to be born again in a spiritual sense as his sons and daughters so as to return to God's presence as his spiritually begotten children (Mosiah 5:7–9; Alma 5:14). The process of being born of the spirit begins when one is baptized and receives the GIFT OF THE HOLY GHOST. Since the HOLY GHOST is a member of the GODHEAD, the effects of the spiritual death, or separation between man and God, is lessened individually when one is truly born of the Spirit.

Birth as spirit beings and birth as mortals have already occurred to all of mankind on the earth. The spiritual rebirth necessary for salvation in the presence of God requires considerable additional individual effort through obedience to the gospel of Jesus Christ.

BIBLIOGRAPHY
Clark, J. Reuben, Jr. *Man—God's Greatest Miracle.* Salt Lake City, 1956.
Smith, Joseph Fielding. *Man, His Origin and Destiny,* p. 354. Salt Lake City, 1954.

HELEN LANCE CHRISTIANSON

BLASPHEMY

Blasphemy denotes sacrilegious actions, speech, or thoughts that mock or revile God. A person blasphemes who, understanding the gravity of this behavior, willfully belittles or maligns God, the Godhead, or that which is of them, such as the commandments, covenants, ordinances, revelation, scriptures, and prophets.

Under the Law of Moses, blasphemy—understood anciently to be mainly the unauthorized uttering of the ineffable name of Jehovah (YHWH)—was a heinous offense punishable by stoning (Ex. 20:7; Lev. 24:10–16). Charges of blasphemy figure twice in the Book of Mormon—in Sherem's false accusations against Jacob (Jacob 7:7) and in Korihor's insolent speech before the chief judge (Alma 30:30). In these cases, and generally, blasphemy embraced many forms of impiety, whether directed against God, against his servants (Acts 13:45), against the king (1 Kgs. 21:10), or in some cases against holy places or things, including the law (Acts 6:13). However, when blasphemies were spoken in relative ignorance, the gift of mercy could mitigate the requirements of justice (1 Tim. 1:13).

If a person with spiritual knowledge intentionally blasphemes God or the divine, the sin is most serious. For those who have entered into the NEW AND EVERLASTING COVENANT, blasphemy in extreme form is a sin against the HOLY GHOST wherein one assents anew unto the death of Christ and the shedding of his innocent blood. This is called the unpardonable sin against the Holy Ghost (Matt. 12:31–32; D&C 132:27).

Emphasizing the gravity of the sin of blasphemy for those who claim to be his followers, Christ revealed that when he comes to purge the world he will commence with those "who have professed to know my name and have not known me, and have blasphemed against me in the midst of my house" (D&C 112:26).

Latter-day Saints are to refrain from blasphemy and the taking of the name of God in vain. Profanity and acrimony diminish spirituality and must be avoided: "But now ye also put off all these; anger, wrath, malice, blasphemy, filthy communication out of your mouth" (Col. 3:8). People are not defiled, Jesus emphasized, by what goes into the mouth, but by what comes from the heart: "For out of the heart proceed evil thoughts, murders, adulteries, fornications, thefts, false witness, blasphemies" (Matt. 15:19). Accordingly, Latter-day Saints are enjoined to avoid all forms of evil speaking of God, of the Lord's anointed, and, by implication, of all that is his, for "in nothing doth man offend God, or against none is his wrath kindled, save those who confess not his hand in all things, and obey not his commandments" (D&C 59:21).

BIBLIOGRAPHY

Hinckley, Gordon B. "Take Not the Name of God in Vain." *Ensign* 17 (Nov. 1987):44–48.

GARY L. BROWNING

BLESSING ON FOOD

Blessings on food are prayers to thank God for providing sustenance and to ask his blessings both on the food and on those who share it. In Mormon homes such blessings precede each meal and may be given by any member of a dining party, adult or child. In private these prayers are spoken orally, but may be spoken silently by individuals dining in public. All blessings on the food are addressed to God in the name of Jesus Christ. They are spoken from the heart as there is no prescribed prayer.

Latter-day Saints follow the patterns established by Christ and his disciples in blessings on food. When feeding the multitudes, Christ gave thanks for sustenance (Matt. 15:35–36) and blessed it (Matt. 14:19). Paul taught that food was to be received with prayer and thanksgiving (1 Tim. 4:3–5).

Biblical examples of praying over food are the basis for the Jewish, Catholic, and Protestant traditions of blessings on food or saying grace. Converts to Mormonism tended to continue these traditions from their prior faiths, and to be bolstered by the Latter-day

Saint instruction on prayer: All things are to be done "with prayer and thanksgiving." Food and all "good things which come of the earth . . . are made for the benefit and the use of man, both to please the eye and to gladden the heart, . . . to strengthen the body and enliven the soul. . . . And in nothing doth man offend God, or against none is his wrath kindled, save those who confess not his hand in all things" (D&C 59:7, 17–19, 21).

Petitioning God for blessings on the food to be eaten is typical of Mormon table blessings. This may include requests for nourishment and good health, for strength to do one's work and God's will and to be of service. Other blessings on the diners or on those who prepared the meal are also deemed appropriate.

In many cultures, breaking bread or sharing a meal with others is an act of hospitality. According to Latter-day scripture such sharing may also be a foretaste of the future Messianic banquet (D&C 58:8). Because family meals provide opportunities for sharing the deepest spiritual concerns and rejoicings, it is especially appropriate to begin such occasions with prayer and the invocation of the Spirit. In LDS families this prayer is customarily spoken at the beginning of the meal only, and not also following the meal, as is the custom among some people of other religions. Because there is no prescribed form for Latter-day Saint blessings on food, such blessings enable families daily to express their own feelings, thoughts, and words in intimate prayer and fellowship two or three times a day.

CHRISTINE QUINN CHRISTENSEN

BLESSINGS

The term "blessings" is used in two different ways in The Church of Jesus Christ of Latter-day Saints. In a broad traditional sense as used in many cultures, the word applies to all good things that come in a person's life—the wonders of nature, the joys of family, the benefits of liberty and education—anything and everything that enriches life. Such blessings are often pointed to as a manifestation of God's love for his children. Latter-day Saint writings are interspersed with this usage. In more specific terminology, blessings refer to ordinances performed under priesthood authority.

A priesthood blessing may be given only by those who have been ordained to the Melchizedek Priesthood. In the Church, most boys at the age of twelve have the Aaronic Priesthood conferred upon them and are ordained to the office of deacon. At age fourteen, they are usually ordained teachers, and at age sixteen, priests. If the priesthood bearer continues to show faithfulness and worthiness, then at age eighteen, or anytime thereafter, he may receive the Melchizedek Priesthood with ordination to the priesthood office of elder. An elder in the Melchizedek Priesthood has authority to perform most priesthood functions in the Church, including giving priesthood blessings.

Each priesthood ordination, from deacon to apostle, is a type of priesthood blessing and is characterized, as are all priesthood blessings, by (1) the LAYING ON OF HANDS by those in authority, (2) an invocation of the authority of the priesthood and the name of Jesus Christ, and (3) such words of blessing as follow the impressions of the Spirit.

This third element, that of spiritual impressions, is vital for any priesthood blessing. A fundamental doctrine of the Church is a belief that a worthy priesthood bearer, when giving a priesthood blessing, will receive promptings from the HOLY SPIRIT regarding what is to be spoken—not necessarily the exact words, but ideas or thoughts that he will then express as clearly as he can in his own words. This is the essence of a priesthood blessing, and distinguishes it from a PRAYER. A prayer seeks to communicate with God, either vocally or silently, and is rooted in the faith that God will hear the words or the thoughts and feelings and then, in his infinite wisdom and power, will respond. A priesthood blessing is based on trust that the priesthood holder, while speaking the blessing, will receive spiritual promptings regarding what is to be spoken and thus his words represent the will of God.

In the Church, formal priesthood blessings include the following:

BLESSING OF CHILDREN. When babies are just a few weeks old, they are usually given a priesthood blessing for the special purpose of conferring a name by which the baby will be known and bestowing promises based on spiritual impressions regarding the baby's future life. A quality of prophecy attends this process. If a baby's father is a worthy holder of the Melchizedek Priesthood, he will usually pronounce the blessing, but it may be given by a grandfather, a family friend, or any other qualified priesthood holder chosen by the baby's parents. Babies are usually blessed in the presence of the congregation at a fast and testimony meeting. However, the blessing may be given at other times and places, such as in a hospital or home, if there is a special need.

CONFIRMATION FOLLOWING BAPTISM. Two ordinances are required for admission to Church membership. The first is BAPTISM. The second, CONFIRMATION, is performed shortly following baptism and is a type of priesthood blessing. Two or more men who hold the Melchizedek Priesthood place their hands on the head of the person who has been baptized and, with one of the men serving as voice, the baptized person is confirmed a member of the Church and given the GIFT OF THE HOLY GHOST. Additional words of counsel or admonition are then expressed according to spiritual promptings.

SETTING APART TO CHURCH ASSIGNMENTS. Customarily, whenever any person is called to serve as a teacher or officer in any of the Church organizations, and always when a person is called to be a missionary or temple worker, persons holding proper priesthood authority place their hands on the person's head and the individual is set apart to the assignment. One of the priesthood bearers pronounces the blessing and expresses whatever counsel or thoughts he is impressed to say.

ADMINISTERING TO THE SICK. Blessings of health or comfort are given to one who is sick or injured. Two Melchizedek Priesthood men normally give this blessing in accord with James 5:14. The head of the sick person is anointed with a few drops of olive oil consecrated for this purpose. The two priesthood bearers then gently place their hands on the head of the afflicted person and the one sealing the anointing expresses promises of healing or comfort as he is impressed. Many incidents of dramatic and even miraculous healings have been recorded in Church history. Any worthy Melchizedek Priesthood bearer, when requested, may give such a blessing.

PATRIARCHAL BLESSINGS. Each organized stake in the Church has one or more patriarchs called to give patriarchal blessings to stake members. Normally this blessing is given just once in a person's life, usually when a person is young, most often in the teenage years. However, the blessing may be given at any age from childhood to advanced years. The patriarchal blessing is a lifetime blessing of guidance, warning, encouragement, and reassurance. Men serving as patriarchs are spiritually mature high priests in the Melchizedek Priesthood who have been ordained especially for the sacred calling of giving patriarchal blessings.

FATHER'S AND HUSBAND'S BLESSINGS. Every Melchizedek Priesthood bearer who is a husband or father has the authority, through worthiness, to give a priesthood blessing on special occasions or in times of special need to members of his family—a husband's blessing to his wife or a father's blessing to a son or daughter. Such blessings may be suggested by the husband or father or requested by the one desiring the blessing. They are blessings of love, counsel, and encouragement. Like all priesthood blessings, these are given by the laying on of hands on the head of the one receiving the blessing.

SPECIAL BLESSINGS OF COUNSEL AND COMFORT. All priesthood officers in the Church, from General Authorities through stake presidencies and ward bishoprics to home teachers, have authority to give blessings of counsel or comfort to Church members within their jurisdiction. These are official priesthood blessings given in the same manner and with similar spiritual promptings as other priesthood blessings. Persons desiring such a blessing usually request it of one of the local priesthood officers in the area where they reside.

BIBLIOGRAPHY
Brockbank, Bernard P. *Commandments and Promises of God.* Salt Lake City, 1983.
Kimball, Spencer W. *Faith Precedes the Miracle.* Salt Lake City, 1972.
McKay, David O. *Gospel Ideals.* Salt Lake City, 1976.
Monson, Thomas A. *Pathways to Perfection.* Salt Lake City, 1973.

BRUCE B. CLARK

BLOOD ATONEMENT

The doctrines of the Church affirm that the ATONEMENT wrought by the shedding of the blood of Jesus Christ, the Son of God, is efficacious for the sins of all who believe, repent, are baptized by one having authority, and receive the Holy Ghost by the laying on of hands. However, if a person thereafter commits a grievous sin such as the shedding of innocent blood, the Savior's sacrifice alone will not absolve the person of the consequences of the sin. Only by voluntarily submitting to whatever penalty the Lord may require can that person benefit from the atonement of Christ.

Several early Church leaders, most notably Brigham Young, taught that in a complete theocracy the Lord could require the voluntary shedding of a murderer's blood—presumably by capital punishment—as part of the process of atonement for such grievous sin. This was referred to as "blood atonement." Since such a theocracy has not been operative in modern times, the practical effect of the idea was its use as a rhetorical device to heighten the awareness of Latter-day Saints of the seriousness of murder and other major sins. This view is not a doctrine of the Church and has never been practiced by the Church at any time.

Early anti-Mormon writers charged that under Brigham Young the Church practiced "blood atonement," by which they meant Church-instigated violence directed at dissenters, enemies, and strangers. This claim distorted the whole idea of blood atonement—which was based on voluntary submission by an offender—into a supposed justification of involuntary punishment. Occasional isolated acts of violence that occurred in areas where Latter-day Saints lived were typical of that period in the history of the American West, but they were not instances of Church-sanctioned blood atonement.

BIBLIOGRAPHY

McConkie, Bruce R. "Blood Atonement Doctrine." In *Mormon Doctrine,* 2nd ed. Salt Lake City, 1966.

Penrose, Charles W. *Blood Atonement, As Taught by Leading Elders of The Church of Jesus Christ of Latter-day Saints.* Salt Lake City, 1884.

Peterson, Paul H. "The Mormon Reformation," pp. 176–99. Ph.D. diss., Brigham Young University, 1981.

Smith, Joseph Fielding. "The Doctrine of Blood Atonement." In *Answers to Gospel Questions,* Vol. 1, pp. 180–91. Salt Lake City, 1957.

LOWELL M. SNOW

BORN IN THE COVENANT

Latter-day Saints make several formal COVENANTS with God such as baptism, confirmation, ordination to the priesthood, and eternal marriage, commonly called temple marriage. A temple marriage or sealing refers to the ceremony in which a man and a woman are married (sealed) to each other for TIME AND ETERNITY in a temple by the authority of the holy priesthood. Children born to the couple after this marriage are automatically sealed to their parents eternally and are spoken of as having been born in the covenant.

Children born to parents not members of the Church or to members who have not been married (sealed) in a temple by priesthood authority are not born in the covenant. However, if these parents subsequently are sealed in temple covenants they can have their children sealed to them, and can secure the same eternal family ties as if all were born in the covenant.

For the eternal blessings of being sealed as a family member to be valid, each must remain faithful to his or her covenants.

[*See also* Salvation for the Dead.]

RALPH L. COTTRELL, JR.

BORN OF GOD

Born of God or "born again" refers to the personal spiritual experience in which repentant individuals receive a forgiveness of sins and a witness from God that if they continue to live the COMMANDMENTS and endure to the end, they will inherit ETERNAL LIFE. The scriptures teach that just as each individual is "born into the world by water, and blood, and the spirit," so must one be "born again" of water and the Spirit and be cleansed by the blood of Christ (John 3:5; Moses 6:59). To be born of God implies a sanctifying process by which the old or natural man is supplanted by the new spiritual man who enjoys the companionship of the Holy Ghost and hence is no longer disposed to commit sin (Col. 3:9–10; Mosiah 3:19; *TPJS*, p. 51). When individuals are born again they are spiritually begotten sons and daughters of God and more specifically of Jesus Christ (Mosiah 5:7; 27:25). The Book of Mormon prophet $Alma_1$ calls this inner transformation a "mighty change in your hearts" (Alma 5:14).

LDS scripture and literature contain numerous examples of individuals who have undergone this process of spiritual rebirth. Enos relates that after "mighty prayer and supplication" the Lord declared that his sins had been forgiven (Enos 1:1–8). After King Benjamin's discourse, the people said that the Spirit had "wrought a mighty change in us, or in our hearts," and that they had "no more disposition to do evil, but to do good continually" (Mosiah 5:2). Of his conversion experience, Alma$_2$ says, "Nevertheless, after wading through much tribulation, repenting nigh unto death, the Lord in mercy hath seen fit to snatch me out of an everlasting burning, and I am born of God" (Mosiah 27:28). Similar experiences are recounted about King Lamoni and his father (Alma 19, 22). In an account written in 1832, the Prophet Joseph Smith describes his first vision as being significant not only for opening a new DISPENSATION of the gospel, but also for his personal conversion. He writes, "The Lord opened the heavens upon me and I saw the Lord and he spake unto me saying Joseph my son thy sins are forgiven thee. [A]nd my soul was filled with love and for many days I could rejoice with great joy and the Lord was with me" (PJS 1:6–7).

Mormon explains the "mighty change" that must occur if one is to be born of God. The first fruit of repentance is the BAPTISM of water and fire, which baptism "cometh by faith unto the fulfilling of the commandments." Then comes a REMISSION OF SINS that brings a meekness and lowliness of heart. Such a transformation results in one's becoming worthy of the companionship of the Holy Ghost, who "filleth with hope and perfect love, which love endureth by diligence unto prayer" (Moro. 8:25–26).

LDS scriptures teach that spiritual rebirth comes by the GRACE of God to those who adhere to the principles and ordinances of the gospel of Jesus Christ, namely, faith, repentance, baptism, and reception of the GIFT OF THE HOLY GHOST. For the process to be genuine, however, one must be diligently engaged in good works, for as James says, "faith without works is dead; . . . by works [is] faith made perfect" (James 2:20, 22). A mere confession of change, or receiving baptism or another ordinance, does not necessarily mean that one has been born of God.

Other Christian faiths also emphasize the importance of being "born again." Unlike many of these, Latter-day Saints do not believe this experience alone is sufficient for SALVATION. Instead, the process of spiritual rebirth signals to Latter-day Saints the beginning of a new life abounding with faith, grace, and good works. Only by ENDURING TO

THE END may the individual return to the presence of God. Those who receive the ordinance of baptism and are faithful in keeping the commandments may enjoy the constant presence of the Holy Ghost who, like fire, will act as a sanctifier, and will witness to the hearts of the righteous that their sins are forgiven, imparting hope for eternal life.

Persons who have experienced this mighty change manifest attitudinal and behavioral changes. Feeling their hearts riveted to the Lord, their obedience extends beyond performance of duty. President Harold B. Lee taught, "Conversion must mean more than just being a 'card-carrying' member of the Church with a tithing receipt, a membership card, a temple recommend, etc. It means to overcome the tendencies to criticize and to strive continually to improve inward weaknesses and not merely the outward appearances" (*Ensign,* June 1971, p. 8). Latter-day Saints believe that individuals who are truly born of God gladly give a life of service to their fellow beings—they share the gospel message, sacrifice their own time, energy, and resources for the benefit of others, and in general hold high the light of Christ, being faithful to all the commandments.

BIBLIOGRAPHY

Cannon, Elaine, and Ed J. Pinegar. *The Mighty Change.* Salt Lake City, 1978.

ED J. PINEGAR

BROTHERHOOD

While members of other Christian denominations may speak metaphorically of all humankind being brothers and sisters and children of God, Latter-day Saints believe it literally in the sense that a father in heaven and a MOTHER IN HEAVEN created spirit children in a PREMORTAL existence. Those spirit children, born into this or other worlds as mortal men and women, are therefore all of the same "generation" and are literally brothers and sisters, children of deity. Among them is Jesus Christ, who is distinct from other men and women in that he is the Firstborn Son of God in the spirit and the Only Begotten of the Father in the flesh.

An important LDS doctrine based on this belief is the concept of equal opportunity for salvation. Since all mortals are offspring of deity, all have equal access to saving grace and may, through good works and moral progression while living as mortals, become saved by that grace. This doctrine of literal kinship is a major driving force behind the Church's proselytizing activities: Latter-day Saints believe that they have an obligation to teach the gospel of Jesus Christ to all the world because all its inhabitants are their brothers and sisters.

Latter-day Saints also believe in the brotherhood of the priesthood, similar to the sisterhood of the Relief Society; a special bond exists among the members of both an individual priesthood quorum and the entire body of the priesthood. As explained in scripture and instructions from Church leaders, this bond obligates priesthood holders to act as shepherds for one another and to be actively concerned for the welfare of other members and their families. In practice, this obligation is largely discharged through monthly home teaching, a system whereby quorum members visit one another, assessing needs and delivering a spiritual message.

Because stakes and wards of the LDS Church are operated by a lay clergy, most active members, both men and women, serve in some unpaid Church calling. The service rendered by priesthood holders in their ecclesiastical positions is often labor-intensive and provides an opportunity for close interaction. This system fosters a feeling of brotherhood of service among priesthood holders.

The most common title used by Latter-day Saints in referring to themselves and to each other is "Brother" or "Sister," though General Authorities of the Church are most often referred to by their more formal titles of "Elder" or "President."

BIBLIOGRAPHY

Brown, Hugh B. "The Gospel Is for All Men." *IE* 72 (June 1969):31–34.

Johnson, P. Wendel. "The How of Brotherhood." *IE* 72 (Sept. 1969):70–75.

Oaks, Dallin H. "Brother's Keeper." *Ensign* 16 (May 1986):20.

Taylor, Henry D. "Am I My Brother's Keeper?" *Ensign* 2 (July 1972):74–75.

TIMOTHY W. SLOVER

BUFFETINGS OF SATAN

An individual who receives extensive spiritual knowledge, enters into sacred COVENANTS, and then turns away from those promises to the

Lord may be left to the buffetings of Satan until complete REPENTANCE has occurred. This sin differs in nature and category from one committed in ignorance. Paul alluded to such in 1 Corinthians 5:1–5, but a clearer understanding of the doctrine is found in latter-day REVELATION (see *DS* 2:96–98).

To the Prophet Joseph Smith the Lord revealed the situation of some who had broken the covenants by which they had entered the United Order. That revelation reads, "The soul that sins against this covenant, and hardeneth his heart against it, shall be dealt with according to the laws of my church, and shall be delivered over to the buffetings of Satan until the day of redemption" (D&C 82:20–21; cf. 78:12; 104:9–10). The same principle applies to persons whose temple marriage is sealed by the HOLY SPIRIT OF PROMISE, and who later transgress and break their covenants. The revelation states that they "shall be delivered unto the buffetings of Satan unto the day of redemption, saith the Lord God" (D&C 132:26).

Elder Bruce R. McConkie, a latter-day apostle, explained that to be "turned over to the buffetings of Satan is to be given into [Satan's] hands; it is to be turned over to him with all the protective power of the priesthood, of righteousness, and of godliness removed, so that Lucifer is free to torment, persecute, and afflict such a person without let or hindrance. When the bars are down, the cuffs and curses of Satan, both in this world and in the world to come, bring indescribable anguish typified by burning fire and brimstone. The damned in hell so suffer" (*MD,* "Buffetings of Satan"; see also McConkie, Vol. 2, p. 335).

The term "buffetings of Satan" used in latter-day revelation is associated with punishment for the violation of covenants and is distinct from the "buffet" or "buffeted" used occasionally in the New Testament, which refers to the suffering, maltreatment, and persecution to which the Savior, Paul, and other church members were often subjected by people (Matt. 26:67; 1 Cor. 4:11; 2 Cor. 12:7).

[*See also* Damnation; Hell.]

BIBLIOGRAPHY

McConkie, Bruce R. *Doctrinal New Testament Commentary,* 3 vols. Salt Lake City, 1965–1973.

DENNIS D. FLAKE

BURNINGS, EVERLASTING

Moses described God as a "consuming fire" (Deut. 4:24), his glory consuming everything corrupt and unholy (D&C 63:34; 101:23–24). The Prophet Joseph Smith explained, "God Almighty Himself dwells in eternal fire; flesh and blood cannot go there, for all corruption is devoured by the fire," but a resurrected being, "flesh and bones quickened by the Spirit of God," can (*TPJS,* pp. 326, 367; cf. Luke 24:36–43; 1 Cor. 15:50). Heaven, not hell, is the realm of everlasting burnings, a view contrasting with the popular conception of hell as a place of fire, brimstone, and searing heat. Heat is a characteristic of God's glory (D&C 133:41–44).

Only those cleansed from physical and moral corruption can endure immortal glory (3 Ne. 27:19; Moses 6:57; *TPJS,* p. 351). Hence, Isaiah rhetorically asked, "Who among us shall dwell with the devouring fire? who among us shall dwell with everlasting burnings?" (Isa. 33:14). Joseph Smith taught, "All men who are immortal (i.e., resurrected beings in any of the DEGREES OF GLORY) dwell in everlasting burnings" (*TPJS,* pp. 347, 361, 367). Resurrected bodies are qualitatively different according to their glory (1 Cor. 15:39–44; D&C 88:28–32).

Describing a vision of the CELESTIAL KINGDOM, Joseph Smith reported, "I saw the transcendent beauty of the gate through which the heirs of that kingdom will enter, which was like unto circling flames of fire; also the blazing throne of God, whereon was seated the Father and the Son" (D&C 137:2–3).

RODNEY TURNER

C

CALLING AND ELECTION

An exhortation to make one's "calling and election sure" is found in Peter's writings (2 Pet. 1:3–10), and is associated with the "more sure word of prophecy" (2 Pet. 1:16–19). The Prophet Joseph Smith explained that "the more sure word of prophecy means a man's knowing that he is sealed up unto eternal life, by revelation and the spirit of prophecy, through the power of the Holy Priesthood" (D&C 131:5).

Peter said that the acquisition and exercise of faith, virtue, knowledge, temperance, patience, godliness, brotherly kindness, and charity are necessary to make one's "calling and election sure" and to obtain a fulness of the blessings of God (2 Pet. 1:5–7; cf. *TPJS,* p. 305).

In addition to acquiring these qualities of character, those who would have their calling and election made sure must receive the ordinances of the gospel, including the temple ordinances (D&C 131:2–3; 132:19–20).

Having one's calling and election made sure is not attained easily. Speaking of this, the Prophet Joseph Smith taught that "When the Lord has thoroughly proved [a person], and finds that the [person] is determined to serve Him at all hazards, then the [person] will find his[/her] calling and election made sure" (*TPJS,* p. 150). The Prophet indicates that this was the case with ancient prophets such as Isaiah, Ezekiel, John, Paul and others (*TPJS,* p. 151).

BIBLIOGRAPHY
Doxey, Roy W., comp. *The Latter-day Prophets and the Doctrine and Covenants,* Vol. 4, pp. 406–409. Salt Lake City, 1965.
McConkie, Bruce R. *Doctrinal New Testament Commentary,* Vol. 3, pp. 323–53. Salt Lake City, 1973.

ROY W. DOXEY

CELESTIAL KINGDOM

The Church of Jesus Christ of Latter-day Saints teaches of three degrees of glory in the AFTERLIFE—the celestial, terrestrial, and telestial. Jesus alluded to these when he said, "In my Father's house are many mansions" (John 14:2). Paul likened them to the sun, moon, and stars, with the highest or celestial being typical of the sun (1 Cor. 15:40–41; cf. D&C 76:50–98). The celestial kingdom was seen in vision by John the Revelator, Paul, and the Prophet Joseph Smith (Rev. 4:6; 2 Cor. 12:2; *TPJS,* pp. 106–107). This earth in its "sanctified, immortal, and eternal state" will become a celestial sphere (D&C 88:19–20; 130:9).

Celestial glory comes to those "who received the testimony of Jesus, and believed on his name and were baptized after the manner of his burial, . . . and who overcome by faith, and are sealed by the Holy Spirit of promise, which the Father sheds forth upon all those who are just and true" (D&C 76:51–53). Within the celestial glory are three levels, and to obtain the highest requires a temple marriage or sealing.

Inhabitants of the highest celestial degree inherit "thrones, kingdoms, principalities, and powers," and dwell with God and Jesus Christ forever (D&C 76:54–70; 132:19–20).

[*See also* Degrees of Glory; Telestial Kingdom; Terrestrial Kingdom.]

SUSAN EASTON BLACK

CEREMONIES

Ceremony and ritual are key concepts for understanding religious behavior. In LDS parlance the word "ordinance" embraces most offi-

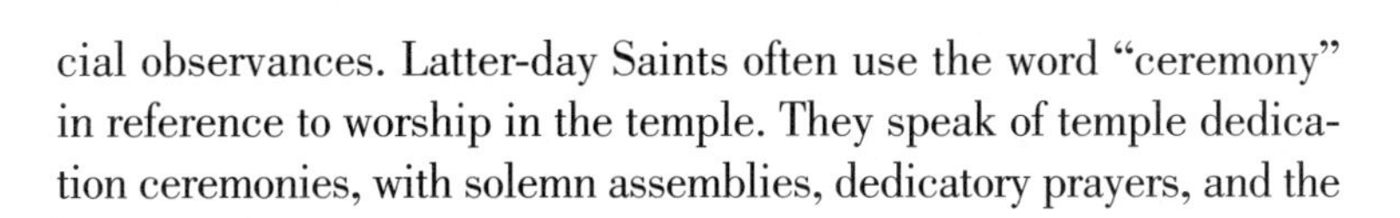

cial observances. Latter-day Saints often use the word "ceremony" in reference to worship in the temple. They speak of temple dedication ceremonies, with solemn assemblies, dedicatory prayers, and the hosanna shout.

In LDS self-awareness, a sequence of ordinances, with temple ceremonies as the apex, constitute the main axis of religious existence. These ordinances are called by Joseph Smith the "rites of salvation," (*TPJS*, p. 191). They define the character and interactions of priesthood, Church organization, authority, living revelation, family structure, kinship linkages, and moral responsibility.

In the discourse of social science, by contrast, ceremony usually refers to any cultural performance that identifies or changes one's social status. Ceremony that concerns the divine or sacred is called ritual.

Comparative study of diverse cultures and peoples suggests several generalizations on ritual that Latter-day Saints would call ordinances or sacred ceremonies.

First, ritual is symbolic. The central values, premises, and assumptions of a way of life are encoded in ceremony. A whole system of thought may be expressed in a simple gesture, a placement of hands, a posture. For Latter-day Saints the blessing and passing of the sacrament, beginning with the presiding priesthood authorities, reactivates each member's covenant relationship with Jesus Christ and the entire complex of living prophets, priesthood authority, revelation, and the influences of the Holy Spirit.

Second, it identifies sacred or set-apart space and time and marks fundamental transformations of social relationships. For Latter-day Saints the Sabbath is sacred time when even the preparation of food should be done with an eye single to the glory of God and with "singleness of heart" (D&C 59:13). The temple stands as the epitome of sacred space and time, the place of the divine name and presence, and embodies the enduring covenants of marriage, family, and sealing.

Third, ritual perpetuates the community through sacred drama. It marks and engenders spiritual birth and rebirth. Regular participation regenerates sentiments of attachment. In this view ceremony is to the reproduction of family and community what DNA is to the biological individual. Among Latter-day Saints such ceremonies include the blessing and naming of infants, priesthood ordinations, patriarchal blessings and father's blessings by the laying on of hands, administering to the sick with consecrated olive oil, and the setting apart of persons to a variety of callings of teaching and service.

Fourth, ritual and other LDS social ceremonies memorialize key events in their historical formation. The historical consciousness of Latter-day Saints is celebrated in periodic commemorations, pageants, dedications, and group memorial services of key events in the restoration.

Fifth, ritual is often countercultural, defining and contrasting the principles of the religious community with those of surrounding societies. LDS emphasis on the "gathering" of disciples to a geographic and spiritual Zion, and the ceremonial renewal of responsibilities in periodic testimony bearing enhance discipleship, and are counterbalances to the disruptions of a secular world of increasingly fragile and fleeting relationships.

Sixth, ritual provides moral authority and constancy to cope with rapid change and social upheaval. It is the cement that unites individuals in common cause. As the Church undergoes geometric expansion, it draws together peoples of all backgrounds and provides the basis for communication and trust amid national, cultural, and ethnic diversity.

No society or group exists without both social and sacred ceremony. Among Latter-day Saints the fundamental importance of ceremony, and of divine authority in its performance, are given expression in a unique latter-day scripture: "In the ordinances . . . the power of godliness is manifest. And without the ordinances thereof, and the authority of the priesthood, the power of godliness is not manifest unto men in the flesh" (D&C 84: 20–21).

BIBLIOGRAPHY

Alexander, Bobby C. "Ceremony." In *The Encyclopedia of Religion,* ed. Mircea Eliade, Vol. 3, pp. 179–83. New York, 1987.

Morris, Brian. *Anthropological Studies of Religion: An Introductory Text.* New York, 1987.

JOHN P. HAWKINS

CHARITY

Charity is a concept found in many cultures, its meaning ranging from a general selfless love of humanity to the specific alms-giving that is often its focus in modern times. Latter-day Saints take their understanding of charity from the Book of Mormon: "Charity is the pure love of Christ, and it endureth forever; and whoso is found possessed of it at the last day, it shall be well with him" (Moro. 7:47; cf. Ether 12:34; 2 Ne. 26:30).

As the love of Christ, charity is characterized as selfless and self-sacrificing (1 Cor. 13:5), emanating from a pure heart, a good conscience, and faith unfeigned (1 Tim. 1:5). Thus, more than an act, charity is an attitude, a state of heart and mind (1 Cor. 13:4–7) that accompanies one's works and is proffered unconditionally (D&C 121:45). It follows, but surpasses in importance, faith and hope (1 Cor. 13:13).

This may have been what Jesus was trying to teach Peter in John 21:15–17, wherein he asks Peter three times if he "loves" him, and, to Peter's affirmative answers, responds, "Feed my sheep" and "Feed my lambs," teaching that the true love of Christ always goes out to others. Loving all of God's children and being willing to sacrifice for them are the depth and breadth of the pure love of Christ. This "bond of perfectness and peace" (D&C 88:125; Col. 3:14) becomes the foundation of all human relationships (cf. 1 Cor. 13). The everlasting love of charity is intended to be an integral part of one's nature: one is to cleave unto it (Moro. 7:46) and be clothed in it (D&C 88:125). In fact, *all* things are to be done in charity. Charity is everlasting; it covers sins (1 Pet. 4:8), it casts out all fears (Moro. 8:17), and it is a prerequisite for entering the kingdom of Heaven (Ether 12:34; Moro. 10:21).

Throughout its history, the law of the LDS Church has been that its members are to do all things with charity. Since its inception in 1842, the LDS Relief Society has had the motto Charity Never Faileth (1 Cor. 13:8; Moro. 7:46). The concept of charity is fundamental to the teachings and the procedures of the Church, being the very core of all it does, including missionary work, welfare services, temple work, tithes and offerings, and home and visiting teaching. As the spiritual welfare of the individual member of the Church is contingent upon charity, so is the welfare of Zion dependent upon the charity in the hearts of Latter-day Saints (2 Ne. 26:28).

BIBLIOGRAPHY
Benson, Ezra Taft. "To the Elderly in the Church." *Ensign* 19 (Nov. 1989):4–8.
Hansen, W. Eugene. "Love." *Ensign* 19 (Nov. 1989):23–24.
Holland, Jeffrey R. "He Loved Them unto the End." *Ensign* 19 (Nov. 1989):25–26.

ADDIE FUHRIMAN

CHASTENING

Latter-day Saints view chastening as a manifestation of God's love and concern. "For whom the Lord loveth he chasteneth, and scourgeth every son whom he receiveth" (Heb. 12:6). Like other religious peoples, they sometimes see death, famine, pestilence, and other human calamities as "acts of God" because he allows them to happen as functions of natural forces. However, Latter-day Saints tend to focus less on the punitive nature of such events and more on the possible positive results, such as HUMILITY, REPENTANCE, instruction, and spiritual change. To "chasten" denotes "to make chaste."

God loves all mankind and works to bring his children back to dwell with him. No one can endure God's presence who has not been purified to become like him. For this reason, Latter-day Saints view life on this earth as a period of testing and training, a time to instruct, refine, and purify the individual, making the child of God more like the Father.

The Book of Mormon tells of God allowing natural disasters to chasten people because whole communities had forgotten him, broken his commandments, and desecrated holy things (Hel. 12:3). The Doctrine and Covenants teaches that many will be blessed if they willingly turn their hearts to God and accept the call to repent and put their lives in order (D&C 93:38–52; cf. Heb. 12:5–11).

The Prophet Joseph Smith stands as an example to Latter-day Saints as one loved, yet chastened by the Lord. To carry out his mission effectively, he had to learn many lessons. Sometimes the Lord merely reminded him to humble himself and become more submissive. Other times, as when he allowed Martin Harris to take the first 116 manuscript pages of the Book of Mormon, which were subsequently lost, the Lord withdrew the power of translation and allowed Joseph to suffer the oppression of darkness. When Joseph was incarcerated in the Liberty Jail, the Lord counseled that all his experiences would be for his good (D&C 122:7). It was, indeed, during and after this difficult period that Joseph received some very significant revelations.

GLADYS CLARK FARMER

CHASTITY, LAW OF

In the law of chastity, the Lord commands restraint in exercising the body's sexual and procreative powers. As revealed in scripture, this law forbids all sexual relationships outside of marriage. Authorities of The Church of Jesus Christ of Latter-day Saints also condemn perverse or coercive sexual acts within marriage.

"Thou shalt not commit adultery," declares the Lord in the Decalogue (Ex. 20:14). Elsewhere in scripture, he prohibits fornication, homosexuality, incest, and bestiality (Ex. 22:16; Lev. 18:6–23). Teaching in both the eastern and western hemispheres, Jesus denounced unchastity in thought as well as deed (Matt. 5:27–28; 3 Ne. 12:27–28). The apostle Paul warned that if the Saints succumbed to sexual sin they would not "retain God in their knowledge" (Rom. 1:26–29). The Lord affirmed in the Book of Mormon that he "delight[s] in the chastity of women," condemning infidelity of husbands as an offense against wives and children (Jacob 2:28, 31–35). The prophet Abinadi indicted the priests of King Noah for harlotry and for failure to live and teach the Mosaic law that prohibits adultery (Mosiah 12:29; 13:22). Corianton was taught by his father, $Alma_2$, that sexual sin is "most abominable above all sins save it be the shedding of innocent blood or denying the Holy Ghost" (Alma 39:5). Mormon lamented the utter degeneracy of soldiers who raped female prisoners, "depriving them of that which was most dear and precious above all things, which is chastity and virtue" (Moro. 9:9).

In latter-day revelation, Church leaders are directed to excommunicate adulterers if they refuse to repent. The Doctrine and Covenants reproves adulterous desires as a denial of the faith, disqualifying offenders from the companionship of the Spirit (D&C

42:23–26; 63:16). The Prophet Joseph Smith beheld in vision that unrepentant adulterers and whoremongers will be with liars and sorcerers in the TELESTIAL KINGDOM (D&C 76:103).

Church leaders have repeatedly stressed obedience to the law of chastity. In an official pronouncement in 1942, the First Presidency promised "the exaltations of eternities" to those who remain chaste, deploring sexual immorality as a destroyer of individuals and nations. "The doctrine of this Church," they stated, "is that sexual sin—the illicit sexual relations of men and women—stands, in its enormity, next to murder. The Lord has drawn no essential distinctions between fornication, adultery, and harlotry or prostitution. Each has fallen under His solemn and awful condemnation" (*CR* 112 [Oct. 1942]:10–12). Sexual violations desecrate much that is holy, including divinely given procreative powers, the sanctity of life, marriage, and family. President David O. McKay said chastity is "the most vital part of the foundation of a happy marriage and . . . the source of strength and perpetuity of the race" (*CR* 137 [Apr. 1967]:8). Church leaders recognize only one standard of chastity for both men and women. Speaking in 1980, President Spencer W. Kimball affirmed: "Total chastity before marriage and total fidelity after are still the standard from which there can be no deviation without sin, misery, and unhappiness" (*CR* 150 [Oct. 1980]:4).

The law of chastity applies not only to behavior but also to dress, speech, and thought. Latter-day Saints are counseled to dress modestly, to use dignified language in speaking of bodily functions, and to cultivate virtuous thoughts. Accordingly, they are to avoid anything pornographic in literature, movies, television, and conversation. Though many outside the Church regard masturbation as normal, LDS leaders teach that the practice is wrong, one that feeds base appetites and may lead to other sinful conduct. Similarly, unmarried couples who engage in petting or fondling are breaking the law of chastity, and stimulating impulses that may lead to other sin.

Chastity fosters personal peace and confidence (see D&C 121:45). Referring specifically to unchastity, Alma wrote that "wickedness never was happiness" (Alma 41:10). The Church teaches that those guilty of infidelity lose the Spirit of the Lord, and bring upon themselves and their families jealousy, grief, anger, and distrust.

Persons guilty of unchastity may receive forgiveness through full

REPENTANCE. Because unchastity violates baptismal and explicit temple vows, penitent offenders must confess such sins to their bishop, branch president, or other appropriate Church leader. After prayerfully considering the transgression, the Church leader may—especially in cases of adultery, fornication, or homosexuality—convene a disciplinary council to help the transgressor through repentance and to protect the integrity of the Church. Depending on the offense and the spiritual maturity of the offender, a disciplinary council may excommunicate, disfellowship, place on probation, or exonerate the person.

Disciplinary councils usually require transgressors to seek forgiveness from individuals whom they have drawn into sexual sin and from spouses betrayed through infidelity. Transgressors are also to seek forgiveness from God through prayerful reformation of their lives, forsaking unchaste actions and thoughts. God promises that he will not remember the sins of those who repent fully (Isa. 1:18; D&C 58:42–43). However, recurrence of the transgression can cause the weight of the former sin to return (D&C 82:7), and more serious consequences to follow (D&C 42:26).

Living the law of chastity does not mean asceticism. Rather, it means to "bridle all [our] passions, that [we] may be filled with love" (Alma 38:12). Within marriage, physical intimacy strengthens the divinely ordained bond between husband and wife. By protecting the soul against carnality, chastity safeguards the joys of marriage in this life and exaltation in the life to come. Only the morally clean may enter the temple, where Latter-day Saints solemnly covenant to keep themselves chaste so that they may receive God's greatest blessing, eternal life (D&C 14:7). Through receiving temple ordinances and remaining worthy, a husband and wife may reach a perfect union sealed by the HOLY SPIRIT OF PROMISE, thus achieving a marriage that endures beyond the grave, blessed with spirit offspring in the eternities (D&C 132:19; cf. 131:1–4).

BIBLIOGRAPHY

Benson, Ezra Taft. *The Teachings of Ezra Taft Benson,* pp. 277–86. Salt Lake City, 1988.

Kimball, Spencer W. *The Miracle of Forgiveness,* pp. 61–89. Salt Lake City, 1969.

McKay, David O. *Gospel Ideals,* pp. 458–76. Salt Lake City, 1953.

BRYCE J. CHRISTENSEN

CHILDREN

[*This entry consists of three articles:*

Roles of Children
Blessing of Children
Salvation of Children

The first article explores the roles of children from leaving their heavenly parents to their roles and activities within an earthly family. The second article relates to an ordinance within the Church usually performed a few weeks after the birth of children when they are given the names by which they shall be known on the records of the Church, and normally a blessing is given at the same time. The last article discusses the innocence of children until they reach the age of accountability; that their salvation is assured until that time.]

ROLES OF CHILDREN

Latter-day Saints believe that children are SPIRIT sons and daughters of God who have come to earth with their own divine inheritances and identities. Parents, with the support of the Church, are responsible for nurturing the divine and righteous attributes of their children and for helping them develop love for God and fellow beings. Through love and prayerful guidance, parents can help children learn that they have a potential for greatness and goodness, and that life on earth has purpose and eternal consequences. Parents and children can establish family bonds that may endure forever.

God has commanded parents to teach their children "to understand the doctrine of repentance, faith in Christ the son of the living God, and of baptism and the gift of the Holy Ghost"; they are also to "teach their children to pray, and to walk uprightly before the Lord" (D&C 68:25, 28). Childhood is a period of preparation and practice in which children must learn to distinguish good from evil, so that when they reach the age of ACCOUNTABILITY and are baptized (usually at eight years), they will be ready to exercise their AGENCY wisely and assume the responsibilities of membership in the Church. Children should learn to serve God and other people, and should prepare for responsibilities they will have as adults.

The Church teaches that children learn gospel values, doctrines, and behavioral applications most effectively in the home. They learn at a very young age to pray individually and as part of the family. In many homes during family prayer, families kneel together while one member prays, and small children take their turn with the help of their parents. In addition to regular individual and family prayers and blessings on the food at each meal, children learn that they can pray whenever they want to express gratitude or need divine help. They can receive priesthood BLESSINGS from their fathers or home teachers when they need inspirational help or guidance.

Latter-day Saints are encouraged to help their children read and study the scriptures daily, and many do this as a family activity at a specified time each day. LDS families are also counseled to hold a family home evening once each week. All family members, including young children, can be given opportunities to conduct these meetings, prepare and present lessons, lead music, read scriptures, answer questions, offer prayers, and provide refreshments. Within this framework of support and cooperation, children take part in making decisions and solving family problems, and they learn to internalize values as they develop autonomy, initiative, and competence. LDS children also learn the gospel in less formal settings as families work, play, and eat together. These activities provide occasions to teach gospel values and create bonds of trust.

Through its programs the Church supports the parents and the home. It provides training, materials, and other adult role models for children, thereby reinforcing gospel principles taught by the family. Children participate with their families during weekly worship services called sacrament meetings, at which they may partake of the sacrament, participate in congregational singing, and give as well as listen to gospel-related talks. During the monthly fast and testimony meeting, members, including children, may bear individual TESTIMONY to the ward congregation.

Primary is an organized program of religious instruction and activity in the Church for children ages eighteen months to twelve years. Its purpose is to teach children the gospel of Jesus Christ and help them learn to live it. Participating in Primary helps children prepare for BAPTISM and other ordinances.

In Primary, held each Sunday, children develop skills and gain competence in communication, leadership, gospel scholarship, and social relationships through many gospel-centered activities. They offer prayers, recite scriptures, and give gospel-related talks. They sing songs written specifically for children, listen to stories, and participate in activities such as dramatizations, role plays, and games. In smaller age-grouped classes, they receive scripturally based lessons designed for their level of understanding. Primary leaders and teachers encourage the children to study and learn the Articles of Faith. Each year the Primary children prepare a sacrament meeting presentation in which they share with the congregation the scriptural concepts they have studied.

Periodic weekday activities help children apply the gospel principles they learn on Sunday and encourage them to interact informally with their peers and leaders. The Primary sponsors quarterly activity days for all children that provide wholesome fun by involving them in physical, creative, cultural, and service activities. Ten- and eleven-year-old girls and boys participate in achievement days twice a month during which they set goals and are recognized as they learn skills in hospitality, arts and crafts, sports and physical fitness, health and personal grooming, outdoor fun and skills, service and citizenship, family skills, and safety and emergency preparedness. In some areas, boys participate in Church-sponsored Scouting programs for their achievement day activities.

The Church provides resources specifically designed to teach children. Age-appropriate scripture-based lesson manuals, a children's songbook, teaching guides, and training videos are available for leaders and teachers. The *Friend,* a monthly magazine written specifically for children, is available through subscription in most English-speaking countries. Excerpts are translated and compiled in international magazines for children living in other parts of the world.

BIBLIOGRAPHY
Family Guidebook. Salt Lake City, 1980.
Primary Handbook. Salt Lake City, 1985.

MICHAELENE P. GRASSLI

BLESSING OF CHILDREN

The blessing of infants is normally performed during a fast and testimony meeting. The father who holds the Melchizedek Priesthood, or another bearer of that priesthood selected by the family, usually pronounces a name and blessing upon a child within a few weeks after its birth. Either may be assisted by other Melchizedek Priesthood bearers. Older children may be blessed at the time of the conversion of their family. Under special circumstances children may be blessed at home or in a hospital.

The precedent for blessing children was set by the Savior in both Palestine and the New World. Both the New Testament (Mark 10:16) and the Book of Mormon (3 Ne. 17:21) describe Jesus blessing little children. In a revelation concerning the government of the Church, the Prophet Joseph Smith received specific directions on this ordinance: "Every member of the Church of Christ having children is to bring them unto the elders before the church, who are to lay their hands upon them in the name of Jesus Christ, and bless them in his name" (D&C 20:70).

The blessing ordinance thus described is neither the infant baptism performed in many other Christian churches nor simply a christening and prayer on the child's behalf. Instead, the priesthood bearer seeks to exercise his right to receive revelation from God in the child's behalf. The fixed portions of the ordinance are the addressing of Heavenly Father, the invoking of the Melchizedek Priesthood authority by which the blessing is spoken, giving the child its name, and closing in the name of Jesus Christ. The giving of the name formally identifies the child on the records of the Church as part of what may become an eternal family unit.

The blessing itself is to be given as dictated by the Spirit and may contain prophecy concerning the child's future, a statement of gifts or promises, and instruction or promises to the parents or siblings of the child.

BIBLIOGRAPHY

Smith, Joseph F. "Blessing and Naming Infants." *Gospel Doctrine,* 12th ed. pp. 191–92. Salt Lake City, 1961.

LOWELL BANGERTER

SALVATION OF CHILDREN

In Latter-day Saint doctrine children are to be instructed in the principles of the gospel and baptized when eight years of age (D&C 68:25–27). They are then responsible to adhere to the teachings of the Church relative to obtaining SALVATION. Before that time they are considered "infants" or "little children" and are not required to be baptized. They are considered "alive in Christ" and are "whole" (Moro. 8:8–12; JST Matt. 18:10–11).

Although children, with all the rest of mankind, feel the mortal "effects" of Adam's transgression, they (and all others) do not have any mystical stain of original sin upon them. Adults must have their own personal sins remitted by repentance and baptism (John 3:5; Acts 2:38; Moses 6:57–62), but "the Son of God hath atoned for original guilt, wherein the sins of the parents [both Adam's and their mortal parents'] cannot be answered upon the heads of the children, for they are whole from the foundation of the world" (Moses 6:54).

The prophet Mormon taught: "Listen to the words of Christ; . . . the curse of Adam is taken from them in me, that it hath no power over them. . . . It is solemn mockery before God, that ye should baptize little children" (Moro. 8:8–9). The Lord instructed Joseph Smith that "little children are redeemed from the foundation of the world through mine Only Begotten; wherefore, they cannot sin, for power is not given unto Satan to tempt little children, until they begin to become accountable before me" (D&C 29:46–47).

This unconditional benefit of Christ's atonement saves all little children regardless of race, color, or nationality, for "all children are alike unto me" (Moro. 8:17). They all begin their mortal lives pure and innocent (D&C 93:38), and "little children also have eternal life" (Mosiah 15:25).

If they die while in this state of innocence and purity, they return to that God who gave them life, saved, and fit for his company. They are in a "blessed" condition, for God's "judgment is just; and the infant perisheth not that dieth in his infancy" (Mosiah 3:16, 18). The Prophet Joseph Smith saw in vision "that all children who die before they arrive at the years of accountability are saved in the celestial kingdom of heaven" (D&C 137:10; *TPJS,* p. 200).

All that is said of infants and little children applies also to those who may be adults in physical body but are not accountable mentally (D&C 29:49–50).

Concepts outlined in scripture and by the prophets clearly demonstrate the marvelous uniting of the laws of justice and mercy because of the Atonement: none are eternally disadvantaged by non-

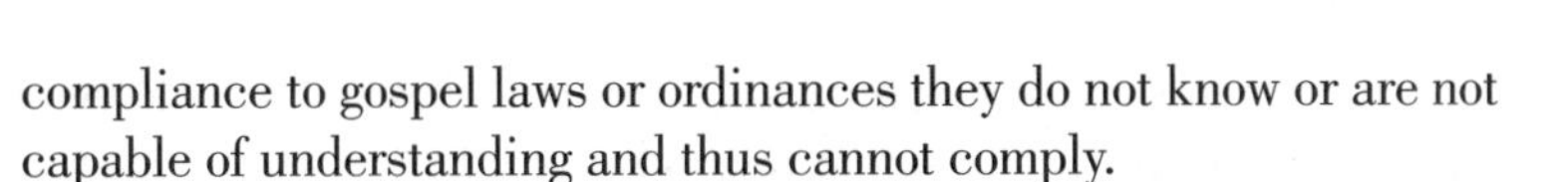

compliance to gospel laws or ordinances they do not know or are not capable of understanding and thus cannot comply.

CALVIN P. RUDD

COMMANDMENTS

Latter-day Saints believe that commandments are divine directives for righteous living; bring happiness and spiritual and temporal blessings; and are part of God's way to redeem his children and endow them with ETERNAL LIFE. Therefore, commandments provide not only a test of faith, obedience, and love for God and Jesus Christ but also an opportunity to experience love from God and joy both in this life and in the life to come. Commandments are received by REVELATION directly from deity or through his prophets. Written accounts of such revelations are contained in the scriptures, which include the Bible, the Book of Mormon, the Doctrine and Covenants, and the Pearl of Great Price.

At the organization of the Church on April 6, 1830, Joseph Smith was designated a seer, translator, prophet, apostle, and elder. On that occasion, the Lord said to the Church, "Thou shalt give heed unto all [Joseph Smith's] words and commandments which he shall give unto you as he receiveth them, walking in all holiness before me; for his word ye shall receive, as if from mine own mouth, in all patience and faith" (D&C 21:4–5; cf. D&C 1:37–38; 5:10; 68:34). Based upon these admonitions, members of the Church accept righteous instruction from those authorized by God as commandments binding upon the Church and upon individuals.

To the Church in 1831 the Lord restated the "first and great" commandment (cf. Matt. 22:37–38): "Wherefore, I give unto them a commandment, saying thus: Thou shalt love the Lord thy God with all thy heart, with all thy might, mind, and strength; and in the name of Jesus Christ thou shalt serve him" (D&C 59:5). This reiteration was followed by the previously established divine injunctions not to steal, commit adultery, or kill (D&C 59:6).

In the Doctrine and Covenants, section 42, which the Lord identified as the "law of the Church" (D&C 42:2, 59), verses 19–27 reaffirm many admonitions from the ten commandments. These basic commandments have been reiterated in successive DISPENSATIONS, or eras, in essentially the same form (Ex. 20:3–17; Deut. 5:6–21; Mosiah 12:34–36; D&C 42:19–27; cf. Matt. 5:17–48).

In Old Testament times, because the prohibition of certain outward acts was emphasized, the consequences of disobedience were seemingly stressed more than spiritual and physical redemption through obedience. With a different emphasis the New Testament and the Book of Mormon accentuate the purifying process of obedience. Christ made it clear that the commandments were to include not only the deeds of men and women but also their thoughts and motives. In the Sermon on the Mount, he contrasted the old law and the new. For instance, to look upon a woman with lust in one's heart was defined as a type of adultery (Matt. 5:28). To become angry with neighbors placed one in danger of judgment (Matt. 5:21–22). Rather than seeking vengeance and "an eye for an eye," Jesus' followers were to turn the other cheek and go the extra mile (Matt. 5:38–42). To sum up the new law, Christ said, "Ye have heard that it hath been said, Thou shall love thy neighbour, and hate thine enemy. But I say unto you, love your enemies, bless them that curse you, do good to them that hate you, and pray for them which despitefully use you, and persecute you; . . . Be ye therefore perfect, even as your Father which is in heaven is perfect" (Matt. 5:43–44, 48; cf. 3 Ne. 12:43–48).

To those listeners in the Western Hemisphere who survived the destruction of A.D. 34, the resurrected Christ explained the relationship between the law and the gospel: "Think not that I am come to destroy the law or the prophets. I am not come to destroy but to fulfil; for verily I say unto you, one jot nor one tittle hath not passed away from the law, but in me it hath all been fulfilled. And behold, I have given you the law and the commandments of my Father, that ye shall believe in me, and that ye shall repent of your sins, and come unto me with a broken heart and a contrite spirit" (3 Ne. 12:17–19). Christ's new law clearly requires that not only outward acts but also inner thoughts and feelings conform to the spirit of the law (cf. Alma 12:12–14; D&C 88:109).

In the Church today, the Lord has emphasized that his commandments include the responsibility of self-direction: "Behold, it is not meet that I should command in all things; for he that is compelled in all things, the same is a slothful and not a wise servant; wherefore he receiveth no reward. Verily I say, men should be anxiously engaged in a good cause, and do many things of their own free will, and bring to pass much righteousness; for the power is in them, wherein they are agents unto themselves" (D&C 58:26–28). When the "law of the Church" was received in 1831 (D&C 42), this individual responsibility was also stressed: "Thou shalt love thy wife with all thy heart" (42:22), and "Thou shalt not speak evil of thy neighbor, nor do him any harm" (42:27). Later, the Lord said, "Thou shalt not steal; neither commit adultery, nor kill, nor do anything like unto it" (D&C 59:6). It is apparent that God requires an awareness of one's AGENCY and in effect grants each the power to direct oneself. As one lives in accord with the commandments and thereby becomes more sensitive to the promptings of the HOLY GHOST, outward observances become less important and the perfection of one's thoughts and motives comes to occupy one's attention.

Thus is it that Latter-day Saints find fulfillment and happiness in obedience not only to specific commandments such as the Word of Wisdom (D&C 89) and the law of tithing (D&C 119) but also to the counsel from inspired leaders given in Church conferences and in approved written sources, such as official Church publications.

BIBLIOGRAPHY

Richards, Stephen L. "Keep the Commandments." *IE* 52 (May 1949):273, 345–48.
Sill, Sterling W. "Keep the Commandments." *Ensign* 3 (Jan. 1973):82–83.

DIX S. COONS

COMMUNION

Communion refers to partaking of the Lord's Supper. The more common term among members of The Church of Jesus Christ of Latter-day Saints is sacrament (D&C 59:9). *Eucharistia* is the Greek term that meant "thanksgiving" among early Christians.

Partaking of the sacrament is the central act of worship and COVENANT renewal and resembles the simple commemorative meal described in the New Testament (cf. Matt. 26:26–28; Mark 14:22–24; Luke 22:19–20; Acts 2:42, 46). Postbiblical doctrines of transubstantiation (real presence) and of a "mere sign" are absent from the LDS teachings. All members of the Church, including unbaptized children, are encouraged to partake of the bread and water as emblems in remembrance of the body and blood of Jesus Christ (see D&C 27). The communion sought is a communion of spirit as envisioned in the sacrament prayers (Moro. 4–5; 3 Ne. 18; D&C 20:77, 79).

PAUL B. PIXTON

CONDESCENSION OF GOD

The Book of Mormon prophet Nephi$_1$ (c. 600 B.C.) was asked by an angel, "Knowest thou the condescension of God?" (1 Ne. 11:16). Nephi was then shown in a vision a virgin who was to become "the mother of the Son of God, after the manner of the flesh" (verse 18). He next beheld the virgin with a child whom the angel identified as "the Lamb of God, yea, even the Son of the Eternal Father" (11:21). Then Nephi understood that the condescension of God is the ultimate manifestation of God's love through Jesus Christ (11:20–22). Such condescension denotes, first, the love of GOD THE FATHER, who deigned to sire a son, born of a mortal woman, and then allow this Son to suffer temptations and pain (Mosiah 3:5–7), "be judged of the world," and be "slain for the sins of the world" (1 Ne. 11:32–33). Second, it signifies the love and willingness of God the Son (Jesus Christ) to die for mankind.

The word "condescension" implies "voluntary descent," "submission," and "performing acts which strict justice does not require." This definition is particularly applicable to Jesus in the portrayal of him by prophets who lived before his birth and who affirmed: "God himself shall come down" to make an atonement (Mosiah 15:1); "the God of Abraham, and of Isaac, and the God of Jacob, yieldeth himself . . . into the hands of wicked men" (1 Ne. 19:10); "the great Creator . . . suffereth himself to become subject unto man in the flesh" (2 Ne. 9:5); and "he offereth himself a sacrifice for sin" (2 Ne. 2:7). "The Lord Omnipotent," said King Benjamin, "shall come down from heaven among the children of men, and shall dwell in a tabernacle of clay" (Mosiah 3:5).

In fulfillment of these prophecies, Jesus descended from the realms of glory for the purposes of experiencing mortal infirmities that he might have mercy and compassion according to the flesh and of taking upon himself the sins, transgressions, pains, and sicknesses of men in order to satisfy the demands of justice and gain victory over death, thereby redeeming his people (Mosiah 15:8–9; Alma 7:11–13). Christ's selfless sacrifice merits profound gratitude and endearing love from all who are recipients of his supernal offering.

BIBLIOGRAPHY

McConkie, Bruce R. "Behold the Condescension of God." *New Era* 14 (Dec. 1984):34–39.

BYRON R. MERRILL

CONFESSION OF SINS

Confession of sins is a necessary beginning step in the process of repenting and gaining forgiveness. It is a test of true repentance: "By this ye may know if a man repenteth of his sins—behold, he will confess them and forsake them" (D&C 58:43).

The need for repentance has existed from the time of Adam. The Lord instructed Adam: "Wherefore teach it unto your children, that all men, everywhere, must repent, or they can in nowise inherit the Kingdom of God, for no unclean thing can dwell there, or dwell in his presence" (Moses 6:57). The Bible states that "if we say that we have no sin, we deceive ourselves, and the truth is not in us" (1 Jn. 1:8). There are two categories of sin, those of commission and those of omission: "All unrighteousness is sin" (1 Jn. 5:17), and "To him that knoweth to do good, and doeth it not, to him it is sin" (James 4:17). Except for Jesus Christ, everyone who has lived past early childhood has sinned (1 Jn. 3:5; 2 Cor. 5:21).

At least three confessions may need to be made to help the sinner repent: To the Lord, to proper ecclesiastical officers, and to the injured party. Latter-day Saint doctrine holds that all must confess their sins to the Lord, from whom alone ultimate forgiveness can come. In addition, major sins (such as adultery, fornication, robbery, embezzlement, fraud, false swearing, and comparable transgressions), which may have a bearing upon Church membership, must be confessed to ecclesiastical officers such as bishops. Church officers are counseled to respond to confessions with confidentiality and understanding, and also to encourage members to seek the Lord's forgiveness, forsake transgression, and make restitution. Transgressors are taught to make proper reconciliation with and restitution to those they have injured. Effective confession requires a "broken heart and contrite spirit" (D&C 59:8) and a willingness to humble oneself and do all that is required for complete forgiveness.

Transgressions of lesser gravity that have offended others, such as marital or social differences, minor outbursts of anger, petty disagreements, and the like, are to be confessed to the injured party often resolving the matter without involving ecclesiastical authority. Public confession is not required unless the transgression has been against the public (D&C 42:88–93).

The Church has no set time or stated formula as to when confession takes place. Periodic interviews with ecclesiastical officers may be suitable occasions, or a special appointment can be made.

Confession helps lift the burden and leads toward peace, freedom, and happiness. After warning his hearers of excruciating pain and punishments that follow unrepented sins, the Lord said: "Confess your sins, lest you suffer these punishments" (D&C 19:20). Repentant persons find substantial psychological as well as spiritual strength in proper confession.

BIBLIOGRAPHY

Kimball, Spencer W. *The Miracle of Forgiveness,* pp. 177–89. Salt Lake City, 1989.

DONG SULL CHOI

CONFIRMATION

Confirmation in The Church of Jesus Christ of Latter-day Saints is a sacred ordinance essential for salvation. This ordinance follows baptism by immersion for the remission of sins and is efficacious only through faith in the Lord Jesus Christ and repentance. It is administered by the laying on of hands by men having authority, one of whom performs the ordinance and blesses the candidate. By this process one becomes a member of the Church and is given the gift of the Holy Ghost (Acts 2:37–38; 19:1–7). Baptism and confirmation are administered to persons at least eight years of age, the age of ACCOUNTABILITY (D&C 68:25–27).

The scriptures attest to the administering of the ordinance of confirmation in New Testament times. When Peter and John went to Samaria and found certain disciples who had received John's baptism in water, they "laid their hands on them, and they received the Holy Ghost" (Acts 8:17; see also verses 14–22).

Confirmation may be performed only by those holding the Melchizedek Priesthood. The Book of Mormon records that Jesus "touched with his hand the disciples whom he had chosen, one by one, even until he had touched them all, and spake unto them as he touched them. [Thereby] he gave them power to give the Holy Ghost" (3 Ne. 18:36–37; Moro. 2:1–3). The Doctrine and Covenants specifies: "And whoso having faith you shall confirm in my church, by the laying on of the hands, and I will bestow the gift of the Holy Ghost upon them" (D&C 33:15).

The ordinance of confirmation is usually performed at a baptismal service or fast and testimony meeting. One or more bearers of the Melchizedek Priesthood lay their hands upon the head of the newly baptized person, and the one who is "voice," calling the person by name, says words to this effect: "In the name of Jesus Christ, and by the authority of the holy Melchizedek Priesthood, I confirm you a member of The Church of Jesus Christ of Latter-day Saints and say unto you, 'receive the Holy Ghost.'" Words of blessing follow as the Spirit of the Lord may dictate, invoking divine guidance, comfort, admonition, instruction, or promise. The initiates are often reminded that through this gift they will discern right from wrong and that the Spirit will be, as it were, a lamp to their feet.

The receiving of the gift of the Holy Ghost may or may not be apparent immediately, although the *right* to receive this gift is conferred at confirmation. The admonition to receive the Holy Ghost is interpreted to include living in a receptive way for the enlightenment of the Spirit. Joseph Smith taught, "No man can receive the Holy Ghost without receiving revelations. The Holy Ghost is a revelator" (*TPJS*, p. 328). One is admonished likewise to seek earnestly for spiritual gifts (1 Cor.

12:1–11, 31; D&C 46:9–26) and the "fruits of the Spirit," including love, joy, peace, and longsuffering (Gal. 5; Moro. 7:45–48).

The scriptures sometimes refer to the sanctifying influence of the Holy Ghost as the "baptism of fire" (Matt. 3:11; 3 Ne. 19:13; Morm. 7:10). Confirmation begins that process. It is seen as a lifetime quest formally renewed each Sabbath in the partaking of the sacrament, whose prayers end with the plea that those who have taken upon themselves the name of Jesus Christ "may always have his Spirit to be with them" (Moro. 4:3).

Once individuals have been confirmed as members of the Church and have received the gift of the Holy Ghost, they may retain this gift by maintaining a state of worthiness with corrections as needed, through an ongoing process of repentance and discipleship.

BIBLIOGRAPHY
Talmage, James E. *AF,* pp. 156–57. Salt Lake City, 1968.

RULON G. CRAVEN

CONTENTION

Ranging from hostile words spoken at home to international conflicts, contention is so prevalent in the world that people tend to think of it as normal, inevitable, and perhaps even necessary. In the Book of Mormon, however, Jesus states, "He that hath the spirit of contention is not of me, but is of the devil, who is the father of contention, and he stirreth up the hearts of men to contend with anger, one with another" (3 Ne. 11:29). Whether at home, at church, in business, or in the community, "such things should be done away" (3 Ne. 11:30). This is fundamental to the teachings of Jesus Christ.

Latter-day Saints place great value on directing their energy in positive ways: "Use boldness, but not overbearance; and also see that ye bridle all your passions, that ye may be filled with love" (Alma 38:12). Thus, scriptures admonish the faithful to "contend for the faith" (Jude 1:3; 1 Thes. 2:2), but not to the point of quarreling or arguing. Contention is especially detrimental at home (Mosiah 4:14) and over doctrine (1 Cor. 11:16; 3 Ne. 11:28).

Jesus taught not only that contention should cease, but anger too, along with derision, contempt, and scorn. Having such feelings places a person in danger of the judgments of the Church and of God (see Matt. 5:22; see also 3 Ne. 12:22, where the phrase "without a cause" is absent).

When people get into difficulties and disagreements with one another, the scriptures furnish wise counsel. If a person feels bad feelings, or discovers that someone has bad feelings against him or her, it is that person's responsibility to go "quickly" and be reconciled (3 Ne. 12:23–25). Implicit in this injunction is the recognition that "we are members one of another" (Eph. 4:25). A troubled relationship is shared by all persons involved and is not just the responsibility of the one who feels hurt or angry. The nature of the reconciliation depends upon the specifics of each situation. Rather than relying on human understanding or formulaic solutions, the Saints are taught to seek divine counsel and to trust the direction of the Lord, the reconciler of all (Prov. 3:5–6; D&C 112:10).

Standing in the way of most solutions to contention is pride: "Only by pride cometh contention" (Prov. 13:10). "The central feature of pride," declared Ezra Taft Benson, "is enmity—enmity toward God and . . . [toward] our fellowmen." Underlying the solution to contention must be the desire for harmony between people which can come only as a person "yields to the enticings of the Holy Spirit . . . and becometh a saint through the atonement of Christ the Lord" (Mosiah 3:19). Atonement and reconciliation with God allow and evoke forgiveness and reconciliation among people.

BIBLIOGRAPHY

Ashton, Marvin J. "No Time for Contention." *Ensign* 8 (May 1978):7–9.

Benson, Ezra T. "Beware of Pride." *Ensign* 19 (May 1989):4–7.

Thornock, A. Lavar. "Contention—and How to Eliminate It." *Ensign* 10 (Aug. 1980):11–15.

CELIA HOKANSON

CONVERSION

From its beginnings to the present day, the Church has had a strong missionary orientation. It teaches that conversion is essentially a process of REPENTANCE and personal spiritual experience (*see* TESTIMONY).

THE NATURE OF CONVERSION. A number of theories have been advanced by sociologists to explain why people are likely to convert to another religious denomination. Glenn M. Vernon indicated that conversion involves several subprocesses, which must be accounted for, including (1) the manner in which the convert becomes aware of the group possessing the ideology; (2) the acceptance of new religious definitions; and (3) the integration of the new convert into the group. John Lofland and Rodney Stark proposed that conversion is a problem-solving process in which the individual uses organizational facilities, programs, and ideologies to resolve various life problems. More recently, David A. Snow, Louis A. Zurcher, and Sheldon Ekland-Olson have emphasized structural proximity, availability, and affective interaction with members of the new denomination as the most powerful influences in determining who will join. Roger A. Straus has proposed that religious conversion is an active accomplishment by the person who converts. Straus thinks that previous theories focus too heavily on the idea that conversion is something which happens to a person as a result of circumstances external to himself. Similarly, C. David Gartrell and Zane K. Shannon propose that conversion should be characterized as a rational choice based on the recruit's evaluation of the social and cognitive outcomes of converting or not converting.

Recovery from crisis, social proximity to members of the Church, and personal problem solving are certainly involved to some extent in at least some conversions. However, research about people who have converted to many churches (Snow and Phillips; Heirich) including The Church of Jesus Christ of Latter-day Saints (Seggar and Kunz), has failed to provide much support for the problem-solving theory of Lofland and Stark. Research by David A. Snow and Cynthia L. Phillips and by Max Heirich provides more evidence of the influence of social networks in conversion.

Most scientific theories, however, lack any significant reference to the influence of the HOLY SPIRIT in conversion, which is the dominant element in the Latter-day Saint understanding of conversion. The visitation of Jesus Christ to Paul on the road to Damascus (Acts 9:1–9) does not fit into any secular theoretical categories. Paul was not seeking a new faith to solve problems in his life. He did not begin to serve

Christ in order to be accepted by his friends. He persecuted Christians because he thought they had fallen away from the true faith. As a religious man, he recognized the voice of God when it spoke to him.

Similar conversion stories are told in the Book of Mormon. For example, as $Alma_2$ and the sons of King $Mosiah_2$ were going about teaching that the religion of their fathers was not true, they were stopped by the angel of the Lord, who asked why they persecuted the believers. $Alma_2$ was struck dumb and fell to the ground unable to move. While his father and others fasted and prayed in his behalf for two days and two nights, $Alma_2$ suffered excruciating pains and torment and finally called upon Jesus Christ for mercy to take away his sins. Immediately, the pain left and his soul was filled with exquisite joy (Alma 36:6–22). Alma arose and proclaimed that he had been reborn through the spirit of the Lord. Alma and the sons of Mosiah spent the rest of their lives preaching of Christ and doing many good works (Mosiah 27:8–31; cf. the spiritual rebirth of the people of Zarahemla at the time of King Benjamin in Mosiah 4–5).

Most conversions are not as dramatic as those of Paul and $Alma_2$ and the sons of Mosiah. The conversion of $Alma_1$ is closer to the kind experienced by most people who join the Church (Mosiah 17:2–4; 18:1). When Abinadi called him and the other priests of the wicked king Noah to repentance, $Alma_1$ knew in his heart that Abinadi spoke the truth. He repented of his sins and began to keep the commandments, with which he was already basically familiar. This wrought a significant change in his life.

From these and other scriptural accounts of the conversion process, it is evident that conversion "implies not merely mental acceptance of Jesus and his teaching but also a motivating faith in him and his gospel—a faith which works a transformation, an actual *change* in one's understanding of life's meaning and in his allegiance to God—in interest, in thought, and in conduct" (Romney, p. 1065). Conversion involves a newness of life, which is effected by receiving divine forgiveness that remits sins (*see* BORN OF GOD). It is characterized by a determination to do good continually, forsaking all sins, and by the healing of the soul by the power of the Holy Spirit, being filled with peace and joy (cf. Romney, p. 1066).

THE PROCESS OF CONVERSION TO THE CHURCH OF JESUS CHRIST OF LATTER-DAY SAINTS. The three subprocesses proposed by Vernon fit quite well the three most obvious aspects of conversion to the Church. The first is "the manner in which the convert becomes aware of the group possessing the ideology." This corresponds to what is referred to in LDS missionary circles as "finding." People come into contact with missionaries in many ways. The most effective source is referral by current Church members who invite friends or family relatives to meet with the missionaries to be taught about the gospel. A second way is for missionaries to knock on doors to invite people to learn about the Church. They also may talk with people they meet on the street or in any other form of normal social contact. Missionaries occasionally set up booths at fairs or expositions. The Church has advertised through the broadcast and print media, offering Church literature. It also operates several visitors centers, usually associated with a Church temple or historical site. Two of the best known are Temple Square in Salt Lake City, Utah, and at historic Nauvoo, Illinois. All these visitors centers offer interested people the opportunity to accept teaching visits by missionaries.

The second of Vernon's subprocesses—acceptance of new religious definitions—corresponds to the second major missionary activity, teaching. Missionaries teach the basic principles of God's plan of salvation. They invite those they teach to learn more by studying the Bible and the Book of Mormon on their own. They encourage, inform, teach, and testify. Study is an important part of the conversion process, for the mind plays a role as the investigator learns to understand and ponder the wisdom, logic, and ethic of gospel principles. As B. H. Roberts once stated, "It is frequently the case that a proper setting-forth of a subject makes its truth self-evident. . . . To be known, the truth must be stated and the clearer and more complete the statement is, the better opportunity will the Holy Spirit have for testifying to the souls of men that the work is true" (Vol. 2, pp. vi-vii).

Prospective converts are invited to seek through prayer a spiritual witness from the Holy Ghost to let them know the truth. As Roberts stated regarding the Book of Mormon, "[The Holy Ghost] must ever be the chief source of evidence for the truth of the Book of Mormon. All other evidence is secondary to this, the primary and infallible. No arrangement of evidence, however skillfully ordered; no argument, however adroitly made, can ever take its place" (pp. vi–vii). A quotation from the Book of Mormon is generally used to invite the prospective convert to seek this spiritual manifestation of the truthfulness of the Book of Mormon and of the gospel message: "And when ye shall receive these things, I would exhort you that ye would ask God, the Eternal Father, in the name of Christ, if these things are not true; and if ye shall ask with a sincere heart, with real intent, having faith in Christ, he will manifest the truth of it unto you, by the power of the Holy Ghost" (Moro. 10:4).

Most converts to the Church do not seem to have personal characteristics that predispose them to conversion. While those who begin looking into the Church tend to be younger than the average population and tend somewhat more often to be women, these factors do not predict who will ultimately accept BAPTISM. Those who seek baptism do not tend to have more personal problems than those who do not, nor do they differ significantly from others in personality traits or personal dispositions.

Conversion to the Church is usually not precipitous. The process begins with the first signs of interest, and may continue for many years, even after baptism. It is not simply a matter of accepting and believing the teachings of the Church. Many who do accept baptism indicate that they do not fully understand the teachings, but that they have come to feel that accepting baptism is the right thing to do. Most of them achieve a more complete understanding and acceptance of Church doctrine as they become integrated into membership. Such integration is the third process mentioned by Vernon.

Becoming a member of the Church has broader implications than simply adopting a new set of religious beliefs. For many new members it means adopting a new lifestyle quite different from the one to which they were accustomed. For nearly all new members, it also means that they become part of a new social network of friends and acquaintances. In some cases, the new Church member is rejected and ostracized by family and former friends. This social transition is made easier if the new convert has previously developed friends and acquaintances among members of the Church.

MISSIONARY WORK IN THE CHURCH. Those who have been converted usually want to share their newfound understanding with others (cf. Perry, pp. 16–18). Paul, Alma_1, and Alma_2 passionately taught the truth of Christ's saving mission throughout the remainder of their lives following their conversions. To the convert who loves people, there is a balance to be achieved between having genuine tolerance for the beliefs of others and fulfilling the desire and obligation to share with them the joy of conversion. The major Jewish and Christian religions have gone through phases when the proselytizing spirit was dominant and other periods when the desire to proselytize was restrained (Marty and Greenspahn).

The Church of Jesus Christ of Latter-day Saints has actively proselytized from its beginnings. Its leaders and members have accepted a mandate to proclaim the restored gospel to "every nation, and kindred, and tongue, and people" (Rev. 14:6; D&C 133:37), to all who will listen. Soon after the formal organization of the Church, Samuel Smith, a brother of Joseph Smith, traveled from place to place offering the Book of Mormon to any who would receive it. Missionaries were soon bringing in converts from the United States, Canada, England, Scandinavia, and Western Europe.

After the main body of members moved to the Intermountain West, the missionary work continued. Increasingly the missionary responsibility was given to young men who had not yet married. Their converts continued to migrate to the American West until well into the twentieth century, in spite of the fact that around the turn of the century Church leaders began to encourage converts to remain where they were and to build up the Church in their homelands.

The Church growth rate since 1860 has never been less than 30 percent for any ten-year period. Since 1950, Church growth has accelerated, advancing to more than 50 percent in each ten-year period from 1950 to 1980 (Cowan).

In recent years the Church has become less and less a church confined to the western United States. As late as 1960, more than half of Church members were located in the Intermountain West, with only 10 percent outside the United States. In 1980, nearly one-third of Church members lived outside the United States, with only about 40 percent in the Intermountain West. In 1989 less than one convert in four was an American citizen.

By far the greatest convert growth outside the United States has been in Latin America, particularly in Mexico, Brazil, Chile, Peru, and Argentina. There has also been considerable increase in the number of baptisms in Asia and the Philippines. In 1979 there were three missions in the Philippines; this increased to twelve by 1990, and the number of convert baptisms per year tripled in that same period. New missions were opened in eastern Europe in 1989 and 1990. In 1990 the Church had more than 40,000 full-time missionaries in 257 missions around the world.

Latter-day Saints believe, as stated by President Marion G. Romney: it may be that "relatively few among the billions of earth's inhabitants will be converted. Nevertheless . . . there is no other means by which the sin-sick souls of men can be healed or for a troubled world to find peace" (p. 1067).

BIBLIOGRAPHY

Burton, Theodore M. "Convince or Convert?" In *BYU Speeches of the Year.* Provo, Utah, 1964.

Cowan, Richard O. *The Church in the Twentieth Century.* Salt Lake City, 1985.

Gartrell, C. David, and Zane K. Shannon. "Contacts, Cognitions, and Conversion: A Rational Choice Approach." *Review of Religious Research* 27 (Sept. 1985):32–48.

Heirich, Max. "Change of Heart: A Test of Some Widely Held Theories About Religious Conversion." *American Journal of Sociology* 83 (Nov. 1977):653–80.

Lofland, John, and Rodney Stark. "Becoming a World-Saver: A Theory of Conversion to a Deviant Perspective." *American Sociological Review* 30 (1965):862–75.

Marty, Martin E., and Frederick E. Greenspahn, eds. *Pushing the Faith: Proselytism and Civility in a Pluralistic World.* New York, 1988.

Perry, L. Tom. "When Thou Art Converted, Strengthen Thy Brethren," *Ensign* 4 (Nov. 1974):16–18.

Roberts, B. H. *New Witnesses for God,* Vol. 2, pp. vi–vii. Salt Lake City, 1926.

Romney, Marion G. "Conversion." *IE* 66 (1963):1065–67.

Seggar, John, and Phillip Kunz. "Conversion: Evaluation of a Step-like Process for Problem-solving." *Review of Religious Research* 13 (Spring, 1972):178–84.

Snow, David A., and Cynthia L. Phillips. "The Lofland-Stark Conversion Model: A Critical Reassessment." *Social Problems* 27 (Apr. 1980):430–47.

Snow, David A.; Louis A. Zurcher, Jr.; and Sheldon Ekland-Olson. "Social Networks and Social Movements: A Microstructural Approach to Differential Recruitment." *American Sociological Review* 45 (Oct. 1980):787–801.

Straus, Roger A. "Religious Conversion as a Personal and Collective Accomplishment." *Sociological Analysis* 40 (Summer, 1979):158–65.

Vernon, Glenn M. *Sociology of Religion,* pp. 101–112. New York, 1962.

KAY H. SMITH

COUNCIL IN HEAVEN

The Council in Heaven, sometimes called the Grand Council, refers to a meeting of God the Father with his spirit sons and daughters to discuss the terms and conditions by which these spirits could come to earth as physical beings. The terms "Council in Heaven" and "Grand Council" do not appear in the scriptures, but are used by the Prophet Joseph Smith in referring to these premortal activities, allusions to which are found in many scriptures (Job 38:4–7; Jer. 1:5; Rev. 12:3–7; Alma 13:3–9; D&C 29:36–38; 76:25–29; Moses 4:1–4; Abr. 3:23–28; cf. *TPJS,* pp. 348–49, 357, 365; *T&S* 4 [Feb. 1, 1843]:82).

One purpose of the heavenly council was to allow the spirits the opportunity to accept or reject the Father's PLAN OF SALVATION, which proposed that an earth be created whereon his spirit children could dwell, each in a PHYSICAL BODY. Such a life would serve as a probationary state "to see if they [would] do all things whatsoever the Lord their God shall command them" (Abr. 3:25). The spirits of all mankind were free to accept or reject the Father's plan but they were also responsible for their choice. The Creation, the Fall, mortality, the Atonement, the Resurrection, and the final judgment were contemplated and explained in the council (*TPJS,* p. 220, 348–50; *MD,* pp. 163–64; *see also* FIRST ESTATE). The plan anticipated mistakes from inexperience and sin and provided remedies. Many spirits were foreordained to specific roles and missions during their mortal experience, conditional upon their willingness and faithfulness in the premortal sphere and their promised continued faithfulness upon the earth. The Prophet Joseph Smith explained, "Every man who has a calling to minister to the inhabitants of the world was ordained to that very purpose in the Grand Council of heaven before this world was. I suppose I was ordained to this very office in that Grand Council" (*TPJS,* p. 365; cf. 1 Pet. 1:20; Jer. 1:5; Abr. 3:22–23).

Although spoken of as a single council, there may have been multiple meetings where the gospel was taught and appointments were made. Jesus and the prophets were foreordained in the council. A redeemer was to perform a twofold mission in redeeming mankind from the physical and spiritual deaths brought about by the FALL OF ADAM and also in providing redemption, upon repentance, for sins committed by individuals. At a certain point in the council, the Father asked, "Whom shall I send [as the Redeemer]?" Jesus Christ, known then as the great I AM and as Jehovah, answered, "Here am I, send me," and agreed to follow the Father's plan (Moses 4:1–4; Abr. 3:27). As a counter-measure, Lucifer offered himself and an amendment to the Father's plan of saving mankind that would not respect their AGENCY. The substitute proposal was also designed to exalt Lucifer above the throne of God. The Father's response was, "I will send the first" (meaning Jehovah). Lucifer rebelled and became Satan, or "the devil." A division developed among the spirits, and no spirits were neutral (*DS* 1:65–66). There was war in heaven (Rev. 12:7–8), and the third of the hosts who followed Lucifer were cast out (Rev. 12:4; D&C 29:36). These rebellious spirits, along with Lucifer, were thrust down to the earth without physical bodies (Rev. 12:9; cf. Isa. 14:12–17). The Prophet Joseph Smith explained: "The contention in heaven was—Jesus said there would be certain souls that would not be saved; and the devil said he could save them all, and laid his plans before the grand council, who gave their vote in favor of Jesus Christ. So the devil rose up in rebellion against God, and was cast down, with all who put up their heads for him" (*TPJS*, p. 357). Heavenly Father and the faithful spirits in heaven wept over them (D&C 76:25–29). Satan and his followers are still at war with those spirits who have been born into mortality (Rev. 12:9; cf. "War in Heaven," p. 788).

BIBLIOGRAPHY

Bible Dictionary. "War in Heaven." In LDS Edition of the King James Version of the Bible, p. 788. Salt Lake City, 1977.

McConkie, Joseph F. "Premortal Existence, Foreordinations and Heavenly Councils." In *Apocryphal Writings and the Latter-day Saints*, ed. W. Griggs, pp. 173–98. Provo, Utah, 1986.

JOHN L. LUND

COVENANT ISRAEL, LATTER-DAY

God established a COVENANT with Abraham, reaffirming it with Isaac and Jacob and then with the children of Israel. In the LDS view, this covenant has been renewed repeatedly and then breached, largely because God's people, after receiving his COMMANDMENTS and promises, have fallen into apostasy and disbelief. Today, as prophesied anciently, this covenant has been restored through the Prophet Joseph Smith and is included in the NEW AND EVERLASTING COVENANT of the gospel (D&C 22:1; cf. Jer. 31:31–34; 32:36–40).

The term "Covenant Israel" refers to ancient Israel, to the New Testament era, and to modern times. Anciently God stated, "I will establish my covenant between me and thee [Abraham] and thy seed after thee . . . for an everlasting covenant, to be a God unto thee, and to thy seed" (Gen. 17:7). Yet this covenant was conditional. Those who would be "his people" had to prove themselves through obedience and faithful commitment to the laws and ordinances of the covenant (cf. Abr. 2:6–11). Later, Jehovah said through Moses, "If ye will obey my voice indeed, and keep my covenant, then ye shall be a peculiar treasure unto me above all people. . . . And ye shall be unto me a kingdom of priests, and an holy nation" (Ex. 19:5–6).

Because ancient Israel rejected God's word and thereby lost his promises, the prophet Hosea warned:

> The Lord hath a controversy with the inhabitants of the land, because there is no truth, nor mercy, nor knowledge of God in the land. By swearing, and lying, and killing, and stealing, and committing adultery, . . . my people are destroyed. . . . I will also reject thee, that thou shalt be no priest to me: seeing thou hast forgotten the law of thy God, I will also forget thy children [Hosea 4:1–6; cf. Amos 8:11–12; Isa. 24:1–6; Jer. 2:11–13].

In New Testament times, Jesus Christ lamented a similar apostasy: "O Jerusalem, Jerusalem, thou that killest the prophets, and stonest them which are sent unto thee, how often would I have gathered thy children together, even as a hen gathereth her chickens, . . . and ye would not!" (Matt. 23:37–38; cf. 3 Ne. 10:4–6). Covenant Israel was meant to be expanded in Old Testament times (Abr. 2:9–11; 1 Ne. 17:36–40), and again in the New Testament era, to include all followers of Christ, both literal descendants of Abraham and gentiles who became part of Abraham's lineage by adoption. "Know ye therefore that they which are of faith, the same are the children of Abraham. . . . For as many of you as have been baptized into Christ have put on Christ. There is neither Jew nor Greek, . . . for ye are all one in Christ Jesus. And if ye be Christ's, then are ye Abraham's seed, and heirs according to the promise" (Gal. 3:7, 27–29; cf. Rom. 4:12–13; Eph. 2:11–12).

The same doctrine applies today: Membership in latter-day covenant Israel, The Church of Jesus Christ of Latter-day Saints, is not limited to a certain lineage but is open to all who willingly accept and abide by its covenantal terms through the LAW OF ADOPTION. Latter-day Saints accept God's covenant with Abraham and his lineage, a covenant reestablished at the time of Joseph Smith (D&C 110:12). Known as the "new and everlasting covenant" (D&C 22:1; Jer. 31:31–34; 32:36–40), it is included in the fulness of the gospel of Jesus Christ. It is considered "new" in each age when it is given to God's people, yet it is "everlasting" because the conditions and promises never change. Further, covenant Israel implies a community willing to accept God's complete law, which is based in latter-day revelation of the same covenant that was revealed in the Old and New Testaments. This requires an acknowledgment that God has spoken to both ancient and latter-day prophets and continues to do so.

Covenants and accompanying ordinances of the gospel of Jesus Christ are the essence of religious life. LDS teaching holds that all of God's commandments are based in covenant. Thus the ordinances of BAPTISM, receiving the GIFT OF THE HOLY GHOST, and the sacrament, as well as keeping the Sabbath day holy and temple worship—including eternal marriage—embody covenants with promises, obligations, and opportunities for blessings. These covenants are mutual promises between God in heaven and men and women on earth. Those willing to abide by such agreements are considered part of covenant Israel, with all the attendant blessings and opportunities. Thus the Church teaches that any law or commandment from God to his children, that helps ensure their SALVATION and ETERNAL LIFE is part of the "everlasting covenant."

The Prophet Joseph Smith taught that "the ancients . . . obtained from God promises of such weight and glory, that our hearts are often filled with gratitude that we are even permitted to look upon them. . . . If we are the children of the Most High, . . . and embrace the same covenant that they embraced, and are faithful to the testimony of our Lord as they were, we can approach the Father in the name of Christ as they approached Him, and for ourselves obtain the same promises" (*TPJS*, pp. 65–66).

[*See also* Abrahamic Covenant.]

JAMES B. MAYFIELD

COVENANTS

The word "covenant" in the Bible is a translation of the Hebrew *berith* and of the Greek *diathēkē*. The Book of Mormon concept seems close to the Hebrew indication of any formalized relation between two parties, such as a bond, pact, or agreement. As such, the term is used for nonaggression pacts between nations (Gen. 26:26–31), a promise of landownership (Gen. 15:18–21), a bond for free slaves (Jer. 34:8–9), or an oath of secrecy (2 Kgs. 11:4). The Greek *diathēkē* is a more legalistic term, implying a formal will, a legal bequest (Gal. 3:17). In the New Testament the term is often translated as "testament," but clearly is used for the same kind of bond as "covenant" (cf. Heb. 7:22; 8:6; Anderson, p. 5). This legal aspect is also clear in the Doctrine and Covenants (e.g., D&C 132:7), where certain organizational issues are couched in covenantal terms (e.g., D&C 82:11–12). The English term "covenant," meaning "coming together," stresses the relational aspect. In other languages the terms used may have more legal connotations.

Members of The Church of Jesus Christ of Latter-day Saints speak of themselves as a "covenant people," both collectively and individually. Entering into righteous and authorized covenants with God is one of the most important aspects of their lives. They see their covenants as modern counterparts of covenant making in biblical times.

Most covenants mentioned in scripture are made by God with mankind, either with individuals or a group. In a group covenant, like that of ancient Israel or of the Nephites, the leader or king "cuts the covenant" (as it is said in Hebrew) for, and in behalf of, his people, who in turn affirm their entrance into the covenant by a collective oath or by REPENTANCE (for example, 2 Chr. 34:29–32). This covenant may be reaffirmed and reestablished, as occurs in King Benjamin's speech (Mosiah 1–6; *see* Ricks, 1984). When such covenants are established, the collective bond with God holds as long as people are obedient to the commandments stated or implied in the covenant. Yet a gradual shift of emphasis from collective toward individual covenant making is discernible from the Old to the New Testament. It is also within the Book of Mormon and in the teachings of the Church. Some tension between the association with the "elect" (Ps.

89:3–4; D&C 88:130–133) and the more general covenant for all mankind (Isa. 55:3) remains. Individual covenants, in any event, are essential in LDS doctrine and religion, both in sacred history and in present practice.

In covenant making, God takes the initiative with a conditional promise, specifying attainable blessings and setting the terms for people to receive them. Sometimes a sign is given to commemorate the pact, like the tables of the covenant (Deut. 9:9–11). Revelations (Jer. 11:1–5) and miracles (Deut. 5:1–6) sometimes accompany covenants. One enters the covenant, usually through a ritual, a visible sign. Blood sacrifices ("the blood of the covenant," Ex. 24:8), the "salt covenant" (Num. 18:19; 2 Chr. 13:5), the circumcision of boys (Acts 7:8), baptism (D&C 22:1; Mosiah 18:7–11), the sacrament (Heb. 8:6; 3 Ne. 18:1–14), the conferral of the priesthood with its "oath and covenant" (D&C 84:33–42), marriage (D&C 132) and other temple rites, all these revealed rituals are called sacraments or ordinances, which have been given as covenants. They serve as a signal that individuals enter into or reaffirm personal covenants with the Lord. As God is bound by his promises (D&C 82:10), covenant making has to be guided by revelation and performed through the authority of the priesthood. Otherwise, God is not truly made party to the accord and agreement. Since covenant rites are essential for man's salvation and EXALTATION, the role of the priesthood in administering these covenantal sacraments is crucial. Without priesthood authority, there are no everlasting covenants. Still, these overt covenant obligations are always directly related to the general commandment of loving God and one's neighbor, called the "covenant of the heart" (Heb. 10:16; Jer. 31:31–34; Isa. 55:3).

The Lord's covenants essentially cover the whole PLAN OF SALVATION. God's promise is to send a Savior for all humans, asking on their part for their obedience to the will of the Lord. Each covenant reflects aspects of the "fulness of his gospel" (D&C 133:57). Though various dispensations may have their specific focus, such as Israel's "covenant of works" and Paul's "covenant of grace," Latter-day Saints categorize all divine covenants under the unity of one gospel. As a consequence, all covenants are always new, everlasting, and continually renewed.

Latter-day Saints enter into an eternal covenant with God at baptism, wherein they promise to take upon them the name of Jesus Christ, to keep his commandments, to bear one another's burdens, to stand as a witness of God at all times, to repent, and to serve and remember Christ always (*see* BAPTISMAL COVENANT; Mosiah 18:8–10; D&C 20:37). They renew this covenant by partaking of the sacrament of the Lord's Supper. Other covenants involving obligations of faithfulness, magnifying one's calling, sacrifice, obedience, righteousness, chastity, and consecration are made when one is ordained to the Melchizedek Priesthood, when one receives the temple ENDOWMENT, and when a man and woman enter into eternal marriage.

Many commentaries stress the one-sidedness of scriptural covenants. Since the Lord's promises greatly exceed human obligations, the blessings of deity significantly overshadow the efforts demanded (see Mosiah 2:21), even though a notion of reciprocity is always present. Something is demanded in return, as a covenant is essentially two-sided; before anything else, it is a relation, the means by which God and man become reconciled in the atonement afforded to all by Jesus Christ.

A covenant is a special relationship with the Lord into which a person or a group may enter. The terms have been set by the Lord both for the rewards (blessings, salvation, exaltation) and the efforts demanded (obedience to rules and commandments). A covenant is fulfilled when people keep their promises and endure to the end in faith, with the Lord giving blessings during life, and salvation and exaltation upon completion.

A broken covenant results from a willful breach of promise, that is, transgression of commandments. By breaking this relationship, a person forfeits blessings. These can be restored in full only by repentance and reentering the covenant. Covenants comfort the righteous (Dan. 9:4) and lift the hearts of the oppressed (Ps. 74:20–21), but shame the unrepentant (Ezek. 16:60–63).

Latter-day Saints hold that the first personal covenants were made in PREMORTAL LIFE, later to be taken again on earth. In the sacred history of the earth, covenants have been made by God with Adam and Eve and with all the ancient patriarchs and prophets and their wives. For example, God made covenants of various kinds with Enoch; Abraham and Sarah; Moses; the kings of Israel and Judah, including David, Solomon, and Josiah (2 Chr. 34:29–32); and many of the prophets. Jesus Christ instituted the sacrament as a covenant establishing a personal relationship with his individual followers (Heb. 8:6), his blood replacing the old sacrificial "blood of the everlasting covenant" (Heb. 13:20). Through Joseph Smith, the everlasting covenants were established anew (*see* NEW AND EVERLASTING COVENANT; D&C 1:15, 22; 22:1; 132).

For each respective group of covenant people, this meaningful relation with the deity is also an identity marker, singling out people or a group from among their peers. Often outward signs are used: circumcision (Gen. 17:2–14), the Sabbath day (Ex. 31:12–17), endogamy or prohibitions on marriage outside the group (Ezra 10:3), greetings (D&C 88:131–133), and dietary proscriptions, such as the food taboos of Leviticus or the latter-day health code of the Word of Wisdom (D&C 89).

Among Christian churches historically, the focus on making covenants has risen since the Reformation. In John Calvin's Geneva the notion of covenant was crucial (Lillback, 1987), a tradition that was passed on to many Protestant denominations, including the Puritans (van Pohr, 1986). In early American ecclesiastical history, covenants were also crucial, and the New England Puritans clearly saw themselves as the covenant people of the Lord (Miller, 1966). This concept has remained important in American culture and is a vital and essential part of LDS religion.

BIBLIOGRAPHY

Anderson, Richard L. "Religious Validity: The Sacramental Covenants in 3 Nephi." In *By Study and Also by Faith,* ed. J. Lundquist and S. Ricks, Vol. 2, pp. 1–51. Salt Lake City, 1990.

Cooper, Rex E. *Promises Made to the Fathers: Mormon Covenant Organization.* Salt Lake City, 1990.

Lillback, P. A. *The Binding of God: Calvin's Role in the Development of Covenant Theology.* Ann Arbor, Mich., 1987.

Miller, P. *Life of the Mind in America from the Revolution to the Civil War.* London, 1966.

Pohr, J. van. *The Covenant of Grace in Puritan Thought.* AAR Studies in Religion 45. Atlanta, Georgia, 1986.

Ricks, Stephen D. "The Treaty/Covenant Pattern in King Benjamin's Address (Mosiah 1–6)." *BYU Studies* 24 (Spring 1984):151–62.

WOUTER VAN BEEK

CURSINGS

Cursings are the opposite of BLESSINGS and may be expressed as (1) the use of vulgar or profane language by people; (2) words or actions by God or his representatives expressing divine displeasure with or warning against wickedness; or (3) God's chastisement of mankind.

Cursing in the form of profane language employing names of deity literally "in vain" has been present in most societies. Since thought is expressed in language, vulgar and blasphemous language corrupts its user by establishing vulgar or profane thought patterns. The statement "Among the wicked, men shall lift up their voices and curse God and die" (D&C 45:32) illustrates both a cause and a consequence regarding profane language, with its effect on and relationship to spiritual life. Cursing that invokes the name of deity is a form of BLASPHEMY and, in biblical times, was punishable by stoning (Lev. 24:16). Cursing of parents was also cause for offenders to be put to death in ancient Israel (Ex. 21:17; Matt. 15:4).

Cursing may be the expression of divine displeasure, warning, or exclusion from God's blessing. Just as blessings are obtained by RIGHTEOUSNESS, cursings result from breaking God's law and failing to keep his commandments (Deut. 11:26–28; D&C 104:1–8; 124:48). Intelligent human beings are largely responsible for their own circumstances, and President Brigham Young said the most severe cursings come upon "those who know their Master's will, and do it not" (*JD* 1:248). Sinning against light and knowledge has more serious consequences than sinning in ignorance (see Mosiah 2:36–37; cf. Alma 32:19–20; 39:6). $Alma_2$ gives an example wherein the same land was simultaneously blessed for those who acted righteously and cursed for those who did not (Alma 45:16).

Curses may be pronounced by God, or they may be invoked by his authorized servants, as was the case with Moses (Deut. 27–30); Elijah (1 Kgs. 17:1; 21:20–24); Peter (Acts 5:1–10); Paul (Acts 13:9–12); and Joseph Smith (D&C 103:25; cf. 124:93). However, the Lord's earthly agents are sent forth primarily to bless and not to curse (Matt. 5:44; Rom. 12:14).

Not all curses have totally negative consequences. As God only does good, his cursings are for "the sake" of improving the person cursed (Gen. 3:17; Deut. 23:5), even though the immediate consequence may be extremely unpleasant. When there is need for correction, the Lord has instructed his servants to reprove "with sharpness," but afterward to show forth an "increase of love" (D&C 121:43).

Some cursings are given first as warnings rather than a more severe immediate chastisement (2 Ne. 1:21, 22); and, like blessings, they sometimes require a long time for their full consequences to be realized. After being invoked, cursings may often be lessened or lifted entirely by subsequent righteousness. Mormon describes an experience of the Lamanites: "And they began to be a very industrious people; yea, and they were friendly with the Nephites; therefore, they did open a correspondence with them, and the curse of God did no more follow them" (Alma 23:18).

Cursings may affect all temporal and spiritual aspects of our lives because all things are governed by law. Lands, crops, handiwork, employment, children, missionary endeavor, interpersonal relationships, and relationships with God are all subject to both cursing and blessing—depending upon individual and collective righteousness or lack of it.

SHERWIN W. HOWARD

D

DAMNATION

"Damnation" is a term derived from the Latin *damnum,* meaning "injury" and "loss," and often connotes deprivation of what should have been possessed. Just as there are varying degrees and types of SALVATION, coupled with ETERNAL PROGRESSION in some areas (D&C 76:96–98; 131:1–4), so are there varying degrees and types of damnation. In LDS doctrine, to be damned means to be stopped, blocked, or limited in one's progress. Individuals are damned whenever they are prevented from reaching their full potential as children of God. Damnation is falling short of what one might have enjoyed if one had received and been faithful to the whole law of the gospel. In this sense, all who do not achieve the highest degree of the CELESTIAL KINGDOM are damned, even though they are saved in some degree of glory. They are damned in the sense that they will not enjoy an eternal increase or the continuation of the family unit in eternity (D&C 132:4, 19). In this context, damnation does not necessarily refer to eternal suffering in hell with the devil, for loss of blessings is in itself a type of hell and damnation. LDS perspectives on this subject include biblical scriptures enriched and clarified by additional revelation; hence, damnation has a wider application than may seem apparent in modern usage (*see* DEGREES OF GLORY; EXALTATION; HEIRS).

In the scriptures, damnation usually refers to the judgment or condemnation that will be pronounced by Jesus Christ on the wicked at the end of the world (Matt. 25:41–46). "Damnation" is an English equivalent of the Hebrew *rasha,* which implies being wicked, impious, ungodly, or guilty, and the Greek *krino,* which implies being put under condemnation. While the word "damnation" appears regularly in the King James Version of the Bible, (i.e., in the New Testament) it is not found in several modern versions, which use words like "doom" or "condemnation" instead.

Many Jews and Christians reject the idea of damnation as an outmoded theological concept, but some Orthodox Jews and conservative Christians hold to a belief in final and eternal damnation. Conservative Christians generally believe that God himself will condemn unrepentant sinners based on justice as merited by the recipients (Matt. 12:41–42; John 12:48; Rom. 3:8). They hold, further, that Christ, the Redeemer, came to save rather than to condemn (John 3:17) and that he alone frees the individual from final damnation (Rom. 8:1–2).

Damnation comes as the result of not believing in the gospel (Mark 16:16), of not accepting additional light and knowledge (Alma 12:9–11), of believing in false doctrines (2 Pet. 2:1), of being slothful and having to be commanded in all things (D&C 58:26–29), and of refusing to humble oneself, repent, and live according to gospel principles. The Prophet Joseph Smith explained, "God had decreed that all who will not obey His voice shall not escape the damnation of hell. What is the damnation of hell? To go with that society who have not obeyed His commands" (*TPJS,* p. 198; cf. pp. 322–23).

Damnation also results from partaking of the Lord's sacrament unworthily (1 Cor. 11:29), taking pleasure in unrighteousness (2 Thes. 2:12), engaging in adulterous relationships (1 Tim. 5:11–12), rejecting the law of the Church (D&C 42:60), neglecting the covenant of eternal marriage (D&C 132:4), altering the holy word of God (Morm. 8:33), and rejecting Jesus Christ (D&C 49:5). If persons do these things and do not repent, they are left without the protection of the law of God and without the spiritual nourishment that they could have enjoyed, and as a result they suffer damnation.

Damnation is not to be equated with never-ending torment or punishment. An early revelation to Joseph Smith explains, "It is not written that there shall be no end to this torment, but it is written *endless torment.* Again, it is written *eternal damnation;* wherefore it is more express than other scriptures, that it might work upon the hearts of the children of men" (D&C 19:6–7; *see also* ENDLESS AND ETERNAL). President Brigham Young explained, "We believe that all will be damned who do not receive the gospel of Jesus Christ; but we do not believe that they will go into a lake which burns with brimstone and fire, and suffer unnamed and unheard of torments, inflicted by cruel and malicious devils to all eternity. The sectarian doctrine of final rewards and punishments is as strange to me as their bodiless, partless, and passionless God. Every man will receive according to the deeds done in the body, whether they be good or bad. All men, excepting those who sin against the Holy Ghost, who shed innocent blood or who consent thereto, will be saved in some kingdom; for in my father's house, says Jesus, are many mansions" (*JD* 11:125–26).

Ultimate and total damnation comes only to the devil and his angels, who rebelled in the FIRST ESTATE, and to the sons of perdition, who are damned eternally and denied entrance into any kingdom of glory hereafter (D&C 76:32–34). The sons of perdition are those guilty of unpardonable sin against the Holy Ghost (D&C 132:27; cf. Mark 3:29), which includes the willful denial of the "Only Begotten Son of the Father, having crucified him unto themselves and put him to an open shame" (D&C 76:35).

BIBLIOGRAPHY

Kimball, Spencer W. "Marriage and Divorce." In *1976 Speeches of the Year,* p. 154. Provo, Utah, 1977.

Lee, Harold B. "Spiritual Rebirth and Death." *IE* 50 (Nov. 1947):716, 752, 754.

Stuy, Brian, ed. Discourse by George Q. Cannon. In *Collected Discourses,* 3 vols.; Vol. 2, pp. 64–76. Sandy, Utah, 1987–1989.

RICHARD NEITZEL HOLZAPFEL

DEATH AND DYING

At death, the spirit and body separate and "the spirits of all men, whether they be good or evil, are taken home to that God who gave them life" (Alma 40:11; cf. Eccl. 12:7). Alma$_2$ describes how the spirits of the "righteous are received into a state of happiness, which is called paradise, a state of rest, a state of peace, where they shall rest from all their troubles and from all care, and sorrow" (Alma

40:12; *see* PARADISE; SPIRIT WORLD). In contrast, the wicked, who "chose evil works rather than good," suffer fear of the wrath of God (Alma 40:13; *see* SPIRIT PRISON). Both those who reside in paradise and those in the spirit prison await the RESURRECTION and the judgment of God (*see* JUDGMENT DAY, FINAL).

RESURRECTION FROM DEATH. Through the atonement of Christ, all mortals will be resurrected irrespective of personal righteousness. Their spirits will have their PHYSICAL BODIES restored to them, and thus there will be a permanent unity of the spirit with an immortal, incorruptible body (John 5:28–29; Alma 11:42–45). Except for the resurrection of Christ, "this flesh must have laid down to rot and to crumble to its mother earth, to rise no more," and the spirits of men would have become devils, subject to Satan for eternity (2 Ne. 9:7–9).

NATURE OF DEATH. The scriptures teach that death does not change one's personality (Alma 34:34). Individual identities are eternal (D&C 18:10; 93:29). Thus all those who have been obedient to God's commandments in any time of the world can look forward to reunions with loved ones and associations with ancestors and descendants. Latter-day Saints believe that death need not terminate personal awareness or interpersonal relationships. For the righteous, family ties can continue beyond death because of sealings in the temple. Thus, family members who have received the gospel in mortality conduct family history research and perform necessary vicarious ordinances in the temple for deceased family members. Many Latter-day Saints feel a closeness to ancestors from generations past because they have studied their lives, and some have served as proxies for them in temple ordinances (see Moses 6:45–46). Grieving parents know that children who die before reaching the age of ACCOUNTABILITY, and others such as the mentally disabled, receive eternal love and salvation through the grace of Christ and are restored to a completeness to continue in familial relationships (Moro. 8:17, 22; D&C 137:10).

Nevertheless, Latter-day Saints do not embrace death willingly, nor do they seek it. Suicide is condemned but judgment of it is left with the Lord (Ballard, pp. 6–9). Abortion also is considered a serious sin under most circumstances and can cause much sorrow.

The best preparation for death is to repent and live righteously.

Those who feel that their lives are in jeopardy with sickness may receive BLESSINGS from the elders of the Church, who, holding the priesthood of God, "shall pray for and lay their hands upon them in my name; and if they die they shall die unto me, and if they live they shall live unto me" (D&C 42:44). Those who face extreme suffering in a terminal illness may call upon the Lord for comfort or relief from pain, and rely upon him to prolong or shorten their days upon the earth. To allow a person who is terminally ill to pass away, rather than maintaining a vegetative existence through artificial systems of support, is not the spiritual equivalent of failing to save the life of a person facing death under other circumstances. The Lord is, however, the ultimate giver and taker of life.

To Latter-day Saints, as to all people, death can be tragic, unexpected, or even a blessed release from suffering. The loss of loved ones is an occasion for mourning. However, in LDS doctrine, death is also an occasion for hope, a birth into the next life, a step in the PLAN OF SALVATION that began in the premortal existence and leads, if one is righteous, to eternal life with God in the CELESTIAL KINGDOM. The grieving of the faithful is appropriately marked by sorrow and hope, not despair and depression. Yet the loss of a loved one is to be taken neither lightly nor coldly. Grief and love are compatible—if not essential—emotions of the faithful. And Latter-day Saints who face death themselves, while experiencing uncertainty and concern for those left behind, can find hope in the plan of salvation and the Lord's promise that "those that die in me shall not taste of death, for it shall be sweet unto them" (D&C 42:46).

DEATH OF INFANTS. Joseph and Emma Smith struggled with personal losses, including the death of several of their children. Joseph wrote: "I have meditated upon the subject, and asked the question, why it is that infants, innocent children, are taken away from us, especially those that seem to be the most intelligent and interesting. The strongest reasons that present themselves to my mind are these: . . . they were too pure, too lovely, to live on earth . . . [but] we shall soon have them again" (*TPJS*, pp. 196–97).

DEATH OF YOUTH. Joseph Smith commented on the untimely death of youth at the funeral of young Ephraim Marks: "[This occasion] calls to mind the death of my oldest brother, Alvin, who died in New

York, and my youngest brother, Don Carlos Smith, who died in Nauvoo. It has been hard for me to live on earth and see these young men upon whom we have leaned for support and comfort taken from us in the midst of their youth. Yes, it has been hard to be reconciled to these things. . . . Yet I know we ought to be still and know it is of God" (*TPJS,* p. 215). The Prophet also found great comfort in the gospel's affirmation of the relationship of mortality to eternity: "We have reason to have the greatest hope and consolations for our dead of any people on the earth; for we have seen them walk worthily in our midst, and seen them sink asleep in the arms of Jesus; and those who have died in the faith are now in the celestial kingdom of God" (*TPJS,* p. 359).

Mourning not only is appropriate; it is also one of the deepest expressions of pure love: "Thou shalt live together in love, insomuch that thou shalt weep for the loss of them that die" (D&C 42:45). $Alma_1$ taught that as part of the BAPTISMAL COVENANT the saints are "to mourn with those that mourn; yea, and comfort those that stand in need of comfort" (Mosiah 18:9). Mourning can heighten our faith and our hopes. The Prophet Joseph Smith said, "The expectation of seeing my friends in the morning of the resurrection cheers my soul and makes me bear up against the evils of life. It is like their taking a long journey, and on their return we meet them with increased joy" (*TPJS,* p. 296).

FUNERALS. LDS funerals are solemn and grieving occasions but also project a spirit of hope based on anticipation of reunion with the deceased after this life. They are usually held in an LDS chapel or a mortuary under the direction of the bishop of the ward (Packer, p. 18). Funerals open and close with sacred music and prayer, sometimes involving congregational singing or a choir (Packer, p. 19). Some LDS hymns describe life after death as a return to the presence of God (*Hymns,* p. 292), or as a condition of rest from mortal cares, and often include a reminder of the travails of mortality as temporary: "And should we die before our journey's through, happy day, all is well. We then are free from toil and sorrow too; with the saints we shall dwell" (*Hymns,* p. 30).

The funeral includes reminiscences and eulogies as well as talks about the ATONEMENT, the Resurrection, life after death, and related doctrines that comfort and inspire the bereaved. Some families choose to have members or friends of the family talk about the life of the deceased or sing an appropriate hymn. A prayer on behalf of the family by one of its members before the public service begins is customary.

GRAVESIDE SERVICES. Following the funeral, a simple graveside dedication service traditionally is held, attended only by family and intimate friends. One who holds the Melchizedek Priesthood, usually a member or close friend of the family, dedicates the grave, asking God to protect it from the elements or other disturbance as a hallowed resting place until the resurrection.

Local law in some countries may dictate cremation rather than burial, but in the absence of such a law, burial is preferred because of its doctrinal symbolism (Packer, p. 19). Circumstances also may dictate a memorial service or a graveside service only. Bishops are counseled to show regard for family wishes in keeping with the spiritual and reverent nature of the occasion (Packer, pp. 19–20).

SUMMARY. Even as death began with the Fall, it will end with the Atonement, through which all are resurrected and the earth itself becomes immortal (D&C 29:22–29; 1 Cor. 15:19–26; Rev. 21:1–4). The hope engendered in Latter-day Saints by this long-range view of the loving Savior, triumphant over death, was reflected in a letter from Joseph Smith to the Church in 1842: "Now what do we hear in the gospel which we have received? A voice of gladness! A voice of mercy from heaven: and a voice of truth out of the earth; glad tidings for the dead; a voice of gladness for the living and the dead; glad tidings of great joy" (D&C 128:19). Although it brings grief to those left behind, death is part of "the merciful plan of the great Creator" (2 Ne. 9:6), it is "a mechanism of rescue" (Packer, p. 21)—an essential step in the Lord's "great plan of happiness" (Alma 42:8).

[*See also* Afterlife.]

BIBLIOGRAPHY

Ballard, M. Russell. "Suicide: Some Things We Know, and Some We Do Not." *Ensign* 17 [Oct. 1987]:6–9.

Barlow, Brent A. *Understanding Death.* Salt Lake City, 1979.

Hinckley, Gordon B. "The Empty Tomb Bore Testimony." *Ensign* 18 (May, 1988):65–68.

Hymns of the Church of Jesus Christ of Latter-day Saints. Salt Lake City, 1985.

Kimball, Spencer W. "Tragedy or Destiny?" *IE* 69 (Mar. 1966):178–80, 210–14, 216–17.
Madsen, Truman G. "Distinctions in the Mormon Approach to Death and Dying." In *Deity and Death,* ed. Spencer J. Palmer, pp. 61–74. Provo, Utah.
Packer, Boyd K. "Funerals—A Time for Reverence." *Ensign* 18 (Nov. 1988):18–21.

L. KAY GILLESPIE

DEGREES OF GLORY

The Church of Jesus Christ of Latter-day Saints has an optimistic view of the eternal rewards awaiting mankind in the hereafter. Members of the Church believe that there are "many mansions" (John 14:2) and that Christ's ATONEMENT and RESURRECTION will save all mankind from death, and eventually will reclaim from hell all except the sons of perdition (D&C 76:43–44). The saved, however, are not placed into a monolithic state called HEAVEN. In the resurrection of the body, they are assigned to different degrees of glory commensurate with the law they have obeyed. There are three kingdoms of glory: the celestial, the terrestrial, and the telestial. The apostle Paul spoke of three glories, differing from one another as the sun, moon, and stars differ in brilliance. He called the first two glories celestial and terrestrial, but the third is not named in the Bible (1 Cor. 15:40–41; cf. D&C 76:70–81, 96–98.) The word "telestial" is an LDS term, first used by the Prophet Joseph Smith and Sidney Rigdon in reporting a vision they received on February 16, 1832 (D&C 76; *Webster's Third New International Dictionary* defines telestial glory as "the lowest of three Mormon degrees or kingdoms of glory attainable in heaven"; *see also* CELESTIAL KINGDOM; TELESTIAL KINGDOM; TERRESTRIAL KINGDOM).

At the final JUDGMENT, all except the devil, his ANGELS, and those who become sons of perdition during mortal life will be assigned to one of the three kingdoms of glory. The devil and his followers will be assigned a kingdom without glory (D&C 76:25–39; 88:24, 32–35).

LDS SCRIPTURE SOURCES. Although the Bible contains references to varying levels of resurrection and heaven (1 Cor. 15:39–58; 2 Cor. 12:2), LDS understanding of the subject comes mainly through revelations given to the Prophet Joseph Smith. The first revelation dealing directly with this matter was received February 16, 1832, and is called "The Vision" (D&C 76). Concerning the circumstances of receiving this revelation, Joseph Smith explained:

> Upon my return from Amherst [Ohio] conference, I resumed the translation of the Scriptures. From sundry revelations which had been received, it was apparent that many important points touching the salvation of man, had been taken from the Bible, or lost before it was compiled. It appeared self-evident from what truths were left, that if God rewarded every one according to the deeds done in the body the term "Heaven," as intended for the Saints' eternal home, must include more kingdoms than one. Accordingly . . . while translating St. John's Gospel, myself and Elder Rigdon saw the following vision [*HC* 1:245].

Later revelations, especially Doctrine and Covenants 88, 131, 132, 137, and 138, have added information on this subject.

THE CELESTIAL GLORY. The celestial kingdom is reserved for those who receive a testimony of Jesus and fully embrace the gospel; that is, they have faith in Jesus Christ, repent of their sins, are baptized by immersion by one having authority, receive the HOLY GHOST by the LAYING ON OF HANDS, and endure in RIGHTEOUSNESS. All who attain this kingdom "shall dwell in the presence of God and his Christ forever and ever" (D&C 76:62). There are, however, different privileges and powers within this kingdom. "In the celestial glory there are three heavens or degrees; and in order to obtain the highest, a man must enter into this order of the priesthood (meaning the new and everlasting covenant of marriage); and if he does not, he cannot obtain it. He may enter into the other, but that is the end of his kingdom; he cannot have an increase" (D&C 131:1–4). "Increase" in this instance means the bearing of spirit children after mortal life (*see* ETERNAL LIVES, ETERNAL INCREASE). Joseph Smith explained, "Except a man and his wife enter into an everlasting covenant and be married for eternity . . . by the power and authority of the Holy Priesthood, they will cease to increase when they die; that is, they will not have any children after the resurrection" (*TPJS*, pp. 300–301). Latter-day Saints believe that those who attain the highest level in the celestial kingdom become gods, receive exaltation, and are joint heirs with Christ of all that the Father has (cf. Rom. 8:14–17; D&C 76:50–70; 84:33–39; 132:19–25).

There is no scriptural explanation of those who go to the two lower categories of the celestial kingdom except that they "are not gods, but are angels of God forever and ever," ministering servants who "remain separately and singly, without exaltation, in their saved condition, to all eternity" (D&C 132:16–17).

THE TERRESTRIAL GLORY. The inhabitants of the terrestrial kingdom are described as the honorable people of the earth who received a testimony of Jesus but were not sufficiently valiant in that testimony to obey all the principles and ordinances of the gospel (D&C 76:71–80). Also, those of "the heathen nations" who "died without law," who are honorable but who do not accept the fulness of the gospel in the postearthly spirit world, are candidates for the terrestrial glory (D&C 45:54; 76:72). In the hereafter, they receive the presence of the Son, but not the fulness of the Father. The glory of the terrestrial kingdom differs from the celestial as the light we see from the moon differs from that of the sun in glory. There is no mention of different degrees or levels in the terrestrial kingdom, but it is reasonable that there, as in the celestial and telestial kingdoms, individuals will differ from one another in glory (see D&C 76:97–98).

THE TELESTIAL GLORY. Those who on earth are liars, sorcerers, whoremongers, and adulterers, who receive not the gospel, or the testimony of Jesus, or the prophets, go to the telestial kingdom. They are judged unworthy of being resurrected at the second coming of Christ and are given additional time in "hell" to repent and prepare themselves for a later resurrection and placement into a kingdom of lesser glory. During this period, they learn to abide by laws they once rejected. They bow the knee and confess their dependence on Jesus Christ, but they still do not receive the fulness of the gospel. At the end of the MILLENNIUM, they are brought out of hell and are resurrected to a telestial glory. There "they shall be servants of the Most High; but where God and Christ dwell they cannot come, worlds without end" (D&C 76:112). However, they do receive "of the Holy Spirit through the ministration of the terrestrial" (verse 86). Though differing in glory from the terrestrial and celestial kingdoms as the light we perceive from the stars differs from that from the moon and the sun, the glory of the telestial kingdom still "surpasses all understanding" (verse 89; see D&C 76:81–90, 98–112; 88:100–101).

OPPORTUNITY FOR ALL. The Church holds that all mankind, except the sons of perdition, will find a place in one of the kingdoms of glory in the hereafter and that they themselves choose the place by the lives they live here on earth and in the post-earthly spirit world. Even the lowest glory surpasses all mortal understanding. Everyone is granted AGENCY (D&C 93:30–32). All have access to the revelatory power of the LIGHT OF CHRIST, which, if followed, will lead them to the truth of the gospel (John 1:1–13; Alma 12:9–11; Moro. 7:14–19; D&C 84:45–48). Everyone will hear the gospel of Jesus Christ, either on earth or in the postearthly spirit world, and have ample opportunity to demonstrate the extent of their acceptance (D&C 138; cf. 1 Pet. 4:6). Those who do not have a chance to receive the gospel on this earth, but who would have fully accepted it had they been able to hear it, and who therefore do receive it in the spirit world, are heirs of the celestial kingdom of God (D&C 137:7–8). They will accept the saving ordinances performed for them by proxy in a temple on the earth (*see* SALVATION FOR THE DEAD). Christ, victorious and gracious, grants to all the desires of their hearts, allowing them to choose their eternal reward according to the law they are willing and able to abide.

BIBLIOGRAPHY

Dahl, Larry E. "The Vision of the Glories." In *Studies in Scripture,* ed. R. L. Millet and K. P. Jackson, Vol. 1, pp. 279–308. Sandy, Utah, 1984.

Smith, Joseph Fielding. *DS,* Vol. 2, pp. 20–24. Salt Lake City, 1955.

Talmage, James E. *AF,* pp. 375–94. Salt Lake City, 1968.

LARRY E. DAHL

DEVILS

In LDS discourse, the term "devil" denotes anyone who promotes the cause of EVIL, but it is especially applied to those unembodied spirits who rebelled against God in the PREMORTAL LIFE and were cast down from HEAVEN to this earth. The devil, who leads them, is also known by the personal names of Lucifer in the premortal existence and Satan since being cast down.

The name Lucifer means "light bearer" in Latin and is a translation of the Hebrew *Heylel ben Shakhar,* which means "herald son of dawn" or "morning star." In the PREMORTAL LIFE, Lucifer was an ANGEL having authority in the presence of God. He played a prominent role in the COUNCIL IN HEAVEN. After the Father in Heaven offered the plan of righteousness to help his children become as he is, Lucifer countered with an alternative plan.

The Father's plan was to save and exalt all of his obedient children. To be obedient, they must keep his commandments and do good. In the Father's plan, it was foreknown that many would reject exaltation and therefore would receive lesser glories.

Lucifer's plan proposed to "save" all of the Father's children by forcing each to obey the Father's law in all things. Lucifer desired that he be rewarded for this great feat of saving everyone by having the Father's honor and glory given to him personally. Because mortals can be saved only in their own freely chosen repentance, Lucifer's proposal was rejected. In the ensuing war in heaven, he gained the allegiance of a third of the Father's spirit children. Lucifer and his followers were then cast out of heaven to earth, where he became Satan and they all became devils (Moses 4:1–3; D&C 29:36–37; 76:25–38).

The name Satan comes from a Hebrew root meaning "to oppose, be adverse," hence "to attack or to accuse" (see Rev. 12:10). On this earth the role of Satan and his fellow devils is to attack the working of righteousness and to destroy it wherever possible (Moses 4:4; D&C 10:20–23; 93:39).

Righteousness is the condition or action of accomplishing the greatest possible happiness for all beings affected. The attainment of full righteousness is possible only with the help of an omniscient and omnipotent being. This full righteousness is the special order of the celestial kingdom where the Father dwells. When the Father's will is done and his order is in place, every person and every thing attains, or is attaining, the potential he, she, or it has for development and happiness. This righteousness is the good of "good and evil." It is to be contrasted with those human desires that are contrary to the Father's order and will.

A good (righteous) person is an agentive being who chooses and accomplishes only righteousness. No mortal is intrinsically and perfectly good, nor can a mortal alone rise to that standard (Matt. 19:17). But mortals can do righteous acts and become righteous through the salvation provided by Jesus Christ. Christ is the fountain of all righteousness (Ether 12:28). The children of God can achieve the Father's order of righteousness through Christ if they choose that order in explicit rejection of evil.

Evil is any order of existence that is not righteous. A state of affairs, an act, or a person not in the order of righteousness is thus evil. Letting one's neighbor languish in abject poverty while one has plenty, or stealing, or desiring harm for another person are all evils. Satan promotes evil everywhere he can, to thwart the righteousness of God (see D&C 10:27). Thus, Satan tempts people to do evil instead of the Father's will. Satan himself is not necessary to evil, but he hastens and abets evil wherever he can.

Satan's first targets on earth were Adam and Eve in the Garden of Eden. Knowing that the Father had commanded Adam and Eve not to partake of the forbidden fruit on penalty of death, Satan sought to destroy the Father's work by enticing Adam and Eve to partake of it anyway. Satan's success marked the beginning of the world (as distinct from the creation of the earth), of Satan's kingdom on this earth (see JST Matt. 1:55).

By obeying Satan, Adam and Eve opened the way for him to have partial dominion over them, over the earth, and over all of their children (*see* FALL OF ADAM). Examples of his partial dominion over the earth granted by the Father are his ability to possess the bodies of animals (Matt. 8:28–32) and to use water to destroy people (D&C 61:14–19). Satan gained the power to tempt those who are accountable to do evil (D&C 29:39), to communicate with individuals to teach them things (usually but not always lies), to possess their bodies, to foster illness and disease, and to cause mortal death. He promotes sin, the doing of evil, which brings SPIRITUAL DEATH to the sinner and misery to all those affected. In each of these opportunities, Satan's power is limited: He can do only what he has specific permission from God to do (D&C 121:4; Luke 8:30–33). His power may be taken away by individuals as they hearken to God and as they correctly use the holy priesthood to limit his operations (D&C 50:13–35).

What Satan did not realize in Eden was that what he did in attempting to destroy the Father's work was actually the very thing needed to fulfill the Father's plan (Moses 4:6). People could not demonstrate their love of God and their willingness to do the work of righteousness sufficiently to qualify them for exaltation unless they were subject to, and able to overcome, evil *and* devil adversaries, such as Satan and his hosts (2 Ne. 2:11–22).

On earth Satan is thus the father of deception, lies, and sin—of all evils—for he promotes them with vigor. He may appear as a counterfeit angel of light or as the prince of darkness, but his usual manifestations to mortals come as either evil revelation to one's heart and mind or indirectly through other persons. His mission is to tempt everyone to choose evil so that each accountable human being's choices can serve as an adequate basis for a final judgment.

This earth life is a mortal probation for all those who have the opportunity to accept and live by the new and everlasting covenant while in the mortal flesh. Those who do not have a full opportunity in this earth life will have their probation extended through the SPIRIT WORLD existence that follows it. By the time of RESURRECTION, each of the Father's children will have made a final choice between good and evil, and each will be rewarded with the good or the evil chosen during the probation (Alma 41:10–15).

When Satan tempts a person to do evil, there are limits to what Satan can accomplish. He can put before a person any kind of evil opportunity, but that evil is enticing only if the person tempted already desires that thing. When people are tempted, it is actually by their own lusts (James 1:12–15).

Satan has power on earth only as individual persons give it to him by succumbing to his TEMPTATIONS (*TPJS*, p. 187). The agency of human beings is to choose righteousness through the Holy Spirit of God or to choose selfishness through the flesh by succumbing to Satan's temptations (2 Ne. 2:26–29). (Human flesh is not evil, but Satan may tempt humans through their flesh.) Individuals who repent in this life are nevertheless tempted by Satan until their death; then Satan has no power over them ever again. Those who die unrepentant are still in Satan's power in the SPIRIT PRISON (Alma 34:34–35). All except the sons of perdition will eventually accept Christ and obey him, and thereby escape the dominion of Satan (D&C 76:110). Thus is the Father's plan of agency fulfilled.

Satan's three temptations of the Savior may be seen as paradigmatic of all human temptation (see David O. McKay, *Gospel Ideals*,

p. 154, Salt Lake City, 1953). The temptation to create bread and eat it when he should not represents the human temptation of the flesh, to sate the senses unrighteously. The temptation to cast himself down from the temple and to be saved by angels when he should not represents the human temptation of social acclaim. The temptation to receive the kingdoms of this world when he should not represents the temptation to have unrighteous dominion or power over others. The Savior did not yield to any of these temptations because his heart was pure and he knew that the way of righteousness lay only in doing the Father's will in all things.

All accountable mortals are tempted, even as our Savior was tempted. As mortals succumb, Satan gains power and earth life becomes a hell. Every person may resist temptation by choosing good over evil. But misinformation, evil cultural traditions (D&C 93:39), despair, and desperate human need all make the choosing of good difficult, even if the person does not particularly desire a given evil (cf. 2 Ne. 28 for an extensive description of the ploys of Satan).

Through Jesus Christ and the partaking of his new and everlasting covenant, mortals have the opportunity to gain power to choose good over evil unerringly and always. As they do so, they are able to establish the righteousness of God and thus heaven on earth (Moses 7:18; D&C 50:34–35).

Human beings resist Satan and evil by controlling their desires—that is, (1) by not desiring the evil that Satan proffers; (2) by gaining more knowledge so that they will be able to see that Satan's temptations are not what they really want; and (3) by having their hearts purified by Jesus Christ so that they will no longer desire any evil but desire instead to do the Father's will in all things (Moro. 7:48; cf. the Savior's answers in Matt. 4:1–10).

The great help in resisting temptation is the HOLY SPIRIT. It is Satan's business to dwell in and with all individuals who do not have the Holy Spirit with them, sometimes even gaining total possession of a person's body, so that he or she loses agency for a time. Partial possession may also occur, for whenever a human being becomes angry, he or she is at least partially possessed by Satan (James 1:20).

In his role as the destroyer, Satan can cause illness and death, but only with permission from God. He cannot take people before their time unless they disobey God and thus forfeit their mission (Job 1:6–12).

As the father of lies, Satan has a disinformation campaign. He spreads false notions about himself, about God, about people, about salvation—all for the purpose of defeating acts of faith in Jesus Christ. Mortals believe his lies because the lies are pleasing to the carnal mind and because they promote or support the selfish desires of the individual who believes them. About himself, Satan tells people that there is no devil, that such an idea is wild imagination (2 Ne. 28:22). About God, Satan desires human beings to believe either that he does not exist or that he is some distant, unknowable, or forbidding being. He tells people that they are to conquer in this world according to their strength and that whatever anyone does is no crime (Alma 30:17). Favorite lies about salvation are either that it comes to everyone in spite of anything one does (Alma 21:6) or that it is reserved only for a special few insiders (Alma 31:17). These erroneous creeds of the fathers, fastened upon their children in the form of false creeds, are called in the scriptures "the chains of hell" (Alma 12:11; D&C 123:7–8).

Secret combinations are another devilish device for spreading misery and obstructing the cause of righteousness (Ether 8:16–26; Hel. 6:16–32). Satan tempts selfish individuals to use others to their own oppressive advantage. Secrecy is essential to prevent retaliation by the victims and just execution of the laws against such combinations. Secret combinations involve personal, economic, educational, political, or military power that controls or enslaves some persons for the pleasure and profit of others.

Satan also has influence over the spirits of wicked persons who have passed from mortality by death and who inhabit the spirit prison (sometimes called Hades). The inhabitants of this prison do not yet suffer cleansing pain, which will later come, but continue to be subject to Satan's lies and temptations (Alma 40–41). They also have the opportunity to hear the servants of Christ (D&C 138:28–37), and if they did not have the opportunity on earth, they now may repent unto exaltation. If they did have the opportunity on earth but did not use it, the spirit prison opportunity again allows them to reject Satan and his lies and temptations, but with the reward of a lesser glory (D&C 76:71–79).

During the MILLENNIUM, Satan will be bound (Rev. 20:2). He will still be on earth, attempting to tempt every person, as he has since the Fall of Adam, but he will be bound because no one will hearken to his temptations (1 Ne. 22:26).

Toward the end of the Millennium, Satan will be loosed (D&C 88:110–15) because people will again hearken to him. But he will be vanquished and sent from this earth to outer darkness, where he and his followers, both spirits and resurrected sons of perdition (Satan is Perdition, "the lost one"), will dwell in the misery and darkness of selfishness and isolation forever.

BIBLIOGRAPHY

For a more complete treatment of the concept of the devil from an LDS point of view, see LaMar E. Garrard, "A Study of the Problem of a Personal Devil and Its Relationship to Latter-day Saint Beliefs" (Master's thesis, Brigham Young University, 1955). Especially valuable is his compilation of quotations from early General Authorities of the LDS Church concerning the topic. Jeffrey Burton Russell's four companion works *The Devil: Perceptions of Evil from Antiquity to Primitive Christianity* (Ithaca, N.Y., 1977), *Satan: The Early Christian Tradition* (Ithaca, N.Y., 1981), *Lucifer: The Devil in the Middle Ages* (Ithaca, N.Y., 1984), and *Mephistopheles: The Devil in the Modern World* (Ithaca, N.Y., 1986) constitute a comprehensive history of the concept of the devil traced through literature, art, and philosophy from ancient times to the modern day. The presentation is a thorough and scholarly treatment but does not derive from an LDS frame of thought.

CHAUNCEY C. RIDDLE

DISCERNMENT, GIFT OF

The gift of discernment consists of the spiritual quality or skill of being able to see or understand, especially that which is hidden or obscure. This ability is shared in a general way by all of God's children, but "discerning of spirits" is one of the GIFTS OF THE SPIRIT that comes, under certain circumstances, specially from God (1 Cor. 12:10; D&C 46:23). The fuller gift of discerning in all spiritual matters—to know whether their occurrence is of God or not—is given by the Lord to "such as God shall appoint and ordain to watch over the church" (D&C 46:27). To possess this gift is to receive divinely revealed understanding of opposing spirits—the spirit of God and the spirit of the DEVIL. Persons possessing such a gift also correctly perceive the right course of action (D&C 63:41).

Not only can the power of discernment distinguish good from evil (Moro. 7:12–18), the righteous from the wicked (D&C 101:95), and false spirits from divine (D&C 46:23), but its more sensitive operation can also make known even "the thoughts and intents of the heart" of other persons (Heb. 4:12; D&C 33:1). "The gift of discernment [embodies] the power to discriminate . . . between right and wrong . . . [and] arises largely out of an acute sensitivity to . . . spiritual impressions . . . to detect hidden evil, and more importantly to find the good that may be concealed. The highest type of discernment . . . uncovers [in others] . . . their better natures, the good inherent within them" (Richards, p. 371).

Every Latter-day Saint has spiritual leaders who, by virtue of their callings, are entitled to the gift of discernment to enable them to lead and counsel correctly. "The gift of discernment is essential to the leadership of the Church [of Jesus Christ of Latter-day Saints]. I never ordain a bishop or set apart a president of a stake without invoking upon him this divine blessing, that he may read the lives and hearts of his people and call forth the best within them. The gift and power of discernment . . . [are] essential equipment for every son and daughter of God. . . . The true gift of discernment is often premonitory. A sense of danger should be heeded to be of value" (Richards, p. 371).

BIBLIOGRAPHY

Richards, Stephen L. "The Gifts of the Spirit." *IE* 53 [May 1950]:371.

Smith, Joseph Fielding, ed. *TPJS*, pp. 202–215. Salt Lake City, 1938.

LEON R. HARTSHORN

DISCIPLESHIP

Like many other Christians, Latter-day Saints believe that only the transformational discipleship of those who believe in and follow Jesus Christ leads to a fulness of joy and peace in this life and ETERNAL LIFE in the world to come. Hence, true disciples are those who make the resurrected, revealing Christ the center of their lives, as did the faithful referred to in the New Testament who sat at the feet, followed in the footsteps, mourned the death, and rejoiced in the resurrection of Christ.

"Faith in the Lord Jesus Christ"—the first principle of the GOSPEL as stated in the fourth ARTICLE OF FAITH—is the explicit foundation of discipleship. From this principle all other principles and ordinances of the gospel derive their efficacy, power, and harmony.

Through his perfect earthly life and infinite atoning sacrifice, Jesus Christ became not only the model and mentor but also the Savior and Redeemer and mankind's advocate with the Father. The atonement, meaning "at-one-ment," empowered the plan whereby all men and women can eventually become like Father in Heaven and MOTHER IN HEAVEN. Through the atonement, Christ took upon himself not only the original transgression of Adam and Eve but also the personal sins of mankind, as well as the consequences of weaknesses and mistakes—including those transmitted through the generations—that are manifested in the lives even of individuals trying to follow in his footsteps. As the savior of mankind, Jesus sets the example and lovingly makes the blessings of the ATONEMENT and personal guidance available to anyone who comes to him with a broken (teachable) heart and a contrite (repentant) spirit (3 Ne. 9:20–22; 12:19–20).

The commitment to become a disciple of Christ is an unconditional one of "heart, might, mind and strength" (D&C 4:2). It centers a person's life on Christ, making Jesus the supreme law-giver, the frame of reference through which all else is viewed. Christ's influence then begins to direct a person's words, acts, and even thoughts, enabling that individual to become a partaker of the divine nature (2 Pet. 1:4), line upon line, precept upon precept.

While some believe that full discipleship comes about almost instantaneously, Latter-day Saints view the commitment at baptism as the beginning of a lifelong process that involves an upward spiral of learning, committing, and doing on increasingly higher planes. The heart of this process is learning to educate and obey the conscience, the repository of the Spirit of Christ given to every person (John 1:9; Moro. 7:16). As individuals obey the general commandments given through his appointed prophets, they become more attuned to hear the "still small voice" of the Holy Ghost (1 Ne. 17:45) that communicates specific personal direction and leads individuals to full discipleship.

The educated conscience, schooled by prayerful study of the scriptures, selfless service, and the making and keeping of God's COVENANTS, becomes a growing source of intrinsic security and well-being, the basis for decision making, the essence of personal FREEDOM. "If ye continue in my word," said Christ, "then are ye my disciples indeed; And ye shall know the truth, and the truth shall make you free" (John 8:31–32). As a person begins to see more as the Lord sees, to acquire more of the "mind of Christ" (1 Cor. 2:16), that individual is empowered to become independent of all other influences and to rise above childhood, genetic, and environmental tendencies.

The fruits that naturally grow out of this divine center are described as characteristics of disciples in both ancient and modern scripture. Disciples receive and obey the Lord's commandments (D&C 41:5); they are "submissive, meek, humble, patient, full of love, willing to submit to all things which the Lord seeth fit to inflict upon [them]" (Mosiah 3:19); they remember the poor and needy, the sick and afflicted (D&C 52:40); they act as a light to others (3 Ne. 15:12), love others as Christ loves (John 13:34–35), and are willing to forsake all to follow him (Luke 14:33) and to lay down their lives for his sake (D&C 103:28).

The role of The Church of Jesus Christ of Latter-day Saints in the process of discipleship is, as Paul observed of the former-day Church, "for the perfecting of the saints" (Eph. 4:12), and for helping members bridge the gap between theory and practice in becoming true disciples.

While one can go to church without being active in the gospel, for Latter-day Saints it is not possible to be a full disciple of Christ without being active in his Church. The Church teaches the GOSPEL, administers its ordinances, and provides opportunities to bring both temporal and spiritual blessings to others. The Church is the KINGDOM OF GOD on earth for which the disciple prays and works while seeking to unify it with God's kingdom in Heaven (Matt. 6:10). Gospel principles and ordinances empower the disciple of Christ, line upon line, to become even as he is.

BIBLIOGRAPHY
Covey, Stephen R. *The Divine Center.* Salt Lake City, 1987.
Hafen, Bruce C. *The Broken Heart.* Salt Lake City, 1989.
Maxwell, Neal A. *Deposition of a Disciple.* Salt Lake City, 1976.
——. *Even As I Am.* Salt Lake City, 1982.

STEPHEN R. COVEY

DISPENSATION OF THE FULNESS OF TIMES

The Dispensation of the Fulness of Times is the final dispensation for this earth. Dispensations are periods of time in which the gospel of Jesus Christ is administered by holy prophets called and ordained by God to deliver his message to the inhabitants of the world. The central work of the "dispensation of the fulness of times" consists of bringing together all gospel ordinances and truths of past dispensations and some items unique to the last days. Paul spoke of a future time when all things that are in heaven and on earth would at last be gathered together, and he called it the "dispensation of the fulness of times" (Eph. 1:10).

This dispensation began with the Prophet Joseph Smith's first vision, and all revelations and divine gifts of former dispensations continually flow into it. Concerning this, Joseph Smith wrote on September 6, 1842: "It is necessary in the ushering in of the dispensation of the fulness of times, which dispensation is now beginning to usher in, that a whole and complete and perfect union, and welding together of dispensations, and keys, and powers, and glories should take place, and be revealed from the days of Adam even to the present time" (D&C 128:18).

David W. Patten, a member of the Quorum of the Twelve Apostles, said in 1838: "The dispensation of the fullness of times is made up of all the dispensations that ever have been since the world began, until this time. . . . All [the prophets] received in their time a dispensation by revelation from God, to accomplish the great scheme of restoration, . . . the end of which is the dispensation of the fulness of times, in the which all things shall be fulfilled that have been spoken of since the earth was made" (*HC* 3:51).

Revelation and restoration characterize the fulness of times. Priesthood, keys (authorization to act), ordinances, covenants, and teachings of past dispensations have been, or will yet be, restored, and this can occur only by revelation. Heavenly messengers ministered to Joseph Smith and Oliver Cowdery, giving them authority, keys, doctrines, and ordinances of past dispensations that had been lost to the world because of fragmentation, abuse, and apostasy. The Doctrine and Covenants records several instances in which these two men saw, talked with, and received authority from resurrected ancient prophets. On May 15, 1829, John the Baptist ordained them to the Aaronic Priesthood (D&C 13). Shortly thereafter, Peter, James, and John, three of Christ's original apostles, conferred the Melchizedek Priesthood on them (D&C 27:12). On April 3, 1836, in the Kirtland Temple, Moses gave them "the keys of the gathering of Israel from the four parts of the earth, and the leading of the ten tribes from the land of the north" (D&C 110:11); Elias committed the keys of the dispensation of the GOSPEL OF ABRAHAM (D&C 110:12); and Elijah fulfilled the promise of Malachi 4:5–6 by bestowing on them the sealing power to "turn the hearts of the . . . children to the fathers" and make available the saving gospel ordinances to all who have lived on earth (D&C 110:13–15). As part of the restoration, the Book of Mormon, a scriptural witness of Jesus Christ and his dealings with ancient people of the Western Hemisphere, was translated by Joseph Smith by divine power. These events were part of the gathering "together in one all things in Christ" (Eph. 1:10; D&C 27:7–13). The priesthood has been revealed "for the last time," and those who now hold the keys do so "in connection with all those who have received a dispensation at any time from the beginning of the creation" (D&C 112:30–31).

Of things unique to the Dispensation of the Fulness of Times, the Prophet Joseph Smith wrote, "Those things which never have been revealed from the foundation of the world, but have been kept hid from the wise and prudent, shall be revealed unto babes and sucklings in this, the dispensation of the fulness of times" (D&C 128:18). Although the PLAN OF SALVATION is the same in every dispensation, the fulness of times will see the accomplishment of specific and unique events, including the rebuilding of the old Jerusalem; building the New Jerusalem; preaching the gospel to every nation, kindred, tongue, and people; the gathering of Israel; and the second coming of Jesus Christ. Everything necessary to usher in the

MILLENNIUM comes under the purview of the dispensation of the fulness of times, which will continue until Christ has subdued all his enemies and has perfected his work (D&C 76:106; *TPJS*, pp. 231–32).

BIBLIOGRAPHY

Matthews, Robert J. "The Fulness of Times." *Ensign* 19 (Dec. 1989):46–51.

McConkie, Bruce R. *A New Witness for the Articles of Faith*, pp. 137, 320. Salt Lake City, 1985.

RAND H. PACKER

DISPENSATIONS OF THE GOSPEL

The term "dispensation" is translated in the New Testament from the Greek *oikonomia*, denoting an idea of stewardship and of ordering affairs of a household. "Dispensations" are also time periods in which the Lord placed on the earth the necessary knowledge, priesthood, and keys of authority to implement his PLAN OF SALVATION for his children. This plan, along with priesthood, was first given to Adam (Moses 5:4–12; 6:62–68; D&C 84:16–18; *TPJS*, pp. 157, 167), but as a consequence of later apostasy and fragmentation among his descendants, it did not remain constantly upon the earth. Hence, from time to time the Lord called new prophets and again revealed the plan and bestowed the necessary priesthood authority, creating a new dispensation.

Each new dispensation, or period of restored truth, presents men and women with a divine stewardship in performing the Lord's work on earth. The recipients become custodians and coworkers with God in bringing to pass his purposes. They work according to his orderly and revealed design. His plan takes into account human weaknesses and provides for times of renewal following apostasy, just as it provides for a redemption from individual failings through repentance and obedience (D&C 121:31–32). The concepts of stewardship and orderliness are important themes in LDS theology.

Prophets are stewards who preach and organize the work of redemption in each dispensation. It has become traditional in some unofficial LDS commentaries to refer to seven major dispensations named after the principal prophet of each: Adam, Enoch, Noah,

Abraham, Moses, Jesus Christ (who led the dispensation of the meridian of time), and Joseph Smith (who introduced the DISPENSATION OF THE FULNESS OF TIMES; see Acts 3:21). However, this list does not take into account other dispensations, such as those among the Jaredites, the Nephites, and the ten lost tribes of Israel.

Rarely have gospel dispensations been universal, reaching all nations, although that is the ideal (e.g., Abr. 2:11). More often, one people has been responsive, while other nations have languished in ignorance and unbelief. However, the Adamic dispensation would at first have been communicated to the entire family of Adam early in his time (see Moses 5:12), and again in the final dispensation, the fulness of times, the gospel "shall be preached unto every nation, and kindred, and tongue, and people" (see D&C 133:37; cf. 90:9–11). The meridian of time was given the same mandate (Matt. 28:19–20), but we have no record that the gospel reached every nation in that period.

Several fundamentals are common to all dispensations: priesthood authority, BAPTISM by immersion and the LAYING ON OF HANDS for the GIFT OF THE HOLY GHOST, the sealing power (D&C 128:9–11), and temple worship. Basic gospel doctrines, including the FALL OF ADAM, faith in Jesus Christ, repentance, and the need for an infinite ATONEMENT, were taught in each era from Adam's day onward whenever there were living prophets selected by the Lord (Moses 5:4–12; D&C 112:29–32).

Some prophets have been given keys and responsibility over specific aspects of God's plan for this earth. In the sense of dispensation or stewardship, each of these assignments could with propriety be called a special dispensation. Joseph Smith taught that Adam, as "the father of all living," stands as the head of the patriarchal order of priesthood for this earth under Christ (*TPJS,* p. 158; D&C 78:16) and holds the keys from generation to generation. Whenever the gospel is revealed anew, it is under the direction of Adam. Noah, the "father of all living" after Adam, is also known as Gabriel and stands next to Adam in priesthood authority (*TPJS,* pp. 157, 167). Moses holds keys of the gathering of Israel (D&C 110:11); and Elijah, of sealing the generations (D&C 2; 110:13–16; JS—H 1:38–39). John the Baptist had a special role of messianic preparation (JST Matt. 11:13–15; 17:10–14). Peter, James, and John received the keys of the Melchizedek Priesthood (*TPJS,* p. 158) from Jesus, Moses, and Elias (Elijah). Moroni holds responsibility for the Book of Mormon (D&C 27:5). Each of these prophets has received a dispensation of keys for which he holds a stewardship and will give an account to the Lord (D&C 27:5–13). In a future gathering, all who hold keys will give a stewardship report to Adam, and he, to Christ (*TPJS,* p. 157; cf. JST Luke 3:8–9).

In establishing the final dispensation, the Lord prepared Joseph Smith by sending prophets from previous dispensations to confer their keys upon him (see D&C 110; 112:32; 128:20–21). Thus, in the dispensation of the fulness of times, all things will be "gathered together into one" (Eph. 1:10; D&C 27:13). Since the final dispensation is a culmination of all that has come before, Joseph Smith is revered as a preeminent figure under Jesus Christ (D&C 128:18; 135:3).

Every dispensation, beginning with Adam's, has been a dispensation of the gospel of salvation through Jesus Christ. That is, in each dispensation the same plan of redemption through the Savior and the necessary holy priesthood have been revealed by God in a similar and consistent manner.

The general consistency of the plan does not preclude differences in revealed counsel and direction appropriate to the diversity in times and cultures of different dispensations. Circumcision, for example, important in previous dispensations as a sign of a covenant, was not essential in later dispensations. Blood SACRIFICES required in Old Testament times to anticipate the Atonement were fulfilled in Christ, with new redemptive emblems of bread and wine being prescribed by Jesus. Latter-day Saints have a strong recognition of change and progress in sacred history. Personal growth and its implications for the development of a perfected Zion society are essential in LDS eschatology (*see* ETERNAL PROGRESSION). This view of progress is evidenced in the concept that the final dispensation builds upon previous ones and achieves the goals of all of them with the celestialization of the earth. The earth then will become a glorious residence for those of all dispensations who have been resurrected and perfected in Christ (D&C 88:17–26).

A definite priesthood line of authority is an essential component of the LDS understanding of dispensations. Thus, Moses and Elijah visited Peter, James, and John at the Mount of Transfiguration to restore certain keys of authority, and as already noted, these and many other ancient prophets visited Joseph Smith to give him the same authority.

Although the Lord's Church in successive dispensations ceased to function on earth because of apostasy, the work of the Lord in each dispensation is open-ended, leading to the final dispensation. The Lord's work that was not completed in an earlier dispensation will continue into the final dispensation, which is appropriately called "the fulness of times." In this last dispensation, some ideals never before reached on the earth will be accomplished (i.e., gathering of Israel, the second coming of Jesus Christ, and the MILLENNIUM).

BIBLIOGRAPHY

Arrington, F. L. "Dispensationalism." In *Dictionary of Pentecostal and Charismatic Movements,* ed. Stanley M. Burgess and Gary B. McGee. Grand Rapids, Mich., 1988.

Hunter, Milton R. *The Gospel Through the Ages.* Salt Lake City, 1945.

Matthews, Robert J. "The Fulness of Times." *Ensign* 19 (Dec. 1989):46–51.

Roberts, B. H., ed. *A Comprehensive History of The Church of Jesus Christ of Latter-day Saints,* Introduction. Salt Lake City, 1930.

COURTNEY J. LASSETTER

DOCTRINE

[*This entry consists of five articles:*

Meaning, Source, and History of Doctrine
Distinctive Teachings
LDS Doctrine Compared with Other Christian Doctrines
Harmonization of Paradox
Treatises on Doctrine

For related articles, see, generally, Articles of Faith; Gospel of Jesus Christ; Jesus Christ; and Plan of Salvation, Plan of Redemption. *For articles of a philosophical nature, see* Knowledge *and* Truth, *among others.*]

MEANING, SOURCE, AND HISTORY OF DOCTRINE

MEANING OF DOCTRINE. The word "doctrine" in the scriptures means "a teaching" as well as "that which is taught." Most often in the Church it refers to the teachings or doctrine of Jesus Christ, understood in a rather specific sense. Scripturally, then, the term "doctrine" means the core message of Jesus Christ—that Jesus is the Messiah, the Redeemer. All other teachings are subordinate to those by which all people "know how to come unto Christ and be saved"—that is, to the "points of doctrine," such as faith, repentance, baptism, and receiving the gift of the Holy Ghost. At one time, stressing the preeminence and foundational nature of this message, Jesus taught, "And whoso shall declare more or less than this, and establish it for my doctrine, the same cometh of evil, and is not built upon my rock" (3 Ne. 11:40).

In the King James Version (KJV) of the Old Testament, the word "doctrine" occurs six times (Deut. 32:2; Job 11:4; Prov. 4:2; Isa. 28:9, 29:24; Jer. 10:8), usually as a translation of the Hebrew word *leqakh*, meaning "instruction" or, more literally, "what is to be received." In the KJV New Testament it is used some fifty times, most often in reference to the teaching or instruction of Jesus Christ, less frequently to the teachings of others.

The "doctrine of Jesus Christ," which the Savior's listeners found "astonishing" (Matt. 7:28) and "new" (Mark 1:27) and which he attributed to the Father (John 7:16–19), is synonymous with his central message, the GOSPEL OF JESUS CHRIST. In Paul's words, it was the good news that the kingdom of God is at hand and that God "hath reconciled us to himself by Jesus Christ" (2 Cor. 5:18).

The apostles, following the death and resurrection of the Savior, continued to teach this essential message (Acts 13:12; 1 Tim. 6:1). They used the word "doctrine" most often in reference to what a person must believe and do in order to be saved (Acts 2:41–47; 1 Tim. 4:16; Heb. 6:1–3).

Most occurrences of the term "doctrine" in the New Testament are in the singular and refer to the "doctrine of Jesus Christ." The plural "doctrines" usually refers to the teachings of men and devils, false and vain teachings contrary to or denying the Savior's "doctrine." Jesus' message comes from the Father and has its content in Jesus Christ, the Messiah and Redeemer, the way of salvation. The "doctrine" of Jesus Christ is the foundation upon which all other teachings, principles, and practices rest.

The Book of Mormon and the Doctrine and Covenants use the

word "doctrine" in the same way. In the singular it always refers to the "doctrine of Jesus Christ" or to the "points of his doctrine" and means "that which will ensure the salvation of those who accept and act upon it." In the plural, it refers to the false teachings of devils or others (2 Ne. 3:12; 28:9; D&C 46:7). The Book of Mormon uses "doctrine" in this special sense as the "doctrine of Jesus Christ" or the gospel (twenty-eight times). Jesus attributed his teaching to the Father: "This is my doctrine, . . . that the Father commandeth all men, everywhere, to repent and believe in me. And whoso believeth in me, and is baptized, the same shall be saved; and they are they who shall inherit the kingdom of God" (3 Ne. 11:32–33). Later he declared, "This is the gospel which I have given unto you—that I came into the world to do the will of the Father, . . . and my Father sent me that I might be lifted up upon the cross; . . . that whoso repenteth and is baptized in my name shall be filled; and if he endureth to the end, behold, him will I hold guiltless before the Father at that day when I shall stand to judge the world" (3 Ne. 27:13–16; cf. D&C 76:40–42).

Thus, the "doctrine of Jesus Christ" is the only teaching that can properly be called "doctrine." It is fixed and unchanging. It cannot be modified or contradicted, but merely amplified as additional truths that deepen understanding and appreciation of its meaning are revealed. It is the basis on which the test of faith is made, and the rock or foundation of all other revealed teachings, principles, and practices.

Some of these other teachings comprise what is sometimes referred to as the PLAN OF SALVATION, which is understood as the larger historical setting in which the "doctrine of Jesus Christ" is situated and hence best understood. This is the plan worked out by the Father from the beginning, centering on the ATONEMENT of Jesus Christ as the necessary means by which all individuals are saved and exalted. All other revealed teachings are either aspects of the doctrine of Jesus Christ or extensions, elaborations, or appendages of it. The Prophet Joseph Smith taught, "The fundamental principles of our religion are the testimony of the Apostles and Prophets, concerning Jesus Christ, that He died, was buried, and rose again the third day, and ascended unto heaven; and all other things which pertain to our religion are only appendages to it" (*TPJS*, p. 121).

Some of the "appendages" that are explicitly identified in the scriptures as part of the doctrine of Jesus Christ are (1) faith in the Lord Jesus Christ, the Son of God; (2) repentance of all sins; (3) baptism by immersion for the remission of sins; (4) the gift of the Holy Ghost by the laying on of hands by those in authority; (5) enduring in righteousness to the end; and (6) the resurrection of all human beings to be judged by Christ (3 Ne. 9:1–16; 11:23–39; 19:7–28; 27:13–21; D&C 10:62–69; 33:10–15; 39:5–6; 76:40–43). Additional teachings, or "things we know" (D&C 20:17), that are closely associated with this foundation include knowledge about the nature of GOD, the creation and the FALL OF ADAM, AGENCY, continuing REVELATION, an open canon and the continual search for the truth of all things, PREMORTAL LIFE, the gathering of Israel, the role of a COVENANT people, sharing the gospel, HOPE and CHARITY, the establishment of Zion, the second coming of Christ, Christ's reign on earth for a thousand years, temple ordinances for the living and the dead, the preaching of the gospel in the postearth SPIRIT WORLD, the need for priesthood, degrees of glory in the hereafter, eternal marriage, and the concept of ultimate EXALTATION in the presence of God to share his glory and life.

In addition to its scriptural use, the word "doctrine" has a broad meaning in Mormon vernacular, where it is used to mean virtually everything that is, or has been, taught or believed by the Latter-day Saints. In this sense, doctrinal teachings answer a host of questions. Some relate closely to the core message of the gospel of Jesus Christ; others are farther removed and unsystematically lap over into such disciplines as history, psychology, philosophy, science, politics, business, and economics. Some of these beliefs qualify as official doctrine and are given to the Saints as counsel, exhortation, reproof, and instruction (2 Tim. 3:16). Continual effort is made to harmonize and implement these principles and doctrines into a righteous life. Other teachings, ones that lack official or authoritative standing, may also be widespread among Church members at any given time.

SOURCE OF DOCTRINE. God is the source of doctrine. It is not devised or developed by man. It is based on eternal truth and is revealed by God to man. It can be properly understood only by revelation through the Spirit of God (1 Cor. 2:11–14; Jacob 4:8).

God dispenses eternal truths "line upon line, precept upon precept" (2 Ne. 28:30). At times, he has revealed the fulness of the gospel, and those who have accepted and lived it were received into his presence. When people have ignored or rejected his gospel, God has on occasion withheld his Spirit, and people have had to live in a state of spiritual darkness.

God reveals as much light as humankind is willing to abide. Hence, varying amounts of true doctrine have existed on the earth at different periods of time, and people on earth during the same era have enjoyed differing amounts of truth. In this sense, there can be said to be a history of doctrine—that is, an account of how, over time, humankind has either grown or declined in the knowledge of the things of God, man, and the world. Joseph Smith taught, "This is the principle on which the government of heaven is conducted—by revelation adapted to the circumstances in which the children of the kingdom are placed" (*TPJS,* p. 256).

Many factors influence how much God reveals, to whom, and under what circumstances. These include (1) who takes the opportunity to ask the Father in the name of Christ; (2) how much faith those seeking knowledge have; (3) what they ask for; (4) what is good for them to receive (D&C 18:18); (5) how willing they are to obey what is given (Alma 12:9–11); (6) what the will and wisdom of God require, for he gives "all that he seeth fit that they should have" (Alma 29:8); (7) whether the faith of people needs to be tested (Mormon was about to write more, but "the Lord forbade it, saying: I will try the faith of my people" [3 Ne. 26:8–11]); and (8) how spiritually prepared people are to receive the revelation (for example, Jesus taught through parables in order to protect those who were not ready to understand [Luke 8:10; D&C 19:22]). The eternal truths constituting the gospel do not change, and eventually all who are exalted in the kingdom of God will understand them and apply them fully. However, mankind's knowledge and understanding of these truths change, as do the policies and practices appropriate to concurrent levels of understanding and obedience.

Inasmuch as God's house "is a house of order . . . and not a house of confusion" (D&C 132:8), there must be one who can speak for God for the whole Church and also settle differences. In The Church of Jesus Christ of Latter-day Saints, the living prophet is the only one authorized to "receive revelations and commandments" binding on the entire Church (D&C 28:1–7; 43:1–7; 128:11). From the time the Church was organized, there has been—and always will be—"a prophet, recognized of God and his people, who will continue to interpret the mind and will of the Lord" (Spencer W. Kimball, *Ensign* 7 [May 1977]:78). Ordinarily, the prophet acts in concert with his counselors in the First Presidency and the Quorum of the Twelve Apostles—those who hold, with the Prophet, the "keys of the kingdom" (D&C 81:2; 112:30)—with the principle of quorum unanimity and common consent of the members of the Church giving power and validity to their decisions (D&C 26:2; 107:27–31). Acting collectively and under the inspiration of God, these leaders are authorized to determine the position of the Church at any given time on matters of doctrine, policy, and practice. This is the proper channel through which changes come. Latter-day Saints believe that God "will yet reveal many great and important things pertaining to the Kingdom of God" (A of F 9). It is expected that such revelations will involve an expanded understanding of doctrine.

Many individuals write or preach their views. Some, by study and obedience, may learn truths that go beyond the stated position of the Church, but this does not authorize them to speak officially for the Church or to present their views as binding on the Church. There are many subjects about which the scriptures are not clear and about which the Church has made no official pronouncements. In such matters, one can find differences of opinion among Church members and leaders. Until the truth of these matters is made known by revelation, there is room for different levels of understanding and interpretation of unsettled issues.

HISTORY OF DOCTRINE. The doctrine of the Church was revealed principally through the Prophet Joseph Smith, though subsequent additions and clarifications have been made. These truths are part of the fulness of the gospel of Jesus Christ, known on earth in earlier times but now lost, necessitating a restoration by revelation.

The Prophet Joseph Smith received and shared his doctrinal understanding line upon line, from the time of his first vision in 1820 to his death in 1844. In many instances, his own understanding was progressively enhanced. In other matters, he learned certain principles early but only taught them as his followers were able and willing to accept them. Concerning the hereafter, for example, he said, "I could explain a hundred fold more than I ever have of the glories of the kingdoms manifested to me in the vision, were I permitted, and were the people prepared to receive them" (*TPJS,* p. 305).

There is no simple pattern or predictable sequence in the growth of Joseph Smith's knowledge. Much of his doctrinal understanding gradually unfolded through revelations that he received in response to various contemporary issues and circumstances facing the infant but quickly expanding Church. Other teachings emerged quite spontaneously. His perceptions grew in completeness and detail, but they did not lose their historical footing in past dispensations or their undeviating goal of bringing people to Christ.

One important catalyst in this process was Joseph Smith's systematic examination of the Bible, which yielded inspired biblical interpretations and textual restorations. Also, many sections of the Doctrine and Covenants are revelations answering questions that arose in this process (e.g., D&C 76, 91, 132).

Joseph's teachings about the Godhead illustrate the previous points. At first, he simply taught that God the Father and the Son were separate personages, without mentioning explicitly the nature of their bodies, even though 3 Nephi 11:15 (translated in 1829) made it clear that Jesus' resurrected body was tangible. Later, in Nauvoo, Joseph declared that "there is no other God in heaven but that God who has flesh and bones" (*TPJS,* p. 181, a comment made in 1841 on the biblical text in John 5:26), and that both the Father and the Son have bodies of "flesh and bones as tangible as man's" (D&C 130:22). Two months before his death, Joseph, for the first time in a recorded public sermon—indeed, in his crowning sermon about the nature of God, the King Follett Discourse—taught that God is an exalted man. And two weeks before his death he spoke of a "plurality of Gods," expanding one's understanding in Genesis 1 of the Hebrew plural *elohim,* or "gods" (Joseph had studied Hebrew in 1835), explaining that "there are Gods many and Lords many, but to us only one, and we are to be in subjection to that one," and declaring that for fifteen years he had always preached "the plurality of Gods" (*TPJS,* pp. 370–71; cf. 1 Cor. 8:5–6).

Similarly, Joseph's teachings relating to such things as the nature of man, his premortal existence, his agency, and his eternal potential of GODHOOD also gradually unfolded to him and to those around him.

He learned in December 1830 that "all the children of men" were created "spiritually, before they were naturally upon the face of the earth" (Moses 3:5). A revelation in 1833 indicated that a component of each individual existed before his or her spiritual creation, a component called INTELLIGENCE, which "was not created or made, neither indeed can be" (D&C 93:29). During the period 1835–1842, while translating the book of Abraham, Joseph Smith learned that Abraham had seen into the premortal world and beheld myriads of "intelligences that were organized before the world was," in the presence of God (Abr. 3:22). Many were "noble and great" and chose to follow Christ. To this was added in 1841 that "at the first organization in heaven we were all present, and saw the Savior chosen and appointed and the plan of salvation made, and we sanctioned it" (*TPJS,* p. 181).

The Prophet's teachings on the atonement of Jesus Christ, creation, foreordination, salvation for the dead, priesthood, temple ordinances, eternal marriage, exaltation, and many other subjects can all be shown to have followed similar courses of development during his ministry (Cannon, Dahl, and Welch).

By 1844, the basic doctrinal structure of the Church was in place. Since that time, however, there have been official pronouncements clarifying doctrinal understanding or adapting doctrinal applications to particular circumstances. Some are now included in the Doctrine and Covenants; others are published as official messages of the First Presidency (cf. *MFP*). Over the years, various procedures and practices have received greater or lesser emphasis as changes have occurred in economic conditions, political circumstances, intellectual atmosphere, Church growth, and many other areas. The essential doctrine of the Church, however, has remained constant amid such change.

Certain Church leaders have written extensively of their understanding of the doctrines of the Church and, as a consequence, have had a significant influence on what many members believe (*see* TREATISES ON DOCTRINE below). These have included Parley P. Pratt, Orson Pratt, James E. Talmage, John A. Widtsoe, B. H. Roberts, Joseph Fielding Smith, and Bruce R. McConkie. Their writings evidence some differences of opinion on unsettled issues, just as different schools of thought exist among Church members in general on certain issues. Examples include efforts to reconcile current scientific teachings and revealed truths, to ponder the nature of uncreated intelligence, and to define eternal progression. Latter-day Saints have faith that answers will eventually be revealed, and are urged, in the meantime, to seek knowledge by all available means and to show tolerance toward those espousing differing opinions on such subjects.

BIBLIOGRAPHY

Cannon, Donald Q.; Larry E. Dahl; and John W. Welch. "The Restoration of Major Doctrines Through Joseph Smith: The Godhead, Mankind, and the Creation." *Ensign* 19 (Jan. 1989):27–33; and "The Restoration of Major Doctrines Through Joseph Smith: Priesthood, the Word of God, and the Temple." *Ensign* 19 (Feb. 1989):7–13.

Lyon, T. Edgar. "Doctrinal Development of the Church During the Nauvoo Sojourn, 1839–1846." *BYU Studies* 15 (Summer 1975):435–46.

M. GERALD BRADFORD
LARRY E. DAHL

DISTINCTIVE TEACHINGS

Few religious doctrines are unique in the strict sense, but many are rare enough to be considered distinctive features of this or that religion or denomination. Several doctrines of the Latter-day Saints are distinctive in this sense, although in most cases other Christians have at some time held identical or similar beliefs. Latter-day Saints insist that their distinctive doctrines were revealed by God in earlier DISPENSATIONS headed by Adam, Enoch, Noah, and so forth down to the time of Christ. Thus, while they may be distinct among modern denominations, these newly revealed doctrines were shared with the one true Church of Jesus Christ in ancient times.

Unique to LDS theology in modern times is a view of the GODHEAD as consisting of three separate beings, two possessing bodies of flesh and bone and one possessing a spirit body. An official declaration concerning the Godhead states: "The Father has a body of flesh and bones as tangible as man's; the Son also; but the Holy Ghost has not a body of flesh and bones, but is a personage of Spirit" (D&C 130:22). Latter-day Saints take the Bible, both Old and New Testaments, in a literal, anthropomorphic sense, attributing to God both a human form and emotions. They accept both a "oneness" and "threeness" of the Godhead as taught in the Bible. However, they reject the traditional doctrine of the Trinity, and believe instead that the Godhead is one in mind, purpose, and testimony, but three in number. Thus, they believe that God is spirit in the sense that he is infused with spirit, and in the sense that the Holy Ghost is a spirit, but they do not limit the Father or the Son to incorporeality.

Latter-day Saints identify Jehovah, the God of the Old Testament, specifically as Jesus Christ. They believe that the God of Abraham, Isaac, and Jacob, the God who walked with Enoch and who talked with Moses on Mount Sinai, was the premortal Jesus Christ, or God the Son, acting as the agent of his Father.

Latter-day Saints also have distinct doctrines about the nature of the universe and how it began. Because they believe that spirit and matter are actually the same thing in different degrees of refinement (see D&C 131:2), Latter-day Saints perceive the universe in terms of two realms, the physical and the spiritual, but these are not antithetical. They deny the spirit/matter dichotomy and insist that both spirit and matter make up a single eternal universe.

Moreover, Latter-day Saints understand "in the beginning" to mean "in the beginning of our part of the story," or in the premortal state "when God began to create our world." They do not believe in an absolute beginning, for in LDS theology spirit, matter, and element are all eternal. Creations may progress from lower to higher orders, and it is God's work and glory to bring this development about (Moses 1:39), but there never was a time when matter did not exist. Latter-day Saints reject the common idea of an ex nihilo creation—that God made everything that exists out of nonexistence. They teach instead that God created everything out of pre-existing but unorganized materials. He organized pre-existing elements to create worlds, and he organized pre-existing intelligence to beget spirits. The spirits of all human beings existed as God's spirit children before their mortal birth on earth.

LDS eschatology also offers several distinct doctrines. For example, Latter-day Saints believe in a temporary state between DEATH and RESURRECTION that the scriptures call the spirit world. This temporary spirit world includes Paradise, where the spirits of the righteous await their glorious resurrection, and Hell, where the spirits of the wicked suffer for their sins while they await resurrection to a lesser degree of glory (Alma 40:11–14; cf. Luke 16:22–23). LDS doctrine teaches that every human being will be resurrected. Many were resurrected soon after Jesus' resurrection; the remaining righteous will be resurrected at the second coming of Christ, and the wicked at the end of Christ's one-thousand-year reign on earth. Hell is a temporary condition, which will yield up its captive spirits at the Resurrection, just as death will yield up its bodies (2 Ne. 9:10–14; cf. Rev. 20:13–14). In the Resurrection all suffering comes to an end (D&C 76:84, 88–89), and all human beings except the sons of perdition will be saved in one of three kingdoms, or degrees of glory: the celestial, the terrestrial, or the telestial (D&C 76:1–19; 88:29–32; cf. 1 Cor. 15:4–42).

Distinctive LDS doctrines concerning the nature of the Church include the belief that the Church of Jesus Christ has been on earth many times, beginning with father Adam, in much the same form it has now and with the same doctrines. The Church and gospel of Jesus Christ are eternal. They were revealed to the people of Adam, Enoch, Noah, Abraham, Moses, Jared, Lehi, and others. Adam knew the gospel, was baptized by immersion in the name of Jesus Christ, and received the gift of the Holy Ghost, just as the Saints in all other dispensations. At times humanity has rejected or distorted the gospel and fallen into apostasy. But eventually the gospel has been restored to its original purity through prophets called to begin a new dispensation. Most recently this same eternal gospel has been restored through the modern Prophet Joseph Smith. Thus the establishment of The Church of Jesus Christ of Latter-day Saints was not the result of a long religious evolution, nor was it merely the restoration of primitive Christianity, but it was the final restoration to earth of an eternal gospel of Jesus Christ revealed to humanity many times since the beginning.

What distinguishes "the true and living Church" from all other churches is possession of the priesthood keys of the kingdom of heaven (see Matt. 16:19). The belief that possession of the apostolic keys is necessary in the true Church is not unique to Latter-day Saints, but the insistence that one of those keys necessarily bestows the gifts of prophecy and revelation is. To hold the keys of the kingdom as Peter did is to be a prophet, seer, and revelator like Peter. And in order to be "true and living" a church must receive these apostolic keys as exercised and transmitted through the hands of its living prophets. As a tree is alive only when its branches are connected to its trunk and roots, so a church is alive only when it is connected by an open channel of revelation to its divine source. Where ecclesiastical leaders have no such prophetic link with the heavens, a church may even teach true doctrines, but it can not be "true and living" (see D&C 1:30; 27:12–13), for it lacks the necessary communication with its own divine roots.

With such emphasis placed on the need for living prophets, it follows that the word of God is primarily the word as spoken to and communicated by the prophets. The written words, the scriptures, are always important as historical precedent and as a record of what the Lord has said to his people in the past, but they are supplemental and secondary to what he may say now through his living prophet. Since Latter-day Saints believe in the genuine gift of prophecy, it follows that the revelations received by modern prophets should be esteemed as highly as those received by ancient ones. Hence, the LDS canon of scripture can never be closed: "We believe all that God has revealed, all that He does now reveal, and we believe that He will yet reveal many great and important things pertaining to the Kingdom of God" (A of F 9).

The Latter-day Saints are also unique in several aspects of their concept of salvation. While most of the LDS doctrines would be familiar to other Christians—for example, the doctrines of the Atonement, justification, sanctification, and grace—there are several distinct features found among the Latter-day Saints. They make a distinction between generic "salvation," which to them means that through the atonement of Christ one is delivered from the grave and from the power of Satan and hell to enter a degree of glory, and "exaltation," which means that through the atonement of Christ and personal obedience to the principles and ordinances of the gospel of Jesus Christ one is raised to the highest degree of glory to share the powers and privileges of God, to sit on his throne and reign in eternity (see D&C 76:1–119; 88:22–23; cf. Rev. 1:6; 3:21). To be exalted is to become like God.

Faithful Latter-day Saints receive in the LDS temples the ordinances and knowledge necessary for celestial exaltation. One part of these sacred rites is called the temple ENDOWMENT because it constitutes a major part of the overwhelming gift extended to humanity through the atonement of Christ. Another temple ordinance is the sealing of husbands and wives, parents and children into families that will endure for time and for eternity. The celestial kingdom will consist of God's heavenly family linked together in love as husbands and wives, parents and children, and brothers and sisters forever. As single individuals, human beings may be saved in lesser degrees of glory, but only families can be exalted.

Not everyone has had the opportunity in mortal life to hear the gospel of Christ and receive all the ordinances of exaltation. Latter-day Saints teach that God has provided for all to hear the gospel so they can accept or reject its blessings. Those who do not have that opportunity in mortality will receive it in the spirit world. The New Testament teaches that Jesus himself visited the spirit world after his death on the cross and preached to the spirits there: "For Christ also hath once suffered for sins, the just for the unjust, that he might bring us to God, being put to death in the flesh, but quickened by the Spirit: By which also he went and preached unto the spirits in prison" (1 Pet. 3:18–19). The purpose of his preaching ministry to the spirits is revealed in the next chapter: "For this cause was the gospel preached also to them that are dead, that they might be judged according to men in the flesh, but live according to God in the spirit" (1 Pet. 4:6). This doctrine has been amplified and explained in latter-day revelation (D&C 137, 138; *see* SALVATION FOR THE DEAD).

Other areas in which the views of the Latter-day Saints differ noticeably from those of the contemporary religious world are the concepts of TIME AND ETERNITY, the LIGHT OF CHRIST, the GIFT OF THE HOLY GHOST, the positive estimate of the Creation and of the physical earth, the eternal necessity of ordinances, the centrality of the ABRAHAMIC COVENANT for modern Christians, and the concept of heaven as a CELESTIAL KINGDOM located upon this renewed and glorified earth.

BIBLIOGRAPHY

Keller, Roger R. *Reformed Christians and Mormon Christians: Let's Talk.* Ann Arbor, Mich., 1986.

Madsen, Truman G. "Are Christians Mormon?" *BYU Studies* 15 (Autumn 1974):73–94.

McConkie, Bruce R. *MD.* Salt Lake City, 1966.

Robinson, Stephen E. *Are Mormons Christians?*, chaps. 6–8. Salt Lake City, 1991.

Talmage, James E. *AF.* Salt Lake City, 1924.

ALMA P. BURTON

LDS DOCTRINE COMPARED WITH OTHER CHRISTIAN DOCTRINES

As biblical scholar W. D. Davies once pointed out, LDS doctrine can be described as biblical Christianity separated from hellenized Christianity, a conjunction of first-century Judaism and Christianity. Latter-day Saints accept the Bible and its apostolic teachings as God's word, but reject many later interpretations of the Bible that express Greek philosophical concerns—they accept John and Paul but reject Augustine. For example, Latter-day Saints accept both the threeness of God and the oneness of God as biblical teachings. The Father, Son, and Holy Spirit are three divine personages who together constitute one GODHEAD. But Mormons reject the attempts of post-biblical, nonapostolic Christianity to define how the oneness and the threeness of God are related. They accept the biblical doctrine of the Trinity, but reject the philosophical doctrine of the Trinity as defined at the Council of Nicaea and later. In short, Latter-day Saints reject the authority and conclusions of theologians and philosophers to define or interpret what the Bible, apostles, or prophets have not. They accept biblical Christianity, but not its extension in extrabiblical creeds and traditions.

To those Christians who have welded the Bible to its later interpretation and cannot separate Plato and Augustine from Peter and Paul, and cannot think of "true" Christianity in first-century categories, LDS doctrine may seem iconoclastic in separating biblical texts from their later "traditional" interpretation. Nevertheless, Latter-day Saints feel that New Testament Saints would have been just as uncomfortable with the philosophical creeds of later Christianity as they themselves are.

LDS rejection of much postbiblical Christianity is based on belief in an ancient apostasy that is both predicted and chronicled in the New Testament (e.g., 2 Thes. 2:1–5; 3 Jn. 9–10). Apostolic authority ceased just after the New Testament period, and without apostolic leadership and authority the Church was soon overwhelmed by alien intellectual and cultural pressures. The simple affirmations of biblical faith were turned into the complex propositions of theology. Though subsequent churches were still "Christian," in the LDS view they no longer possessed the *fulness* of the GOSPEL OF JESUS CHRIST or apostolic authority. Latter-day Saints would agree with

Catholics and "high church" Protestants that apostolic authority is essential in the true church but would also agree with other Protestants that apostolic authority was lacking in medieval orthodoxy. A close parallel is presented by Protestant rejection of Roman Catholic claims to binding apostolic authority. While Latter-day Saints trace the Apostasy to roughly the second century and reject subsequent orthodoxy, most Protestants would place it somewhere nearer the fifteenth century and then reject subsequent Catholicism.

Protestants who denied the necessity of apostolic succession, or who did not believe its links were severed by the Reformation, generally held that the fulness of the gospel could be achieved by reforming the Roman Church. Latter-day Saints, who insist on the necessity of apostolic succession but believe its links were severed early, see a reformation as inadequate for recovering the fulness of the gospel and reestablishing original Christianity. Only a total restoration of apostolic doctrines and authority could reestablish the pure Christianity of the first century. The Church of Jesus Christ of Latter-day Saints sees itself as constituting this Restoration.

LDS rejection of hellenistic philosophy in matters of doctrine accounts for many characteristic differences between Latter-day Saints and other Christians. For example, Latter-day Saints reject the Platonic spirit–matter dichotomy, which holds that spirit and matter are opposed and inimical to each other. They believe instead that spirit is refined matter and that both spirit and matter are eternal, being neither created nor destroyed. The Prophet Joseph Smith taught that "there is no such thing as immaterial matter. All spirit is matter, but it is more fine or pure, and can only be discerned by purer eyes" (D&C 131:7).

Thus, for Latter-day Saints there is no ultimate incompatibility between spirit and matter or between the spiritual and the physical realms. In LDS theology, the physical elements are coeternal with God. The idea that physical matter is transitory, corrupt, or incompatible with spiritual or eternal life is rejected. Latter-day Saints usually define "spiritual" as "infused with spirit" rather than as "nonphysical." This unitary understanding of spirit and matter allows them to accept the Father and the Son as the concrete, anthropomorphic beings represented in scripture and reject the definition of God as the abstract, "totally other" nonbeing of philosophical theology.

For Latter-day Saints, God *exists* in the normal sense in association with time and space, rather than in the abstract Platonic sense of beyond time and space. The traditional disparagement of matter and of the physical state of being is not well grounded biblically, and Latter-day Saints believe it is a product of hellenistic thought. They also think the concept of a God "without body, parts or passions" dismisses too much of the biblical data or allegorizes it excessively.

Since Mormons believe that the elements are eternal, it follows that they deny the ex nihilo creation. Rather, the universe was created (organized) out of preexisting elements that God organized by imposing physical laws. The Prophet Joseph Smith also taught that intelligence is also eternal and uncreated: "The intelligence of spirits had no beginning, neither will it have an end. . . . Intelligence is eternal and exists upon a self-existent principle" (*TPJS*, pp. 353–54).

Just as God organized preexisting matter to create the universe, so he organized preexisting intelligence to create the spirits that eventually became human beings. Consequently, Latter-day Saints do not view God as the *total* cause of what human beings are. Human intelligence is uncreated by God, and therefore independent of his control. Thus Mormons insist that human beings are free agents in the fullest sense, and deny both the doctrines of prevenient and irresistible grace, which make God's choice determinative for SALVATION or damnation. God will not coerce independent, self-existent wills. Though he desires the exaltation of all, and offers it equally to all, its achievement requires individual cooperation, a covenant relationship. In this way, LDS theology escapes the classical dilemma of predestination and theodicy imposed by believing that God created all things from nothing and is therefore solely responsible for the final products. Their radical doctrine of individual free agency also allows the Latter-day Saints to deny the theory of human depravity. The Fall of Adam did not totally incapacitate humans from doing any good thing—they remain able to choose and to perform either good or evil. Moreover, Latter-day Saints accept the concept of the "fortunate Fall" (*mea culpa).* The Fall was a necessary step in the progress of humanity: "Adam fell that men might be; and men are, that they might have joy" (2 Ne. 2:25).

A positive view of the physical universe and of man also allows Latter-day Saints to anticipate a physical afterlife, the CELESTIAL

KINGDOM, a community of physically resurrected beings transformed and perfected. Unlike many ancient church fathers, they do not long to escape the realm of the flesh, but rather to sanctify it. Hence, in the LDS view, even the physical relationships of family and marriage can continue in the eternities in a sanctified state. Thus there is little asceticism and no celibacy in LDS theology, which sees in both of these tendencies a denial of the goodness of God's physical creation (Gen. 1:31); and LDS theology avoids the traditional disparagement of the human body and the contempt for human sexuality that are largely due to the neoplatonism of late antiquity.

While common ground for Latter-day Saints and other Christians is an acceptance of the Bible and its teachings, issues of interpretation aside, Mormonism agrees with "high church" orthodoxy against conservative Protestantism on the doctrine of the sufficiency of scripture. Though they accept the Bible, Latter-day Saints, like Roman Catholics and the Eastern Orthodox, for example, do not believe that the biblical text alone is sufficient for salvation. Biblical teaching, while true and accepted, has been imperfectly preserved and can be fully reconstituted only through supplemental REVELATION. This is not because New Testament Christianity was defective, but because New Testament Christianity is only partially preserved in the modern Bible. Those doctrines that were not preserved must be *restored;* consequently, Mormons deny both biblical inerrancy and sufficiency. Since the apostles and prophets of earliest Christianity received direct revelation from God (see, e.g., Acts 10:9–16, 28), Latter-day Saints believe that any church claiming the fulness of the gospel must also enjoy this gift.

This crucial principle of continuing revelation is illustrated in the experience of the Prophet Joseph Smith, whose visions and revelations form the foundation of LDS doctrine. As the *magisterium* of the church is fundamental for Roman Catholics, and the scriptures are the *fontes* for Protestants, for Latter-day Saints the highest authority in religious matters is continuing revelation from God given through the living apostles and prophets of his Church, beginning with Joseph Smith and continuing to the present leadership.

Latter-day Saints insist that both the canon of scripture and the structure of theology are always open-ended, and can always be added upon by God through revelation to his prophets (A of F 9).

Through this means they have received clarification of biblical doctrines that are disputed in other denominations, for example, Christ's ministry to the dead in 1 Peter 3:18 and 4:6 (see D&C 128; 137; 138). Also through modern revelation Latter-day Saints have received some distinctive doctrines that are not explicitly found in the Bible. In these cases modern revelation has not rehabilitated a doctrine that is unclear, but has restored a doctrine that was entirely lost.

Latter-day Saints share with most Christians the conviction that salvation comes only through the ATONEMENT OF JESUS CHRIST, which is representative, exemplary, and substitutionary in nature. Christ is the mediator of humanity to the Father instead of fallen Adam; he sets an example for humans to emulate; and he takes mankind's place in suffering for sins.

Latter-day Saints are monophysite in their christology; that is, they believe Christ has only one nature, which is simultaneously both human and divine. This is possible because the human and the divine are not mutually exclusive categories in LDS thought, as in the duophysite christology of much orthodoxy. As Lorenzo Snow said, "As man now is, God once was: As God now is, man may be" (Snow, p. 46). Most Christians would agree with the first half of this couplet as applied to the person of Christ, but Latter-day Saints apply it also to the Father. The second half of the couplet is more orthodox in the denominational sense than either Protestants or Catholics, for Latter-day Saints share the ancient biblical doctrine of deification (*apotheosis*) with Eastern Orthodoxy. Several of early Christianity's theologians said essentially the same thing as Lorenzo Snow. Irenaeus said, "If the word became a man, it was so men may become gods" (Against Heresies, 4. Pref), and Athanasius maintained that "[Christ] became man that we might be made divine" (On the Incarnation, 54). Yet Latter-day Saints combine both halves of the couplet to reach what they feel is the only possible conclusion—human and divine are not mutually exclusive categories. Mormons insist that the two categories are one: Humans are of the lineage of the gods. Latter-day Saints would agree entirely with C. S. Lewis in *Mere Christianity:*

> He said (in the Bible) that we were "gods" and He is going to make good His words. If we let Him—for we can prevent Him, if we choose—He

will make the feeblest and filthiest of us into a God or goddess, dazzling, radiant, immortal creature, pulsating all through with such energy and joy and wisdom and love as we cannot now imagine [p. 175].

BIBLIOGRAPHY

Dodds, Erwin. *Pagan and Christian in an Age of Anxiety.* New York, 1970.

Keller, Roger. *Reformed Christians and Mormon Christians: Let's Talk.* Ann Arbor, Mich., 1986.

Lash, Symeon. "Deification." In *The Westminster Dictionary of Christian Theology,* ed. A. Richardson and J. Bowden. Philadelphia, 1983.

Madsen, Truman, ed. *Reflections on Mormonism: Judaeo-Christian Parallels.* Salt Lake City, 1978.

Robinson, Stephen E. *Are Mormons Christian?* Salt Lake City, 1991.

Snow, Eliza R. *Biography and Family Record of Lorenzo Snow.* Salt Lake City, 1884.

STEPHEN E. ROBINSON

HARMONIZATION OF PARADOX

Because Latter-day Saints reject the influences of Neoplatonism on original Christian theology, they are not on the horns of the dilemmas posed by some of the paradoxes in traditional Christian theology. This is not to say, however, that LDS ethical life and religious thought are free of paradox. LDS perspective tends to harmonize many paradoxes through its views that opposition is necessary in all things and that God and mankind are in the same order of reality but at different stages of knowledge and progression.

As used in ordinary discourse, "paradox" usually refers to a statement that on its face is unbelievable because it is apparently self-contradictory or is contrary to well-established facts, common sense, or generally received belief. While many paradoxes are no doubt false, not all necessarily are. Indeed, in the history of human thought, many brash paradoxes have overthrown a generally received but false belief, eventually to become widely accepted themselves—"some time a paradox, but now time gives it proof" (*Hamlet* 3.1.115).

Classical Christian theology is in many ways paradoxical. This is often the result of the unstable theological blending that occurred in the early centuries of Christianity when (a) insights that came from personal Judeo-Christian revelation were (b) interpretatively recast within an impersonal Neo-platonic view of reality. To mention a few:

1. (a) The loving God who is profoundly touched by the feelings of our infirmities is (b) without passions or outside influences.

2. (a) The God who acts in human history and responds to personal prayers is (b) timeless and unchangeable.
3. (b) The God without body or parts became (a) embodied in the person of Jesus of Nazareth.
4. The God who is (b) absolutely unlimited and good, and who created all things out of nothing (a) created a world abounding with evils.
5. (a) The Godhead consists of three perfect and separate persons who (b) collectively constitute one metaphysical substance.

Latter-day Saint doctrine, while affirming (a) the Judeo-Christian dimensions of the foregoing propositions regarding God, rejects (b) the Neo-platonic framework and metaphysic within which Judeo-Christian revelation has historically been interpreted. Accordingly, LDS understanding of Christian doctrine does not manifest those paradoxes that are generated by the union of these two incompatible sets of beliefs.

Latter-day Saint thought builds bridges between entities and quantities that are normally thought to be incongruous. Reality is not seen as a dichotomy but as a graded continuum: Thus, SPIRIT is understood to be a form of matter, but a highly refined form; and time is part of eternity. A corporeal God is omnipresent through the light that emanates from him and that is in and through all things (D&C 88: 12–13).

In ethical discourse, the axiomatic and eternal principle of AGENCY demands that there be "an opposition in all things" (2 Ne. 2:11) to ensure that meaningful choices can be made—not only between good and evil but also from among an array of righteous alternatives (*see* EVIL). Weakness exists that it may bring strength (Ether 12:27). Thus, Latter-day Saint moral life ranges between options that are often paradoxical: the imperatives of improving oneself or serving other people; spending time at home or rendering Church service; favoring individuality or institutionality; obtaining wealth or giving to the poor; finding one's life by losing it in service to others (Matt. 10:39).

Such tensions, however, do not impede LDS action, nor are they transcended through mysticism, irony, or resignation (whether optimistically or pessimistically). They are embraced in a series of interrelated gospel principles that guide LDS life, including

- personal revelation (by the Holy Ghost each individual can tell what leads to Christ [Moro. 7:12–13; 10:5–6])
- the mandate to act (knowledge of what is right comes by doing it [John 7:17])
- the making of voluntary covenants (people obligate themselves by what they agree to do)
- an extended concept of self (helping others is tantamount to helping oneself)
- the atonement of Jesus Christ (his judgment will encompass both divine grace and human works, retributive justice and compassionate mercy)
- the eternal relativity of kingdoms and progression (with all their differences, all people are on the same pathway to perfection).

For Latter-day Saints, the paradoxes of knowledge are generally resolved under the concept of "continuing revelation" (*see* REVELATION). While Latter-day Saints are inclined to hold that each truth is self-consistent and coherent with all other truth, they also acknowledge the imperfection of human understanding. Mortal attempts to comprehend or express divine truths are inherently liable to error for at least two reasons: (1) the linguistic-conceptual frameworks within which such facts are expressed and interpreted are culturally conditioned and manifestly inadequate; and (2) mankind's awareness of the facts is fragmentary and incomplete, "for as the heavens are higher than the earth, so are my ways higher than your ways, and my thoughts than your thoughts" (Isa. 55:8–9), and in mortality "man doth not comprehend all the things which the Lord can comprehend" (Mosiah 4:9). But by revelation, human knowledge may increase: "No man knoweth of [God's] ways save it be revealed unto him" (Jacob 4:8). "The natural man receiveth not the things of the Spirit of God, . . . neither can he know them, because they are spiritually discerned" (1 Cor. 2:14).

Thus where definitively clear revelation appears to contradict generally received opinion, common sense, or well-established facts, Latter-day Saints give priority to revelation and trust that time will give proof to what now seems paradoxical or that within God's more complete comprehension of things there may be mediating principles by which two apparently conflicting partial truths may be reconciled. This trust and hope for further revelation quiets such unsearchable paradoxes as how God's complete knowledge can be reconciled with mankind's agency, how scriptural and scientific accounts of creation can be harmonized, or how, in general, study and faith, reason and revelation, symbolic vision and practical literal-mindedness can all be accommodated concurrently. LDS doctrine is resistant to extremes: Its authoritativeness has not been transformed into abstractions or absolutes; nor have its revelations wandered into mysticism or vagueness. In such ways, the doctrines of the eternal gospel maintain their own set of tensions in a mortal world.

BIBLIOGRAPHY

Hafen, Bruce C. "Love Is Not Blind: Some Thoughts for College Students on Faith and Ambiguity." In *BYU Speeches of the Year,* pp. 8–17. Provo, Utah, 1979.

DAVID L. PAULSEN

TREATISES ON DOCTRINE

Doctrinal works—that is, periodicals, tracts, and books—have been numerous in the LDS tradition, reflecting the lay character of the ministry, the large corpus of scripture, and continuing concern with right belief as well as right conduct.

Official letters, including doctrinal expositions, of the First Presidency are published in *Messages of the First Presidency,* ed. James R. Clark, 6 vols. (Salt Lake City, 1965–1975). Influential tracts and pamphlets have been compiled in *Handbook of the Restoration* and in *Scrapbook of Mormon Literature,* comp. Ben E. Rich, 2 vols. (Chicago, n.d.).

In addition to volumes on Joseph Smith's teachings (*TPJS, WJS*), there are doctrinal statements in *Journal of Discourses* (1980). Compilations of discourses of the Presidents of the Church, all published in Salt Lake City, include Brigham Young, *Discourses of Brigham Young,* ed. John A. Widtsoe (1954); John Taylor, *The Gospel Kingdom,* ed. G. Homer Durham (1987); *Discourses of Wilford Woodruff,* ed. G. Homer Durham (1946); *Teachings of Lorenzo Snow,* comp. Clyde J. Williams (1984); Joseph F. Smith, *Gospel Doctrine* (1939); Heber J. Grant, *Gospel Standards* (1941); George Albert

Smith, *Sharing the Gospel with Others* (1948); David O. McKay, *Gospel Ideals* (1953); Joseph Fielding Smith, *Doctrines of Salvation,* comp. Bruce R. McConkie, 3 vols. (1954–1956); Harold B. Lee, *Stand Ye in Holy Places* and *Ye Are the Light of the World* (1974); *Teachings of Spencer W. Kimball,* ed. Edward L. Kimball (1982); and *Teachings of Ezra Taft Benson* (1988).

Following is a list of books that have made significant contributions to the understanding of doctrine (unless otherwise noted, these works were published in Salt Lake City): Parley P. Pratt, *A Voice of Warning* (New York, 1837) and *Key to Theology* (1856); Orson Pratt, *An Interesting Account of Several Remarkable Visions and of the Late Discovery of Ancient American Records* (Edinburgh, 1840); Orson Spencer, *Spencer's Letters* (Liverpool and London, 1852); John Taylor, *Mediation and Atonement* (1882) and *The Government of God* (1884); Franklin D. Richards and James Little, *A Compendium of the Doctrines of the Gospel* (1882); B. H. Roberts, *The Gospel* (Liverpool, 1888), *Mormon Doctrine of Deity* and *Jesus Christ: The Revelation of God* (1903) and *The Seventy's Course in Theology,* 5 vols. (1907–1912); James E. Talmage, *Articles of Faith* (1899) and *Jesus the Christ* (1915); Orson F. Whitney, *Gospel Themes* (1914) and *Saturday Night Thoughts* (1921); Joseph F. Smith, *Gospel Doctrine* (1919); Brigham Young, *Discourses of Brigham Young,* ed. John A. Widtsoe (1926); John A. Widtsoe, *Priesthood and Church Government* (1939), *A Rational Theology* (1945), and *Evidences and Reconciliations,* 3 vols. in 1 (1960); Joseph Smith, *Teachings of the Prophet Joseph Smith,* comp. by Joseph Fielding Smith (1938); Orson Pratt, *Orson Pratt's Works,* ed. Parker P. Robison (1945), and *Masterful Discourses of Orson Pratt,* ed. N. B. Lundwall (1946); Milton R. Hunter, *The Gospel Through the Ages* (1945); Daniel H. Ludlow, ed., *Latter-day Prophets Speak* (1948); J. Reuben Clark, Jr., *On the Way to Immortality and Eternal Life* (1949); *Writings of Parley P. Pratt,* ed. Parker P. Robison (1952); Bruce R. McConkie, *Mormon Doctrine* (1958, rev. 1966); Spencer W. Kimball, *The Miracle of Forgiveness* (1969); and George Q. Cannon, *Gospel Truth,* ed. Jerreld Newquist, 2 vols. (1972, 1974).

Shorter treatises include Oliver Cowdery, "General Charge to the Twelve" (1835); Quorum of the Twelve, "A Proclamation to the World" (1845); Lorenzo Snow, "Law of Tithing" (1899); James E.

Talmage, "The Honor and Dignity of the Priesthood" (1914); J. Reuben Clark, Jr., "The Charted Course of the Church in Education" (1938) and "When Are the Writings or Sermons of Church Leaders Entitled to the Claim of Scripture?" (1954); Harold B. Lee, "Priesthood . . . Core of All Activity" (1961) and "Priesthood Correlation" (1961); Spencer W. Kimball, "When the World Will Be Converted" (1974), "Lengthening Our Stride" (1974), and "Becoming Pure in Heart" (1978); N. Eldon Tanner, "Church Administration" (1979).

ELEANOR KNOWLES

E

ELECT OF GOD

The elect of God are those who are heirs to all that the Father has. Although the faithful have always been the elect of God, even before Abraham, the present concept that God elects or chooses individuals or groups to whom he makes promises of eternal SALVATION, and in turn requires of them certain obligations, has its roots in the COVENANT God made with Abraham. In ancient times Abraham's descendants were considered the elect, especially through Isaac and Jacob (Israel). For disobedience, the Israelites were eventually scattered throughout the world. However, God has not forgotten his covenant with their fathers. Biblical, Book of Mormon, and latter-day prophets have declared that ultimately the Israelite people will be gathered from their dispersion and restored to favor with God (cf. Amos 9:13–15). All persons who are not literally of Israel can be brought into the elect lineage of Abraham by the LAW OF ADOPTION when they accept the gospel (Abr. 2:10; D&C 84:33–34; Gal. 3:26–29; 4:5–7).

The GOSPEL OF JESUS CHRIST, restored to the earth through the Prophet Joseph Smith, inaugurated the restoration and the gathering of the elect from the four quarters of the earth (D&C 33:6; 110:11). When scattered children of Israel hear the gospel message of salvation, they are invited to come into the fold of Christ, his Church, by

REPENTANCE, BAPTISM, and receiving the HOLY GHOST by the LAYING ON OF HANDS (*MD*, p. 201).

To enjoy the fulness of the covenant BLESSINGS and the eternal felicity of God in the presence of Abraham, Isaac, and Jacob, the elect must be faithful in keeping all the covenants required of them by the Lord. Some may choose not to be so devoted, whereas others pursue such excellence in faithfulness that their CALLING AND ELECTION are made sure (cf. 2 Pet. 1:10). These become "the elect according to the covenant" (JS—M 1:22) and are made partakers of the same eternal reward that was extended to Abraham. That is, they are assured of EXALTATION in God's presence with Abraham, Isaac, and Jacob (Luke 13:28; D&C 132:29–32, 37).

BIBLIOGRAPHY
Richards, LeGrand. *Israel, Do You Know!* Salt Lake City, 1954.

ARTHUR A. BAILEY

ELIAS, SPIRIT OF

The "spirit of Elias" is a LDS concept that refers to the preparatory power that initiates gospel restoration following periods of apostasy. The Prophet Joseph Smith explained, "The spirit of Elias is to prepare the way for a greater revelation of God, which is the Priesthood of Elias, or the Priesthood unto which Aaron was ordained. And when God sends a man into the world to prepare for a greater work, holding the keys of the power of Elias, it was called the doctrine of Elias, even from the early ages of the world. . . . We find the Apostles endowed with greater power than John [the Baptist]: their office was more under the spirit and power of Elijah than Elias" (*TPJS*, pp. 335–36).

John the Baptist was the forerunner of Jesus Christ in the meridian of time (Matt. 11:12–14; 17:12; JST John 1:21–24). He "was ordained by the angel of God . . . to make straight the way of the Lord before the face of his people, to prepare them for the coming of the Lord" (D&C 84:28). By authority of the Aaronic Priesthood, John preached repentance and baptism for the remission of sins, in preparation for the coming of one mightier who would baptize with the HOLY GHOST.

On May 15, 1829, John the Baptist, as a resurrected being, ordained Joseph Smith and Oliver Cowdery to the Aaronic Priesthood preparatory to Christ's second coming. Describing this ordination, Joseph Smith stated:

> An angel . . . laid his hands upon my head, and ordained me to a Priest after the order of Aaron, and to hold the keys of this Priesthood, which office was to preach repentance and baptism for the remission of sins, and also to baptize. But I was informed that this office did not extend to the laying on of hands for the giving of the Holy Ghost; that office was a greater work, and was to be given afterward; but that my ordination was a preparatory work, or a going before, which was the spirit of Elias [*TPJS,* p. 335].

Later, Peter, James, and John conferred upon Joseph Smith and Oliver Cowdery the Melchizedek Priesthood (D&C 27:12), and still later (April 3, 1836) Elijah conferred additional keys upon them (D&C 110:13–16).

Joseph Smith further explained:

> The spirit of Elias is first, Elijah second, and Messiah last. Elias is a forerunner to prepare the way, and the spirit and power of Elijah is to come after, holding the keys of power, building the Temple to the capstone, placing the seals of the Melchizedek Priesthood upon the house of Israel, and making all things ready; then Messiah comes to His Temple, which is last of all. . . . Elijah was to come and prepare the way and build up the kingdom before the coming of the great day of the Lord, although the spirit of Elias might begin it [*TPJS,* pp. 335, 340].

A. JAMES HUDSON

ELIJAH, SPIRIT OF

For members of The Church of Jesus Christ of Latter-day Saints, the spirit of Elijah is the spirit of family kinship and unity. It is the spirit that motivates the concern to search out ancestral family members through family history; and, on their behalf, to perform proxy baptisms, temple ENDOWMENTS, and sealing ordinances (*HC* 6:252). This is seen as fulfillment of the prophecy of Malachi that in the last days Elijah "will turn the heart [in Hebrew, the innermost part, as the soul, the affections] of the fathers to the children, and the heart of the children to their fathers" (Mal. 4:5–6).

The appearance of Elijah to the Prophet Joseph Smith and Oliver Cowdery in the Kirtland Temple in 1836 inaugurated anew this spirit (D&C 110:13). The spirit of Elijah is active in the impetus anyone feels toward finding and cherishing family members and family ties past and present. In the global sense, the spirit of Elijah is the spirit of love that may eventually overcome all human family estrangements. Then the priesthood power can bind generations together in eternal family relationships and "*seal* the children to the fathers and fathers to the children" within the gospel of Jesus Christ (*WJS*, p. 329).

BIBLIOGRAPHY

Smith, Joseph Fielding. "Elijah the Prophet and His Mission." *Utah Genealogical and Historical Magazine* 12 (Jan. 1921): 1–20.

MARY FINLAYSON

ENDLESS AND ETERNAL

The terms "endless" and "eternal" have at least two connotations each in The Church of Jesus Christ of Latter-day Saints. They are used both as adjectives and as nouns. The adjectival forms, fitting the more traditional viewpoint, denote a concept of time without beginning or end. In a second, less familiar usage, the phrase "endless and eternal" functions as a noun, another name for God (Moses 1:3; 7:35)—in the manner of "Alpha and Omega," or "the Beginning and the End."

In a revelation dated March 1830 (now D&C 19), the Prophet Joseph Smith learned that phrases such as "endless punishment" and "eternal life" have qualitative as well as quantitative implications. The word "endless," for example, has sometimes been employed by God for greater impact "that it might work upon the hearts of the children of men" (D&C 19:7). Consequently, the term "endless punishment" may or may not imply a duration of time—that there will be no end to such punishment—but it clearly does imply that the punishment (or blessing) is associated with the Eternal One. "Eternal punishment is God's punishment. Endless punishment is God's punishment" (D&C 19:11–12). In like manner, the concept of eternal life referred to in scripture (e.g., John 17:3) implies more than life lasting forever; it also connotes a quality of life like that of God, as well as life with God (*DS* 2:8, 228).

BIBLIOGRAPHY

Doxey, Roy W., comp. *Latter-day Prophets and the Doctrine and Covenants,* Vol. 1, pp. 204–208. Salt Lake City, 1963.

Ludlow, Daniel H. *A Companion to Your Study of the Doctrine and Covenants,* Vol. 1, p. 142. Salt Lake City, 1978.

ARTHUR R. BASSETT

ENDOWMENT

An endowment generally is a gift, but in a specialized sense it is a course of instruction, ordinances, and COVENANTS given only in dedicated temples of The Church of Jesus Christ of Latter-day Saints. The words "to endow" (from the Greek *enduein*), as used in the New Testament, mean to dress, clothe, put on garments, put on attributes, or receive virtue. Christ instructed his apostles to tarry at Jerusalem "until ye be endued with power from on high" (Luke 24:49), a promise fulfilled, at least in part, on the day of Pentecost (Acts 2). In modern times, a similar revelation was given: "I gave unto you a commandment that you should build a house, in the which house I design to endow those whom I have chosen with power on high; for this is the promise of the Father unto you; therefore I command you to tarry, even as mine apostles at Jerusalem" (D&C 95:8–9).

Though there had been preliminary and preparatory spiritual outpourings upon Latter-day Saints in Ohio and Missouri, the endowment in its full sense was not received until the Nauvoo Temple era. As he introduced temple ordinances in 1842 at Nauvoo, the Prophet Joseph Smith taught that these were "of things spiritual, and to be received only by the spiritual minded" (*TPJS*, p. 237). The endowment was necessary, he said, to organize the Church fully, that the

Saints might be organized according to the laws of God, and, as the dedicatory prayer of the Kirtland Temple petitioned, that they would "be prepared to obtain every needful thing" (D&C 109:15). The endowment was designed to give "a comprehensive view of our condition and true relation to God" (*TPJS*, p. 324), "to prepare the disciples for their missions in the world" (p. 274), to prevent being "overcome by evils" (p. 259), to enable them to "secure the fulness of those blessings which have been prepared for the Church of the Firstborn" (p. 237).

The endowment of "power from on high" in modern temples has four main aspects. First is the preparatory ordinance, a ceremonial washing and anointing, after which the temple patron dons the sacred clothing of the temple.

Second is a course of instruction by lectures and representations. These include a recital of the most prominent events of the Creation, a figurative depiction of the advent of Adam and Eve and of every man and every woman, the entry of Adam and Eve into the Garden of Eden, the consequent expulsion from the garden, their condition in the world, and their receiving of the PLAN OF SALVATION leading to the return to the presence of God (Talmage, pp. 83–84). The endowment instructions utilize every human faculty so that the meaning of the gospel may be clarified through art, drama, and symbols. All participants wear white temple robes symbolizing purity and the equality of all persons before God the Father and his Son Jesus Christ. The temple becomes a house of revelation whereby one is instructed more perfectly "in theory, in principle, and in doctrine" (D&C 97:14). "This completeness of survey and expounding of the gospel plan makes temple worship one of the most effective methods of refreshing the memory concerning the entire structure of the gospel" (Widtsoe, 1986, p. 5).

Third is making covenants. The temple endowment is seen as the unfolding or culmination of the covenants made at BAPTISM. Temple covenants give "tests by which one's willingness and fitness for righteousness may be known" (Widtsoe, p. 335). They include the "covenant and promise to observe the law of strict virtue and chastity, to be charitable, benevolent, tolerant and pure; to devote both talent and material means to the spread of truth and the uplifting of the [human] race; to maintain devotion to the cause of truth; and to seek in every way to contribute to the great preparation that the earth may be made ready to receive . . . Jesus Christ" (Talmage, p. 84). One also promises to keep these covenants sacred and to "trifle not with sacred things" (D&C 6:12).

Fourth is a sense of divine presence. In the dedicatory prayer of the temple at Kirtland, Ohio, the Prophet Joseph Smith pleaded "that all people who shall enter upon the threshold of the Lord's house may feel thy power, and feel constrained to acknowledge that thou hast sanctified it, and that it is thy house, a place of thy holiness" (D&C 109:13). Of temples built by sacrifice to the name of the Lord Jesus Christ, dedicated by his authority, and reverenced in his Spirit, the promise is given, "My name shall be here; and I will manifest myself to my people in mercy in this holy house" (D&C 110:8). In the temples there is an "aura of deity" manifest to the worthy (Kimball, pp. 534–35). Through the temple endowment, one may seek "a fulness of the Holy Ghost" (D&C 109:15). Temple ordinances are seen as a means for receiving inspiration and instruction through the Holy Spirit, and for preparing to return to the presence of God.

In Nauvoo, the Prophet Joseph taught for the first time that it is the privilege of Latter-day Saints to act as agents in behalf of their kindred dead. After receiving their own temple endowment, Latter-day Saints return to the temple frequently to participate in the endowment ceremony as proxies for, and in behalf of, deceased persons. Consistent with the law of agency, it is believed that those so served have complete freedom in the spirit world to accept or reject the spiritual blessing thus proffered them (*HC* 5:350).

[*See also* Baptism for the Dead; Salvation for the Dead.]

BIBLIOGRAPHY

Kimball, Spencer W. *Teachings of Spencer W. Kimball,* ed. Edward L. Kimball. Salt Lake City, 1982.

Packer, Boyd K. *The Holy Temple.* Salt Lake City, 1980.

Talmage, James E. *House of the Lord.* Salt Lake City, 1968.

Widtsoe, John A. *Priesthood and Church Government.* Salt Lake City, 1939.

——. *Temple Worship.* Salt Lake City, 1986.

ALMA P. BURTON

ENDURING TO THE END

Enduring to the end, or remaining faithful to the laws and ordinances of the GOSPEL OF JESUS CHRIST throughout life, is a fundamental requirement for SALVATION in the KINGDOM OF GOD. This belief distinguishes Latter-day Saints from many other Christian denominations, which teach that salvation is given to all who simply believe and confess that Jesus is the Christ. Latter-day Saints believe that to be saved a person must have faith in Jesus Christ, demonstrate REPENTANCE of sins, submit to BAPTISM by immersion, and receive the GIFT OF THE HOLY GHOST by the LAYING ON OF HANDS by those holding the true priesthood authority, and then remain faithful to all COVENANTS, continue in RIGHTEOUSNESS, and endure faithfully to the end of mortal life (Heb. 3:6–14; 6:4–15; Mark 13:13). This enduring faithfulness makes it possible for a person to receive fully the grace of Christ. The Doctrine and Covenants states, "If you keep my commandments and endure to the end you shall have eternal life, which gift is the greatest of all the gifts of God" (D&C 14:7).

The Book of Mormon prophet $Nephi_1$ taught the principle of enduring to the end as a requirement of salvation: "After ye have repented of your sins, and witnessed unto the Father that ye are willing to keep my commandments, by the baptism of water, and have received the baptism of fire and of the Holy Ghost, . . . and after this should deny me, it would have been better for you not to have known me. . . . He that endureth to the end, the same shall be saved" (2 Ne. 31:14–15; cf. Heb. 6:4–6). As Nephi explains, enduring to the end involves having faith, hope, and charity; faithfully following the example of Jesus Christ; and always abounding in good works (cf. Alma 7:23–24): "Unless a man shall endure to the end, in following the example of the Son of the living God, he cannot be saved. . . . Wherefore, ye must press forward with a steadfastness in Christ, having a perfect brightness of hope, and a love of God and of all men. Wherefore, if ye shall press forward, feasting upon the word of Christ, and endure to the end, . . . ye shall have eternal life" (2 Ne. 31:16, 20).

Enduring to the end includes being willing and prepared to endure faithfully the trials of life, as did Job, Stephen (Acts 7), Paul (2 Tim. 4:5–7), Peter (1 Pet. 1–4), and $Moroni_2$ (Moroni 1:1–3). The

Lord spoke this reassurance to the Prophet Joseph Smith after several months of incarceration in Liberty Jail: "My son, peace be unto thy soul; thine adversity and thine afflictions shall be but a small moment; And then, if thou endure it well, God shall exalt thee on high; thou shalt triumph over all thy foes" (D&C 121:7–8).

BIBLIOGRAPHY
Ashton, Marvin J. "If Thou Endure It Well." *Ensign* 14 (Nov. 1984):20–22.
Maxwell, Neal A. "Endure It Well." *Ensign* 20 (May 1990):33–35.

JOHN M. MADSEN

ETERNAL LIFE

The scriptures clearly state that eternal life comes from God through his son Jesus Christ (John 3:16; 14:6; Heb. 5:9; 2 Ne. 31:20–21; Alma 11:40; Ether 3:14; D&C 45:8), and is the "greatest of all the gifts of God" (D&C 14:7; *see also* EXALTATION; GODHOOD). To Latter-day Saints the phrase "eternal life" refers not only to everlasting life but also and more particularly to the quality of life God lives. Eternal life is available to all people who have lived on earth who accept this gift by their obedience to God's laws and ordinances.

God's work, and the source of his glory, is bringing to pass "the immortality and eternal life" of his children (Moses 1:39). In other words, God works to enable his children's return to his presence so that they may both live with him and live as he lives.

So allied is Christ with the Father that the scriptures sometimes define eternal life as "knowing" them: "This is life eternal, that they might know thee the only true God, and Jesus Christ, whom thou hast sent" (John 17:3; D&C 132:24).

Knowing Christ in this world comes by receiving him and his law (D&C 132:23–24). Jeremiah spoke for the Lord: "I will put my law in their inward parts, and write it in their hearts. . . . And they shall teach no more every man his neighbour . . . saying, Know the Lord: for they shall all know me" (Jer. 31:33–34). As stated in the Gospel of John, one begins to know Christ and his will by searching the scriptures, for, as Jesus affirmed, "they are they which testify of me" (John 5:39).

Having the law written in one's heart implies an acceptance that prompts action; indeed, the scriptures mention many actions that one must take in order to receive the gift of eternal life. To enter the path leading toward eternal life, one must exercise faith in Christ (John 3:36; 6:47; Moro. 7:41), repent, be baptized for the remission of one's sins (2 Ne. 31:17–18), and receive the gift of the Holy Ghost. The scriptures state that once on the path, the believer must strive to keep the COMMANDMENTS (2 Ne. 31:19–20; Alma 7:15–16)—that is, to do the works of RIGHTEOUSNESS (D&C 59:23), primary among which is charity (1 Cor. 13; Matt. 25:34–36). The believer must also ENDURE TO THE END (2 Ne. 31:20–21; D&C 50:5; cf. Paul's phrase "patient continuance in well doing," Rom. 2:7), and make covenants in connection with temple ordinances (D&C 124:55; 128:12).

While in mortality, individuals may come to a stage of knowing the Father and the Son that allows the Lord to promise them eternal life. This occurrence is described in scripture as receiving the HOLY SPIRIT OF PROMISE (D&C 88:3–4) and the Second Comforter (John 14:16; D&C 88:2–4; *see also* JESUS CHRIST, SECOND COMFORTER); having the more sure word of prophecy (D&C 131:5); and having one's CALLING AND ELECTION made sure (2 Pet. 1:10; D&C 131:5).

God invites all people to seek and ask earnestly for eternal life, and reassures all who do so that they will not be given a stone (cf. Matt. 7:7–11). They are promised "revelation upon revelation, knowledge upon knowledge," which brings an understanding of "peaceable things—that which bringeth joy, that which bringeth life eternal" (D&C 42:61). Those who will receive eternal life in its fullest come forth in the first RESURRECTION (Mosiah 15:21–25) and inherit the highest degree of glory in the CELESTIAL KINGDOM (D&C 76:50–59; 88:4; 101:65).

The Prophet Joseph Smith was at a loss for words to capture the eternal splendor of God the Father and of his son Jesus Christ, "whose brightness and glory defy all description" (JS—H 1:17). Language can describe the glories of eternal life only inadequately through metaphors of overwhelmingly bright light or fire (Ex. 24:17; Acts 26:13–15; Rev. 21:23; 1 Ne. 1:8–10; D&C 110:1–4; cf. "shine as the brightness of the firmament," Dan. 12:3); pure truth (John 14:6; Ether 4:12; D&C 84:45–48; 93:36; Moses 7:29–40); glass or crystal (Rev. 4:6; D&C 130:9); and timelessness (Ps. 90:4; 2 Pet. 3:8;

Rev. 10:6; Alma 40:8; D&C 88:110). Paul points out how far eternal life exceeds the descriptive ability of language when he says, "Eye hath not seen, nor ear heard, neither have entered into the heart of man, the things which God hath prepared for them that love him" (1 Cor. 2:9).

[*See also* Immortality and Eternal Life.]

BIBLIOGRAPHY
Monson, Thomas S. *Pathways to Perfection.* Salt Lake City, 1976.

CATHERINE CORMAN PARRY

ETERNAL LIVES, ETERNAL INCREASE

"Eternal lives" is a term that refers to the right and power to beget children after the resurrection, granted to those who are exalted in the highest degree of the CELESTIAL KINGDOM. This is an aspect of ETERNAL PROGRESSION. "In the celestial glory there are three heavens or degrees; and in order to obtain the highest, a man must enter into this order of the priesthood [meaning the new and everlasting covenant of marriage]; And if he does not, he cannot obtain it. He may enter into the other, but that is the end of his kingdom; he cannot have an increase" (D&C 131:1–4).

This distinctive doctrine of The Church of Jesus Christ of Latter-day Saints was taught by Joseph Smith and was especially articulated on May 16–17, 1843, at Ramus, Illinois, where he often visited and preached. Conversing on spiritual topics with a small party of friends, the Prophet Joseph Smith shed light on the concept of eternal increase: "Except a man and his wife enter into an everlasting covenant and be married for eternity, while in this probation, by the power and authority of the Holy Priesthood, they will cease to increase when they die; that is, they will not have any children after the resurrection. But those who are married by the power and authority of the priesthood in this life, and continue without committing the sin against the Holy Ghost, will continue to increase and have children in the celestial glory" (*TPJS,* pp. 300–301). Doctrine and Covenants, section 131, is largely concerned with this subject, and was first included in 1876.

A husband and wife who are married in the new and everlasting covenant and sealed by the HOLY SPIRIT OF PROMISE under the proper priesthood authority are promised that they shall inherit "thrones, kingdoms, principalities, and powers," and their "glory shall be a fulness and a continuation of the seeds forever and ever" (D&C 132:19). They are likened to gods, having no end. They share in the promises of eternal posterity made to Abraham and Sarah: "Both in the world and out of the world should they continue as innumerable as the stars" (D&C 132:30).

Brigham Young, in 1862, spoke of eternal lives, stating that the opportunity to become heirs to all things, and to become a "King of kings and Lord of lords, . . . is promised to the faithful, and are but so many stages in that ceaseless progression of eternal lives. . . . There will be no end to the increase of the faithful" (*JD* 10:5). He described such a situation as a pleasing one, creating happiness beyond mortal comprehension. In 1864 he elaborated: "In like manner, every faithful son of God, becomes, as it were, Adam to the race that springs from his loins, when they are embraced in the covenants and blessings of the Holy Priesthood . . . in the progress of eternal lives. . . . We have not yet received our kingdoms, neither will we, until we have finished our work on the earth, passed through the ordeals, are brought up by the power of the resurrection, and are crowned with glory and eternal lives" (*JD* 10:355).

Latter-day Saints believe that all worthy men and women, through righteous living and being sealed by the power of the priesthood, will in ETERNAL LIFE inherit, with Adam and Eve, Abraham and Sarah, and all the faithful, those same blessings and enjoy a continuation of seeds forever, or eternal increase.

SHIRLEY S. RICKS

ETERNAL PROGRESSION

The principle of eternal progression cannot be precisely defined or comprehended, yet it is fundamental to the LDS worldview. The phrase "eternal progression" first occurs in the discourses of Brigham Young. It embodies many concepts taught by Joseph Smith, especially in his King Follett Discourse. It is based on the proposition that "there is no such thing as principle, power, wisdom, knowledge, life, position, or anything that can be imagined, that remains stationary—they must increase or decrease" (Young, *JD* 1:350).

Progression takes many forms. In one sense, eternal progression refers to everything that people learn and experience by their choices as they progress from PREMORTAL LIFE, to MORTALITY, to postmortal spirit life, and to a resurrected state in the presence of God. Personal progression is possible in each of these states, but not the same kind of progression. Progression apparently occurred in the premortal life, for most spirits there chose to follow Christ and some were noble and great, while others chose to follow Lucifer. Entering mortality affords opportunities for further progression. Obtaining a PHYSICAL BODY is a crucial step, enabling a person to experience physical sensations of all kinds and to progress in knowledge and understanding, all of which will rise with the person in the Resurrection (D&C 130:18). Brigham Young taught that even in mortality, "We are in eternity" (*JD* 10:22), and the object of this existence is "to learn to enjoy more, and to increase in knowledge and experience" (*JD* 14:228). "When we have learned to live according to the full value of the life we now possess, we are prepared for further advancement in the scale of eternal progression—for a more glorious and exalted sphere" (*JD* 9:168).

Life is never static. "One must progress or retrograde. One cannot stand still. Activity is the law of growth, and growth, progress, is the law of life" (A. Bowen, in *Christ's Ideals for Living,* O. Tanner, ed., Salt Lake City, 1980, p. 368). A person's attitude about "'eternal progression' will largely determine his philosophy of life . . . exalting, increasing, expanding and extending broader and broader until we can know as we are known, see as we are seen" (Young, *JD* 16:165).

At the Resurrection and Judgment, people will be assigned a DEGREE OF GLORY. Further progress is believed possible within each degree. Marriage and family life, however, continue only in the CELESTIAL KINGDOM, allowing "eternal increase" through having spirit children (*see* ETERNAL LIVES, ETERNAL INCREASE). "All this and more that cannot enter into our hearts to conceive is promised to the faithful, and are but so many stages in that ceaseless progression of eternal lives" (Young, *JD* 10:5).

No official Church teaching attempts to specify all the ways in which God progresses in his exalted spheres; "there is no end to [His] works, neither to [His] words" (Moses 1:38). God's glory and power are enhanced as his children progress in glory and power (see Moses 1:39; Young, *JD* 10:5). Ideas have been advanced to explain how God might progress in knowledge and still be perfect and know all things (*see* FOREKNOWLEDGE OF GOD; OMNIPOTENCE OF GOD).

The concept of eternal progression is a salient feature of the gospel of Jesus Christ, readily distinguishable from traditional Christian theology. The philosophical views of the Middle Ages were basically incompatible with such a concept, and the idea of progress that emerged in the eighteenth-century Enlightenment was that of social evolution (Bury, *The Idea of Progress,* London, 1932). The traditional Christian view has held that those in heaven enter "a state of eternal, inactive joy. In the presence of God they would worship him and sing praises to him eternally, but nothing more" (Widtsoe, p. 142). Latter-day Saints, however, constantly seek personal and righteous improvement not only by establishing Zion in this world, but by anticipating the continuation of progression eternally.

BIBLIOGRAPHY

Widtsoe, John A. "Is Progress Eternal or Is There Progress in Heaven?" *IE* 54 (Mar. 1951):142; see also *Evidences and Reconciliations,* pp. 179–85, Salt Lake City, 1960.

LISA RAMSEY ADAMS

EVIL

[*The LDS concept of evil is also explained in the article on* Devils. *The following article discusses a view of the purposes of evil and presents an LDS response to traditional discussions of the problem of evil.*]

In ordinary discourse, the term "evil" has a very wide definition and, along with the term "bad," is used in English most often to refer to morally wrong intentions, choices, and actions of agents (moral evil); to the operations of nonhuman nature such as disease, earthquakes, volcanic eruptions, and tornadoes (natural evil); and to the human and animal pain and suffering (psychological evil) that moral and natural evils may cause. In more technical philosophical discourse, it is applied also to inherent human limitations and defects (metaphysical evil).

The term is used with additional meanings in LDS scripture and discourse. In the Old Testament, the term is translated from the Hebrew term, *ra'*, and its cognates, whose applications range widely from (1) what tastes nasty or is ugly, displeasing, or sad, through (2) moral wickedness and the distress, misery, and tragedy that ensue from it, to (3) willful disobedience of God and his intentions for human beings. The latter two senses of the term predominate in the New Testament and in latter-day scriptures. Given its widely variant meanings, the precise meaning of evil must be ascertained from its context.

LDS scripture further illuminates biblical suggestions about God's purposes for his children and, thereby, helps to clarify one fundamental sense of evil. God disclosed to Moses: "This is my work and my glory—to bring to pass the immortality [resurrection, with everlasting bodily duration] and eternal life [Godlike quality or mode of being] of man" (Moses 1:39). Thus, anything inconsistent with, contrary to, or opposed to the achievement of these ends would be evil.

There seems to be no basis in latter-day scripture for either the privative or relativistic views of evil advocated by some philosophers. In the fifth century, St. Augustine, puzzled by the existence of evil in a world that was created by God, concluded that evil must not be a substance or a positive reality in its own right, but only the absence of good (*privatio boni*). Yet, in the Old and New Testaments, evil is depicted as menacingly real, a view shared by latter-day scripture. Nor is there any scriptural evidence that good and evil are simply matters of personal preference. Rejecting this kind of relativism, Proverbs declares, "There is a way which seemeth right unto a man, but the end thereof are the ways of death" (Prov. 14:12); and Isaiah warns, "Woe unto them that call evil good, and good evil; that put darkness for light, and light for darkness; that put bitter for sweet, and sweet for bitter!" (Isa. 5:20). Relativism is also rejected in latter-day scripture (2 Ne. 28:8).

Nonbelievers and believers alike often question why God would allow evil of any kind to exist. The question becomes especially acute within an Augustinian worldview that affirms God to be the ex nihilo or absolute creator of whatever exists other than himself. On that premise it appears that God is the *ultimate* source or cause of all evil, or, at least, a knowing accessory before the fact, and thus omniresponsible for all evils that occur.

Latter-day Saints reject the troublesome premise of creation ex nihilo (out of nothing), affirming rather that there are actualities that are coeternal with God. These coeternal actualities include INTELLIGENCES (sometimes perceived as primal selves or persons), chaotic matter (or mass energy), and laws and principles (perhaps best regarded as the properties and relations of matter and intelligences). Given this plurality of uncreated entities, it does not follow, within an LDS worldview, that God is the ultimate source of evil. Evil is traceable, alternatively, to the choices of other autonomous agents (such as Lucifer, the Devil) who are also coeternal with God, and, perhaps, even to recalcitrant properties of uncreated chaotic matter.

Though on the basis of latter-day revelation it is evident that God is neither the source nor the cause of either moral or natural evil, the question still arises as to why he does not prevent or eliminate it. The ancient philosopher Epicurus posed the problem in the form of a dilemma: Either God is unwilling to prevent the evil that occurs or he is unable to prevent it. If he is unable, then he is not omnipotent; if he is unwilling, then he is not perfectly good. Epicurus' statement of the dilemma is based on two assumptions: (1) a perfectly good being prevents all the evil it can; and (2) an omnipotent being can do anything and, hence, can prevent all evil.

From an LDS perspective the first assumption appears to be false. A perfectly good being would certainly wish to maximize the good, but if, in the nature of things, allowing an experience of evil were a necessary condition of achieving the greatest good, a perfectly good being would allow it. For example, it seems evident that the existence of OPPOSITION and TEMPTATION is a necessary condition for the expression of morally significant FREEDOM and the development of genuinely righteous personalities (see 2 Ne. 2:11–16; Moses 6:55).

Latter-day Saints would also reject the second assumption. Since there are realities that are coeternal with God, his omnipotence must be understood not as the power to bring about any state of affairs absolutely, but rather as the power to bring about any state of affairs consistent with the natures of coeternal realities. This insight makes possible an instrumentalist view of evil. With Epicurus' basic assumptions thus modified by latter-day revelation, it seems possible to construct a coherent LDS concept of the nature, use, and existence of evil.

DAVID L. PAULSEN

EXALTATION

To Latter-day Saints, exaltation is a state that a person can attain in becoming like God—SALVATION in the ultimate sense (D&C 132:17). Latter-day Saints believe that all mankind (except the sons of perdition) will receive varying DEGREES OF GLORY in the AFTERLIFE. Exaltation is the greatest of all the gifts and attainments possible. It is available only in the highest degree of the CELESTIAL KINGDOM and is reserved for members of the Church of the Firstborn. This exalted status, called ETERNAL LIFE, is available to be received by a man and wife. It means not only living in God's presence, but receiving power to do as God does, including the power to bear children after the resurrection (*TPJS,* pp. 300–301; D&C 132:19). Blessings and privileges of exaltation require unwavering faith, repentance, and complete obedience to the GOSPEL OF JESUS CHRIST.

In a revelation to the Prophet Joseph Smith, the Savior stated the following conditions: "Strait is the gate, and narrow the way that leadeth unto the exaltation and continuation of the lives, and few there be that find it, because ye receive me not in the world neither do ye know me" (D&C 132:22).

All Church ordinances lead to exaltation, and the essential crowning ordinances are the ENDOWMENT and the eternal marriage covenant of the temple (D&C 131:1–4, 132).

MARGARET MCCONKIE POPE

F

FAITH IN JESUS CHRIST

Faith in Jesus Christ is the first principle of the GOSPEL OF JESUS CHRIST (A of F 4). One who has this faith believes him to be the living Son of God, trusts in his goodness and power, repents of one's sins, and follows his guidance. Faith in the Lord Jesus Christ is awakened as individuals hear his gospel (Rom. 10:17). By faith they enter the gate of REPENTANCE and BAPTISM, and receive the GIFT OF THE HOLY GHOST, which leads to the way of life ordained by Christ (2 Ne. 31:9, 17–18). Those who respond are "alive in Christ because of [their] faith" (2 Ne. 25:25). Because God's way is the only way that leads to salvation, "it is impossible to please him" without faith (Heb. 11:6). Faith must precede miracles, signs, gifts of the Spirit, and righteousness, for "if there be no faith . . . God can do no miracle" (Ether 12:12). The Book of Mormon prophet Moroni$_2$ summarized these points:

> The Lord God prepareth the way that the residue of men may have faith in Christ, that the Holy Ghost may have place in their hearts, according to the power thereof; and after this manner bringeth to pass the Father, the covenants which he hath made unto the children of men. And Christ hath said: If ye will have faith in me ye shall have power to do whatsoever thing is expedient in me. And he hath said: Repent all ye ends of the earth, and come unto me, and be baptized in my name, and have faith in me, that ye may be saved [Moro. 7:32–34].

Although in common speech people speak of having faith in people, principles, or things, faith in its eternal sense is faith in, and only in, Jesus Christ. It is not sufficient to have faith in just anything; it must be focused on "the only true God, and Jesus Christ" whom he has sent (John 17:3). Having faith means having complete confidence in Jesus Christ alone to save humankind from sin and the finality of death. By his grace "are ye saved through faith" (Eph. 2:8). If "Christ be not risen," then "your faith is also vain" and "ye are yet in your sins" (1 Cor. 15:14, 17). To trust in the powers of this world is to "trust in the arm of flesh" and, in effect, to reject Christ and his gospel (2 Ne. 4:34).

Paul explained, "Now faith is the substance [or assurance] of things hoped for, the evidence [the demonstration or proof] of things not seen" (Heb. 11:1). Mortals must live by faith, since divine realities are veiled from their physical senses. The invisible truths of the gospel are made manifest by the Holy Spirit and are seen in the lives of people who live by faith, following the daily directions of that Spirit. Though most mortals have not seen the spiritual realities beyond this physical world, they can accept such premises in faith, based on personal spiritual witness(es) and the scriptural record of former and latter-day special witnesses whom God has called and who have experienced these realities firsthand.

True faith is belief plus action. Faith implies not only the mental assent or cognition of belief but also its implementation. Beliefs in things both spiritual and secular impel people to act. Failure to act on the teachings and commandments of Christ implies absence of faith in him. Faith in Jesus Christ impels people to act in behalf of Christ, to follow his example, to do his works. Jesus said, "Not every one that saith unto me, Lord, Lord, shall enter into the kingdom of heaven; but he that *doeth* the will of my Father which is in heaven" (Matt. 7:21; italics added). James further emphasized that "faith, if it hath not works, is dead, being alone. Yea, a man may say, Thou hast faith, and I have works: shew me thy faith without thy works, and I will shew thee my faith by my works" (James 2:17–18; *see also* GRACE).

Righteousness leads to greater faith, while sin and wickedness diminish faith. "The just [man] shall live by his faith" (Hab. 2:4). Violating the commandments of God brings a loss of the Spirit of the

Lord and a loss of faith, for faith in Jesus Christ is incompatible with disobedience. The Book of Mormon prophet $Alma_2$ characterized the words of Christ as a seed that is tested as people plant it in their hearts and nourish it. If they desire to see the seed grow, they must give it room and nourish it with their faith. If it is a good seed, it will swell and grow, and they will know that it is good. However, if they neglect the seed, it will wither away. But if they will "nourish the word . . . by [their] faith with great diligence," it will grow into a tree of life, and they will taste its fruit, which is eternal life (Alma 32:26–43).

Faith may be nurtured and renewed through scripture study, prayer, and works consistent with the commandments of the gospel. Because those who act on faith, repent, and are baptized receive a remission of sins, they have reason to hope for eternal life (Moro. 7:41). With this hope, their faith in Jesus Christ further inspires individuals to minister to each other in CHARITY, even as Christ would have done (Moro. 7:44), for the "end of the commandment is charity out of . . . faith unfeigned" (1 Tim. 1:5). "Charity is the pure love of Christ, and it endureth forever" (Moro. 7:47). Thus, faith, or "steadfastness in Christ," enables people to ENDURE TO THE END, continuing in faith and charity (2 Ne. 31:20; 1 Tim. 2:15; D&C 20:29). True faith is enduring and leads to an assurance that one's efforts have not gone unnoticed and that God is pleased with one's attitude and effort to implement the principles of the gospel of Jesus Christ in one's personal life.

While Alma explained how faith leads to knowledge, modern LDS commentary also points out how certain kinds of knowledge strengthen faith (*MD*, pp. 261–67). The knowledge that God exists, a correct understanding of his character, and a reassurance that he approves of one's conduct can help one's faith "become perfect and fruitful, abounding in righteousness" ("Lectures on Faith," pp. 65–66).

The restoration of the gospel in modern times was initiated by an act of faith by the youthful Joseph Smith. Reading the Bible, he was struck by the encouragement of James to all who lack wisdom that they should "ask in faith, nothing wavering" (James 1:6). The visions that came to Joseph Smith in answer to his prayers are evidence that prayers are "answered according to [one's] faith" (Mosiah 27:14).

Though God delights to bless his children, he "first, [tries] their faith, . . . then shall the greater things be made manifest" (3 Ne. 26:9). But there will be "no witness until after the trial of your faith" (Ether 12:6), and "without faith you can do nothing" (D&C 8:10). "Signs come by faith, not by the will of men" (D&C 63:10).

Because faith involves the guidance of the Holy Ghost to individuals, it leads them by an invisible hand to "the unity of the faith" (Eph. 4:13). Through the strength of others and increased confidence in the Lord's way, faith provides a shield against the adversary (Eph. 6:16). Similarly, faith has been described as part of one's armor, serving as a "breastplate of faith and love" (1 Thes. 5:8) in protecting the faithful from evil.

BIBLIOGRAPHY

Benson, Ezra Taft. *The Teachings of Ezra Taft Benson,* pp. 65–69. Salt Lake City, 1988.

Kimball, Spencer W. *Faith Precedes the Miracle.* Salt Lake City, 1973.

"Lectures on Faith." In *The Lectures on Faith in Historical Perspective,* ed. L. Dahl and C. Tate, pp. 29–104. Provo, Utah, 1990.

DOUGLAS E. BRINLEY

FALL OF ADAM

Latter-day Saints recognize the fall of Adam and Eve as an actual event that occurred in the Garden of Eden and has affected the entire earth and everyone in the human family. The Fall was a necessary step in the eternal progress of mankind and introduced the conditions that made the mission of Jesus Christ absolutely necessary for SALVATION. The four standard works and the teachings of many prominent leaders of the Church are the sources for the LDS doctrine of the Fall. These sources dwell at length on the beneficial effects of the Fall as part of God's "great plan of happiness" (Alma 42:8) for his children and testify that Adam and Eve are to be honored for their actions (*see* PLAN OF SALVATION, PLAN OF REDEMPTION; PURPOSE OF EARTH LIFE).

The creation of the earth was a multistep process in which the fall of Adam and Eve and their expulsion from the Garden of Eden were the final necessary steps in bringing about the mortal condition.

Without the Fall, Adam and Eve would have had no children (2 Ne. 2:23); hence, the human family would not have come into existence upon this earth under the conditions and circumstances in the garden. The prophet Lehi explained, "Adam fell that men might be" (2 Ne. 2:25), and Enoch declared, "Because that Adam fell, we are" (Moses 6:48).

After the Fall, Adam and Eve were taught the gospel of Jesus Christ and rejoiced in their situation. Adam blessed God, saying, "Because of my transgression my eyes are opened, and in this life I shall have joy, and again in the flesh I shall see God" (Moses 5:10). And Eve was glad, saying, "Were it not for our transgression we never should have had seed, and never should have known good and evil, and the joy of our redemption, and the eternal life which God giveth unto all the obedient" (Moses 5:11).

The Fall was not an accident, not an obstruction to God's plan, and not a wrong turn in the course of humanity. "The Lord . . . created the earth that it should be inhabited" by his children (1 Ne. 17:36), and since Adam and Eve would have had no children in their Edenic condition, the Fall was a benefit to mankind. It was part of the Father's plan, being both foreknown to him and essential to the human family. All these things were "done in the wisdom of him who knoweth all things" (2 Ne. 2:24).

The Fall brought two kinds of death upon Adam, Eve, and their posterity: the separation of the spirit and the physical body, which the scriptures call the "temporal death" (Alma 11:42–43); and being shut out of God's presence, which is called SPIRITUAL DEATH (2 Ne. 9:6; D&C 29:41). Jesus Christ redeems all mankind unconditionally from the two deaths brought by the fall of Adam (*see* ORIGINAL SIN), raises all mankind from the grave, and restores them to God's presence for a judgment (Hel. 14:16–17). The Atonement also redeems individuals from the consequences of their own sins on conditions of repentance.

The Book of Mormon explains, "The natural man is an enemy to God, and has been from the Fall of Adam, and will be, forever and ever, unless he yields to the enticings of the Holy Spirit, and putteth off the natural man and becometh a saint through the Atonement of Christ the Lord" (Mosiah 3:19; cf. Alma 22:14; 42:9–15). God "created Adam, and by Adam came the fall of man. And because of the fall of man came Jesus Christ, . . . and because of Jesus Christ came the redemption of man" (Morm. 9:12; cf. 2 Ne. 9:6).

The Doctrine and Covenants states that the Fall occurred as a result of transgression: "The devil tempted Adam, and he partook of the forbidden fruit and transgressed the commandment. . . . Wherefore, I, the Lord God, caused that he should be cast out from the Garden of Eden, from my presence, because of his transgression, wherein he became spiritually dead" (D&C 29:40–41). Thereafter, God sent angels to teach Adam and his seed "repentance and redemption, through faith on the name of mine Only Begotten Son" (D&C 29:42; cf. Moses 5:6–8).

The Fall was not a sin against chastity. Adam and Eve were "man and wife" and were commanded by God to multiply (Gen. 1:27–28; Moses 3:21–25; Abr. 5:14–19). Joseph Fielding Smith, an apostle explained, "The transgression of Adam did *not* involve sex sin as some falsely believe and teach. Adam and Eve were married by the Lord while they were yet immortal beings in the Garden of Eden and before death entered the world" (*DS* 1:114–15; cf. *JC*, pp. 29–31).

An inseparable relationship between the Fall of Adam and the ATONEMENT OF JESUS CHRIST is established in ancient and modern scripture. Paul's summation is, "For as in Adam all die, even so in Christ shall all be made alive" (1 Cor. 15:22). Latter-day revelation further emphasizes that Christ will redeem all things from death and the effects of the Fall.

The Prophet Joseph Smith taught that Adam's role was "to open the way of the world" (*TPJS*, p. 12); thus, he was the first man to enter mortality, and the fall of Adam has a mortal effect upon the entire earth. The earth shall die (D&C 88:25–26), but through the atoning power of Jesus Christ "the earth will be renewed and receive its paradisiacal glory" (A of F 10). "All things shall become new, even the heaven and the earth, and all the fulness thereof, both men and beasts, the fowls of the air, and the fishes of the sea; and not one hair, neither mote, shall be lost, for it is the workmanship of mine hand" (D&C 29:24–25; cf. 101:24–26; Isa. 51:6).

As Lehi declared, "If Adam had not transgressed he would not have fallen, but he would have remained in the Garden of Eden. And all things which were created must have remained in the same state in which they were after they were created; and they must have remained forever, and had no end" (2 Ne. 2:22; cf. Moses 3:9). Various interpretations have been suggested concerning the nature of life on the earth before the Fall and how the Fall physically affected the world, but these go beyond the clearly stated doctrine of the Church. The Church and the scriptures are emphatic, however, that the Fall brought the two kinds of death to Adam and his posterity.

BIBLIOGRAPHY

McConkie, Joseph Fielding, and Robert L. Millet, eds. *The Man Adam.* Salt Lake City, 1990.

Packer, Boyd K. "The Law and the Light." In *The Book of Mormon: Jacob Through Words of Mormon, to Learn With Joy*, pp. 1–31. Provo, Utah, 1990.

Smith, Joseph Fielding. *Man, His Origin and Destiny.* Salt Lake City, 1954.

ROBERT J. MATTHEWS

FASTING

The practice of periodic abstinence from food and drink for devotional purposes has been documented since early times. The Bible and the Book of Mormon attest to fasting in its several forms, public or private, institutionalized or spontaneous. In a revelation to the Prophet Joseph Smith, the Lord commanded the Latter-day Saints to "continue in prayer and fasting from this time forth" (D&C 88:76).

Church members fast together generally on the first Sunday of each month, in preparation for fast and testimony meeting. They usually abstain from food and drink for two consecutive meals, attend Church services, and donate a fast offering for the care of the needy. Additionally, an individual, family, or congregation may fast for a specific cause such as one who is sick or otherwise afflicted. An individual may desire the intimate communication with deity engendered by a prayerful fast when preparing for a difficult task or significant change in the circumstances of life. A person may fast when seeking spiritual enlightenment or guidance in decision making, strength to overcome weakness or endure trial, comfort in sorrow, or help at other times of special need.

General principles of the fast include prayerful preparation concerning the subject of the fast and frequent contemplation and meditation throughout to achieve oneness in purpose and spirit with the Lord; a quiet, humble, and cheerful conduct befitting one seeking blessing or spiritual enlightenment (Matt. 6:16–18; cf. 3 Ne. 13:16–18); and a prayer of gratitude and thanksgiving when ending the fast.

Rich blessings are promised to those who fast and help the needy (Isa. 58:8–9). Self-control, communion with the Lord, and spiritual strength and power accompany compliance with the law. The spirit of the fast is aptly represented in latter-day scripture: "Verily, this is fasting and prayer, or in other words, rejoicing and prayer" (D&C 59:14).

BIBLIOGRAPHY

Ricks, Stephen D. "Fasting in the Bible and Book of Mormon." In *Book of Mormon: The Keystone Scripture,* ed. Paul R. Cheesman. Provo, Utah, 1988, pp. 127–36.

Smith, Joseph F. *Gospel Doctrine,* 10th ed. Salt Lake City, 1956.

DAWN M. HILLS

FEAR OF GOD

In ancient scripture the phrase "fear of God" typically signified faith, reverence, and trust. Fear of God, so defined and felt, tends to diminish other forms of fear that arise in the absence of genuine faith. Thus, modern REVELATION admonishes against fearing to do good (D&C 6:33), fearing enemies (D&C 122:9; 136:17), fearing Satan (Moses 1:20), and fearing death (D&C 101:36). An undergirding principle permeates Latter-day Saint practice: "If ye are prepared ye shall not fear" (D&C 38:30). In the spiritual realm, unpreparedness can lead to what the scriptures call "a certain fearful looking for of judgment" (Heb. 10:27).

Latter-day Saints are sometimes described, because of an assumed overemphasis on works, as living in "fear and trembling." The phrase is Paul's (Phil. 2:12). Actually, Mormons aspire to follow Paul's teaching and practice to be "anxiously engaged in a good cause," but that anxiety is related to freedom and responsibility (see D&C 58:27). They strive to find and fulfill their callings and fear to fall short of the divine purpose in their lives. They are constantly charged to magnify their callings and not to be weary in well-doing. Modern revelation promises that on condition of "persuasion, by long-suffering, by gentleness and meekness, and by love unfeigned" (D&C 121:41), "[their] confidence [shall] wax strong in the presence of God" (D&C 121:45). This parallels the promise of John: "Perfect love casteth out fear" (1 Jn. 4:18).

JOHN R. CHRISTIANSEN

FIRST ESTATE

First estate refers to the unspecified period of time otherwise known as PREMORTAL LIFE. The words "first estate" in Jude 1:6 are the King James translation of the Greek *arché*. In other English versions the word is translated as "principality," "domain," "dominion," "appointed spheres," "responsibilities," and "original rank." In the context of Jude 1:6 each of these implies that certain intelligent beings existed in significant positions in the pre-earth life and fell from their favored status with God.

Latter-day Saints believe that all MANKIND were begotten as individual spirit children of God, with individual agency, prior to being born into MORTALITY. Using this agency, a third part of these spirits followed Lucifer and rebelled against God and the PLAN OF SALVATION that God proposed to bring about the eventual EXALTATION of his children through the atoning sacrifice of Jesus Christ. Because of their rebellion, these spirits "kept not their first estate" (Jude 1:6) and were subsequently cast out of heaven, being denied the opportunity of having a mortal body on this earth (D&C 29:36–38; Moses 4:1–4; Abr. 3:26–28; cf. Rev. 12:4, 7–9). All the remaining spirits proved themselves sufficiently faithful to be permitted the privilege of experiencing earth life with a PHYSICAL BODY (Abr. 3:22–26).

[*See also* Birth; Second Estate.]

ALEXANDER L. BAUGH

FIRST PRINCIPLES OF THE GOSPEL

The first principles and ordinances of the gospel are "first, Faith in the Lord Jesus Christ; second, Repentance; third, Baptism by immersion for the remission of sins; fourth, Laying on of hands for the gift of the Holy Ghost" (A of F 4). The resurrected Savior taught that these principles constitute his "gospel": "Repent, all ye ends of the earth, and come unto me and be baptized in my name, that ye may be sanctified by the reception of the Holy Ghost, that ye may stand spotless before me at the last day. Verily, verily, I say unto you, this is my gospel" (3 Ne. 27:20–21; cf. Acts 2:37–38). These four principles prepare one to *enter* the "strait and narrow path which leads to eternal life" (2 Ne. 31:17–18).

First, faith in Jesus Christ often begins with a desire to believe (Alma 32:26–28), which may be kindled by hearing or reading others' true testimonies of Christ and his atonement. One nourishes faith by patient obedience to God's commandments. Faith then grows through a process that includes REPENTANCE, baptism for REMISSION OF SINS, increased confidence in Christ, and eventually a Christlike nature (Hafen, pp. 141–200).

Repentance involves (1) realization of guilt; (2) godly sorrow and suffering; (3) confession for relief from the hurtful effects of sin; (4) restitution, as far as it is possible; (5) replacement of sin with obedience to God's requirements; and (6) acceptance of Christ's atoning sacrifice. Through the Atonement, if one repents, Christ's mercy satisfies the demands of justice.

Baptism, the third principle and first essential ordinance, is the fruit of repentance and is required of all who would be saved in the KINGDOM OF GOD (John 3:3–5; cf. 2 Ne. 9:23). Baptism has several purposes. It is a symbolic washing and cleansing of sins and is prerequisite to membership in the Church. When followed by the reception of the Holy Ghost, it is the doorway to personal SANCTIFICATION (Moro. 6:1–4). The prescribed method of baptism is by immersion in water by a priest in the Aaronic Priesthood or by one who holds the Melchizedek Priesthood. "The symbolism of the rite is preserved in no other form" (*AF,* p. 137).

Being "born of the Spirit," or receiving the GIFT OF THE HOLY GHOST, entitles one to the continual help, guidance, and comfort of the Holy Ghost. "The special office of the Holy Ghost is to enlighten and ennoble the mind, to purify and sanctify the soul, to incite to good works, and to reveal the things of God" (*AF*, p. 167). When asked how the Church differed from the other religions of the day, Joseph Smith replied that "we differed in mode of baptism, and the gift of the Holy Ghost . . . [and] that all other considerations [of differences from other churches] were contained in the gift of the Holy Ghost" (*HC* 4:42). The gift of the Holy Ghost is conferred by the LAYING ON OF HANDS by a holder of the Melchizedek Priesthood.

Summarizing the process from faith and repentance to sanctification, the Book of Mormon prophet Mormon stated, "And the first fruits of repentance is baptism; and baptism cometh by faith unto the fulfilling the commandments; and the fulfilling the commandments bringeth remission of sins; and the remission of sins bringeth meekness, and lowliness of heart; and because of meekness and lowliness of heart cometh the visitation of the Holy Ghost, which Comforter filleth with hope and perfect love, which love endureth by diligence unto prayer, until the end shall come, when all the saints shall dwell with God" (Moro. 8:25–26).

These four principles and ordinances of the gospel are "first" because they both initiate and enable the process of development from a spiritual rebirth to a divine nature.

BIBLIOGRAPHY

Hafen, Bruce C. *The Broken Heart: Applying the Atonement to Life's Experiences.* Salt Lake City, 1989.

Kimball, Spencer W. *The Miracle of Forgiveness.* Salt Lake City, 1969.

MARIE KARTCHNER HAFEN

FOREKNOWLEDGE OF GOD

Modern scripture speaks unequivocally of the foreknowledge of God: "All things are present before mine eyes" (D&C 38:2). It affirms that God has a fulness of truth, a "knowledge of things as they are, and as they were, and as they *are to come*" (D&C 93:24, emphasis added).

Divine foreknowledge includes the power to know even the thoughts and intents of the human heart: "There is none else save God that knowest thy thoughts and the intents of thy heart" (D&C 6:16). Divine foreknowledge is at least, in part, knowledge of his own purposive plans for the cosmos and for humankind, plans that "cannot be frustrated, neither can they come to naught" (D&C 3:1). "Known unto God are all his works from the beginning of the world" (Acts 15:18; Abr. 2:8). These include the conditions of the PLAN OF SALVATION. For example, "God did elect or predestinate that all those who would be saved, should be saved in Christ Jesus, and through obedience to the Gospel" (*TPJS*, p. 189). It is likewise foreknown that all humankind will die, be resurrected, and be brought to judgment.

In scripture, the root terms for divine knowing connote more than a subject-object, cognitive relationship; they imply a close, direct, participative, affective awareness. Divine foreknowledge is the knowledge of a Heavenly Father, not knowledge of a metaphysical abstraction. Scriptures that speak of divine foreknowledge emphasize God's understanding of an experience with his people and their destiny rather than the content and logic of that knowledge. Anyone seeking to understand divine foreknowledge must begin by recognizing that scripture does not directly address the question as it has been formulated in philosophy and theology, where the emphasis is on the content and logic of knowledge. The scriptures are explicit that God knows all and that we can trust him. They have not been explicit about what that means philosophically or theologically. Consequently, short of new revelation, any answer to the theological question of God's foreknowledge can be only speculative.

In an attempt to reconcile divine foreknowledge and human freedom, major Jewish and Christian theologians and philosophers have offered three alternatives. In the first, both horns of the dilemma are affirmed: "Everything is foreseen, and freedom of choice is given." This is the position of Rabbi Akiba and Maimonides (Aboth 3, 19; Yad, Teshuvah 5:5), as well as of Augustine and Anselm (*City of God* 5.9–10; *The Harmony of the Foreknowledge, the Predestination, and the Grace of God with Free Choice* 1.3). Maimonides argues that though it is logically impossible for human foreknowledge of one's actions to be compatible with freedom, God's foreknowledge, which is of a different and mysterious kind, is compatible with freedom.

In the second, God's foreknowledge is limited. Since people are free, God knows the possibilities and probabilities of human choice, but not the inevitabilities. God is omniscient in knowing all that can be known; but not in knowing beforehand exactly how people will use their freedom, since that cannot be known because future, contingent events do not exist. This is the view of the Talmudist Gersonides (Levi Ben Gershon, 1288–1344; Milhamot Adonai, III, 6) and, with some modifications, of Charles Hartshorne and process philosophers.

In the third, humans are not genuinely free. Freedom is an illusion that arises from human ignorance of divine cause and necessity. All that individuals do is actually determined and predetermined. God both pre-knows and pre-causes all that occurs. This is the view of Spinoza and Calvin.

Historically, most Latter-day Saints have taken the first general position: everything is foreseen and freedom remains. Some have taken the second, that God's foreknowledge is not absolute. The third alternative, that human freedom is illusory, is incompatible with LDS belief in genuine free agency and responsibility. Praise and blame, accountability and judgment, are meaningless unless humans are free. Any doctrine of foreknowledge that undercuts this principle violates the spirit and letter of LDS scripture.

Consequently divine foreknowledge, however it is finally defined, is not predestination. What God foresees is not, for that reason, divinely caused, even though it is in some sense known (Talmage, p. 317). Divine foreknowledge is the background of *foreordination.* But, again, foreordination is not pre-causation. Rather, "foreordination is a conditional bestowal of a role, a responsibility, or a blessing which, likewise, foresees but does not fix the outcome" (Maxwell, p. 71).

BIBLIOGRAPHY

Hartshorne, Charles, and William L. Reese. *Philosophers Speak of God.* Chicago, 1953.

Maxwell, Neal A. "A More Determined Discipleship." *Ensign* 9 (Feb. 1979):69–73.

Talmage, James E. *The Vitality of Mormonism,* pp. 317 ff. Boston, 1919.

JAMES E. FAULCONER

FOREORDINATION

Foreordination is the premortal selection of individuals to come forth in MORTALITY at specified times, under certain conditions, and to fulfill predesignated responsibilities. In LDS interpretation, "foreordained" does not mean predetermined. It is the outcome of voluntary choice, not the violation or abrogation of it. The idea of preexistence and premortal preparation for earth life is hinted at in biblical sources, and evidence of it appears in some early Jewish-Christian sources. But it has been less prominent in later thought.

Abraham was told that he was included among the valiant SPIRITS and was therefore chosen or *foreordained* before his birth to be a leader in God's kingdom on earth (Abr. 3:22–23). The Lord likewise informed Jeremiah, "Before I formed thee in the belly I knew thee; and . . . I ordained thee a prophet unto the nations" (Jer. 1:5). $Alma_2$ taught that priests belonging to a "holy order" were foreordained "according to the foreknowledge of God, on account of their exceeding faith and good works" (Alma 13:1, 3). The Prophet Joseph Smith concluded that "every man who has a calling to minister to the inhabitants of the world was ordained to that very purpose in the Grand Council of heaven before this world was" (*TPJS*, p. 365). And in addition to these foreordinations to priesthood callings, many spirits may have been foreordained to specific nations and generations, which Paul characterized as the "bounds of habitation" (Acts 17:26), as well as to families and to varied assignments, work, or missions on earth.

While each of these selections is ultimately based on the omniscience and foreknowledge of God, several factors may influence one's earthly circumstances. Foreordination comes as a blessing or reward for premortal righteousness and valiant commitment to Jesus Christ. BIRTH into the house of Israel and heirship to all the blessings of Abraham, Isaac, and Jacob are often seen as the birthright of dedicated souls (see Eph. 1:4–5; Rom. 9:4). These rights and blessings may still be obtained by any and all who elect to receive them, whether in this life or the next. People sooner or later will manifest, as Elder B. H. Roberts, of the Seventy, taught, "the strength of that intelligence and nobility to which their spirits had attained in the heavenly kingdom before they took bodies upon earth" (T. Madsen, *Defender of the Faith* [Salt Lake City, 1980], p. 2). The Doctrine and Covenants teaches that men and women may come to God through RIGHTEOUSNESS and diligence and thus become numbered with those who are "sons [and daughters] of Moses and of Aaron and the seed of Abraham, and the church and kingdom, and the elect of God" (D&C 84:34).

Through faithfulness on earth, whatever one's premortal foreordination or prior covenants, one may, as Paul taught, become "adopted" into the favored lineage: "They are not all Israel, which are of Israel" (Rom. 9:6). Many, that is, may be foreordained to high missions in mortality, but may, through sin, rebellion, or sloth, fail in their foreordinations and give up their blessings. Obedience to the COVENANTS and ordinances of the gospel is a primary factor in determining ultimate election to the chosen lineage.

Latter-day Saints further believe that the times, places, and circumstances of birth into mortality may be the outcome of former covenants and decisions as well as that which would be best, in divine wisdom, to provide both opportunities and challenges for the individual's growth and development. Additionally, foreordination may also be based on God's own purposes and plans to bless all of his children. The specifics of these factors remain unclear. As a result, a person's premortal character can never be judged by his or her present station in life. Some of the most bitter and arduous circumstances may be, in the perspective of eternity, the most blessed, and perhaps even the situations that men and women elected and agreed to enter. Foreordination does not preclude the exercise of agency. Foreordination is a *conditional* preappointment to or bestowal of certain blessings and responsibilities.

Following Augustine and Calvin, some have interpreted the word "predestine" in Romans 8:29–30 and Ephesians 1:4–5 as meaning divine precausation. In this view, God is the ultimate causal agent, whereas man is always and only an effect. Latter-day Saints reject this interpretation. They believe that neither the Greek nor related scriptural sources lead to this view. Paul's usage of this term refers to being foreordained to divine sonship through Christ. Furthermore, since God knows "all things, for all things are present before [his] eyes" (D&C 38:1–2), he anticipates our choices. However, he does not make the choices for us. Knowing our potential, he foreordains those who will help to bring about his purposes. Latter-day Saints extend this concept to embrace foreordination to any divinely appointed ministry or function.

BIBLIOGRAPHY
Maxwell, Neal A. "Meeting the Challenges of Today." *Speeches of the Year*, pp. 149–56. Provo, Utah, 1978.
Top, Brent L. *The Life Before.* Salt Lake City, 1988.
Winston, David. "Preexistence in the Wisdom of Solomon and Mormon Sources." In *Reflections on Mormonism*, ed. Truman Madsen, pp. 13–35. Salt Lake City, 1978.

BRENT L. TOP

FREEDOM

The gospel of Jesus Christ does not represent freedom merely as a philosophic concept or abstract possibility, but establishes it at the foundations of the creation of the world and as the fundamental condition of God's dealings with his children. As a general expression the word "freedom" refers to AGENCY, liberty, independence, and autonomy. Freedom, or the genuine possibility of choosing, necessarily defines the most basic condition of human beings in the temporal world.

Latter-day Saint scriptures teach that the premortal life was an environment of choice in which God proposed to his spirit children a PLAN OF SALVATION for their growth and advancement (see Job 38:6–7; 2 Ne. 2:17; D&C 29:36; Abr. 3:22–28). In earth life, with bodies of flesh and bone and vast new possibilities of action, God's children would be free to make choices within the whole spectrum of good and evil. They would also experience the necessary consequences of those choices. "And we will take of these materials, and we will make an earth whereon these may dwell; And we will prove them herewith, to see if they will do all things whatsoever the Lord their God shall command them" (Abr. 3:24–25).

God promised those who would do his will that they would be redeemed from their errors and sins and gain eternal life. Satan opposed the Father's plan, aware that this more extensive freedom involved the risk of spiritual death, where some would be separated from the Father by their sins, would not repent, and thus could not return to dwell in his kingdom. To avert such a separation, Satan proposed an environment without freedom and hence without sin. Consequently, all would return to the Father, but without moral improvement or advancement (*see* DEVILS). The "honor" for their return would belong to Satan (Isa. 14:13; Moses 4:1).

A majority of God's spirit children joyfully elected freedom over bondage, knowledge over ignorance, advancement over stagnation, and even danger over security; so the temporal world was created, with freedom as its unconditional ground. The temporal world is an environment of choices and thus of moral action and ACCOUNTABILITY as people are summoned to do the will of God. Men and women may not evade or escape their freedom, for reality always appears as a set of choices informed by some kind of understanding of good, the outcome of which defines in some measure the course of human events. The Book of Mormon says of this decision,

> Wherefore, men are free according to the flesh; and all things are given them which are expedient unto man. And they are free to choose liberty and eternal life, through the great Mediator of all men, or to choose captivity and death, according to the captivity and power of the devil; for he seeketh that all men might be miserable like unto himself [2 Ne. 2:27].

FREEDOM AND HUMAN CHOICE. Latter-day Saints understand, however, that not all of God's children will find themselves in situations of equal freedom. All people are born into a world created by the acts and beliefs of those who lived before them. These differences are preserved in the traditions, institutions, and practices that have been handed down. While God gives everyone the LIGHT OF CHRIST that draws each to the good, the traditions and practices into which some are born may conceal the truth and lead such people into harmful and sinful acts. For these, God will have mercy (Alma 9:15–16).

Still others are born into situations where the truth is widely known and the opportunity to do good is broadly available. Yet they do evil in the face of the truth and thus create consequences that reduce their choices, distance themselves from the Spirit of God, and bring upon themselves unhappiness, destruction, and the darkness of Satan's power (Gal. 5:13–25). Furthermore, they do not suffer alone from the consequences of their choices. The ill-used freedom of some can result in the undeserved suffering of others, and while this is unjust, the risk of unwarranted suffering is necessarily present in a world where evil exists. Nevertheless, this condition too serves God's purpose, for some adversity humbles people before God (Alma 32:12–16). Through earthly trials men and women are tried and tested, but thereby progress and unfold the talents and gifts that God has given them (2 Ne. 2:11; Alma 62:41; D&C 122:1–9). When a whole people choose darkness over light, however, they create a legacy of confinement for following generations that sometimes has to be divinely corrected (e.g., Gen. 6:5–7; Lev. 18:24–30; Moses 8:22–30; Hel. 10:11–12).

On the other hand, those who choose good are made more free by a larger presence of the HOLY GHOST in their lives, and a greater power to know and do God's will (John 7:16–18; 8:29–32; Alma 19:33). Therefore, the good choices of some can bless the lives of others. As a consequence of the righteous works of a few (see Gal. 5–6), previously limited lives can expand to enjoy new and positive opportunities, while old injustices and grievances are brought to settlement. In the measure that the institutions and beliefs of a people embody truth and virtue and oppose corruption and depravity, an environment of greater freedom develops. A fulness is achieved when God establishes his kingdom on earth and reveals to humankind knowledge, power, gifts, and ordinances that open up the way to complete salvation and exaltation. The city of Enoch, as well as the righteous people living in America for 200 years after the visit of the resurrected Savior (see 4 Ne. 1), established high-water marks in the history of human freedom. In this sense, then, God not only calls individuals to live righteous lives, but summons them as his people to make covenants with him and to justly exercise his power as a community of the faithful. Freedom, therefore, should not be seen as merely a possibility of individuals, for it opens up to its fulness only within the kingdom of the righteous (see D&C 138, esp. verse 18).

FREEDOM AND GOVERNMENT. The scriptures further teach that God instituted governments to bless humankind on the earth. Good government must do more than preserve order; it must protect freedom, ensure justice, and secure the general welfare. "And the law of the land which is constitutional, supporting that principle of freedom in maintaining rights and privileges, belongs to all mankind, and is justifiable before me" (D&C 98:5). God proclaims, "I, the Lord God, make you free, therefore ye are free indeed; and the law also maketh you free" (D&C 98:8). The law protects individuals and their liberties from the arbitrary and deleterious acts of others. The genuine rule of law requires that all be equally subject to rules that are prospective, widely known, and publicly arrived at through mechanisms of government that have been and continue to be consensually agreed upon. The law secures peace by proscribing choices injurious to others, ensures justice by holding all accountable to the law in accordance with fair procedures, and secures the general welfare through the passage of laws that regulate and coordinate social intercourse to the benefit of all. In exchange for these advantages, citizens must fulfill their obligations to sustain and support the government. In the end, the environment of freedom is enhanced and expanded through good government.

Nevertheless, governments are often oppressive and act to restrict freedom and establish privileges for the few by arbitrarily setting up public rules and applying them unevenly without proper safeguards. The abuse of political power is most offensive and bondage nearly complete when freedom of conscience and its expression in free speech are restricted and the right to worship God openly according to one's own beliefs is abridged. In the end, Latter-day Saints believe that the claims of government should be limited to its own proper domain and not allowed to encroach upon the province of freedom to act according to moral conscience. To avoid such political evil, Latter-day Saints are encouraged not only to support constitutional government and the processes it establishes but also to work for laws that bring about freedom and encourage virtue. In this larger sense, the scriptures summon those who follow Jesus to go the extra mile, to give more than they receive, to do good without thought of what they might gain in return. Thus, as citizens, Latter-day Saints are obligated to go beyond the pursuit of self-interest; they are committed to serve others, to bring about the common good, and to secure the general welfare of the people.

BIBLIOGRAPHY

Oaks, Dallin H. "Free Agency and Freedom." In *The Book of Mormon: Second Nephi, The Doctrinal Structure,* ed. M. Nyman and C. Tate, pp. 1–17. Salt Lake City, 1989.

DAVID E. BOHN

FULNESS OF THE GOSPEL

The phrase "fulness of the gospel" refers to the whole doctrine of redemption demonstrated and taught in the ministry and life of Jesus Christ. It "consists in those laws, doctrines, ordinances, powers, and authorities needed to enable men to gain the fulness of salvation" (*MD*, p. 333).

Fulness is a term sometimes used in the scriptures to describe Christ himself, regarding both his stature as the Son of God and what he offered mankind. John, in bearing witness of the Savior, said, "And of his fulness have all we received, and grace for grace" (John 1:16). To receive the fulness the Savior offered is to accept him as the one who made salvation possible for all through the Atonement and to follow his teachings. Thus, to experience a fulness of joy requires one to keep God's commandments (D&C 93:27).

Christ himself declared the fulness of his gospel: "For I came down from heaven, not to do mine own will, but the will of him that sent me. And this is the Father's will . . . , that every one which seeth the Son, and believeth on him, may have everlasting life; and I will raise him up at the last day" (John 6:38–40).

Latter-day Saints believe that every prophet, from whatever dispensation, prophesied of Christ. But the phrase fulness of the gospel implies that periods have occurred when the gospel was not on the earth in its fulness, either in doctrine or in ordinance. The Book of Mormon was described by a heavenly messenger to Joseph Smith in 1820 as "giving an account of the former inhabitants of this continent," and "the fulness of the everlasting Gospel was contained in it, as delivered by the Savior" (JS—H 1:34).

President Ezra Taft Benson explains: "The Book of Mormon contains the fulness of the gospel of Jesus Christ (D&C 20:9). That does not mean it contains every teaching, every doctrine ever revealed. Rather, it means that in the Book of Mormon we will find the fulness of those doctrines required for our salvation. And they are taught plainly and simply so that even children can learn the ways of salvation and exaltation" (Benson, pp. 18–19).

Nephi$_1$, a Book of Mormon prophet living centuries before the coming of Christ, indicated that the fulness of the gospel would not always be on the earth. In a vision of the Lord's future ministry, he saw that parts of the gospel would be altered and tampered with. Nephi wrote, speaking of the Bible, "When it proceeded forth from the mouth of a Jew it contained the fulness of the gospel of the Lord, of whom the Twelve apostles bear record." But men have taken away from the Bible "many parts which are plain and most precious; and also many covenants of the Lord have they taken away," which resulted in a loss of the gospel (cf. 1 Ne. 13:24–29).

Latter-day Saints believe that this apostasy and corruption of the scriptures necessitated a later restoration of the fulness of the gospel through prophets called of God. This restoration began with the first vision of 1820 to the Prophet Joseph Smith and continued with subsequent revelations, including modern scripture and priesthood authority, which remain today in The Church of Jesus Christ of Latter-day Saints.

BIBLIOGRAPHY

Benson, Ezra Taft. *A Witness and a Warning.* Salt Lake City, 1988.

DEAN B. FARNSWORTH

G

GARMENTS

The word "garment" has distinctive meanings to Latter-day Saints. The white undergarment worn by those members who have received the ordinance of the temple ENDOWMENT is a ceremonial one. All adults who enter the temple are required to wear it. In LDS temples, men and women who receive priesthood ordinances wear this undergarment and other priestly robes. The garment is worn at all times, but the robes are worn only in the temple. Having made COVENANTS of righteousness, the members wear the garment under their regular clothing for the rest of their lives, day and night, partially to remind them of the sacred covenants they have made with God.

The white garment symbolizes purity and helps assure modesty, respect for the attributes of God, and, to the degree it is honored, a token of what Paul regarded as taking upon one the whole armor of God (Eph. 6:13; cf. D&C 27:15). It is an outward expression of an inward covenant, and symbolizes Christlike attributes in one's mission in life. Garments bear several simple marks of orientation toward the gospel principles of OBEDIENCE, TRUTH, life, and DISCIPLESHIP in Christ.

An agency of the Church manufactures these garments in contemporary, comfortable, and lightweight fabrics. They are available for purchase through Church distribution centers.

Scripture, as well as legends from many lands and cultures, points toward the significance of sacral clothing. A biblical tradition teaches that Adam and Eve, prior to their expulsion from Eden, wore sacred clothing. "Unto Adam also and to his wife did the Lord God make coats of skins, and clothed them" (Gen. 3:21). These were given in a context of REPENTANCE and forgiveness, and of offering SACRIFICE and making covenants.

In antiquity, priestly vestments were part of widespread tradition. The Targums (Aramaic paraphrases of the Old Testament) teach that these garments were "precious garments" or "glorious garments" or "garments of honor." Rabbi Eleazer called them "coats of glory." A rabbinic source asks: "And what were those garments?" The answer is, "The vestments of the High Priesthood, with which the Almighty clothed them because Adam was the world's first-born" (Kasher, *Encyclopedia of Biblical Interpretation,* Vol. 1, p. 137). In Moses' time those who officiated in the Tabernacle wore a certain kind of garment: "And [Moses] put upon [Aaron] the coat, and girded him with the girdle, and clothed him with the robe, and put the ephod upon him, and he girded him with the curious girdle of the ephod, and bound it unto him therewith" (Lev. 8:7; see Testament of Levi 8). Latter-day Saints similarly wear temple garments in connection with their priesthood functions.

The clergy and many of the committed in almost all major faiths wear special clothing. For Latter-day Saints, among whom there is no professional ministry, men and women from all walks of life share in the callings, responsibilities, and blessings of the priesthood. Their sacred clothing, representing covenants with God, is worn under rather than outside their street clothes.

In a Messianic passage Isaiah declared: "I will greatly rejoice in the Lord, my soul shall be joyful in my God; for he hath clothed me with the garments of salvation, he hath covered me with the robe of righteousness" (Isa. 61:10). In the current dispensation, the principle has been reaffirmed in prophetic idiom: "Zion must increase in beauty, . . . and put on her beautiful garments" (D&C 82:14). Latter-day Saints believe that all such clothing is symbolic of the submission, sanctification, and spotless purity of those who desire to serve God and Christ and ultimately regain their eternal presence (D&C 61:34; 135:5).

BIBLIOGRAPHY
Nibley, Hugh W. *Sacred Vestments,* 38 pages. Provo, Utah, 1984.
Packer, Boyd K. *The Holy Temple.* Salt Lake City, 1980.

EVELYN T. MARSHALL

GETHSEMANE

The name Gethsemane (derived from Hebrew "oil press") is mentioned twice in the Bible, both in the New Testament (Matt. 26:36; Mark 14:32); in each case, it is called a "place" (Greek *chorion,* "piece of land") to which Jesus Christ and his apostles retired after their last supper together. The fourth gospel calls the area "a garden" (John 18:1). For Latter-day Saints, Gethsemane was the scene of Jesus' greatest agony, even surpassing that which he suffered on the cross, an understanding supported by Mark's description of Jesus' experience (Mark 14:33–39).

According to Luke 22:43–44, Jesus' anguish was so deep that "his sweat was as it were great drops of blood falling down to the ground," an observation that harmonizes with the view that Jesus suffered most in Gethsemane during his ATONEMENT. Even though these verses are missing in some of the earliest extant manuscripts of Luke's gospel, their content is confirmed in modern revelation (e.g., D&C 19:18). The evidence for Jesus' extreme agony in Gethsemane is buttressed by a prophecy in the Book of Mormon and a statement by the resurrected Savior recorded in the Doctrine and Covenants. About 125 B.C., a Book of Mormon king, Benjamin, recounted in an important address a prophecy of the coming MESSIAH spoken to him by an angel during the previous night. Concerning the Messiah's mortal experience, the angel declared that "he shall suffer temptations, and pain of body, hunger, thirst, and fatigue, even more than man can suffer, except it be unto death; for behold, blood cometh from every pore, so great shall be his anguish for the wickedness and the abominations of his people" (Mosiah 3:7). The Doctrine and Covenants gives the following poignant words of the resurrected Jesus: "Behold, I, God, have suffered these things for all, that they might not suffer if they would repent; . . . which suffering caused myself, even God, the greatest of all, to tremble because of pain, and to bleed at every pore, and to suffer both body and spirit" (D&C 19:16, 18).

Modern LDS leaders have emphasized that Jesus' most challenging experience came in Gethsemane. Speaking in a general conference of the Church in 1982, Marion G. Romney, a member of the First Presidency, observed that Jesus suffered "the pains of all men, which he did, principally, in Gethsemane, the scene of his great agony" (*Ensign* 12 [May 1982]:6). Church President Ezra Taft Benson wrote that "it was in Gethsemane that Jesus took on Himself the sins of the world, in Gethsemane that His pain was equivalent to the cumulative burden of all men, in Gethsemane that He descended below all things so that all could repent and come to Him" (Benson, p. 7).

While tradition locates Gethsemane on the lower slopes of the Mount of Olives, the exact spot remains unknown. Luke associates it with the Mount of Olives (Luke 22:39), and John notes that it lay across the Kidron brook (John 18:1), which flows from the north along Jerusalem's east side. The particular use of "place" (Greek *topos*) to describe the spot in the gospels of Luke and John suggests that the location was bound up with Jesus' destiny and consequently possesses a sacred character (Luke 22:40; John 18:2). It was a spot that Jesus and his disciples customarily visited (Luke 22:39), which allowed Judas and the others to find him on the night of his arrest (John 18:2).

BIBLIOGRAPHY

Benson, Ezra Taft. *Come Unto Christ.* Salt Lake City, 1983.

Maxwell, Neal A. "The New Testament—A Matchless Portrait of the Savior." *Ensign* 16 (Dec. 1986):20–27.

Wilkinson, John. *Jerusalem as Jesus Knew It,* pp. 125–31. London, 1978.

S. KENT BROWN

GIFT OF THE HOLY GHOST

The gift of the HOLY GHOST is the right or privilege of receiving divine manifestations, spiritual gifts, and direction from the Holy Ghost. This gift is conferred upon members of the Church by the LAYING ON OF HANDS following BAPTISM. It is considered one of the essential ordinances of the GOSPEL OF JESUS CHRIST and an absolute prerequisite of SALVATION.

The Holy Ghost is the third member of the GODHEAD, while the gift of the Holy Ghost consists of the privilege to receive inspiration, manifestations, and other spiritual gifts and blessings from that member of the Godhead (*TPJS*, p. 199). Among the most important spiritual blessings associated with the gift of the Holy Ghost is the sanctifying or cleansing power of the Holy Ghost, whereby men and women are BORN OF GOD. Through this BAPTISM OF FIRE AND OF THE HOLY GHOST, individual hearts and desires are cleansed and spirits made pure as the culmination of the process of repentance and baptism (2 Ne. 31:13, 17; 3 Ne. 27:20). Other important manifestations of the Holy Ghost include bearing witness of Jesus Christ and of divine truths, providing spiritual guidance and warning as appropriate, and enabling discernment of right and wrong.

The gift of the Holy Ghost is understood to be the key to all of the "spiritual gifts" found in the Church, including the gifts of prophecy and REVELATION, of healing, of speaking in tongues, and of the translation and interpretation of tongues. These distinctive GIFTS OF THE SPIRIT normally are manifested only among those who have received the gift of the Holy Ghost and who qualify by their needs and their worthiness for such divine assistance, even as the original apostles of Christ received these gifts only after the Holy Ghost came upon them on the Day of Pentecost (Acts 2:1–17).

In LDS practice, the gift of the Holy Ghost is given by the laying on of hands as indicated in the New Testament (see Acts 8:17–18; 19:2–6; 2 Tim. 1:6; Heb. 6:2), normally immediately following or within a few days of the baptism by water. A bearer of the Melchizedek Priesthood (usually joined by a few others holding the same priesthood) lays his hands upon the head of the newly baptized member, calls the person by name, confirms him or her a member of the Church, and says, "Receive the Holy Ghost." The exact wording of this ordinance is not prescribed, but it always involves the CONFIRMATION of membership, the bestowal of the gift of the Holy Ghost, and a reference to the priesthood authority by which the ordinance is performed. These basic components of the ordinance often are followed by a verbal BLESSING that offers counsel and direction to the new member. In proxy temple ordinance work for deceased persons, the same basic confirmation follows the ordinance of baptism for the dead.

The New Testament account of how the Saints in Samaria received the gift of the Holy Ghost makes clear that bestowal of this gift requires a higher authority than is needed for performing baptisms (see Acts 8:14–17).

When Jesus Christ visited the Nephites, he first gave authority to baptize (3 Ne. 11:22), and in a subsequent visit he gave authority to bestow the Holy Ghost, as he touched and spoke to each of the twelve disciples individually (3 Ne. 18:36–37). Whereas baptisms can be performed by priests in the Aaronic Priesthood, the Holy Ghost can be conferred only by bearers of the higher or Melchizedek Priesthood (Moro. 2:2; JS—H 1:70). John the Baptist referred to this fundamental distinction between the two priesthoods: "I indeed baptize you with water unto repentance: but he that cometh after me is mightier than I . . . he shall baptize you with the Holy Ghost, and with fire" (Matt. 3:11).

The gift of the Holy Ghost is formally bestowed upon an individual only once, but the spiritual benefits associated with this gift can and should be continuous during a lifetime. Latter-day Saints are taught to strive to live so as to have the Holy Ghost as a "constant companion" to strengthen them and help them choose the right (D&C 121:46). The granting of the gift alone, however, does not insure these inspirations. The actual reception of the Holy Ghost is conditional upon the humility, faith, and worthiness of the individual who has had the gift bestowed on him or her. President Joseph F. Smith taught that the gift of the Holy Ghost confers upon worthy and desirous members "the right to receive . . . the power and light of truth of the Holy Ghost, although [they] may often be left to [their] own spirit and judgment" (*GD*, pp. 60–61).

The gift of the Holy Ghost is referred to by the Prophet Joseph Smith as one of the basic principles and ordinances of the gospel, being integrally linked to faith in Jesus Christ, repentance, and baptism by immersion for the REMISSION OF SINS (*see* A of F 4; FIRST PRINCIPLES OF THE GOSPEL). Together these four constitute the "first principles" of the gospel of Jesus Christ (*see* 3 Ne. 27:19–21; GOSPEL OF JESUS CHRIST) and the only means whereby men and women can be cleansed of all sin—to become pure and spotless and worthy to enter the presence of God.

The Holy Ghost continues to aid in the process of spiritual purification through "the baptism by fire," which has been described in these words: "By the power of the Holy Ghost—who is the Sanctifier (3 Ne. 27:19–21)—dross, iniquity, carnality, sensuality, and every evil thing is burned out of the repentant soul as if by fire; the cleansed person becomes literally a new creature of the Holy Ghost. . . . He is born again" (*MD*, p. 73). The Savior referred to this spiritual rebirth when he told Nicodemus, "Except a man be born of water and of the Spirit, he cannot enter into the kingdom of God" (John 3:5).

A single experience of being "born again" does not alone insure salvation. It is also necessary for a person to "endure to the end," an essential element of the gospel of Christ (2 Ne. 31:20; 3 Ne. 27:16–17). The prophet $Nephi_1$ taught that ENDURING TO THE END requires that one "feast upon the words of Christ," following the guidance of the Holy Ghost in "all things what ye should do" (2 Ne. 32:3–5). The gift of the Holy Ghost thus ensures that divine guidance and spiritual renewal take place throughout one's life, provided that the requisite repentance and humility are manifested.

BIBLIOGRAPHY

Lampe, G. W. H. "Holy Spirit." In *The Interpreter's Dictionary of the Bible,* Vol. 2, pp. 626–39. Nashville, Tenn., 1962.

Shepherd, M. H., Jr. "Hands, Laying on of." In *The Interpreter's Dictionary of the Bible,* Vol. 2, pp. 521–22. Nashville, Tenn., 1962.

Talmage, James E. *AF*, pp. 157–70.

BRUCE DOUGLAS PORTER

GIFTS OF THE SPIRIT

The seventh Article of Faith of The Church of Jesus Christ of Latter-day Saints reads: "We believe in the gift of tongues, prophecy, revelation, visions, healing, interpretation of tongues, and so forth." All such heavenly endowments come as gifts of the Spirit—that is, through the grace of God and the operation and power of the HOLY GHOST. As prerequisites to obtaining such gifts, a person must receive the ordinances of baptism and the bestowal of the GIFT OF THE HOLY GHOST from an authorized priesthood holder, must earnestly seek to obtain the gift or gifts, and must make sincere efforts to keep the Lord's COMMANDMENTS.

Clearly the Spirit can grant any gift that would fill a particular need; hence, no exhaustive list is possible, but many gifts have been promised the Church. Through the New Testament, readers are familiar with the six specified above: the two related to the gifts of tongues and their interpretation, or the power to speak in a language not previously learned and the ability to interpret such speech; the gift of prophecy, exhibited sometimes in the predictive sense but more often in the sense that "the testimony of Jesus is the spirit of prophecy" (Rev. 19:10); revelation, or the heaven-inspired receipt of knowledge, wisdom, or direction; visions, or visual spiritual manifestations such as prophets have received in all ages and as Joel predicted for many others in the latter days (Joel 2:28–29); healing, or the power to "lay hands on the sick" that they may recover (Mark 16:18).

Scripturally, gifts of the Spirit are among the signs that "follow them that believe" (Mark 16:17). Eager to receive such promised gifts but lacking in understanding, some of the early converts to the Church (1831–32) became caught up in "spiritual" excesses that were common to revivalist campground meetings, with which they were familiar. In early days in Kirtland, Ohio, the Prophet Joseph Smith observed, "many false spirits were introduced . . . many ridiculous things were entered into . . . [that would] cause the Spirit of God to be withdrawn" (*TPJS,* pp. 213–14). In congregations around Kirtland, Parley P. Pratt specifically noted "disgusting" spiritual operations, "unseemly gestures," people falling "into ecstasies, and . . . drawn into contortions . . . fits" (Pratt, p. 61). Joseph Smith condemned such practices as unnatural and without useful purpose, since they communicated no intelligence (*TPJS,* pp. 204, 214). Thus dissociating the Church from the spiritual extravagances of frontier Christianity, the authorities moved swiftly against such erroneous practices, reclaiming those members whom they could and excommunicating those who persisted in their error.

In the doctrinal unfolding of the infant Church, Joseph Smith received revelations relating to spiritual gifts, notably that of March 8, 1831 (now D&C 46). Having first warned against deception by false spirits, the revelation set out the gifts much as Paul and $Moroni_2$ did for the first-century and the Nephite churches, respectively (see 1 Cor. 12; Moroni 10). Mentioned besides the six above were knowledge; wisdom; faith to be healed; the working of miracles; knowledge of the ways in which gifts may be administered; and the DISCERNMENT of spirits, whether they are of God or of the devil. Listed too was the gift of the Spirit's witness of Jesus Christ and his atonement for the sins of the world, and, for some, the gift of believing the words of one who declares that witness (D&C 46:14).

The revelation promises at least one gift to every faithful Latter-day Saint. Bishops and other presiding officers, by virtue of their callings to watch over the Church, may receive multiple gifts, including the special gift of discernment to detect false from true spirits. On the latter point, Joseph Smith cautioned about "the common error of considering all supernatural manifestations to be of God," warning that evil spirits as well as heavenly ones can, for example, speak in tongues and interpret them; and that in their deception they may even give recognition to the Savior and his authorized servants (*TPJS*, pp. 206–13, 229; also Luke 4:33–35; Acts 16:16–18).

Many early LDS journals recount experiences with spiritual gifts: In 1830 Newel Knight saw a vision of heaven apparently similar to what the martyr Stephen described ("Newel Knight's Journal," pp. 52–53). In Kirtland in 1831, Chloe Smith, who had been languishing near death, was instantly restored to health under Joseph Smith's ministration (Pratt, pp. 66–67). At a meeting in Ontario, Canada, in 1833, Lydia Bailey (later Knight) spoke in tongues (*Journal History*, Oct. 19, 1833). Following Heber C. Kimball's prophetic promise in 1836 that a son would be born to Parley and Thankful Pratt, childless after ten years of marriage, a son was born a year later (Pratt, pp. 130–31, 165). Then as now, both leaders and the general membership were blessed with such gifts.

Gifts of the Spirit are to be sought for their beneficial effect rather than for their remarkable character (see 1 Cor. 14). In fact, as Joseph Smith observed, only one or two of the gifts are visible when in operation. In its commonly understood sense, the gift of tongues is one such, but President Joseph F. Smith stressed its more practical aspect: "I needed the gift of tongues once, and the Lord gave it to me. I was in a foreign land, sent to preach the gospel to a people whose language I could not understand. Then I sought earnestly for the gift of tongues, and by this gift and by study, in a hundred days after landing upon those islands I could talk to the people in their language as I now talk to you in my native tongue. This was a gift that was worthy of the gospel. There was a purpose in it" (Smith, p. 201). In this way, the gift is frequently enjoyed by LDS missionaries today.

Throughout the world, Latter-day Saints report a variety of spiritual gifts in the normal course of their lives. Faithful members commonly receive through the Spirit the gift of the testimony of Jesus Christ and his restored gospel—and those individual testimonies constitute the strength of the Church; the gift of knowledge of spiritual things is enjoyed widely; daily, priesthood bearers lay hands on the heads of sick family members or friends, as requested (see James 5:14–15), and bring them heaven's healing powers, frequently with instant effect; men, women, and young persons receive revelation as needed for the benefit of themselves, their families, or those whom they serve in Church callings. Virtually all of these activities and others of comparable spiritual significance go on in the privacy of home and heart without any public awareness of them.

All spiritual gifts are needed in the Church (1 Cor. 12), but that some are more to be desired than others is evident from Paul's writings: One is to seek the best gifts. Of special significance for all who desire "a more excellent way" (1 Cor. 12:31) is to receive and develop the gift of CHARITY. This "pure love of Christ" is a fundamental mark of true DISCIPLESHIP, a prerequisite to ETERNAL LIFE, and a quality one is therefore to pray and work for with all energy of heart (Moroni 7:47–48; 10:21; Ether 12:34). Paul's masterful exposition on charity (1 Cor. 13) further defines this attribute and confirms love as the great commandment and the Christian's crucial need. Disciples are to manifest this gift and also desire others (1 Cor. 14:1), working by the power of God and by the gifts of the Spirit (Moro. 10:25).

BIBLIOGRAPHY

"Newel Knight's Journal." In *Scraps of Biography*. Salt Lake City, 1883.

Pratt, Parley P. *Autobiography of Parley Parker Pratt*. Salt Lake City, 1967.

Smith, Joseph F. *Gospel Doctrine*. Salt Lake City, 1977.

H. GEORGE BICKERSTAFF

GOD

Latter-day Saints declare, "We believe in God, the Eternal Father, and in His Son, Jesus Christ, and in the Holy Ghost" (A of F 1). Joseph Smith offered the following clarification: "The Father has a body of flesh and bones as tangible as man's; the Son also; but the Holy Ghost has not a body of flesh and bones, but is a personage of Spirit" (D&C 130:22; *see* GOD THE FATHER; HOLY GHOST; JESUS CHRIST).

The Father, Son, and Holy Ghost are three separate and distinct beings who constitute one GODHEAD. Generally speaking, the Father is the Creator, the Son is the Redeemer, and the Holy Ghost is the Comforter and Testifier (cf. *MFP* 5:26–34; *TPJS*, p. 190). Many scriptural passages illustrate the distinct character of the members of the Godhead. For example, at the baptism of Jesus, while he was in the water, the Father's voice was heard from heaven, and the Holy Ghost descended "like a dove" and rested upon the Son (Matt. 3:13–17; *see* JESUS CHRIST: BAPTISM). All three persons were manifested separately and simultaneously. Also, Jesus said, "My Father is greater than I" (John 14:28), and in another place declared, "The Father judgeth no man, but hath committed all judgment unto the Son" (John 5:22). Further, Jesus pointed to the Father and himself as two separate witnesses of the divinity of his work (John 5:32–37; 8:12–18). On the Mount of Transfiguration the heavenly Father identified the mortal Jesus to Peter, James, and John as "my beloved Son" (Matt. 17:5). Moreover, the Son often prayed to his Father. In Gethsemane he prayed to the Father while in deep anguish (Mark 14:32–39; cf. Luke 22:40–46; D&C 19:16–19), and on the cross he cried out to the Father, "My God, my God, why hast thou forsaken me?" (Matt. 27:46; Mark 15:34; cf. Ps. 22:1). All of these passages clearly show that the Father is a being distinct from the Son. Although they are one in mind and purpose, they are two separate individuals and bear testimony of one another (cf. 3 Ne. 11:7–11).

The way in which the Godhead is one is illustrated by Jesus' prayer that his disciples would be one, even as he and the Father are one (John 17:21–22; cf. 3 Ne. 11:27, 32–36; 28:10–11). Here he was praying for his disciples' unity of mind, purpose, and testimony, not for the merger of their identities into a single being. He prayed that they would be one in desire, purpose, and objective, exactly as he and his Father are (*TPJS,* p. 372; *see* UNITY).

The Father, as God, is omnipotent, omniscient, and, through his spirit, omnipresent (*see* LIGHT OF CHRIST). He is merciful and gracious, slow to anger, abundant in goodness. His course is one eternal round. He is a God of truth and no respecter of persons. He personifies love.

Though Latter-day Saints extensively use the scriptures to learn about God, their fundamental knowledge concerning him is based upon the Prophet Joseph Smith's first vision, the Prophet's subsequent revelatory experiences, and individual personal REVELATION. While mankind may reason or speculate concerning the existence of God, and his nature, the principal way by which they can know about God is dependent upon his revealing himself to them (*see* TESTIMONY OF JESUS CHRIST).

Before A.D. 325, the date of the first Christian ecumenical council at Nicaea, the nature of God was debated by philosophers and people of faith. Since then, the concept of God has been the subject of ecumenical councils, philosophical discussions, and creeds. None of these is the source of the LDS understanding of God. To be sure, many classical arguments for the existence of God have been advanced, including the ontological arguments of Anselm, the five "proofs" of St. Thomas Aquinas, the teleological argument of Descartes, the ethical argument of Leibniz, and the postulates of practical reason of Kant. As impressive as any of these might be as achievements of the human intellect, none of them is the source of faith in God for Latter-day Saints, whose faith is based upon personal testimony grounded in personal experience.

The last chapter of the Book of Mormon records this promise: "And when ye shall receive these things [of God], I would exhort you that ye would ask God, the Eternal Father, in the name of Christ, if these things are not true; and if ye shall ask with a sincere heart, with real intent, having faith in Christ, he will manifest the truth of it unto you, by the power of the Holy Ghost. And by the power of the Holy Ghost ye may know the truth of all things" (Moro. 10:4–5). The personal witness that one receives in answer to prayer is called a TESTIMONY. Latter-day Saints teach that through this source a person can receive a sure witness that God lives, a confirmation regarding the various principles that the scriptures teach, and clarification where it is needed.

Belief in God, or a measure of faith in him, is essential to finding the reality of his existence. Inasmuch as God exists, and human beings are his children, it is important for men and women to know these facts because such knowledge is a component of ETERNAL LIFE (John 17:3). Individuals need to know that they are themselves eternal beings, that they are dependent upon God for their earthly existence (cf. Mosiah 2:21), and that their future condition depends on how they relate to God and keep his commandments (*see* COMMANDMENTS; OBEDIENCE).

God loves his children and has provided the means for them to realize their divine potential (*see* GODHOOD). God has given humankind the program for his children as a whole (*see* PLAN OF SALVATION, PLAN OF REDEMPTION), and through the gift of the Holy Ghost he gives special guidance to individuals as they seek it. God revealed his will to prophets in ancient times and to apostles in the meridian of time, and he continues to reveal himself to living prophets and apostles in the latter days.

Learning of God's existence creates the desire to know him, and know what he would have one do or be. As one's faith and knowledge of God increase, one desires more and more to keep God's commandments and feel close to him. The Prophet Joseph Smith taught that knowing the true character of God forms the basis for the faith that leads to salvation (*Lectures on Faith* 4:1). Jesus promised that the Comforter, or Holy Ghost, would be sent to one who keeps God's commandments (John 14:26). The ideal is to enjoy that influence continuously.

The Prophet Joseph Smith said, "It is the first principle of the Gospel to know for a certainty the character of God, and to know that we may converse with him as one man converses with another, and that he was once a man like us: yea, that God himself, the Father of us all, dwelt on an earth, the same as Jesus Christ himself did" (*TPJS*, pp. 345–46). Further, "God himself was once as we are now, and is an exalted man, and sits enthroned in yonder heavens! That is the great secret. If the veil were rent today, and the great God who holds this world in its orbit, and who upholds all worlds and all things by his power, was to make himself visible,—I say, if you were to see him today, you would see him like a man in form—like yourselves in all the person, image, and very form as a man; for Adam was created in the very fashion, image and likeness of God, and received instruction from, and walked, talked and conversed with him, as one man talks and communes with another" (*TPJS*, p. 345).

Thus, all humans must learn from God who they are, where they came from, why they are on earth, where they are going, and what their eternal potential is, by studying the scriptures and receiving personal revelation. All things center in God.

BIBLIOGRAPHY

"The Father and the Son: A Doctrinal Exposition by the First Presidency and the Twelve." *MFP* 5:26–34.

Kimball, Spencer W. *The Teachings of Spencer W. Kimball,* ed. Edward L. Kimball. Salt Lake City, 1982.

McConkie, Bruce R. *A New Witness for the Articles of Faith.* Salt Lake City, 1985.

Smith, Joseph Fielding. *DS* 1:1–55. Salt Lake City, 1954.

Talmage, James E. *AF,* pp. 29–51. Salt Lake City, 1965.

DAVID H. YARN, JR.

GOD THE FATHER

[*This entry is composed of four articles:*

Overview
Names and Titles
Glory of God
Work and Glory of God

The first article is an introduction to doctrines about God the Father and the sources where they may be found. The second article lists the main names and titles by which God is known in LDS scripture. The third article offers a brief discussion of the Glory of God. The concluding article in this entry elaborates on the concept of the purposes of God in relation to mankind.]

OVERVIEW

Latter-day Saints commonly refer to God the Eternal Father as Elohim, a Hebrew plural (*'elohim*) meaning *God* or *gods,* and to his Son Jesus Christ as Jehovah (*see* JEHOVAH, JESUS CHRIST).

Distinguishing between the persons of the Father and the Son is not possible with more ambiguous terms like "God"; therefore, referring to the Father as "Elohim" is a useful convention as long as one remembers that in some passages of the Hebrew Bible the title *'elohim* does not refer exclusively to the person of God the Father. A less ambiguous term for God the Father in LDS parlance might be "Ahman" (cf. D&C 78:15, 20), which, according to Elder Orson Pratt, is a name of the Father (*JD* 2:342).

In Church theology, the doctrine of the nature of God is established more clearly by the First Vision of the Prophet Joseph Smith than by anything else. Here, Joseph Smith saw for himself that the Father and the Son were two separate and distinct beings, each possessing a body in whose image and likeness mortals are created. For Latter-day Saints, no theological or philosophical propositions about God can override the primary experience of the Prophet.

In one sense, it creates a slight distortion to focus on one member of the Godhead and discuss his characteristics in isolation from those of the other two, for Father, Son, and Holy Ghost are one in mind, one in purpose, and one in character (John 10:30; 17:11, 21–23). Most of what can be said of the Father is also true of the Son and vice versa. The Prophet Joseph Smith said that the Son does nothing for which the Father is not the exemplar (*TPJS*, p. 312; cf. John 5:19–20).

Yet God the Father is not one in substance with the Son or the Holy Spirit, but is a separate being. The Father existed prior to the Son and the Holy Ghost and is the source of their divinity. In classical terms, LDS theology is subordinationist; that is, it views the Son and the Holy Ghost as subordinate to and dependent upon God the Eternal Father. They are his offspring. Thus Joseph Smith referred to the Father as "God the first" to emphasize his priority in the Godhead (*TPJS*, p. 190). The Son and the Holy Spirit were "in the beginning, with God," but the Father alone existed before the beginning of the universe as it is known. He is ultimately the source of all things and the Father of all things, for in the beginning he begot the Son, and through the instrumentality of his agent, the Son, the Father accomplished the creation of all things.

Latter-day Saints perceive the Father as an exalted Man in the most literal, anthropomorphic terms. They do not view the language of Genesis as allegorical; human beings are created in the form and image of a God who has a physical form and image (Gen. 1:26). The Prophet Joseph Smith explained, "The Father has a body of flesh and bones as tangible as man's; the Son also; but the Holy Ghost has not a body of flesh and bones, but is a personage of Spirit" (D&C 130:22). Thus, "God is a Spirit" (John 4:24) in the sense that the Holy Ghost, the member of the Godhead who deals most often and most directly with humans, is a God and a spirit, but God the Father and God the Son are spirits with physical, resurrected bodies. Latter-day Saints deny the abstract nature of God the Father and affirm that he is a concrete being, that he possesses a physical body, and that he is in space and time. They further reject any idea that God the Father is "totally other," unknowable, or incomprehensible. In LDS doctrine, knowing the Father and the Son is a prerequisite to eternal life (John 17:3; D&C 88:49). In the opinion of many Latter-day Saints, the concept of an abstract, incomprehensible deity constitutes an intrusion of Greek philosophical categories upon the biblical record.

The Father, Elohim, is called the Father because he is the literal father of the spirits of mortals (Heb. 12:9). This paternity is not allegorical. All individual human spirits were begotten (not created from nothing or made) by the Father in a premortal state, where they lived and were nurtured by Heavenly Parents. These spirit children of the Father come to earth to receive mortal bodies; there is a literal family relationship among humankind. Joseph Smith taught, "If men do not comprehend the character of God, they do not comprehend themselves" (*TPJS*, p. 343). Gods and humans represent a single divine lineage, the same species of being, although they and he are at different stages of progress. This doctrine is stated concisely in a well-known couplet by President Lorenzo Snow: "As man now is, God once was: as God now is, man may be" (*see* GODHOOD). This principle is clearly demonstrated in the person of Jesus Christ, a God who became mortal, and yet a God like whom mortals may become (Rom. 8:29; 2 Cor. 3:18). But the maxim is true of the Father as well. As the Prophet Joseph Smith said, "God himself was once as we are now, and is an exalted man, and sits enthroned in yonder heavens! That is the great secret" (*TPJS*, p. 345). Thus, the Father became the Father at some time before "the beginning" as humans know it, by experiencing a mortality similar to that experienced on earth. There has been speculation among some Latter-day Saints on the implications of this doctrine, but nothing has been revealed to the Church about conditions before the "beginning" as mortals know it. The important points of the doctrine for Latter-day Saints are that Gods and humans are the same species of being, but at different stages of development in a divine continuum, and that the heavenly Father and Mother are the heavenly pattern, model, and example of what mortals can become through obedience to the gospel (*see* MOTHER IN HEAVEN). Knowing that they are the literal offspring of Heavenly Parents and that they can become like those parents through the gospel of Jesus Christ is a wellspring of religious motivation. With God as the literal Father and with humans having the capacity to become like him, the basic religious questions "Where did I come from?," "Why am I here?," and What is my destiny?" are fundamentally answered.

Latter-day Saints also attribute omnipotence and omniscience to the Father. He knows all things relative to the universe in which mortals live and is himself the source and possessor of all true power manifest in it. This is part of what it means to be exalted, and this is why human beings may safely put their faith and trust in God the Father, an exalted being. Nevertheless, in most things dealing with this world, the Father works through a mediator, his Son, Jesus Christ. With few exceptions, scriptural references to God, or even to the Father, have Jesus Christ as the actual subject, for the Father is represented by his Son. On those few recorded occasions when the Father has plainly manifested himself, he has apparently limited his personal involvement to bearing witness of the Son, as at the baptism of Jesus (Matt. 3:17), at the transfiguration (Matt. 17:5), in his witness to the Nephites and Lamanites (3 Ne. 11:7), and in Joseph Smith's First Vision (JS—H 1:17). Christ is the agent of the Father, and since he alone, by his atonement, has made access to the Father possible, Latter-day Saints worship and pray to the Father and offer all other sacred performances to him in the name of the Son, Jesus Christ (Moses 5:8).

Another important personal attribute of the Father is his perfect love (1 Jn. 4:8). Because of this love, it is the nature of the Father to improve everything and everyone to the extent that they will allow.

Out of preexisting chaos, matter unorganized, the Father created an orderly universe. Out of preexisting intelligence, he begat spirit children. Even those of his children who will not cooperate and obey, and who cannot therefore become like him, he still saves, if they will allow it, and places them in lesser kingdoms of glory (D&C 76:42–43; *see* SALVATION): "For behold, this is my work and my glory—to bring to pass the immortality and eternal life of man" (Moses 1:39). The love of the Father is not limited to those who worship and obey him, although their rewards will be greatest, but it is extended to all of his children. The Father's work, and his glory, is to love and to lift all of his children as far as they will allow him. Latter-day Saints believe it is the intention of the Father to make all human beings as happy as they possibly can be. To that end, the Father authored the PLAN OF SALVATION. The Father desires that all human beings be exalted like himself, receive the powers and the joys that he possesses, and experience a fulness of joy in eternity. The limiting factor is the degree to which humans, by exercising their faith and obedience and by making wise choices, will permit the Father to bless them in achieving this goal. Sometimes having faith in God means having faith that the Father's plan will do what it is designed to do—to bring maximum happiness to human beings. Nevertheless, Latter-day Saints believe, in contrast to some other views, that the Father will never violate individual agency by forcing his children to exaltation and happiness. Coercion in any degree, even in the form of predestination to the celestial kingdom, is abhorrent to the nature of the Father. All relationships to him or associations with him are voluntary.

BIBLIOGRAPHY

Cannon, Donald Q., and Larry E. Dahl. *The Prophet Joseph Smith's King Follett Discourse: A Six Column Comparison of Original Notes and Amalgamations.* Provo, Utah, 1983.

McConkie, Bruce R. *A New Witness for the Articles of Faith,* pp. 58–65. Salt Lake City, 1985.

Smith, Joseph Fielding. *DS,* Vol. 1, pp. 1–17.

STEPHEN E. ROBINSON

NAMES AND TITLES

Known names and titles of God the Eternal Father are limited in number, especially when compared to the names applied to Jesus

Christ (*see* JESUS CHRIST, NAMES AND TITLES OF). Latter-day Saints understand the Godhead to consist of three separate individuals: the Father; Jesus Christ, his Son; and the Holy Ghost (D&C 130:22). Therefore, when the need exists to distinguish God the Father from the other two members of the Godhead, Church members select from the names found in scripture.

GOD. Among Latter-day Saints, the title "God" generally identifies God the Father. Occasionally, God may refer to the unified Godhead of the Father, Son, and Holy Ghost (cf. 2 Ne. 31:21; D&C 20:28) and at times to each member individually (*AF*, pp. 159–63). This characteristic makes the attempt to distinguish the Father from Jesus Christ in scripture very difficult at times. Significantly, Jesus' declarations that he and the Father are "one," and to know one is to know the other, indicate that the unity or "oneness" of the Godhead—in purpose and mind and testifying of one another—is of primary worth and seems to diminish the importance of making distinctions among its members. The scriptures teach that a person will come to know the Father by first knowing Christ (John 14:6–23; D&C 84:35–38; 93:1–22; 132:12). Jesus' instructions that his believers are to be "one" with him as he is "one" with the Father are basic to his doctrine (cf. John 17:1–26; 3 Ne. 11:32–36).

FATHER, FATHER IN HEAVEN. The name-title "Father in Heaven" refers to the director of creation and Father of the spirits of all mankind (*MFP* 5:26–27). Jesus used the terms "my Father," "our Father," and "the Father" when teaching about and praying to his Father. The Aramaic word *'abba* (father) has carried over into English translations of the New Testament (Mark 14:36; Rom. 8:15; Gal. 4:6). In the Book of Mormon, the resurrected Jesus continually used the title "Father" when referring to the Father in Heaven (e.g., 3 Ne. 11:11; 19:20–23). In some instances, however, Father may refer to the Son (*see* JESUS CHRIST, FATHERHOOD AND SONSHIP OF). According to both the New Testament and Book of Mormon, faithful souls who are converted to Jesus Christ and who make personal covenants with him are spiritually reborn, becoming "his sons and his daughters" (e.g., Mosiah 5:7; cf. 1 Cor. 4:15; 2 Cor. 6:18; *MFP* 5:27–31).

GOD THE FATHER. The combination of the title "God" and the appellative "Father" specifies the Father of Jesus Christ and of all spirits. Latter-day Saints worship God the Father and Jesus Christ and pray to the Father in the name of Christ as directed by the Lord (D&C 88:64).

ELOHIM. The commonly used term for "God" or "gods" in the Hebrew Bible is *'elohim,* a plural form whose singular is *'eloah* or *'el* and has the meaning of "lofty one" or "exalted one." Early Church leaders adopted the policy of designating God the Father by the exalted name-title "Elohim" (cf. *MFP* 5:26). This terminology has continued down to the present.

JEHOVAH, LORD, LORD GOD. The term "Lord," printed with capital letters in many English versions of the Old Testament, is a substitute for the name Jehovah (*yhwh* in the Hebrew Bible). Even though Latter-day Saints identify Jesus Christ as Jehovah (3 Ne. 15:3–5; cf. D&C 110:1–4; *see* JEHOVAH, JESUS CHRIST), they utilize the title "Lord" for both the Father and the Son, as is common throughout scripture. The title "Lord God" in the Hebrew Bible is a compound of *'elohim* preceded by either *yhwh* (Jehovah) or *adonai* (lord or master). This combined name-title refers mainly to Jehovah in the Old Testament. In the New Testament, the Book of Mormon, and in other latter-day scriptures, "Lord God" can mean either the Father (e.g., Moses 4:1–4) or the Son (Mosiah 3:21).

AHMAN. In two revelations to Joseph Smith (D&C 78:20; 95:17), Jesus Christ referred to himself as "the Son Ahman," allowing the possibility that "Ahman" may be a word meaning God, and one of the names of the Father (*see* AHMAN). The name also appears in a compound place name, Adam-ondi-Ahman (D&C 116:1; 117:8, 11).

MAN OF HOLINESS. Adam learned by revelation that one of the names of God the Father is "Man of Holiness" (Moses 6:57). Enoch also recorded God's words: "Behold, I am God; Man of Holiness is my name; Man of Counsel is my name; and Endless and Eternal is my name" (Moses 7:35; *see* ENDLESS AND ETERNAL).

In the Bible and latter-day scripture, other titles for God carry valuable meaning: "Father of Spirits," "God of all other Gods," "Endless," "The Living God," and "Lord of Sabaoth [Hebrew for "Hosts"], which is by interpretation, the creator of the first day, the beginning and the end" (D&C 95:7).

BIBLIOGRAPHY
Talmage, James E. *AF*. Salt Lake City, 1915.

GLADE L. BURGON

GLORY OF GOD

Glory is an intrinsic attribute and emanation of God, which LDS scriptures associate with divine law and with the power and Spirit that "proceedeth forth from the presence of God to fill the immensity of space" (D&C 88:7–13). Prominent terms for this "spirit of glory" (1 Pet. 4:14) are the Spirit of God, the HOLY SPIRIT, the Spirit of the Lord, the light of truth, the LIGHT OF CHRIST, and the Spirit of Christ. This all-pervading Spirit is so pure and refined that it is not perceptible to mortals under ordinary circumstances (D&C 131:7–8; *TPJS*, pp. 207, 301–332). Yet on occasion, the prophets testify, the innate glory has been visibly manifest as flaming spiritual fire (Ex. 24:17; Acts 2:3; Hel. 5:43–45; 3 Ne. 17:24; 19:13–14; *HC* 1:30–32). Moses and Jesus were transfigured by the same glorifying power (Ex. 34:29–35; Matt. 17:2).

Because glory radiates from God, he is described as "a consuming fire" (Deut. 4:24; cf. Isa. 33:14). God may withhold or conceal his glory (*TPJS*, pp. 162, 181, 325). But he may also radiate such transcendent light and heat that no mortal flesh can endure his presence (Mal. 4:1; D&C 133:41, 49; *HC* 1:17, 37). Only when clothed by the Spirit can anyone endure the glorious presence of God (Moses 1:2, 11; D&C 67:11).

The spirit of glory permeates God's creations (D&C 63:59; 88:41). Therefore, they are kingdoms of glory, and to behold any or the least of his creations is to behold a portion of his glory (Moses 1:5; Ps. 19:1; D&C 88:45–47; *TPJS*, p. 351). Since God's works are endless, his glory is ever-increasing (Abr. 3:12; Moses 1:38; 7:30). His "work and glory" are to bring to pass the immortality and eternal life of his children (Moses 1:39). As Jesus' submission to the will of his Father glorified both himself and his Father, so does the obedience of his children glorify both themselves and God (John 13:31; 17:1). Oneness with God is achieved through this relationship of glory (John 17:21–23; D&C 88:60).

The degree to which mortal men and women acquire and live the moral and spiritual principles of light and truth inherent in divine INTELLIGENCE determines the degree to which they will be filled with the glory of God when resurrected and, therefore, the sphere of glory they will inherit in eternity (D&C 88:22–32; 93:20, 28; 130:18–19; *TPJS*, p. 366).

RODNEY TURNER

WORK AND GLORY OF GOD

A revelation received by Moses between his experience at the burning bush (Ex. 3:1–4:17) and his return to Egypt (Ex. 4:20; cf. Moses 1:26) describes the work and glory of God as "to bring to pass the immortality and eternal life of man" (Moses 1:39). One of the most frequently quoted passages of scripture in LDS sermons, this declaration elucidates the chief object of God's actions on behalf of his children.

Earlier in this vision, Moses had "beheld many lands; and each land was called earth, and there were inhabitants on the face thereof" (Moses 1:29). Then the Lord told him that "as one earth shall pass away, and the heavens thereof even so shall another come; and there is no end to my works" (1:38). After receiving this expansive, orienting view of God's creations, Moses asked the Lord, "Tell me, I pray thee, why these things are so, and by what thou madest them?" (1:30).

The Lord answered the first question by explaining that "this is my work and my glory—to bring to pass the immortality and eternal life of man" (Moses 1:39). Creating worlds and populating them with his children are major parts of God's "work." He creates earths as dwelling places for his spirit children, where they receive physical bodies and learn to walk by faith. Whereas IMMORTALITY is neverending life, ETERNAL LIFE means to become like God (*see* GODHOOD). Thus, God's "glory" consists in mankind's attainment of everlasting glory, the ultimate being eternal life.

In answer to Moses' second question (i.e., "by what thou madest them?"), the Lord stated that worlds were created by the power of the "Only Begotten Son, who is full of grace and truth" (Moses 1:32). This passage underscores the view that the creative acts of God, which include all inhabitable worlds (Moses 1:33; cf. John 1:1–2), are done through the Only Begotten as God's agent, and are done in grace and truth for the benefit of his children.

DENNIS L. LARGEY

GODHEAD

[*For discussions about the three members of the Godhead and their divine attributes and manifestations in the world, see* GOD; GOD THE FATHER; JESUS CHRIST; HOLY GHOST; HOLY SPIRIT; GIFT OF THE HOLY GHOST. *See also* GODHOOD; ENDLESS AND ETERNAL; INTELLIGENCE; FOREKNOWLEDGE OF GOD; OMNIPOTENCE OF GOD.]

Latter-day Saints believe in God the Father; his Son, Jesus Christ; and the Holy Ghost (A of F 1). These three Gods form the Godhead, which holds the keys of power over the universe. Each member of the Godhead is an independent personage, separate and distinct from the other two, the three being in perfect unity and harmony with each other (*AF,* chap. 2).

This knowledge concerning the Godhead derives primarily from the Bible and the revelations of the Prophet Joseph Smith. For example, the three members of the Godhead were separately manifested at the baptism of Jesus (Matt. 3:16–17) and at the stoning of Stephen (Acts 7:55–56). Joseph Smith commented, "Peter and Stephen testify that they saw the Son of Man standing on the right hand of God. Any person that had seen the heavens opened knows that there are three personages in the heavens who hold the keys of power, and one presides over all" (*TPJS,* p. 312).

On June 16, 1844, in his last Sunday sermon before his martyrdom, Joseph Smith declared that "in all congregations" he had taught "the plurality of Gods" for fifteen years: "I have always declared God to be a distinct personage, Jesus Christ a separate and distinct personage from God the Father, and that the Holy Ghost was a distinct personage and a Spirit: and these three constitute three distinct personages and three Gods" (*TPJS,* p. 370). The two earliest surviving accounts of Joseph's first vision do not give details on the Godhead, but that he consistently taught that the Father and the Son were separate personages is clearly documentable in most periods of his life (e.g., D&C 76:23 [1832]; 137:3 [1836]; his First Vision, JS—H 1:17 [recorded 1838]; D&C 130:22 [1843]). While the fifth lecture on faith (1834) does not identify the Holy Ghost as a "personage," it affirms that "the Father, Son, and Holy Spirit constitute the Godhead" (cf. Millet, pp. 223–34).

Although the three members of the Godhead are distinct personages, their Godhead is "one" in that all three are united in their thoughts, actions, and purpose, with each having a fulness of knowledge, truth, and power. Each is a God. This does not imply a mystical union of substance or personality. Joseph Smith taught:

> Many men say there is one God; the Father, the Son and the Holy Ghost are only one God. I say that is a strange God anyhow—three in one, and one in three! It is a curious organization anyhow. "Father, I pray not for the world, but I pray for those that thou hast given me . . . that they may be one as we are." . . . I want to read the text to you myself—"I am agreed with the Father and the Father is agreed with me, and we are agreed as one." The Greek shows that it should be agreed. "Father, I pray for them which thou hast given me out of the world, . . . that they all may be agreed," and all come to dwell in unity [*TPJS*, p. 372; cf. John 17:9–11, 20–21; also cf. *WJS*, p. 380].

The unity prayed for in John 17 provides a model for the LDS understanding of the unity of the Godhead—one that is achieved among distinct individuals by unity of purpose, through faith, and by divine will and action. Joseph Smith taught that the Godhead was united by an "everlasting covenant [that] was made between [these] three personages before the organization of this earth" relevant to their administration to its inhabitants (*TPJS*, p. 190). The prime purpose of the Godhead and of all those united with them is "to bring to pass the immortality and eternal life of man" (Moses 1:39; Hinckley, p. 49–51).

Each member of the Godhead fulfills particular functions in relation to each of the others and to mankind. God the Father presides over the Godhead. He is the Father of all human spirits and of the physical body of Jesus Christ. The human body was formed in his image.

Jesus Christ, the Firstborn son of God the Father in the spirit and the Only Begotten son in the flesh, is the creative agent of the Godhead and the redeeming mediator between the Father and mankind. By him God created all things, and through him God revealed the laws of salvation. In him shall all be made alive, and through his atonement all mankind may be reconciled with the Father.

The Holy Ghost is a personage of spirit who bears witness to truth. The Father and the Holy Ghost bear witness of the Son, and the Son and the Holy Ghost bear witness of the Father (3 Ne. 11:32; cf. John 8:18). Through the Holy Ghost, revelations of the Father and of the Son are given.

The LDS doctrine of the Godhead differs from the various concepts of the Trinity. Several postbiblical trinitarian doctrines emerged in Christianity. This "dogmatic development took place gradually, against the background of the emanationist philosophy of Stoicism and Neoplatonism (including the mystical theology of the latter), and within the context of strict Jewish monotheism" (*ER* 15:54). Trinitarian doctrines sought to elevate God's oneness or unity, ultimately in some cases describing Jesus as *homoousious* (of the same substance) with the Father in order to preclude any claim that Jesus was not fully divine. LDS understanding, formulated by latter-day revelation through Joseph Smith, rejects the idea that Jesus or any other personage loses individuality by attaining Godhood or by standing in divine and eternal relationships with other exalted beings.

BIBLIOGRAPHY

Hinckley, Gordon B. "The Father, Son, and Holy Ghost." *Ensign* 16 (Nov. 1986):49–51.

Millet, Robert L. "The Supreme Power over All Things: The Doctrine of the Godhead in the Lectures on Faith." In *The Lectures on Faith in Historical Perspective,* ed. L. Dahl and C. Tate, pp. 221–40. Provo, Utah, 1990.

Roberts, B. H. "The Doctrine of the Church in Respect of the Godhead." *IE* 1 (Aug. 1898):754–69.

PAUL E. DAHL

GODHOOD

Logically and naturally, the ultimate desire of a loving Supreme Being is to help his children enjoy all that he enjoys. For Latter-day Saints, the term "godhood" denotes the attainment of such a state—one of having all divine attributes and doing as God does and being as God is. Such a state is to be enjoyed by all exalted, embodied, intelligent beings (*see* ETERNAL PROGRESSION; EXALTATION; GOD; PERFECTION). The Church of Jesus Christ of Latter-day Saints teaches that all resurrected and perfected mortals become gods (cf. Gen. 3:22; Matt. 5:48). They will dwell again with GOD THE FATHER, and live and act like him in endless worlds of happiness, power, love, glory, and knowledge; above all, they will have the power of procreating endless lives. Latter-day Saints believe that Jesus Christ attained godhood and that he marked the path and led the way for others likewise to become exalted divine beings by following him (cf. John 14:3).

The LDS conception of godhood is central to their understanding of why God creates and acts. Latter-day Saints believe in a God who "cleaves unto" other eternal INTELLIGENCES (D&C 88:40) and wants to make them happy. Joseph Smith observed, "Happiness is the object and design of our existence; and will be the end thereof, if we pursue the path that leads to it; and this path is virtue, uprightness, faithfulness, holiness, and keeping all the commandments of God" (*TPJS*, p. 255). Happiness is the goal of existence, and God created this world in order to promote happiness (2 Ne. 2:25). Because he loves the world, he gave his "only begotten Son" (John 3:16). God gives commandments to help mankind achieve happiness. Joseph Smith wrote: "In obedience there is joy and peace unspotted, unalloyed; and as God has designed our happiness—and the happiness of all His creatures, he never has—He never will institute an ordinance or give a commandment to His people that is not calculated in its nature to promote that happiness which He has designed, and which will not end in the greatest amount of good and glory to those who become the recipients of his law and ordinances" (*TPJS*, pp. 256–57). The Book of Mormon refers to God's plan of salvation as "the great plan of happiness" (Alma 42:8). In this sense, God creates in order to increase the total happiness in the universe.

As the Supreme Being in the universe, God has the greatest capacity for happiness. Thus, to maximize joy in others, God desires them to be as much like him as possible. "For behold, this is my work and my glory—to bring to pass the immortality and eternal life of man" (Moses 1:39; cf. Ps. 16:11). This latter-day scripture is understood to mean that God's goal is to help men and women share in the kind of eternal life he lives. Joseph Smith wrote: "God . . . was more intelligent, [and he] saw proper to institute laws whereby [his children] could have a privilege to advance like himself. The relationship we have with God places us in a situation to advance in knowledge. He has power to institute laws to instruct the weaker intelligences, that they may be exalted with himself, so that they might have one glory upon another, and all that knowledge, power, glory, and intelligence, which is requisite in order to save them in the world of spirits" (*TPJS*, p. 354).

All of God's spirit children have within them a divine nature with the potential to become like him. To become more like God, individuals must gain increased light and truth and follow all the commandments that God has given. They must know God (John 17:3; D&C 88:49) and see him (1 Jn. 3:2). Those who achieve this level of perfection will become joint-heirs with Christ: "For as many as are led by the Spirit of God, they are the sons of God. . . . And if children, then heirs; heirs of God, and joint-heirs with Christ; if so be that we suffer with him, that we may be also glorified together" (Rom. 8:14–17). "All that [the] Father hath" shall be given to them (D&C 84:37–38). In biblical terms, those who are worthy to share in all the power and glory that God himself has are called "gods": "Ye are gods; and all of you are children of the most High" (Ps. 82:6; John 10:34–38). Latter-day scriptures refer to several persons, including Abraham, Isaac, and Jacob, who once lived on earth and who are now resurrected beings and have become gods (D&C 132:37).

Most people are accustomed to using the term "God" to identify only one being, the Father. But the scriptures sometimes use the term to designate others as well. In this sense, while the faithful worship only one God in spirit and in truth, there exist other beings who have attained the necessary intelligence and righteousness to qualify for the title "god." Jesus Christ is a god and is a separate personage, distinct from God the Father (*see* GODHEAD).

People qualify themselves for this rank and degree of exaltation by bringing themselves fully in line with all that God has commanded them to do: "Here, then, is eternal life—to know the only wise and true God; and you have got to learn how to be Gods yourselves, and to be kings and priests to God, . . . namely, by going from one small degree to another, and from a small capacity to a great one; from grace to grace, from exaltation to exaltation, until you attain to the resurrection of the dead, and are able to dwell in everlasting burnings, and to sit in glory, as do those who sit enthroned in everlasting power" (*TPJS*, pp. 346–47).

Joseph Smith also wrote, "Every man who reigns in celestial glory is a God to his dominions" (*TPJS*, p. 374). This does not mean that any person ever would or could supplant God as the Supreme Being in the universe; but it does mean that through God's plan and with his help, all men and women have the capacity to participate in God's eternal work. People participate in this work by righteous living, by giving birth to children in mortality and helping them live righteous lives, and by bringing others to Christ. Moreover, Latter-day Saints believe that those who become gods will have the opportunity to participate even more fully in God's work of bringing eternal life to other beings. God is referred to as "Father in Heaven" because he is the father of all human spirits (Heb. 12:9; cf. Acts 17:29), imbuing them with divine potentials. Those who become like him will likewise contribute to this eternal process by adding further spirit offspring to the eternal family.

Latter-day Saints believe that God achieved his exalted rank by progressing much as man must progress and that God is a perfected and exalted man: "God himself was once as we are now, and is an exalted man, and sits enthroned in yonder heavens! That is the great secret. If the veil were rent today, and the great God who holds this world in its orbit, and who upholds all worlds and all things by his power, was to make himself visible,—I say, if you were to see him today, you would see him like a man in form—like yourselves in all the person, image, and very form as a man; for Adam was created in the very fashion, image and likeness of God, and received instruction from, and walked, talked and conversed with him, as one man talks and communes with another" (*TPJS*, p. 345).

Much of the LDS concept of godhood is expressed in a frequently cited aphorism written in 1840 by Lorenzo Snow, fifth President of the Church. At the time, Snow was twenty-six years old, having been baptized four years earlier. He recorded in his journal that he attended a meeting in which Elder H. G. Sherwood explained the parable of the Savior regarding the husbandman who hired servants and sent them forth at different hours of the day to labor for him in his vineyard. Snow continued, as recorded in his sister's biography of him: "The Spirit of the Lord rested mightily upon me—the eyes of my understanding were opened, and I saw as clear as the sun at noonday, with wonder and astonishment, the pathway of God and man. I formed the following couplet which expresses the revelation, as it was shown me. . . . As man now is, God once was: As God now is, man may be" (Eliza R. Snow, p. 46).

BIBLIOGRAPHY
Snow, Eliza R. *Biography and Family Record of Lorenzo Snow.* Salt Lake City, 1884.
Snow, LeRoi C. "Devotion to a Divine Inspiration." *IE* 22 (1919):653–62.
Widtsoe, John A. *Evidences and Reconciliations,* pp. 65–67. Salt Lake City, 1960.

K. CODELL CARTER

GOSPEL OF ABRAHAM

On April 3, 1836, the keys of the "dispensation of the gospel of Abraham" were committed to the Prophet Joseph Smith and Oliver Cowdery in the Kirtland Temple as part of the restoration of all things in the DISPENSATION OF THE FULNESS OF TIMES (D&C 110:12). It was promised that through latter-day recipients of the gospel and their seed, all generations who accept it shall be blessed (*HC* 2:434–36). This renewed the promise that was given anciently to Abraham (Gen. 12:1–3; Abr. 2:6, 9–11; cf. Gal. 3:7–9, 29).

Latter-day Saints teach that Adam, Enoch, Noah, Abraham and many others headed DISPENSATIONS OF THE GOSPEL. Divine blessings and commandments were bestowed appropriate to the circumstances of the faithful people of God in each dispensation.

The gospel dispensation of Abraham includes the patriarchal order of the priesthood and the eternal marriage covenant (D&C 131:1–4; 132:28–30), by which the ABRAHAMIC COVENANT is perpetuated from generation to generation among the faithful. Abraham was given a promise of innumerable posterity both in the world and out of the world. This promise is renewed for all who obey the gospel of Jesus Christ and receive the priesthood covenant of celestial marriage, "and by this law is the continuation of the works of [the] Father" among mankind both in time and eternity (D&C 132:31–33). The restoration of all things included the restoration of the keys to Joseph Smith to make it possible in modern times for all who do the works of Abraham to inherit the covenant and blessings of Abraham.

JOEL A. FLAKE

GOSPEL OF JESUS CHRIST

[This entry is discussed below under two headings:

The Gospel in LDS Teaching
Etymological Considerations for "Gospel"

The first division outlines the Latter-day Saint conception of the gospel of Jesus Christ, the fundamental teaching of the Church, as it is presented in scripture and in the teachings of the modern prophets. The second explores the complex history of the term and its possible meanings, particularly in Greek-speaking New Testament times.]

THE GOSPEL IN LDS TEACHING

JESUS CHRIST and his apostles and prophets have repeatedly announced the "good news" or "gospel" that by coming to Christ, a person may be saved. The Father is the author of the gospel, but it is called the gospel of Jesus Christ because, in agreement with the Father's plan, Christ's ATONEMENT makes the gospel operative in human lives. Christ's gospel is the only true gospel, and "there shall be no other name given nor any other way nor means whereby salvation can come unto the children of men, only in and through the name of Christ, the Lord Omnipotent" (Mosiah 3:17; cf. Acts 4:12).

Even though Latter-day Saints use the term "gospel" in several ways, including traditional Christian usages, the Book of Mormon and other latter-day scriptures define it precisely as the way or means by which an individual can come to Christ. In all these scriptural passages, the gospel or doctrine of Christ teaches that salvation is available through his authorized servants to all who will (1) believe in Christ; (2) repent of their sins; (3) be baptized in water as a witness of their willingness to take his name upon them and keep his COMMANDMENTS; (4) receive the Holy Ghost by the LAYING ON OF HANDS; and (5) endure to the end. All who obey these commandments and receive the BAPTISM OF FIRE AND OF THE HOLY GHOST and endure in faith, hope, and charity will be found guiltless at the last day and will enter into the kingdom of heaven (Alma 7:14–16, 24–25; Heb. 6:1–2).

THE PLAN OF SALVATION. President Brigham Young taught that the "Gospel of the Son of God that has been revealed is a plan or system of laws and ordinances, by strict obedience to which the people who inhabit this earth are assured that they may return again into the presence of the Father and the Son" (*JD,* 13:233). The gospel of Jesus Christ is a key part of the PLAN OF SALVATION (or plan of redemption), which provides an opportunity for all people to obtain ETERNAL LIFE. Because of the FALL OF ADAM, which has passed upon all individuals by inheritance, all are subject to a physical death and a SPIRITUAL DEATH (2 Ne. 9:4–12; D&C 29:39–45; 1 Cor. 15:12–22) and cannot save themselves. God, the loving Father of all spirits, has declared that it is his work and glory "to bring to pass the immortality and eternal life of man" (Moses 1:39). For this purpose he provided a savior, Jesus Christ, who, because of his perfect LOVE, his sinlessness, and his being the Only Begotten of the Father in the flesh, was both willing and able to offer himself as a sacrifice for the sins of the world (John 3:16). Through his atonement, Christ redeemed all men, women, and children unconditionally from the two deaths occasioned by the transgression of Adam and Eve, and will also redeem them from their own sins, if they accept and obey his gospel (Moses 6:62; D&C 20:17–25; 76:40–53).

BASIC ELEMENTS. Modern revelations state that the Book of Mormon contains "the fulness of the gospel" (D&C 20:9; 27:5; 42:12). Of all the standard works, the Book of Mormon contains the most detailed exposition of the gospel. In three separate passages the basic elements of the gospel are explained by a prophet or by Jesus himself (2 Ne. 31:2–32:6; 3 Ne. 11:31–41; 27:13–21). Each of these passages is framed by the affirmation that "this is my doctrine" or "this is my gospel." The revelations to the Prophet Joseph Smith confirm these Book of Mormon statements of the gospel in every detail (see D&C 18:17–23; 19:29–31; 20:25–29).

These core texts repeat the basic elements of the gospel message several times in slightly varied ways. Joseph Smith referred to them in abbreviated form as "the first principles and ordinances of the Gospel" (A of F 4).

1. Faith. LDS teaching emphasizes FAITH IN JESUS CHRIST as the first principle of the gospel. The priority of faith is twofold. The individual who accepts the gospel must start with faith in Jesus Christ, believing in him and his power to save people from their

sins. Without faith, no one would be strongly motivated to repent and to live the rest of the gospel principles. Faith is also fundamental to the other elements of the gospel in that each of them is dependent on acts of faith in important ways. In this sense, Nephi$_1$ compares living the gospel to entering a strait and narrow path that leads to eternal life. The gate by which one can enter this path is repentance and baptism. With the guidance of the Holy Ghost, one can follow the path, exercising faith and enduring to the end. Thus, faith in Jesus Christ is a link between what one does to enter the gate and what must be done thereafter. One cannot have entered the gate by repenting and making baptismal covenants "save it were by the word of Christ with unshaken faith in him, relying wholly upon the merits of him who is mighty to save" (2 Ne. 31:19). After starting on this strait and narrow path, one cannot reach salvation except by "press[ing] forward with a steadfastness [faith] in Christ . . . feasting upon the word of Christ" (2 Ne. 31:20), which includes those things that the HOLY GHOST tells one to do (2 Ne. 32:3, 5).

2. Repentance. The centrality of faith is emphasized by the way the gospel is presented in the Book of Mormon, with faith usually mentioned in the center and the call to REPENTANCE at the first. Individuals must forsake their sins and offer up "a sacrifice . . . [of] a broken heart and a contrite spirit." This requires that the sinner come down into the depths of HUMILITY and become "as a little child" (3 Ne. 9:20–22).

3. Baptism. The gospel emphasizes the absolute need for baptism for those accountable and capable of sin. Like repentance, baptism is also a commandment, and candidates for salvation must be baptized in order to obey the commandment (see 2 Ne. 31:6–7).

   This essential ordinance is a witness to the Father that the repentant individual has covenanted with God to keep his commandments and has taken upon himself or herself the name of Christ. Faith in Jesus Christ, repentance, and baptism are the gate by which one enters into the way that leads to eternal life (2 Ne. 31:13–15). Because infants are incapable of sin or of making such covenants, parents are instructed to prepare them for baptism by the time they reach eight years of age, the age of ACCOUNTABILITY established in revelation (D&C 68:25–28).

4. The Holy Ghost. While water baptism symbolizes purification and rising from death to life, the actual cleansing or REMISSION OF SINS comes by obedience, and as a gift from God "by fire and by the Holy Ghost" (2 Ne. 31:17; Matt. 3:11), by which the individual is BORN OF GOD, having become a "new creature" (Mosiah 27:24–26; 1 Pet. 1:23). This spiritual experience is a witness from the Father and the Son that the sacrifice of the penitent has been accepted. After Jesus had taught the Nephites and they were baptized, "the Holy Ghost did fall upon them, and they were filled with the Holy Ghost and with fire" (3 Ne. 19:13; cf. Acts 2:4).

   The GIFT OF THE HOLY GHOST, administered by the laying on of hands by one having authority, includes the promise "If ye will enter in by the way, and receive the Holy Ghost, it will show unto you all things what ye should do" (2 Ne. 32:5). This gift is a constant companion by which the individual receives "the words of Christ" directly for guidance in his or her own life, in addition to inspired instruction from Church leaders (2 Ne. 32:3; see also John 14:26; 16:13).

5. Endure to the End. "Enduring to the end" is the scriptural phrase describing the subsequent life of a member of Christ's church who has embraced the first principles of the gospel and has entered the gate that leads to eternal life. Once on this strait and narrow path, the member must press forward in faith, and continue in obedience to all the commandments of God.

   Faith is linked with hope and charity. Receiving a remission of sins generates a hope of salvation. This is more than a desire, and gives a feeling of assurance. Such hope grows continually brighter through the workings of the Holy Ghost if one is consistently obedient (Ether 12:4). Charity, the "pure love of Christ," is characteristic of those who obey the commandments (Moro. 7:3–4, 47). Such persons reflect to others the same kind of pure love that they experience from the Lord.

6. Salvation. In addition to receiving daily blessings, Jesus Christ promises that those who comply with all of the principles and ordinances will receive eternal life. As revealed to the Prophet

Joseph Smith, salvation entails becoming an heir to the fulness of the CELESTIAL KINGDOM (D&C 76:50–70).

All LDS standard works contain clear statements of the gospel of Jesus Christ (see D&C 10:63–70; 11:9–24; 19:29–32; 20:37; 33:10–13; 39:6; 68:25; Moses 5:14–15, 58; 6:50–53). Latter-day Saints find the same concept in many New Testament passages (Matt. 3:11; 24:13–14; Acts 2:38; 19:4–6; Rom. 1:16), although frequently only a few of the six key elements are specifically mentioned in any one passage. This is also true of the Book of Mormon. For example, the promise "They that believe in him shall be saved" (2 Ne. 2:9) may be understood as a merism (an abbreviation of a formula retaining only the first and last elements) that implicitly invokes all six components even though they are not mentioned individually. Another merism states that believing in Jesus and enduring to the end is life eternal (2 Ne. 33:4; cf. v. 9).

OTHER MEANINGS. Although emphasis is placed on truths necessary for salvation, LDS usage of the term "gospel" is not confined to the scriptural definition. Latter-day Saints commonly refer to the entire body of their religious beliefs as "the gospel." By the broadest interpretation, all TRUTH originating with God may be included within the gospel. President Joseph F. Smith said:

> In the theological sense, the gospel means more than just the tidings of good news, with accompanying joy to the souls of men, for it embraces every principle of eternal truth. There is no fundamental principle, or truth anywhere in the universe, that is not embraced in the gospel of Jesus Christ, and it is not confined to the simple first principles, such as faith in God, repentance from sin, baptism for the remission of sins, and the laying on of hands for the gift of the Holy Ghost, although these are absolutely essential to salvation and exaltation in the kingdom of God [pp. 85–86].

Notwithstanding this wide range of meanings associated with the gospel, as President Smith explained, the saving truths encompassed by the first principles are indispensable and must be followed to obtain salvation. They are the central focus of the Church's teachings and practices. Latter-day Saints are under strict command to share the fundamental, first principles of the gospel with others so that all may have an equal chance to obtain salvation. Proselytizing efforts of individual members and full-time missionaries are intended to invite others to come to Christ through obedience to gospel principles and ordinances.

President Ezra Taft Benson has similarly explained that "the gospel can be viewed from two perspectives. In the broadest sense, the gospel embraces all truth, all light, all revealed knowledge to mankind. In a more restrictive sense the gospel means the doctrine of the Fall . . . [and] atonement." Clarifying the restrictive sense, he explained:

> When the Savior referred to his gospel, He meant the . . . laws, covenants, and ordinances that men must comply with to work out their salvation. He meant faith in the Lord Jesus Christ, repentance from all sin, baptism by immersion by a legal administrator for the remission of our sins, and the receipt of the gift of the Holy Ghost, and finally he meant that one should be valiant in his testimony of Jesus until the end of his days. This is the gospel Jesus preached [p. 30].

Those who die without hearing the gospel while in MORTALITY will receive this opportunity in the SPIRIT WORLD. The necessary ordinances of baptism and the laying on of hands for the gift of the Holy Ghost will be performed on behalf of the dead by living members in Latter-day Saint temples. The deceased will decide for themselves whether to accept or reject the ordinances performed in their behalf (*see* SALVATION FOR THE DEAD).

ETERNAL NATURE OF THE GOSPEL. Latter-day Saints believe that the gospel has always existed and will continue to exist throughout the eternities. The Prophet Joseph Smith said, "The great Jehovah contemplated the whole of the events connected with the earth, pertaining to the plan of salvation, before it rolled into existence, or ever 'the morning stars sang together' for joy" (*TPJS*, p. 220). The eternal nature of the gospel was also emphasized by President John Taylor, who declared that "the gospel is a living, abiding, eternal, and unchangeable principle that has existed co-equal with God, and always will exist, while time and eternity endure, wherever it is developed and made manifest" (p. 88).

LDS scriptures explain that after the Lord had taught Adam and Eve the Plan of Salvation and the gospel (Moses 5:4–11), Adam was "caught away by the Spirit of the Lord" into the water where he was baptized. Following his baptism, the "Spirit of God descended upon him, and thus he was born of the Spirit" (Moses 6:48–68). In later describing this experience, Enoch explained that God called upon Adam with his own voice, teaching him the same gospel set out in other scriptures:

> If thou wilt turn unto me, and hearken unto my voice, and believe, and repent of all thy transgressions, and be baptized, even in water, in the name of mine Only Begotten Son, who is full of grace and truth, which is Jesus Christ, the only name which shall be given under heaven, whereby salvation shall come unto the children of men, ye shall receive the gift of the Holy Ghost [Moses 6:52].

Latter-day scripture records that Adam and Eve taught their children the gospel, but that Satan came among them and persuaded some to love him more than God (Moses 5:13; *see* DEVILS). Thus it has been with the descendants of Adam and Eve, and in this situation, the Lord called upon people everywhere to believe in the Son and to repent of their sins that they might be saved. This gospel message was a "firm decree" sent forth "in the world, until the end thereof," and was preached from the beginning by ANGELS, by the voice of God, and by the Holy Ghost (Moses 5:12–15, 58–59).

Latter-day Saints understand the history of the world in terms of periods of faithfulness and of apostasy. Although there have been many times when the gospel of Jesus Christ has been lost from the earth, it has repeatedly been restored through prophets sent to declare new DISPENSATIONS OF THE GOSPEL. The gospel has been given to successive generations and will maintain its efficacy forever. The restoration of the fulness of the gospel to Joseph Smith initiated the "last dispensation," or the DISPENSATION OF THE FULNESS OF TIMES, and he was promised that the gospel will never again be taken from the earth. The gospel of Jesus Christ continues to be the only means given under heaven whereby men and women can come to their Savior and be saved, and is the standard against which all people will be judged (*see* JUDGMENT DAY, FINAL).

ETYMOLOGICAL CONSIDERATIONS FOR "GOSPEL"

The English word "gospel" is derived from the Old English *godspel* (god story). It was chosen by English translators of the New

Testament as a translation of the Greek *euaggelion* (Latin, *evangelium*) or "good news." The term is used in the New Testament principally to refer to the message of salvation through Jesus Christ, often referred to as the "gospel of Jesus Christ" (Mark 1:1) or the "gospel of the Kingdom of God" (Mark 1:14; Luke 8:1). The gospel or "good news" in the New Testament is the "glad tidings" to all that if they will come to Christ and keep his commandments, they will be saved (Matt. 7:21; Mark 16:15–16). Paul uses *euaggelion* more than other New Testament writers, adopting both noun and verb forms of the Greek term. The practice of referring to written accounts of the life and ministry of Jesus as "gospels" arose among Christians in the first century and was well established by the second.

Although latter-day scriptures give a more definite and formulaic concept of the gospel, their teaching is consistent with and enhanced by scholarly reflections on the possible etymologies of the New Testament term. Both Hebrew and Greek antecedents occur in verb and derivative noun forms, the primary sense referring to the delivery of messages, particularly good news—victory in battle being a common example. This is expanded in Isaiah by application to the herald who announces the return of exiles to Jerusalem, proclaiming the good news of prosperity and deliverance and the kingship of Jehovah (Isaiah 52:7; see Friedrich, p. 708).

Ancient Greek usage of *euaggelion* included the ideas of liberation from enemies and deliverance from demonic powers. It can refer to oracular sayings, but more precisely to their fulfillment. This cluster of meanings made *euaggelion* an appropriate term for New Testament writers who understood the gospel as the means by which men can escape the evil powers of this world and as the fulfillment of ancient prophecies of a coming Messiah.

Religious usage of *euaggelion* before Christian times was common to the popular imperial cults in which the worship of Greek and Roman emperors was believed to bring wealth and power in various forms. When first used by Christians, this language must have been ironic, having the effect of forcing its hearers and readers to compare Caesar on his throne and Christ on the cross, and to make the corresponding choice between the universal pursuit of power and wealth (material benefits) in this world and the singular *way* of faith, repentance, and the Spirit taught by Jesus. This implicit comparison becomes explicit when three New Testament gospels report Jesus' instruction to "render unto Caesar the things that are Caesar's, and to God the things that are God's" (Mark 12:17; cf. Matt. 22:21 and Luke 20:25). Paul uses the same irony when he calls the gospel a mystery (see Friedrich, pp. 712, 723–25; Eph. 6:19). The disappointment of some with Jesus as Messiah was precisely that he was not the kind of savior worshiped in the cults of emperors.

The Book of Mormon uses the terms "gospel" and "doctrine" interchangeably, in a way that is consistent with New Testament usage, at least to the extent that both imply communications that can be reduced to verbal statements. The New Testament term "doctrine" (*didaskalia*) means "teaching" and refers either to the doctrine of Christ, or to the vain teachings of people or devils. Similarly, Book of Mormon writers use both "gospel" and "doctrine" to refer to a teaching that can be reduced to a set of statements or "points of . . . doctrine" (1 Ne. 15:14; Hel. 11:22).

BIBLIOGRAPHY

Benson, Ezra Taft. *Teachings of Ezra Taft Benson.* Salt Lake City, 1988.

Collins, Raymond F. "Gospel." *Encyclopedia of Religion,* Vol. 6, pp. 79–82. New York, 1987.

Friedrich, Gerhard. "Euaggelizomai, Euaggelion, . . ." In *Theological Dictionary of the New Testament,* Gerhard Kittel, ed., Vol. 2, pp. 707–737. Grand Rapids, Mich., 1964.

Nibley, Hugh. "Prophets and Glad Tidings." In *CWHN* 3: 259–67.

Piper, O. A. "Gospel," In *Interpreter's Dictionary of the Bible,* Vol. 2, pp. 442–48. Nashville, Tenn., 1962.

Roberts, B. H. *The Gospel: An Exposition of Its First Principles and Man's Relationship to Deity.* Salt Lake City, 1966.

Smith, Joseph F. *GD,* pp. 85–86, 95–106.

Talmage, James E. *AF,* pp. 52–170.

Taylor, John. *Gospel Kingdom,* Salt Lake City, 1964.

Yarn, David H., Jr. *The Gospel: God, Man, and Truth.* Salt Lake City, 1965.

NOEL B. REYNOLDS

GRACE

One of the most controversial issues in Christian theology is whether salvation is the free gift of unmerited grace or is earned through good WORKS. Paul's statement that "a man is justified by faith without the deeds of the law" (Rom. 3:28) is frequently cited to support the former view, while James's statement that "faith without works is dead" (James 2:20) is often quoted in favor of the latter view. The LDS doctrine that salvation requires *both* grace and works is a revealed yet commonsense reconciliation of these contradictory positions.

C. S. Lewis wrote that this dispute "does seem to me like asking which blade in a pair of scissors is most necessary" (p. 129). And in one way or another almost all Christian denominations ultimately accept the need for both grace and works, but the differences in meaning and emphasis among the various doctrinal traditions remain substantial.

LDS doctrine contains an affirmative sense of interaction between grace and works that is unique not only as to these concepts but also reflects the uniqueness of the restored gospel's view of man's nature, the FALL OF ADAM, the ATONEMENT, and the process of salvation. At the same time, the LDS view contains features that are similar to basic elements of some other traditions. For example, the LDS insistence that such works as ordinances be performed with proper priesthood authority resembles the Catholic teaching that its sacraments are the requisite channels of grace. Also the LDS emphasis on the indispensability of personal faith and REPENTANCE in a direct relationship with God echoes traditional Protestant teachings. The LDS position "is not a convenient eclecticism, but a repossession [through the Restoration] of a New Testament understanding that reconciles Paul and James" (Madsen, p. 175).

The Church's emphasis on personal responsibility and the need for self-disciplined obedience may seem to de-emphasize the role of Christ's grace; however, for Latter-day Saints, obedience is but one blade of the scissors. All of LDS theology also reflects the major premise of the Book of Mormon that without grace there is no salvation: "For we know that it is by grace that we are saved, after all we can do" (2 Ne. 25:23). The source of this grace is the atoning sacrifice of Jesus Christ: "Mercy cometh because of the atonement" (Alma 42:23).

The teachings of Christian theology since the Middle Ages are rooted in the belief that, primarily because of the effects of the Fall and original sin, humankind has an inherently evil nature. In both the Catholic and the Protestant traditions, only the grace of God can overcome this natural evil. Various Christian writers have disputed the extent to which the bestowal of grace completely overcomes man's dark nature. In the fifth century, reflecting his personal struggle with what he believed to be his own inherent evil nature, Augustine saw grace as the only escape from the evil of earthly pleasures and the influence of the worldly "city of man." In the thirteenth century Thomas Aquinas was more sanguine, recognizing the serious wounding caused by original sin, but also defending man's natural potential for good.

In the early sixteenth century, Martin Luther, through his reading of Paul and reacting against the sale of indulgences, concluded that faith, God's unilateral gift to chosen individuals, is the true source of grace and, therefore, of justification before God. Luther thus (perhaps unintentionally) broke the medieval church's control over grace, thereby unleashing the political force of the protestant reformation. For Luther, man's individual effort can in no way "earn" or otherwise be part in the righteousness infused by grace. Even the good works demonstrated in a life of obedience to God are but the visible *effects* of grace. This idea later influenced the development of the Puritan ethic in America. John Calvin, Luther's contemporary, developed a complete doctrine of predestination based on Luther's idea that God unilaterally chooses those on whom he bestows the gifts of faith and grace.

The Catholic response to Luther's challenge rejected predestination and reaffirmed both that grace is mediated by church sacraments and that grace cannot totally displace human AGENCY. At the same time, Catholic thought underscored the primacy of God's initiative. "Prevenient grace" operates upon the human will before one turns to God; yet, once touched by grace, one is still free to cooperate or not. The interaction between divine grace and human freedom is not totally clear; however, grace is increased as one obeys God's commandments, and grace raises one's natural good works to actions of supernatural value in a process of spiritual regeneration.

In recent years, some Protestant theologians have questioned the way an exclusive emphasis on unmerited grace negates a sense of personal responsibility. Dietrich Bonhoeffer, for example, condemned the idea of "cheap grace," which falsely supposes that because "the account has been paid in advance . . . everything can be had for nothing" (*The Cost of Discipleship,* 1963, p. 45). John MacArthur was concerned that contemporary evangelism promises sinners that they "can have eternal life yet continue to live in rebellion against God" (*The Gospel According to Jesus,* 1988, pp. 15–16). And Paul Holmer wrote that stressing the dangers of works is "inappropriate if the listeners are not even trying! Most Church listeners are not in much danger of working their way into heaven" ("Law and Gospel Reexamined," *Theology Today* 10 [1953–54]:474).

Some Latter-day Saints have shared similar concerns about the limitations of a one-sided view of the grace-works controversy, just as they have shared the Catholic concern about a doctrine of grace that undercuts the fundamental nature of free will. Latter-day Saints see Paul's writing about the inadequacy of works and "the deeds of the law" (Rom. 3:27–28) as referring mainly to the inadequacy of the ritual works of the Law of Moses, "which had been superseded by the higher requirements of the Gospel [of Jesus Christ]"; thus, Paul correctly regarded many of "the outward forms and ceremonies" of the Law of Moses as "unessential works" (*AF,* p. 480). As the prophet Abinadi declared in the Book of Mormon (c. 150 B.C.), "Salvation doth not come by the law alone; and were it not for the atonement, which God himself shall make for the sins and iniquities of his people, . . . they must unavoidably perish, notwithstanding the law of Moses" (Mosiah 13:28).

In a broader sense, LDS devotion to the primary role of grace while concurrently emphasizing self-reliance stems from a unique doctrinal view of man's nature and destiny. As noted by Reformation scholar John Dillenberger, "In stressing human possibilities, Mormonism brought things into line, not by abandoning the centrality of grace but by insisting that the [real] powers of humanity . . . reflected the actual state of humanity as such. . . . Mormonism brought understanding to what had become an untenable problem within evangelicalism: how to reconcile the new power of humanity with the negative inherited views of humanity, without abandoning the necessity of grace." In this way, Dillenberger concluded, "perhaps Mormonism . . . is the authentic American theology, for the self-reliance of revivalist fundamentalist groups stood in marked contrast to their inherited conception of the misery of humanity" (p. 179).

In LDS teachings, the fall of Adam made Christ's redemption

necessary, but not because the Fall by itself made man evil. Because of transgression, Adam and Eve were expelled from Eden into a world that was subject to death and evil influences. However, the Lord revealed to Adam upon his entry into mortality that "the Son of God hath atoned for original guilt"; therefore, Adam's children were not evil, but were "*whole* from the foundation of the world" (Moses 6:54). Thus, "every spirit of man was *innocent* in the beginning; and God having redeemed man from the fall, men became again, in their infant state, *innocent* before God" (D&C 93:38).

As the descendants of Adam and Eve then become accountable for their own sins at age eight, all of them taste sin as the result of their own free choice. "All have sinned, and come short of the glory of God" (Rom. 3:23). One whose cumulative experience leads her or him to love "Satan more than God" (Moses 5:28) will eventually become "carnal, sensual, and devilish" (Moses 5:13; 6:49) by nature. On the other hand, one who consciously accepts Christ's grace through the Atonement by faith, repentance, and baptism yields to "the enticings of the Holy Spirit, and putteth off the natural man and becometh a saint through the Atonement of Christ the Lord" (Mosiah 3:19). In this way, the individual takes the initiative to accept the grace made available by the Atonement, exercising faith through a willing "desire to believe" (Alma 32:27). That desire is often kindled by hearing others bear testimony of Christ. When this word of Christ is planted and then nourished through obedience interacting with grace, as summarized below, the individual may "become a saint" by nature, thereby enjoying eternal (meaning godlike) life.

Grace is thus the source of three categories of blessings related to mankind's salvation. First, many blessings of grace are *unconditional*—free and unmerited gifts requiring no individual action. God's grace in this sense is a factor in the Creation, the Fall, the Atonement, and the plan of salvation. Specifically regarding the Fall, and despite death and other conditions resulting from Adam's transgression, Christ's grace has atoned for original sin and has assured the resurrection of all humankind: "We believe that men will be punished for their own sins, and not for Adam's transgression" (A of F 2).

Second, the Savior has also atoned *conditionally* for personal sins. The application of grace to personal sins is conditional because it is available only when an individual repents, which can be a demanding form of works. Because of this condition, mercy is able to satisfy the demands of justice with neither mercy nor justice robbing the other. Personal repentance is therefore a *necessary* condition of salvation, but it is not by itself *sufficient* to assure salvation (*see* JUSTICE AND MERCY). In addition, one must accept the ordinances of BAPTISM and the LAYING ON OF HANDS to receive the GIFT OF THE HOLY GHOST, by which one is born again as the spirit child of Christ and may eventually become sanctified (cf. D&C 76:51–52; *see also* GOSPEL OF JESUS CHRIST).

Third, after one has received Christ's gospel of faith, repentance, and baptism unto forgiveness of sin, relying "wholly upon the merits of him who is mighty to save," one has only "entered in by the gate" to the "strait and narrow path which leads to eternal life" (2 Ne. 31:17–20). In this postbaptism stage of spiritual development, one's best efforts—further works—are required to "endure to the end" (2 Ne. 31:20). These efforts include obeying the Lord's commandments and receiving the higher ordinances performed in the temples, and continuing a repentance process as needed "to retain a remission of your sins" (Mosiah 4:12).

In the teachings of Martin Luther, such works of righteousness are not the result of personal initiative but are the spontaneous effects of the internal grace one has received, wholly the fruits of the gracious tree. In LDS doctrine by contrast, "men should . . . do many things of their own free will, and bring to pass much righteousness. For the power is in them, wherein they are agents unto themselves" (D&C 58:27–28). At the same time, individuals lack the capacity to develop a Christlike nature by their own effort. The perfecting attributes such as hope and charity are ultimately "bestowed upon all who are true followers . . . of Jesus Christ" (Moro. 7:48) by grace through his atonement. This interactive relationship between human and divine powers in LDS theology derives both from the significance it attaches to free will and from its optimism about the "fruits of the spirit" (Gal. 5:22–25) among the truly converted, "those who love me and keep all my commandments, *and* him that seeketh so to do" (D&C 46:9).

God bestows these additional, perfecting expressions of grace conditionally, as he does the grace that allows forgiveness of sin. They are given "after all we can do" (2 Ne. 25:23)—that is, in addition to our best efforts. In general, this condition is related less to obeying particular commandments than it is to one's fundamental spiritual character, such as "meekness and lowliness of heart" (Moro. 8:26) and possessing "a broken heart and a contrite spirit" (Ps. 51:17; 3 Ne. 9:20; Hafen, chap. 9). Or, as Moroni wrote at the end of the Book of Mormon, "If ye shall deny yourselves of all ungodliness, and love God with all your might, mind, and strength, then is his grace sufficient for you, that by his grace ye may be perfect in Christ; . . . then are ye sanctified in Christ by the grace of God, through the shedding of the blood of Christ" (Moro. 10:32–33).

BIBLIOGRAPHY

Dillenberger, John. "Grace and Works in Martin Luther and Joseph Smith." In *Reflections on Mormonism: Judaeo-Christian Parallels,* ed. Truman G. Madsen. Provo, Utah, 1978.

Hafen, Bruce C. *The Broken Heart: Applying the Atonement to Life's Experiences.* Salt Lake City, 1989.

Holmer, Paul L. "Law and Gospel Re-examined." *Theology Today* 10 (1953–1954):474.

Keller, Roger R. *Reformed Christians and Mormon Christians: Let's Talk!* Urbana, Ill., 1986.

Lewis, C. S. *Mere Christianity.* New York, 1943.

Madsen, Truman G. *Reflections on Mormonism,* p. 175. Provo, Utah, 1978.

McDonald, William, ed. "Grace." In *New Catholic Encyclopedia,* Vol. 6. New York, 1967.

Millet, Robert L. *By Grace Are We Saved.* Salt Lake City, 1989.

Rahner, Karl, ed. *The Teaching of the Catholic Church.* Regensburg, Germany, 1965.

BRUCE C. HAFEN

H

HEAVEN

Significant meanings of the word "heaven" are (1) the place where God resides (Matt. 6:9; Alma 18:30); (2) the eternal dwelling place of the righteous in the hereafter (Matt. 6:20; 1 Pet. 1:4); and (3) the type of life enjoyed by heavenly beings. A desire for heaven—to eventually live in a better world than the present one—is the basis of a hope that motivates Latter-day Saints (cf. Ether 12:4; D&C 25:10).

Although the specific word "heaven" is regularly used in the day-to-day literature of the Church, it is not as frequently used as it no doubt would be if there were not substitute terms. The revealed nomenclature involving the hereafter in latter-day scripture is precise in detailing the varied conditions that exist in the afterlife. Hence in LDS literature there are many words that refer to life beyond mortality, such as PARADISE, the CELESTIAL KINGDOM, the TERRESTRIAL KINGDOM, the TELESTIAL KINGDOM, or the DEGREES OF GLORY.

In the future, this earth will be renewed and receive a paradisiacal glory (A of F 10; Isa. 65:17–25; D&C 88:25–26). This change of the earth will be associated with the millennial reign of the Savior, and the earth will eventually become a "new heaven and a new earth" (D&C 29:23). The earth will ultimately be "like unto crystal and will be a Urim and Thummim to the inhabitants who dwell thereon" (D&C 130:9). When this occurs, both the Father and the

Son will rule over this planet and those who dwell upon it. This earth will be a heaven to its celestial inhabitants. Speaking of conditions of the future life, the Prophet Joseph Smith explained, "That same sociality which exists among us here will exist among us there, only it will be coupled with eternal glory, which glory we do not now enjoy" (D&C 130:2).

The doctrinal emphasis on the eternal nature of the family and the implementation of gospel principles into home and family relationships have frequently led leaders of the Church to characterize the faithful family as a foretaste of "heaven here on earth" (Monson, p. 69).

[*See also* Afterlife; Kingdom of God: In Heaven.]

BIBLIOGRAPHY

McDannell, Colleen, and Bernhard Lang. *Heaven: A History.* New Haven and London, 1988.

Monson, Thomas S. "Hallmarks of a Happy Home." *Ensign* 18 (Nov. 1988):69–72.

ARTHUR WALLACE

HEIRS

[*This entry consists of two parts:* Heirs of God *and* Joint-Heirs with Christ. *The first part explains that by obedience to the commandments of God a person can become an heir of God. The second part emphasizes that the gospel of Jesus Christ also provides the way for one to become a joint-heir with Jesus Christ, and obtain the special inheritance of the Church of the Firstborn.*]

HEIRS OF GOD

The doctrine of becoming an heir of God through the gospel of Jesus Christ was noted by Paul (Rom. 8:14–17; Gal. 3:26–29; 4:1–7; *see also* CALLING AND ELECTION). In this connection, The Church of Jesus Christ of Latter-day Saints teaches that all humans are spirit sons and daughters of God, with the potential of inheriting all that the Father has (D&C 84:33–38). Every member of the human family is a child of God. However, through obedience to the gospel of Jesus Christ, including having faith, love, charity, and participating in temple ordinances and sealings, men and women can become heirs of God in a special way. Such persons are called the "children of Christ, his sons and his daughters," being "spiritually begotten" by him (Mosiah 5:7). They will be exalted in the CELESTIAL KINGDOM. Members of the Church make several COVENANTS with God, beginning with baptism and continuing through the temple ENDOWMENT and marriage, by which they promise to obey God's commandments and to consecrate to him all that they possess in order to become heirs through Christ in the Father's kingdom. Such may eventually be exalted by God and be given many divine powers, including eternal increase.

Promises of inheritance are extended also to those who die without a knowledge of the gospel, for they shall have opportunity in the SPIRIT WORLD to hear the message of redemption, and have the essential ordinances of the gospel performed in their behalf in the temples of the Church.

[*See also* Salvation for the Dead.]

JOSEPH GRANT STEVENSON

JOINT-HEIRS WITH CHRIST

Joint-heirs with Christ identifies those persons who attain the highest degree of the CELESTIAL KINGDOM. Latter-day Saints regard Jesus Christ as the firstborn spirit child of God the Father and the Only Begotten of the Father in the flesh. Because of this priority, he is the natural heir of the Father. Through strict obedience to the Father's will, progressing from grace to grace by obeying the gospel and its ordinances and making the infinite ATONEMENT, Jesus became the Savior of all mankind and also heir to all that the Father has. Those who accept Jesus Christ as their redeemer, repent of their sins, obey the ordinances of the gospel, and live in willing obedience with the Holy Spirit as their guide, can also become heirs of God and joint-heirs with Jesus Christ. In the eternities, they can inherit the same truth, power, wisdom, glory, and EXALTATION possessed by God the Father and by the Son (see D&C 84:38).

The scriptures set forth the Father's plan of salvation for becoming joint-heirs with Christ. This includes taking the name of Christ upon oneself and living a Christlike life. Obeying the gospel means keeping the ordinances and ceremonies as well as living the moral law. Having started on the course of salvation, each individual is expected to continue to serve the Lord with a pure heart to the end of the mortal life. Through the GRACE of Jesus Christ and the blood that he shed, the willing and obedient are redeemed and sanctified.

All people are spirit children of God and recipients of his love, but only through accepting and living the gospel of Jesus Christ are individuals born again, spiritually begotten, and adopted into the family of God in a special relationship as the "sons and daughters" of Christ (Mosiah 5:7; Gal. 4:5–7; Rom. 8:14–17; *see also* BORN OF GOD; LAW OF ADOPTION). Through the gospel, one becomes a joint-heir with Christ, a member of the Church of the Firstborn, and a partaker of the fulness of God's glory.

N. GAYLON HOPKINS

HELL

The term "hell" as used in the King James Version of the Bible is the English translation of four words in the original biblical languages: Hebrew *sheol* and Greek *hades*, *geenna* (Heb. *gehenna*), and a noun implied in the verb *tartar.* These terms generally signify the abode of all the dead, whether righteous or disobedient, although *geenna* and *tartaróō* are associated with a place of punishment. The derivation and literal meaning of *sheol* are unknown, but words in Hebrew derived from it bear the idea of "hollowness."

Latter-day scriptures describe at least three senses of hell: (1) that condition of misery which may attend a person in mortality due to disobedience to divine law; (2) the miserable, but temporary, state of disobedient spirits in the SPIRIT WORLD awaiting the Resurrection; (3) the permanent habitation of the sons of perdition, who suffer the second SPIRITUAL DEATH and remain in hell even after the resurrection.

Persons experiencing the first type of hell can be rescued from suffering through repentance and obedience to the laws and ordinances of the gospel of Jesus Christ because of the ATONEMENT of Jesus Christ. The Savior suffered so that he could deliver everyone from hell (Alma 7:11–13; 33:23). Those who do not repent, however, may experience the pains of hell in this life as well as in the next (D&C 76:104; 1 Ne. 16:2; Alma 40:14). The Prophet Joseph Smith described the true nature of hell: "A man is his own tormenter and his own condemner. Hence the saying, They shall go into the lake that burns with fire and brimstone. The torment of disappointment in the mind of man is as exquisite as a lake burning with fire and brimstone" (*TPJS,* p. 357). Thus, hell is both a place, a part of the world of spirits where suffering and sorrow occur, and a state of mind associated with remorseful realization of one's own sins (Mosiah 2:38; Alma 36:12–16).

A second type, a temporary hell of the postmortal spirit world, is also spoken of as a SPIRIT PRISON. Here, in preparation for the Resurrection, unrepentant spirits are cleansed through suffering that would have been obviated by the atonement of Christ had they repented during mortality (D&C 19:15–20; Alma 40:13–14). At the last resurrection this hell will give up its captive spirits. Many of these spirits will enter into the TELESTIAL KINGDOM in their resurrected state (2 Ne. 9:10–12; D&C 76:84–89, 106; Rev. 20:13). References to an everlasting hell for these spirits are interpreted in light of the Doctrine and Covenants, which defines ENDLESS AND ETERNAL as referring not to the length of punishment, but rather referring to God's punishment because he is "endless" and "eternal" (19:4–13). Individual spirits will be cleansed, will cease to experience the fiery torment of mind, and will be resurrected with their physical bodies.

The Savior's reference to the "gates of hell" (Hades, or the spirit world; Matt. 16:18) indicates, among other things, that God's priesthood power will penetrate hell and redeem the repentant spirits there. Many have been, and many more will yet be, delivered from hell through hearing, repenting, and obeying the gospel of Jesus Christ in the spirit world after the death of the body. LDS doctrine emphasizes that after his mortal death Jesus Christ went to the spirit world and organized the teaching of the gospel there (D&C 138; cf. Luke 23:43; 1 Pet. 3:18–20). The Athanasian Creed and some forms of the "Apostles'" Creed state that Christ "descended into hell." LDS teaching is that Jesus entered the spirit world to extend his redemptive mission to those in hell, upon conditions of their repentance (*see* SALVATION FOR THE DEAD).

A third meaning of "hell" (second spiritual death) refers to the realm of the devil and his angels, including those known as sons of perdition (2 Pet. 2:4; D&C 29:38; 88:113; Rev. 20:14). It is a place for those who cannot be cleansed by the Atonement because they committed the unforgivable and unpardonable sin (1 Ne. 15:35; D&C 76:30–49). Only this hell continues to operate *after* the Resurrection and Judgment.

BIBLIOGRAPHY

"Descent of Christ into Hell." In *Oxford Dictionary of the Christian Church*, p. 395. New York, 1983.

Nibley, Hugh W. "Christ Among the Ruins." *Ensign* 13 (July 1983):14–19.

M. CATHERINE THOMAS

HOLINESS

In LDS thought, as in most religions, it is God who invests a person, place, or object with holiness: "For I am able to make you holy, and your sins are forgiven you" (D&C 60:7). Thus the temples of the Church are said to be holy because they are dedicated to Deity who has manifested himself within them. Latter-day Saints speak of the sabbath as holy because God has put his spirit into that day. The wooded area where Joseph Smith received his first vision is spoken of as the sacred grove because the Father and the Son appeared there. Marriage and other priesthood ordinances are considered holy because God is directly and personally a party to such covenants. The scriptures are holy because they contain the word of God.

Although they infrequently use the term "holy" (an exception is in a beloved hymn which beseeches God, "More holiness give me"), Latter-day Saints strive for a measure of holiness and PERFECTION in MORTALITY: "Man may be perfect in his sphere; . . . individual perfection is relative. . . . The law of the Gospel is a perfect law and the sure effect of full obedience thereto is perfection" (Talmage, p. 169).

The process of becoming holy is based on three doctrines: JUSTIFICATION, which satisfies the demands of justice for the sins of the individual through the ATONEMENT OF JESUS CHRIST; purification, made possible by that same atonement and symbolized in the sacrament of the bread and water, requiring the constant cleansing of oneself from earthly stains and imperfections; and SANCTIFICATION, the process of being made holy. Having purified oneself of imperfections to the greatest degree possible, one is invested, over a lifetime, with holiness from God. $Alma_2$ is an example of one recognized by God as holy (Alma 10:7–9).

These principles are summarized in the next to the last verse of the Book of Mormon: "And again, if ye by the grace of God are perfect in Christ, and deny not his power, then are ye sanctified in Christ by the grace of God, through the shedding of the blood of Christ, which is in the covenant of the Father unto the remission of your sins, that ye become holy, without spot" (Moro. 10:33).

BIBLIOGRAPHY
Lee, Harold B. *Stand Ye in Holy Places.* Salt Lake City, 1974.
Talmage, James E. *The Vitality of Mormonism,* p. 169. Boston, 1919.

ELOUISE M. BELL

HOLY GHOST

The Church of Jesus Christ of Latter-day Saints teaches that the Holy Ghost is a spirit man, a spirit son of GOD THE FATHER. It is fundamental Church doctrine that God is the Father of the spirits of all men and women, that Jesus is literally God's Son both in the spirit and in the flesh, and that the Holy Ghost is a personage of spirit separate and distinct from both the Father and the Son. The Holy Ghost is the third member of the Eternal GODHEAD, and is identified also as the HOLY SPIRIT, Spirit of God, Spirit of the Lord, and the comforter. All three members of the Godhead were manifested at Jesus' baptism (Mark 1:9–12). Regarding them the Prophet Joseph Smith taught: "The Father has a body of flesh and bones as tangible as man's; the Son also; but the Holy Ghost has not a body of flesh and bones, but is a personage of Spirit. Were it not so, the Holy Ghost could not dwell in us" (D&C 130:22). In a figurative sense, the Holy Ghost dwells in the hearts of the righteous Saints of all DISPENSATIONS (D&C 20:18–21).

Joseph Smith also stated that an "everlasting covenant was made between three personages before the organization of this earth, and relates to their dispensation of things to men on the earth; these personages . . . are called God the first, the Creator; God the second, the

Redeemer; and God the third, the witness or Testator" (*TPJS,* p. 190).

Latter-day Saints understand that by obedience to the laws and ordinances of the gospel Adam received the Holy Ghost and thus learned that redemption from the Fall will come through Christ to all who accept him (Moses 5:6–9). Thus, the gospel was preached from the beginning, being declared by ANGELS, by the voice of God, and by the GIFT OF THE HOLY GHOST (Moses 5:58–59; cf. 2 Pet. 1:21). Nephi$_1$ (c. 600 B.C.) testified that the Holy Ghost is "the gift of God unto all those who diligently seek him, as well in times of old as in the time that he should manifest himself unto the children of men. . . . For he that diligently seeketh shall find; and the mysteries of God shall be unfolded unto them, by the power of the Holy Ghost, as well in these times as in times of old, and as well in times of old as in times to come" (1 Ne. 10:17–19).

Joseph Smith taught that the influence of the Holy Ghost, which is the convincing power of God of the truth of the gospel, can be received before BAPTISM, but the gift, or constant companionship, of the Holy Ghost, which comes by the LAYING ON OF HANDS, is obtained only after baptism (*TPJS,* p. 199). "You might as well baptize a bag of sand as a man," he said, "if not done in view of the remission of sins and getting of the Holy Ghost. Baptism by water is but half a baptism, and is good for nothing without the other half—that is, the baptism of the Holy Ghost" (*TPJS,* p. 314). Thus, a person is expected to receive the witness of the Holy Ghost to the truthfulness of the gospel of Jesus Christ, of scripture, and of the words of the living prophets before baptism; the full outpouring of the Spirit does not come, however, until the person has complied with the command to be baptized. Only after baptism can the gift be conferred by one in authority (Moro. 10:3–5; D&C 76:52). And even then the Holy Ghost cannot be received by someone who is not worthy of it, since the Holy Ghost will not dwell in the heart of an unrighteous person. Thus, the actual companionship of the Holy Ghost may be received immediately after baptism or at a subsequent time, when the one receiving the promise becomes a fit companion for that holy being. Should the individual cease thereafter to be clean and obedient, the Holy Ghost will withdraw (1 Cor. 3:16–17).

The Holy Ghost is a sanctifier. Because no unclean thing can dwell in a divine presence, the whole system of salvation centers on the process of sanctification; people are saved to the extent that they are sanctified. Sanctification and holiness are inseparable. "To be sanctified is to become clean, pure, and spotless; to be free from the blood and sins of the world; to become a new creature of the Holy Ghost, one whose body has been renewed by the rebirth of the Spirit. Sanctification is a state of saintliness, a state attained only by conformity to the laws and ordinances of the gospel" (*MD,* p. 675).

The Holy Ghost is a revelator. The Prophet Joseph Smith taught that "no man can receive the Holy Ghost without receiving revelations" (*TPJS,* p. 328). To enjoy the companionship of the Holy Ghost is to enjoy the spirit of REVELATION (D&C 8:2–3). Without revelation there can be no competent witness of Christ or his gospel (Rev. 19:10). The Holy Ghost is the source of all saving knowledge. Those who sincerely and prayerfully seek this knowledge are promised that everything expedient will be revealed to them (D&C 18:18). Nephi testified that Christ manifests himself "unto all those who believe in him, by the power of the Holy Ghost; yea, unto every nation, kindred, tongue, and people, working mighty miracles, signs, and wonders, among the children of men according to their faith" (2 Ne. 26:13; cf. 1 Cor. 2:11–13; D&C 76:116).

The Holy Ghost is a teacher. All who will be saved must be tutored by the Holy Ghost. The things of the Spirit can only be understood when taught and learned by the Spirit (D&C 50:11–24). The divine commission to teach the truths of salvation rests with the Holy Ghost. Jesus was filled with the power of the Holy Ghost (Luke 4:1). "He spake not as other men, neither could he be taught; for he needed not that any man should teach him" (JST Matt. 3:25). The Father gave Christ the Spirit without measure (John 3:34). Angels also speak by the power of the Holy Ghost (2 Ne. 32:3). Such is the standard for all who go forth in Christ's name. "Ye are not sent forth to be taught," the Savior said to the early Latter-day Saints, "but to teach the children of men the things which I have put into your hands by the power of my Spirit; and ye are to be taught from on high. Sanctify yourselves and ye shall be endowed with power, that ye may give even as I have spoken" (D&C 43:15–16).

Describing the influence of the Holy Ghost as it fell upon him and Oliver Cowdery, the Prophet Joseph Smith said, "We were filled with the Holy Ghost, and rejoiced in the God of our salvation. Our minds being now enlightened, we began to have the scriptures laid open to our understandings, and the true meaning and intention of their more mysterious passages revealed unto us in a manner which we never could attain to previously, nor ever before had thought of" (JS—H 1:73–74; cf. Alma 5:46). The Holy Ghost also brings to remembrance that which has previously been learned (John 14:26), directs that for which one should pray (D&C 46:30), and makes known what is to be spoken in preaching and teaching (D&C 84:85).

The Holy Ghost is the Comforter. A distinctive characteristic of the truths of salvation is that they are attended by a spirit of comfort and peace. It is the office of the Holy Ghost to lift burdens, give courage, strengthen faith, grant consolation, extend hope, and reveal whatever is needed to those having claim on his sacred companionship (Moses 6:61).

Jesus taught that no sin is greater than the sin against the Holy Ghost (Matt. 12:31–32). A latter-day revelation explains, "The blasphemy against the Holy Ghost, which shall not be forgiven in the world nor out of the world, is in that ye commit murder wherein ye shed innocent blood, and assent unto my death, after ye have received my new and everlasting covenant, saith the Lord God" (D&C 132:27). Joseph Smith observed further that such a one rejects the Son after the Father has revealed him, denies the truth, and defies the PLAN OF SALVATION. "From that time he begins to be an enemy. . . . He gets the spirit of the devil—the same spirit that they had who crucified the Lord of Life—the same spirit that sins against the Holy Ghost. You cannot save such persons; you cannot bring them to repentance; they make open war, like the devil, and awful is the consequence" (*TPJS*, p. 357–58; cf. D&C 76:31–38, 43–48).

The Holy Ghost is such an uplifting power and source of necessary gospel knowledge that to have his constant companionship and influence is the greatest gift a person can receive in mortality (cf. D&C 121:46). It is reported that on one occasion, when the Prophet Joseph Smith was asked, "Wherein [the LDS Church] differed from the other religions of the day," he replied, that it was in "the gift of the Holy Ghost by the laying-on of hands, . . . [and] that all other considerations were contained in the gift of the Holy Ghost" (*HC* 4:42).

BIBLIOGRAPHY
McConkie, Bruce R. *A New Witness for the Articles of Faith,* chaps. 28–31. Salt Lake City, 1985.
McConkie, Joseph Fielding, and Robert L. Millet. *The Holy Ghost.* Salt Lake City, 1989.

JOSEPH FIELDING MCCONKIE

HOLY OF HOLIES

In ancient times, through divine instruction to Moses, the Holy of Holies was made the center of the tabernacle (Ex. 25–27). It was a fifteen-foot cube formed by hanging veils made of goat hair, ram skins, and other dyed skins. Some were embroidered with figures of cherubim in blue, purple, and scarlet. The Holy of Holies was designated as the repository for a chest called the ark of the covenant. This chest, constructed of gold-plated acacia wood, was the place of the stone tablets inscribed by the hand of God, and the resting place for the mercy seat. Fashioned in one piece of fine gold, this seat, with cherubim engraven above it, formed the visible throne for the presence of God. Once a year, on the day of atonement, the high priest entered the Holy of Holies and sprinkled sacrificial blood over the mercy seat as expiation for Israel's sins. Though the ark has disappeared, this ritual was continued in the temples of Zerubbabel and Herod.

A latter-day Holy of Holies has been dedicated in the great temple in Salt Lake City. It is a central chamber adjoining the celestial room. Beyond its sliding doors are six steps to similar doors, symbolic of the veil that guarded the Holy of Holies in ancient times. The sanctuary is of circular design with a domed ceiling. The appointments include inlaid wood, gold leaf, stained glass, and unique lighting. The presiding high priest, the President of the Church, controls access to this sanctuary.

BIBLIOGRAPHY
Encyclopedia Judaica, Vol. 15, cols. 681–82, 748–49. Jerusalem, 1971.
Talmage, James E. *House of the Lord,* pp. 162–63. Salt Lake City, 1974.

LYSLE R. CAHOON

HOLY SPIRIT

The Holy Spirit is a term often used to refer to the HOLY GHOST. In such cases the Holy Spirit is a personage. Ghost is an Old English word meaning spirit. The scriptures use this term to designate the third member of the GODHEAD (Alma 11:44) and to speak of the Spirit's power to testify (Alma 7:16), to grant knowledge (Alma 5:46; D&C 76:116), to persuade (Mosiah 3:19), to indicate remission of sins (D&C 55:1), and to sanctify (Alma 5:54). The term Holy Spirit is the core of the phrase HOLY SPIRIT OF PROMISE denoting the Holy Ghost's sanction of every ordinance performed in righteousness. The influence or spirit that emanates from Jesus Christ, which is also called the LIGHT OF CHRIST, is holy, but is neither the Holy Spirit nor a personage.

JERRY A. WILSON

HOLY SPIRIT OF PROMISE

The Holy Spirit of Promise is one of many descriptive name-titles of the HOLY GHOST and refers to a specific function of the Holy Ghost. In John 14:16, the Savior, who had been a comforter to his disciples, assured them that after his departure into heaven they would receive another comforter: "And I will pray the Father, and he shall give you another Comforter, that he may abide with you for ever." The next verse speaks of this Comforter as "the Spirit of truth," who "dwelleth with you, and shall be in you" (verse 17). The Lord subsequently identified this promised Comforter as the Holy Ghost (verse 26). Doctrine and Covenants 88:3 reiterates and clarifies: "Wherefore, I now send upon you another Comforter, even upon you my friends, that it may abide in your hearts, even the Holy Spirit of promise; which other Comforter is the same that I promised unto my disciples, as is recorded in the testimony of John."

The Holy Spirit of Promise is the power by which ordinances and other righteous acts performed on this earth, such as baptism and eternal marriage, are ratified, validated, and sealed in heaven as well as on earth. Paul taught the Ephesians that after acting on their faith in Christ they "were sealed with that Holy Spirit of promise," which was the surety of their "inheritance until the redemption of the purchased possession" (Eph. 1:12–14). The sealing of earthly COVENANTS and performances is conditional and depends upon the recipient's personal commitment and worthiness. If a person who has received the Holy Spirit of Promise subsequently becomes unrighteous, the seal is broken until full repentance and forgiveness occur (*DS* 1:55; 2:94–99).

The necessity of sealing by the Holy Ghost is emphasized in the following passage: "All covenants, contracts, bonds, obligations, oaths, vows, performances, connections, associations, or expectations, that are not made and entered into and sealed by the Holy Spirit of promise, . . . are of no efficacy, virtue, or force in and after the resurrection from the dead; for all contracts that are not made unto this end have an end when men are dead" (D&C 132:7). Earthly representatives of the Lord, such as bishops and elders may be deceived by an unworthy person, but no one can deceive the Holy Spirit, who will not ratify an ordinance received unworthily. This safeguard is attached to all blessings and covenants associated with the gospel of Jesus Christ.

The ultimate manifestation of the Holy Spirit of Promise is in connection with having one's CALLING AND ELECTION made sure—that is, receiving "the more sure word of prophecy" testifying that an individual is sealed up to ETERNAL LIFE (D&C 131:5). The Holy Spirit of Promise validates this blessing or seals it upon the person. Referring to the Holy Spirit of Promise the Lord says, "This Comforter is the promise which I give unto you of eternal life, even the glory of the celestial kingdom" (D&C 88:4; cf. *MD*, pp. 361–62).

BIBLIOGRAPHY

McConkie, Bruce R. *Doctrinal New Testament Commentary*, Vol. 3, pp. 333–37. Salt Lake City, 1973.

LAWRENCE R. FLAKE

HOPE

The concept of hope plays a vital role in Latter-day Saint thought. Firmly centered in Christ and his resurrection, it is the "hope of eternal life" (Titus 1:2) repeatedly alluded to by Paul. It is the opposite of the despair found among those who are "without Christ, having no hope, and without God in the world" (Eph. 2:12). As the Book of Mormon prophet Moroni writes, "If ye have no hope, ye must needs be in despair" (Moro. 10:22). For those, however, who accept Christ's atonement and resurrection, there comes a "brightness of hope" (2 Ne. 31:20) through which all who believe in God "might with surety hope for a better world" (Ether 12:4).

The scriptures employ the term "hope" in a variety of ways. Some usages suggest desire, such as the statement in Article of Faith 13 that "we believe all things, we hope all things, we have endured many things, and hope to be able to endure all things." Others denote firm expectation, such as Paul's description of Abraham "who against hope believed in hope, that he might become the father of many nations" (Rom. 4:18). Still others make it an integral part of faith, such as the scriptural observations that "faith is the substance of things hoped for, the evidence of things not seen" (Heb. 11:1).

Regardless of their form, the individual variations of meaning all center on the confidence or trust in God that springs from knowledge that mankind is saved through the Atonement ("for we are saved by hope," Rom. 8:15). Hence, hope is inseparably connected with faith. Book of Mormon passages add insight to New Testament teachings by expanding on this interactive relationship: "How is it that ye can attain unto faith, save ye shall have hope?" (Moro. 7:40); "hope cometh of faith" (Ether 12:4); "without faith there cannot be any hope" (Moro. 7:42).

In combination with faith, hope leads to knowledge of the truth about Jesus Christ ("if ye have faith, ye hope for things which are not seen, which are true" [Alma 32:21]). It is also an essential attitude for individual salvation ("man must hope, or he cannot receive an inheritance in the place which thou hast prepared" [Ether 12:32]).

Paul's praise of "faith, hope, and charity" (1 Cor. 13:13) as basic Christian virtues expands understanding of these concepts with its intimation that faith and hope are prerequisites to developing charity—a Christlike love of others. This type of love cannot grow out of despair or disbelief. Using the same triadic concept, the Book of Mormon describes their relationship to repentance, baptism, and the Gift of the Holy Ghost, all required for salvation in the kingdom of

God (2 Ne. 31:16–21). Hope is integral to the gospel formula: through steadfastness in Christ (faith), a perfect brightness of hope, and love of God (charity), the baptized can endure to the end and be saved. Having these attributes is also necessary for service in the Lord's kingdom: "If you have not faith, hope, and charity, you can do nothing" (D&C 18:19; cf. D&C 4:5).

Paul observed that the writings of ancient prophets were given "that we through patience and comfort of the scriptures might have hope" (Rom. 15:4; cf. Ps. 16:9; Prov. 10:28; 14:32; Jer. 17:7; Joel 3:16). The Prophet Joseph Smith claimed that Latter-day Saints "have the greatest hope . . . for our dead of any people on the earth" if they have died in the faith (*TPJS,* p. 359). He was referring to their possession of another testament of Christ (the Book of Mormon) and to additional latter-day scriptures that contain newly revealed truth about the purpose of mortal existence, the state of life after death, the eternity of the marriage covenant, and the plan of salvation generally. This additional knowledge gives Latter-day Saints special reason for hope in this life and for life in the worlds to come.

JAMES K. LYON

HUMILITY

True humility is the recognition of one's imperfection that is acquired only as one joyfully, voluntarily, and quietly submits one's whole life to God's will (Micah 6:8; James 4:6; Mosiah 4:10; Morm. 5:24; Ether 6:17). This includes obeying in love his every commandment, repenting of sins, honoring with endurance his every COVENANT, and striving for greater PERFECTION with self-discipline. Humility can result only from faithful submission to the teachings of Jesus Christ. Seeds of humility can be experienced in spontaneous moments of overwhelming gratitude, awe, and reverence when individuals recognize God's hand in the beauty of a sunset, the power of a waterfall, the miracle of life, or the magnitude and glory of human creations. Thus humility is not only a state of being but a process of obeying and reconciling one's life to God's providence as it is made known through his scriptures, prophets, creations, and answers to prayer.

Those seeking to be humble are counseled to pursue knowledge of God's glory, to experience his goodness and love, to receive a REMISSION OF SINS, and to "retain in remembrance, the greatness of God, and your own nothingness, and his goodness and long-suffering towards you" (Mosiah 4:11).

The Church promotes understanding of humility by encouraging members to study the scriptures and writings of Church leaders who pair this virtue with other virtues such as being meek, patient, loving, and submissive (Mosiah 3:19); gentle, long-suffering, diligent in obeying God's commandments, and full of hope and charity (Alma 7:23, 24); faithful and prayerful (D&C 105:23); repentant (Moro. 8:10); wise (Alma 32:12); able to bear adversity and weaknesses (Ether 12:27); joyful and pure in heart (Hel. 3:35); knowledgeable (D&C 4:6); self-disciplined; and teachable and broken-hearted. A lifestyle void of humility exhibits undesirable qualities: PRIDE (Hel. 4:12), haughtiness (Isa. 2:11), wickedness (2 Ne. 28:14), guile (D&C 124:97), jealousy (D&C 67:10), evil (2 Chr. 36:12), hate, envy, anger, arrogance, inordinate ambition, fault-finding, and self-righteousness.

Latter-day Saints with a TESTIMONY pursue humility as a duty, believing it is God's will to seek this virtue. "God will have a humble people. We can either choose to be humble or we can be compelled to be humble" (Benson, 1989, p. 6). As the foundation for spiritual progress, humility disposes people to hear God's word, to be receptive to inspiration, revelation, and spiritual wisdom. It befits members to accept callings in the Church. Humility must accompany REPENTANCE before BAPTISM (D&C 20:37), approaching the divine with "a broken heart and contrite spirit" (2 Ne. 2:7; 3 Ne. 12:19; D&C 20:37). To seek humility is to ask it of God, to recognize it as fruit of a spiritual life (2 Chr. 33:12). Divine grace, strength, and forgiveness are promised to the humble (1 Pet. 5:5; 3 Ne. 4:33; Ether 9:35; D&C 1:28; 104:23). Scripture warns the proud of impending afflictions, temptations, and even destruction (Isa. 10:33; 2 Chr. 12:7; Mosiah 3:18; Morm. 5:24; D&C 5:28, 32). Adversity and weaknesses can humble individuals, bringing them closer to God. TRIALS often develop spirituality and humility. However, Church leaders emphasize that good conduct and humility without covenants and ordinances will neither redeem nor exalt (Packer, p. 82).

Latter-day Saints are enjoined to imitate Jesus, who was meek and lowly, following not only his example and teachings but also those of his prophets as they walk in his footsteps. "Only Jesus Christ is uniquely qualified to provide that hope, that confidence and that strength to . . . rise above our human failings. To do that, we must . . . live by his laws and teachings" (Benson, 1983, p. 6). To become humble like Jesus, to become his disciples, individuals must take up their crosses, trust in him, approach perfection through wise choices, and submissively endure to the end (D&C 122:7). Christ's pattern of humility was unblemished. Though members aspire to this perfection, they are to keep perspective on their fallibility by balancing unfulfilled aspirations to emulate Christ with positive recognition of his gifts to them, of their worth as God's children, and of their progress toward humility over a lifetime. In the face of social pressures for self-interested individuality, the Church stresses selflessness and humility as keys for returning to God. Persons who would attain the fulness of the immortalizing promises of the ATONEMENT must persist in achieving humility in spite of obstacles and societal ethics that distract from this goal (Mosiah 3:19).

The desire for humility is nourished by an understanding acceptance of the greatness of the Savior's sacrifice to provide SALVATION and RESURRECTION for all. As people comprehend God's love for them, hearts and minds will be humbled and drawn into closer unity with him and with all fellow beings.

BIBLIOGRAPHY

Benson, Ezra Taft. "Jesus Christ: Our Savior and Redeemer." *Ensign* 13 (Nov. 1983):6–8.

——. "To the Elderly in the Church." *Ensign* 19 (May 1989):4–8.

Maxwell, Neal A. *Meek and Lowly*. Salt Lake City, 1987.

Packer, Boyd K. "The Only True Church." *Ensign* 15 (Nov. 1985):80–82.

ALICE T. CLARK

I

IMMORTALITY

"Immortality is to live forever in the resurrected state with body and spirit inseparably connected" (*MD*, p. 376). The FALL OF ADAM brought death, and the ATONEMENT OF JESUS CHRIST brought life. Immortality is as broad as the Fall; since all creatures die, all will be given everlasting life (1 Cor. 15:22).

In the Garden of Eden, Adam and Eve were not subject to death until the Fall. When they partook of the forbidden fruit, they were ushered out of God's presence; mortality and its consequent death descended upon them, and subsequently upon all mankind and all other living things.

That humans became mortal was a necessary step in the Lord's eternal PLAN OF SALVATION for his children. The conditions of mortality, however, left mankind subject to death and incapable on its own of reclaiming the dead from the grave. Jesus Christ, the Only Begotten of the Father in the flesh, was the only one capable of redeeming the human family from the effects of the Fall, thus providing for a RESURRECTION of the PHYSICAL BODY.

The individual spirit that inhabits and gives life to the mortal physical body is not subject to the same death that is common to mortality. All spirits are immortal (cf. Alma 42:9; *TPJS*, p. 207; *see also* SOUL; SPIRIT).

The Lord himself died a physical death in order to bring about the resurrection of all the dead and to grant immortality to all mankind. The prophet Lehi said, "Wherefore, how great the importance to make these things known unto the inhabitants of the earth, that they may know that there is no flesh that can dwell in the presence of God, save it be through the merits, and mercy, and grace of the Holy Messiah, who layeth down his life according to the flesh, and taketh it again by the power of the Spirit, that he may bring to pass the resurrection of the dead, being the first that should rise" (2 Ne. 2:8).

During his earthly life, Jesus Christ raised several from the dead; however, they were restored only to mortal life. By his later atonement and resurrection of his physical, tangible body (Luke 24:36–40), Jesus provided the means by which every person will be resurrected to immortal life, with a tangible body of flesh and bones, even as he has. Paul taught, "For as in Adam all die, even so in Christ shall all be made alive" (1 Cor. 15:22), and "When this corruptible shall have put on incorruption, and this mortal shall have put on immortality, then shall be brought to pass the saying that is written, Death is swallowed up in victory" (1 Cor. 15:54; cf. Rom. 6:5).

Immortality is a free gift for all mankind. Amulek, a Book of Mormon prophet, taught that "this restoration shall come to all, both old and young, both bond and free, both male and female, both the wicked and the righteous; . . . every thing shall be restored to its perfect frame, as it is now, or in the body, . . . that they can die no more; their spirits uniting with their bodies, never to be divided" (Alma 11:44–45). Immortality, or the resurrection from the dead, will be given to all forms of life, for God glorifies himself "by saving all that His hands had made, whether beasts, fowls, fishes or men" (*TPJS,* p. 291; D&C 29:24–25).

Although sometimes used interchangeably, the words "immortality" and "eternal life" are not synonymous. All who obtain eternal life will also have immortality, but not all who receive immortality will have eternal life. The term "eternal life" has reference to the type or quality of life that God has, which is given only to the faithful, and includes much more than living forever. "And thus did I, the Lord God, appoint unto man the days of his probation—that by his natural death he might be raised in immortality unto eternal life, even as many as would believe" (D&C 29:43).

[*See also* Immortality and Eternal Life.]

BIBLIOGRAPHY

Smith, Joseph Fielding. *Doctrines of Salvation,* Vol. 2, pp. 4–13. Salt Lake City, 1955.

Talmage, James E. *AF,* pp. 87–93. Salt Lake City, 1952.

DAN W. ANDERSEN

IMMORTALITY AND ETERNAL LIFE

The Church of Jesus Christ Latter-day Saints teaches that the work and glory of God is to bring to pass both the IMMORTALITY and the ETERNAL LIFE of men and women (Moses 1:39; 2 Ne. 10:23–25). These two conditions in the AFTERLIFE are not necessarily synonymous, though each is given as a consequence of the ATONEMENT OF JESUS CHRIST.

Immortality is to live forever in a resurrected condition without death that was introduced to this world through the FALL OF ADAM and Eve (2 Ne. 2:22–23). Through Jesus Christ's atonement, all living things will receive a resurrection, the spirit and the flesh uniting never again to be separated, and will live forever in an immortal state (2 Ne. 2:8–9; 9:13; Alma 11:45). Immortality is a free gift from God because of unconditional GRACE, and does not require works of OBEDIENCE. "For as in Adam all die, even so in Christ shall all be made alive" (1 Cor. 15:22).

"Eternal life" is a higher state than immortality alone and means to live forever in a resurrected condition in the presence of God, and to become like God. It likewise is available only through the grace of Jesus Christ and is the greatest of all gifts that God bestows upon his children (D&C 14:7). Eternal life is EXALTATION into the type and quality of life that God lives. Receiving eternal life is conditional, predicated upon obedience to the fulness of gospel law and ordinances (D&C 29:43–44; 130:20–21). It requires voluntary obedience to all of the ordinances and principles of the gospel, beginning with FAITH in Jesus Christ and continuing through BAPTISM, the LAYING ON

OF HANDS for the GIFT OF THE HOLY GHOST, and the COVENANTS of the ENDOWMENT and marriage in the temple, and of ENDURING TO THE END.

BIBLIOGRAPHY

Smith, Joseph Fielding. *Man, His Origin and Destiny*, pp. 271–72. Salt Lake City, 1954.

LEAUN G. OTTEN

INDIVIDUALITY

It is LDS doctrine that every human being has an eternal identity, existing from the premortal state and continuing forever (Abr. 3:22–23). Moreover, all individuals are responsible for their own choices, and all will stand before the Lord to present an accounting of their lives at the Judgment Day (A of F 2; Moro. 10:27). This, however, does not mean that individuals are autonomous or alone. All individuals are spirit children of God the Father, who organized them into relationships in order to maximize their growth and happiness through loving and serving one another.

LDS teachings make clear that living the gospel of Jesus Christ means voluntarily submitting the self to the will of God. Joseph F. Smith, felt that it shows "a stronger characteristic of individuality" to bring the self into harmony with God than to be separate from him (*JD* 25:245). An individual must voluntarily obey God's will to achieve righteousness (John 7:16), and God's will requires service to others in one's family and community (Matt. 20:26–27). Paradoxically, "he that loseth his life for [Christ's] sake shall find it" (Matt. 10:39); and as David O. McKay stated, "A man's duties to himself and to his fellow men are indissolubly connected" (p. 289). The Church cannot force individuals to become one with God and others. That must be done "only by persuasion, by long-suffering, by gentleness and meekness, and by love unfeigned; by kindness" (D&C 121:41–43).

The ultimate objectives of The Church of Jesus Christ of Latter-day Saints are as inclusive and extensive as can be imagined, both individually and collectively—namely, to attain ETERNAL LIFE for all individuals and eternal continuity for families and to maintain a supportive, unified community of Saints on earth who live the fulness of the gospel of Jesus Christ. The scale and profundity of these objectives are equal to the depth of commitment they require. Christ promises righteous men and women that they shall be joint-heirs with him, inheritors of "all that my Father hath" (D&C 84:33–39; Rom. 8:14–18). Having offered the riches of eternity, the Savior may require the faithful to voluntarily sacrifice all their earthly possessions, including life itself, in order "to produce the faith necessary unto life and salvation" (*Lectures on Faith,* Lecture 6, paragraph 7). Latter-day Saints express this principle in a beloved hymn: "I'll go where you want me to go, dear Lord, . . . I'll be what you want me to be" (*Hymns,* p. 270).

Salvation is both an individual and a collective matter. Individuals are punished for their own sins, but the personal choices that foster growth and exaltation necessarily involve other people. The atonement of Jesus Christ is relational: "No man cometh unto the Father, but by me," the Savior said, and people demonstrate their love for him by keeping his commandments (John 14:6, 15). The BAPTISMAL COVENANT is both personal and social: it involves personal willingness to remember Christ always, and it encourages members to "bear one another's burdens" (Mosiah 18:8).

While the singular focus of the Church on achieving its ultimate objectives unifies its members in ways that contrast markedly with organizations having internally competing objectives, there are limits to the diversity in individual beliefs and practices that the Church can tolerate and still achieve its mission. Neither Joseph Smith's oft-quoted statement that "I teach the people correct principles and they govern themselves" (*JD* 10:57–58) nor Lehi's insistence that people are free to choose liberty and eternal life or captivity and death (2 Ne. 2:26–27) means that the Church can ignore internal challenges to its integrity or principles (Matt. 18:17; 2 Thes. 3:14–15; D&C 42:24, 74–93). Severe cases of disruption and violation may be subjected to disciplinary procedures and may result in disfellowshipment or even excommunication.

Christ affirms great diversity and individuality in gospel service. Each person has abilities to perform Christlike service that others may not be able to perform. Jesus taught that personal spiritual gifts and talents are to be cultivated and shared: "the best gifts" are given "that all may be profited thereby" (D&C 46:8–12; *see also* GIFTS OF THE SPIRIT).

Organizations may in a measure constrain behavior, and the Church has a constraining influence on individuals insofar as they choose to conform or fulfill the requirements for holding callings or a temple recommend. However, there is ample room for the expression of individuality and appreciation for those who may take a novel approach to the righteous fulfillment of their responsibilities. God counsels his children to use their gifts creatively and intelligently in his service: "It is not meet that I should command in all things; for he that is compelled in all things, the same is a slothful and not a wise servant" (D&C 58:26–28). Moreover, most Church constraints, such as the law of chastity or the directive to avoid addictive substances, are intended to free the individual for a happier life. Voluntarily following Jesus Christ is the ultimate liberty, and sin, the ultimate captivity (John 8:32; 2 Ne. 2:26–27).

Latter-day Saints are taught that they and all the rest of the human family are eternal children of a loving Heavenly Father. Their individuality is priceless and eternal. The recognition that the Church is enriched by a diversity of individual endowments, experiences, and interests always has been fundamental to the LDS faith. The concluding sentence of the Articles of Faith celebrates the diverse individual paths that are part of the righteous life: "If there is anything virtuous, lovely, or of good report or praiseworthy, we seek after these things."

[*See also* Unity.]

BIBLIOGRAPHY

Brown, Victor, Jr. "Differences." *Ensign* 8 (July 1978):8–11.

Dahl, Larry E., and Charles D. Tate, Jr., eds. *The Lectures on Faith in Historical Perspective.* Provo, Utah, 1990.

Higbee, Kenneth. "On Doing Your Own Thing." *New Era* 5 (Apr. 1975):18–20.

McKay, David O. "Each Individual Must Work Out His Own Salvation." *Instructor* 96 (1961):289–90.

Packer, Boyd K. *Teach Ye Diligently.* Salt Lake City, 1975.

Talmage, James E. "Practical Religion." *AF*, chap. 24.

HOWARD M. BAHR

INTELLIGENCE

According to latter-day scripture, "The glory of God is intelligence, or, in other words, light and truth" (D&C 93:36). Mankind, too, may be glorified by gaining intelligence (D&C 93:28–30). As Christ did not receive a fulness of intelligence at first but continued from "grace to grace" until he received a fulness (D&C 93:11–13, 27–28), so it is with all persons. Whatever principles of intelligence they gain in mortality will rise with them in the Resurrection (D&C 130:18–19).

To gain increased intelligence, individuals must be agents to act for themselves (D&C 93:30), which means that they must be tried and tempted (D&C 29:39), and at the same time, the works of the Lord must be plainly manifest to them (D&C 93:31) so that they will have choice. In PREMORTAL LIFE, men and women were intelligent beings (Abr. 3:21–22) who were given AGENCY by God (Moses 4:3; D&C 29:36). In mortality, they are also given agency by God (D&C 101:78), to gain knowledge of good and evil (Moses 5:11). Intelligence increases as individuals forsake evil and come to the Lord, calling on his name, obeying his voice, and keeping his commandments (D&C 93:1–2, 28, 37). Intelligence is lost through disobedience, hardening of hearts, and clinging to false traditions (Mark 8:21; D&C 93:39).

Intelligence, however defined, is not created or made (D&C 93:29); it is coeternal with God (*TPJS*, pp. 353–54). Some LDS leaders have interpreted this to mean that intelligent beings—called intelligences—existed before and after they were given spirit bodies in the premortal existence. Others have interpreted it to mean that intelligent beings were organized as spirits out of eternal intelligent matter, that they did not exist as individuals before they were organized as spirit beings in the premortal existence (Abr. 3:22; *JD* 7:57; 2:124). The Church has taken no official position on this issue.

[*See also* Intelligences.]

BIBLIOGRAPHY

Roberts, B. H. "Immortality of Man." *IE* 20 (Apr. 1907):401–423.

DENNIS J. PACKARD

INTELLIGENCES

The word "intelligences" (plural) occurs frequently in LDS literature, having reference to the period of the premortal existence of mankind. The term has received two interpretations by writers within the Church: as the literal spirit children of Heavenly Parents and as individual entities existing prior to their spirit birth. Because latter-day revelation has not clarified the meaning of the term, a more precise interpretation is not possible at present.

The scriptural source for the word "intelligences" is the book of Abraham 3:21–22. The Lord instructed the patriarch Abraham regarding the premortal experiences of all who have been or ever will be upon the earth. Among those events was the COUNCIL IN HEAVEN, at which the Father's PLAN OF SALVATION for his children was discussed. Abraham wrote of this, "Now the Lord had shown unto me, Abraham, the intelligences that were organized before the world was; . . . for he stood among those that were spirits, and he saw that they were good; and he said unto me: Abraham, thou art one of them" (Abr. 3:22–23). The Prophet Joseph Smith spoke of intelligences as follows: "God himself, finding he was in the midst of spirits and glory, because he was more intelligent, saw proper to institute laws whereby the rest could have a privilege to advance like himself. The relationship we have with God places us in a situation to advance in knowledge. He has power to institute laws to instruct the weaker intelligences, that they may be exalted with himself, so that they might have one glory upon another, and all that knowledge, power, glory, and intelligence, which is requisite in order to save them" (*TPJS*, p. 354).

Concerning man's premortal existence, the Lord revealed to Joseph Smith, "Man was also in the beginning with God. Intelligence, or the light of truth, was not created or made, neither indeed can be" (D&C 93:29). "Intelligence," as used here, is singular, and it is not clear from this passage if it refers to individual, conscious identity. As noted, Abraham referred to the spirit offspring of God as organized intelligences, apparently using the word "intelligences" to mean "spirits." Church authorities have indicated that spirit birth was not the beginning. Spencer W. Kimball, then a member of the Quorum of the Twelve, wrote, "Our spirit matter was eternal and co-existent with God, but it was organized into spirit bodies by our Heavenly Father" (*The Miracle of Forgiveness*, p. 5, Salt Lake City, 1969). Marion G. Romney, of the First Presidency, speaking of people's divine origin as children of God, stated, "Through that birth process, self-existing intelligence was organized into individual spirit beings" (*Ensign* 8 [Nov. 1978]:14). Bruce R. McConkie, an apostle, wrote:

> Abraham used the name *intelligences* to apply to the spirit children of the Eternal Father. The intelligence or spirit element became intelligences after the spirits were born as individual entities (Abr. 3:22–24). Use of this name designates both the primal element from which the spirit offspring were created and also their inherited capacity to grow in grace, knowledge, power, and intelligence itself, until such intelligences, gaining the fulness of all things, become like their Father, the Supreme Intelligence [*MD*, p. 387].

While the revelations leave no doubt as to the existence of intelligent matter prior to its being organized as spirits, speculation sometimes arises regarding the nature of premortal existence and whether there was individual identity and consciousness prior to birth as a spirit. Some hold that the terms "intelligence" and "intelligences" have reference to a form of prespirit conscious self-existence, which included individual identity, variety, and agency (so reasoned B. H. Roberts, pp. 401–423). Others maintain that while these characteristics, attributes, and conditions are eternal, they essentially came together for each individual at the spirit birth. The question of whether prespirit intelligence had individual identity and consciousness remains unanswered. Elder Joseph Fielding Smith gave this caution in 1936:

> Some of our writers have endeavored to explain what an intelligence is, but to do so is futile, for we have never been given any insight into this matter beyond what the Lord has fragmentarily revealed. We know, however, that there is something called intelligence which always existed. It is the real eternal part of man, which was not created or made. This intelligence combined with the spirit constitutes a spiritual identity or individual [p. 10].

No formal pronouncements have been made by the leading councils of the Church to clarify what additional meanings and attributes may be assigned to the word "intelligences," beyond that which identifies intelligences as spirit children of God.

[*See also* First Estate; Intelligence; Premortal Life; Spirit Body.]

BIBLIOGRAPHY

McConkie, Bruce R. *Mormon Doctrine,* pp. 386–87. Salt Lake City, 1966.

Roberts, B. H. "Immortality of Man." *IE* 10 (Apr. 1907):401–423.

Smith, Joseph Fielding. *Progress of Man.* Salt Lake City, 1936.

PAUL NOLAN HYDE

J

JEHOVAH, JESUS CHRIST

The Godhead consists of three separate and distinct beings: the Father, Son, and Holy Ghost (D&C 130:22; A of F 1). While some Christians do not equate Jesus Christ and Jehovah in their theologies, biblical passages indicate that relationship, and latter-day scriptures often refer to Jesus Christ, the Son, as Jehovah (e.g., D&C 110:3–4; Moro. 10:34).

The name Jehovah is an anglicized rendering of the tetragrammaton YHWH, a proper noun in biblical Hebrew that identifies God. Following a Jewish tradition that avoided pronouncing God's name, translators of the King James Version rendered almost all occurrences of YHWH as "Lord." Latter-day Saints view many other occurrences of "Lord" as references to Jehovah, both in the New Testament and in LDS scripture.

Since his PREMORTAL LIFE, Jesus Christ has functioned as the constant associate of the Father working under his direction. In 1916 the First Presidency and the Quorum of the Twelve Apostles issued a doctrinal statement on the relationship between the Father and the Son: "Jesus the Son has represented and yet represents Elohim His Father in power and authority. This is true of Christ in His preexistent, antemortal, or unembodied state, in the which He was known as Jehovah; also during His embodiment in the flesh; . . . and since that period in His resurrected state" (*MFP* 5:31–32).

Throughout scripture, several roles of Jehovah-Jesus Christ are specifically identified.

CREATOR. Jehovah as Creator is attested throughout the Old Testament (e.g., Ps. 24:1–2). Speaking to Moses, God said, "Worlds without number have I created; . . . and by the Son I created them, which is mine Only Begotten" (Moses 1:33). John and others acknowledged Jesus as the Word, the Creator: "In the beginning was the Word; . . . all things were made by him; and without him was not any thing made" (John 1:1–3, 14; cf. Eph. 3:9; Col. 1:16). Similarly, the Book of Mormon teaches, "The Lord Omnipotent who reigneth, who was, and is from all eternity to all eternity, shall come down from heaven among the children of men. . . . And he shall be called Jesus Christ, the Son of God, the Father of heaven and earth, the Creator of all things from the beginning" (Mosiah 3:5–8; cf. 2 Ne. 9:5; 3 Ne. 9:15).

LAWGIVER. To Moses, Jehovah identified himself by the title "I AM THAT I AM"—a variation on the verbal root of YHWH (Ex. 3:14). This title was claimed by Jesus in mortality: "Before Abraham was, I am" (John 8:58; cf. John 4:26). After his resurrection, Jesus told hearers in the Americas, "Behold, I am he that gave the law, and I am he who covenanted with my people Israel; therefore, the law in me is fulfilled, for I have come to fulfil the law" (3 Ne. 15:5; cf. Matt. 5:17).

REDEEMER, DELIVERER, AND ADVOCATE. Jehovah delivered the children of Israel from Egypt. Paul taught that this same being would redeem mankind from sin and death (cf. 1 Cor. 10:1–4). This point is made clear in the Book of Mormon: "The God of our fathers, who were led out of Egypt, . . . yea, the God of Abraham . . . yieldeth himself . . . as a man, into the hands of wicked men . . . to be crucified" (1 Ne. 19:10; cf. 2 Ne. 9:1–26; Mosiah 13:33–35). When the Savior appeared to the Prophet Joseph Smith in the Kirtland Temple on April 3, 1836, "his voice was as the sound of the rushing of great waters, even the voice of Jehovah, saying: I am the first and the last; I am he who liveth, I am he who was slain; I am your advocate with the Father" (D&C 110:3–4).

JUDGE. The Book of Mormon prophet $Moroni_2$ drew attention to "the great Jehovah, the Eternal Judge" (Moro. 10:34), reaffirming what the Psalmist and others had said (e.g., Ps. 9:7–8; Isa. 33:22). Jesus Christ proclaimed that he was the judge: "For the Father . . . hath committed all judgment unto the Son" (John 5:22, 27; cf. Acts 10:42).

IN HIS NAME. In the beginning, men began "to call upon the name of the Lord" (Gen. 4:25, 26; cf. Moses 5:8; 6:4). In Moses's time Jehovah instructed the priests to "put my name upon the children of Israel" (Num. 6:27; cf. Deut. 28:10). Before the coming of Christ, Book of Mormon people took upon themselves his name (Mosiah 5:8–12; Alma 34:38; *see* JESUS CHRIST, TAKING THE NAME OF, UPON ONESELF). In all dispensations, the name of Christ is the only name "whereby salvation can come unto the children of men" (Isa. 43:3, 11; Mosiah 3:17; Acts 4:12; cf. Moses 5:7–9).

Divine names and titles, especially in the Bible, are occasionally ambiguous. The distinction between the Father and the Son is sometimes unclear. For example, the Hebrew term *Elohim*—a title usually applied to the Father by Latter-day Saints—often refers to Jehovah in the Bible (e.g., Isa. 12:2). Furthermore, people prayed to Jehovah as if he were the Father. In some cases, ambiguity may be due to the transmission of the text; in others, it may be explained by divine investiture wherein Christ is given the authority of the Father: "Thus the Father placed His name upon the Son; and Jesus Christ spoke and ministered in and through the Father's name; and so far as power, authority, and Godship are concerned His words and acts were and are those of the Father" (*MFP* 5:32).

BIBLIOGRAPHY

Talmage, James E. *JC*, pp. 32–41.

DAVID R. SEELY

JESUS CHRIST

[*This entry consists of twelve articles:*

Overview
Prophecies About Jesus Christ

Firstborn in the Spirit
Only Begotten in the Flesh
Birth of Jesus Christ
Baptism of Jesus Christ
Ministry of Jesus Christ
Crucifixion of Jesus Christ
Resurrection of Jesus Christ
Forty-Day Ministry and Other Post-Resurrection
Appearances of Jesus Christ
Latter-day Appearances of Jesus Christ
Second Coming of Jesus Christ

These titles are self-explanatory and each emphasizes a major feature about Jesus Christ. The long list of topics illustrates his importance in the doctrines of the Church, and the large amount of information available through the scriptures and the teachings of latter-day prophets.]

OVERVIEW

Jesus Christ is the central figure in the doctrine of The Church of Jesus Christ of Latter-day Saints. The Prophet Joseph Smith explained that "the fundamental principles of our religion are the testimony of the Apostles and Prophets, concerning Jesus Christ, that He died, was buried, and rose again the third day, and ascended into heaven; and all other things which pertain to our religion are only appendages to it" (*TPJS,* p. 121). Latter-day Saints believe that complete salvation is possible only through the life, death, resurrection, doctrines, and ordinances of Jesus Christ and in no other way.

Christ's relationship to mankind is defined in terms of his divine roles in the three phases of existence—premortal, mortal, and postmortal.

PREMORTAL JESUS. In the premortal life, Jesus Christ, whose main title was JEHOVAH, was the firstborn spirit child of God the Father and thus the eldest brother and preeminent above all other spirit children of God. In that FIRST ESTATE, he came to be more intelligent than all other spirits, one "like unto God" (Abr. 3:19, 24), and served as the representative of the Father in the creation of "worlds without number" (Heb. 1:1–3; D&C 76:24; Moses 1:33; 7:30). LDS leaders have declared that all REVELATION since the FALL OF ADAM has been by, and through, Jehovah (Jesus Christ) and that whenever the Father has appeared unto man, it has been to introduce and bear record of the Son (JST John 1:19; *DS* 1:27). He was known to Adam, and the patriarchs from Adam to Noah worshiped him in humble reverence. He was the Almighty God of Abraham, Isaac, and Jacob, the God-Lawgiver on Sinai, the Holy One of Israel. Scriptural records affirm that all the prophets from the beginning spoke or wrote of the time when Jehovah would come to earth in the form of man, in the role of a MESSIAH. Peter said, "to him give all the prophets witness" (Acts 2:25–31; 10:43). Jacob taught that "none of the prophets have written, nor prophesied, save they have spoken concerning this Christ" (Jacob 7:11; cf. Mosiah 3:5–10; 13:33; 3 Ne. 20:24).

MORTAL JESUS. Jehovah was born into this life in Bethlehem of Judea and grew up as Jesus of Nazareth. He came in condescension—leaving his station as the Lord Omnipotent to undertake a mission of pain and humiliation, having everlasting consequences for mankind (see 1 Ne. 11; Mosiah 3:5–10; *see also* CONDESCENSION OF GOD). His life was one of moral perfection—he was sinless and completely submissive to the will of the Father (John 5:30; 2 Cor. 5:21; Heb. 4:15; 1 Pet. 2:22; Mosiah 15:2). Jesus is the model and exemplar of all who seek to acquire the divine nature. As taught by Joseph Smith, the Savior "suffered greater sufferings, and was exposed to more powerful contradictions than any man can be." Through all of this, "he kept the law of God, and remained without sin" (*Lectures on Faith*, Lecture 5, paragraph 2). The risen Lord asked the Nephites, "What manner of men ought ye to be? Verily I say unto you, even as I am" (3 Ne. 27:27; cf. 12:48).

Jesus was more, however, than sinlessness, goodness, and love. He was more than a model and teacher, more than the embodiment of compassion. He was able to accomplish his unique ministry—a ministry of reconciliation and salvation—because of who and what he was. President Ezra Taft Benson stated, "The Church of Jesus Christ of Latter-day Saints proclaims that Jesus Christ is the Son of God in the most literal sense. The body in which He performed His mission in the flesh was fathered by that same Holy Being we worship as God, our Eternal Father. Jesus was not the son of Joseph, nor was He begotten by the Holy Ghost. He is the Son of the Eternal Father!" (Benson, p. 4). From Mary, a mortal woman, Jesus inherited mortality, including the capacity to die. From his exalted Father he inherited immortality, the capacity to live forever. The Savior's dual nature—man and God—enabled him to make an infinite atonement, an accomplishment that no other person, no matter how capable or gifted, could do (cf. Alma 34:9–12). First, he was able, in GETHSEMANE, in some majestic but incomprehensible manner, to assume the burdens and effects of the sins of all mankind and, in doing so, to engage suffering and anguish beyond what a mere mortal could endure (2 Ne. 9:21; Mosiah 3:7; D&C 18:11; 19:16; Taylor, p. 148). Second, he was able to submit to physical death, to willingly lay down his life and then take up his body again in the RESURRECTION (John 5:26; 10:17, 18; 2 Ne. 2:8).

POSTMORTAL JESUS. Latter-day Saints believe that between his death on the cross at Calvary and his resurrection, Jesus' spirit entered the SPIRIT WORLD, a postmortal place of the disembodied, those awaiting and preparing for the reunion of their bodies and spirits. Peter taught that Christ went into this realm to preach to the spirits in prison (1 Pet. 3:18–20; 4:6). A modern revelation explains that Jesus did not go himself among the wicked and disobedient who had rejected the truth. Rather, he ministered to the righteous in PARADISE and organized and empowered them to teach those spirits who remained in darkness under the bondage of sin and ignorance (see D&C 138:29–32). Thus, the Messiah's mission to "preach good tidings unto the meek," to "bind up the brokenhearted, to proclaim liberty to the captives, and the opening of the prison to them that are bound" (Isa. 61:1; Luke 4:18–19) extended after death into the life beyond (*see* SALVATION FOR THE DEAD; SPIRIT PRISON).

Jesus "broke the bands of death"; he was the "first fruits of them that slept" (1 Cor. 15:20; Alma 11:40–41). He rose from the tomb with an immortal, glorified body and initiated the first resurrection or the resurrection of the just, the raising of the righteous dead who had lived from the days of Adam to the time of Christ (Matt. 27:52–53; Mosiah 15:21–25; Hel. 14:25–26; 3 Ne. 23:7–13). Jesus Christ will come again to earth in power and glory. The first resurrection, begun at the time of Christ's resurrection, will resume as the righteous dead from the meridian of time to his second coming return with him in resurrected and immortal glory. This second advent will also signal the beginning of the MILLENNIUM, a thousand years of earthly peace during which Satan will be bound and have no power over the hearts of those who remain on earth (Rev. 20:1–2; 1 Ne. 22:26). Joseph Smith taught that "Christ and the resurrected Saints will reign over the earth during the thousand years. They will not probably dwell upon the earth [constantly], but will visit it when they please, or when it is necessary to govern it" (*TPJS*, p. 268). During this era, Jesus will reveal himself, and, in the words of Isaiah, "the earth shall be full of the knowledge of the Lord, as the waters cover the sea" (Isa. 11:9; Heb. 2:14).

Jesus Christ is the God of the whole earth and invites all nations and people to come unto him. His mortal ministry, as described in the New Testament, was primarily among the Jews. Following his death and resurrection he appeared to his "other sheep," groups of scattered Israelites. First, as described in the Book of Mormon, he ministered to the Nephites in America. He taught them his gospel and authorized them to officiate in his name. He then visited the lost tribes, the ten northern tribes of Israel, which were scattered at the time of the Assyrian captivity in 721 B.C. (John 10:16; 3 Ne. 15:12–16; 17:4). In addition to the appearances recorded in the Bible and the Book of Mormon, which are ancient scriptural witnesses of the Redeemer, Joseph Smith testified that Jesus Christ, in company with his Eternal Father, appeared to him near Palmyra, New York, in the spring of 1820 to open the DISPENSATION OF THE FULNESS OF TIMES (JS—H 1:1–20). On subsequent occasions the risen Savior has visited and revealed himself to his latter-day prophets and continues to direct his latter-day Church and kingdom (*see* JESUS CHRIST: LATTER-DAY APPEARANCES OF).

Latter-day Saints center their worship in, and direct their prayers to, God the Eternal Father. This, as with all things—sermons, testimonies, prayers, and sacraments or ordinances—they do in the name of Jesus Christ (2 Ne. 25:16; Jacob 4:4–5; 3 Ne. 18:19; D&C 20:29; Moses 5:8). The Saints also worship Christ the Son as they acknowledge him as the source of truth and redemption, as the light and life of the world, as the way to the Father (John 14:6; 2 Ne. 25:29; 3 Ne. 11:11). They look to him for deliverance and seek to be like him (see D&C 93:12–20; McConkie, 1978, pp. 568–69). In emphasizing the transforming power of Christ's example, President David O. McKay observed that "no man can sincerely resolve to apply to his daily life the teachings of Jesus of Nazareth without sensing a change in his own nature" (*IE* 65 [June 1962]:405).

Jesus Christ brought to pass the bodily resurrection of all who have lived or who will yet live upon the earth (1 Cor. 15:21–22; Alma 11:40–42). Because he overcame the world, all men and women may—by exercising faith in him, trusting in his merits, and receiving his grace—repent of their sins and know the peace of personal purity and spiritual wholeness (John 14:27; Phil. 4:7; 2 Ne. 2:8; 25:23; Enos 1:1–8; Mosiah 4:1–3). Those who have learned to rely on the Lord and lean upon his tender mercies "sing the song of redeeming love" (Alma 5:26). Nephi$_1$, the Book of Mormon prophet-leader, exulted, "I glory in my Jesus, for he hath redeemed my soul from hell" (2 Ne. 33:6). "We talk of Christ, we rejoice in Christ, we preach of Christ, we prophesy of Christ, . . . that our children may know to what source they may look for a remission of their sins" (2 Ne. 25:26). A latter-day apostle has written:

> I believe in Christ;
> He stands supreme!
> From him I'll gain my fondest dream;
> And while I strive through grief and pain,
> His voice is heard: Ye shall obtain.
> I believe in Christ; so come what may,
> With him I'll stand in that great day
> When on this earth he comes again
> To rule among the sons of men.
> [Bruce R. McConkie, "I Believe in Christ," no. 134, *Hymns*, 1985]

BIBLIOGRAPHY

Benson, Ezra Taft. *Come Unto Christ.* Salt Lake City, 1983.

Dahl, Larry E., and Charles D. Tate, eds. *The Lectures on Faith in Historical Perspective.* Provo, Utah, 1990.

McConkie, Bruce R. *The Promised Messiah.* Salt Lake City, 1978.

——. *The Mortal Messiah,* 4 vols. Salt Lake City, 1979–1981.

——. *The Millennial Messiah.* Salt Lake City, 1982.

Talmage, James E. *Jesus the Christ.* Salt Lake City, 1972.

Taylor, John. *The Mediation and Atonement of Our Lord and Savior Jesus Christ.* Salt Lake City, 1882.

ROBERT L. MILLET

PROPHECIES ABOUT JESUS CHRIST

Prophecies concerning the birth, mortal ministry, and post-Resurrection ministry of Jesus Christ permeate the Bible. Moreover, the latter-day scriptures used by members of The Church of Jesus Christ of Latter-day Saints—the Book of Mormon, which bears the modern subtitle "Another Testament of Jesus Christ," the Doctrine and Covenants, and the Pearl of Great Price—contain numerous prophetic utterances about the MESSIAH that in general are clearer than those in the Bible. For Latter-day Saints, these four volumes of scripture constitute the principal sources for the prophecies about Jesus' life and mission. This article reviews the prophecies concerning Jesus most often referred to by Latter-day Saints.

The New Testament teaches that the divinity of Jesus Christ was recognized by some during his own lifetime, as well as by God's ancient prophets. For example, Andrew announced to his brother Simon Peter that he had found the Messiah (John 1:41). The Book of Mormon prophets Abinadi and $Nephi_2$, son of $Helaman_2$, taught that all of God's prophets, including Moses and Abraham, "have testified of the coming of Christ" (Mosiah 13:33; Hel. 8:16–22; cf. Jacob 4:4).

The scriptures are rich in prophetic detail concerning the birth of Jesus. Isaiah declared, "Behold, a virgin shall conceive, and bear a son, and shall call his name Immanuel" (Isa. 7:14), a passage that Matthew cited as having reference to Jesus (Matt. 1:22–23). Micah poetically pronounced, "Bethlehem Ephratah, though thou be little among the thousands of Judah, yet out of thee shall he come forth unto me that is to be ruler in Israel; whose goings forth have been from of old, from everlasting" (Micah 5:2). Among Book of Mormon people, $Nephi_1$ foretold that "even six hundred years from the time that my father [Lehi] left Jerusalem," the Savior would be raised up (1 Ne. 10:4; 19:8). Samuel the Lamanite (c. 6 B.C.) told a doubting generation of the signs to be given in the Western Hemisphere that would accompany the birth of Christ (Hel. 14:2–8). These included the appearance of a new star and two days and one night without darkness (Hel. 14:4–5).

Some prophecies of the Messiah's birth were fulfilled when the angel of the Lord announced to shepherds near Bethlehem: "Unto you is born this day in the city of David a Saviour, which is Christ the Lord" (Luke 2:11). On the other side of the world, the day before his birth, the Lord announced to his prophet $Nephi_3$ that he should be of "good cheer; for behold, the time is at hand, and on this night shall the sign be given, and on the morrow come I into the world, to show unto the world that I will fulfill all that which I have caused to be spoken by the mouth of my holy prophets" (3 Ne. 1:13).

Latter-day Saints believe that the mission of Jesus Christ has been known since earliest times. The angel of the Lord declared to Adam that the Son was "the Only Begotten of the Father from the beginning," and that Adam would "be redeemed, and all mankind, even as many as will," if they "repent and call upon God in the name of the Son forevermore" (Moses 5:8–9). The message that Jesus Christ is the Advocate, the Redeemer, and the Intercessor, and that "There is no other way nor means whereby man can be saved, only through the atoning blood of Jesus Christ" (Hel. 5:9), has been repeated by God's representatives in all ages (see Moses 5:14–15; Isa. 53:4–5; Acts 4:12; 2 Ne. 2:9–10; 9:6–7; Mosiah 4:8; 5:8; Alma 11:40; D&C 45:3).

Events of Jesus' mortal life and ministry are found in numerous prophecies. In the Joseph Smith Translation of the Bible (JST), an insightful passage states "that Jesus grew up with his brethren, and waxed strong, and waited upon the Lord for the time of his ministry to come . . . [and] needed not that any man should teach him" (JST Matt. 3:24–25). $Nephi_1$ saw in a vision, and King Benjamin learned from an angel, that the Savior would perform healings, cast out devils, and raise the dead (1 Ne. 11:31; Mosiah 3:5–6). According to New Testament writers, Jesus' triumphal ride into Jerusalem on a beast of burden was foreknown by Zechariah (Zech. 9:9; Matt. 21:5; John 12:14–15), as was his betrayal for thirty pieces of silver (Zech. 11:12–13; Matt. 27:9–10). From the angel, King Benjamin learned that blood would come "from every pore, so great shall be his [Jesus'] anguish for the wickedness and the abominations of his people" (Mosiah 3:7). Christ's rejection by his own people was prophesied both by himself and by others (e.g., Ps. 69:8; Mosiah 15:5; 3 Ne. 9:16; John 1:11).

Many years before the event, prophets such as Enoch and $Nephi_1$ saw the Lord lifted up on the cross (Moses 7:47, 55; 1 Ne. 11:33). Isaiah prophesied that the suffering servant would make "his grave with the wicked, and with the rich in his death" (Isa. 53:9). The Book of Mormon prophet Abinadi (c. 150 B.C.) associated that passage in Isaiah with Jesus (Mosiah 15), and its fulfillment was recorded by Luke (23:32–33). Matthew tells of the physical disturbances that occurred at the moment Jesus gave up his life (Matt. 27:50–54), events that Zenos saw in a vision hundreds of years earlier (1 Ne. 19:10–12).

Christ foretold his own death and resurrection when he answered a demand for a sign: "Destroy this temple [physical body], and in three days I will raise it up" (John 2:19). Jesus' eventual victory over death was known by the ancients, for God told Enoch that "righteousness will I send down out of heaven; and truth will I send forth out of the earth, to bear testimony of mine Only Begotten; his resurrection from the dead; yea, and also the resurrection of all men" (Moses 7:62). Later, inspired men in the Americas learned of this event. Nephi$_1$, Jacob, Benjamin, and Samuel proclaimed the time when Christ "layeth down his life according to the flesh, and taketh it again by the power of the Spirit, that he may bring to pass the resurrection of the dead, being the first that should rise" (2 Ne. 2:8; cf. 1 Ne. 10:11; Mosiah 3:10; Hel. 14:15–17).

Jesus Christ's ministry to the SPIRIT PRISON (1 Pet. 3:18–19) was anticipated by Isaiah when he recorded that "after many days shall [the prisoners gathered in the pit] be visited" (Isa. 24:22). Section 138 of the Doctrine and Covenants records a vision of this event, received by a modern prophet, President Joseph F. Smith, when he saw "the hosts of the dead, both small and great . . . awaiting the advent of the Son of God into the spirit world, to declare their redemption from the bands of death" (D&C 138:11, 16).

The righteous of earlier ages have looked forward to the second coming of Jesus Christ. Jesus told his disciples to "watch therefore, for ye know neither the day nor the hour wherein the Son of man cometh" (Matt. 25:13; cf. D&C 49:6–7), and indicated that he would come "as a thief" in the night (1 Thess. 5:2; Rev. 3:3; 16:15). He revealed to Joseph Smith that a universal revelation would be given so that "all flesh shall see me together" (D&C 101:23; cf. Isa. 40:5). Isaiah foresaw events of the second coming (Isa. 63–66), as did Daniel, Micah, Zechariah, and Malachi (Dan. 7:13; Micah 1:3; Zech. 12:10; 13:6; Mal. 3:12). When the resurrected Lord appeared among the Nephites, he spoke about his eventual triumphant return to earth, quoting Malachi, chapters 3 and 4 (3 Ne. 24–25).

The Prophet Joseph Smith clarified and added to prophecies of the events surrounding Jesus' second coming, including the restoration of the gospel (D&C 133:36–37), the resurrection of the dead (D&C 88:95–102), the beginning of the Millennium (D&C 43:30–31), and the binding of Satan for a thousand years (D&C 45:55). Both ancient and modern prophets foretold that, at the end of a thousand years of peace, Satan would be loosed and the final battle between good and evil would be waged (Rev. 20:7–8; D&C 43:31). John the Revelator and the ancient prophet Ether, who both saw in vision all of these events, beheld the renewal of the earth and the establishment of the New Jerusalem (Rev. 21; Ether 13:1–10). This city will have "no need of the sun, neither of the moon, to shine in it: for the glory of God did lighten it, and the Lamb is the light thereof" (Rev. 21:23).

BIBLIOGRAPHY

Jackson, Kent P. "The Beginnings of Christianity in the Book of Mormon." In *The Book of Mormon: The Keystone Scripture,* ed. P. Chessman. Provo, Utah, 1988.

Matthews, Robert J. "The Doctrine of the Atonement—The Revelation of the Gospel to Adam." In *Studies in Scripture,* ed. R. Millet and K. Jackson, Vol. 2, pp. 111–29. Salt Lake City, 1985.

——. *A Bible! A Bible!* Salt Lake City, 1990.

McConkie, Bruce R. *The Promised Messiah.* Salt Lake City, 1978.

——. *The Millennial Messiah.* Salt Lake City, 1982.

GARY LEE WALKER

FIRSTBORN IN THE SPIRIT

Fundamental to the teachings of The Church of Jesus Christ of Latter-day Saints is the concept that all human beings were born as spirit sons and daughters of heavenly parents before any were born as mortals to earthly parents. Latter-day Saints believe that the eldest and firstborn spirit child of God is Jehovah and that it was he who was later born with a physical body to Mary as Jesus Christ. That is, Jehovah of the Old Testament became Jesus Christ of the New Testament when he was born into mortality. The Psalmist refers to the Messiah as the firstborn (Ps. 89:27), and the apostle Paul speaks of Jesus as the "firstborn among many brethren" (Rom. 8:29; cf. Heb. 2:17) and as the "firstborn of every creature" (Col. 1:15). Perhaps the most authoritative statement on the subject is from the Savior himself, who declared to the Prophet Joseph Smith, "I was in the beginning with the Father, and am the Firstborn" (D&C 93:21). In 1909 the First Presidency of the Church declared:

> The Father of Jesus is our Father also. Jesus Himself taught this truth, when He instructed His disciples how to pray: "Our Father which art in heaven," etc. Jesus, however, is the firstborn among all the sons of God—the first begotten in the spirit, and the only begotten in the flesh. He is our elder brother, and we, like Him, are in the image of God. All men and women are in the similitude of the universal Father and Mother, and are literally the sons and daughters of Deity [*MFP* 4:203].

JERRY C. GILES

ONLY BEGOTTEN IN THE FLESH

Ancient and modern scriptures use the title Only Begotten to emphasize the divine nature of Jesus Christ. Latter-day Saints recognize Jesus as literally the Only Begotten Son of God the Father in the flesh (John 3:16; D&C 93:11; Moses 6:52). This title signifies that Jesus' physical body was the offspring of a mortal mother and of the eternal Father (Luke 1:35, 1 Ne. 11:18). It is LDS doctrine that Jesus Christ is the child of Mary and GOD THE FATHER, "not in violation of natural law but in accordance with a higher manifestation thereof" (*JC*, p. 81).

The fact of Jesus' being the literal Son of God in the flesh is crucial to the ATONEMENT, which could not have been accomplished by an ordinary man. Because of the FALL OF ADAM, all mankind are subject to physical death and are shut out from the presence of God. The human family is unable to save itself. Divine law required the sacrifice of a sinless, infinite, and eternal being—a God—someone not dominated by the Fall, to redeem mankind from their lost and fallen condition (Alma 34:9–14; cf. 42:15). This price of redemption was more than any mortal person could pay, and included the spiritual sufferings and physical agony in GETHSEMANE (Luke 22:44; Mosiah 3:7; D&C 19:18). To complete the Atonement by physical death and RESURRECTION, it was necessary that Jesus be able to lay down his physical body and also be able to take it up again. He could do this only because he had life in himself, which he inherited from God his

Father (John 5:26; 10:17–18). Christ inherited the ability to die from his mortal mother and the power to resurrect himself from his immortal Father. Dying was for him a voluntary, deliberate act for mankind, made possible only because he was the Only Begotten of the Father (D&C 20:18–26).

BIBLIOGRAPHY
McConkie, Bruce R. *The Promised Messiah*, pp. 467–73. Salt Lake City, 1978.

GERALD HANSEN, JR.

BIRTH OF JESUS CHRIST

Latter-day Saint scripture affirms unequivocally that the birth of Jesus Christ was the mortal advent on earth of an actual God, a second and distinct member of the GODHEAD. Adam was assured redemption through the Only Begotten of the Father, and every true prophet had a hope of Christ's glory (Moses 5:6–10; Jacob 4:4).

Biblical prophecies and accounts of Jesus' birth are confirmed and enlarged in latter-day scripture. While Matthew's birth narrative emphasizes Christ's kingship (drawing attention to the magi, King Herod, and Bethlehem, the city of King David) and Luke's account accents Jesus' humility and holiness (mentioning the lowly manger, the shepherds, and the heavenly choirs), the Book of Mormon focuses on his coming as a fulfillment of a loving God's plan that was established from before the foundation of the world.

The time of Jesus' birth, along with the purposes of his mortal ministry, were established in the PREMORTAL LIFE (*see* COUNCIL IN HEAVEN; Moses 4:1–4; 1 Ne. 10:2–4; Mosiah 3:5–10). A detailed vision of the anticipated Savior's birth was recorded by Nephi$_1$, a Book of Mormon prophet, shortly after 600 B.C. (1 Ne. 11:7–24). He foresaw a virgin in the city of Nazareth who was carried away in the spirit, and then saw the virgin again with a child in her arms, whom an angel identified as the Son of God. Nephi described Christ's coming as the CONDESCENSION OF GOD, which may be understood in two respects: first, in that God the Father, a perfected and glorified personage of flesh and bones, condescended to become the father of a mortal offspring, born of Mary; and second, in that Jesus (Jehovah), the God who created worlds without number (Moses 1:32–33; John 1:1–4, 14; Heb. 1:1–2), willingly submitted himself to all the trials and pains of mortality (Mosiah 3:5–8; *MD*, p. 155).

For Latter-day Saints, the paternity of Jesus is not obscure. He was the literal, biological son of an immortal, tangible Father and Mary, a mortal woman. Jesus is the only person born who deserves the title "the Only Begotten Son of God" (John 3:16; Benson, p. 3; *see* JESUS CHRIST: ONLY BEGOTTEN IN THE FLESH). He was not the son of the Holy Ghost; it was only through the HOLY GHOST that the power of the Highest overshadowed Mary (Luke 1:35; 1 Ne. 11:19).

The place where the nativity should occur was a point of public controversy in Jesus' day (John 7:40–43). The Book of Mormon prophet $Alma_2$, about 83 B.C., foretold that Christ's birthplace would be "at Jerusalem which is the land of our forefathers" (Alma 7:10), referring to the region surrounding the city itself: "Christ was born in a village some six miles from the city of Jerusalem . . . in what we now know the ancients themselves designated as "the land of Jerusalem"" (*CWHN* 6:102).

The Bible and the Book of Mormon report the appearance of great signs in the Western Hemisphere at the time of the birth of the Messiah for the benefit of the faithful. For example, about 6 B.C. Samuel the Lamanite prophesied that lights would appear in heaven and that there would be no darkness during the night when Christ was born (Hel. 14:3–7). On the day when Samuel's five-year prophecy was about to expire and the unbelievers were accordingly about to execute those who had believed his words, Samuel's prophecies of the Savior's birth were fulfilled (3 Ne. 1:4–23). In the New World, as in the Old, "angels did appear unto men, wise men, and did declare unto them glad tidings of great joy" (Hel. 16:14).

BIBLIOGRAPHY

Benson, Ezra Taft. *Come Unto Christ.* Salt Lake City, 1983.
Brown, Raymond E. *The Birth of the Messiah.* Garden City, N.Y., 1977.
McConkie, Bruce R. *The Mortal Messiah,* Vol. 1, pp. 313–66. Salt Lake City, 1981.

ANDREW C. SKINNER

BAPTISM OF JESUS CHRIST

At the commencement of his public ministry, Jesus went from Galilee to the Jordan, where he was baptized by John the Baptist. He did thereby "humble himself before the Father" and witness to him "that he would be obedient to him" (2 Ne. 31:7). For Latter-day Saints this event shows that Jesus by his own example taught that all people must be baptized by immersion by one having authority. All persons must also receive the HOLY GHOST in order to obtain the testimony of Jesus (see John 1:32–34; Rev. 1:2; 19:10) and enter into the kingdom of heaven.

Jesus was baptized by immersion by John, who was ordained when eight days old by an angel of God to "make straight the way of the Lord" (D&C 84:28). As Jesus came up out of the water, John saw the heavens open and the spirit of God descending upon Jesus, and the voice of GOD THE FATHER declared to John, "This is my beloved Son, in whom I am well pleased" (Matt. 3:17). Thereafter John bore record that Jesus was the Son of God (John 1:33–34; D&C 93:15–17). At the baptism of Jesus all three members of the GODHEAD were manifest, thus revealing the separate identities of the Father, the Son, and the Holy Ghost.

Many have wondered why Jesus needed baptism, since he was without sin. Some have seen this as "an act of simple submissive obedience on the part of the Perfect One" (A. Edersheim, *Life and Times of Jesus the Messiah* [reprinted, Grand Rapids, Mich., 1971], p. 280); others have suggested that Jesus still faced "a possibility of a subtle sin: the sin of shrinking from what might lie ahead" and thus was baptized to fortify himself with "utter consecration" and to express to his nation "the urgency of commitment" (*Interpreter's Bible*, Vol. 8, p. 78).

However, Latter-day Saints understand from the Bible and the Book of Mormon that Jesus was baptized "to fulfill all righteousness," which means that Jesus humbled himself before the Father, witnessed to the Father that he would obey him, and thereby showed mankind the narrowness of the gate leading to ETERNAL LIFE (2 Ne. 31:6–9). In submitting to baptism Jesus "set the example" for all mankind, for if Jesus, being holy, was baptized "to fulfil all righteousness . . . how much more need have we, being unholy, to be baptized?" (2 Ne. 31:5; see also *AF*, chap. 6). Those who follow his example and his gospel with full purpose of heart, with honesty before God, and "with real intent, repenting of [their] sins," are promised that they will receive the BAPTISM OF FIRE AND OF THE HOLY GHOST, and be able to "speak with the tongue of angels, and shout praises" to God (2 Ne. 31:13).

BIBLIOGRAPHY
Farley, S. Brent. "The Baptism and Temptation of Jesus." In *Studies in Scripture,* ed. K. Jackson and R. Millett, Vol. 5, pp. 175–87. Salt Lake City, 1986.
McConkie, Bruce R. *The Mortal Messiah,* Vol. 1, pp. 399–404. Salt Lake City, 1979.

J. PHILIP SCHAELLING

MINISTRY OF JESUS CHRIST

The central role played by Jesus' mortal ministry in Latter-day Saint doctrine and belief is well expressed in Joseph Smith's statement that "the fundamental principles of our religion are the testimony of the Apostles and Prophets, concerning Jesus Christ, that He died, was buried, and rose again the third day, and ascended into heaven; and all other things which pertain to our religion are only appendages to it" (*TPJS,* p. 121; *HC* 3:30).

Latter-day Saints share with many other Christians the acceptance of the four New Testament gospels and Acts 1:1–11 as essentially accurate historical accounts of the earthly ministry of Jesus Christ. While not biblical inerrantists, their confidence in the biblical record is strengthened in two unique ways: First, they believe specific elements of Christ's earthly ministry to have been revealed beforehand to pre-Christian prophets. These REVELATIONS agree with subsequent accounts in the gospels. Second, they believe that the risen Jesus himself has affirmed many details of that biblical account. Thus, the Book of Mormon and other texts of the specifically Latter-day Saint canon are regarded as "proving to the world that the holy scriptures are true" (D&C 20:11; cf. 1 Ne. 13:39).

That God's Son would come to earth and take upon himself a physical body, for example, was foreknown by many prophets (1 Ne. 13:42; Enos 1:8; Mosiah 3:5; Hel. 8:13–22; Ether 3:15–17). The approximate date of his coming was also known (1 Ne. 10:4; 19:8; 2 Ne. 25:19; Hel. 14:2). Several ancient believers were privileged to see him before his mortal advent (2 Ne. 2:4; 11:2; Alma 19:13; Ether 3:14; 9:22; D&C 107:49, 54; Moses 1:2; 7:4; Abr. 2:6–11; cf. Isa. 6:1–3). His name-title, Jesus Christ, (i.e., "Savior Anointed") was known long beforehand, as were the name and virginity of his mother and the place of his birth (1 Ne. 11:13–14, 18–20; 2 Ne. 25:19; Mosiah 3:8; Alma 7:10; Ether 3:14; Moses 6:52, 57; 7:50; cf. Micah 5:2). Ancient prophets foresaw his baptism, predicting even its location and specific details of the mission of John the Baptist (1 Ne. 10:8–10). Nephi$_1$ knew that the Savior would call twelve apostles to assist in his ministry (1 Ne. 11:34–36; 12:9; 13:26, 40–41; 14:20, 24, 27), and King Benjamin prophesied of his many miracles (Mosiah 3:5–6). Jesus' atoning death by crucifixion was well known to pre-Christian prophets, who understood that it would be accompanied by three days of darkness preceding his resurrection (1 Ne. 10:11; 11:33; 19:10; 2 Ne. 25:14; Mosiah 3:9–10; Alma 7:11; Hel. 14:14, 20, 27; Moses 7:55). Indeed, sacrificial practices from Adam onward, including the rituals of the Law of Moses, prefigured Christ and, furthermore, were recognized as doing so by many who performed them (Jacob 4:5; Moses 5:5–7).

Later LDS scriptures, including the words of the risen Jesus himself, confirm such details of the New Testament record as the unity of the Sermon on the Mount (3 Ne. 12–14) and the authenticity of some of his separate sayings (3 Ne. 15:12–24). His pain in the garden of GETHSEMANE is attested (D&C 19:18; cf. Mosiah 3:7), as are his crucifixion (D&C 20:23; 21:9; 35:2; 45:52; 46:13; 53:2), his resurrection on the third day (Morm. 7:5; D&C 18:12; 20:23), and his identity as the long-awaited suffering Savior (3 Ne. 11:10–11). His earthly agonies are said to qualify him as an intercessor between God and man (D&C 45:4; cf. Isa. 53:12). In such texts as Doctrine and Covenants section 7 and the Joseph Smith Translation of the Bible (JST), Latter-day Saints believe that they have been granted more complete information on Jesus' Palestinian ministry. (Interestingly, the JST anticipates modern scholarly emphasis on the individual character of the New Testament gospels by labeling each one as the "testimony" of its respective author. This same view seems to underlie Doctrine and Covenants 88:141.)

Gospel accounts inform and underscore LDS understanding of the earthly ministry of Jesus, in whom Latter-day Saints see God physically present among his people. Not only did Jesus perform miracles, expressing thereby his power over both demons and natural elements, but he explicitly affirmed his unity of purpose with the Father (John 14:8–10; 17:21) and his identity as the Jehovah of the Old Testament (John 8:56–59). While Moses ascended the mountain to receive the old law, Jesus ascended a mount to proclaim a new one (cf. 3 Ne. 15:4–5). Moses himself was present at the transfiguration (Matt. 17:1–8). LDS scriptures further affirm the New Testament gospels' warm portrait of Jesus' compassion for sinners, his concern for the poor, and his love for children. They portray him as a popular teacher who taught with parables, preached in synagogues, confronted hypocrisy, and won the love and admiration of many of his hearers.

Latter-day Saints recall, too, the reaction of Jesus' hearers to the Sermon on the Mount: "For he taught them as one having authority, and not as the scribes" (Matt. 7:29). Just as he did not call upon the power of others to perform miracles, Jesus needed no precedents to justify his teachings. In himself he had power over death—both over the death of others (as in the healing of Lazarus, the daughter of Jairus, and the son of the widow of Nain) and his own death (John 5:26; 10:17–18). Thus, Latter-day Saints join with other Christians in an acceptance of Jesus of Nazareth as their redeemer from death. But he is also the source of priesthood authority, who called and empowered ordinary, untrained men to serve him in a newly organized church and, acting for him in his capacity as "the good Shepherd," to "feed his sheep" (John 21:15–17) through both teaching and priesthood ordinances. They reject claims of a dichotomy between the priestly and the prophetic in his ministry. They note that he taught the necessity of baptism and submitted to that requirement himself (John 3:1–5; Matt. 3:15). They recall that he reverenced the temple of his day and expected others to do likewise (Luke 2:41–50; John 2:13–17).

LDS understanding of the role of faith and works in salvation is grounded in the insistence of Jesus that love for him will express itself in obedience to his COMMANDMENTS (John 14:15; cf. John 15:14; Matt. 5–7). His call for his followers to be perfect (Matt. 5:48) is rendered plausible by the fact that he overcame the same temptations that beset them (Heb. 4:15–16; Matt. 4:1–11; Luke 4:1–13) and that he suffered for their transgressions (Mosiah 3:7; Isa. 53:3–12). Indeed, Latter-day Saints are informed by their scriptures that it is at least partially because of the experience gained and the empathy achieved during his earthly sojourn that Jesus knows how to minister to the needs of those who trust in him (Alma 7:12; D&C 62:1; 88:6).

BIBLIOGRAPHY

McConkie, Bruce R. *The Mortal Messiah,* 4 vols. Salt Lake City, 1979–1981.

Talmage, James E. *JC.* Salt Lake City, 1915.

Taylor, John. *The Mediation and Atonement of Jesus Christ.* Salt Lake City, 1882; repr. 1964.

DANIEL C. PETERSON

CRUCIFIXION OF JESUS CHRIST

Crucifixion was the form of execution suffered by Jesus Christ on Calvary as the necessary conclusion to his voluntary infinite atoning sacrifice begun in GETHSEMANE (*see* ATONEMENT). Many people supported and followed Jesus, but a small group of influential Judaean leaders, who disagreed with his doctrines and felt threatened by his popularity, succeeded in having the Roman governor, Pontius Pilate, condemn him to death.

LDS scriptures give prophetic witness that crucifixion would be the method of the Savior's death (e.g., 1 Ne. 19:10–13; 2 Ne. 10:3–5; Mosiah 3:9; 15:7; Moses 7:55). Israelites did not crucify. They did hang executed bodies ignominiously "on a tree" for part of a day (Deut. 21:22–23; cf. Acts 5:30), but for crucifixion it was necessary to invoke Roman law and practice.

Crucifixion was a form of execution probably begun by the Persians and used in Egypt and Carthage. The Romans perfected it as a torture designed to produce maximum pain and a slow death. Reserved for the vilest of criminals and rarely administered to Roman citizens, crucifixion was customarily preceded by flogging the back, buttocks, and legs with a short whip consisting of leather thongs with small iron balls or sharp pieces of sheep bone attached. The weakened victim was then made to carry at least a portion of the cross to the site of crucifixion. Romans commonly used large nails to fix the wrists and palms to the cross bar and the feet to the vertical portion of the cross. The nails inflicted terrible pain but caused no immediate life-threatening injury. A person could live in agony for hours or even days. The body's position made breathing difficult since hanging by the arms kept the chest expanded so that exhaling required the active use of the diaphragm. If the sufferer pushed with his feet, he elevated his body, placing the chest in a more natural position and making it easier to breathe. Soldiers sometimes hastened death by breaking the legs of the victim, making it almost impossible to push the body high enough to breathe.

After Jesus had hung on the cross for several hours, he forgave the soldiers who had crucified him (Luke 23:34; JST Luke 23:35) and voluntarily gave up his life (cf. John 10:18), commending his spirit into his Father's hands. The Romans broke the legs of the two who were crucified with Jesus, but believing that he was already dead, they merely thrust a spear into his side (John 19:33–34).

BIBLIOGRAPHY

Edwards, William D.; Wesley J. Gabel; and Floyd E. Hosmer. "On the Physical Death of Jesus Christ." *Journal of the American Medical Association,* 255 (1986):1455–63.

Hengel, Martin. *Crucifixion.* Philadelphia, 1977.

MERRILL C. OAKS

RESURRECTION OF JESUS CHRIST

Latter-day Saints view the resurrection of Jesus Christ as the most glorious event of all time. Having the power to lay down his body and to "take it again" (John 10:18), the Savior conquered death for himself and all mankind (1 Cor. 15:22). LDS faith in the literal and physical resurrection of Jesus is greatly strengthened by ancient and modern testimonies of many witnesses.

The Book of Mormon contains prophecies of the resurrection of Jesus years before the actual event. The prophet Nephi$_1$ declared, "Behold, they will crucify him; and . . . he shall rise from the dead" (2 Ne. 25:13; also 1 Ne. 19:10). In the Bible Jesus himself prophesied that on "the third day he shall be raised again" (Matt. 17:23).

The third day did come, and Jesus became the "firstfruits of them that slept" (1 Cor. 15:20), his spirit permanently reuniting with his body in a glorified, immortal state. His resurrected body was not subject to pain, disease, or death. It could pass through walls; it could defy the earthly laws of gravity; but it was a tangible "glorious body" (Phil. 3:21) composed of flesh and bones. Jesus said to his disciples, "Behold my hands and my feet, that it is I myself: handle me, and see; for a spirit hath not flesh and bones, as ye see me have" (Luke 24:39). He then ate broiled fish and honeycomb in their presence as a further witness of his corporeal nature.

Latter-day Saints firmly distinguish themselves from those who deny the physical resurrection of Jesus or claim that his divine nature is solely spiritual, with his postmortal appearances being merely temporary physical or mystical manifestations (Nibley, pp. 156–59). They find such doctrine inconsistent with the words of Paul, who taught that the resurrected Christ "dieth no more" (Rom. 6:9), meaning that his resurrected body would never again be separated from his spirit (James 2:26; Alma 11:45).

In his resurrected state, Jesus retained the prints of nails in his hands and feet as a special manifestation to the world. Such marks, however, are only temporary. After all have confessed that he is the Christ, his resurrected body will, like those of all mankind, be restored to its "proper and perfect frame" (Alma 40:23).

Once resurrected, Jesus "gained the keys . . . to open the graves for all men" (*DS* 1:128), and with those keys he opened the gates of the resurrection: The "graves were opened" and "many saints did arise and appear unto many" (Matt. 27:52; 3 Ne. 23:11).

Christ's resurrection was not hidden. Witnesses of this event were both legion and varied: the women at the tomb (Luke 24:1–10); Mary in the garden (John 20:11–18); ten apostles together (Luke 24:36–43); eleven apostles, including doubting Thomas (John 20:24–29); two disciples on the road to Emmaus (Luke 24:13–24); "above five hundred brethren at once" (1 Cor. 15:6); and Paul on the road to Damascus (Acts 9:3–9). Of all these records, none is more profound than that of his appearance to the Nephites, where, one by one, 2,500 men, women, and children "did see with their eyes and did feel with their hands, and did know of a surety . . . that it was he" (3 Ne. 11:15). To these accounts, Latter-day Saints add modern appearances of the resurrected Lord to Joseph Smith and others (e.g., JS—H 1:17; D&C 76:22–23).

Jesus Christ will yet appear in the latter days and testify, "These wounds are the wounds with which I was wounded in the house of my friends" (D&C 45:52; cf. Zech. 13:6), visiting all kingdoms over which he is creator (D&C 88:51–61). Honest and credible witnesses of all ages have testified, and will yet testify, as did the angelic messengers of old, "He is risen" (Matt. 28:6).

BIBLIOGRAPHY

Nibley, Hugh W. "Easter and the Prophets." *The World and the Prophets,* in *CWHN* 3:154–62.

Romney, Marion G. "The Resurrection of Jesus." *Ensign* 12 (May 1982):6–9.

TAD R. CALLISTER

FORTY-DAY MINISTRY AND OTHER POST-RESURRECTION APPEARANCES OF JESUS CHRIST

After his RESURRECTION, Jesus spent much of the next forty days with his disciples, "speaking of the things pertaining to the kingdom of God" (Acts 1:3) and opening "their understanding, that they might understand the scriptures," namely, what is "in the Law of Moses, and in the prophets, and in the Psalms concerning [him]" (Luke 24:44–45). As part of Jesus' ministry, these forty days are important to Latter-day Saints. In addition, a major section of the Book of Mormon is devoted to his post-resurrection ministry in the Western Hemisphere.

The New Testament mentions the forty-day ministry but provides only limited detail. For example, during this time Jesus appeared to the Twelve with Thomas present (John 20:26–29), spoke of "things pertaining to the kingdom of God" (Acts 1:3), "and many other signs truly did Jesus in the presence of his disciples, which are not written in this book" (John 20:30). Paul mentions that on one occasion Jesus "was seen of above five hundred brethren at once" (1 Cor. 15:6). Finally, before his ascension Jesus commanded the apostles to go "into all the world, and preach the gospel to every creature" (Mark 16:15–16; cf. Matt. 28:18–20; Luke 24:47–48; John 21:15–17; Acts 1:4–5).

Over forty accounts outside scripture claim to tell what Jesus said and did during his forty-day ministry. Latter-day Saints believe that some of these accounts, like the apocrypha, contain things "therein that are true," but in addition contain "many things . . . that are not true" (D&C 91).

These accounts report the following: Jesus teaches the apostles the gospel they should preach to the world. He tells of a PREMORTAL LIFE and the creation of the world, adding that this life is a probationary state of choosing between good and evil, and that those who choose good might return to the glory of God. He foretells events of the LAST DAYS, including the return of Elijah. He also tells the disciples that the primitive church will be perverted after one generation, and teaches them to prepare for tribulation. These apocryphal accounts state that Christ's resurrection gives his followers hope for their own resurrection in glory. Besides salvation for the living, SALVATION FOR THE DEAD is a major theme, as are the ordinances: BAP-

TISM, the sacrament or eucharist, ordination of the apostles to authority, their being blessed one by one, and an initiation or ENDOWMENT (cf. Luke 24:49; usually called "mysteries"), with an emphasis on GARMENTS, marriage, and prayer circles. These accounts, usually called secret (Greek, *apokryphon;* Coptic, *hep*), are often connected somehow to the temple, or compared to the Mount of Transfiguration. Sometimes the apostles are said to ascend to heaven where they see marvelous things. Whether everything in such accounts is true or not, the actions of the apostles after the post-resurrection visits of Jesus contrast sharply with those before.

Many people dismiss accounts outside the New Testament with the labels apocrypha, pseudepigrapha, fiction, or myth. Some ascribe them to psychological hallucinations that the trauma of Jesus' death brought on the disciples. Others discard such traditions because sects later branded as "heresies" championed them. Most ignore them. Latter-day Saints generally tend to give thoughtful consideration to them, primarily because of the long, detailed account in the Book of Mormon of Christ's post-resurrection ministry among the Nephites and Lamanites "who had been spared" (3 Ne. 11–28).

Many elements found in the Old World forty-day literature also appear in 3 Nephi in the Book of Mormon. This account tells how his Father announced Jesus to some of the surviving Nephites and Lamanites, and how he descended from heaven to the temple at Bountiful to minister to the multitude there for three days. The people "did see with their eyes and did feel with their hands, and did know of a surety and did bear record" that Jesus had risen from the dead (3 Ne. 11:13–17). Jesus chose twelve disciples, gave them authority to perform ordinances, and commanded them to teach all the people (3 Ne. 11:18–41; 18:36–39; 19:4–13; Moro. 2). He declared his doctrine, forbidding disputation about it: "The Father commandeth all men, everywhere, to repent and believe in me. And whoso believeth in me, and is baptized, the same shall be saved" (3 Ne. 11:32–33). Jesus' teachings, including a version of the Sermon on the Mount very similar to the one contained in the New Testament, comprise "the law and the commandments" for the people (3 Ne. 12:19). Jesus healed their sick, blessed their children, and prayed for the multitude (3 Ne. 17:2–25; 19:5–36). Many were transfigured when ANGELS descended to minister to them (3 Ne. 17:22–25;

19:14–16). Jesus instituted the ordinances of baptism and the sacrament of bread and wine (3 Ne. 11:22–29; 18:1–14, 26–35; 19:10–13; 20:3–9), and taught the multitude how to live their lives free from sin (3 Ne. 18:12–25). He also taught that sin prevents participation in the ordinances, but no one is forbidden to attend the synagogue or to repent and come to him (3 Ne. 18:25–33). He described the future in terms of COVENANTS made with the house of Israel, quoting Old Testament prophecies of Moses (Deut. 18:15–19 = 3 Ne. 20:36–38; Gen. 12:3; 22:18 = 3 Ne. 20:25, 27), Isaiah (Isa. 52:1–3, 6–8, 9–10, 11–15 = 3 Ne. 20:36–40, 32, 34–35, 41–45; Isa. 52:8–10 = 3 Ne. 16:18–20; Isa. 52:12, 15 = 3 Ne. 21:29, 8; Isa. 54 = 3 Ne. 22), Micah (Micah 4:12–13; 5:8–15 = 3 Ne. 20:18–19, 16–17; 21:12–18), and Habakkuk (Hab. 1:5 = 3 Ne. 21:9), that the remnants of Israel will be gathered when the prophecies of Isaiah begin to be fulfilled and when the remnants begin to believe in Christ, the Book of Mormon itself being a sign of the beginning of these events (3 Ne. 16:4–20; 20:10–23:6; 26:3–5). After inspecting their records, Jesus gave them additional prophecies that they had not had (Mal. 3–4 = 3 Ne. 24–25), and "did expound all things" to their understanding (3 Ne. 20:10–26:11).

Even more sacred things said and done by Jesus during his three-day visit to the Western Hemisphere were not included in the present record (3 Ne. 26:6–12). His post-resurrection ministries to the people of Nephi and to the Old World disciples were only two of several he performed and of which records were made (3 Ne. 15:11–16:3; cf. D&C 88:51–61; *TPJS,* p. 191). Latter-day Saints hope to prepare themselves to receive the fuller accounts that are yet to come (2 Ne. 29:11–14; D&C 25:9; 101:32–35; 121:26–33; A of F 9).

BIBLIOGRAPHY

Brown, S. Kent, and C. Wilfred Griggs. "The Forty-Day Ministry of Christ." *Ensign* 5 (Aug. 1975):6–11, also in *Studies in Scripture,* ed. K. Jackson, Vol. 6, pp. 12–23. Salt Lake City, 1987.

Nibley, Hugh W. "Evangelium Quadraginta Dierum." *Vigiliae Christianae* 20 (1966):1–24, reprinted in *CWHN* 4:10–44.

For comparisons with the Book of Mormon, see H. Nibley, "Christ Among the Ruins," *Ensign* 13 (June 1983):14–19, in *CWHN* 8:407–34; and *Since Cumorah, CWHN* 7. Specialized studies include H. Nibley, "The Early Christian Prayer Circle," *BYU Studies* 19 (1978):41–78, in *CWHN* 4:45–99.

For the primary sources, see the references in the preceding works; English translations of many are found in Edgar Hennecke and Wilhelm Schneemelcher, *New Testament Apocrypha,* 2 vols., Philadelphia, 1965, and James M. Robinson, *The Nag Hammadi Library,* San Francisco, 1978, rev. ed. 1988.

JOHN GEE

LATTER-DAY APPEARANCES OF JESUS CHRIST

As shown in the New Testament and the Book of Mormon, after his resurrection, Jesus Christ can, and also does, appear to people in this latter-day DISPENSATION OF THE GOSPEL. When these sacred manifestations are for personal instruction, they are not spoken of openly. However, when it is appropriate, the divine communication is made public. It is a principle of the gospel that the Lord Jesus Christ can, and will, manifest himself to his people, including individual members, "in his own time, and in his own way, and according to his own will" (D&C 88:68).

The most important appearance of the Savior in this dispensation occurred when he and the Father came to Joseph Smith in the spring of 1820. This theophany, commonly called the First Vision, revealed the separate nature of these two members of the GODHEAD and ushered in the DISPENSATION OF THE FULNESS OF TIMES and the restoration of all things.

In 1832, Jesus Christ again appeared in a vision to Joseph Smith and Sidney Rigdon. Both men saw and conversed with him (D&C 76:14) and also witnessed a vision of the kingdoms to which mankind will be assigned in the life hereafter. The Lord also appeared to Joseph Smith and Oliver Cowdery in April 1836 in the Kirtland Temple shortly after its dedication and manifested his acceptance of this first latter-day temple (D&C 110:1–10).

A revelation pertaining to the salvation for the dead was given to Joseph Smith in an earlier appearance of Jesus Christ and the Father in the Kirtland Temple on January 21, 1836: "The heavens were opened upon us, and I beheld . . . the blazing throne of God, whereon was seated the Father and the Son" (D&C 137:1, 3). Joseph Smith said that visions were given to many in the meeting and that "some of them saw the face of the Savior" (*HC* 2:382).

Joseph Smith also recorded other occasions when Church members beheld the Savior. On March 18, 1833, he wrote of a significant meeting of the School of the Prophets: "Many of the brethren saw a heavenly vision of the Savior, and concourses of angels, and many other things, of which each one has a record of what he saw" (*HC* 1:335). He wrote of a similar experience of Zebedee Coltrin (*HC* 2:387), and on another occasion he reported that "the Savior made His appearance unto some" at a meeting the week after the dedication of the Kirtland Temple (*HC* 2:432).

Appearances of Jesus Christ have not been restricted to the early days of the Church. In 1898 the Savior appeared to Lorenzo Snow, the fifth President of the Church, and gave him important instructions regarding the Church (*My Kingdom Shall Roll Forth,* pp. 68–70, Salt Lake City, 1980). The sixth President of the Church, Joseph F. Smith, saw the Savior in a vision in 1918, as recorded in Doctrine and Covenants section 138. This vision showed the Savior's visit to the spirits of the dead while his body was in the tomb between the time of his crucifixion and resurrection. In 1985, Ezra Taft Benson, the thirteenth President of the Church, said, "Today in Christ's restored church, The Church of Jesus Christ of Latter-day Saints, He is revealing Himself and His will—from the first prophet of the Restoration, even Joseph Smith, to the present" (p. 4).

It is a teaching of latter-day revelation that individual members can have a personal visit from the Savior, and see his face, and receive instruction from him, when they are prepared, and when the Lord chooses to grant such an experience (D&C 93:1; *see* JESUS CHRIST, SECOND COMFORTER).

BIBLIOGRAPHY

Benson, Ezra Taft. "Joy in Christ." *Ensign* 16 (Mar. 1986):4.

JOEL A. FLAKE

SECOND COMING OF JESUS CHRIST

In Jewish and Christian thought there are two basic ways of viewing the coming of the MESSIAH. Some consider promises of a Messiah and a millennial era symbolic of a time when men will finally learn to live in peace and harmony and the world will enter a new age of enlightenment and progress; no one individual nor any one specific event will usher in this age. The Church of Jesus Christ of Latter-day Saints opposes this view and agrees with the many other Jewish and Christian groups who affirm that there is an actual Messiah, that he will come at some future time to the earth, and that only through his coming and the events associated therewith will a millennial age of peace, harmony, and joy begin. Jews look for the first coming of the Messiah; Latter-day Saints and other Christians for the second coming of Jesus Christ.

The scriptures, both biblical and modern, abundantly testify that the era just preceding the second advent of the Savior will be "perilous" (2 Tim. 3:1) and filled with "tribulation" (Matt. 24:29). At that time "the devil shall have power over his own dominion" (D&C 1:35). The resulting judgments upon the wicked are part of the preparations for the MILLENNIUM.

The righteous as well as the unenlightened will experience these times of tribulation. LDS sources teach that the Lord will gather the righteous together in "holy places" (D&C 101:22), which include Zion and her stakes (D&C 115:6). These places are described in terms of "peace," "refuge," and "safety for the saints of the Most High God" (D&C 45:66). The promise is that God "will not suffer that the wicked shall destroy the righteous. Wherefore, he will preserve the righteous by his power . . . Wherefore, the righteous need not fear" (1 Ne. 22:16–17).

Attempts to predict the time of the coming of the Messiah are legion in both Jewish and Christian traditions. Latter-day Saints consider the second coming "near, even at the doors" (D&C 110:16). But they also accept the decree of scripture that "the hour and the day [of Christ's coming] no man knoweth, neither the angels in heaven, *nor shall they know until he comes*" (D&C 49:7 [italics added]; cf. Matt. 24:36).

With many other Christians, Mormons believe the second coming will be preceded by the battle of Armageddon and by Christ's appearance on the Mount of Olives (*see* LAST DAYS). Of this event the Doctrine and Covenants says:

> And then shall the Jews look upon me and say: What are these wounds in thine hands and in thy feet? Then shall they know that I am the Lord; for I will say unto them: These wounds are the wounds with which I was wounded in the house of my friends. I am he who was lifted up. I am Jesus that was crucified. I am the Son of God. And then shall they weep because of their iniquities; then shall they lament because they persecuted their king [D&C 45:51–53; cf. Zech. 13:6].

"From that day forward," it has been proclaimed, "the Jews as a nation become holy and their city and sanctuary become holy. There also the Messiah establishes his throne and seat of government" (Clark, p. 258).

Before Christ's coming in glory, "there shall be silence in the heaven for the space of half an hour; and immediately after shall the curtain of heaven be unfolded . . . and the face of the Lord shall be unveiled" (D&C 88:95). This apparently is the time when "all flesh shall see me together" (D&C 101:23; Rev. 1:7).

The Doctrine and Covenants declares that "the earth shall pass away so as by fire" (D&C 43:32). Some have conjectured that this could occur through a nuclear holocaust. Though certain apocalyptic passages may seem to describe the effects of nuclear warfare (e.g., Isa. 34:1–10), a modern REVELATION teaches that the "fire" of the Second Coming is the actual presence of the Savior, a celestial glory comparable to the glory of the sun (D&C 76:70) or a "consuming fire" (Heb. 12:29; cf. Mal. 3:2; 4:1). "So great shall be the glory of his presence that the sun shall hide his face in shame" (D&C 133:49). "The presence of the Lord shall be as the melting fire that burneth, and as the fire which causeth the waters to boil" (D&C 133:41; cf. Isa. 64:2; JS—H 1:37). "Element shall melt with fervent heat" (D&C 101:25) and "the mountains shall flow down at thy presence" (D&C 133:44). The Doctrine and Covenants repeats Isaiah's declaration that "the Lord shall be red in his apparel, and his garments like him that treadeth in the wine-vat" (D&C 133:48; cf. Isa. 63:2).

The apostle Paul wrote to the Thessalonian Saints that those living on the earth at the time of Christ's appearing would be caught up to meet him (1 Thess. 4:16–17). The Doctrine and Covenants, using similar language, adds that these righteous saints will be "quickened" and will join those "who have slept in their graves," who will also "be caught up to meet him in the midst of the pillar of heaven" (D&C 88:96–97; *see* RESURRECTION). Christ will descend to earth "in like manner as ye have seen him go into heaven" (Acts 1:11).

With the coming of Christ, the millennial era of peace, harmony, and RIGHTEOUSNESS will begin. Satan will then have "no power over the hearts of the people, for they dwell in righteousness, and the Holy One of Israel reigneth" (1 Ne. 22:26; *see also* MILLENNIUM).

BIBLIOGRAPHY

Clark, James R., comp. "Proclamation of the Twelve." In *Messages of the First Presidency,* Vol. l, p. 258. Salt Lake City, 1965.

Lund, Gerald N. *The Coming of the Lord.* Salt Lake City, 1971.

McConkie, Bruce R. *The Millennial Messiah: The Second Coming of the Son of Man.* Salt Lake City, 1982.

Smith, Joseph Fielding. *The Signs of the Times.* Salt Lake City, 1964.

GERALD N. LUND

JESUS CHRIST, FATHERHOOD AND SONSHIP OF

Latter-day Saint scriptures refer to Jesus Christ as both the Father and the Son. Most notably in the Book of Mormon, Christ introduced himself to the brother of Jared saying, "I am the Father and the Son" (Ether 3:14); Nephi$_1$ referred to the Lamb of God as "the Eternal Father" (1 Ne. 11:21, 1830 ed.), and the prophet Abinadi said that the Messiah would be "the Father . . . and the Son" (Mosiah 15:3). Such usage has been explained in several ways consistent with the fundamental LDS understanding of the Godhead as three distinct beings.

There is no lack of clarity about Christ's sonship. Jesus is the Son of God in at least three ways. First, he is the firstborn spirit child of God the Father and thereby the elder brother of the spirits of all men and women as God the Father, known also by the exalted name-title Elohim, is the father of the spirits of all mankind (Num. 16:22; Heb. 12:9; John 20:17). Thus, when Christ is called the Firstborn (e.g., Rom. 8:29; Col. 1:15; D&C 93:21), Latter-day Saints accept this as a possible reference to Christ's spiritual birth. Second, he is the literal physical son of God, the Only Begotten in the Flesh (e.g., John 1:14; 3:16; 2 Ne. 25:12; Jacob 4:11; D&C 29:42; 93:11; Moses 1:6; 2:26). Third, spiritually he is also a son by virtue of his submission unto the will of the Father (Heb. 5:8).

Jesus Christ is also known by the title of Father. The meaning of scriptures using this nomenclature is not always immediately clear, primarily owing to the fact that Christ and his Father are virtually inseparable in purpose, testimony, glory, and power. In most cases, however, the scriptural usage can be explained in several ways:

Christ is sometimes called Father because of his role as Creator from the beginning. Before his mortal birth, and acting under the direction of the Father, Jesus was JEHOVAH, the Lord Omnipotent, through whom God created worlds without number (Moses 1:33; 7:30; John 1:1–3; Heb. 1:2). Because of his creative role, Christ-Jehovah is called "the Father of heaven and earth, the Creator of all things from the beginning" in the Book of Mormon (Mosiah 3:8; see also 2 Ne. 25:16; Alma 11:39; 3 Ne. 9:15). Jesus' role as Creator is similarly attested in the Bible (e.g., John 1:3; Eph. 3:9; Col. 1:16) and the Doctrine and Covenants (e.g., D&C 38:1–3; 45:1; 76:24; 93:9).

Jesus Christ is also known as Father through the spiritual rebirth of mankind (*see* BORN OF GOD). As the foreordained Redeemer, he became the "author of eternal salvation unto all them that obey him" (Heb. 5:9). He is the Savior. No person will come unto the Father except through him and by his name (John 14:6; Acts 4:12; Mosiah 3:17). Those who accept the gospel of Jesus Christ and receive its saving covenantal ordinances, living worthy of its sanctifying and enlightening powers, are "born again" unto Christ and become known as the children of Christ, "his sons and daughters," his "seed" (Mosiah 5:5–8; 15:10–13; 27:25–26; Alma 5:14). Christ thus becomes the Father of their salvation, the Father of life in the Spirit, the Father of the new birth. In a related sense, he is also the Father of all mankind in that the RESURRECTION of the entire human family comes through him (Sperry, p. 35).

Furthermore, Jesus is called Father because of the authority God gave him to act for the Father. He explained in Jerusalem: "I can of mine own self do nothing . . . I am come in my Father's name" (John 5:30, 43). An LDS leader has clarified this: "All revelation since the fall has come through Jesus Christ, who is the Jehovah of the Old Testament. . . . The Father has never dealt with man directly and personally since the fall, and he has never appeared except to introduce and bear record of the Son" (*DS* 1:27). Latter-day Saints understand this to mean that, except when introducing the Son, God always acts and speaks to mankind through Jesus Christ. Accordingly, the Father has placed his name upon the Son, authorized and empowered him to speak even in the first person for him, as though he were the Father. An example of this is when the Lord Jehovah (who would later come to earth as Jesus of Nazareth) spoke to Moses: "Moses, my son; . . . thou art in the similitude of mine Only Begotten; and mine

Only Begotten is and shall be the Savior" (Moses 1:6). Sometimes the Savior has spoken both as the Father (Elohim) and as the Son (Jesus) in the same revelation (e.g., D&C 29:1 and 42; 49:5 and 28).

In addition, Christ is Father in that he literally inherited attributes and powers from his Father (Elohim). From Mary, his mother, Jesus inherited MORTALITY, the capacity to die. From God, his Father, Jesus inherited IMMORTALITY, the capacity to live forever: "As the Father hath life in himself; so hath he given to the Son to have life in himself" (John 5:26; cf. Hel. 5:11). Christ is "the Father because he was conceived by the power of God" (Mosiah 15:3). "This is a matter of his Eternal Parent investing him with power from on high so that he becomes the Father because he exercises the power of that Eternal Being" (McConkie, p. 371).

Christ is also Father in that he spiritually received all that the Father has. "I am in the Father, and the Father in me, and the Father and I are one—the Father because he gave me of his fulness, and the Son because I was in the world" (D&C 93:3–4).

Other explanations are likewise possible. All persons have multiple roles in life. A man can be a father, son, and brother; a woman can be a mother, daughter, and sister. These titles describe roles or functions at a given time, as well as relationships to others. For Latter-day Saints, this is so with the Christ. He has many names and titles. He ministers as both the Father and the Son. After explaining that the God of Abraham, Isaac, and Jacob would come to earth, take a body, and minister as both Father and Son, Abinadi summarized: "And they are one God, yea, the very Eternal Father of heaven and earth" (Mosiah 15:4; see also Mosiah 7:26–27; D&C 93:14). The Father and the Son, the Spirit and the flesh, the God and the man—these titles, roles, and attributes are blended wondrously in one being, Jesus Christ, in whom "dwelleth all the fulness of the Godhead bodily" (Col. 2:9).

BIBLIOGRAPHY

"'The Father and the Son': A Doctrinal Exposition of the First Presidency and the Twelve," June 30, 1916. In *MFP* 5:26–34. Salt Lake City, 1971.

McConkie, Bruce R. *The Promised Messiah,* chaps. 4, 9, 20. Salt Lake City, 1978.

Smith, Joseph Fielding. *DS* 1:26–34. Salt Lake City, 1954.

Sperry, Sidney B. *Answers to Book of Mormon Questions,* pp. 31–38. Salt Lake City, 1967.

ROBERT L. MILLET

JESUS CHRIST, NAMES AND TITLES OF

Since Jesus Christ is the central focus both in Church devotion and in scripture, he is naturally known under many names and titles, including the following:

JESUS. The Hebrew *yeshua'* or *yehoshua'*, meaning "Jehovah saves," is transliterated into English as the name Joshua. In Greek, it became *Iesous,* thence *Iesus* in Latin and *Jesus* in English. Since Jesus was actually Jehovah performing saving work, his name *yeshua'*, "Jehovah saves," coincides precisely.

MESSIAH. This title comes from the Hebrew *meshiach,* "anointed one." Among the Israelites, prophets, priests and kings were anointed, designating them as rightful successors. Commonly, "messiah" referred to a figure awaited by Israel to be her king. Applied to Jesus, the title retains its full sense of "anointed" prophet, priest, and king.

CHRIST. Greek for Messiah (anointed one) is *Christos,* Christ in English. Thus, "Jesus Christ" joins a name and a title, and means Jesus the Messiah.

SON OF GOD. Jesus was not the son of any mortal man. His biological father was God, the Father. As Son of God, Jesus represents the Father and acts as his agent in all things.

SON OF MAN. From his mother Jesus inherited mortality. Hebrew *ben 'adam* denotes "a son of Adam," that is, any mortal man (Dan. 8:17). Thus, as a son of Adam, Jesus represents Adam's children, acting as their agent with the Father. As both Son of God and Son of Man, Jesus stands between God and man as mediator. With the definite article, *the* Son of Man described an expected apocalyptic heavenly figure, identified with the Messiah (Dan. 7:13). Jesus is the son of the archetypal Man, the perfect heavenly Man, the Eternal Father (Moses 6:57; 7:35). In this sense, "Son of Man" equals "Son of God" and conveys an intentional ambiguity, reflecting both Jesus' mortal and immortal parentage.

SON OF DAVID. Jews expected the Messiah to belong to David's lineage. Prophets had foretold that a son (descendant) of David would restore Israel's kingdom to its former zenith (see Isa. 11:1–9; Jer.

23:5–6). According to Matthew 1:1–16, Jesus was descended from David. "Son of David" refers particularly to Jesus' messiahship in its political aspect as Davidic king.

JEHOVAH. Latter-day Saints believe that Jesus was Jehovah himself, God of Israel, not son of Jehovah (Isa. 41:14; 43:11, 14; Mosiah 3:5; 3 Ne. 11:14; 15:5). The name Jehovah vocalized thus is not found in ancient texts, but is a modern convention. In ancient times, the Hebrew text had no vowels; thus the consonants in God's name were *yhwh*. Jews avoided pronouncing these consonants when reading aloud, substituting *'adonai,* a word meaning "the Lord." Following this practice, King James translators usually rendered *yhwh* as "the Lord." In medieval Hebrew texts, the vowels from *'adonai* were added to the consonants *yhwh* to remind Jewish readers to say "*'adonai.*" English translators adopted this convention, creating the artificial form "Jehovah." Latter-day Saints accept Jehovah as a name for the premortal Christ because this is the common English form for *yhwh.*

EL. *'El* is not a name, but is the common noun for God in Hebrew (plural, *'elohim*). Latter-day Saints often use Elohim for the Father, allowing a distinction between members of the GODHEAD. Nevertheless, in the Old Testament, El and its cognates, such as Elohim and El Shaddai (God Almighty), usually refer to the premortal Jesus, the god (*'el*) of the Old Testament.

EMMANUEL. Since Jesus was the ancient El, the angel (Matt. 1:23) correctly called his name Emmanuel (Hebrew, *'immanu'el*), meaning El (god) with us.

THE LORD. Since Jews uttered *'adonai* (Lord) instead of the divine name, the Greek Bible (c. 200 B.C.) usually translated *yhwh* as *ho kurios,* "the Lord." Thus, "the Lord," whether *'adonai* or *kurios,* equaled "Jehovah." Not surprisingly, "the Lord" is Jesus' most common title in the New Testament. The confession of the early Church, "Jesus is Lord" could only mean Jesus is Jehovah.

I AM. In Exodus 3:14, Jehovah (Jesus Christ) identified himself as "I AM," perhaps affirming Jesus as the creator who exists independently of his creation. Scholars see connections between this Old Testament title and Jesus' many "I am" statements in the New

Testament, for example, "I am the good Shepherd" (John 10:11, 14), or "Before Abraham was I am" (John 8:58).

FATHER. In at least three senses Jesus is Father: (1) he is the creator of the physical universe; (2) he is the Father's agent in everything pertaining to this creation and its inhabitants; and (3) he is Father of all eternal, resurrected human beings. Jesus Christ begets spiritually and gives ETERNAL LIFE to one "born again," who thus becomes Christ's son or daughter (Mosiah 27:25). Moreover, Latter-day Saints call Christ "elder brother." In the premortal context this is correct, for there Jesus was "the Firstborn" of all spirit children of the Father (D&C 93:21). Nevertheless, "Father" best describes Christ's present and future relationship to mortals who have been spiritually reborn.

SECOND COMFORTER. The Holy Ghost, the Comforter, comforts the faithful with the assurance of inheriting the KINGDOM OF GOD. However, through faith in Christ one can receive a *second* comforter, an appearance of Jesus himself, who assures the individual of his or her place in the kingdom. After a witness from the Spirit, the Second Comforter is a personal witness from the risen Lord (John 14:16–23).

SAVIOR. The most sublime of titles, Savior underscores Jesus' role in the divine plan. Both Old and New Testaments specify that the Savior is God (Isa. 45:21–23; Luke 1:47; etc.). Through agony and death suffered for others, Jesus is able to erase imperfections and bestow worthiness, on condition of repentance. Since imperfect beings cannot reside in God's presence (D&C 1:31), Jesus saves believers from their imperfection, their sins, and their worst selves. (See also, above, the definition of his name, "Jesus.")

THE WORD. As words carry the thoughts of one mind to the minds of others, so Jesus communicates the mind and will of the Father to mortals. Moreover, as words are agents for expression, so from the beginning (John 1:1–3) Jesus is the agent for expressing and accomplishing the Father's will. Christ is both the messenger and the message.

ALPHA AND OMEGA. Equivalent to the Old Testament term "the first and the last" (e.g., Isa. 44:6), alpha and omega are the first and last letters of the Greek alphabet. Just as no letters stand before alpha or after omega, so there are no other gods in this creation other than that represented in Jesus Christ. He encompasses all, from beginning to end; he extends beyond all extremities and categories.

ONLY BEGOTTEN. Jesus Christ is the only being begotten by the Father in MORTALITY. His full title is "the Only Begotten of the Father in the flesh." Since Mormons believe all humans were spiritually begotten by the Father before creation, "Only Begotten" is understood as being limited to mortality.

LAMB OF GOD. In the first Passover, a slain lamb's blood was daubed on Israelites' houses to avert the destroyer. In the New Testament, Jesus is understood as a Passover lamb supplied by God, and Passover stands as a type for the death of Jesus, the Lamb of God, whose blood, through BAPTISM and the sacrament of the Lord's Supper, protects Christians from the destroyer, Satan. According to Moses 5:6–8, animal sacrifices were to be "a similitude of the sacrifice of the Only Begotten of the Father."

STEPHEN E. ROBINSON

JESUS CHRIST, SECOND COMFORTER

The term "Second Comforter" refers to Jesus Christ in his role of ministering personally to his faithful followers (John 14:21–23; D&C 93:1; 130:3). Jesus taught his disciples that the Holy Ghost was a comforter (John 14:26), but he also spoke of a second comforter (John 14:16–21). Latter-day Saints have been given additional understanding about the Second Comforter by the Prophet Joseph Smith:

> After a person has faith in Christ, repents of his sins, and is baptized for the remission of his sins and receives the Holy Ghost (by the laying on of hands), which is the first Comforter, then let him continue to humble himself before God, hungering and thirsting after righteousness, and living by every word of God, and the Lord will soon say unto him, Son, thou shalt be exalted. When the Lord has thoroughly proved him, and finds that the man is determined to serve Him at all hazards, then the man will find his calling and his election made sure, then it will be his privilege to receive the other Comforter, which the Lord hath

> promised the Saints, as is recorded in the testimony of St. John, in the 14th chapter, from the 12th to the 27th verses. . . .
>
> Now what is this other Comforter? It is no more nor less than the Lord Jesus Christ Himself; . . . when any man obtains this last Comforter, he will have the personage of Jesus Christ to attend him, or appear unto him from time to time, and even He will manifest the Father unto him, and they will take up their abode with him, and the visions of the heavens will be opened unto him, and the Lord will teach him face to face, and he may have a perfect knowledge of the mysteries of the Kingdom of God; and this is the state and place the ancient Saints arrived at when they had such glorious visions—Isaiah, Ezekiel, John upon the Isle of Patmos, St. Paul in the three heavens, and all the Saints who held communion with the general assembly and Church of the First Born [*TPJS*, pp. 150–51].

The Lord has counseled his Saints to "seek his face" (D&C 101:37–38). No sinful person can endure his presence, and hence will not obtain the blessing (D&C 67:10–13; JST Ex. 33:11, 20). In God's wisdom, some faithful individuals are blessed with the Second Comforter while remaining in mortality.

[*See also* Calling and Election; Jesus Christ, Latter-day Appearances of.]

BIBLIOGRAPHY

McConkie, Bruce R. *A New Witness for the Articles of Faith,* pp. 492–99, 549. Salt Lake City, 1985.

THOMAS E. SHERRY

JESUS CHRIST, SOURCES FOR WORDS OF

For followers of Jesus Christ, nothing has more authority or significance than his very words. Called *ipsissima verba* or *logia,* they are not colored by paraphrase or interpretation, but represent his exact instructions, whether spoken by Jesus himself in the first person or by another commissioned by him, speaking in the first person—as if God—through the power of the HOLY GHOST (2 Ne. 32:3; 33:10–11; D&C 1:38; cf. Rev. 19:1–10).

The status given Jesus' words goes back to early Christianity. Much current interest in New Testament apocrypha rests in the hope of recovering authentic sayings of Jesus. For example, in the words of a modern editor, "The Gospel of Thomas is not a 'gospel' in the proper sense. . . . it is no other and no less than a collection of 114 logia, the most extensive collection of sayings of Jesus, or sayings attributed to Jesus, that has yet come down to us independently of the New Testament tradition" (Puech, pp. 284–85).

Some ancient and contemporary sources unique to The Church of Jesus Christ of Latter-day Saints augment the known body of Jesus' words. The Church teaches that Jesus Christ is both the God of the Old Testament and the New Testament. Therefore, it views quotes attributed to God in the Old Testament as *ipsissima verba* of Jesus. For example, God's command to Moses to "stretch out thine hand over the sea, and divide it" is considered to be from Jesus Christ (Ex. 14:16; cf. 1 Cor. 10:1–4). Moreover, when ancient prophets quote God in the first person, such as "I the Lord love judgment, I hate robbery for burnt offering" (Isa. 61:8), these words are reckoned as Jesus' *ipsissima verba* (*see* JESUS CHRIST: FIRSTBORN IN THE SPIRIT and JESUS CHRIST, NAMES AND TITLES OF).

As the Prophet Joseph Smith produced under inspiration the Joseph Smith Translation of the Bible (JST), many *logia* were recorded. For instance, after Moses broke the first set of tablets with the Ten Commandments, the Lord commanded him to make another. In current Hebrew manuscripts, God says that he will rewrite what was on the first. But in the JST, the Lord adds, "It shall not be according to the first [tablets], for I will take away the priesthood out of their midst; therefore my holy order, and the ordinances thereof, shall not go before them" (JST Ex. 34:11–12; Deut. 10:1–2; cf. D&C 84:18–27).

The JST also adds *logia* to the New Testament. As background to Jesus' illustration of not putting new wine into old bottles, the JST adds, "Then said the Pharisees unto him, Why will ye not receive us with our baptism, seeing we keep the whole law? But Jesus said unto them, Ye keep not the law. If ye had kept the law, ye would have received me, for I am he who gave the law. I receive not you with your baptism, because it profiteth you nothing. For when that which is new is come, the old is ready to be put away" (JST Matt. 9:18–21). Such passages, although not in any extant Greek text, are accepted by Latter-day Saints as true sayings of Jesus.

In addition to accepting biblical scripture, the Church has canonized other scriptures which preserve *ipsissima verba* of Jesus Christ: the Pearl of Great Price, the Book of Mormon, and the Doctrine and Covenants.

In the Pearl of Great Price, the Book of Moses—an excerpt from the JST—preserves the declaration well known among Latter-day Saints, "For behold, this is my work and my glory—to bring to pass the immortality and eternal life of man" (Moses 1:39). The Book of Abraham also contains teachings of Jehovah, or Christ. In chapter 3, Jehovah compares the nature of the universe to the variety of spirits, or intelligences, that inhabit the universe. Recounting God's dealings with people inhabiting the American continent, the Book of Mormon also preserves sayings given to their prophets. In addition to specific words from "the Son" recorded by $Nephi_1$ (2 Ne. 31:12, 14) and others (e.g., $Moroni_2$ in Ether 12:26–28), Jesus' words spoken to the people of the Western Hemisphere soon after his resurrection also appear. Besides a discourse similar to the Sermon on the Mount recorded in Matthew 5–7 (3 Ne. 12–14), the risen Jesus spoke of baptism (3 Ne. 11), the sacrament (chap. 18), the gathering of Israel, and the helping role of the Gentiles (chaps. 16, 20–21).

The Doctrine and Covenants records sayings of Christ directed to people of the contemporary world: "Hearken, O ye people of my church, . . . verily I say: Hearken ye people from afar; and ye that are upon the islands of the sea, listen together," are words spoken in 1831 (D&C 1:1). This volume comprises an extensive collection of the words of Jesus Christ as a voice of warning and instruction on how to prepare both the earth and one's own heart for his second coming.

An additional contemporary source for the words of Christ resides in statements of the Presidents of the Church. The Lord has declared that "his word ye shall receive, as if from mine own mouth" (D&C 1:38; 21:5). Thus, whenever the President of the Church speaks officially within his office and calling, his words are considered by Latter-day Saints to have the same authority as words of the Lord himself.

[*See also* Jesus Christ in the Scriptures.]

BIBLIOGRAPHY
Millet, Robert L. "The Formation of the Canonical Gospels." In *Apocryphal Writings and the Latter-day Saints,* ed. W. Griggs. Provo, Utah, 1986.
Puech, Henri-Charles. "Gnostic Gospels and Related Documents." In *New Testament Apocrypha,* ed. Edgar Hennecke and Wilhelm Schneemelcher, Vol. 1, pp. 231–362. Philadelphia, 1963.

J. PHILIP SCHAELLING

JESUS CHRIST, TAKING THE NAME OF, UPON ONESELF

It is a doctrine of The Church of Jesus Christ of Latter-day Saints that the only way to obtain salvation is to take the name of Jesus Christ upon oneself. This is categorically stated in several latter-day revelations. Although not specifically stated in the Bible, the concept is implied in Paul's declaration to "put on Christ" (Rom. 13:14; Gal. 3:27); Peter's statement that Jesus Christ is the only name given "among men, whereby we must be saved" (Acts 4:12; Ex. 15:2; 1 Sam. 2:1; Ps. 27:1); and the Lord's instruction to Moses to "put my name upon the children of Israel" (Num. 6:27; cf. Jer. 15:16). The taking of the name of Christ upon oneself in this dispensation begins with being baptized into his Church and keeping the commandments.

The Lord declared to the Prophet Joseph Smith that all persons desiring a place in the kingdom of the Father must take upon themselves the name of Christ (D&C 18:24–25, 27). Amulek, in the Book of Mormon, counseled the wayward Zoramites to "take upon you the name of Christ" (Alma 34:38). The resurrected Jesus promised, "Whoso taketh upon him my name, and endureth to the end, the same shall be saved at the last day" (3 Ne. 27:5–6; cf. Mosiah 25:23; 26:18). Abraham was told by the Lord, "I will take thee, to put upon thee my name" (Abr. 1:18).

Sacred covenant making is associated with taking the name of Jesus upon oneself. King Benjamin said, "There is no other name given whereby salvation cometh; therefore, I would that ye should take upon you the name of Christ, all you that have entered into the covenant with God that ye should be obedient unto the end of your lives" (Mosiah 5:8; cf. 18:8–12; Alma 46:15). The covenants of BAPTISM (D&C 20:37; cf. 2 Ne. 31:13) and of the Lord's Supper (D&C

20:77; Moro. 4:3) require taking the name of Jesus Christ upon oneself. Bruce R. McConkie, a latter-day apostle, stated, "We have taken upon ourselves his name in the waters of baptism. We renew the covenant therein made when we partake of the sacrament [Lord's Supper]. If we have been born again, we have become the sons and daughters of the Lord Jesus Christ" (McConkie, p. 393).

Dallin H. Oaks, also an apostle, further explained that "we take upon us the name of Christ when we are baptized in his name, when we belong to his Church and profess our belief in him, and when we do the work of his kingdom. There are other meanings as well, deeper meanings that the more mature members of the Church should understand and ponder" (Oaks, p. 80). The "deeper meanings" are identified as inheriting the fulness of God's glory and obtaining EXALTATION in the celestial kingdom (Oaks, pp. 81–83).

BIBLIOGRAPHY

McConkie, Bruce R. "Jesus Christ and Him Crucified." In *BYU Devotional Speeches of the Year,* pp. 391–405. Provo, Utah, 1976.

Oaks, Dallin H. "Taking Upon Us the Name of Jesus Christ," *Ensign* 15 (May 1985):80–83.

PAUL R. WARNER

JESUS CHRIST, TYPES AND SHADOWS OF

Latter-day Saints believe that many events, persons, and objects in the Old Testament and other scriptures were "types" or foreshadowings of Jesus Christ. Jesus taught, for instance, that manna had anticipated him, the true heavenly bread (John 6:30–35), and that Jonah's three days in the fish signified his death and burial (Matt. 12:38–41).

Paul affirmed that the water produced from a rock by Moses pointed to the spiritual nourishment to come through Jesus (Ex. 17:6; 1 Cor. 10:4); furthermore, he asserted that the first Adam prefigured Jesus, the second Adam, who brought life to his spiritual offspring in contrast to Adam who brought death (Rom. 5:12–21; 1 Cor. 15:45). Similarly, the inheritances of Ishmael and Isaac foreshadowed differences between the old covenant and the new (Gal. 4:22–31).

According to Hebrews 7:15, the Messiah came "after the similitude of Melchizedek," (Hebrew, "King of Righteousness") who prefigured the roles of priest and king. The genealogy of Jesus in Matthew 1:2–17 was written to prove that Jesus was both descended from and foreshadowed by David as king over Israel. Some LDS leaders have taught that the lives of many prophets have served as types of Christ (McConkie, pp. 448–53).

Prototypes and intimations can also be found in the symbolism of ancient Israel's sacred ceremonies. For example, the scapegoat and purification rites of the Day of Atonement signify Christ's salvation wrought by suffering and death (Heb. 9:7–14). Further, the Feast of Tabernacles, with its harvest and light associations, teaches of the Messianic reign (2 Bar. 29:4–8; John 8:12).

Book of Mormon passages add impetus to the notion of scriptural types. Amulek observed that "the whole meaning of the [Mosaic] law . . . point[ed] to that great and last sacrifice . . . [of] the Son of God" (Alma 34:14). Moreover, Abraham's offering of Isaac was called a "similitude of God and [the sacrifice of] his Only Begotten Son" (Jacob 4:5). God showed to ancient Israel "many signs, and wonders, and types, and shadows . . . concerning [Christ's] coming" (Mosiah 3:15). The prophet Alma called the Liahona a God-given compass, a "type" of Christ, who guides toward eternal life (Alma 37:38–46). In the broad sense, "all things . . . given of God . . . unto man, are the typifying of [Christ]" (2 Ne. 11:4).

The Pearl of Great Price also teaches that all creation bears record of Christ (Moses 6:63). This includes the sun, which points to him, the light of the world (see D&C 88:5–13). Similarly, every revealed ordinance exhibits a symbolic linkage to one element or another of Jesus' ministry. For example, just as the daily sacrifices of Jerusalem's temple foreshadowed Christ's sacrifice (Heb. 7:26–28), so Latter-day Saints see gospel ordinances as pointing to him and to the way back into his presence.

BIBLIOGRAPHY

McConkie, Bruce R. *The Promised Messiah*, pp. 374–453. Salt Lake City, 1978.

Read, Lenet H. "Symbols of the Harvest: Old Testament Holy Days and the Lord's Ministry." *Ensign* (Jan. 1975):32–36.

LENET HADLEY READ

JESUS CHRIST IN THE SCRIPTURES

[*This entry consists of four articles:*

Jesus Christ in the Bible
Jesus Christ in the Book of Mormon
Jesus Christ in the Doctrine and Covenants
Jesus Christ in the Pearl of Great Price

Jesus Christ is the central focus in all scriptures accepted by Latter-day Saints. Jesus Christ in the Bible *details how Jesus is seen as the central figure—both in prophecy and in its fulfillment—in the Old and New Testaments. The article* Jesus Christ in the Book of Mormon *treats the pivotal prophetic interest in Christ manifested in the Book of Mormon, including his post-resurrection appearance to people in the Western Hemisphere.* Jesus Christ in the Doctrine and Covenants *illuminates the fundamental dominance of the person of Jesus in latter-day revelation. The article* Jesus Christ in the Pearl of Great Price *summarizes Jesus' place both in ancient prophetic expectation and in its latter-day fruition.*]

JESUS CHRIST IN THE BIBLE

Latter-day Saints view Jesus Christ as the central figure of the entire Bible. The Old and New Testaments are divinely inspired records that reveal the mission of Jesus as Creator, God of Israel, Messiah, Son of God, Redeemer, and eternal King. The Bible contains history, doctrinal teachings, and prophecy of future events, with Jesus Christ as the main subject in every category.

The Old Testament contains an account of the Creation, and of the dealings of God with the human family from Adam to about 400 B.C. The promise of a messiah is a generally pervading theme. The New Testament chronicles principal events in the earth life of Jesus the Messiah from his birth through death, resurrection, and ascension into heaven, with a promise that he will return to earth to judge the world and then reign as king. Latter-day Saints identify Jesus as Jehovah, the Creator, the God of Adam, of Abraham, of Moses, and of Israel. Jesus is Jehovah come to earth as the promised Messiah (*see* JEHOVAH, JESUS CHRIST). Hence, the dealings of God with the human family throughout the Old Testament and New Testament periods form a record of the premortal and the mortal Jesus Christ.

THE HISTORICAL JESUS. Latter-day Saints take the biblical message about Jesus literally (*see* JESUS CHRIST: MINISTRY OF). The historical Jesus is the Jesus of the Bible: the Only Begotten Son of God in the flesh, born of the Virgin Mary in Bethlehem, baptized by John the Baptist. He performed a variety of miracles, was a teacher of the gospel who occasionally spoke in parables, and "went about doing good" (Acts 10:38). He chose twelve apostles, organized a church, gathered many followers, and was rejected by the Jewish rulers. His attitudes toward Samaritans, women, political leaders (e.g., Herod, Caesar), ritual law, and prayer were rather revolutionary for his day. He suffered at GETHSEMANE, bled at every pore, was crucified, died, was resurrected from the dead, and subsequently ascended into heaven from the Mount of Olives. Latter-day Saints consider both the historical portion of the record of the life of Jesus, and the prophetic portion, to be accurate. The promises that this same Jesus will come again in glory, in person to judge the world, then reign on the earth as King of Kings, are future realities that are taken literally.

PORTRAYAL OF JESUS THROUGH CEREMONY. Throughout the Bible, the mission of Jesus Christ is portrayed in ceremonies that are types and symbols of actual events. To the Old Testament prophets, animal sacrifices prefigured and typified the coming of Jesus to shed his blood and sacrifice his life for the sins of mankind. Because lambs were frequently offered, Jesus is spoken of in the New Testament as the Lamb of God (John 1:29, 36; cf. 1 Ne. 11:21).

For the animal sacrifice to symbolize Jesus' sacrifice, it had to be from among the firstlings of the flock (meaning the first male born to its mother) without blemish, offered without a bone being broken, and its blood had to be shed. Each of these points had a counterpart in Jesus' life on earth. Even details of the Passover service, requiring the blood of the lamb to be placed on the door post so that the angel of death might pass over that house (Ex. 12:3–24, 46), prefigured the mission and saving power of Jesus, the Lamb of God, who was crucified at the time of the annual Passover celebration. Paul, understanding this symbolism, exclaims, "For even Christ our passover is sacrificed for us" (1 Cor. 5:7).

The Law of Moses is identified by Paul as "our schoolmaster to bring us unto Christ" (Gal. 3:24). To do that, it foreshadowed and typified Christ. When he worked out the Atonement, Christ fulfilled all the law; therefore the law had an end in him, and was replaced by the fulness of the gospel (3 Ne. 9:17; cf. Matt. 5:17–18; Heb. 10:1). LDS understanding of the role of the law of Moses and of other Old Testament ordinances is clearly spoken by the Book of Mormon prophet Nephi about 600 B.C.:

> Behold, my soul delighteth in proving unto my people the truth of the coming of Christ; for, for this end hath the Law of Moses been given; and all things which have been given of God from the beginning of the world, unto man, are the typifying of him [2 Ne. 11:4; cf. Jacob 4:5].

When Jesus ate the Passover meal with the Twelve at the Last Supper, he gave them bread representing his flesh, which would be broken, and wine representing his blood, which would be shed. Believers were commanded to partake of this symbolic ceremony often: "This do in remembrance of me" (Luke 22:17–20; cf. 3 Ne. 18:3–13; 20:8–9).

OLD TESTAMENT FORESHADOWINGS. The writers of the four Gospels saw things in the Old Testament that foreshadowed the actual events in Jesus' life. Matthew (1:23) cites Isaiah 7:14: "A virgin shall conceive, and bear a son, and shall call his name Immanuel," a name meaning "God with us." He likewise cites Hosea 11:1, "I . . . called my son out of Egypt" (Matt. 2:15).

John (13:8–11) notes that the betrayal of Jesus by a friend was spoken of in earlier scripture (Ps. 41:9). John (19:24) also cites the dealing of the soldiers for Jesus' robe as a fulfillment of Psalm 22:18, and the sponge with vinegar pressed to Jesus' lips (John 19:28–30) as having been alluded to in Psalm 69:21. John (19:33–36) also notes that Jesus' legs were not broken on the cross, in harmony with Exodus 12:46.

Isaiah prophesied that in Israel a son would be born of the lineage of David, who would be called the "mighty God," the "Prince of Peace" (Isa. 9:6–7). The Messiah's mission as redeemer, suffering for the sins of mankind, is portrayed in Isaiah 53 and 61.

THE GOD OF ISRAEL IS JESUS OF NAZARETH. Revelation to the Prophet Joseph Smith shows that, beginning with Adam, there have been several gospel DISPENSATIONS on the earth. The prophets in each of these dispensations knew of Christ, taught his gospel (including the ceremonies and ordinances), and held the holy priesthood, which was called "the Holy Priesthood, after the Order of the Son of God" (D&C 107:3; cf. Alma 13:1–16). These ancient prophets not only knew of the future coming of Jesus as the Messiah, but they also knew that the God whom they worshiped, Jehovah, would come to earth and become that Messiah (cf. Mosiah 13:33–35). As noted earlier, in Isaiah 7:14 the name Immanuel identifies Jesus as God. New Testament passages illustrate this concept.

Jesus directed his listeners to search the scriptures, for "they are they which testify of me" (John 5:39). He told the Jewish rulers that Moses "wrote of me" (John 5:45–46; cf. John 1:45; 1 Cor. 10:1–4). Later he informed them that "Abraham rejoiced to see my day: and he saw it, and was glad" (John 8:56). When asked how he and Abraham could have known each other when their lives on earth were separated by so much time, Jesus replied, "Before Abraham was, I am" (John 8:58). The Greek term here translated "I am" is identical with the Septuagint phrase in Exodus 3:14 that identifies Jehovah as "I AM."

That Jesus' audience understood that he had plainly told them he was none other than Jehovah, also known as I AM, the God of Abraham and of Moses, is evident, for "then took they up stones to cast at him" (John 8:59) because they supposed that he had blasphemed. A further demonstration that they understood Jesus' assertion that he was God come to earth is shown later when they "took up stones again to stone him," and Jesus asked: "For which of [my] works do ye stone me?" Their reply was "for blasphemy; and because that thou, being a man, makest thyself God" (John 10:31–33).

After his resurrection Jesus went through the passages of the Old Testament with his disciples, "beginning at Moses and all the prophets," expounded to them "in all the scriptures the things concerning himself" (Luke 24:27), and showed them "in the Law of Moses, and in the prophets, and in the psalms" the prophecies pertaining to his mission (Luke 24:44; *see* JESUS CHRIST: PROPHECIES ABOUT).

Peter wrote that the ancient prophets "searched diligently" and had the "Spirit of Christ," which "testified beforehand the sufferings of Christ," and that these prophets did "minister [in their day] the things, which are now reported" about Jesus Christ (1 Pet. 1:10–12).

And Paul declared that in all his teachings about Jesus, he had said "none other things than those which the prophets and Moses did say should come" (Acts 26:22).

Extensive prophecies that Jesus will come again to the earth as Judge and King are recorded in Matthew (16:27; 24:1–51) and Joseph Smith—Matthew (1:1–55) (*see* JESUS CHRIST: SECOND COMING OF JESUS CHRIST). Latter-day Saints believe that just as Old Testament foreshadowing and prophecies of Christ were fulfilled in his first coming, so will prophecies of his second coming be literally fulfilled.

CLARIFICATIONS FROM LATTER-DAY REVELATION. The foregoing items from the Bible, coupled with confirmatory and illuminating statements in latter-day revelation, lead members of the Church to see both the Old and the New Testaments as reliable records about the premortal, mortal, postmortal, and future millennial mission of Jesus Christ. Latter-day Saints fully accept the biblical message about Jesus Christ, and, in addition, because of other sacred scriptures that strengthen and supplement the biblical report, they appreciate the mission of Jesus in a wider sense than is possible from the Bible alone. For example, Jesus spoke to Jewish hearers about "other sheep," not of the Jews, whom he would visit and who would "hear my voice" (John 10:16). Many have supposed that these were the Gentiles. However, in the Book of Mormon the resurrected Jesus specifically identifies these other sheep as a branch of the house of Israel on the American continent whom he was visiting, personally showing them his body and vocally teaching them his gospel (3 Ne. 15:13–24). The Book of Mormon thus explains a passage about the Savior beyond what the Bible offers, and also enlarges the concept of Jesus' ministry.

Latter-day revelation also provides a deeper appreciation for events that occurred on the Mount of Transfiguration than is available in the Bible alone. That which the New Testament offers is accepted as historically correct, but incomplete. One learns from latter-day revelation that on the mount, Jesus, Moses, and Elijah gave the keys of the priesthood to Peter, James, and John in fulfillment of the Savior's promise in Matthew 16:19 (*TPJS,* p. 158). The three apostles also saw a vision of the future glorification of the earth (D&C 63:2–21). These points are lacking in the biblical account. Moses and Elijah (called Elias) "appeared in glory, and spake of [Jesus'] decease which he should accomplish at Jerusalem" (Luke 9:30–31), which shows that they knew him and knew of his mission.

Jesus' ministry is also clarified in other instances in latter-day revelation. John 3:23 suggests that Jesus personally performed baptisms in water, but this is largely negated by John 4:2, which states that it was in fact not Jesus, but his disciples, who performed the baptisms. Through the Joseph Smith Translation of the Bible, the text of John 4:2–3 is clarified to assert that Jesus did indeed perform water baptisms, but not as many as did his disciples. Topics discussed in the latter work include Jesus at the temple at age twelve; his precocious childhood; his temptations in the wilderness; his parables; his ability to redeem little children; and his compassion for people.

BIBLIOGRAPHY

McConkie, Bruce R. *Doctrinal New Testament Commentary,* 3 vols. Salt Lake City, 1965, 1970, 1973.

——. *The Promised Messiah; The Mortal Messiah; The Millennial Messiah,* 6 vols. Salt Lake City, 1978, 1979, 1980, 1981, 1982.

Matthews, Robert J. "A Greater Portrayal of the Master." *Ensign* 13 (Mar. 1983):6–13.

Talmage, James E. *Jesus the Christ.* Salt Lake City, 1963.

ROBERT J. MATTHEWS

JESUS CHRIST IN THE BOOK OF MORMON

The main purpose of the Book of Mormon is to convince all people "that Jesus is the Christ, the Eternal God, manifesting himself unto all nations" (title page). Through the spiritual experiences of its writers, many of whom were prophets and eyewitnesses of Christ's glory, the Book of Mormon communicates clear, personal knowledge that Jesus Christ lives. It explains his mission from the Creation to the final judgment, and expresses his pure and atoning love for all mankind.

The Book of Mormon is an intimate scripture. It exhorts each reader "to come unto Christ, and lay hold upon every good gift," mindful that "every good gift cometh of Christ" (Moro. 10:18, 30).

The book is singularly focused. In the words of $Nephi_1$, "We talk of Christ, we rejoice in Christ, we preach of Christ, we prophesy of Christ" (2 Ne. 25:26). Only by Jesus' sacrifice can the repentant "answer the ends of the law" (2 Ne. 2:7). "There is no other head whereby ye can be made free. There is no other name given whereby salvation cometh" (Mosiah 5:8).

All Book of Mormon prophets proclaimed the same word of Jesus Christ (Jacob 4:5). In visions, public speeches, and personal statements they typically declared (1) that Jesus is the Son of God, the Creator, the Lord God Omnipotent, the Father of heaven and earth, and the Holy One of Israel, (2) who would come and did come down to earth to live as a mortal born of Mary, a virgin, (3) to heal the sick, cast out devils, and suffer temptation, (4) to take upon himself the sins of the world and redeem his people, (5) to be put to death by crucifixion and rise from the dead, (6) to bring to pass the resurrection of all mankind, and (7) to judge all people in the last day according to their works (1 Ne. 11–14; Mosiah 3:5–27; Alma 33:22).

The personality and attributes of Jesus are expressed in the Book of Mormon (see Black, pp. 49–64). He is a person who invites, comforts, answers, exhorts, loves, cries, is troubled over the sins of mankind, and is filled with joy. He welcomes all who will come unto him. He patiently pleads with the Father on behalf of all who have become saints through his atoning blood. He is a true and merciful friend. He visits those who believe in him. He heals those who weep at the thought of being separated from him. With hands still bearing the wounds of his death, he touches, is touched, and gives power. He remembers all his covenants and keeps all his promises. He is all-powerful, judging the world and vanquishing the wicked. He is "the light, and the life, and the truth of the world" (Ether 4:12).

Book of Mormon prophets who taught extensively of Christ before his birth include the brother of Jared (Ether 3); Lehi (1 Ne. 10; 2 Ne. 2); $Nephi_1$ (1 Ne. 11, 19; 2 Ne. 25, 31–33); Jacob (2 Ne. 9); Abinadi (Mosiah 13–16); Benjamin (Mosiah 3–5); $Alma_2$ (Alma 5, 7, 12–13, 33, 36, 42); Amulek (Alma 34); Samuel the Lamanite (Hel. 14); and $Nephi_3$ (3 Ne. 1). The apex of the Nephite record is the appearance of the resurrected Lord Jesus Christ to a congregation of 2,500 men, women, and children who had gathered at their temple in the land Bountiful. For three days, Jesus personally ministered among them (3 Ne. 11–28). The Book of Mormon ends with testimonies of Jesus by Mormon (Morm. 7; Moro. 7) and his son $Moroni_2$ (Ether 4; Moro. 10). Some 101 appellations for Jesus are found in the

3,925 references to Christ in the Book of Mormon's 6,607 verses (Black, pp. 16–30).

In addition to his visitations in 3 Nephi, Jesus appeared to Lehi (1 Ne. 1:9), $Nephi_1$, Jacob (2 Ne. 11:2–3), King Lamoni (Alma 19:13), Mormon (Morm. 1:15), $Moroni_2$ (Ether 12:39), and the brother of Jared (Ether 3:14). Each bore personal testimony of Jesus Christ. Many others heard his voice.

From visions and revelations received before he left Jerusalem about 600 B.C., Lehi knew the tender mercies of the promised Messiah. To him the Messiah would be the Redeemer who would restore the fallen, lost, and displaced. In one vision, Lehi read a heavenly book that "manifested plainly of the coming of a Messiah, and also the redemption of the world" (1 Ne. 1:19). This knowledge focused all subsequent Nephite preaching and interpretation on the mission of the Savior. It was also revealed to Lehi that in six hundred years "a prophet would the Lord God raise up among the Jews—even a Messiah, or, in other words, a Savior of the world" (1 Ne. 10:4), the same pleading and merciful servant of whom other prophets had written, including Zenos in his allegory of the Lord's olive tree representing Israel (Jacob 5). Being "grafted in" to that tree was interpreted by Lehi as "com[ing] to the knowledge of the true Messiah" (1 Ne. 10:14).

From the prophecies of Isaiah as well as from his own visions, Lehi knew that a prophet would prepare the way of the Lord before his coming (1 Ne. 10:8; cf. Isa. 40:3) and that "after he had baptized the Messiah with water, he should behold and bear record that he had baptized the Lamb of God, who should take away the sins of the world" (1 Ne. 10:10). Furthermore, Isaiah spoke of the Lord's servant being "despised and rejected, . . . wounded for our transgressions, bruised for our iniquities, . . . brought as a lamb to the slaughter" (Isa. 53:3–7); and Lehi prophesied that the Jews would slay the Messiah, adding that the Redeemer would rise from the dead (1 Ne. 10:11).

$Nephi_1$ asked the Lord for a greater understanding of his father's visions, especially for a clearer understanding of the Tree of Life. He acquired a love for the CONDESCENSION OF GOD that would bring the Son of God down to dwell in the flesh, born of a beautiful virgin. Christ's goodness stands in sharp contrast with his rejection and crucifixion (1 Ne. 11:13–33; 19:10; cf. Deut. 21:22). $Nephi_1$ (who himself knew what it meant to be persecuted for righteousness' sake) referred more than sixty times to the divine offering of this sacrificial Lamb of God (1 Ne. 11:21). As ruler and teacher of his people, Nephi emphasized that they should follow the rule of Christ, the only true Savior who would ever come, the sole source of their life and law, and the only one in whom all things would be fulfilled (2 Ne. 25:16–18, 25–27).

In connection with his calling as a priest and teacher, Jacob, the brother of $Nephi_1$, expounded on the atonement of Christ. He told how Christ would suffer and die for all mankind so that they might become subject to him through his "infinite atonement," which overcomes the Fall and brings resurrection and incorruptibility (2 Ne. 9:5–14).

Certain terms such as "Messiah" (anointed) and "Lamb of God" were used often by Lehi, $Nephi_1$ and Jacob as designations for Christ before it was revealed by an angel that the Messiah's "name shall be Jesus Christ, the Son of God" (2 Ne. 25:19; cf. 2 Ne. 10:3; Mosiah 3:8). The name Jesus, like Joshua, derives from the Hebrew root *yasha'*, meaning "to deliver, rescue, or save"; and *christos* is the Greek equivalent of the Hebrew *mashiyach,* meaning "anointed" or "Messiah" (*see* JESUS CHRIST, NAMES AND TITLES OF). Thus, the Nephites used the intimate yet freely spoken name of the mortal Jesus as their name for God, while the ineffable YHWH (*see* JEHOVAH, JESUS CHRIST) appears only twice in the book (2 Ne. 22:2; Moro. 10:34).

Some, such as Sherem, whose cultural roots lay in the monotheistic world of Jerusalem, resisted the worship of the Messiah, alleging that this violated the Law of Moses (Ex. 20:3; Jacob 7:7; *see* ANTICHRISTS). Nephi had previously declared that the Father, Son, and Holy Ghost were "one God" (2 Ne. 31:21), but Nephite challengers continued to attack the proposition that Jesus was God, to deny that his atonement could be efficacious in advance of its occurrence, and to argue that there could not be many Gods who were still one God (e.g., Mosiah 17:8; Alma 11:28). Abinadi and others gave inspired explanations (Mosiah 14–16; *see* JESUS CHRIST, FATHERHOOD AND SONSHIP), but until the resurrected Jesus appeared, announced by and praying to the Father, such issues were not firmly put to rest.

About 124 B.C., King Benjamin received from an angel a succinct declaration of the atoning mission of Christ (Mosiah 3:2–27). It places central attention on the atoning blood of Christ and corroborates that Jesus would sweat blood from every pore in anguish for his people (Mosiah 3:7; see also Luke 22:43–44; D&C 19:18; Irenaeus, *Against Heresies* 22.2; *see* GETHSEMANE). Christ's blood will atone for the sins of all those who repent or have ignorantly sinned (see Mosiah 3:11, 15, 16, 18). When Benjamin's people passionately cried out in unison for God to "apply the atoning blood of Christ that we may receive forgiveness of our sins" (Mosiah 4:2), Benjamin gave them the name of Christ by covenant, the only name "whereby salvation cometh" (Mosiah 5:7–8).

$Alma_2$, the judicial and religious defender of the freedom of belief (c. 100–73 B.C.), taught faith in Jesus Christ as the master of personal CONVERSION. Alma had tasted the transforming joy that came when he called upon the name of Jesus Christ for mercy (Alma 36:18), and in his subsequent sermons he described how the "image of God" might be "engraven upon your countenances" (Alma 5:19), and how the word of God is to be planted in each convert's soul, where, if nourished, it will spring up as an everlasting tree of life (Alma 32:40; 33:22–23; for a similar image, see the early Christian *Odes of Solomon* 11:18).

About 30 B.C. a group of Lamanites were converted to Christ when God's light shone and his voice spoke out of an enveloping cloud of darkness (Hel. 5:33–43). Twenty-five years later, a prophet named Samuel the Lamanite foretold that more significant signs of light would appear at the time of Jesus' birth and that massive destruction and darkness would be seen at his death (Hel. 14:2–27). Five years after Samuel, $Nephi_3$ heard the voice of Jesus declaring that he would come into the world "on the morrow," and the signs of Jesus' birth were seen; thirty-three years and four days after that, all the land heard the voice of Christ speaking through the thick darkness on the Western Hemisphere that accompanied his crucifixion and death (3 Ne. 9).

Within that same year, they saw the resurrected Jesus Christ come down out of heaven (3 Ne. 11:8). The resurrected Christ appeared to a congregation of righteous Nephites at their temple and allowed them to feel the wounds in his hands and feet, and thrust their hands into his side (3 Ne. 11:15). They heard the voice of the Father saying, "Behold my Beloved Son, in whom I am well pleased, in whom I have glorified my name—hear ye him" (3 Ne. 11:7).

For three days, Jesus was with these people. He called and ordained twelve disciples, and taught his gospel of faith, repentance, baptism, and the gift of the Holy Ghost. As the one who had given and fulfilled the Law of Moses, he gave the people commandments of obedience, sacrifice of a broken heart, brotherly love and reconciliation, faithfulness to one's spouse, chastity, integrity, charity, and consecration (*see* ENDOWMENT). He taught them to fast and pray, in secret and in their families. He healed their sick, and in the presence of angels and witnesses he blessed the parents and their children. They entered into a sacred covenant with him, and he promised that if they would do his will and keep his commandments they would always have his spirit to be with them, would personally know the Lord and would be welcomed into his presence at the last day (3 Ne. 14:21–23; see Welch, pp. 34–83).

As revealed in the Book of Mormon, Jesus wants all people to become like him and their Father in Heaven. Jesus said, "Therefore, what manner of men ought ye to be? Verily I say unto you, even as I am" (3 Ne. 27:27). He invited all, saying, "I would that ye should be perfect even as I, or your Father who is in heaven is perfect" (3 Ne. 12:48). His constant and loving purpose was to make that possible.

BIBLIOGRAPHY

Black, Susan E. *Finding Christ Through the Book of Mormon.* Salt Lake City, 1987.

Charlesworth, James H. "Messianism in the Pseudepigrapha and the Book of Mormon." In *Reflections on Mormonism,* ed. T. Madsen, pp. 99–137. Provo, Utah, 1978.

Roberts, B. H. "Christ in the Book of Mormon." *IE* 27 (1924):188–92.

Scharffs, Stephen. "Unique Insights on Christ from the Book of Mormon." *Ensign* 18 (Dec. 1988):8–13.

Welch, John W. *The Sermon at the Temple and the Sermon on the Mount.* Salt Lake City, 1990.

JOHN W. WELCH

JESUS CHRIST IN THE DOCTRINE AND COVENANTS

The Doctrine and Covenants is a unique collection of revelations and inspired writings bearing witness to the modern world that Jesus Christ lives. Unlike the other standard works of The Church of Jesus

Christ of Latter-day Saints, the revelations in the Doctrine and Covenants were received in modern times by latter-day prophets and therefore are not translations of ancient documents. The central figure of the Doctrine and Covenants is indeed Jesus Christ. He identifies himself repeatedly throughout its pages with various titles expressing his Godhood and his redeeming power.

The Doctrine and Covenants presents more than sixty names or titles for Jesus. When referring to himself or his work, the Lord uses at least eighteen descriptive titles, including "Lord" (more than 300 times); "Jesus Christ" (81 times); "Redeemer" (24 times); "Savior" and "Jesus" (19 times each); "Alpha and Omega" and "Only Begotten" (13 times each); "the Beginning and the End" (12 times); "Eternal" (11 times); "Jehovah" (6 times); "Advocate," "Endless," and "Bridegroom" (5 times each); "Lawgiver" and "I Am" (3 times each). These titles invoke special respect for Jesus Christ. "Behold, I am from above . . . I am over all, and in all, and through all . . . and the day cometh that all things shall be subject unto me. Behold, I am Alpha and Omega, even Jesus Christ" (D&C 63:59–60; *see also* JESUS CHRIST, NAMES AND TITLES OF).

Jesus affirms his role as the Creator. "Thus saith the Lord your God, even Jesus Christ, the Great I Am, Alpha and Omega, the beginning and the end, the same which looked upon the wide expanse of eternity, . . . before the world was made . . . I am the same which spake, and the world was made, and all things came by me" (D&C 38:1–3).

A unique reference is made to Jesus as the Son AHMAN. "Ahman" could be an expression in the Adamic language (D&C 78:20; 95:17; see also *JD* 2:342). Another unique passage identifies Christ as the Lord of Sabaoth, Hebrew for "hosts"—both of heaven and earth; therefore he is "creator of the first day, the beginning and the end" (D&C 95:7).

In one memorable passage Jesus describes his suffering as the Redeemer of mankind. The autobiographical details expressed here are found nowhere else in scripture: "Which suffering caused myself, even God, the greatest of all, to tremble because of pain, and to bleed at every pore, and to suffer both body and spirit—and would that I might not drink the bitter cup, and shrink" (D&C 19:18). He "suffered these things for all, that they might not suffer if they would repent" (19:16). True to his character, the Savior gives glory and honor to his Father in Heaven: "Nevertheless, glory be to the Father, and I partook and finished my preparations unto the children of men" (D&C 19:19; cf. 78:4). Because he made the sacrifice, Christ can intercede with the Father for the penitent: "I am Christ, and in mine own name, by the virtue of the blood which I have spilt, have I pleaded before the Father for them" (D&C 38:4; cf. 45:1–4).

Jesus refers to himself as the Bridegroom, drawing attention to his parable of the virgins recorded in Matthew 25, when he prophesied of his second coming: "Be faithful, praying always, having your lamps trimmed and burning, and oil with you, that you may be ready at the coming of the Bridegroom" (D&C 33:17).

In modern revelation the Lord also gives comfort: "Be of good cheer, and do not fear, for I the Lord am with you, and will stand by you" (D&C 68:6); and "Be thou humble; and the Lord thy God shall lead thee by the hand, and give thee answer to thy prayers (D&C 112:10). Jesus also warns mankind of the necessity to be humble, stating that "although a man may have many revelations, and have power to do many mighty works, yet if he boasts in his own strength, and sets at naught the counsels of God, and follows after the dictates of his own will and carnal desires, he must fall and incur the vengeance of a just God upon him" (D&C 3:4).

In several sections of the Doctrine and Covenants, the Lord testifies that he is the one who gives scripture through inspiration, and he commands that his words be studied (D&C 1:29; 3:16–20; 11:22; 20:8–9; 84:57). In summary he says, "Search these commandments, for they are true and faithful, and the prophecies and promises which are in them shall all be fulfilled" (D&C 1:37).

The Lord explains perplexing scriptural passages and concepts in the Gospel of John, 1 Corinthians, Revelation, and Isaiah (D&C 7; 77; 86; 113). Scriptural concepts concerning sacred history, priesthood, and patriarchal lineage are emphasized by him in other revelations (D&C 84:6–28; 107:1–14, 40–57). He also restored fragments of lost scriptures (e.g., D&C 7; 93:7–17).

The Lord tells why he gives these revelations to mankind: "I give unto you these sayings that you may understand and know how to worship, and know what you worship, that you may come unto the

Father in my name, and in due time receive of his fulness" (D&C 93:19).

The voice of Jesus Christ in the Doctrine and Covenants is the word of the Lord comforting and encouraging his Saints; testifying of his own divinity and sacred mission; warning the world of judgments to come; declaring his majesty and power; and promising forgiveness and mercy to the penitent. Latter-day Saints accept these revelations as latter-day proclamations of the mind and will of the Lord Jesus Christ.

BIBLIOGRAPHY

Maxwell, Neal A. "The Doctrine and Covenants: The Voice of the Lord." *Ensign* 8 (Dec. 1978):4–7.

CLARK V. JOHNSON

JESUS CHRIST IN THE PEARL OF GREAT PRICE

The standard work of scripture called the Pearl of Great Price contains selected materials ranging from the time of Adam to the present, including words of Adam, Enoch, Noah, Abraham, Moses, Jesus Christ, and Joseph Smith. It presents some 300 references to Jesus Christ, including such names and titles as Beginning and the End, Beloved Son, Creator, God, Jehovah, Jesus, Jesus Christ, King of Zion, Lord, Lord God, Messiah, Only Begotten, Rock of Heaven, Savior, Son, and Son of Man. A particular contribution is the fact that Jesus Christ has been the focus of every DISPENSATION from Adam to Joseph Smith.

JESUS THE CREATOR. Jesus is identified as the Creator under the aegis of God the Father in Moses, chapters 2 and 3. The book of Abraham adds the clarification that Jesus did not act alone but with a council of intelligent spirits, among whom was Abraham (Abr. 3:23).

SATAN'S REBELLION. In the premortal estate the Father chose Jesus to become the Only Begotten and Redeemer. Satan rebelled against the Father's choice and became the archenemy of Jesus and of all who follow him (Moses 4:1–4; *also see* FIRST ESTATE).

ADAM AND EVE AND THE PLAN OF SALVATION. Adam and Eve (Moses 1:34; 4:26; 5:5–9) were the first to be taught and to accept the Father's PLAN OF SALVATION on this earth. Adam was commanded by

God to make an offering of the firstlings of his flocks. After many days, an angel of the Lord asked why he offered sacrifices. When Adam confessed his lack of understanding, the angelic visitor explained, "This thing is a similitude of the sacrifice of the Only Begotten of the Father, which is full of grace and truth. . . . In that day the Holy Ghost fell upon Adam, which beareth record of the Father and the Son, saying: I am the Only Begotten of the Father from the beginning, henceforth and forever, that as thou hast fallen thou mayest be redeemed, and all mankind, even as many as will" (Moses 5:7–9).

The ATONEMENT of Jesus Christ has applied to mankind from the beginning. Adam believed in the coming of Christ, was baptized in his name, and received the GIFT OF THE HOLY GHOST and the priesthood keys of a dispensation (Moses 6:51–68; D&C 107:41–42).

ENOCH, A WITNESS OF THE SON OF MAN. Enoch preached faith in Jesus Christ, repentance, baptism, receiving the gift of the Holy Ghost, growing in the knowledge of God, justification, and sanctification, all to be achieved through the atoning blood of Christ (Moses 6:46–62).

Enoch was a prophetic witness of the Lord Jesus Christ and knew that Jesus was the God of the ancient prophets, the Redeemer and Savior, the Son of the "Man of Holiness" who is God the Father. He saw, in vision, the coming of the Savior in the meridian of time, his crucifixion, and his triumphal ascension unto the Father (Moses 7:47, 53, 55). Enoch the seer (Moses 6:36) saw also the coming of the "Son of Man, in the last days, to dwell on the earth in righteousness for the space of a thousand years" (Moses 7:65).

NOAH, PREACHER OF DELIVERANCE THROUGH CHRIST. Noah pleaded with the people saying, "Believe and repent of your sins and be baptized in the name of Jesus Christ, the Son of God, even as our fathers, and ye shall receive the Holy Ghost, that ye may have all things made manifest; and if ye do not this, the floods will come in upon you" (Moses 8:24).

ABRAHAM. Abraham was visited by Jehovah (Abr. 1:16) and knew him as the one "like unto God," the Creator, the Son of Man, and the opponent of Satan (Abr. 3:24–28).

MOSES, DELIVERER, AND TYPE OF CHRIST. After Moses had been tried by a confrontation with the devil and had twice stood in the presence of God (Moses 1:2–39), he was told, "And now, Moses, my son, I will speak unto thee concerning this earth upon which thou standest; and thou shalt write the things which I shall speak" (Moses 1:40). Moses was also told that he was in the "similitude" of the Only Begotten, the Savior, who was full of grace and truth (Moses 1:6). When Moses was confronted by the powers of darkness, he called upon God for strength and in the name of the Only Begotten commanded Satan to depart (Moses 1:20–22). Moses served the God of Israel, whom he knew was the Messiah, the Only Begotten, the Savior, and the Creator of "worlds without number" (Moses 1:32–33).

MATTHEW, RECORDER OF THE LORD'S MINISTRY. In a discourse to his disciples three days before his crucifixion, Jesus counseled them on how to survive the forthcoming destruction of Jerusalem and how future disciples should survive a similar devastation to come in the latter days as a prelude to his second coming (Matt. 24). Joseph Smith's translation of that discourse is presented as Joseph Smith—Matthew.

JOSEPH SMITH. The Prophet Joseph Smith learned by divine experience that there are both a Savior, who is Son, and a God who is Father. This he learned in his first vision when a pillar of light appeared "above the brightness of the sun" and fell upon him. In that light he saw "two Personages, whose brightness and glory defy all description, standing above [him] in the air. One of them spake unto [him], calling [him] by name and said, pointing to the other—This is My Beloved Son. Hear Him!" In this vision, Joseph Smith talked to the Father and to the Lord Jesus Christ (JS—H 1:15–17). The Prophet later wrote, "I had actually seen a light, and in the midst of that light I saw two Personages, and they did in reality speak to me; and though I was hated and persecuted for saying that I had seen a vision, yet it was true (JS—H 1:25).

In the ARTICLES OF FAITH, Joseph Smith declared Jesus' position as a member of the GODHEAD, outlined the first principles of the gospel of Jesus Christ, and affirmed that Christ will come again to reign personally upon the earth.

BIBLIOGRAPHY
Peterson, H. Donl. *The Pearl of Great Price: A History and Commentary,* pp. 20, 74–75. Salt Lake City, 1987.

JAMES R. HARRIS, SR.

JOY

The Prophet Joseph Smith declared, "Happiness is the object and design of our existence; and will be the end thereof, if we pursue the path that leads to it" (*TPJS,* p. 255). The concept of true joy to be experienced in this life and in the life to come lies at the core of LDS thought. The Book of Mormon prophet Lehi taught, "Adam fell that men might be; and men are, that they might have joy" (2 Ne. 2:25; cf. Alma 42:8).

Latter-day Saints believe in a PREMORTAL LIFE in which all lived with God, the literal father of the spirits of humankind. Part of God's plan for the growth and progress of his children—the goal of which is to help everyone become as God himself is and to know the joy that he knows—involves a mortal experience. Therein people obtain a physical body, the power of procreation, and an independence and AGENCY that allow experiences of diverse kinds and thereby enhance the powers of self-determination.

In this light, Latter-day Saints view the physical body, the mortal environment, the procreative power, and the freedom of choice as essential elements of joy. Thus, Heavenly Father created this earth and sent his children to it that they might know joy. In this profound sense, joy and happiness arise from combinations of experience, responsibility and service, and pain and grief, along with pleasure and enjoyment. At the center of God's plan to make maximum joy accessible to his children is the ATONEMENT of Christ (2 Ne. 2:10–14, 22–27).

One can identify aspects of joy that are available in this life. First are the simple joys of being aware of and appreciating the gifts of life, the earth, and personal agency (e.g., taste, smell, beauty, music). A second is the joy of using these gifts to create opportunities or to develop relationships (e.g., marriage, parenting, charity). A third is the joy of coming to understand how mortality fits into the divine purpose or plan of the Heavenly Father (*see* PLAN OF SALVATION, PLAN OF REDEMPTION). This understanding derives from learning of God's plan for his children's salvation and using it as a framework for comprehending and assimilating life's experiences. Another is the joy of accepting Christ as Savior and feeling his acceptance and approval of one's efforts. This joy is accompanied by the power and beauty of Christ's spirit in one's life. In this connection, the Book of Mormon describes a scene wherein "the spirit of the Lord came upon them, and they were filled with joy, having received a remission of their sins, and having peace of conscience" (Mosiah 4:3; cf. John 15:10–12).

LDS doctrine teaches that joy is obtained only by RIGHTEOUSNESS (Mosiah 4:3, 20). Consequently, Latter-day Saints view God's COMMANDMENTS as loving counsel from a wise Father—a Father whose goal is human happiness. They believe that lives which conform to God's will and are governed by his standards will create the most joyful response to all of life's circumstances, bringing both a fulfillment in life's accomplishments and a sweet resolve in life's sorrows.

BIBLIOGRAPHY

Eyre, Richard M. *The Discovery of Joy.* Salt Lake City, 1974.

——. *Teaching Children Joy.* New York, 1986.

Hanks, Marion D. "Joy Through Christ." *Ensign* 2 (July 1972):104–106.

Romney, Marion G. "Joy and Happiness." *Ensign* 3 (Sept. 1973):2–3.

RICHARD M. EYRE

JUDGMENT

All humankind shall stand before Jesus, "and he shall separate them from one another, as a shepherd divideth his sheep from the goats" (Matt. 25:32). The verb "separate" reflects the Lord's determination of exact boundaries between good and evil, since he "cannot look upon sin with the least degree of allowance" (D&C 1:31). The Greek New Testament word for judgment (*krino*) means to separate or to decide, and refers not only to God's decisions but to those made by man as well (Matt. 7:1–2).

Amulek warned that this life is the time to prepare to meet God (Alma 34:32). MORTALITY requires basic decisions of a moral and spiritual character, in which individuals are free to choose for themselves yet are accountable to God for their choices. In turn, God will render a perfect and just decision to determine blessings or punishments. In the judgment there will be a perfect restoration of joy for righteous living and of misery for evil (Alma 41:3–5). After death is not the time to repent: "Ye cannot say, when ye are brought to that awful crisis, that I will repent, that I will return to my God; . . . for that same spirit which doth possess your bodies at the time that ye go out of this life . . . will have power to possess your body in that eternal world" (Alma 34:34).

Judgment applies to "the whole human family" (Morm. 3:20; cf. John 5:25–29; *TPJS,* p. 149). Every soul will come before the bar of God through the power of the ATONEMENT and the RESURRECTION (Jacob 6:9). Indeed, as Christ was lifted up on the cross, he will raise all men before him in judgment (3 Ne. 27:14–15; *TPJS,* p. 62). Christ has been given the responsibility for judgment. He taught, "The Father judgeth no man, but has committed all judgment unto the Son" (John 5:22). Others have been given some role in judgment, such as the Twelve apostles in Palestine and the Twelve disciples among the Nephites as described in the Book of Mormon (Morm. 3:18–19). Individuals will also judge themselves either by having a perfect knowledge of their joy and righteousness or by having a perfect knowledge of their guilt and unrighteousness (2 Ne. 9:14, 46). All have the assurance, however, that final judgment is in the hands of Christ (2 Ne. 9:41).

Three sets of records will be used in judgment: the records kept in heaven, the records kept on earth (D&C 128:6–7), and the records embedded in the consciousness of each individual (*MD,* p. 97; cf. Alma 11:43). Individuals are judged according to their works, thoughts, words, and the desires of their hearts (Alma 12:14; D&C 137:9).

There can be no pretense or hypocrisy in the manner in which people accept and live the gospel (2 Ne. 31:13). The Lord will judge members of the Church as to whether they have sought to deny themselves all ungodliness (Moro. 10:32) and whether they have served others with their whole soul (D&C 4:3). Other criteria for judgment include their concern for the needs of others, both spiritual and physical, and the use they make of the light and talents that they have been given (D&C 82:2–3). To merit God's approval, everyone must live and serve according to his will (Matt. 7:21–23) and do all things the Lord commands (Abr. 3:26). Yet, since all have sinned and come short of the glory of God (Rom. 3:23), except Jesus only, all are dependent on the Atonement and on repentance to escape the demands of justice (*see* JUSTICE AND MERCY).

Judgment is an expression of the love of God for his children and is exercised mercifully. Mercy takes into account the variety and differing circumstances of human life. For instance, many of God's expectations are relative to the opportunity that individuals have had to know the gospel. Nevertheless, "mercy cannot rob justice," and those who rebel openly against God merit punishment (Alma 42:25; Mosiah 2:38–39; 2 Pet. 2:9). Although the "Lord's arms of mercy are extended to all" (Alma 5:33), only those who repent have claim on mercy through the Son (Alma 12:33–34). God's judgment reflects the truth that he is "a perfect, just God, and a merciful God also" (Alma 42:15). Eventually all persons will acknowledge that God's judgment is just: "every nation, kindred, tongue, and people shall see eye to eye and shall confess before God that his judgments are just" (Mosiah 16:1).

The principle of judgment was operative in the premortal estate, is continuously operative during mortal life, and will continue in the spirit world and beyond, through resurrection and final judgment. In the premortal state Satan and "a third part" of God's children were denied the opportunity of mortality because they rebelled against God (Abr. 3:24–28; D&C 29:36–38). In mortal life nations and peoples have been destroyed or scattered when they have become ripened in iniquity and the judgments of God have thereby come upon them (1 Ne. 17:37).

Judgment during mortality is a continuous process to assess people's worthiness to participate in the saving ordinances of the gospel and to serve in the Church. This is done by means of interviews with local Church leaders. Priesthood leaders are called upon to judge the deeds of member's who transgress God's commandments to determine their standing in the Church. Judgment also occurs at death as individuals are received into the SPIRIT WORLD either in happiness or in misery (Alma 40:9–14).

In LDS doctrine, individual destiny after the final judgment is not limited to either HEAVEN or HELL. Although the wicked will be thrust into hell (D&C 76:106); nevertheless, all humankind (except those who deny the Holy Ghost and become sons of perdition) will be redeemed when Christ perfects his work (D&C 76:107). Thus, nearly everyone who has lived on the earth will eventually inherit a degree of glory, it being that amount of heavenly bliss and glory that they have the capacity and the qualifications to receive.

Concerning those who die without an opportunity to hear the gospel, the Lord revealed to Joseph Smith that "all who have died without a knowledge of this gospel, who would have received it if they had been permitted to tarry, shall be heirs of the celestial kingdom of God; also all that shall die henceforth without a knowledge of it, who would have received it with all their hearts, shall be heirs of that kingdom" (D&C 137:7–8). Little children who die also receive the full blessings of salvation (Moro. 8:11, 22). All mankind will be taught the gospel, either on earth or in the spirit world. All necessary ordinances will be performed on the earth vicariously by living proxies in the temple for those who did not have the opportunity to receive the gospel while in this life, so that they may accept or reject the gospel in the spirit world and be judged on the same basis as those who receive the gospel on earth and remain faithful (1 Pet. 4:6). Such doctrine is not only just; it is also a merciful expression of the pure love of Christ (*TPJS*, p. 218; Moro. 7:44–47).

[*See also* Baptism for the Dead; Plan of Salvation, Plan of Redemption; Purpose of Earth Life; Salvation for the Dead; Spiritual Death.]

BIBLIOGRAPHY

McConkie, Bruce R. *MD*, pp. 398–99, 400–408. Salt Lake City, 1966.

Smith, Joseph Fielding, comp. *TPJS*, pp. 216–23. Salt Lake City, 1938.

DEAN JARMAN

JUDGMENT DAY, FINAL

A purpose of the final judgment is to judge every person, to provide a separation of the faithful from the wicked, and to make available the promised blessings of eternal reward to God's faithful children. Jesus Christ is the judge.

The concept of a final judgment requires that it be deferred until the entire mortal experience is completed. The PLAN OF SALVATION teaches of a partial judgment at the time of death, when the spirit leaves the mortal body and enters the world of spirits (Alma 40:11–14), of another partial judgment at the time of resurrection, when the spirit and the physical body are permanently resurrected and reunited (Alma 11:45); and of a final judgment (Rev. 20:12; D&C 38:5) that will consign individuals to an eternal status (D&C 29:27–29; 3 Ne. 26:4). Thus, this final judgment will take place following the reuniting of body and spirit in the RESURRECTION (Alma 11:44; 12:12). By that time, every person will have been given an opportunity to receive an understanding of the gospel of Jesus Christ (1 Pet. 3:19–20; Luke 4:18; Isa. 42:7).

At the Judgment, each person will be required to give an accounting of the use of his or her moral agency during mortality (D&C 101:78). The final judgment is the final point of eternal accountability for all voluntary actions, words, thoughts, desires, and works of the individual. The full significance of such an accounting cannot be adequately assessed unless it is realized that all judgments granted from the seat of God's justice are of infinite scope and eternal consequence (3 Ne. 26:4; D&C 76:112).

Every person born to mortality will be brought to a final judgment (Morm. 3:18–20). No mortal act, no matter how righteous or wicked, will provide exemption from this judgment.

Each individual is to be judged according to the degree of knowledge and opportunity available during mortal probation (2 Ne. 2:10). On the basis of records kept both on earth and in heaven (Rev. 20:12; 2 Ne. 29:11; D&C 128:7), each individual will be judged according to works, desires, and intent of the heart (Mosiah 4:6; 1 Ne. 15:33; D&C 33:1; 137:7–9; Alma 41:3) and assigned to an eternal kingdom. In this solemn responsibility, the Savior will apply both justice and mercy, such that every individual will know and declare that his or her reward is just (2 Ne. 9:46; Mosiah 27:31). Every soul will recognize that the record presented is true and that the Judgment constitutes a proper decision (Mosiah 16:1; 29:12) at the hand of a loving yet impartial judge (Mosiah 29:12–13; Alma 41:3–7; cf. *TPJS*, p. 218).

Not all, however, will be held equally responsible for personal mortal acts. Speaking of the Judgment, the Prophet Joseph Smith taught that God "will judge them, 'not according to what they have not, but according to what they have,' those who have lived without law, will be judged without law, and those who have a law, will be judged by that law" (*TPJS*, p. 218).

Each brings his or her own record to this judgment, as stated by Church President John Taylor: "Because that record that is written by the man himself in the tablets of his own mind—that record that cannot lie—will in that day be unfolded before God and angels, and those who shall sit as judges" (*JD* 11:79; cf. Alma 41:7). Jesus Christ will be at the judgment bar, for he is the judge of both the living and the dead (Alma 11:44; Moro. 10:34; D&C 76:68).

Others will also participate in the process, but the final judgment rests with Christ. The twelve apostles of the Lamb will judge the righteous among the twelve tribes of Israel (D&C 29:12; Matt. 19:28; 1 Ne. 12:9–10), and the twelve Nephite disciples will judge the Nephites (3 Ne. 27:27). Still other prophets and righteous Saints have been appointed to help judge the works and deeds of their fellow sojourners in mortality (1 Cor. 6:2; Morm. 3:18–20). Thus, "there will be a whole hierarchy of judges who, under Christ, shall judge the righteous. He alone shall issue the decrees of damnation for the wicked" (McConkie, p. 520).

The Lord Jesus Christ earned the right to judge every earthly soul as he ensured the plan of redemption through the Atonement (3 Ne. 27:14–16; Alma 42:23). That this responsibility was explicitly given to the Son by the Father (John 5:22, 27) is attested in the Book of Mormon: "My Father sent me that I might be lifted up upon the cross; . . . that I might draw all men unto me, that as I have been lifted up by men even so should men be lifted up by the Father, to stand before me, to be judged of their works" (3 Ne. 27:14). Evidence of the Father's divine trust is shown in giving Jesus the responsibility of pronouncing eternal judgment on the Father's own children. Christ will judge in accordance with the will of the Father (John 5:30).

The basis of justice carried out at the final judgment lies in the agency granted to mortals so that "every man may be accountable for his own sins in the day of judgment" (D&C 101:78). There would be little value to agency without accountability. Just as Cain was counseled by the Lord, "If thou doest well, shalt thou not be accepted?" (Gen. 4:7), so each person has full option in making moral choices.

As a result of this final judgment, the wicked will be eternally separated from the righteous (D&C 76; Alma 41:5). This separation will be the desired state for both, for neither the wicked nor the righteous could enjoy the constant presence of others so unlike themselves. As stated by Moroni, "Ye would be more miserable to dwell with a holy and just God, under a consciousness of your filthiness before him, than ye would to dwell with the damned souls in hell" (Morm. 9:4). And to the righteous, judgment will bring fulfillment of the promise that "they who have believed in the Holy One of Israel, they who have endured the crosses of the world, and despised the shame of it, they shall inherit the kingdom of God, which was prepared for them from the foundation of the world, and their joy shall be full forever" (2 Ne. 9:18).

BIBLIOGRAPHY

Ludlow, Daniel H., ed. *Latter-day Prophets Speak,* pp. 50–60. Salt Lake City, 1948.

McConkie, Bruce R. *The Millennial Messiah.* Salt Lake City, 1982.

Young, Brigham. *Discourses of Brigham Young,* ed. John A. Widtsoe, pp. 382–86. Salt Lake City, 1941.

DONALD N. WRIGHT

JUSTICE AND MERCY

Justice and mercy are attributes of deity. They are also eternal principles. The "justice of God" (Alma 41:2; 42:14) is a principle so fundamental that without it, "God would cease to be God" (Alma 42:13). Of equivalent significance is God's mercy, which, broadly, is the ultimate source of all of the blessings of the human race and, specifically, is the principle that allows mankind's redemption. The competing demands of justice's claim for punishment and mercy's claim for forgiveness are reconciled by the unifying power of the ATONEMENT OF JESUS CHRIST.

On one hand, justice rewards righteousness. "And when we obtain any blessing from God, it is by obedience to that law upon which it is predicated" (D&C 130:21, see also D&C 82:10). On the other, justice requires penalties as a consequence of disobedience to the laws of God, for "I the Lord cannot look upon sin with the least degree of allowance" (D&C 1:31). Just as obedience to divine law leads to blessings, justice affixes a punishment to each violation of the Lord's commandments (Alma 42:17–18, 22), and men and women will be "punished for their own sins" (A of F 2). Each person will thus be judged according to his or her works (Rom. 2:5–6; 3 Ne. 27:14; Alma 41:2–6), although the degree of accountability varies according to the extent of each person's knowledge and culpability (2 Ne. 9:25; Mosiah 3:11). Yet the principle of mercy allows the atonement of Jesus Christ to pay the demands of justice on a repentant transgressor's behalf in a way that reconciles the principles of mercy and justice.

Not just any person may invoke mercy on behalf of another: "Now there is not any man that can sacrifice his own blood which will atone for the sins of another . . . therefore there can be nothing which is short of an infinite atonement which will suffice for the sins of the world" (Alma 34:11–12). Jesus Christ alone can achieve such an infinite atonement "once for all" (Hebrews 10:10) because of his nature as the actual son of God in the flesh and because he was himself without sin (*see* ATONEMENT OF JESUS CHRIST; JESUS CHRIST: ONLY BEGOTTEN IN THE FLESH).

Mercy is not extended arbitrarily. To protect individuals from the undeserved effects of sins for which they are not responsible, the Atonement unconditionally paid the penalty for the transgression of Adam and Eve in the Garden of Eden. It pays similarly for sins committed in ignorance (Mosiah 3:11; see also Moses 6:54). However, the Atonement removes the penalty for personal sins for which one is accountable only on the condition of individual repentance.

In this way, the concepts of justice, mercy, and the Atonement retain both a specific integrity and a logically consistent relationship: "The plan of mercy could not be brought about except an atonement should be made; therefore God himself atoneth for the sins of the world, to bring about the plan of mercy, to appease the demands of justice, that God might be a perfect, just God, and merciful God also. . . . But there is a law given, and a punishment affixed, and a repentance granted; which repentance mercy claimeth; otherwise, justice claimeth the creature. . . . For behold, justice exerciseth all his demands, and also mercy claimeth all which is her own; and thus, none but the truly penitent are saved" (Alma 42:13, 15, 22, 24).

Mercy is thus rehabilitative, not retributive or arbitrary. The Lord asks repentance from a transgressor, not to compensate the Savior for paying the debt of justice, but to induce the transgressor to undertake a meaningful process of personal development toward a Christlike nature.

At the same time, mercy depends ultimately on the Lord's extension of unmerited grace. Even though conditioned on repentance for personal sins, mercy is never fully "earned" by its recipients. Repentance is a necessary, but not a sufficient, condition of salvation and exaltation. "For we know that it is by grace that we are saved, after all we can do" (2 Ne. 25:23). The unearned nature of mercy is demonstrated by the Atonement's having unconditionally compensated for the disabilities imposed on mankind by the FALL OF ADAM. Adam and Eve and their posterity were utterly powerless to overcome the physical and spiritual deaths that were introduced by the Fall. Moreover, transgressors do not "pay" fully for their sins through the process of repentance. Even though repentance requires restitution to the extent of one's ability, most forms of restitution are beyond any person's ability to achieve. No matter how complete our repentance, it would all be to no avail without a mediator willing and able to pay our debt to justice, on condition of our repentance. Thus, even with sincere and complete repentance, all are utterly dependent on Jesus Christ.

Through the atonement of Jesus Christ, justice and mercy are interdependent and interactive, demonstrating that God cannot be just without being merciful, nor merciful without being just.

BIBLIOGRAPHY

Hafen, Bruce C. "Justice, Mercy, and Rehabilitation." In *The Broken Heart*, pp. 143–54. Salt Lake City, 1989.

Oaks, Dallin H. "The Atonement and the Principles of Justice and Mercy." Unpublished manuscript, from May 1, 1985, General Authority training meeting.

Roberts, B. H. *The Atonement*. Salt Lake City, 1911.

Taylor, John. *Mediation and Atonement*. Salt Lake City, 1882.

BRUCE C. HAFEN

JUSTIFICATION

Although the word "justify" has several meanings, its main meaning in the latter-day scriptures is inseparably intertwined with the concepts of GRACE (Rom. 3:28; Gal. 2:16; 2 Ne. 2:5; Mosiah 14:11; D&C 20:30; Moses 6:60), FAITH, REPENTANCE, RIGHTEOUSNESS, and SANCTIFICATION.

Justification is a scriptural metaphor drawn from the courts of law: a judge justifies an accused person by declaring or pronouncing that person innocent. Likewise, God may treat a person as being "not guilty" of sin. All mortals individually need to be justified because they fall short of perfect obedience to God, becoming "carnal, sensual, and devilish" through transgression (Moses 5:13; Mosiah 16:3), are "cut off" from God, and are in jeopardy of becoming "miserable forever" (2 Ne. 2:5). In this plight, they of themselves cannot be justified through subsequent obedience to the law and cannot change their own nature to become obedient. Furthermore, they are severed from the source of the divine power that can change, or sanctify, them (2 Ne. 9:5–9).

However, through the ATONEMENT OF JESUS CHRIST, when men, women, or children have faith in Jesus, are truly penitent, call upon his name, and are baptized, they become eligible for the redeeming grace extended through Jesus Christ. In this sense they become justified. This is given as a gift by grace, since fallen man must rely "alone upon the merits of Christ" (1 Ne. 10:6; Moro. 6:4). The faith by which one receives this grace manifests itself in an active determination to follow Christ in all things. It is demonstrated by obedience to the commandments to repent and be baptized, followed by a life of submission, obedience, and service to God and others (2 Ne. 31:16–20; Moro. 8:25–26; *see* GOSPEL OF JESUS CHRIST).

Justification directly opens the way to sanctification by establishing a "right" relationship of mortals with God. Thus, God, without denying justice, can bless them with the sanctifying power of the Holy Ghost (Mosiah 5:1–2; 3 Ne. 27:20). Justification starts the believer on the path toward righteousness.

Because justified, and even sanctified, persons can fall from that state of grace, believers are admonished to "take heed and pray always" (D&C 20:30–33) and to meet together often to fast and partake of the sacrament of the Lord's Supper, thereby renewing and personally reviewing their covenants with God, including baptism and its cleansing effect (Moro. 6:5–6), and to endure to the end (D&C 53:7).

The person whom God justifies has not yet necessarily received the promise of eternal life (*see* HOLY SPIRIT OF PROMISE; JESUS CHRIST, SECOND COMFORTER). To obtain that promise, the justified must continue in the path of faith, wherein nothing can separate the faithful from the love of God.

BIBLIOGRAPHY
Anderson, Richard L. *Understanding Paul.* Salt Lake City, 1983.
Sperry, Sidney B. *Paul's Life and Letters,* pp. 171–78. Salt Lake City, 1955.

COLIN B. DOUGLAS

K

KINGDOM OF GOD

IN HEAVEN

The kingdom of God in HEAVEN is the place where God lives. It is a CELESTIAL KINGDOM, organized under "the divinely ordained system of government and dominion in all matters, temporal and spiritual" (*JC,* p. 789). It is a purposeful state of existence, composed of intellectual and physical effort. It is a place of perfect order, ETERNAL PROGRESSION, everlasting family, and a fulness of joy.

The Savior taught his disciples to pray, "Our Father which art in heaven, . . . Thy kingdom come. Thy will be done in earth, as it is in heaven" (Matt. 6:9–10). The kingdom of God is set up on the earth to prepare for the kingdom of God in heaven (D&C 65:5–6). The Lord revealed to the Prophet Joseph Smith that this earth shall be "sanctified from all unrighteousness, that it may be prepared for the celestial glory, . . . that bodies who are of the celestial kingdom may possess it forever and ever" (D&C 88:17–20). When this occurs, this glorified celestial earth will become the kingdom of heaven for the Saints who have lived upon it, and then shall the meek and the righteous inherit it (Matt. 5:5; D&C 88:25–26; 130:9; *TPJS,* p. 181).

The purpose of The Church of Jesus Christ of Latter-day Saints is to help prepare its members to live forever in the kingdom of God in heaven.

GEORGE W. PACE

ON EARTH

The kingdom of God on earth exists wherever the priesthood of God is (*TPJS*, pp. 271–74). At present it is The Church of Jesus Christ of Latter-day Saints. The Church was established by divine authority to prepare its members to live forever in the celestial kingdom or kingdom of God in heaven. Its nature is ecclesiastical and nonpolitical. It "asserts no claim to temporal rule over nations; its scepter of power is that of the Holy Priesthood, to be used in the preaching of the gospel and in administering its ordinances for the salvation of mankind living and dead" (*JC*, p. 788).

The kingdom of God on the earth is the stone, spoken of by Daniel, that in the latter days would roll forth to fill the earth and never be destroyed (Dan. 2:34–45). It is the kingdom that the Savior prayed would come (Matt. 6:10), and he taught us to pray in like manner. In the meridian of time Jesus set up the kingdom of God on earth, called and ordained apostles and prophets, bestowed the necessary priesthood authority (Matt. 16:19; John 15:16), and charged them with the responsibilities of the Church. After an apostasy removed that priesthood from earth, the authority to reestablish the kingdom of God on the earth was given to the Prophet Joseph Smith by heavenly messengers. Through Joseph Smith the Lord said:

> The keys of the kingdom of God are committed unto man on the earth, and from thence shall the gospel roll forth unto the ends of the earth, as the stone which is cut out of the mountain without hands shall roll forth, until it has filled the whole earth. . . . Call upon the Lord, that his kingdom may go forth upon the earth, that the inhabitants thereof may receive it, and be prepared for the days to come, in the which the Son of Man shall come down in heaven, clothed in the brightness of his glory, to meet the kingdom of God which is set up on the earth. Wherefore, may the kingdom of God go forth, that the kingdom of heaven may come [D&C 65:2, 5–6].

GEORGE W. PACE

KNOWLEDGE

Latter-day Saints believe that certain forms of knowledge are essential for salvation and eternal life (John 17:3). The Prophet Joseph

Smith taught that "a man is saved no faster than he gets knowledge, for if he does not get knowledge, he will be brought into captivity," and thus human beings have a need for "revelation to assist us, and give us knowledge of the things of God" (*TPJS*, p. 217). One of the purposes of the priesthood, which is the authority to administer the gospel, is to make this saving "knowledge of God" available to all (D&C 84:19). Those who die without a chance to obtain a knowledge of the gospel of Jesus Christ will be given opportunity to receive and accept the gospel in the life after death to become "heirs of the Celestial Kingdom" (D&C 128:5; 137:7–9; 138:28–34; *see* SALVATION FOR THE DEAD).

Knowledge makes possible moral agency and freedom of choice (John 8:32; 2 Ne. 2:26–27; Hel. 14:30–31; Moro. 7:15–17). Those who receive knowledge are responsible to live in accordance with it. Those who sin after having received knowledge of the truth by revelation bear greater condemnation than those who sin in ignorance (Heb. 10:26–27; 2 Pet. 2:20–21; Mosiah 2:36–39; Alma 24:30), while mercy is extended to those who sin in ignorance, or without knowledge of the truth (Mosiah 3:11; Alma 9:14–17; Hel. 7:23–24).

Knowledge is one of the gifts of the spirit that all people are commanded to seek (1 Cor. 12:8; Moro. 10:9–10; D&C 46:17–18). Knowledge of the truth of the gospel of Christ is conveyed as well as received by the power of the Holy Ghost (Moro. 10:5; 1 Cor. 2:9–16; D&C 50:19–21). Similarly, knowledge of the mysteries of God also comes through personal revelation. Shared knowledge of the things of God is available in the scriptures and other teachings of his prophets.

Knowledge is closely associated in scripture with other virtues such as meekness, long suffering, temperance, patience, godliness, kindness, and charity (2 Pet. 1:5–7; D&C 4:6; 107:30–31; 121:41–42). It is intimately related to truth; genuine knowledge is truth (D&C 93:24). Knowledge is understood to be an active, motivating force rather than simply a passive awareness, or collection of facts. This force is seen, for example, in acts of faith (Alma 32:21–43) and obedience (1 Jn. 2:4). The word "knowledge" is also used to refer to vain or false knowledge, and to the pride that often comes with knowledge based on human learning unaccompanied by righteousness and the spirit and knowledge of God (1 Cor. 8:1–2; 2 Tim. 3:7; 2 Ne. 9:28–29).

All people are encouraged to seek deeply and broadly to gain knowledge of both heavenly and earthly things (D&C 88:77–80). Such knowledge comes by study of the works of others, and also by faith (D&C 88:118). The LDS Church has traditionally encouraged and supported the pursuit of knowledge and education by its members. Knowledge gained through study and also by faith is obtained "line upon line and precept upon precept" (D&C 98:11–12; 128:21). All knowledge gained in this life stays with those who attain it and rises with them in the resurrection, bringing some advantage in the life to come (D&C 130:18–19). The next life holds the promise of "perfect knowledge" or understanding (2 Ne. 9:13–14).

BIBLIOGRAPHY

Reynolds, Noel B. "Reason and Revelation." In *A Thoughtful Faith: Essays on Belief by Mormon Scholars,* ed. P. Barlow, pp. 205–224. Centerville, Utah, 1986.

RICHARD N. WILLIAMS

L

LAST DAYS

The term "last days" refers to the current period of time, the preparatory era before the second coming of the Christ. This period is marked by prophetic signs (D&C 45:37–40). "The end of the world" is not the end of the earth, but the end of evil and the triumph of righteousness (JS—H 1:4). At the conclusion of these last days, the Lord Jesus Christ will come again and personally reign upon the renewed "paradisiacal" earth (A of F 10).

During the last days, many marvelous events will occur that are signs that this preparatory period has begun (Isa. 29:14). These include the restoration of the gospel of Jesus Christ, the preaching of his gospel among all nations, the coming forth of modern scripture, and the gathering of scattered Israel. The restoration of the gospel before the coming of the Lord (Acts 3:19–21) includes the revealing anew of lost truths, priesthood power, temple worship, and the full organization of the Church of Jesus Christ, including apostles and prophets.

Christ prophesied that his gospel would be preached "in all the world for a witness unto all nations; and then shall the end come" (Matt. 24:1, 4). The Savior also foretold to Enoch that in the last days righteousness would come "down out of heaven," and truth will come "forth out of the earth" to bear testimony of Jesus Christ and of "his resurrection from the dead" (Moses 7:62). The Book of Mormon,

Doctrine and Covenants, and Pearl of Great Price have come forth in partial fulfillment of these prophecies. Additional sacred writings are yet to come forth (cf. 2 Ne. 29:13; Ether 4:5–7).

A further sign will be the gathering of Israel. The house of Joseph is to be gathered to the "tops of the mountains" of the Western Hemisphere (Isa. 2:2) and to "stakes" (centers of strength) in many lands (*HC* 3:390–91). The house of Judah will gather by the millions to Jerusalem and its environs in fulfillment of prophecy (Wilford Woodruff in Ludlow, p. 240; *DS* 3:257–59). Another gathering will bring the lost tribes of Israel "from the north countries," to join with the house of Joseph (*DS* 3:306).

In contrast to these preparatory events, the prophecies state that in the last days gross wickedness will cover the earth (2 Tim. 3:1–7). Ancient and modern prophets have written that the world's latter-day inhabitants will "defile the earth" (Isa. 24:5) and become as wicked as Sodom and Gomorrah (Wilford Woodruff in Ludlow, p. 224) and as those of the time of Noah (*DS* 3:20), and that if Jesus "were here to-day, and should preach the same doctrine He did then, they would put Him to death" (*HC* 6:58).

This wickedness will result in wars of unprecedented destruction (George A. Smith, *CR*, Oct. 1946, p. 149), parents and children seeking each other's lives (Mark 13:12; *HC* 3:391), great increases in crime (Wilford Woodruff in Ludlow, p. 228), the destruction of many cities (Brigham Young in Ludlow, p. 223), and a "desolating scourge" that will reach plague proportions (D&C 29:19).

As the end nears, the earth will be in commotion (D&C 45:26; cf. Joel 2:30–32). There will be severe lightnings and thunderings (D&C 87:6). The waves of the sea will heave themselves beyond their bounds (D&C 88:90). The earth will "reel to and fro as a drunken man" (D&C 49:23). A devastating hailstorm will destroy the crops of the earth (D&C 29:16), causing widespread famine (Brigham Young in Ludlow, p. 223). These judgments and wars will ultimately result in the "full end" of all nations (D&C 87:6).

Immediately preceding the Second Coming, unmistakable signs will appear in the heavens. The sun will be darkened, the moon will turn to blood, the stars will fall, and the powers of heaven will be shaken (D&C 45:42). In addition, the rainbow will be taken from the sky (*HC* 6:254). Finally, a great sign will be seen having the appearance of "seven golden lamps set in the heavens representing the various dispensations of God to man" (Wilford Woodruff in Ludlow, pp. 233–34). There will then be silence in heaven for half an hour, and "immediately after shall the curtain of heaven be unfolded as a scroll is unfolded after it is rolled up, and the face of the Lord shall be unveiled" (D&C 88:95).

As the earth becomes increasingly full of violence and immorality, the righteous will be watching the signs of the times and will call upon the Lord and seek to be worthy to abide the day of his coming (Luke 21:36; Acts 2:21). These faithful disciples of the Lord will experience "very little compared with the terrible destruction, the misery and suffering that will overtake the world" (John Taylor in Ludlow, p. 225; Moses 7:61); moreover, the righteous who fall victim to pestilence and to disease will be saved in the kingdom of God (*HC* 4:11).

To escape these judgments, the faithful will obey the commandments (*DS* 3:33–35; Luke 21:36), honor the priesthood (Wilford Woodruff in Ludlow, pp. 235–36), take the Holy Spirit for their guide (D&C 45:57), and stand in holy places (D&C 45:32). As the polarization of the righteous and the wicked increases, the righteous followers of the Savior will be called "Zion" (both the condition of purity of heart and the community of the pure-hearted). A city, Zion (the New Jerusalem), will be established on the American continent and, together with her outlying stakes, will be a place of refuge (*HC* 3:391). And old Jerusalem will become a holy city (Ether 13:5). From these two capital cities of the millennial era, Jesus Christ will personally rule the renewed, paradisiacal world.

BIBLIOGRAPHY

Ludlow, Daniel H. *Latter-day Prophets Speak.* Salt Lake City, 1951.
Lund, Gerald N. *The Coming of the Lord.* Salt Lake City, 1971.

GRANT E. BARTON

LAW

[*Four different articles treat diverse aspects of LDS beliefs and experience with law. Two of the articles are grouped below:*

Overview
Divine and Eternal Law

The Overview *discusses the LDS concept of law in general and of divine and eternal law in particular.* Divine and Eternal Law *summarizes and describes the references in LDS scripture to the central role of law as pertaining to God.*

The experience of Latter-day Saints and the Church in the courts is reported in Legal and Judicial History *in another volume. Regarding LDS views on specific aspects of civil law, see also* Freedom. *For information on other law-related topics, see* Justice and Mercy. *Commandments and gospel principles are often referred to as "laws"; on these subjects, see such entries as* Commandments *and* Obedience.]

OVERVIEW

Three types of laws exist: spiritual or divine laws, laws of nature, and civil laws. Latter-day Saints are deeply and consistently law-oriented, because laws, whether spiritual, physical, or civil, are rules defining existence and guiding action. Through the observance of laws, blessings and rewards are expected, and by the violation of laws, suffering, deprivation, and even punishment will result.

Basic LDS attitudes toward law and jurisprudence are shaped primarily by revelations contained in the Doctrine and Covenants, and by explanations given by the Presidents of the Church. God is, by definition, a god of order: "Behold, mine house is a house of order, saith the Lord God, and not a house of confusion" (D&C 132:8). God and law are inseparable, for if there is no law, there is no sin; and if there is no sin, there is no righteousness, "and if these things are not there is no God" (2 Ne. 2:13). Law emanates from God through Christ. Jesus said, "I am the law, and the light" (3 Ne. 15:9), and God's word is his law (D&C 132:12).

In an 1832 revelation, Joseph Smith learned that law is a pervasive manifestation of God's light and power: "The light which is in all things . . . is the law by which all things are governed" (D&C 88:12–13). In connection with both spiritual law and natural law, no space or relationship occurs in which law is nonexistent. "There are many kingdoms; for there is no space in the which there is no kingdom; . . . and unto every kingdom is given a law; and unto every law there are certain bounds also and conditions" (D&C 88:37–38).

There are as many laws as there are kingdoms, which reflect greater or lesser light and truth. Some laws are higher, and some are lower. The kingdom of God operates in accordance with higher laws befitting God's exalted station, while the earth and all mortality and other kingdoms belong to lower spheres and therefore operate under different laws. The degree of glory that a person or thing can abide depends on how high a law he, she, or it is able to abide (D&C 88:22–25).

Lower laws are subsumed in higher laws. If people keep the laws of God, they have "no need to break the laws of the land" (D&C 58:21). Similarly, when the Law of Moses was fulfilled by Jesus Christ, it was subsumed in him.

Existence is a process of progressively learning to obey higher law. Obeying and conforming to law are understood as a sign of growth, maturity, and understanding, and greater obedience to law produces greater freedom (D&C 98:5) and associated blessings (D&C 130:20–21).

At all levels, the principles of AGENCY and ACCOUNTABILITY are in effect: People may choose which laws to obey or to ignore, but God will hold them accountable and reward them accordingly (D&C 82:4). This is not viewed as a threat; law's purpose is not to force or punish but to guide and provide structure.

In the divine or spiritual sphere, law is not the product of a philosophical or theoretical search for what is right or good. It emanates from deity and is revealed through Jesus Christ and his prophets.

Spiritual laws given by God to mankind are commonly called COMMANDMENTS, which consist variously of prohibitions ("thou shalt not"), requirements ("thou shalt"), and prescriptions ("if a man"). The commandments are uniformly coupled with promised blessings for faithful compliance. Thus, Latter-day Saints describe themselves as covenant people who may be rewarded now, and in the hereafter, for their faithfulness. Many such COVENANTS are bilateral in character; that is, members make personal commitments in a variety of formal ordinances to keep in accord with certain commandments.

Spiritual laws, or God's commandments, are generally understood to have been purposefully decreed by a loving Heavenly Father, who desires to bring to pass the exaltation of his spirit children. Thus, "there is a law, irrevocably decreed in heaven before the foundations of this world, upon which all blessings are predicated" (D&C 130:20). Latter-day Saints believe that God knows or stipulates all types of acts and forbearances required by all individuals in order for them to attain that blessed eternal state of exaltation and that he has revealed these requirements to humankind through his servants. No law given of God is temporal (D&C 29:34).

"Irrevocability" in the foregoing quotation connotes permanence and unchangeability. Since God cannot lie, the commandments and promises contained in his covenants with people will not be revoked, though he can revoke a specific commandment to individuals when they have disobeyed (D&C 56:3–6). The fundamentals are not situational and do not ebb and flow with changing concepts of morality or theology outside the Church. The President of the Church is a prophet of God who receives revelations and inspiration to interpret and apply those basic principles as human circumstances change.

In accordance with the principle of agency, God commands, but he does not compel. No earthly mechanism exists for the enforcement of God's laws. The prophet teaches the members correct principles, and they are expected to govern themselves. Missionary work and education of Church members are carried out so that people may make informed choices. They are taught that making an informed choice results either in a blessing (current or deferred) or an undesirable consequence (current or deferred). Ignorance of the law is considered a legitimate excuse. Because of the atonement of Jesus Christ, repentance is not required of those "who have ignorantly sinned" or "who have died not knowing the will of God concerning them" (Mosiah 3:11), even though failure to abide by the commandment may result in the loss of blessings that would flow from proper conduct. In most cases, violators of divine law can escape the punishment connected with the offense by repentance, the demands of justice having been satisfied by the atonement of Christ in the interest of all (*see* JUSTICE AND MERCY).

BIBLIOGRAPHY

Firmage, Edwin B., and Christopher L. Blakesley. "J. Reuben Clark, Jr.: Law and International Order." *BYU Studies* 13 (Spring 1973):273–346.

Garrard, LaMar E. "God, Natural Law, and the Doctrine and Covenants." In *Doctrines for Exaltation*, pp. 55–76. Salt Lake City, 1989.

JOHN S. WELCH

DIVINE AND ETERNAL LAW

LDS revelation emphasizes the existence and indispensability of law. The relation of divine law to other species of law has not been given systematic treatment in Mormon thought as it has in traditional Christian theology (e.g., the *Summa Theologica* of Thomas Aquinas). But distinctive observations about divine law and eternal law may be drawn from Latter-day scriptures and related sources.

Aquinas identified four categories of law: (1) eternal law, which is coextensive with the divine mind and with the overall purpose and plan of God; (2) natural law, which addresses mankind's proper participation in eternal law but is discovered by reason without the assistance of revelation and promulgation; (3) divine positive law, also a part of the eternal law, which pertains to the sacraments and ordinances necessary to the attainment of mankind's supernatural end made known by revelation; and (4) man-made positive law, which regulates the affairs of mankind not specifically addressed by God's law (e.g., laws that regulate such things as corporations, stocks, bonds, wills, and trusts) or which mandate the natural law with the power of the state.

LDS sources affirm laws roughly corresponding to each of these four types. Unlike traditional Jewish and Christian theologies, which place God outside of, and antecedent to, nature, however, LDS theology places God within nature.

"Divine" laws are instituted by God to govern his creations and kingdoms and to prescribe behavior for his offspring. Such law, in the terms of Acquinas's categories, would be divine positive law (i.e., law existing by virtue of being posited or enacted by God). Some Latter-day Saints believe that "eternal" law is self-existent, unauthored law, which God himself honors and administers as a condition of his perfection and Godhood. It should be noted that the adjectives "divine" and "eternal" do not have fixed usages in writing (*see* TIME AND ETERNITY).

Latter-day scriptures and other sources do not explicitly state that eternal law exists independently or coeternally with God. This characteristic of eternal law is sometimes inferred, however, from two concepts that do have support in scripture and other LDS sources:

1. God is governed (bound) by law. Latter-day scriptures state that "God would cease to be God" if he were to allow mercy to destroy

justice, or justice to overpower mercy, or the plan of redemption to be fulfilled on unjust conditions (Alma 42:13). Scriptures further state that "I, the Lord, am bound when ye do what I say" (D&C 82:10), implying that God by nature and definition—not by any external coercion—is righteous and trustworthy. Some Church writers have said that "[God] himself governs and is governed by law" (*MD,* p. 432) and that "the Lord works in accordance with natural law" (*DS* 2:27). They likewise speak of "higher laws" that account for providence and miracles.

2. Intelligence and truth were not created; they are coeternal with God. "Intelligence, or the light of truth, was not created or made, neither indeed can be. All truth is independent in that sphere in which God has placed it, to act for itself, as all intelligence also; otherwise there is no existence" (D&C 93:29–30). Joseph Smith expanded upon this teaching in his King Follett Discourse, stating that "we infer that God had materials to organize the world out of chaos. . . . Element had an existence from the time he had. The pure principles of element . . . had no beginning, and can have no end. . . . The mind or the intelligence which man possesses is coeternal with God himself" (*TPJS,* pp. 350–53). If truth and intelligence were not created by God and are coeternal with him, it may be that they are ordered by and function according to eternal laws or principles that are self-existent. This may be implied in Joseph Smith's phrase "laws of eternal and self-existent principles" (*TPJS,* p. 181).

Consistent with the eternal laws, God fashions and decrees laws that operate in the worlds he creates and that set standards of behavior that must be observed in order to obtain the blessing promised upon obedience to that law. Joseph Smith taught that "[God] was the first Author of law, or the principle of it, to mankind" (*TPJS,* p. 56).

Latter-day scriptures emphasize the pervasive nature of divine law: "[God] hath given a law unto all things, by which they move in their times and their seasons" (D&C 88:42). "This is the light of Christ . . . which light proceedeth forth from the presence of God to fill the immensity of space—The light which is in all things, which giveth life to all things, which is the law by which all things are governed, even the power of God who sitteth upon his throne" (D&C 88:7, 12–13).

These same sources suggest, however, that divine law operates within the domain to which it inherently pertains or is assigned by God and, therefore, has limits or bounds: "All kingdoms have a law given; and there are many kingdoms; for there is no space in which there is no kingdom; and there is no kingdom in which there is no space, either a greater or a lesser kingdom. And unto every kingdom is given a law; and unto every law there are certain bounds also and conditions" (D&C 88:36–38).

The above references apparently pertain to descriptive law—that is, the divine law that operates directly upon or through physical and biological orders.

Other laws of God are prescriptive. They address the free will of man, setting forth standards and rules of behavior necessary for salvation and for social harmony. Latter-day Saints embrace such prescriptive commands of God as found in the ten commandments and the Sermon on the Mount. Latter-day revelation also confirms that blessings and salvation come through compliance with divine laws: "There is a law, irrevocably decreed in heaven before the foundations of this world, upon which all blessings are predicated—and when we obtain any blessing from God, it is by obedience to that law upon which it is predicated" (D&C 130:20–21). "And they who are not sanctified through the law which I have given unto you, even the law of Christ, must inherit another kingdom, even that of a terrestrial kingdom, or that of a telestial kingdom" (D&C 88:21).

Of these prescriptive laws or commandments of God, LDS teachings tend to emphasize the following characteristics: (1) the extent of the divine laws revealed to mankind may vary from dispensation to dispensation, according to the needs and conditions of mankind as God decrees; (2) they are given through and interpreted by his prophets; (3) they are relatively concise, but "gentle" or benevolent, given to promote the happiness he has designed for his children (*TPJS*, pp. 256–57); and (4) they are efficacious for mankind as God's harmony with eternal law was, and is, efficacious for him, and will bring to pass the exaltation of his righteous children.

BIBLIOGRAPHY
Aquinas, Thomas. *Summa Theologica* 1266–73, trans. the Fathers of the English Dominican Province. London, 1915.
Widtsoe, John A. *A Rational Theology*. Salt Lake City, 1952.

CARL S. HAWKINS
DOUGLAS H. PARKER

LAW OF ADOPTION

The house of Israel in a spiritual and eternal perspective will finally include all who are the true followers of Jesus Christ. Although those of the direct blood lineage of the house of Israel are genealogically the sheep of God's fold, they must fulfill all the spiritual conditions of discipleship. Those not of the blood of Israel can become Israel through adoption (cf. Rom. 8:14; Gal. 3:7, 29; 4:5–7; Matt. 3:9; JST Luke 3:8; Abr. 2:10), through the principles and the ordinances of the gospel: faith in the Lord Jesus Christ; repentance of sins; baptism by water and reception of the HOLY GHOST; and enduring to the end.

In a larger sense, everyone must be adopted into the family of God in order to enjoy the fulness of his blessings in the world to come. As the Only Begotten of the Father in the flesh, Jesus is the only natural heir and therefore the only one whose birthright is the kingdom of his Father. If others are to qualify as joint-heirs with Christ in his Father's kingdom, they must be fully adopted by God.

The adoption process is, in the Prophet Joseph Smith's words, "a new creation by the Holy Ghost" (*TPJS*, p. 150). As summarized in the Doctrine and Covenants, individuals who enter into the COVENANT and "magnify their calling" are "sanctified by the Spirit unto the renewing of their bodies. They become the sons of Moses and of Aaron and the seed of Abraham, and the church and kingdom, and the elect of God" (D&C 84:33–34).

BIBLIOGRAPHY
Irving, Gordon. "The Law of Adoption: One Phase in the Development of Mormon Concept of Salvation, 1830–1900." *BYU Studies* 14 (Spring 1974):291–314.

V. BEN BLOXHAM

LAYING ON OF HANDS

The laying on of hands on the head of an individual as a religious ceremony has served many purposes historically and continues to do so for The Church of Jesus Christ of Latter-day Saints. The most common are the following:

THE SACRIFICIAL CEREMONIES OF ANCIENT ISRAEL. Anciently, in burnt and sin offerings, the offerer laid his hands on the sacrifice prior to its being slain (e.g., Ex. 29:10; Lev. 1:4; 4:4; 2 Chron. 29:23). In the case of the scapegoat, hands were laid on the head, symbolizing transference of the sins of the people to the animal (Lev. 16:21). The hands of the people were laid upon the Levites, and they in turn laid their hands upon the offerings (Num. 8:10–12).

BESTOWAL OF THE GIFT OF THE HOLY GHOST. CONFIRMATION and bestowing of the gift of the Holy Ghost by the laying on of hands follows BAPTISM. The Doctrine and Covenants explains that the one performing the ordinance is acting as proxy for the Lord himself: "I will lay my hand upon you by the hand of my servant Sidney Rigdon, and you shall receive my Spirit, the Holy Ghost, even the Comforter, which shall teach you the peaceable things of the kingdom" (D&C 36:2; cf. Moro. 2:2). This ordinance may be performed only by Melchizedek Priesthood holders, not by those of the lesser or Aaronic Priesthood (D&C 20:58). This explains why John the Baptist, though he performed water baptism, did not bestow the Holy Ghost by the laying on of hands (Matt. 3:11), and it may explain why Philip did not do so for his Samaritan converts (Acts 8:5–17), or Apollos for the Ephesians (Acts 19:6; see also Acts 8:12–20). In Philip's case, he baptized the Samaritans, but Peter and John, who held the higher priesthood, were sent to confer the Holy Ghost, and they laid "their hands on them, and they received the Holy Ghost" (Acts 8:17).

Paul may have referred to this gift when he counseled his companion Timothy to "neglect not the gift that is in thee, which was given thee by prophecy, with the laying on of the hands of the presbytery" (1 Tim. 4:14). On another occasion Paul admonished him to "stir up the gift of God, which is in thee by the putting on of my hands" (2 Tim. 1:6).

BESTOWAL OF THE GIFTS AND RIGHTS OF AN OFFICE. Moses ordained

Joshua as his successor by the laying on of hands (Num. 27:18, 23; Deut. 34:9). Jesus' apostles used this procedure in authorizing seven men to manage practical economic matters in the early church (Acts 6:1–6). Paul and Barnabas were ordained to a missionary journey by the laying on of hands of the "prophets and teachers at Antioch" (Acts 13:3).

The Book of Mormon reports that Jesus conferred upon his disciples the power to give the Holy Ghost by laying his hands upon them (3 Ne. 18:37; Moro. 2:3). The Aaronic Priesthood was conferred on the Prophet Joseph Smith and Oliver Cowdery by the hands of the resurrected John the Baptist (JS—H 1:68–69). All subsequent transmission of authority comes from the President of the Church by the laying on of hands. A REVELATION on priesthood states: "Wherefore, it must needs be that one be appointed of the High Priesthood to preside over the priesthood, and he shall be called President of the High priesthood of the Church . . . From the same comes the administering of ordinances and blessings upon the church, by the laying on of the hands" (D&C 107:65–67). Accordingly, all men and women are installed in any Church office or calling by a setting apart by the laying on of hands of those in authority.

HEALING THE SICK. The laying on of hands to heal the sick was a common practice of Jesus (Mark 5:23; 6:5; 16:18; Luke 13:12–13). Luke records that "all they that had any sick with divers diseases brought them unto him; and he laid his hands on every one of them, and healed them" (Luke 4:40). Jesus did not use this method exclusively. Sometimes a touch was sufficient, or his word only. In the case of a man who was deaf and had a speech impediment, Jesus touched his tongue and his ears (Mark 7:33).

Jesus conferred the power of healing on his followers: "And these signs shall follow them that believe . . . they shall lay hands on the sick, and they shall recover" (Mark 16:18). Ananias laid hands on Paul that he might regain his sight (Acts 9:17–18). Paul thus healed the father of Publius in Malta (Acts 28:8). The Lord commanded that this practice should be continued in the Latter-day Church (D&C 42:43–44).

IMPARTING A BLESSING. Blessings in addition to those for health are given by the laying on of hands. Among these are patriarchal blessings (as when Jacob blessed Ephraim and Manasseh [Gen. 48:14]), blessings for the Lord's protecting care, blessings for success in the Lord's work, blessings of counsel, and the blessing of children. (Matt. 19:15; Mark 10:13, 16; cf. Acts 8:12–20; Moro. 2:2).

C. KENT DUNFORD

LIFE AND DEATH, SPIRITUAL

Unlike physical life and death, over which individuals have little control, spiritual life and death are opposite poles between which a choice is required. Latter-day scripture states that all people "are free to choose liberty and eternal life, through the great Mediator of all men, or to choose captivity and death, according to the captivity and power of the devil" (2 Ne. 2:27). This opposition between life and death is viewed as the fundamental dichotomy of all existence.

At one pole is Jesus Christ, who is described throughout the scriptures as light and life (e.g., John 1:4; 3 Ne. 15:9; D&C 10:70). He is the author both of physical life, as the creator of the earth and its life-sustaining sun (D&C 88:7), and of spiritual life, as the giver of eternal life (3 Ne. 15:9). To choose life is to follow him on a path that leads to freedom and eternal life.

Satan, at the opposite pole, is darkness and death (e.g., Rom. 6:23; Alma 15:17; D&C 24:1). He is the author of temporal death, as the one who enticed Adam and Eve to initiate the Fall, and of spiritual death, as the tempter who induces individuals to separate themselves from God through sin. To choose to follow Satan by succumbing to sin and resisting Christ's entreaties to repent is to choose death.

The freedom to choose effectively between life and death is a result of the redemption of Christ (2 Ne. 2:27), and it is God's work and glory "to bring to pass the immortality and eternal life of man" (Moses 1:39).

The scriptures speak of two SPIRITUAL DEATHS. The first has already come upon all humans as a result of the Fall, separating "all mankind . . . from the presence of the Lord" (Hel. 14:16). The second will be experienced by only those who, having once known Christ, willfully deny him and refuse to repent, being thus "cut off again as to things pertaining to righteousness" (Hel. 14:18). Spiritual death does not mean that a person's spirit literally has died (the spirit is immortal), but that one is in "a state of spiritual alienation from God" (Smith, Vol. 1, p. 45), a death "as to things pertaining unto righteousness" (Alma 12:16; 40:26).

Because little children are not capable of sinning (Moro. 8:10–14), the first spiritual death does not begin for an individual on the earth until the age of ACCOUNTABILITY (eight years of age; D&C 68:27). Generally, as individuals mature they begin to recognize the consequences of their acts and become responsible for them (D&C 18:42). Insofar as they do not harmonize behavior with an understanding of truth and goodness, they create a gulf between themselves and God—that is, spiritual death.

The first step toward overcoming this state was taken, paradoxically, before the Fall occurred: in premortal life. All who have been or will be born on this earth chose both physical and spiritual life when as spirit children of God they chose to follow the Father's plan for earth life. After they reach the age of accountability during earth life, they must again choose.

According to LDS understanding, the choice between spiritual life and death is made at the time of BAPTISM and CONFIRMATION, the ordinances that symbolically reconcile a person to God and initiate a lifetime process of spiritual rebirth. Once baptismal covenants are made and the GIFT OF THE HOLY GHOST is conferred and received, the symbolic rebirth must be made actual through the day-to-day struggle to repent and choose life—Christ and righteousness. The choice is not made once and for all, but many times during a lifetime.

Latter-day Saints do not view righteousness simply as a way to avoid an unpleasant AFTERLIFE and gain a heavenly reward. Following Christ is also the path to happiness in mortal life. As people harmonize their lives with God's laws, they are "blessed in all things, both temporal and spiritual" (Mosiah 2:41). In Christ is life abundant (John 10:10); "if thou wilt enter into life, keep the commandments" (Matt. 19:17).

In an everyday sense, choosing life for the Latter-day Saint should include loving and serving others, praying and studying the words of God daily, sharing knowledge of Christ and his plan with others, speaking the truth, remaining chaste before marriage and faithful after marriage, rearing children with patience and love, and being honest in all things. Enjoying such things constitutes the abundant life.

In the postmortal period, "life" again depends upon Christ's ATONEMENT, which overcomes the first spiritual death by making it possible for all men and women to come into God's presence to be judged. At that point, everyone will be judged worthy of a DEGREE OF GLORY and its quality of life except the sons of perdition. These individuals suffer the second spiritual death for having committed the unpardonable sin, which is denying Christ in the face of full knowledge and truth (D&C 76:30–38; *HC* 6:314).

[*See also* Eternal Life; Opposition; Spiritual Death.]

BIBLIOGRAPHY

Hunter, Howard W. "The Golden Thread of Choice." *Ensign* 19 (Nov. 1989):17–18.

Smith, Joseph Fielding. *DS*, 3 vols.

SUE BERGIN

LIGHT OF CHRIST

The light of Christ refers to the spiritual power that emanates from God to fill the immensity of space and enlightens every man, woman, and child. Other terms sometimes used to denote this same phenomenon are HOLY SPIRIT, "Spirit of the Lord," and "Spirit of Truth," but it is different from the HOLY GHOST. The scriptures are not always precise in the use of such terminology, and several attempts have been made to describe the various aspects of this important manifestation of God's goodness and being.

Jesus Christ is the light and life of the world (John 8:12; 3 Ne. 15:9). This light is described in the Doctrine and Covenants as "the same light that quickeneth your understandings; which light proceedeth forth from the presence of God to fill the immensity of space—the light which is in all things, which giveth life to all things, which is the law by which all things are governed, even the power of God who sitteth upon his throne, who is in the bosom of eternity, who is in the midst of all things (D&C 88:11–13). B. H. Roberts, a seventy, interpreted this to mean that the Light of Christ is a creative power, a governing power, a life-giving power, and an "intelligence-inspiring power" (Roberts, 2:7–8).

This light manifests itself in different ways and degrees. In its "less refined existence," wrote Parley P. Pratt, it is visible as sunlight. It is also the refined "intellectual light of our inward and spiritual organs, by which we reason, discern, judge, compare, comprehend, and remember the subjects within our reach." It is revealed as instinct in animals, reason in man, and vision in the prophets (p. 25).

John A. Widtsoe gave this general description of the emanation of God's power: "God is a personal being of body—a body limited in extent. He cannot, therefore, at a given moment be personally everywhere. . . . By his power, will and word, [he] is everywhere present. . . . The holy spirit permeates all the things of the universe, material and spiritual" (Widtsoe, pp. 68–69).

Since God possesses a fulness of this power and man only a small portion, it becomes a goal of Latter-day Saints to receive more of this light, which for the faithful grows "brighter and brighter until the perfect day" (D&C 50:24). Initially, this "Spirit giveth light to every man that cometh into the world" (D&C 84:46; see also John 1:9; Moro. 7:16). It equips all people with a basic discernment of good and evil, which Latter-day Saints often equate with conscience. By listening to the promptings of the Spirit one is led via faith and baptism to a higher spiritual blessing called the GIFT OF THE HOLY GHOST, "a greater and higher endowment of the same Spirit which enlightens every man that comes into the world" (C. W. Penrose, *JD* 23:350). Continued progression will eventually lead to a fulness of the Spirit, or glorification in the CELESTIAL KINGDOM.

BIBLIOGRAPHY

Pratt, Parley P. *Key to the Science of Theology.* Salt Lake City, 1979.

Roberts, B. H. *Seventy's Course in Theology,* 5 vols. Salt Lake City, 1907–1912; Vol. 3 on the doctrine of deity and Vol. 5 on divine immanence.

Smith, Joseph Fielding. *DS,* Vol. 1, pp. 49–54.

Widtsoe, John A. *A Rational Theology.* Salt Lake City, 1915.

C. KENT DUNFORD

LIGHT AND DARKNESS

Many juxtapositions of light and darkness are identifiable in latter-day scripture. Darkness was apparently the primeval condition (Gen. 1:2; Moses 2:2; Abr. 4:2). Light was introduced by the divine word: "Let there be light: and there was light" (Gen. 1:3; Moses 2:3; Abr. 4:3). It was decreed "good" and was divided from the darkness, light being known as "day" and darkness as "night" (Gen. 1:4–5; Moses 2:4–5; Abr. 4:4–5). The account in Abraham adds that "they (the gods) comprehended the light, for it was bright" (Abr. 4:4; *see also* GODHEAD).

This primeval contrast figures importantly in the early literature of Mesopotamia, as in the ancient Sumerian epic of King Gilgamesh, also in various pre-Socratic philosophies in Greece, especially the oppositional philosophy of Heraclitus. These usages, like those of scripture, refer to light and darkness as physical phenomena of the environment to be apprehended by the senses. Other meanings, literal and metaphorical, equate light with life, love, goodness, righteousness, godliness, virtue, blessedness, happiness, freedom, sweetness, guiltlessness, spiritual-mindedness, intelligence, wisdom, heaven-sent revelation, and so on. Darkness is associated with things deathly, devilish, infernal, fallen, carnal, wicked, corrupt, intemperate, mournful, miserable, bitter, fettered, benighted, and ultimately ill-fated.

Despite their opposition, light and darkness may be confused. Isaiah speaks of persons who "put darkness for light, and light for darkness" (Isa. 5:20). Further, individuals may prefer darkness to light. John cites Christ's condemnation of those who love darkness rather than light because their deeds are evil, which may induce hatred of light (John 3:19–20).

The proportion of light to darkness within one's body is considered a function of the eye and, specifically, the orientation of the eye. Jesus said in the Sermon on the Mount, "The light of the body is the eye; if therefore thine eye be single [here the JST adds "to the glory of God"] thy whole body shall be full of light. But if thine eye be evil, thy whole body shall be full of darkness. If therefore the light that is in thee be darkness, how great is that darkness" (Matt. 6:22–23; cf. JST Matt. 6:22). The Doctrine and Covenants explains, "And if your eye be single to my glory, your whole bodies shall be filled with light, and there shall be no darkness in you; and that body which is filled with light comprehendeth all things" (D&C 88:67). And "the day shall come when you shall comprehend even God, being quickened in him and by him" (D&C 88:49).

Christ is a God-appointed source and giver of light, a revealer of God's glory, a banisher of darkness. The apostle Paul wrote, "For God, who commanded the light to shine out of darkness, hath shined in our hearts, to give the light of the knowledge of the glory of God in the face of Jesus Christ" (2 Cor. 4:6). Peter spoke of Christ who "hath called you out of darkness into his marvellous light" (1 Pet. 2:9). The Book of Mormon describes the epiphanous experience of the Lamanite king Lamoni: "The dark veil of unbelief was being cast away from his mind, and the light which did light up his mind, which was the light of the glory of God, which was a marvelous light of his goodness—yea, this light had infused such joy into his soul, the cloud of darkness having been dispelled, that the light of everlasting life was lit up in his soul" (Alma 19:6; cf. Alma 32:35). In modern revelation Christ has reiterated his divine function as "the light which shineth in darkness," which the darkness cannot comprehend nor extinguish (e.g., D&C 6:21; 88:49).

The interplay of these literal and symbolic meanings is perhaps most graphically portrayed in LDS christology. On the occasion of his birth in Bethlehem, there was a miraculous interruption of the conventional twenty-four-hour light-dark cycle in the Western Hemisphere; it was, in essence, a celebration of light. The Book of Mormon records that "There was no darkness in all that night, but it was as light as though it was mid-day. . . . The sun did rise in the morning again, according to its proper order; and they knew that it was the day that the Lord should be born, because of the sign which had been given (3 Ne. 1:15, 19). In contrast, at the crucifixion of Christ and for three consecutive days "there was thick darkness upon all the face of the land, insomuch that the inhabitants thereof who had not fallen could feel the vapor of darkness; and there could be no light" (3 Ne. 8:20–23).

The same vividness of contrast between light and darkness is seen in Joseph Smith's experiences.

BIBLIOGRAPHY

Madsen, Truman G. "Man Illumined." In *To the Glory of God,* pp. 121–133, ed. C. Tate. Salt Lake City, 1972.

HAROLD L. MILLER, JR.

LOVE

The "pure love of Christ" (Moro. 7:47) is the foundation of true religion. A lawyer once asked Jesus Christ, "Master, which is the great commandment in the law? Jesus said unto him, Thou shalt love the Lord thy God with all thy heart, and with all thy soul, and with all thy mind. This is the first and great commandment. And the second is like unto it. Thou shalt love thy neighbour as thyself. On these two commandments hang all the law and the prophets" (Matt. 22:36–40; cf. Gal. 5:14).

Love is manifest in its perfection in God the Eternal Father and his son Jesus Christ. John declared that "God is love" (1 Jn. 4:8). His love has no portions and no bounds; love given to one does not diminish that given to another. The Father desires to share with his children all that he has—all truth, power, and goodness. He is the Father of all human SPIRITS. He placed human beings upon this earth and provided the plan through which his Only Begotten Son makes it possible for individuals to come back into his presence and receive EXALTATION and ETERNAL LIFE. "For God so loved the world, that he gave his only begotten Son, that whosoever believeth in him should not perish, but have everlasting life" (John 3:16).

Jesus Christ also loved the Father's children, his brothers and sisters, so much that he freely shed his blood and laid down his life to atone for their sins and bring about a universal RESURRECTION. "Greater love hath no man than this, that a man lay down his life for his friends" (John 15:13).

While his death and ATONEMENT were the supreme manifestations of love, his actions during his life in the Holy Land and during his post-resurrection ministry among the Nephites in the Western Hemisphere also exemplify this principle. His heart was filled with compassion for the poor and for all who suffered. He healed the sick, raised the dead, fed the hungry, and blessed the children. Then, when his life was ending and he hung in agony on the cross, he besought God to forgive the soldiers who crucified him (JST Luke 23:34[35]).

Within his example are found all the characteristics of what is called in the scriptures charity or "the pure love of Christ" (Moro. 7:47). Love is kind and long-suffering, humble, "seeketh not her own, is not easily provoked, thinketh no evil, and rejoiceth not in iniquity but rejoiceth in the truth, beareth all things, believeth all things, hopeth all things, endureth all things" (Moro. 7:45; cf. 1 Cor. 13:4–7).

To his disciples Jesus said, "A new commandment I give unto you, that ye love one another; as I have loved you, that ye also love one another. By this shall all men know that ye are my disciples, if ye have love one to another" (John 13:34–35).

Human beings show their love to God through obedience to his COMMANDMENTS (2 Jn. 6). Love of God, according to the prophet $Nephi_1$ of the Book of Mormon, is "most desirable above all things" (1 Ne. 11:22). According to King Benjamin, another Book of Mormon leader, to gain the love of God individuals must put off the natural man, learn to listen to the HOLY GHOST, accept the ATONEMENT OF JESUS CHRIST, and become as children—submissive, meek, humble, patient, and willing to submit to all things, even as a child submits to his father (Mosiah 3:19).

Mormon, another Book of Mormon prophet, declared that the gift of love must be sought: "Pray unto the Father with all the energy of heart," he advised, "that ye may be filled with this love, which he hath bestowed upon all who are true followers of his Son, Jesus Christ" (Moro. 7:48).

Obedience to the first great commandment is not possible without obedience to the second: "If a man say, I love God, and hateth his brother, he is a liar: for he that loveth not his brother whom he hath seen, how can he love God whom he hath not seen? And this commandment have we from him, that he who loveth God love his brother also" (1 Jn. 4:20–21).

As the Savior manifested his love through service, so do human beings. The Saints of God are recognized by the love they show one to another. Love includes kindness, tenderness, understanding, mercy, forgiveness, affection, and ultimately a willingness to sacrifice all that one has, if necessary. The absence of love is a sign of apostasy.

Love is particularly important in the family unit. It begins in the home between husband and wife. "Thou shalt love thy wife with all thy heart, and shalt cleave unto her and none else" (D&C 42:22). This encompasses both a spiritual and a physical fidelity. Then, when husbands and wives as parents govern their households by the principle of love, "the same spirit will be sooner or later diffused through every member of [the] family. . . . Love is the only correct governing principle" (Cannon, p. 383). As David O. McKay, a latter-day prophet, said, "I picture heaven to be a continuation of the ideal home" (*Gospel Ideals,* Salt Lake City, 1953, p. 490).

Love established in the home then extends out to the neighborhood, the state, the nation, and the world and has the power to bind people together and make them one. "Differences of language, of education, of race and of nationality all disappear. Under its influence, prejudices and animosities vanish" (Cannon, p. 299).

The love of the Saints also includes loving those who are considered adversaries. The Savior taught, "Love your enemies, bless them that curse you, do good to them that hate you, and pray for them who despitefully use you and persecute you; that ye may be the children of your Father who is in heaven; for he maketh his sun to rise on the evil and on the good" (3 Ne. 12:44–45; cf. Matt. 5:44–45).

Love of one's enemies does not extend to love of their wickedness but does extend to efforts to turn them from such actions. It includes respect for their significance and potential as children of God.

Jesus prophesied that in the LAST DAYS evil will have great power and the love of many shall wax cold (Matt. 24:12), but the scriptures also promise great blessings "held in reserve for them that love him" (D&C 138:52).

BIBLIOGRAPHY

Beardall, Douglas, and Jewel Beardall, comps. *The Qualities of Love.* Salt Lake City, 1978.

Cannon, George Q. *Gospel Truth.* Jerreld L. Newquist, comp. Salt Lake City, 1987.

Madsen, Truman G. *Four Essays on Love.* Salt Lake City, 1971.

VIVIAN PAULSEN

M

MANKIND

The Church of Jesus Christ of Latter-day Saints views all descendants of Adam and Eve as the children of God—not in an abstract or metaphorical sense, but as actual spirit offspring of GOD THE FATHER and a MOTHER IN HEAVEN. This basic premise has profound implications for the LDS understanding of what human beings are, why they are here on earth, and what they can become.

As children of God, men and women have infinite potential (see 2 Ne. 2:20; Heb. 12:9). As a result of their divine heritage, all people carry the inherent capacity and the predisposition to become as their heavenly parents. Latter-day Saints seek to follow the injunction of Christ to be "perfect, even as your Father which is in heaven is perfect" (Matt. 5:48). Their view of each person's relationship with God stresses that life is as a maturing process, a working toward becoming like God, of becoming worthy to be with God (*see* EXALTATION; GODHOOD). Mortal life may be only a beginning, but the potential is there.

This view of mankind emphasizes the family. Marriage is central to the LDS spiritual experience: "Neither is the man without the woman, neither the woman without the man, in the Lord" (1 Cor. 11:11). Marriage is not intended to last for this life only, but for eternity; therefore, Latter-day Saints marry in the temple for TIME AND ETERNITY. As members of the family of God, Latter-day Saints see the family as the most important arena of life. "No other success,"

President David O. McKay frequently declared, "can compensate for failure in the home" (*Family Home Evening Manual,* "Preface," Salt Lake City, 1966).

The LDS ideal also reaches out toward the universal family of humanity. People with infinite potential have infinite value; all people matter because they are brothers and sisters in the family of God. The LDS perspective affirms the infinite love of God for all mankind, and the essential goodness of human beings and their capacity to improve the world. The conviction that people are responsible for their moral behavior, "agents unto themselves" (D&C 58:28), tends to make Latter-day Saints supporters of political systems that maximize free choices (*see* AGENCY). The intelligence, or inner core of the soul, is seen in LDS theology as self-existent, not created ex nihilo, but having existed always, and thus ultimately responsible for its own decisions and its own destiny as well (*see* INTELLIGENCES).

The vast potential of human beings, as literal spirit children of God, brings to the LDS view of mankind a purposeful and weighty sense of responsibility. Sons and daughters of God have an obligation to develop their divinely given talents, to magnify what God has given them. Latter-day Saints privately, and through the Church, labor to make the most of individuals. They believe that through the ages people are accountable for their responses to God, which determine what they now are and what they will be, and that it is God's work and glory to bring about the exaltation of mankind.

Each human intelligence is born of God as a spirit child, and that spirit child is later born into MORTALITY in a physical body. Spirit is unusually real to the Latter-day Saints, for whom everything that exists has spiritual essence: "All things . . . are spiritual" (D&C 29:34; Moses 3:5). Mortal life thus becomes for Latter-day Saints not only a difficult and risky time, but also a time of infinite opportunities and possibilities, a pivotal step in the eternal process of becoming as wise and good as the heavenly parents.

This sense of possibility and of responsibility tends to make Latter-day Saints strong proponents of all forms of ennobling education: "the glory of God is intelligence" (D&C 93:36). In a world fraught with risk and temptation on the one hand and the possibility of godliness on the other, the wise Latter-day Saint will "seek learning, even by study and also by faith" (D&C 88:118).

Thus, the PURPOSE OF EARTH LIFE is to prepare for eternity through learning and experience. In mortal life Latter-day Saints expect TRIALS, challenges, and tests. But the expectation of difficulty in life holds within it the promise of real happiness, of having life "more abundantly" (John 10:10). The Book of Mormon prophet Lehi summarizes the LDS sense of the challenge and reward of this mortal experience made possible by the fortunate FALL OF ADAM: "Adam fell that men might be; and men are, that they might have joy" (2 Ne. 2:25).

BIBLIOGRAPHY
Madsen, Truman G. *Eternal Man.* Salt Lake City, 1966.
Talmage, James E. *The Vitality of Mormonism.* Boston, 1919.

STEVEN C. WALKER

MEN, ROLES OF

For men in The Church of Jesus Christ of Latter-day Saints, the ideal example of manhood is Jesus Christ, the Savior of all mankind. There is no substitute. All men must transcend cultural biases and variations when they decide to pattern themselves after the Son of God, who is the complete representative of the Father. LDS men ideally strive to follow Christ by serving family and fellowbeings through love, work, priesthood callings, instruction, and example.

The scriptures and the prophets make it clear to Latter-day Saints what the Savior expects of a man. To the Nephites he plainly stated, "For that which ye have seen me do even that shall ye do. . . . Therefore, what manner of men ought ye to be? Verily I say unto you, even as I am" (3 Ne. 27:21, 27). King Benjamin, tutored by an angel, described what has become a characterization of the challenges and potentials of manhood:

> For the natural man is an enemy to God, and has been from the Fall of Adam, and will be, forever and ever, unless he yields to the enticings of the Holy Spirit, and putteth off the natural man and becometh a saint through the atonement of Christ the Lord, and becometh as a child, submissive, meek, humble, patient, full of love, willing to submit to all

> things which the Lord seeth fit to inflict upon him, even as a child doth submit to his father [Mosiah 3:19].

Paul taught about manliness by addressing the husband's role: "Husbands, love your wives, even as Christ also loved the church, and gave himself for it. . . . So ought men to love their wives as their own bodies" (Eph. 5:25, 28). President Brigham Young often expounded on this theme: "Let the father be the head of the family, the master of his own household. And let him treat [the sisters] as an angel would treat them" (*JD* 4:55). "Set that example before your wives and your children, before your neighbors and this people, that you can say: Follow me, as I follow Christ" (*JD* 15:229). "I exhort you, masters, fathers, and husbands, to be affectionate and kind to those you preside over" (*JD* 1:69).

Husbands and fathers are expected to emulate the love of the Savior by teaching, serving, and ministering to their families. It is the man's role to engender and nurture life in benevolent partnership with his wife. It is not the man's role to serve his own selfish interests, declining to marry and to create a family. Obviously, he cannot fulfill his proper role without a loyal wife who is likewise true to her covenants with God.

By ordination to the priesthood, LDS men covenant to magnify their callings and to so live that, after sufficient diligent service to Christ's work, "all that my Father hath shall be given unto [them]" (D&C 84:38). To receive all that the Father has is to be endowed with the power, knowledge, blessings, and loving responsibilities of eternal fatherhood. With this power, however, comes a sacred obligation to act in love as the Heavenly Father does, never in selfishness or lust.

The duty of men is to acquire knowledge *and* love so that everything they do is right and true, patterned after Jesus Christ, for "this is life eternal, that they might know thee the only true God, and Jesus Christ, whom thou hast sent" (John 17:3). The Prophet Joseph Smith taught, "Here, then, is eternal life—to know the only wise and true God; and you have got to learn how to be Gods yourselves . . . namely, by going from one small degree to another, and from a small capacity to a great one; from grace to grace" (*TPJS,* pp. 346–47).

By serving according to the principles of the priesthood, each man should learn how to conduct himself like the Savior, who learned from his Father, for "no power or influence can or ought to be maintained by virtue of the priesthood, only by persuasion, by long-suffering, by gentleness and meekness, and by love unfeigned; by kindness, and pure knowledge, which shall greatly enlarge the soul without hypocrisy, and without guile" (D&C 121:41–42). It is a general responsibility of all men in the Church to serve as home teachers; in addition, each will usually hold another calling, such as an Aaronic Priesthood quorum adviser, a scoutmaster or cubmaster, a Sunday School or Primary teacher, an athletic director, musician, activities chairman, clerk, bishop, stake president, or General Authority.

As it is God's work and glory "to bring to pass the immortality and eternal life of man" (Moses 1:39), so it is the responsibility of men to work while in mortality to help other people progress toward eternal life. Work in its broadest sense becomes a mark of a true man: A man is responsible for seeing that he and his family have sufficient means to live and to develop their talents. He is expected to labor to make the place where he and they live as comfortable as possible. He is also to work to bring spiritual order to the household through family prayer, father's blessings, and gospel study, teaching his children that life's proper priorities are gospel centered. He is taught to pray for, and bless, his family members. He shows them by example how to treat a wife—and women in general and children—with utmost respect (cf. Eph. 5:25; 6:4; D&C 42:22; 75:28). The Church encourages husbands to make every possible effort to keep their families intact and, should divorce occur, to strive to influence their children for good and to pay appropriate respect to their mothers, both to make the best of a difficult situation in this life and to prepare for adjustments in the next.

LDS men are exhorted by their leaders to become strong yet mild, to be ambitious to serve yet selfless in order to add to another's eternal growth, and to measure their success by how they nurture others and how they teach and make possible the progress and growth of others rather than use others to feed their own needs. Men, in other words, are expected to become Christlike natural patriarchs, as exemplified by the Father and by the Son, devoid of harshness, domination, or selfishness.

[*See also* Brotherhood.]

BIBLIOGRAPHY
Hinckley, Gordon B. "What Will the Church Do for You, a Man?" *Ensign* 2 (July 1972):71–73.

VICTOR L. BROWN, JR.

MESSIAH

MESSIAH

Messiah is a Hebrew term signifying "anointed one." The Greek equivalent is *christos,* whence the name Christ. Jesus, the divinely given name of the Savior (Matt. 1:21), derives from the Hebrew *Yeshua* or *Yehoshua* (or Joshua, as it commonly appears in English), from a root meaning "to save." With other Christians, Latter-day Saints agree that implicit in the name Jesus Christ lies the doctrine that he is the Messiah, the Anointed One who saves.

Like the New Testament, the Book of Mormon clearly identifies Jesus as the Messiah (1 Ne. 10:4–17; 2 Ne. 25:16–20; Hel. 8:13–17). It also declares that a knowledge of the Messiah existed "from the beginning of the world" (1 Ne. 12:18; Mosiah 13:33–35) and prophesies details of his life and mission. For example, the Messiah would appear in a body (1 Ne. 15:13), his name would be Jesus Christ (2 Ne. 25:19; Mosiah 3:8), and he would be baptized as an example of obedience (2 Ne. 31:4–9). Moreover, signs would attend his birth, death, and resurrection (2 Ne. 26:3; Hel. 14:2–8, 20–28). In this connection, he would be slain and rise from the dead, bringing to pass the resurrection (1 Ne. 10:11; 2 Ne. 2:8). At the last day, he is to appear in power and glory (2 Ne. 6:14), to reign as king and lawgiver (D&C 45:59; 1 Tim. 6:14–15).

[*See also* Jesus Christ, Names and Titles of.]

DAVID B. GALBRAITH

MESSIANIC CONCEPT AND HOPE

It is LDS doctrine that a knowledge of the role of Jesus Christ as the Messiah has been on the earth from the beginning. God taught Adam and Eve about the Messiah who would redeem mankind. Called "Only Begotten" and "Son of Man," even his name Jesus Christ was revealed (Moses 5:7–11; 6:52–57). These are, of course, the anglicized words meaning "Savior Anointed." God also taught Enoch that the "Messiah, the King of Zion" would die on a cross (Moses 7:53–55).

From other sources it is evident that Hebrew people clearly believed in a redeemer, though characterizations varied. The Bible refers to him through imagery such as "the shepherd, the stone of Israel" (Gen. 49:24), the "tried stone" or "sure foundation" (Isa. 28:16), the "stem of Jesse" and "Branch" (Isa. 11:1; Jer. 33:15–16). He is also called Redeemer, Holy One of Israel, Savior, Lord of Hosts, the First and Last (Isa. 43:1–15; 44:6), and even a servant (Isa. 42:1; 49:3; 50:10; 52:13).

Because biblical prophecy uses the imagery of royalty, some believed that at his first coming the Messiah would save them from political bondage. Jacob foresaw that Shiloh would come, to whom people would gather (Gen. 49:10). Moses prophesied, "There shall come a Star out of Jacob, and a Sceptre shall rise out of Israel" (Num. 24:17). Isaiah envisioned a child born, "and the government shall be upon his shoulder. . . . Of the increase of . . . peace there shall be no end, upon the throne of David, and upon his kingdom" (Isa. 9:6–7). Micah recorded that from Bethlehem "shall he come forth . . . to be ruler in Israel" (Micah 5:2). Jeremiah saw that "a King shall reign . . . and shall execute judgment and justice" (Jer. 23:5). However, such royal prophecies of a king and ruler would find fulfillment in the Messiah's eternal, rather than his mortal, role.

The prophets planted seeds of belief in a Messiah, seeds that would flower during later periods. The Dead Sea scrolls reveal a hope in two Messiahs who would lead a religious revival. Judas Maccabeus' example (d. 160 B.C.), overthrowing the Greeks and reestablishing Jewish independence, spawned hope during the early Roman period (63 B.C.–A.D. 70) that a Messiah would deliver the Jewish nation. Although royalty and battle imagery in the Bible was interpreted to mean political deliverance, those images referred to spiritual salvation. Said Jesus, "My kingdom is not of this world" (John 18:36).

The title Messiah (Hebrew *mashiah;* Greek *christos*) means "anointed one." Among ancient Israelites, persons set apart for God's work were anointed with oil, including prophets, priests, and kings. Jesus, citing a messianic prophecy from Isaiah (61:1), told hearers in

Nazareth, "The Spirit of the Lord is upon me, because he hath anointed me to preach the gospel, . . . to heal the brokenhearted, to preach deliverance to the captives" (Luke 4:18).

Isaiah described the "servant" as one who would be smitten (Isa. 50:6), even "wounded for our transgressions, . . . bruised for our iniquities," and yet "make intercession for the transgressors" (53:3–5, 12). Zechariah added that he would be wounded in the house of his friends (Zech. 12:10; 13:6–7). New Testament authors also understood that Jesus was to suffer before entering his glory (e.g., Luke 24:26; Acts 3:18).

Throughout his ministry Jesus clearly understood his messiahship (cf. 3 Ne. 15:20–23). For instance, when the Samaritan woman acknowledged, "I know that Messias cometh," Jesus responded, "I that speak unto thee am he" (John 4:25–26). Peter declared, "Thou art the Christ [Messiah]" (Matt. 16:16); and Andrew, Peter's brother, announced, "We have found the Messias" (John 1:41). Even devils are reported to have said, "Thou art Christ the Son of God" (e.g., Luke 4:41).

The biblical portrayal of a mortal Messiah reviled rather than ruling, rejected rather than reigning, is amplified in the Book of Mormon. As its modern subtitle indicates, the Book of Mormon is another testament of Jesus Christ, or Jesus the Messiah. Book of Mormon writers taught that all prophets spoke concerning the Messiah (Jacob 7:11; Mosiah 13:33). In approximately 600 B.C., Lehi taught that "redemption cometh in and through the Holy Messiah. . . . Behold he offereth himself a sacrifice for sin . . . that he may bring to pass the resurrection of the dead" (2 Ne. 2:6–10).

Nephi$_1$ wrote that since all are in a fallen state, they must rely on the Messiah, the Redeemer. He learned that the Son of God was willing to come as the Messiah, preach the gospel, serve as an example of righteous living, and be slain for the sins of all (1 Ne. 10:4–6, 11; 11:26–33; 19:9; 2 Ne. 25:11–19; 31:9–16).

King Benjamin described how Jesus Christ would come from heaven to dwell in a mortal body, "working mighty miracles, such as healing the sick . . . [and casting] out devils," suffering temptation and fatigue. Even blood would come "from every pore, so great shall be his anguish for the wickedness and the abominations of his people." Saying that he was only a man and that "he hath a devil, [they] shall scourge him, and shall crucify him" (Mosiah 3:5–10).

Alma$_2$ said of the Messiah's ministry, "He shall go forth, suffering pains and afflictions and temptations of every kind. . . . And he will take upon him death, that he may loose the bands of death which bind his people; and he will take upon him their infirmities . . . that he may know according to the flesh how to succor his people according to their infirmities" (Alma 7:11–12).

More than five centuries before Christ's birth, Jacob wrote, "For this intent have we written these things, that they may know that we knew of Christ, and we had a hope of his glory many hundred years before his coming; and not only we ourselves had a hope of his glory, but also all the holy prophets which were before us" (Jacob 4:4).

BIBLIOGRAPHY

McConkie, Bruce R. *The Promised Messiah.* Salt Lake City, 1978.

D. KELLY OGDEN

MILLENNIUM

As a generic term, "millennium" connotes any period of 1,000 years' duration. In the Judeo-Christian tradition, however, one such period stands preeminent, namely, that future time when peace and righteousness will prevail under the direct providence of God and his MESSIAH.

The prophet Isaiah spoke of this time when "they shall beat their swords into plowshares, and their spears into pruninghooks: nation shall not lift up sword against nation, neither shall they learn war any more" (Isa. 2:4). He further declared that the natural fears and enmities within the animal kingdom will cease, that "the wolf also shall dwell with the lamb, and the leopard shall lie down with the kid" (Isa. 11:6–9; cf. D&C 101:26). Ezekiel prophesied that the Earth, which lost its pristine character as a result of the FALL OF ADAM (cf. Gen. 3:17–19), will return to its paradisiacal state once again (Ezek. 36:35; cf. A of F 10). For the duration of the Millennium, Satan will be bound (Rev. 20:1–3). In place of the diabolical regime of the "prince of this world" (John 12:31; 14:30; D&C 1:35), the Lord Jesus Christ will dwell personally among the inhabitants of earth, ruling over the KINGDOM OF GOD with the aid of righteous mortals and resurrected Saints from all ages (Isa. 35:2; Dan. 7:14, 27).

Christ taught his disciples to pray to the Father for the kingdom to come when his will would be done on earth as it is in heaven (Matt. 6:10). Jesus declared to them that he would be sent again by the Father at the end of the world for a day of JUDGMENT and an era of paradisiacal glory (cf. Matt. 25:31–46; John 5:22–29; Acts 1:3–8). Some early Christians appear to have anticipated the SECOND COMING OF JESUS CHRIST and the onset of the Millennium as imminent, despite the Savior's caution that none but the Father knew the time of his coming, and despite both angelic and apostolic pronouncements concerning events that must precede the Millennium (cf. Matt. 24; Acts 3:19–21; 2 Thes. 2:1–4). Numerous church leaders in the Post-Apostolic (Patristic) period, such as Justin Martyr of Rome, Papias of Hierapolis, Irenaeus of Lyons, and Lactantius, accepted the notion of a literal Millennium following the resurrection of the dead, when a visible and glorious kingdom of Christ would exist on earth. By the late third and fourth centuries, however, church fathers such as Origen (d. c. A.D. 254) and Augustine (d. A.D. 429) had transformed the notion of a literal Millennium into an allegorical or figurative one: The millennial reign of peace for them took place in the hearts of individual men and women and began with the outpouring of the Holy Spirit on the day of Pentecost (cf. Acts 2:16–20). From that time until the sixteenth-century Protestant reformation, belief in a literal millennium was regarded as unorthodox by the institutional church. The restoration of all things in this, the DISPENSATION OF THE FULNESS OF TIMES, affirms that Christ will return for a millennial reign of peace. During the Millennium, members of the Church of Jesus Christ from any era of time will help in the government of the earth under Christ's direction (Dan. 7:27; D&C 103:7; cf. Matt. 5:5).

John the Revelator saw that at the commencement of the Millennium a New Jerusalem would descend to earth from heaven. Traditional Christianity has generally associated this with a renewing of the city where Jesus ministered among the Jews during the meridian of time. However, the revelations given to the Prophet Joseph Smith show that the New Jerusalem in the Western Hemisphere will coexist with the old Jerusalem, each as a hemispheric capital. From them laws, decrees, and leadership in the kingdom of God will emanate. Thus the nuances found in Isaiah 2:3 that "out of Zion shall go forth the law, and the word of the Lord from Jerusalem" telling of two locations are not redundant or merely rhetorical. According to modern scripture, a New Jerusalem will yet be established within the borders of the state of Missouri in North America (D&C 84:2–4; cf. 57:2–3; A of F 10).

The Millennium symbolizes a sabbatical in human history (cf. D&C 77:12; Moses 7:64), analogous to the role of the weekly sabbath (cf. Ex. 20:8–11). The millennial period is patterned after the Lord's period of rest following the six creative periods (cf. Gen. 2:1–3).

Life will go on for those on earth: "And they shall build houses, and inhabit them; and they shall plant vineyards, and eat the fruit of them, . . . and mine elect shall long enjoy the work of their hands" (Isa. 65:21–22). Righteous mortal men and women who die after the beginning of the Millennium "shall not sleep . . . in the earth, but shall be changed in the twinkling of an eye" (D&C 101:31), and children born in this era "shall grow up until they become old" (D&C 63:51; Isa. 65:20). The devil will have no "power to tempt any man," being bound because of the righteousness of the earth's inhabitants, and children will grow up without sin (1 Ne. 22:26; D&C 43:30–31; 45:58; 101:28–31). However, those who are wicked will not be resurrected or returned to the earth until after the millennium of righteousness (D&C 76:81, 85).

Whereas numerous temples will already dot the earth prior to the Millennium, their number and distribution will increase during this time, providing places where priesthood ordinances essential to salvation and eternal life can be performed in uninterrupted calm. The work of preaching the gospel of Jesus Christ to all the inhabitants of the earth will continue under his direction. Meanwhile, a similar teaching program will continue among the spirits of those who have departed this life and are waiting the day of their resurrection (D&C 138). While such spirits may hear the gospel of salvation and accept or reject it in the spirit worlds, mortals on earth will perform saving ordinances such as baptism on their behalf (*see* BAPTISM FOR THE DEAD). Conditions of peace and righteousness will prevail during the Millennium to allow this work to proceed until essential ordinances have been made available to every individual who has lived on earth since the time of Adam and Eve (cf. D&C 138).

[*See also* Last Days; Time and Eternity.]

BIBLIOGRAPHY

Doxey, Roy W. "The Millennium." *Relief Society Magazine* 54 (Jan. 1967):58–63.

Leonard, Glen M. "Early Saints and the Millennium." *Ensign* 9 (Aug. 1979):43–47.

McConkie, Bruce R. *MD,* pp. 492–501. Salt Lake City, 1966.

PAUL B. PIXTON

MORTALITY

Mortality is not viewed as a curse by Latter-day Saints, but as an opportunity and an essential stage in progress toward obtaining EXALTATION. The ultimate purpose of the period of mortality from birth to death is to prepare to meet God with a resurrected body of glory (John 5:25–29; Alma 12:24). Death is a temporary separation of the body and the spirit, and, for those who have striven to live in accordance with God's commandments, is not something to be feared: "Fear not even unto death; for in this world your joy is not full, but in me your joy is full" (D&C 101:36; cf. Mosiah 16:7; D&C 42:46).

Although mortality is a temporary stage of life, it is essential for an individual's ETERNAL PROGRESSION for two reasons. First, it is necessary to receive a PHYSICAL BODY. God the Father, in his perfected state, has a body of flesh and bone, as does the Son (Luke 24:36–39; D&C 130:22). Mortal men and women, as the spirit offspring of God, also gain physical bodies in mortality that are indispensable to their progress, and will rise in the RESURRECTION and be perfected (Job 19:25–26; Luke 24:39). Without a physical body one cannot have a fulness of joy.

Second, this life is a period of development and probation, a time to overcome temptation or inclinations toward sin and corruption (Mosiah 3:19). Such inclinations can be given up through REPENTANCE, the ATONEMENT, and AGENCY (Mosiah 5:2). Mortals experience opposites—good and evil, happiness and bitterness, joy and misery—and have the opportunity to live true to the commandments and teachings of God. OPPOSITION is a fundamental feature of mortality, where human actions and choices are made within the possibility of doing wrong, where acceptance of the commandments and teachings of God is done in the face of opposition and temptation. While Latter-day Saints do not believe that perfection is possible in this life, they believe in working toward it in response to the injunction of Jesus Christ to "Be ye therefore perfect" (Matt. 5:48; cf. 3 Ne. 12:48). Through repentance and obedience they try to resist the temptations that beset them.

Inasmuch as mortal existence is a time of learning in order to make the greatest progress, each individual first must accept by faith the validity of God's commandments and teachings, and then through experience gain a knowledge of their truth. People exercise agency in how they live their lives, even as they respond to the Spirit of Christ, which is given to all born into mortality. Thus all have the ability, when given proper instruction, including associations with those who are examples of the light and truth of the gospel of Jesus Christ, to recognize and understand the laws of God (D&C 84:45–46; Moro. 7:16).

To all who are willing and who make the effort, mortality provides a vast opportunity for learning, for overcoming weaknesses, for repenting of wrongdoing, for correcting mistakes, for increasing in wisdom, and for progressing toward God. Eve recognized this when she declared that were it not for her and Adam's transgression, the human race "never should have known good and evil, and the joy of our redemption, and the eternal life which God giveth unto all the obedient" (Moses 5:11).

[*See also* Birth; Death and Dying; Evil; Fall of Adam; Joy; Life and Death, Spiritual; Mankind; Premortal Life; Purpose of Earth Life.]

BIBLIOGRAPHY

Smith, Joseph Fielding. *DS* 1:56–71.

JAMES P. BELL

MOTHER IN HEAVEN

Latter-day Saints infer from authoritative sources of scripture and modern prophecy that there is a Heavenly Mother as well as a Heavenly Father.

The Church of Jesus Christ of Latter-day Saints rejects the idea found in some religions that the spirits or souls of individual human beings are created ex nihilo. Rather it accepts literally the vital scriptural teaching as worded by Paul: "The Spirit itself beareth witness with our spirit, that we are the children of God." This and other scriptures underscore not only spiritual sibling relationships but heirship with God, and a destiny of joint heirship with Christ (Rom. 8:16–18; cf. Mal. 2:10).

Latter-day Saints believe that all the people of earth who lived or will live are actual spiritual offspring of God the Eternal Father (Num. 16:22; Heb. 12:9). In this perspective, parenthood requires both father and mother, whether for the creation of spirits in the PREMORTAL LIFE or of physical tabernacles on earth. A Heavenly Mother shares parenthood with the Heavenly Father. This concept leads Latter-day Saints to believe that she is like him in glory, perfection, compassion, wisdom, and holiness.

Elohim, the name-title for God, suggests the plural of the Caananite *El* or the Hebrew *Eloah.* It is used in various Hebrew combinations to describe the highest God. It is the majestic title of the ultimate deity. Genesis 1:27 reads, "So God created man in his own image, in the image of God created he him, *male and female* created he them" (emphasis added), which may be read to mean that "God" is plural.

For Latter-day Saints, the concept of eternal family is more than a firm belief; it governs their way of life. It is the eternal plan of life, stretching from life before through life beyond mortality.

As early as 1839 the Prophet Joseph Smith taught the concept of an eternal mother, as reported in several accounts from that period. Out of his teaching came a hymn that Latter-day Saints learn, sing, quote, and cherish, "O My Father," by Eliza R. Snow. President Wilford Woodruff called it a REVELATION (Woodruff, p. 62).

> In the heav'ns are parents single?
> No, the thought makes reason stare!
> Truth is reason; truth eternal
> Tells me I've a mother there.
> When I leave this frail existence,
> When I lay this mortal by,
> Father, Mother, may I meet you
> In your royal courts on high? [Hymn no. 292]

In 1909 the First Presidency, under Joseph F. Smith, issued a statement on the origin of man that teaches that "man, as a spirit, was begotten and born of heavenly parents, and reared to maturity in the eternal mansions of the Father," as an "offspring of celestial parentage," and further teaches that "all men and women are in the similitude of the universal Father and Mother, and are literally the sons and daughters of Deity" (Smith, pp. 199–205).

Belief that there is a Mother in Heaven who is a partner with God in creation and procreation is not the same as the heavy emphasis on Mariology in the Roman tradition.

Today the belief in a living Mother in Heaven is implicit in Latter-day Saint thought. Though the scriptures contain only hints, statements from presidents of the Church over the years indicate that human beings have a Heavenly Mother as well as a Heavenly Father.

BIBLIOGRAPHY

Wilcox, Linda P. "The Mormon Concept of a Mother in Heaven." In *Sisters in Spirit*, ed. Maureen U. Beecher and Lavina F. Anderson. Urbana, Ill., 1987.

Woodruff, Wilford. *The Discourses of Wilford Woodruff*, ed. G. Homer Durham. Salt Lake City, 1968.

ELAINE ANDERSON CANNON

MYSTERIES OF GOD

"Mysteries of God" is a scriptural phrase in which the word "mysteries" refers to knowledge about God that is often hidden from mortal understanding. It does not refer to something incomprehensible in principle. Like many people of other religions, Latter-day Saints deem a knowledge of some mysteries to be necessary (D&C 76:5–10), and acquire such knowledge in part through ordinances and in part through REVELATION (cf. *TPJS*, p. 324).

As found both in the Bible and in latter-day scripture, the term "mystery" describes a doctrine revealed only to the faithful but not given to the "world" or to the uninitiated. (Matt. 13:11; 1 Cor. 2:7; Eph. 3:1–7; 1 Ne. 10:11; D&C 42:61, 65).

The terms "mystery," "mysteries," "mystery of God," and "mysteries of Godliness" appear more than a dozen times in the New Testament, always with the sense of something known to God but unknown to humans who have not yet been divinely instructed. Although none of these terms appears in the Old Testament, the word "secrets" in Daniel 2:28 ("But there is a God in heaven that revealeth secrets") and the term "secret" in Amos 3:7 ("Surely the Lord God . . . revealeth his secret unto his servants the prophets") are equivalent to "mysteries," especially because they are associated with divine revelation (cf. D&C 76:10).

The Book of Mormon prophet $Nephi_1$ (c. 570 B.C.) equated the plain and precious truths of the gospel with the mysteries of God, noting that those who were stiff-necked and hard of heart, including some members of his own family, found them difficult to believe. But the faithful accepted such truths willingly, under the heart-softening influence of the HOLY GHOST (1 Ne. 2:11–16; 10:17–22; 15:1–11). Nephi and his followers believed that Jesus Christ would come, that men and women should be baptized and receive the Holy Ghost, and that God speaks to those who inquire, answering their prayers. In fact, Nephi cites his knowledge of these mysteries in the opening statement of his record as part of his qualification to write it (1 Ne. 1:1).

In latter-day scripture the word "mysteries" typically has three interrelated meanings. First, the mysteries consist of significant truths about God and his works. Second, faithful, obedient members of the Church will be given this sacred knowledge through revelation. Finally, those who are not made partakers of this special understanding will not attain the same glory as those who are. Understanding the mysteries of God is a gospel privilege for the reverent who serve God faithfully (D&C 76:1–10; cf. 1 Ne. 10:17–19; Moses 1:5).

The Prophet Joseph Smith was given the "keys of the mysteries and the revelations" (D&C 28:7; 35:18) in connection with the Melchizedek Priesthood (D&C 84:19; 107:18–19). Thus, obtaining the hidden truths is bound up with the power of the Melchizedek Priesthood, "which priesthood administereth the gospel and holdeth the key of the mysteries of the kingdom, even the key of the knowledge of God" (D&C 84:19).

Paradoxically, the term "mystery" encapsulates a dual meaning, both to reveal and to conceal. For the initiated, it designates something believable and understandable. For the nonbeliever its significance is obscure. In other words, the belief and faith of the potential knower determine in great part whether the knowledge is comprehensible or not (Alma 12:9–11).

The knowledge alluded to in the phrases "mysteries of God" or "mysteries of Godliness" may be received in ways other than exclusively verbal. Throughout history, divine knowledge also has been communicated in ceremonies, rites, purifications, and so on. Such is the case in the temples of the Latter-day Saints, where faithful members of the Church gain knowledge and understanding of heavenly truths as they receive ordinances by covenant.

The broad meaning of "Godliness" embraces the state of being like God, of approximating God's nature or qualities. The possibility is suggested in the so-called Law of the Harvest. Just as apple seeds produce apple trees, so the offspring of deity, human beings, when they are fully mature—that is, holy, knowledgeable and virtuous—are like their divine parents.

Jesus' statement in John 17:3, uttered as he petitioned his Father, takes on a more profound meaning in light of the scriptural references to the mysteries of God: "And this is life eternal, that they might know thee the only true God, and Jesus Christ, whom thou hast sent." The "knowing" to which the Savior refers is that higher knowledge often designated "the mysteries of God" or "the mysteries of Godliness."

BIBLIOGRAPHY

Brown, Raymond E. *The Semitic Background of the Term "Mystery" in the New Testament.* Facet Books Biblical Series 21. Philadelphia, 1968.

Welch, John W. "The Calling of a Prophet." In *The Book of Mormon: The Keystone Scripture,* ed. P. Cheesman. Provo, Utah, 1988.

CLARK D. WEBB

N

NEW AND EVERLASTING COVENANT

The new and everlasting covenant is the gospel of Jesus Christ. The sum of all gospel COVENANTS that God makes with mankind is called "*the* new and everlasting covenant" and consists of several individual covenants, each of which is called "*a* new and *an* everlasting covenant." It is "new" when given to a person or a people for the first time, and "everlasting" because the gospel of Jesus Christ and PLAN OF SALVATION existed before the world was formed and will exist forever (*MD*, pp. 479–80).

Baptism, marriage, and all other covenants from God necessary for salvation are new and everlasting (D&C 22:1; 45:9; 66:2; 132:4–7). Holy covenants have been introduced anew in each of the DISPENSATIONS OF THE GOSPEL from Adam to Joseph Smith, and have been available whenever the gospel of Jesus Christ has been upon the earth. Therefore, these covenants are spoken of as everlasting. Covenants of salvation and exaltation are everlasting in the sense also that once entered into they are forever binding and valid only if they are not broken by transgression.

All covenants between God and mankind are part of the new and everlasting covenant (D&C 22; 132:6–7). Thus, celestial marriage is *a* new and *an* everlasting covenant (D&C 132:4) or the new and everlasting covenant of *marriage*. Some covenants, such as baptism, have force in all dispensations. Other covenants are made for special purposes in particular dispensations; circumcision as a sign of a covenant is of this type (*MD*, p. 479). The same eternal covenant conditions may be established through other ritual signs at other times.

Covenants and promises instituted by God are governed by certain stipulations and conditions that he has set and that his children must comply with to make the covenant or promise valid (*DS* 1:152–160). The Lord's house is a house of order, and all things are done according to law (D&C 130:20–21; 132:8–11):

> For all who will have a blessing at my hands shall abide the law which was appointed for that blessing, and the conditions thereof, as were instituted from before the foundation of the world.
>
> And as pertaining to the new and everlasting covenant, it was instituted for the fulness of my glory. . . .
>
> And verily I say unto you, that the conditions of this law are these: All covenants, contracts, bonds, obligations, oaths, vows, performances, connections, associations, or expectations, that are not made and entered into and sealed by the Holy Spirit of promise, of him who is anointed, both as well for time and for all eternity, . . . by revelation and commandment through the medium of mine anointed, . . . are of no efficacy, virtue, or force in and after the resurrection from the dead; for all contracts that are not made unto this end have an end when men are dead [D&C 132:5–7].

The Lord has said, "I, the Lord, am bound when ye do what I say; but when ye do not what I say, ye have no promise" (D&C 82:10).

BIBLIOGRAPHY

Smith, Hyrum M., and Janne M. Sjodahl. *Doctrine and Covenants Commentary*, pp. xiv, 822. Salt Lake City, 1972.

D. CECIL CLARK

O

OBEDIENCE

Obedience in the context of the gospel of Jesus Christ means to comply with God's will, to live in accordance with his teachings and the promptings of his Spirit, and to keep his COMMANDMENTS. Disobedience means to do anything less, whether it be to follow Satan and his will, to live in accordance with one's own selfish wants and desires, or to be a "slothful" person who must be "compelled in all things" (D&C 58:26).

Part of God's purpose in designing mortal life for his children was to "prove them herewith, to see if they will do all things whatsoever the Lord their God shall command them" (Abr. 3:25; cf. D&C 98:14). Passing such a test is necessary for one to progress to become like God because he, himself, lives in accordance with law and principles of justice (Alma 42:22–26; *see* GODHOOD). Thus, obedience to divine law is essential to ETERNAL PROGRESSION, and those who live obediently in this life will "have glory added upon their heads for ever and ever" (Abr. 3:26).

The importance of obedience is further emphasized by the fact that God permits sorrows and suffering on this earth in part to help teach obedience. Thus Jesus Christ, the exemplar, learned "obedience by the things which he suffered" (Heb. 5:8; cf. Alma 7:12), and the Lord's people "must needs be chastened until they learn obedience, if it must needs be, by the things which they suffer" (D&C

105:6). On the other hand, God has also promised that he will provide a way for his children to obey him (cf. 1 Ne. 3:7).

In the LDS view, although it can sometimes be difficult to be obedient because it requires making difficult choices among alternatives, it does bring BLESSINGS in this life and in eternity. In fact, all blessings depend upon obedience: "When we obtain any blessing from God, it is by obedience to that law upon which it is predicated" (D&C 130:21). Disobedience may result in the loss of blessings in this world and may bring curses or punishments in the next life as well. Therefore, when God gives a commandment, he frequently specifies both the blessings that come from obedience and the curses or punishments that come from disobedience. Accordingly, the commandment to "honour thy father and thy mother" specifies the potential blessing "that thy days may be long upon the land which the Lord thy God giveth thee" (Ex. 20:12); and the commandment to Book of Mormon peoples to serve God on the American continent came with the promise of being "free from bondage" or, in the case of noncompliance, the curse of being "swept off" (Ether 2:8–12; *see* AGENCY).

God also recognizes the need to obey the laws of governments. Thus he states: "Let no man break the laws of the land, for he that keepeth the laws of God hath no need to break the laws of the land. Wherefore, be subject to the powers that be, until he reigns whose right it is to reign" (D&C 58:21–22). Joseph Smith reiterated this principle: "We believe in . . . obeying, honoring, and sustaining the law" (A of F 12).

The purest and best motivation for obedience to godly law is LOVE: "If ye love me, keep my commandments" (John 14:15). However, because God wants his children to grow spiritually, he neither requires nor desires unwilling or begrudged compliance, nor "blind obedience." Every person has the right, and even the responsibility, to learn whether a commandment, prompting, or teaching comes from God. However, because God also requires faithful response—"the heart and a willing mind" (D&C 64:34)—from his children, he does sometimes require obedience of the type wherein one complies humbly with his teachings, promptings, or commandments even before totally understanding the reasons for them. Adam gave such obedience when commanded by the Lord to offer the firstlings of his flocks. "After many days," when an angel asked him why he was offering such sacrifice, Adam replied: "I know not, save the Lord commanded me." The angel then taught Adam the reason for the offering: It represented the atoning SACRIFICE that Jesus Christ would eventually make on behalf of all human beings (Moses 5:5–8).

God does not hold people responsible or punish them for disobedience to laws and commandments that they have not had opportunity to learn and understand. King Benjamin taught that Christ's "blood atoneth for the sins of those who have fallen by the transgression of Adam, who have died not knowing the will of God concerning them, or who have ignorantly sinned" (Mosiah 3:11).

As with Adam, men and women who willingly obey the commandments of God because they love him will receive greater KNOWLEDGE and understanding of God and his purposes. Disobedience brings no such growth in knowledge or understanding, and may result in loss of previously gained knowledge and ability or opportunity to make further choices (D&C 1:33). In other words, it can result in both spiritual and temporal captivity for the disobedient. Thus, Jacob taught the Nephites that they were free to choose "liberty and eternal life" or to choose "captivity and death" (2 Ne. 2:27).

BIBLIOGRAPHY

Packer, Boyd K. "Obedience." *BYU Speeches of the Year.* Provo, Utah, 1971.

CHERYL BROWN

OMNIPOTENCE OF GOD; OMNIPRESENCE OF GOD; OMNISCIENCE OF GOD

The Church of Jesus Christ of Latter-day Saints uses the familiar terms "omnipotent," "omnipresent," and "omniscient" to describe members of the GODHEAD.

OMNIPOTENCE.

The Church affirms the biblical view of divine omnipotence (often rendered as "almighty"), that GOD is supreme, having power over all things. No one or no force or happening can frustrate or prevent him from accomplishing his designs (D&C 3:1–3). His power is sufficient to fulfill all his purposes and promises, including his promise of eternal life for all who obey him.

However, the Church does not understand this term in the traditional sense of absoluteness, and, on the authority of modern REVELATION, rejects the classical doctrine of creation out of nothing. It affirms, rather, that there are actualities that are coeternal with the persons of the Godhead, including elements, intelligence, and law (D&C 93:29, 33, 35: 88:34–40). Omnipotence, therefore, cannot coherently be understood as absolutely unlimited power. That view is internally self-contradictory and, given the fact that evil and suffering are real, not reconcilable with God's omnibenevolence or loving kindness.

OMNIPRESENCE. Since Latter-day Saints believe that God the Father and God the Son are gloriously embodied persons, they do not believe them to be bodily omnipresent. They do affirm, rather, that their power is immanent "in all and through all things" and is the power "by which all things are governed" (D&C 88:6, 7, 13, 40–41). By their knowledge and power, and through the influence of the Holy Ghost, they are omnipresent.

OMNISCIENCE. Latter-day Saints differ among themselves in their understanding of the nature of God's knowledge. Some have thought that God increases endlessly in knowledge as well as in glory and dominion. Others hold to the more traditional view that God's knowledge, including the FOREKNOWLEDGE of future free contingencies, is complete. Despite these differing views, there is accord on two fundamental issues: (1) God's foreknowledge does not causally determine human choices, and (2) this knowledge, like God's power, is maximally efficacious. No event occurs that he has not anticipated or has not taken into account in his planning.

BIBLIOGRAPHY

Roberts, B. H. "The Doctrine of Deity." *Seventy's Course in Theology,* third year. Salt Lake City, 1910.

DAVID L. PAULSEN

OPPOSITION

Opposition and AGENCY are eternal and interrelated principles in the theology of The Church of Jesus Christ of Latter-day Saints. Agency is man's innate power to choose between alternative commitments and finally between whole ways of life. Opposition is the framework within which these choices and their consequences are possible.

In his account of the FALL OF ADAM, Lehi teaches that the philosophy of opposites is at the heart of the plan of redemption. Had Adam and Eve continued in a state of premortal innocence, they would have experienced "no joy, for they knew no misery; doing no good, for they knew no sin" (2 Ne. 2:23). Hence, Lehi concludes, "it must needs be, that there is an opposition in all things . . . [otherwise] righteousness could not be brought to pass, neither wickedness, neither holiness nor misery, neither good nor bad" (2 Ne. 2:11).

Latter-day Saints understand that contrast and opposition were manifest in PREMORTAL LIFE as well as on Earth (Abr. 3:23–28; Moses 6:56) and that the distinction between good and evil is eternal. Prior to earth life the spirits of all men had opportunities to choose God and demonstrate love for him by obeying his LAW (Matt. 22:37) or to yield to satanic proposals for rebellion and coercion (2 Ne. 2:11–15; cf. Luke 16:13; 2 Ne. 10:16). Different, indeed opposite, consequences followed these choices (Abr. 3:26).

Scripture relates the principle of opposition to crucial states of human experience. Among them are life and death, knowledge and ignorance, light and darkness, growth and atrophy.

LIFE AND DEATH. As a consequence of Adam and Eve's partaking of the fruit of the tree of knowledge of good and evil, they and all their posterity became subject to physical death and to the afflictions and degeneration of the mortal body (2 Ne. 9:6–7). They also became subject to spiritual death, which means spiritual separation from God because of sin. However, through Christ, provision had already been made for their redemption (2 Ne. 2:26), the overcoming of both deaths, and the return to the presence of God. In the span of eternity, the worst form of death is subjection to Satan and thereby exclusion from the presence of God (2 Ne. 2:29). Christ came to bring life, abundant life, everlasting life with God (John 10:28; 17:3; D&C 132:23–24).

KNOWLEDGE AND IGNORANCE. Opposition was, and is, a prerequisite of authentic KNOWLEDGE, "for if they never should have bitter they could not know the sweet" (D&C 29:39; cf. 2 Ne. 2:15). Such knowledge is participative. Because "it is impossible for a man to be saved in ignorance" (D&C 131:6), the Prophet Joseph Smith taught, "A man is saved no faster than he gets [such] knowledge" (*TPJS*, p. 217; cf. 357). One may aspire to all truth (D&C 93:28), but not without confronting the heights and depths of mortal experience, either vicariously or actually.

LIGHT AND DARKNESS. Latter-day Saints find a parallel between light and darkness, the concept of the "two ways," and the idea of the warring "sons of darkness" and "sons of light" apparent in the dead sea scrolls. Jesus teaches that "if therefore the light that is in thee be darkness, how great is that darkness!" (Matt. 6:23) and that "he who sins against the greater light shall receive the greater condemnation" (D&C 82:3). Finally, the sons and daughters of God are to reach the point where "there shall be no darkness in [them]" (D&C 88:67).

GROWTH AND ATROPHY. The principle of opposition also implies that people cannot be tested and strengthened unless there are genuine alternatives (Abr. 3:23–25) and resistances. Life is a predicament in which there are real risks, real gains, real losses. From such tests emerge responsibility, judgment, and soul growth. Latter-day Saints believe that this encounter with choice and conditions for progression will continue forever. It follows that in the gospel framework, once one is committed, there is no such thing as neutrality or standing still. Joseph Smith taught, "If we are not drawing towards God in principle, we are going from Him" (*TPJS*, p. 216).

One may err in religion by attempting to reconcile the irreconcilable; so one may assume opposition when there is none. In some forms of Judaism and Christianity, for example, the view prevails that the flesh and the spirit are opposed and antithetical. Paul is often cited in this connection. But a close reading of Paul and other writers shows that "flesh" most often applies to man bound by sin, and "spirit" to one regenerated through Christ. Thus, it is not the flesh, but the vices of the flesh that are to be avoided. And it is not the earth, but worldliness (wickedness) that is to be transcended (JST Rom. 7:5–27). Similarly, Latter-day Saints do not finally pit faith against reason, or the spirit against the senses, or the life of contemplation against the life of activity and service. Only when these are distorted are they opposed, for when the self is united under Christ, they are reconciled.

In the plan of redemption, opposition is not obliterated but overcome: evil by good, death by life, ignorance by knowledge, darkness by light, weakness by strength.

BIBLIOGRAPHY

Roberts, B. H. *The Gospel.* Liverpool, 1888.

——. *Comprehensive History of the Church.* Vol. 2, pp. 403–6. Salt Lake City, 1930.

KAY P. EDWARDS

ORIGINAL SIN

While The Church of Jesus Christ of Latter-day Saints teaches that the transgression of Adam and Eve brought death into the world and made all mortals subject to temptation, suffering, and weakness, it denies that any culpability is automatically transmitted to Adam and Eve's offspring. All mortals commit sin, but they will be punished "for their own sins, and not for Adam's transgression" (A of F 2).

IN OTHER FAITHS. The doctrine of original sin as taught traditionally states that, due to the FALL OF ADAM, infants are born tainted with actual sin, resulting in the "privation of sanctifying grace"; this dogma "does not attribute to the children of Adam any properly so-called responsibility for the act of their father," nor is it a voluntary sin "in the strict sense of the word," yet it is a "real sin" (S. Harent, "Original Sin," in *Catholic Encyclopedia,* 1911 ed., Vol. 11, p. 315). All people, according to this doctrine, except the Virgin Mary and Jesus Christ, inherit an actual, existing personal guilt. A corollary of this belief is the doctrine of infant baptism, holding that infants are to be baptized to remove this sin because those who die without baptism remain unsanctified and forever excluded from heaven and the presence of God.

The doctrine of original sin derives from an interpretation given to the writings of Paul, particularly Romans 5:12–21, by some theologians of the second and third centuries. More than any other,

Augustine in the fifth century transformed Paul's teachings on the Fall into the doctrine of original sin. His views were adopted as doctrine and formally canonized by the decrees of the Council of Trent in the sixteenth century. According to this view, Adam's sin is considered "original" because it arose with the "origin" of man.

Protestantism largely accepts this doctrine. John Calvin stated: "We believe that all the posterity of Adam is in bondage to original sin, which is a hereditary evil" (R. Reed, *The Gospel as Taught by Calvin* [Grand Rapids, Mich., 1979], p. 33). Protestant views emphasize the inherited nature of the sin, reflecting the German word for "original sin," *Erbsunde* (literally "inherited sin"). Rabbinic Judaism teaches of two inclinations, one evil and one good; and some Jews consider "circumcision as a means of escaping damnation" (Samuel Cohon, *Essays in Jewish Theology* [Cincinnati, Ohio, 1987], p. 265).

IN LDS DOCTRINE. Latter-day Saints believe that infants inherit certain effects of the Fall, but not the responsibility for any sin as a result of Adam's or Eve's transgression. From the foundation of the world, the atonement of Jesus Christ makes amends "for the sins of those who have fallen by the transgression of Adam" (Mosiah 3:11). Therefore, baptism is not needed until children reach a state of accountability, generally at the age of eight years, for little children cannot sin and are innocent (*see* CHILDREN: SALVATION OF CHILDREN). They are redeemed from the beginning by the grace of Jesus Christ (D&C 29:46–47), whose atonement cleanses them of the effects of the Fall (D&C 137:10). The Prophet Mormon wrote the following words of Christ: "Little children are whole, for they are not capable of committing sin; wherefore the curse of Adam is taken from them in me, that it hath no power over them" (Moro. 8:8).

In one account in the Pearl of Great Price, Adam learned that he had been forgiven for his transgression in the Garden of Eden, and that "the Son of God hath atoned for original guilt, wherein the sins of the parents cannot be answered upon the heads of the children" (Moses 6:54). However, as a consequence of the Fall, evil is present in the world and all "children are conceived in sin, [and] so when they begin to grow up, sin conceiveth in their hearts, and they taste the bitter, that they may know to prize the good" (Moses 6:55). Begetting children in marriage is not a sin (cf. Heb. 13:4), but the propensity for sin is inherited.

No mortal person bears the burden of repenting for Adam's transgression. Nevertheless, all inherit the effects of the Fall: All leave the presence of God at birth, all are subject to physical death, and all will sin in some measure. From the moment of conception, the body inherits the seed of mortality that will eventually result in death, but only as a person becomes accountable and chooses evil over good do personal sins result in further separation from God. Thus Adam was counseled: "Wherefore teach it unto your children, that all men, everywhere, must repent, or they can in nowise inherit the kingdom of God, for no unclean thing can dwell there" (Moses 5:57).

BIBLIOGRAPHY

Haag, Herbert. *Is Original Sin in Scripture?* New York, 1969.
McConkie, Bruce R. *A New Witness for the Articles of Faith,* pp. 81–104. Salt Lake City, 1985.

BYRON R. MERRILL

ORIGIN OF MAN

The view of the "origin of man" in The Church of Jesus Christ of Latter-day Saints differs significantly from that in most other modern traditions. Its prime concern is to affirm that humans were created as SPIRITS by and in the image of God, which determined their form and nature long before they became earthly organisms. Questions about what biological or cultural mechanisms might have produced *Homo sapiens* and over what period of time that often dominate secular discussions are of limited interest for Latter-day Saints.

The clearest presentation of the Church position may be a 1909 statement by the First Presidency entitled "The Origin of Man," where four essential points are made: (1) God created humans (Gen. 1:27–28); (2) God created Adam, "the origin of the human family" and "the first man"; (3) creation was sequential: first spiritual, later physical; and (4) each human body displays the characteristics of the individual premortal SPIRIT that inhabits it. Other ideas included in the statement are that humanity was not "a development from the lower orders of creation" but a "fall" from a higher state of existence; that an understanding of all the details about the origin of man is not vital to one's salvation, although the matter is related to several important truths; that the subject cannot be fully clarified by human learning alone; and that only certain relevant facts are now known, to which the Church adheres.

Subsequent official statements indicate that the details of how Adam became "the first man" are considered not to have been revealed clearly enough to settle questions of process. Emphasized instead is an eternal perspective wherein the individual as an "undeveloped offspring of celestial parentage is capable, by experience through ages and aeons, of evolving into a God" (*IE* 28:1091).

Since the rise of Darwinism in 1860, individual Latter-day Saints, both leaders and members, have occasionally participated in public discussion about evolution, since the official position of the Church on man's origin is not definitive in all respects. Mormons have expressed a wide range of views that are reminiscent of the well-known debates among Christians. Since a large number of Latter-day Saints entered careers in science early in this century, some have attempted to reconcile scientific facts and ideas with statements from the scriptures and prophetic leaders that are emphasized in the LDS tradition. Others have argued that in this area science merely offers "theories of men" and should therefore be discounted.

Many sympathetic to science interpret certain statements in LDS scripture to mean that God used a version of evolution to prepare bodies and environmental surroundings suitable for the premortal spirits. For example, one scriptural description of creation says, "the Gods *organized the earth to bring forth* . . . every thing that creepeth upon the earth after its kind" (Abr. 4:25 [emphasis added]). Certain statements of various General Authorities are also used by proponents of this idea to justify their opinions.

Other Latter-day Saints accept a more literal reading of scriptural passages that suggest to them an abrupt creation. Proponents of this view also support their positions with statements from scripture and General Authorities.

While the current state of revealed truth on the LDS doctrine of man's origin may permit some differences of opinion concerning the relationship of science and religion, it clearly affirms that God created man, that the FALL OF ADAM was foreknown of God and was real and significant, and that the ATONEMENT of Christ was foreordained and necessary to reverse the effects of the Fall. Perhaps because these claims embrace the main doctrinal issues relevant to the condition of man, the description of the actual creation process does not receive much attention from the general membership of the Church or from the authorities.

BIBLIOGRAPHY

Jeffrey, Duane E. "Seers, Savants and Evolution: The Uncomfortable Interface." *Dialogue* 8, Nos. 3/4 (1973):41–75.

"Mormon View of Evolution." *IE* 28 (Sept. 1925):1090–91; reprinted in *MFP* 5:244.

"The Origin of Man." *IE* 13 (Nov. 1909):75–81; reprinted in *MFP* 4:199–206.

Packer, Boyd K. "The Law and the Light." In *The Book of Mormon: Jacob Through Words of Mormon, To Learn with Joy,* ed. M. Nyman and C. Tate, pp. 1–31. Salt Lake City, 1990.

JOHN L. SORENSON

P

PARADISE

Paradise is a Persian word (*para-daeza,* meaning "enclosure") that came into Greek and meant a pleasant place, such as a park or garden. Later it came to refer generally in scripture to that place where righteous spirits go after death. The word "paradise" is not found in the Old Testament, but occurs three times in the New Testament: Luke 23:43, where the Savior on the cross says to the thief, "Today shalt thou be with me in paradise"; 2 Corinthians 12:2–4, where Paul alludes to his vision of the third heaven and also to paradise; and Revelation 2:7, which describes the righteous who partake of the Tree of Life in the midst of God's paradise (cf. D&C 77:2, 5). The latter two uses of paradise seem to refer to the highest degree of heaven (the CELESTIAL KINGDOM) rather than to the SPIRIT WORLD. Another sense of paradise pertains to the condition of the Garden of Eden, which was paradisiacal in nature. Article of Faith 10 declares that "the earth will be renewed and receive its paradisiacal glory," which is to say that it will eventually return to the edenic state that existed before the FALL OF ADAM.

The Savior's reference to paradise in Luke 23:43 pertains neither to heaven, nor to a specific place of righteous spirits, but to the spirit world in general, since the thief was not prepared to enter into the abode of the righteous. It is a misconception that this passage justifies "deathbed REPENTANCE," that is, the idea that one can delay repentance until death and still enter a heavenly condition. The gospel of Jesus Christ requires that persons use the gift of mortal life to learn to control appetites, thus preparing themselves to meet God and to acquire the divine nature (Rom. 8:29; Alma 34:32–35). The Prophet Joseph Smith taught that the thief on the cross was to be with Jesus Christ "in the world of spirits" (he did not say paradise or heaven). "Hades, Sheol, paradise, spirits in prison, are all one: it is a world of spirits. The righteous and the wicked all go to the same world of spirits" (*TPJS,* pp. 309–310).

It is apparent from the scriptures, however, that even though the spirit world is one world, there exists a division between righteous and disobedient spirits. Luke 16:22–26 indicates a division and also a gulf fixed between the place of the righteous (Abraham's bosom) and the place of the wicked (cf. 1 Ne. 15:28–29). Between his death and his RESURRECTION, the Savior visited the spirit world (1 Pet. 3:18–20; 4:6; D&C 138) and bridged the gulf by giving righteous spirits authority to cross the gulf and carry the gospel to the spirits dwelling in darkness. This darkness is sometimes referred to as SPIRIT PRISON, HELL, or even "outer darkness" (Alma 40:13–14).

The Book of Mormon and the Doctrine and Covenants teach that paradise is the part of the spirit world where the righteous, those who in mortality obeyed God's commandments and were faithful to their COVENANTS, await the resurrection. Alma teaches that the spirits of the righteous "are received into a state of happiness, which is called paradise, a state of rest, a state of peace, where they shall rest from all their troubles and from all care, and sorrow" (Alma 40:12). It was in paradise that righteous spirits like Adam, Eve, and Abraham greeted the Savior on his appearance in the spirit world after his crucifixion (D&C 138:38–49). Paradise is a temporary condition. At the resurrection it "must deliver up the spirits of the righteous" (2 Ne. 9:13). Even though the righteous spirits attain to a greater state of rest and happiness (Alma 40:12) than is possible in this life, they look "upon the long absence of their spirits from their bodies as a bondage" (D&C 138:50). When the Savior visited the spirit world, he taught these righteous spirits in paradise and "gave them power to come forth, after his resurrection from the dead, to enter into his Father's kingdom, there to be crowned with IMMORTALITY and ETERNAL LIFE, and continue thenceforth their labor as had been promised by the Lord, and be partakers of all blessings which were held in reserve for them that love him" (D&C 138:51–52). As teaching and missionary work proceed in the spirit prison and ordinances for the dead are performed in temples on the earth, the once uninformed and the disobedient but now repentant and purified spirits may enter into paradise and enjoy association with the righteous and the blessings of the gospel. The Prophet Joseph Smith taught, "There is never a time when the spirit [of man] is too old to approach God. All are within the reach of pardoning mercy, who have not committed the unpardonable sin, which hath no forgiveness, neither in this world, nor in the world to come. There is a way to release the spirits of the dead; that is by the power and authority of the Priesthood—by binding and loosing on earth" (*TPJS*, pp. 191–92).

[*See also* Spirit World.]

BIBLIOGRAPHY

Young, Brigham. *Discourses of Brigham Young,* comp. John A. Widtsoe, pp. 376–81. Salt Lake City, 1946.

M. CATHERINE THOMAS

PERFECTION

Through all generations, God has commanded his children to be perfect. His mandates to Abraham, "Walk before me, and be thou perfect" (Gen. 17:1), and to the Israelites, "Thou shalt be perfect with the Lord thy God" (Deut. 18:13), were one with his charge, "Be ye therefore perfect, even as your Father which is in heaven is perfect" (Matt. 5:48; cf. 3 Ne. 12:48).

Although the Savior's injunction is an unequivocal call to perfection, Latter-day Saints recognize that only he was totally without blemish or stain and was perfect in an infinite and absolute sense. "And being made perfect, he became the author of eternal salvation unto all them that obey him" (Heb. 5:9).

Human beings are required to seek perfection in certain respects that are attainable in mortality only through Christ. The New Testament refers to "them that are perfect" (1 Cor. 2:6; cf. Matt. 19:21; James 3:2; Heb. 12:23), and the Greek word *teleios,* meaning "perfect," also means "complete, whole, fully initiated, mature." Such maturity and completeness consist of receiving the fulness of the gospel, walking by faith in the Lord Jesus Christ, repenting of one's sins, receiving necessary ordinances, being faithful to covenants with the Lord, obeying the Lord and submitting to his will, seeking first the kingdom of God and his righteousness, and having charity, "the bond of perfectness and peace" (D&C 88:125).

Latter-day prophets have taught that men and women can become perfect "in the spheres in which [they] are called to act . . . [and that] we may become as perfect in our sphere as God is perfect in his higher and more exalted sphere" (Smith, p. 252; cf. *JD* 6:99; 2:129; 10:223). Mortal beings have the comforting assurance that God "giveth no commandments unto the children of men, save he shall prepare a way for them that they may accomplish the thing which he commandeth them" (1 Ne. 3:7).

Mormons believe that Jesus Christ provides the means for all humans to become perfect. He is "the way, the truth, and the life: no man cometh unto the Father but by [him]" (John 14:6). Through his atoning sacrifice all men and women can repent and become perfected by having their sins and errors and the desire for sin removed. Ultimately, eternal life and godly perfection are gifts of God (D&C 14:7), rooted in the grace of God, redemption, individual righteousness, and being born of God. Human effort falls short; God's gift of grace compensates for this shortcoming, "for we know that it is by grace that we are saved, after all we can do" (2 Ne. 25:23).

The process by which faithful Saints advance toward perfection is gradual, made step by step. Just as the Savior "continued from grace to grace, until he received a fulness" (D&C 93:13), so God gives his children milk before meat (1 Cor. 3:2; Heb. 5:12; D&C 19:22). "It is not requisite that a man should run faster than he has strength" (Mosiah 4:27). This process is variously described as a "ladder" (*TPJS*, p. 348), a "road" (*DS* 2:18–19), and a "process to be pursued throughout one's lifetime" (Kimball, p. 6). In 1831 the Lord admonished the Saints to "continue in patience until ye are perfected" (D&C 67:13).

Although to many the goal of perfection seems overwhelming, Christ promised, "My yoke is easy, and my burden is light" (Matt. 11:30). While obedience to the commandments is essential, the spirit of perfection is contrary to ever-lengthening checklists of outward acts visible to others. Rather, prophets invite all to "come unto Christ, and be perfected in him, and deny yourselves of all ungodliness; . . . and love God with all your might, mind and strength, then is his grace sufficient for you" (Moro. 10:32). Therein lies the power to overcome sin and discouragement.

The man or woman who seeks the perfection of the Redeemer participates in the Father's work of saving and exalting mankind: "He proceeds to help his frail fellow men in their attempts to progress; thus becoming a partner with God in working out the Plan of Salvation" (Widtsoe, p. 180). Latter-day Saints believe that they must become perfected and one in spirit, as individuals and as a body (Eph. 4:12), in order to inherit the kingdom of God.

[*See also* Sanctification.]

BIBLIOGRAPHY

"Becoming Justified and Sanctified." In *Relief Society Personal Study Guide*, pp. 63–69. Salt Lake City, 1989.

Kimball, Spencer W. "Hold Fast to the Iron Rod." *Ensign* 8 (Nov. 1978):4–6.

Lund, Gerald N. "Are We Expected to Achieve Perfection in this Life?" *Ensign* 16 (Aug. 1986):39–41.

Smith, Joseph F. *Gospel Doctrine*, p. 252. Salt Lake City, 1939.

Widtsoe, John A. *Evidences and Reconciliations*, p. 180. Salt Lake City, 1960.

CAROL LEE HAWKINS

PHYSICAL BODY

Latter-day Saints believe that the physical human body was created by God in his express image, and that one of the most important purposes of earth life is for the spirit children of God to obtain a physical body and grow through the experience of MORTALITY.

The physical body, with all its structures and physiological systems, appetites and passions, strengths and frailties, serves as the mortal housing of the spirit. Before BIRTH, the spirit leaves God's presence and comes to this world to take up a physical body. In mortality, the body is imperfect and will eventually die. In due time, the physical body of every human will be resurrected in its "proper and perfect frame" (Alma 40:23) and the spirit will be restored to it in a state of immortality.

Together, the physical body and the spirit constitute the SOUL (D&C 88:15). The salvation of the soul requires PERFECTION of both body and spirit. GOD THE FATHER and JESUS CHRIST, both perfected and glorified beings, possess tangible resurrected bodies of flesh and bone (D&C 130:22). The Prophet Joseph Smith stated, "No person can have this salvation except through a tabernacle" (*TPJS*, p. 297; see also D&C 93:35). To become like God, his children, too, must obtain physical bodies. "We came to this earth that we might have a body and present it pure before God in the celestial kingdom. The great principle of happiness consists in having a body" (*TPJS*, p. 181).

These beliefs are crucial to LDS understanding of the importance of the physical body. Many religions view the human corporeal nature as a state of constant conflict between the righteous enticings of the spirit and the vices of the flesh, ending only when death frees the spirit from the body. In contrast, Latter-day Saints strive for righteous harmony between the two, seeking perfection and discipline of the spirit along with training and health of the body. Health includes both physical and moral hygiene. The Word of Wisdom and other scriptural admonitions concerning health are intended to be followed to ensure a clean and clear mind and vigorous longevity "unto the renewing of their bodies" (D&C 84:33). CHASTITY, in both deed and thought, and physical and moral health are conditions essential for spiritual sensitivity, receiving a TESTIMONY, and personal REVELATION.

Latter-day Saints view the possession of a body as an eternal privilege and a blessing. The righteous decision to accept the plan of God the Father and come into this world was rewarded with the gift of a human body. Humans are free to choose their actions while in the flesh, and they are privileged to experience the pleasures and pains of being alive. This is a blessing not enjoyed by those who followed Satan's lead and were cast out of God's presence, never to have a mortal body. During Christ's ministry, he found several occasions to cast out DEVILS. In the most notable incident, the spirits requested that Christ not cast them out entirely, but that he allow them to enter the bodies of nearby swine (Mark 5:6–13). For Latter-day Saints this suggests how much the followers of Satan desire a physical body.

RESURRECTION, the ultimate and perfect unification of body and spirit, gives spirits the power to overcome SPIRITUAL DEATH: "For behold, if the flesh should rise no more our spirits must become subject to that angel who fell from before the presence of the Eternal God, and became the devil, to rise no more" (2 Ne. 9:8).

For Latter-day Saints the physical body, in all its developmental, anatomical, and physiological complexities and functions, is evidence of God's creative hand. It is, in itself, miraculous. Furthermore, the day-to-day vitality of the body can be attributed to divine regulation; as expressed by King Benjamin, it is God who "has created you from the beginning, and is preserving you from day to day, by lending you breath, that ye may live and move and do according to your own will, and even supporting you from one moment to another" (Mosiah 2:21).

The upkeep and maintenance of the body are important in LDS belief. Disease is a natural condition that disturbs the normal function of the body's physical processes. When ill or injured, Latter-day Saints exercise faith toward recovery. Worthy priesthood holders, by administering a BLESSING of health, may call upon the power of God to aid in the healing process. At the same time, Latter-day Saints are encouraged to take full advantage of modern medicine and technology in the prevention and cure of sickness and do not find this inconsistent with accepting the blessings of the priesthood, for they see an ultimate unity between SPIRIT and matter.

BIBLIOGRAPHY

Lockhart, Barbara. "The Body: A Burden or a Blessing?" *Ensign* 15 (Feb. 1985):56–60.

Madsen, Truman G. *Eternal Man*, pp. 43–51. Salt Lake City, 1966.

Nelson, Russell M. "Self Mastery." *Ensign* 15 (Nov. 1985):30–32.

KENT M. VAN DE GRAAFF

PLAN OF SALVATION, PLAN OF REDEMPTION

Latter-day Saints believe that eons ago, GOD, in his infinite wisdom and never-ending mercy, formulated a plan whereby his children could experience a physical existence, including mortality, and then return to live in his presence in eternal felicity and glory. This plan, alternately called "the plan of salvation" (Jarom 1:2; Alma 42:5; Moses 6:62), "the plan of redemption" (Jacob 6:8; Alma 12:25; 42:11), and the "great plan of happiness" (Alma 42:8), provided both the way and the means for everyone to receive SALVATION and gain ETERNAL LIFE. Eternal life is God's greatest gift to his children (D&C 6:13), and the plan of salvation is his way of making it available to them. Although the term "plan of salvation" is used repeatedly in latter-day scripture, it does not occur in the Bible, though the doctrines pertaining to it are discoverable in its pages.

The Father is the author of the plan of salvation; JESUS CHRIST is its chief advocate; the HOLY SPIRIT helps carry it out, communicating God's will to men and helping them live properly.

THE PREMORTAL EXISTENCE. Latter-day Saints believe that all humans are spirit children of heavenly parents (*see* GOD THE FATHER; MOTHER IN HEAVEN), and they dwelt with them prior to BIRTH on this earth (Heb. 12:9; cf. Jer. 1:5; Eph. 1:4). In that PREMORTAL LIFE, or FIRST ESTATE, those spirit children could not progress fully. They needed a PHYSICAL BODY in order to have a fulness of joy (D&C 93:33–34), and the spirits also needed to be placed in an environment where, by the exercise of AGENCY, they could prove their willingness to keep God's commandments (Abr. 3:25). On the other hand, if they succumbed to TEMPTATION, they would be shut out from God's presence, for "no unclean thing can dwell with God" (1 Ne. 10:21; Eph. 5:5). To bring those who yielded to temptation back into God's presence, a plan of redemption had to be set in place, and this required a redeemer.

A COUNCIL IN HEAVEN was held of all the spirits, and two individuals volunteered to serve as the redeemer. One was Lucifer, a son of the morning (Isa. 14:12; D&C 76:26), who said he would "redeem all mankind, that one soul shall not be lost," but they would have no choice in the matter. Their agency would be destroyed (Moses 4:1–3). Such a proposal was out of harmony with the plan of the Father, for the agency of mankind is an absolute prerequisite to progress. JEHOVAH, the premortal Jesus Christ, had first stepped forward and volunteered to give his life as payment for all sins. He set no plan or conditions of his own, but said, "Father, thy will be done, and the glory be thine forever" (Moses 4:2). He was selected by the Father.

When Lucifer would not accept the Father's choice, a war in

heaven ensued, and he was cast out for rebellion (Moses 4:3; D&C 76:25), along with those who followed him, numbering about a third of the spirits (Rev. 12:4, 7–9; D&C 29:36–38). After Satan's expulsion, the Father's plan was carried forward. Three events ordained and instituted by God before the creation of the Earth constitute the foundation stones upon which the plan of salvation rests. These are the Creation, the FALL OF ADAM, and the ATONEMENT OF JESUS CHRIST. "These three divine events—the three pillars of eternity—are inseparably woven together into one grand tapestry known as the eternal plan of salvation" (McConkie, p. 81).

THE CREATION. One of the purposes for creating this earth was for God's spirit children to obtain physical bodies and learn to walk by faith. Earth life is the second estate. The scriptures teach that by the power of his Only Begotten Son, the Father has created "worlds without number" (Moses 1:33; cf. John 1:3; Heb. 1:2), but the Lord has revealed to us detailed information only about this world (Moses 1:40).

Ecclesiastes states that "whatsoever God doeth, it shall be forever" (Eccl. 3:14). God does not work for temporal ends (D&C 29:34–35). The scriptures specify that when God created the earth, it was in a paradisiacal and deathless state. If Adam and Eve had not transgressed and fallen, "all things which were created must have remained in the same state in which they were after they were created; and they must have remained for ever, and had no end" (2 Ne. 2:22; cf. Moses 3:9; *DS*, pp. 75–77).

THE FALL. An earth in a deathless and paradisiacal state did not fulfill conditions needed for the progression of God's children (*see* PURPOSE OF EARTH LIFE). The Book of Mormon gives some reasons why the Fall was part of the foreordained plan of God. Agency is of paramount importance in the proving process. Critical to agency are choices or alternatives. Lehi taught that "there must needs be an opposition in all things" (2 Ne. 2:11). But in the state in which Adam and Eve found themselves, there was no such opposition. They had physical bodies, but were in a state of innocence. There was no death, sin, sorrow, or pain. Furthermore, in that state they would have had no children (2 Ne. 2:22–23). It appears that a major reason Lucifer and his followers had access to those on earth is the necessity that everyone be enticed by both good and evil (2 Ne. 2:16).

Eve was beguiled by Satan to partake of the forbidden fruit, exercised her agency and did so. Adam also chose to partake, realizing that if he did not, Eve and he would be separated and the command to multiply and replenish the earth would be thwarted. Therefore, "Adam fell that men might be" (2 Ne. 2:25). "With the eating of the 'forbidden fruit,' Adam and Eve became mortal, sin entered, blood formed in their bodies, and death became a part of life. . . . After Adam fell, the whole creation fell and became mortal. Adam's fall brought both physical and spiritual death into the world upon all mankind" (Bible Dictionary, p. 670; *DS* 1:77; Hel. 14:16–17; *see also* SPIRITUAL DEATH). Later, both Adam and Eve rejoiced in the opportunities that had come to them because of the fall (Moses 5:10–11).

The Fall was part of God's plan for mankind and came as no surprise. "All things have been done in the wisdom of him who knoweth all things" (2 Ne. 2:24). Latter-day Saints affirm that Adam and Eve were actual beings, the first parents, and that the Fall was a literal event both in time and place. Elder Joseph Fielding Smith explained, "If Adam did not fall, there was no Christ, because the atonement of Jesus Christ is based on the fall of Adam" (*DS* 1:120). Elder James E. Talmage wrote, "It has become a common practice with mankind to heap reproaches on the progenitors of the family, and to picture the supposedly blessed state in which we would be living but for the fall; whereas our first parents are entitled to our deepest gratitude for their legacy to posterity" (*AF*, p. 70).

THE ATONEMENT. The Atonement is the crowning phase of the plan of salvation, without which all else would have been without purpose and all would have been lost. Atonement literally means "at-one-ment" and carries the idea of reconciliation, or the reuniting, of the human family with Heavenly Father. Understanding reconciliation necessitates an examination of the operation of the laws of JUSTICE AND MERCY.

God's perfect love, patience, long-suffering, and care for humanity's eternal welfare are the manifestations of his mercy. God is also just and so cannot look upon sin with the "least degree of allowance" (Alma 45:16). Perfect justice requires that every violation of God's law be punished and every act of obedience to the law be rewarded or blessed (D&C 130:20–21). Mercy and justice are basic to God's nature, and neither can be ignored. If the demands of justice were the only consideration and mercy ignored, no one could come back into God's presence, for "all have sinned and come short of the glory of God" (Rom. 3:23). If God were to excuse sin, then mercy would rob justice. Such cannot be. "What, do ye suppose that mercy can rob justice? I say unto you, Nay; not one whit. If so, God would cease to be God" (Alma 42:25).

In the atonement of Jesus Christ, justice and mercy are combined to bring about the plan of redemption. As the Only Begotten Son of a divine Father and a mortal mother, Jesus was subject to the effects of the fall of Adam (mortality, temptation, pain, etc.), but had the power to live a perfect, sinless life (Heb. 3:15; D&C 45:4) and to lay down his life and take it up again (John 5:26; 10:17). In LDS doctrine, the miraculous conception and virgin birth of Jesus Christ are accepted as literally true and absolutely essential to the working of the plan of salvation. Because of his sinless life, justice had no claim on him. Because of his infinite, divine power, he could pay the price of sin for all of God's children and satisfy justice in their behalf (D&C 45:3–5). His was not a human sacrifice, but an infinite, eternal sacrifice (Alma 34:40). He atoned not only for the fall of Adam but also for the individual sins of every person. He extends forgiveness to everyone upon the condition of repentance.

In Gethsemane, Christ took upon himself the burden of the sins of the world and suffered for them in a way that is incomprehensible to mortals. "He suffereth the pains of all men, yea, the pains of every living creature, both men, women, and children, who belong to the family of Adam" (2 Ne. 9:21). This incomprehensible agony was so intense that it caused Jesus, "even God, the greatest of all, to tremble because of pain, and to bleed at every pore, and to suffer both body and spirit" (D&C 19:18; Mosiah 3:7; cf. Luke 22:42). Because he had power over death, Jesus endured (*JC,* p. 613). The shame, suffering, trials, scourging, and crucifixion were such that a mortal, finite being cannot fathom the price required before the Redeemer could say, "It is finished!" (John 19:30). God's great plan of redemption was implemented, and justice was not robbed by mercy, but rather was *paid* in full by the atoning blood of Jesus Christ. This payment for everyone's sins is called the grace of Jesus Christ. Without it, all stand condemned to eternal damnation. Hence, $Nephi_1$ declared, "It is by grace that we are saved, after all we can do" (2 Ne. 25:23). Paul also taught the doctrine of salvation by grace (Eph. 2:8–9)—that is, without Christ's atonement, nothing any mortal could do would suffice.

Some aspects of Christ's atonement are unconditional. All mortal beings will be resurrected and brought back into the presence of God for the judgment regardless of the kind of lives they have lived (1 Cor. 15:22; 2 Ne. 9:12–15; Hel. 14:16–17), thus redeeming all humankind from both the mortal and spiritual deaths occasioned by the fall of Adam. Another unconditional aspect of Christ's mercy applies to young children who are not capable of understanding the difference between good and evil and therefore are not accountable. They cannot sin or be tempted of Satan (D&C 29:47; Moro. 8:8). "They are all alive in [Christ] because of his mercy" (Moro. 8:19; cf. D&C 29:46). LDS doctrine states that all children who die before the age of ACCOUNTABILITY (age eight) are saved in the CELESTIAL KINGDOM (D&C 137:10). Mercy extends also to those who through mental handicaps do not reach the mental age of eight, the level of accountability (D&C 29:50).

However, for those who are mentally accountable, part of their estrangement from God is the direct result of their own sins, in addition to Adam's transgression. Unless something is done in their behalf, they will not be allowed to return to the presence of God after their judgment, for no unclean thing can enter there (1 Ne. 10:21). The Lord has set in place certain principles and ordinances called the gospel, which must be followed to have Christ's full atoning power applied to one's own sins: (1) FAITH IN JESUS CHRIST, (2) REPENTANCE, (3) BAPTISM by immersion for the remission of sins by one having authority, and (4) the GIFT OF THE HOLY GHOST by the LAYING ON OF HANDS (*see* ARTICLES OF FAITH). Paul and others emphasized that humans are saved by GRACE and not by their own WORKS (Eph. 2:8). This is true because no mortals can work perfectly enough to save themselves. No mortals have, or can have, the power to overcome the effects of the fall of Adam, or even their own sins. Everyone must depend on the atoning blood of the Savior for salvation. With equal clarity and firmness, the Savior and his servants have taught that how people live is a condition for bringing the power of the Atonement to bear in their own lives. "Not every one that saith unto me, Lord, Lord, shall enter into the kingdom of heaven; but he that doeth the will of the Father" (Matt. 5:21). "The hearers of the law are [not] just before

God, but the doers of the law shall be justified" (Rom. 1:18; 2:13). "They which do [the works of the flesh] shall not inherit the kingdom of God" (Gal. 5:21). "Behold, [Christ] offereth himself a sacrifice for sin, to answer the ends of the law, unto all those who have a broken heart and contrite spirit; and unto none else can the ends of the law be answered" (2 Ne. 2:7).

THE SPIRIT WORLD AND THE THREE DEGREES OF GLORY. When mortals complete their sojourn on earth and pass through the portal called death, they enter the postmortal SPIRIT WORLD. As part of the plan of salvation, the Lord set a time between death and the RESURRECTION when men and women can continue their progression and further learn principles of perfection before they are brought to the final judgment (Alma 40:6–21). Jesus Christ went to the postmortal spirit world while his body lay in the tomb to preach the gospel to them (1 Pet. 3:19–20; 4:6; D&C 138:11–37) so that those spirits in the postmortal spirit world could hear and accept or reject the gospel. Since baptism, the gift of the Holy Ghost, temple endowment, and sealing are earthly ordinances, Latter-day Saints perform the ordinances vicariously for the dead in their temples (*see* SALVATION FOR THE DEAD). Because individuals differ so widely in their obedience to God's commandments, LDS theology rejects the traditional Christian concepts of the single option of heaven or hell in explaining the final destiny of souls (*see* SOUL). Through a vision given to the Prophet Joseph Smith (D&C 76), the Lord has shown, as he also revealed to Paul, that there are several DEGREES OF GLORY in mankind's eternal reward (D&C 76; cf. 1 Cor. 15:42).

The plan of salvation was created by the Father, brought into reality by the atoning sacrifice of his Beloved Son, and facilitated by the gifts of the Holy Ghost. It embraces the Creation, the Fall, and the Atonement, including the Resurrection, and sweeps across all time from the premortal existence to the final state of IMMORTALITY and eternal life.

BIBLIOGRAPHY

McConkie, Bruce R. *A New Witness for the Articles of Faith,* pp. 81–104, 144–59. Salt Lake City, 1985.

Packer, Boyd K. *Our Father's Plan.* Salt Lake City, 1984.

Taylor, John. *The Mediation and Atonement of Our Lord and Savior Jesus Christ.* Salt Lake City, 1882.

GERALD N. LUND

PRAYER

Prayer marked the beginning of The Church of Jesus Christ of Latter-day Saints when God the Father and his son Jesus Christ appeared in answer to the Prophet Joseph Smith's plea to know which of the neighboring churches he should join. Young Joseph Smith had followed James's invitation: "If any of you lack wisdom, let him ask of God, that giveth to all men liberally. . . . But let him ask in faith, nothing wavering" (James 1:5–6). God answered the boy's sincere and earnest plea (JS—H 1:5–20). And this first vision shows prayer as the way to commune with God and receive REVELATION from him. Faith, sincerity, obedience, and seeking are attributes that lift the soul to God; this is the essential character of prayer for the Latter-day Saint.

Adam and Eve began praying to God after they were cast out of the Garden of Eden. "And Adam and Eve, his wife, called upon the name of the Lord, and they heard the voice of the Lord from the way toward the Garden of Eden, speaking unto them, and they saw him not" (Moses 5:4). Though they were separated from God, communication with him was possible and important, for the Lord commanded, "Thou shalt repent and call upon God in the name of the Son forevermore" (Moses 5:8).

Among Latter-day Saints, this commandment to pray still applies. The Lord instructs, "Ask, and ye shall receive; knock, and it shall be opened unto you" (D&C 4:7; cf. Matt. 7:7). Home teachers, for instance, are to "visit the house of each member, and exhort them to pray vocally and in secret" (D&C 20:47). Other scriptures emphasize these important commandments: "Pray always lest that wicked one have power in you, and remove you out of your place" (D&C 93:49). "Pray always, lest you enter into temptation and lose your reward" (D&C 31:12). "For if ye would hearken unto the Spirit which teacheth a man to pray ye would know that ye must pray; for the evil spirit teacheth not a man to pray, but teacheth him that he must not pray. But behold . . . ye must pray always, and not faint; . . . ye must not perform any thing unto the Lord save in the first place ye shall pray unto the Father in the name of Christ, that he will consecrate thy performance unto thee, that thy performance may be for the welfare of thy soul" (2 Ne. 32:8–9). Thus, the scriptures make clear that prayer is a commandment as well as an opportunity to communicate with God and to receive blessings and direction from him.

The Church uses set prayers only in temple ordinances, in the two sacrament prayers, and in the BAPTISMAL PRAYER. "By revelation the Lord has given the Church . . . set prayers for use in our sacred ordinances. . . . [These] relate to the atonement of the Lord Jesus Christ, his crucifixion, and his burial and resurrection. All of the ordinances in which we use these prayers place us under solemn covenants of obedience to God" (Kimball et al., p. 56). In all other instances, Latter-day Saints express themselves in their own words.

Although few set prayers occur in their worship, Latter-day Saints follow a pattern when praying. Prayers are addressed to the Father in Heaven, following the example set by Christ when instructing his disciples how to pray (Matt. 6:9; 3 Ne. 13:9). His prayer serves as a pattern: Disciples are to praise and thank God, ask for daily physical needs, and plead for the spiritual power to forgive, be forgiven, and resist temptation. Jesus used simple, expressive language in his prayers, avoiding vain repetition and flowery phrases (Matt. 6:5–13; 3 Ne. 13:5–13; 19:20–23, 28–29; cf. 3 Ne. 17:14–17; 19:31–34). More important than the words is the feeling that accompanies prayer. Christ reiterated a clear, prophetic warning: "This people draweth nigh unto me with their mouth, and honoureth me with their lips; but their heart is far from me" (Matt. 15:8; cf. Isa. 29:13). In praising God, in offering thanks, in asking for needs—remembering to pray that God's will be done—language is to be reverent, humble, and sincere. President Spencer W. Kimball commented, "In all our prayers, it is well to use the pronouns *thee, thou, thy,* and *thine* instead of *you, your,* and *yours* inasmuch as they have come to indicate respect" (p. 201). Unnecessary repetition of God's name is avoided, as are idle clichés. Prayers close by stating that the prayer is offered in the name of Jesus Christ, concluding with amen. When someone prays in behalf of a group, the members customarily repeat the final "amen" aloud, expressing acceptance of what has been said. In private, the individual or family members kneel with bowed heads and closed eyes. In public, the one praying usually stands, but also observes behavior appropriate to prayer. A prayer's length is determined somewhat by the occasion, but generally prayers are reasonably concise, expressing thanks and petitioning God for what the group needs, avoiding a sermon or display of verbal skills. For both invocations and benedictions the Church teaches that the one praying should express worship rather than make a display or preach a sermon.

Prayer is both an individual and a family form of worship. Usually, the day begins and ends with prayer. At least once daily, LDS families should pray together. The father, or the mother in his absence, calls on one member to pray for the family. As days pass, each family member has the opportunity to lead family prayer. A blessing on the food that offers thanks to God also precedes each meal, the younger children often offering this simple prayer, at first with the help of a parent. In addition, one is encouraged to pray whenever the desire or need occurs: to give thanks for a special blessing, to ask for help in difficult circumstances, or to speak with God on any matter of concern. Prayers begin and end all formal Church meetings and often begin other occasions for which Latter-day Saints have responsibility, such as Church-sponsored athletic contests, concerts, and plays.

Another practice associated with prayer is the fast observed on the first Sunday of the month. Latter-day Saints abstain from two consecutive meals, ending their FASTING with a fast and testimony meeting, bearing public testimony of God and Christ and giving thanks for God's goodness and blessings. In addition, whenever circumstances dictate, special pleas to God are combined with fasting, occasionally observed by a whole congregation to petition for special blessings outside the ordinary course of events (see D&C 27:18).

The comprehensive scope of prayer has been outlined by the Book of Mormon prophet Alma$_2$: "I would that ye should be humble, . . . asking for whatsoever things ye stand in need, both spiritual and temporal; always returning thanks unto God for whatsoever things ye do receive" (Alma 7:23). Amulek, a noted Book of Mormon teacher, followed these essential qualities of prayer when he counseled men and women to pray about physical needs: "Cry unto [God] when ye are in your fields, yea, over all your flocks. Cry unto him in your houses, yea, over all your household, both morning, mid-day, and evening . . . Cry unto him over the crops of your fields, that ye may prosper in them. Cry over the flocks of your fields, that they may increase" (Alma 34:20–21, 24–25). Thus, a student may pray about studies, a merchant about business, a mother and father about the welfare of their children. Although prayer may be for physical needs, spiritual results may also occur, and vice versa. A student who prays about studies is not likely to cheat on examinations; a merchant who prays about business is not likely to be dishonest.

Alma$_2$ sought still other spiritual blessings:

> O Lord, my heart is exceedingly sorrowful; wilt thou comfort my soul in Christ. O Lord, wilt thou grant unto me that I may have strength, that I may suffer with patience these afflictions which shall come upon me, because of the iniquity of this people. . . . O Lord, wilt thou grant unto us [Alma and fellow missionaries] that we may have success in bringing [our brethren] again unto thee in Christ. Behold, O Lord, their souls are precious, . . . therefore, give unto us, O Lord, power and wisdom that we may bring these, our brethren, again unto thee [Alma 31:31–35].

The intent of Alma's prayer underlies the missionary program of the Church. Alma's disciple Amulek also told his people to "cry unto [God] against the devil, who is an enemy to all righteousness" (Alma 34:23). The spiritual blessings one might pray for include comfort when sorrowing, strength to resist temptation, wisdom to discern good and evil, compassion to forgive others, and understanding of God's will for one's life. An important purpose of prayer is to thank God for life itself and for all that makes life valuable. Ingratitude is an offense against God because it is a failure to recognize his power and love (D&C 59:14–21). Giving thanks is a way of praising God by acknowledging his ever-present hand.

Latter-day Saints are taught that preparation is necessary if one is to communicate effectively with God. A tranquil time and place allow quiet contemplation on the specific requests one may make. Joseph Smith went to a nearby grove to pray for an answer to his question, and received his glorious vision. Job was told, "Prepare thine heart, and stretch out thine hands toward him" (Job 11:13). Alma$_2$ listed the qualities of a heart prepared for prayer: "I would that ye should be humble, and be submissive and gentle; easy to be entreated; full of patience and long-suffering . . . being diligent in keeping the commandments of God. . . . And see that ye have faith, hope, and charity, and then ye will always abound in good works" (Alma 7:23–24). Moroni$_2$ stressed the need for "a sincere heart, . . . real intent, . . . [and] faith in Christ" (Moro. 10:4).

Latter-day Saints believe that relationships with others must also harmonize with Christ's teachings. Christ taught that God's forgiveness could not be obtained unless the sinner were willing to forgive those who had sinned against him (Matt. 6:14–15; Mark 11:25–26). A prepared heart is also a giving heart. Amulek spoke of this quality: "I say unto you, do not suppose that [praying] is all; for . . . if ye turn away the needy, and the naked, and visit not the sick and afflicted, and impart of your substance, if ye have, to those who stand in need—I say unto you, if ye do not any of these things, behold, your prayer is vain, and availeth you nothing" (Alma 34:28).

When one's heart is prepared, God promises answers. The elders of the early Church were promised that "if ye are purified and cleansed from all sin, ye shall ask whatsoever you will in the name of Jesus and it shall be done" (D&C 50:29). In even stronger terms this assurance is repeated to all who pray: "I, the Lord, am bound when ye do what I say; but when ye do not what I say, ye have no promise" (D&C 82:10). However, it is wise to pray that God's will be done, even if it means denial of a request. God warns that asking for what "is not expedient" will turn to one's "condemnation" (D&C 88:64–65).

One answer to a faithful prayer is illustrated through the experience of Oliver Cowdery, an early elder of the Church, when he attempted to help with translating the Book of Mormon. He was told to "study it out in [his] mind" and, if his translation were right, it would be confirmed with a burning in his bosom; if wrong, a "stupor of thought" would come (D&C 9:8–9). When prayers are answered, one experiences peace of mind and assurance that God has heard, even though the answer may be no. The Savior's submissiveness as he prayed in GETHSEMANE shows the way: "Nevertheless not my will, but thine, be done" (Luke 22:42).

BIBLIOGRAPHY

Kimball, Spencer W. *Faith Precedes the Miracle*, pp. 21–58. Salt Lake City, 1972.

——. *The Teachings of Spencer W. Kimball*, ed. Edward L. Kimball, pp. 115–27. Salt Lake City, 1982.

Kimball, Spencer W., *Prayer*. Salt Lake City, 1977.

McConkie, Bruce R. *Doctrinal New Testament Commentary*, Vol. 1, pp. 233–37. Salt Lake City, 1975.

MAE BLANCH

PREACHING THE GOSPEL

Prior to his ascension, the resurrected Savior charged his apostles to "teach all nations, baptizing them in the name of the Father, and of the Son, and of the Holy Ghost: teaching them to observe all things whatsoever I have commanded you" (Matt. 28:19–20). This charge reiterates the call of Abraham (Abr. 2:6, 9–11) and has been unequivocally renewed in the latter days (D&C 110:12): "And the voice of warning shall be unto all people" (D&C 1:4). "This calling and commandment give I unto you concerning all men . . . [they] shall be ordained and sent forth to preach the everlasting gospel among the nations" (D&C 36:4–5). "For, verily, the sound must go forth from this place unto all the world, and unto the uttermost parts of the earth—the gospel must be preached unto every creature, with signs following them that believe" (D&C 58:64). The Church of Jesus Christ of Latter-day Saints responds to this charge by sending missionaries to people of all persuasions throughout the world.

The calling to preach the gospel has a distinctive meaning among Latter-day Saints. All who are in the Church are directly or indirectly indebted to missionaries for their introduction to the gospel. Historically, missionary labor has been carried out by members of the Church who have gone "two by two" (D&C 42:6; 52:10; cf. Luke 10:1; John 8:17) into every land and clime of the free world. LDS missionary labor is not a profession or vocation. It is voluntary and unpaid. The majority of those who presently serve for an average of two years are young men and women, but many older couples of various professions or walks of life also serve. Mission presidents are themselves laymen called to serve usually for three years. At this writing (1991), some 40,000 LDS full-time missionaries are serving.

In addition, there are other modes of preaching the gospel. Members may be called to fulfill stake missions that are coordinated in time spent with their regular occupations or professions. They devote about ten hours per week (usually evenings) to missionary work in their own stake area. The "Every member a missionary" program emphasized by President David O. McKay involves members inviting friends or interested persons into their homes for discussions of gospel principles. A General Missionary Fund is maintained by member contributions, which help some persons in undeveloped countries to supplement their savings and serve full-time missions. Whether laboring at home or abroad, Latter-day Saints are constantly admonished that the witness and testimony of the gospel are only effective if they reflect genuine and continual discipleship of Jesus Christ. The gospel is to be taught in mildness and in meekness, in demonstration of the Spirit, and in love unfeigned (D&C 38:41; 99:2; 121:41).

The command of the Lord to preach the gospel to all nations has a twofold purpose: to bring people to an understanding of the gospel of Jesus Christ, and also to sound the warning voice to leave mankind without excuse.

BIBLIOGRAPHY

Smith, Joseph Fielding. *DS* 1:307–324.

MAX L. PINEGAR

PRE-EXISTENCE (PRE-EARTHLY EXISTENCE)

[*The term "pre-existence," or more accurately, "premortal existence," refers to a period of individual conscious and accountable life before birth into mortality on this earth. It is Latter-day Saint doctrine that living things existed as individual spirit beings and possessed varying degrees of intelligence in an active, conscious spirit state before mortal birth and that the spirit continues to live and function in the mortal body. The revelations teach that premortal spirit bodies have general resemblance to their physical counterparts.*

Articles pertaining to the premortal existence are Birth; Council in Heaven; Devils; First Estate; Foreordination; God the Father; Intelligences; Jehovah, Jesus Christ; Jesus Christ, Firstborn in the Spirit; Mother in Heaven; Premortal Life; Soul; Spirit; Spirit Body.]

PREMORTAL LIFE

Prior to mortal BIRTH individuals existed as men and women in a spirit state and thus coexisted with both the Father and the Son. That period of life is also referred to as the FIRST ESTATE or PRE-EXISTENCE.

The Bible presents the concept that mankind had a preparation period prior to mortal birth. The Lord said to Jeremiah: "Before I formed thee in the belly I knew thee; and before thou camest forth out of the womb I sanctified thee, and I ordained thee a prophet unto the nations" (Jer. 1:5), and the "Preacher" asserted "The spirit shall return unto God who gave it" (Eccl. 12:7). In other scriptures, such as Alma 13:3, it is written that priests were "called and prepared from the foundation of the world according to the foreknowledge of God, on account of their exceeding faith and good works."

There is indeed indication that the INTELLIGENCE dwelling in each person is coeternal with God. It always existed and never was created or made (D&C 93:29). In due time that intelligence was given a SPIRIT BODY, becoming the spirit child of God the Eternal Father and his beloved companion, the MOTHER IN HEAVEN. This spirit, inhabited by the eternal intelligence, took the form of its creators and is in their image (Ballard, p. 140).

To the Prophet Joseph Smith it was revealed that we are all literal spirit sons and daughters of heavenly parents. He received a revelation of information once made known to Moses: "I [God] made the world, and men before they were in the flesh" (Moses 6:51). This likewise reflects the implication in Numbers 16:22 that God is the Father of all, and hence he is "the God of the spirits of all flesh."

Intelligences were organized before the world was, and among these were many great and noble ones, such as Abraham and Moses. God stood in their midst, saw that they were good, and chose them for responsibilities on earth and throughout eternity (Abr. 3:21–23). Jesus, the firstborn spirit, was preeminent among them. "Jesus . . . existed with the Father prior to birth in the flesh; and . . . in the preexistent state He was chosen and ordained to be the one and only Savior and Redeemer of the human race" (*JC*, p. 6).

Revelation indicates that all things, even the earth itself, had a spirit existence before the physical creation. Elder Joseph Fielding Smith wrote, "Not only has man a spirit, and is thereby a living soul, but likewise the beasts of the field, the fowl of the air, and the fish of the sea have spirits, and hence are living souls. . . . The fish, the fowl, the beasts of the field lived before they were placed naturally in this earth, and so did the plants that are upon the face of the earth. The spirits that possess the bodies of the animals are in the similitude of their bodies" (*DS* 1:63–64). The biblical passage that says the Lord God made "every plant of the field before it was in this earth, and every herb of the field before it grew" (Gen. 2:5) is clarified in a parallel scripture with the words: "For I, the Lord God, created all things, of which I have spoken, spiritually before they were naturally upon the face of the earth . . . and I, the Lord God, had created all the children of men and not yet a man to till the ground; for in heaven created I them" (Moses 3:5).

The Prophet Joseph Smith taught that "God himself, finding he was in the midst of spirits and glory, because he was more intelligent, saw proper to institute laws whereby the rest [of the intelligences] could have a privilege to advance like himself" (*TPJS,* p. 354). His plan included sending his sons and daughters to earth (the second estate), to obtain a body of flesh and bones and learn by experience through earthly vicissitudes, with no memory of the first estate and with the agency to fail or succeed.

In a council in heaven to preview earth life, the Lord called before him his spirit children and presented the PLAN OF SALVATION by which they would come to this earth, partake of mortal life with physical bodies, pass through a probation in mortality, and progress to a higher exaltation. The matter was discussed as to how, and upon what principle, the salvation, exaltation, and eternal glory of God's sons and daughters would be brought about (cf. *DS* 1:58). The Firstborn of God volunteered to implement the plan of salvation (Abr. 3:27). Lucifer, who was also a son of the Father, came forward with a counterproposal: "Behold, send me, I will be thy Son, and I will redeem all mankind, that not one soul shall be lost and surely I will do it; wherefore, give me thine honor" (Moses 4:1). Already of exalted status, Lucifer sought to aggrandize himself without regard to the rights and agency of others, seeking to destroy the agency of man (*JC,* p. 7–8). The Father said, "I will send the first" (Abr. 3:27).

This decision led the hosts of heaven to take sides, and a third part rose in rebellion and, with Lucifer, were cast out of heaven. "They were denied the privilege of being born into this world and receiving mortal bodies. . . . The Lord cast them out into the earth, where they became the tempters of mankind" (*DS* 1:65; cf. Jude 1:6).

Elder James E. Talmage wrote, "The offer of the firstborn Son to establish through His own ministry among men the gospel of salvation, and to sacrifice himself, through labor, humiliation and suffering even unto death, was accepted and made the foreordained plan of man's redemption from death, of his eventual salvation from the effects of sin, and of his possible exaltation through righteous achievement" (*JC,* p. 18). Elder Joseph Fielding Smith explained, "God gave his children their free agency even in the spirit world, by which the individual spirits had the privilege, just as men have here, of choosing the good and rejecting the evil, or partaking of the evil to suffer the consequences of their sins" (p. 318–19).

The Book of Mormon prophet $Alma_2$ further explains the opportunities presented to the spirit children of God in the premortal existence: "In the *first place* being left to choose good or evil; therefore they having chosen good and exercising exceedingly great faith, are called with a holy calling . . . on account of their faith, while others would reject the Spirit of God on account of the hardness of their hearts and blindness of their minds, while, if it had not been for this they might have had as great privilege as their brethren. Or in fine, in the *first place* they were on the same standing with their brethren; thus this holy calling being prepared from the foundation of the world for such as would not harden their hearts, being in and through the atonement of the Only Begotten Son" (Alma 13:3–5; *emphasis added*). The "first place" here refers to one's first estate or premortal existence.

The doctrine of FOREORDINATION suggested in the above passage is understood to mean that many may come to earth with preassigned callings and responsibilities. The Prophet Joseph Smith taught, "Every man who has a calling to minister to the inhabitants of the world was ordained to that very purpose in the Grand Council of heaven before this world was" (*TPJS,* p. 365). Abraham was shown the noble and great premortal spirits, and the Lord said to him, "Thou art one of them; thou wast chosen before thou wast born" (Abr. 3:22–23). The apocryphal book of Tobit also suggests the concept that in a premortal life there were assignments that could affect mortality (6:17). However, even though some may be foreordained to special missions on earth, Elder Joseph Fielding Smith stated that "no person was foreordained or appointed to sin or to perform a mission of evil" (*DS* 1:61). Foreordinations and appointments do not proscribe one's agency or free will.

The character of one's life in the SPIRIT WORLD probably influences disposition and desires in mortal life. From among those who were the noble and great ones in that former world, the Lord selected those to be his prophets and rulers on earth in the second estate, for he knew them before they were born, and he knows who will be likely to serve him in mortality. Characteristics of the spirit, which were developed during experiences of the former existence, may play an important part in man's progression through mortal life (cf. *DS* 1:60). "Even before they [the prophets] were born, they, with many others, received their first lessons in the world of spirits and were prepared to come forth in the due time of the Lord to labor in his vineyard for the salvation of souls of men" (D&C 138:56).

This concept that God's spirit children developed some characteristic capabilities, but yet come to earth in forgetfulness, is similar to that expressed in Wordsworth's "Ode, Intimations of Immortality from Recollections of Early Childhood": "Our birth is but a sleep and a forgetting: . . . Trailing clouds of glory do we come from God, who is our home" (verses 58, 64–65). Elder Orson Hyde, an apostle, declared that lack of memory does not mean that mankind did not have a premortal life. He explained that many people leave their homeland to live in another country, yet after a number of years memory of that earlier country can be almost obliterated as though it never existed. "We have forgotten! . . . But our forgetfulness cannot alter the facts" (*JD* 7:315).

Thus, to Latter-day Saints premortal life is characterized by individuality, agency, intelligence, and opportunity for ETERNAL PROGRESSION. It is a central doctrine of the theology of the Church and provides understanding to the age-old question "Whence cometh man?"

BIBLIOGRAPHY

Ballard, Melvin J. *Sermons and Missionary Services of Melvin J. Ballard,* comp. Bryant S. Hinckley, p. 140. Salt Lake City, 1949.

Smith, Joseph Fielding. "Is Man Immortal?" *IE* 19 (Feb. 1916):318–19.

GAYLE OBLAD BROWN

PRIDE

In an address drawing together Book of Mormon and other scriptural teachings regarding pride, President Ezra Taft Benson called it "the universal sin, the great vice" (1989, p. 6). He characterized its central feature as "enmity—enmity toward God and enmity toward our fellowmen" and defined "enmity" as "hatred toward, hostility to, or a state of opposition." He observed that "pride is essentially competitive in nature," arising when individuals pit their will against God's or their intellects, opinions, works, wealth, and talents against those of other people (p. 4). He warned that "pride is a damning sin in the true sense of that word," for "it limits or stops progression" and "adversely affects all our relationships" (p. 6).

The scriptures abound with admonitions against pride. "Pride goeth before destruction" (Prov. 16:18). Pride felled Lucifer (cf. Moses 4:1–3; 2 Ne. 24:12–15; D&C 29:36; 76:28) and destroyed the city of Sodom (Ezek. 16:49–50). In the closing chapters of the Book of Mormon, the prophet Mormon wrote, "Behold, the pride of this nation, or the people of the Nephites, hath proven their destruction" (Moro. 8:27). Three times in the Doctrine and Covenants the Lord uses the phrase "beware of pride," including warnings to Oliver Cowdery, the second elder of the Church, and to Emma Smith, the wife of Joseph Smith (D&C 23:1; 25:14; 38:39). The Lord has said that when he cleanses the earth by fire, the proud shall burn as stubble (3 Ne. 25:1; D&C 29:9; Mal. 4:1).

While most consider pride a sin of the rich, gifted, or learned looking down on others, President Benson warned that it is also common among those looking up—"faultfinding, gossiping . . . living beyond our means, envying, coveting, withholding gratitude . . . and being unforgiving and jealous" (1989, p. 5).

God has commanded the Saints to "seek to bring forth and establish the cause of Zion" (D&C 6:6). When Zion is established, its people will be "of one heart and one mind" and will dwell together in righteousness (Moses 7:18). But "pride is the great stumbling block to Zion" (Benson, 1989, p. 7). Pride leads people to diminish others in the attempt to elevate themselves, resulting in selfishness and contention.

The proud love "the praise of men more than the praise of God" (John 12:42–43) and fear the judgment of men more than that of God (cf. D&C 3:6–7; 30:1–2; 60:2). They do not receive counsel or correction easily but justify and rationalize their frailties and failures, making it difficult for them to repent and receive the blessings of the

Atonement. They have difficulty rejoicing in their blessings, because they are constantly comparing them to see whether they have more or less than someone else. Consequently, they are often ungrateful.

The antidote for pride is humility, "a broken heart and a contrite spirit" (3 Ne. 9:20, 12:19). Men can choose to do those things that will foster the growth of humility: they can choose to confess and forsake their sins, forgive others, receive counsel and chastisement, esteem others as themselves, render service, love God, and submit to his will (Benson, 1989, p. 7). By yielding "to the enticings of the Holy Spirit," the prideful individual can become "a saint through the atonement of Christ" and become "as a child, submissive, meek, humble" (Mosiah 3:19; cf. Alma 13:28).

BIBLIOGRAPHY

Benson, Ezra Taft. "Cleansing the Inner Vessel." *Ensign* 16 (May 1986):4–7.

——. "Beware of Pride." *Ensign* 19 (May 1989):4–7.

Burton, Theodore M. "A Disease Called Pride." *Ensign* 1 (Mar. 1971):26–29.

REED A. BENSON

PURPOSE OF EARTH LIFE

[*This entry consists of two articles:* LDS Perspective *discusses the Mormon understanding of life's purposes, and* Comparative Perspective *contrasts the LDS understanding with that of the major world religions.*]

LDS PERSPECTIVE

Latter-day Saint prophets have affirmed the purpose of life within the framework of three questions: (1) Whence did we come? (2) Why are we here? (3) What awaits us hereafter? The scriptural context of these questions is assurance of the eternal character of the SOUL and of the creation of the earth as a place for the family of God.

All men and women have lived as spirit beings in a premortal state, and all are the spiritual offspring of God (Abr. 3:21–22). In that world all the family of God were taught his plans and purposes. "At the first organization in heaven we were all present, and saw the Savior chosen and appointed and the plan of salvation made, and we sanctioned it" (*TPJS*, p. 181). All the spirit children of God developed various degrees of intelligence and maturity. Those who voluntarily subscribed to the conditions of mortality were embodied and made subject to the Light of Christ "that lighteth every man that cometh into the world" (D&C 93:2). So that earth life may be a probation, a veil of forgetfulness has been drawn over the former life.

In mortality, at least six purposes are opened to mankind:

1. To be given a body, whose experiences and maturation, and eventual permanent resurrection, are essential to the perfecting of the soul. "We came to this earth that we might have a body and present it pure before God in the celestial kingdom" (*TPJS,* p. 181; *see* PHYSICAL BODY; RESURRECTION).
2. To grow in knowledge, and develop talents and gifts (*see* INTELLIGENCE). "If you wish to go where God is, you must be like God, or possess the principles which God possesses, for if we are not drawing towards God in principle, we are going from Him and drawing towards the devil" (*TPJS,* p. 216).
3. To be tried and tested. "We will prove them herewith," says the record of Abraham, "to see if they will do all things whatsoever the Lord their God shall command them" (Abr. 3:25). Through mortality one experiences contrasts and opposites—health and sickness, joy and sadness, blessings and challenges—and thus comes to know to prize the good. "Adam fell that men might be; and men are, that they might have joy" (2 Ne. 2:23). Such joy, as Elder B. H. Roberts of the Seventy wrote, can come only from "having sounded the depths of the soul, from experiencing all emotions of which mind is susceptible, from testing all the qualities and strength of the intellect" (Roberts, p. 439; *see* JOY; MORTALITY).
4. To fill and fulfill the missions and callings that were conferred or preordained (*see* FOREORDINATION; PREMORTAL LIFE). Latter-day Saints often speak of earth life as a second estate and allude to the promise given to and through Abraham that "they who keep their second estate [i.e., fulfill the purposes of mortality] shall have glory added upon their heads for ever and ever" (Abr. 3:26).
5. To exercise agency without memory of the premortal existence, thus to "walk by faith" and have the "realities anticipated in the spirit world renewed and confirmed" (*see* AGENCY).

6. To establish the foundations of eternal family relationships, first as sons and daughters, then as fathers and mothers. The united family is the epitome of the fulfilled and saintly life.

The life to come is the extension and fulfillment of the mortal sojourn: to enter into and live forever in the presence of God. But probation does not end with death. Nor do opportunities to hear, accept, and apply the truths and powers of Christ. Indeed, Joseph Smith taught that even for the faithful, "it is *not all* to be comprehended in this world; it will be a great work to learn our salvation *and exaltation even beyond the grave*" (*TPJS,* p. 348). He added that when the spirit is separated from the body, the process is somewhat impeded, hence the importance of using the time while in mortality, for redemption, and the folly of procrastination of repentance and renewal.

In all this, the continuity of the former life with this one, and in turn this life with the next, is clearly taught. The tendency of much religion, Eastern and Western—to divide life into two worlds and to hold that they are utterly distinct and unlike—is reversed. Life is change, transformation, and exaltation. Mortality is a dress rehearsal for the next world. There, light, glory, and dominion will be conferred in fulness on those who have fulfilled the words of eternal life in this world, and are therefore prepared for eternal life in the world to come.

BIBLIOGRAPHY

Roberts, B. H. "Modern Revelation Challenges Wisdom of Ages to Produce More Comprehensive Conception of the Philosophy of Life." *Liahona the Elders' Journal* 20 (May 8, 1923):433–39.

JAMES P. BELL

COMPARATIVE PERSPECTIVE

Religions tend to present life as meaningful when it conforms to a cosmic plan—a plan that is either intentionally instituted by God or is grounded in the nature of a cosmos that is divine in origin. For Latter-day Saints, the divinely ordered cosmos is the tenor of all scripture. Within this context, latter-day scripture affirms the interrelated themes of the crucial importance of the PHYSICAL BODY, of trials, of the experience of opposition, of the eternality of family, and of the vision of joy and glory in the likeness of God (*see* PURPOSE OF EARTH LIFE: LDS PERSPECTIVE).

Alternative views move in two directions. Some hold that if there is no God and if the ultimate end of all human life is personal annihilation, life has no meaning. This is the position, for example, of Arthur Schopenhauer. Existentialists, who generally assert that humans create their own meaning in a godless and objectively absurd universe, take a similar stance. Others, including some naturalists and humanists, hold that life is worthwhile even if the claims of supernatural religion are false. Marxists, for instance, hold that a purposive society, if not a meaningful cosmos, emerges as an objective entity through the inexorable processes of history.

Some thinkers affirm that life has purpose even if that purpose is shrouded in mystery. Hedonism typically maintains that questions of ultimate meaning cannot be answered and hence should be ignored in favor of calculating maximum pleasure and minimum pain. Confucianism tends not to speak to this issue. It asserts the existence of a spiritual order that is prior to, and superior to, the social order, but focuses on issues of a this-worldly character. Many strands of Judaism take the same approach, believing that the life to come is secondary to the task of establishing and maintaining a sanctified community in this world and looking to a day when, in the words of a venerable Hebrew prayer, "the world shall be perfected under the reign of the Almighty."

Latter-day Saints see life as a three-stage process—a premortal, mortal, and postmortal existence. All stages are essential to the unfolding and perfecting of the self, which is the work and glory of God. The process can be characterized as both this-worldly and other-worldly (*see* GOD: WORK AND GLORY OF; MORTALITY; PRE-EXISTENCE; RESURRECTION).

Plato's "myth of the cave" depicts the human condition as bondage to false beliefs and illusions, which the true philosopher aims to transcend. In the *Phaedo,* Socrates argues that the philosopher "is always pursuing death and dying." The wise man longs for the separation of his soul from his body; for freedom from illness, fatigue, and the deceptions of the senses; and for release into a realm of intuitive contemplation. Gnosticism, a movement akin to Platonism, shared the notion of the fall and hoped-for ascent of a divine soul, but frequently denied the goodness of both the physical universe and the deity who had made it. In the thirteenth century Thomas Aquinas offered a classical enunciation of the Catholic position that man's highest goal, even in this material world, is the "contemplative life," which will be perfected after death. The happiness of the saints will consist in an intellectual "seeing" of the divine essence, vision not in the eye but in the mind. Latter-day scripture affirms both the life of intelligence, defined as light and truth, and the redemption of the soul, defined as both spirit and body. The purpose of life is not escape but transformation—of man, of community, and of the cosmos.

In the major religious traditions of eastern and southern Asia, God (or the gods) sometimes has a marginal role. Hinduism teaches that the deepest human desire is for infinitude, for infinite being, knowledge, and joy. One must therefore seek *mukti*, liberation, from the finitude and limitations that seem to be humanity's natural condition. The word "seem" is crucial because Hinduism insists that behind individual and finite personalities lies Atman-Brahman, the Godhead itself. Men and women are already infinite; liberation consists simply—although it is not so simple!—in recognizing that fact. Buddhism, springing from Hindu soil and often considered a kind of reformation of the older religion, essentially concurs in this diagnosis of the human condition, although its nontheistic forms differ in the way it explains human nature. The Buddha (the title comes from a word meaning roughly "to be enlightened") held that the fundamental human problem is a desire to be separate and that life's purpose is the extinction of that desire, thus enabling men and women to overcome, in this or a series of lives, the selfish cravings that are the chief source of their sufferings and woe. LDS thought rejects both reincarnation and the theory of human suffering as illusory (*see* REINCARNATION).

The notion of soul liberation as the purpose of life is not uncongenial to religions of the Abrahamic tradition, including that of the Latter-day Saints, although it has seldom if ever become the dominant paradigm. The declaration of the Hebrew scriptures that God pronounced the material cosmos "good" has remained normative. For this and other reasons, Jewish, traditional Christian, Muslim, and LDS thought unite in the view that the supremely good God is directly responsible for the general situation in which human beings find themselves. But no tradition emphasizes more than does the LDS that the conditions of mortality were "voluntarily subscribed to" by each individual (*TPJS*, p. 325; cf. D&C 93:30–31). Latter-day Saints likewise agree that eventual union with God implies no loss of finite individual identity, but rather a relationship with him.

A pervasive Christian view is expressed in the Westminster Shorter Catechism of 1647, which declares that "man's chief end is to glorify God, and to enjoy him forever." God created us to bring glory to himself—which was not vanity on his part, since he fully deserves that glory, whereas human beings do not—and will reward those whom he saves with the enjoyment of himself. This can be compared with the position of Islamic tradition that attributes to God the words "I was a hidden treasure but wished to be known, and therefore I created the world." The aim of human beings in Islam is therefore to submit (*aslama*) themselves to the will of God and to glorify him through their actions. Judaism and Islam are closely related in their emphasis upon law and right behavior and in their declaration that obedience to the commandments of God is the purpose of life. Judaism, however, differs from Islam in its belief that the full range of the divine commandments (*mitzvoth*) is incumbent only upon Jews, with non-Jews subject to the few basic "Noachian precepts." Islam, on the other hand, insists that God's demands are identical for all human beings. "I did not create the jinn and mankind," the Koran quotes Allah as saying, "except to serve me."

Some Protestant thinkers have affirmed that human beings exist to manifest the divine attributes, to embody in their own imperfect lives something of God's glory. A similar view occurs in the statement of the Catholic Baltimore Catechism that "God made us to show forth His goodness and to share with us His everlasting happiness in heaven." Latter-day scripture affirms that God will share not only his gifts and blessedness but also his divine nature. Catholic and Protestant forms of Christianity, however, part company; the former holds that God's aims for mankind are ideally realized in a life of sacramental and liturgical worship, whereas the latter emphasizes acceptance of the free grace of Christ. Latter-day Saints affirm that saintly life is impossible without access to the grace of Christ; freely chosen obedience to divinely given covenants, laws, and ordinances in which the atonement and grace of Christ are manifest; and then the giving of oneself in whole-souled discipleship.

BIBLIOGRAPHY

Palmer, Spencer J., and Roger R. Keller. *Religions of the World: A Latter-day Saint View.* Provo, Utah, 1989.

Romney, Thomas C. *World Religions in the Light of Mormonism.* Independence, Mo., 1946.

DANIEL C. PETERSON
HUSTON SMITH

R

REINCARNATION

Reincarnation refers to a theory that one SPIRIT (life or soul) passes from one material body to another through repeated births and deaths, usually of the same species, often with ethical implications; thus the present life is viewed as only one of many. This theory is rejected by The Church of Jesus Christ of Latter-day Saints.

The idea of repeated return or of a continuing, exacting wheel of rebirth is based on the Eastern doctrine of karma. Karma literally means "deeds" or "actions" and, in a limited sense, may refer to a system of cause and effect. According to this belief, all inequalities of birth, society, race, and economic being are products of one's individual karma created by an accumulation of previous behavior. Karma is also seen as a cosmic law of justice. It is an eternally moving wheel of rebirth. Experience is repeatable. An individual spirit can live again and again in a wide variety of guises and forms in the mortal estate.

In Latter-day Saint doctrine, mankind is on the road to IMMORTALITY and ETERNAL LIFE. One moves from one type of existence to another along the way. But this teaching is distinguishable from reincarnation on several counts:

1. In Latter-day Saint belief, there is only one physical death for any one person (Heb. 9:27). Amulek, in the Book of Mormon, taught that man can die only once (Alma 11:45). Reincarnation posits

many deaths, but in Latter-day Saint thought, the RESURRECTION (incarnation) follows death (cf. D&C 29:24–25).

2. In LDS theology, the PHYSICAL BODY is sacred, and its elements are imperishable. The body is prerequisite to becoming like God. In reincarnation, the present physical body is of little or no consequence.
3. In LDS theology, mortality is a time to be tested and proved "to see if [people] will do all things whatsoever the Lord their God shall command them" (Abr. 3:25). In reincarnation, there are many future lives, so there is no urgent need to repent now. Reincarnation contradicts Amulek's admonition that "this life is the time for men to prepare to meet God" (Alma 34:32). The Prophet Joseph Smith said that transmigration of souls (spirits) was not a correct principle (*TPJS,* pp. 104–105).
4. In LDS theology, there is one single, unique historical act of redemption made by Jesus Christ. Through it, Christ becomes the only name under heaven "whereby man can be saved" (D&C 18:23). Reincarnation denies the absolute centrality of Christ's atonement by affirming the theoretical existence of an abundance of equally miraculous deities, who appear in a variety of forms, born again and again.

BIBLIOGRAPHY

Palmer, Spencer J., and Roger R. Keller. *Religions of the World: A Latter-day Saint View.* Provo, Utah, 1990.

SPENCER J. PALMER

REMISSION OF SINS

"Remission of sins" is the scriptural phrase that describes the primary purpose of BAPTISM: to obtain God's forgiveness for breaking his COMMANDMENTS and receive a newness of life. It is fundamental among the FIRST PRINCIPLES AND ORDINANCES OF THE GOSPEL: FAITH in the Lord JESUS CHRIST, REPENTANCE, BAPTISM by immersion for the remission of sins, and LAYING ON OF HANDS for the GIFT OF THE HOLY GHOST. To grant pardon of sins is one manifestation of God's mercy, made possible by the ATONEMENT. It is the blessing sought by those who fervently prayed, "O have mercy, and apply the atoning blood of Christ that we may receive forgiveness of our sins, and our hearts may be purified" (Mosiah 4:2). Having one's sins remitted is a vital part of the developmental process that results in godhood and lies at the heart of the religious experience of a Latter-day Saint.

Baptism for the remission of sins is one of the most prominent themes of the scriptures, being both a requirement and a blessing associated with accepting Christ as the divine Redeemer and Savior of the world and joining his Church. According to LDS scriptures and teachings, the principles and ordinances of the gospel, including baptism for the remission of sins, were taught and practiced by all the prophets from Adam and Enoch (Moses 6:52–60, 64–68; 7:10–11) to the present time. The doctrine was taught before the earthly ministry of Jesus by Benjamin (Mosiah 4:3–4) and John the Baptist (Mark 1:3–4). It was articulated by Christ himself to the Twelve apostles in Jerusalem (Matt. 28:16–20; John 20:21–23) and to the Nephites (3 Ne. 12:2), preached by Peter following Christ's ascension (Acts 2:37–38), and commanded of the Church as part of the restoration (D&C 49:11–14; 84:64). Authority to administer the ordinance of baptism by immersion for the remission of sins is held by bearers of the Aaronic Priesthood (D&C 13; 107:20) as well as by those who hold the Melchizedek Priesthood (D&C 20:38–45).

God commands all but little children and the mentally incompetent to submit to the first principles and ordinances (Moro. 8:11; D&C 29:46–50; 68:27), not as acts of compliance with his sovereignty, but because uncleanliness (sinfulness) is incompatible with godliness. There is no alternative path to exaltation (1 Ne. 15:33; 3 Ne. 27:19; Moses 6:57). Thus, those who do not receive a remission of sins through baptism are not BORN OF GOD and exclude themselves from his kingdom (Alma 7:14–16; D&C 84:74). Remission includes the pardoning of sins by God, who releases sinners with the promise that "their sins and their iniquities will I remember no more" (Heb. 8:12). Remission also includes the repentant person's recognition of God's communication of that forgiveness. Such a realization is accompanied by peace of conscience and feelings of inexpressible joy (Mosiah 4:1–3, 20). Having been "washed [by] the blood of Christ" (Alma 24:13; 3 Ne. 27:19), one is granted relief from the unhappiness that accompanies wickedness (Alma 41:10; 36:12–21) and increases in love for God, knowing that forgiveness is made possible only by the Savior's atoning sacrifice (D&C 27:2; 2 Ne. 9:21–27).

Remission of sins is an achievement made possible through the Atonement and earned through genuine changes in spirit and a discontinuation of behavior known to be wrong. Enos described the process as a "wrestle . . . before God" (Enos 1:2). The essential experience is to recognize one's unworthiness, taste of Christ's love, stand steadfast in faith toward him (Mosiah 4:11), and with contrite heart acknowledge that he was crucified for the sins of the world (D&C 21:9; 3 Ne. 9:20–22). Thus committed to Christ and engaged in repentance, one keeps the commandments by submitting to baptism and receiving the gift of the Holy Ghost. The initial sense of repentance and forgiveness that leads one to the ordinances (3 Ne. 7:25; D&C 20:37) is amplified and confirmed through the BAPTISM OF FIRE administered by the Comforter (2 Ne. 31:17; D&C 19:31). This series of experiences forms the basis for a spiritual testimony of the truthfulness of the GOSPEL OF JESUS CHRIST and a lifelong commitment to Christian living and Church service.

Remission of sins can be lost through recurrent transgression, for "unto that soul who sinneth shall the former sins return, saith the Lord your God" (D&C 82:7). Benjamin therefore enjoins the forgiven to retain their state by righteous living: "For the sake of retaining a remission of your sins from day to day, that ye may walk guiltless before God . . . ye should impart of your substance to the poor, every man according to that which he hath, such as feeding the hungry, clothing the naked, visiting the sick and administering to their relief, both spiritually and temporally, according to their wants" (Mosiah 4:26).

BIBLIOGRAPHY

Kimball, Spencer W. *The Miracle of Forgiveness.* Salt Lake City, 1969.

WILLIAM S. BRADSHAW

REPENTANCE

Repentance is the process by which humans set aside or overcome sins by changing hearts, attitudes, and actions that are out of harmony with God's teachings, thereby conforming their lives more completely to his will. In the words of one latter-day prophet, repentance is "to change one's mind in regard to past or intended actions or conduct" (McKay, p. 14). Paul observes that "all have sinned, and come short of the glory of God" (Rom. 3:23). For this reason, the Lord "gave commandment that all men must repent" (2 Ne. 2:21; Moses 6:57). This means that repentance is required of every soul who has not reached perfection.

Repentance has been central to God's dealings with his children since they were first placed on the earth. Old Testament prophets constantly called the children of Israel individually and collectively to repent and *turn* to God and righteous living from rebellion, apostasy, and sin. In New Testament times, the work of Jesus Christ on earth may be described as a ministry of repentance—that is, of calling on God's children to return to their God by changing their thinking and behavior and becoming more godlike. The Savior taught, "Be ye therefore perfect, even as your Father which is in heaven is perfect" (Matt. 5:48). Christ's apostles were called primarily to preach FAITH in Christ and to declare repentance to all the world (Mark 6:12). In modern times, few topics occur in the Lord's revelations as pervasively as this one. He has given latter-day prophets and all messengers of his gospel repeated instructions to declare "nothing but repentance unto this generation" (D&C 6:9). The Prophet Joseph Smith identified repentance and faith in Jesus Christ as the two fundamental principles of the gospel (A of F 4). And the gospel itself has been called "a gospel of repentance" (D&C 13; 84:27).

In modern as in earlier times, the term "repentance" literally means a turning from sin and a reversing of one's attitudes and behavior. Its purposes are to develop the divine nature within all mortal souls by freeing them from wrong or harmful thoughts and actions and to assist them in becoming more Christlike by replacing the "natural man" (1 Cor. 2:14) with the "new man" in Christ (Eph. 4:20–24).

This process is not only necessary in preparing humans to return and live with God, but it enlarges their capacity to love their fellow beings. Those who have reconciled themselves with God have the spiritual understanding, desire, and power to become reconciled with their fellow beings. God has commanded all humans to forgive each other: "I, the Lord, will forgive whom I will forgive, but of you it is required to forgive all men" (D&C 64:10). As God shows his love by forgiving ("I will forgive their iniquity, and I will remember their sin no more"; Jer. 31:34), his children, as they forgive others, also reflect this love.

True repentance, while seldom easy, is essential to personal happiness, emotional and spiritual growth, and eternal SALVATION. It is the only efficacious way for mortals to free themselves of the permanent effects of sin and the inevitable attendant burden of guilt. To achieve it, several specific changes must occur. One must first recognize that an attitude or action is out of harmony with God's teachings and feel genuine sorrow or remorse for it. Paul calls this "godly sorrow" (2 Cor. 7:10). Other scriptures describe this state of mind as "a broken heart and a contrite spirit" (Ps. 51:17; 2 Ne. 2:7; 3 Ne. 9:20). This recognition must produce an inward change of attitude. The prophet Joel exhorted Israel to "rend your heart, and not your garments" (Joel 2:12–13), thereby bringing the inner transformation necessary to begin the process of repentance.

Some form of CONFESSION is also necessary in repentance. In some cases, the transgressor may need to confess to the person or persons wronged or injured and ask forgiveness; in other cases, it may be necessary to confess sins to a Church leader authorized to receive such confessions; in still other cases, a confession to God alone may be sufficient; and sometimes all three forms of confession may be necessary.

In addition, repentance requires restitution to others who have suffered because of the sin. Whenever possible, this should be done by making good any physical or material losses or injury. Even when this is not possible, repentance requires other, equally significant actions, such as apologies; increased acts of kindness and service toward offended persons; intensified commitment to, and activity in, the Lord's work; or all of these in concert.

Finally, for repentance to be complete, one must abandon the sinful behavior. A change of heart begins the process; a visible outward change of direction, reflected in new patterns of behavior, must complete it (Mosiah 5:2). Failure to alter outward actions means that the sinner has not repented, and the weight of the former sin returns (D&C 82:7; cf. Matt. 18:32–34).

One purpose of repentance is to bless people by affording through forgiveness the one and only way of relieving the suffering that attends sin: "For behold, I, God, have suffered these things for all, that they might not suffer if they would repent; but if they would not repent, they must suffer even as I" (D&C 19:16–17).

The Lord has repeatedly promised that all who repent completely shall find forgiveness of their sins, which in turn brings great joy. The parables of the lost sheep and the lost coin exemplify the joy in heaven over one sinner who repents (Luke 15:4–10); the parable of the prodigal son (or lost son) illustrates the joy in heaven and similar joy in the circle of family and friends and within the repentant son himself over his return from sin (Luke 15:11–32).

Though repentance is indispensable to eternal salvation and to earthly happiness, it is not sufficient by itself to reunite a person with God. Complete repentance first requires faith in the Lord Jesus Christ, which in turn generates strong motivation and power to repent. Both are necessary for, and thus must precede, BAPTISM, the reception of the GIFT OF THE HOLY GHOST, and membership in the Lord's kingdom. After awakening faith in Christ in the hearts of his listeners on the day of Pentecost, Peter exhorted them to "repent, and be baptized every one of you in the name of Jesus Christ for the remission of sins and you shall receive the Holy Ghost" (Acts 2:38). Only with the requisite repentance, symbolized by a "broken heart and a contrite spirit" and the abandonment of former sinful deeds and thought patterns, is one prepared to be baptized, receive the Holy Ghost, and have all previous sins remitted. Through baptism, a repentant person enters the kingdom of God by making covenants to remember Christ always and keep his commandments. The REMISSION OF SINS comes "by fire and by the Holy Ghost" (2 Ne. 31:17; D&C 20:37).

Since repentance is an ongoing process in the mortal effort to become Christlike, the need for it never diminishes. It requires active, daily application as humans recognize and strive to overcome sin and error and in this way ENDURE TO THE END. For this reason, the Lord has instituted a means whereby each person who has repented and entered into the baptismal covenant may renew it by partaking of the sacrament in remembrance of him. This time of self-examination allows one to reflect on the promises made at baptism, which were to take Christ's name upon oneself, to remember him always, and to keep his commandments. Thus, the process of repentance is kept alive by this frequent period of reflection as the participant partakes of symbols of Christ's body and blood in remembrance of his sacrifice to atone for human sin.

Scriptures inform us that "this life is the time for men to prepare to meet God" and that so-called deathbed repentance is usually not effective:

> Ye cannot say, when ye are brought to that awful crisis, that I will repent, that I will return to my God. Nay, ye cannot say this; for that same spirit which doth possess your bodies at the time that ye go out of this life, that same spirit will have power to possess your body in that eternal world. . . . If ye have procrastinated the day of your repentance even until death, behold, ye have become subjected to the spirit of the devil [Alma 34:32–35].

To return to God's presence, mortals must strive during this life to attain Christlike qualities, which can only be gained by turning from sin. To defer such efforts blocks the exercise of faith essential to repentance, prevents the operation of the Holy Ghost, and retards the development of the personal qualities reflected in the "broken heart and contrite spirit" necessary to live in God's presence.

Repentance is one of the most powerful redemptive principles of the restored gospel of Jesus Christ. Without it, there would be no eternal progression, no possibility of becoming Christlike, no relief from the burden of guilt that every human incurs in a lifetime. With it, there is the glorious promise uttered by Isaiah that even for grievous sins there might be forgiveness: "Though your sins be as scarlet, they shall be as white as snow; though they be red like crimson, they shall be as wool" (Isa. 1:18).

BIBLIOGRAPHY

Gillum, Gary P. "Repentance Also Means Rethinking." In *By Study and Also by Faith,* ed. J. Lundquist and S. Ricks, Vol. 2, pp. 406–37. Salt Lake City, 1990.

Kimball, Spencer W. *The Miracle of Forgiveness.* Salt Lake City, 1969.

——. *The Teachings of Spencer W. Kimball,* ed. Kimball, Edward L., pp. 80–114. Salt Lake City, 1982.

McKay, David O. *Gospel Ideals,* pp. 12–14. Salt Lake City, 1953.

JAMES K. LYON

RESURRECTION

Resurrection is the reunion of the SPIRIT with an immortal PHYSICAL BODY. The body laid in the grave is mortal; the resurrected physical body is immortal. The whole of man, the united spirit and body, is defined in modern scripture as the "soul" of man. Resurrection from the dead constitutes the redemption of the soul (D&C 88:15–16).

Although the idea of resurrection is not extensively delineated in the Old Testament, there are some definite allusions to it (e.g., 1 Sam. 2:6; Job 14:14; 19:26; Isa. 26:19; Dan. 12:2). And in the New Testament, the resurrection of Jesus Christ, as the prototype of all resurrections, is an essential and central message: "I am the resurrection and the life" (John 11:25).

The evidence of Christ's resurrection is measurably strengthened for Latter-day Saints by other records of post-Resurrection visitations of the Christ (*see* JESUS CHRIST: FORTY-DAY MINISTRY AND OTHER POST-RESURRECTION APPEARANCES). For example, in the 3 Nephi account in the Book of Mormon, an entire multitude saw, heard, and touched him as he appeared in transcendent resurrected glory. This is accepted by Latter-day Saints as an ancient sacred text. The tendency of some recent scholarship outside the Church to radically separate the "Jesus of history" and the "Christ of faith" and to ascribe the resurrection faith to later interpreters is challenged by these later documents and by modern revelation.

Ancient witnesses, including Paul, came to their assurance of the reality of the Resurrection by beholding the risen Christ. From like witnesses, Latter-day Saints accept the record that at the resurrection of Christ "the graves were opened," in both the Old World and the new, and "many bodies of the saints which slept arose" (Matt. 27:52; 3 Ne. 23:9–10). In the current dispensation, resurrected beings, including John the Baptist, Peter, James, and Moroni$_2$ appeared and ministered to Joseph Smith and Oliver Cowdery.

In the theology of Judaism and some Christian denominations resurrection has often been spiritualized—that is, redefined as a symbol for immortality of some aspect of man such as the active intellect, or of the soul considered to be an immaterial entity. In contrast, scientific naturalism tends to reject both the concept of the soul and of bodily resurrection. Latter-day Saints share few of the assumptions that underlie these dogmas. In LDS understanding, the spirit of each individual is not immaterial, but consists of pure, refined matter: "It existed before the body, can exist in the body; and will exist separate from the body, when the body will be mouldering in the dust; and will in the resurrection, be again united with it" (*TPJS*, p. 207). Identity and personality persist with the spirit, and after the resurrection the spirit will dwell forever in a physical body.

Platonism and gnosticism hold that embodiment is imprisonment, descent, or association with what is intrinsically evil. In contrast, the scriptures teach that the physical body is a step upward in the progression and perfection of all. The body is sacred, a temple (1 Cor. 3:16; D&C 93:35). Redemption is not escape from the flesh but its dedication and transformation. Joseph Smith taught, "We came into this earth that we might have a body and present it pure before God in the Celestial Kingdom" (*TPJS*, p. 181). On the other hand, if defiled, distorted, and abused, the body may be an instrument of degradation, an enemy of genuine spirituality.

In contrast to the view that the subtle powers of intellect or soul must finally transcend the body or anything corporeal, the Prophet Joseph Smith taught that all beings "who have tabernacles (bodies), have power over those who have not" (*TPJS*, p. 190; 2 Ne. 9:8). At minimum, this is taken to mean that intellectual and spiritual powers are enhanced by association with the flesh. It follows that a long absence of the spirit from the body in the realm of disembodied spirits awaiting resurrection will be viewed not as a beatific or blessed condition, but instead as a bondage (D&C 45:17; 138:50). Moreover, "spirit and element [the spirit body and the physical body], inseparably connected, [can] receive a fulness of joy. And when separated, man cannot receive a fulness of joy" (D&C 93:33, 34).

In contrast to the view that the body when buried or cremated has no identifiable residue, Joseph Smith taught that "there is no fundamental principle belonging to a human system that ever goes into another in this world or the world to come" (*HC* 5:339). Chemical disintegration is not final destruction. The resurrected body is tangible, but when the flesh is quickened by the Spirit there will be "spirit in their [veins] and not blood" (*WJS*, p. 270; see also *TPJS*, p. 367).

Resurrection is as universal as death. All must die and all must be resurrected. It is a free gift to everyone. It is not the result of the exercise of faith or accumulated good works. The Book of Mormon prophet Amulek declares, "Now this restoration shall come to all, both old and young, both bond and free, both male and female, both the wicked and the righteous" (Alma 11:44; cf. *TPJS,* pp. 199–200, 294–297, 310–311, 319–321, 324–326).

Not all will be resurrected at the same moment, "but every man in his own order: Christ the firstfruits; afterward they that are Christ's at his coming" (1 Cor. 15:23). "Behold, there is a time appointed that all shall come forth from the dead," Alma writes, to stand embodied before God to be judged of their thoughts, words, and deeds (Alma 40:4).

"All men will come from the grave as they lie down, whether old or young" (*TPJS,* p. 199). And he who quickeneth all things shall "change our vile body, that it may be fashioned like unto his glorious body" (Philip. 3:21). "The body will come forth as it is laid to rest, for there is no growth nor development in the grave. As it is laid down, so will it arise, and changes to perfection will come by the law of restitution. But the spirit will continue to expand and develop, and the body, after the resurrection will develop to the full stature of man" (Joseph F. Smith, *IE* 7 [June 1904]:623–24).

The resurrected body will be suited to the conditions and glory to which the person is assigned in the day of judgment. "Some dwell in higher glory than others" (*TPJS,* p. 367). The Doctrine and Covenants teaches that "your glory shall be that glory by which your bodies are quickened" (D&C 88:28), and three glories are designated (D&C 76). Paul (1 Cor. 15:40) also mentioned three glories of resurrected bodies: one like the sun (celestial), another as the moon (terrestrial), and the third as the stars. In a revelation to Joseph Smith, the glory of the stars was identified as telestial (D&C 76). The lights of these glories differ, as do the sun, the moon, and the stars as perceived from earth. "So also is the resurrection of the dead" (1 Cor. 15:40–42).

In a general sense, the Resurrection may be divided into the resurrection of the just, also called the first resurrection, and the resurrection of the unjust, or the last resurrection. The first resurrection commenced with the resurrection of Christ and with those who immediately thereafter came forth from their graves. In much larger numbers, it will precede the thousand-year millennial reign, inaugurated by the "second coming" of the Savior (D&C 45:44–45; cf. 1 Thes. 4:16–17). At that time, some will be brought forth to meet him, as he descends in glory. This first resurrection will continue in proper order through the MILLENNIUM. The righteous who live on earth and die during the Millennium will experience immediate resurrection. Their transformation will take place in the "twinkling of an eye" (D&C 63:51). The first resurrection includes the celestial and terrestrial glories.

The final resurrection, or resurrection of the unjust, will occur at the end of the Millennium. In the words of the apocalypse, "the rest of the dead lived not again until the thousand years were finished" (Rev. 20:5). This last resurrection will include those destined for the telestial glory and perdition.

Of his visionary glimpses of the Resurrection, the Prophet Joseph Smith remarked, "The same glorious spirit gives them the likeness of glory and bloom; the old man with his silvery hairs will glory in bloom and beauty. No man can describe it to you—no man can write it" (*TPJS*, p. 368). Referring to the doctrine of the Resurrection as "principles of consolation," he pled, "Let these truths sink down in our hearts that, we may even here, begin to enjoy that which shall be in full hereafter." He added, "All your losses will be made up to you in the resurrection, provided you continue faithful. By the vision of the Almighty I have seen it" (*TPJS*, p. 296).

The hope of a glorious resurrection undergirds the radiance that characterized the faith of New Testament Saints as well as those who have since kept that faith alive in the world, including the Saints of the latter days.

BIBLIOGRAPHY

Ballard, Melvin J. "The Resurrection." In *Melvin Ballard . . . Crusader for Righteousness*, ed. Melvin R. Ballard. Salt Lake City, 1966.

Nickelsburg, George W. *Resurrection, Immortality, and Eternal Life in Intertestamental Judaism.* Cambridge, Mass., 1972.

Smith, Joseph F. *GD.*

Talmage, James E. *AF.*

DOUGLAS L. CALLISTER

REVELATION

Receiving personal revelation is a vital and distinctive part of the LDS religious experience. Response to personal revelation is seen as the basis for true faith in Christ, and the strength of the Church consists of that faithful response by members to their own personal revelations. The purpose of both revelation and the response of faith is to assist the children of men to come to Christ and learn to love one another with that same pure love with which Christ loves them.

TYPES OF REVELATION. A DISPENSATION of the GOSPEL OF JESUS CHRIST is a series of personal revelations from God. These revelations may be direct manifestations from God, as in the following typical cases:

1. theophanies (seeing God face-to-face), as in the first vision of the Prophet Joseph Smith, which came at the beginning of the present dispensation (JS—H 1:15–20)
2. revealed knowledge from the Father that Jesus is "the Christ, the Son of the living God" (Matt. 16:13–17; *see also* SPIRIT OF PROPHECY)
3. visitations of angelic persons, such as the appearance of the angel Moroni to Joseph Smith (JS—H 1:30–32)
4. revelations through the Urim and Thummim, by which means Joseph Smith translated the Book of Mormon
5. open visions, as when Joseph Smith and Sidney Rigdon were shown the kingdoms of the hereafter
6. physically hearing the voice of God, as is recorded in 3 Nephi 11
7. receiving the still, small voice of the HOLY SPIRIT, as in the experience of Elijah (1 Kgs. 19)
8. receiving the GIFTS OF THE SPIRIT (D&C 46)
9. having a burning in the bosom as an indication of the will of God, as in the explanation given to Oliver Cowdery (D&C 9:8)
10. dreams (1 Ne. 8:2–32)
11. manifestations of the LIGHT OF CHRIST, by which all men know good from evil (Alma 12:31–32; D&C 84:46–48).

Such direct manifestations of the mind and will of God are known as gifts and are contrasted with signs. Gifts always have a spiritual component, even when they have a physical aspect. Signs are physical manifestations of the power of God and are a form of revelation from God, though they may be counterfeited and misinterpreted. Signs may show that God is at work, but spiritual gifts are required to know how one should respond.

REVELATION TO THE CHURCH. In every dispensation, God appoints his prophet to guide his people. The prophet's purpose is not to be an intermediary between God and others, though a prophet must often do so. His purpose is, rather, to assist others to receive from God the personal revelation that he, the prophet, has taught God's truth, which will show the way to Christ.

The prophet as head of The Church of Jesus Christ of Latter-day Saints and all other persons who preside in the Church, including General Authorities, stake presidents, bishops, general presidencies, and parents, may receive revelation for the benefit of those over whom they preside. These revelations can be passed on to the membership of the Church through conference and other talks and in personal counsel. But each individual is entitled to know by personal revelation that these messages given through presiding authorities are truly from the Savior himself. President Brigham Young expressed concern that the Latter-day Saints would "have so much confidence in their leaders" that they would "settle down in a state of blind self-security," abandoning the responsibility to obtain their own revelation: "Let every man and woman know, by the whispering of the Spirit of God to themselves, whether their leaders are walking in the path the Lord dictates, or not" (*JD* 9:150).

Presiding quorums in the Church are entitled to revelation for the Church on matters of doctrine, policies, programs, callings, and disciplinary actions, as each might be appropriate to a given quorum. Decisions of these quorums are to be made only by the personal, individual revelation of God to each member of that quorum. "And every decision made by either of these quorums must be by the unanimous voice of the same; that is, every member in each quorum must be agreed to its decisions, in order to make their decisions of the same power or validity one with the other" (D&C 107:27).

The scriptures contain the inspired writings of God's appointed prophets and are provided to others for their edification (D&C 68:2–4). By this means, people have received the inspired words recorded in the Old and New Testaments. Through revelation, the Prophet Joseph Smith translated the Book of Mormon and received those things set forth in the Doctrine and Covenants and the Pearl of Great Price. Latter-day Saints anticipate that more prophetic scripture will yet be revealed and that scripture written by past prophets but now lost to the world will be restored (2 Ne. 29:11–14; D&C 27:6). The true meaning of all scripture is to be revealed by the power of the Holy Ghost to the individual reader or hearer (2 Pet. 1:20; D&C 50:17–24).

PERSONAL REVELATION. After baptism and confirmation, each member has the right, when worthy, to the constant companionship of the HOLY GHOST (*see* GIFT OF THE HOLY GHOST). Through that companionship all the gifts of the Spirit are revealed to faithful individuals, who accomplish their mortal works in righteousness through the gifts and power of God revealed to and through them (Moro. 10:25). The challenges of living by personal revelation include (1) distinguishing revelation from God through his Holy Spirit from personal thoughts and desires, and from the influences of Satan (*see* DEVILS); (2) following the teachings and directions of the living prophet of God; and (3) living by every word that proceeds from the mouth of God (Matt. 4:4; John 3:5–8; D&C 50:13–24; 98:11–13; Deut. 8:3).

In modern societies, the idea of divine revelation is widely discounted for many reasons, including the violent acts that some have perpetrated while claiming divine direction. But God has made it known through the restoration of the gospel that revelation is available to all who seek it and that failure to seek spiritual guidance and direction is itself a mistake and a form of wishful thinking. Humans have eternal spirits, and each person experiences the supernatural influences that work upon his or her own spirit. Better than to ignore the spiritual side of oneself is to study one's personal spiritual experiences until they make sense. Those who acknowledge spiritual experiences are called the "honest in heart," and they are candidates for the revealed riches of godliness (D&C 8:1; 97:8).

The fundamental revelation from God is the KNOWLEDGE of good through the Light of Christ (John 1:9). The prophet Lehi taught his children that because of the choices made by Adam and Eve, their descendants receive supernatural knowledge of both good and evil, making a choice between the two necessary in fulfillment of the PURPOSE OF EARTH LIFE. After mortality God returns to each human being eternally the good or evil each chose in life (Alma 41:1–5; 2 Ne. 2:27).

But before any final judgment, each person will be taught the gospel of Jesus Christ by the power of the Holy Spirit. This gospel is the good news that the Son of God will assist all persons to stop doing evil and will save them from the consequences of all the evil they have done if they will believe in him and repent. Acting to accept this revelation constitutes faith in Jesus Christ, which, if it continues, may bring additional revelation from God: more instruction; the gifts of the Spirit; the knowledge imparted through saving ordinances of the NEW AND EVERLASTING COVENANT; angelic visitations; visions; the revelation to know God himself face-to-face; and finally, the revelation to be given the fulness of godhood, to be made joint-heirs with Christ (D&C 121:29).

The LDS concept of individual revelation as fundamental to all human experience helps explain other distinctive LDS teachings. The key to making the proper distinction between supernatural revelation and its counterfeit is that fundamental knowledge of good and evil. Individuals must experiment, being as honest in heart and mind as they can, until they can see clearly what is good and what is evil. Those who learn to distinguish good from evil in this life can then distinguish the good spirit from the evil spirit. They then can distinguish the true gospel of Jesus Christ from its counterfeits, the true path of righteousness from the byways of covenant breaking and bending, and the true and living God from the image of God produced by their own wishful thinking (Moro. 7:5–19).

Joseph Smith taught the Saints how to recognize and receive revelation:

> A person may profit by noticing the first intimation of the spirit of revelation; for instance, when you feel pure intelligence flowing into you, it may give you sudden strokes of ideas, so that by noticing it, you may find it fulfilled the same day or soon; (i.e.) those things that were presented unto your minds by the Spirit of God, will come to pass; and thus by learning the Spirit of God and understanding it, you may grow into

the principle of revelation, until you become perfect in Christ Jesus [*TPJS*, p. 151].

To learn to communicate with others by the gifts of that Holy Spirit makes it possible for one to be a prophet or prophetess of God. Latter-day Saints believe that through divine revelation every child of Christ may, and should, become a prophet or a prophetess to his or her own divinely appointed stewardship (Num. 11:29), holding fast to that which is good and rejecting that which is evil (1 Thes. 5:19–21).

Thus, the human problem is not to *get* revelation, but to *understand* the revelation one receives, to respond only to that which is good, and to minister only that which is good. The servants of Christ are counseled to look to him and to him only for light and TRUTH. They are told not to take counsel from any human being or to hearken to any person unless he or she speaks by the power of the Holy Spirit. Truth, light, righteous power, and salvation come from above, from God himself, through divine revelation, and not from human beings or from below (2 Ne. 28:30–31).

BIBLIOGRAPHY

Backman, Milton V., Jr. *The Heavens Resound,* pp. 284–309. Salt Lake City, 1983.

Oaks, Dallin H. "Revelation." In *Brigham Young University 1981–82 Fireside and Devotional Speeches,* pp. 20–26. Provo, Utah, 1982.

Packer, Boyd K. "Revelation in a Changing World." *Ensign* 19 (Nov. 1989):14–16.

Wright, H. Curtis. "The Central Problem of Intellectual History." *Scholar and Educator* 12 (Fall 1988):52–68.

CHAUNCEY C. RIDDLE

RIGHTEOUSNESS

Righteousness comprises a broad group of concepts and traits. As with the biblical Hebrew *sedek* and the Greek *dikaiosune,* the English word "righteousness" describes the ideal of religious life, with Godlike behavior as the norm. Righteousness is right conduct before God and among mankind in all respects. The scriptures give the following perspectives:

Righteousness is ultimately synonymous with HOLINESS or godliness. Christ himself is known as "the Righteous" (Moses 7:45, 47) and as "the Son of Righteousness" (3 Ne. 25:2). His "ways are righteousness forever" (2 Ne. 1:19).

The state of righteousness is available to mankind through the redemption of Christ as one is BORN OF GOD: "Marvel not that all mankind, yea, men and women . . . must be born again; yea, born of God, changed from their carnal and fallen state, to a state of righteousness, being redeemed of God, becoming his sons and daughters" (Mosiah 27:25).

The terms "righteous" and "righteousness" also apply to mortals who, though beset with weaknesses and frailties, are seeking to come unto Christ. In this sense, righteousness is not synonymous with PERFECTION. It is a condition in which a person is moving toward the Lord, yearning for godliness, continuously repenting of sins, and striving honestly to know and love God and to follow the principles and ordinances of the gospel. Saints of God are urged to do "the works of righteousness" (D&C 59:23) and to "bring to pass much righteousness" (D&C 58:27).

Inherent in the meaning of righteousness is the concept of JUSTIFICATION. It is impossible for finite mortals to live in perfect obedience to God's laws or to atone infinitely for their sins. "For all have sinned," Paul wrote, "and come short of the glory of God" (Rom. 3:23). Christ's ATONEMENT mercifully reconciles the demands of justice (*see* JUSTICE AND MERCY), making it possible for repentant mortals to become "right" with God—"at one" with him.

When Saul of Tarsus saw the resurrected Christ on the road to Damascus, "he trembling and astonished said, Lord, what wilt thou have me to do?" (Acts 9:6). From that moment on, he sought to know the will of God and live accordingly. But he also lamented over mortal weaknesses: "For I know that in me, that is, in my flesh, dwelleth no good thing . . . only in Christ" (JST Rom. 7:19). "There is none righteous, no, not one" (Rom. 3:10). Like all apostles and prophets, however, Paul also taught the glorious message that through the grace of Christ mortals can "put off . . . the old man"—their fallen and sinful selves—and "put on the new man, which after God is created in righteousness and true holiness" (Eph. 4:22, 24).

The scriptures abound in similar exhortations to flee wickedness, accept the Lord's grace, and come unto Christ in righteousness. "O wretched man that I am!" exclaimed Nephi. "Yea, my heart sorroweth because of my flesh; my soul grieveth because of mine iniquities." But recognizing the Savior as "the rock of [his] righteousness," Nephi cried: "O Lord, wilt thou redeem my soul? . . . Wilt thou make me that I may shake at the appearance of sin? . . . Wilt thou encircle me around in the robe of thy righteousness!" (2 Ne. 4:17–35).

Righteousness begins in the heart—the "broken heart." It begins when individuals see themselves where they really are: in a fallen state, as "unworthy creatures" who are unable to pull themselves out of their own sins. As they confront the monumental gulf between "the greatness of God, and [their] own nothingness," their hearts break and they "humble [themselves] even in the depths of humility, calling on the name of the Lord daily, and standing steadfastly in the faith" (Mosiah 4:11).

Righteous souls then seek to become right with the Lord, by asking sincerely for forgiveness. As the Lord blesses such with his grace, they desire to respond with even greater faithfulness, love, and obedience. Although they may not reach perfect righteousness in mortality, their lives are beyond reproach—"as becometh saints" (Eph. 5:3).

Scriptures provide a wealth of insight into the attitudes, behaviors, and beliefs that form the basis of a righteous life (e.g., 2 Pet. 1:4–8; D&C 4:5–6). Notably, in the Sermon on the Mount (Matt. 5–7; cf. 3 Ne. 12–14), Jesus revealed the meaning of righteousness—a pattern that he exemplified by his own life:

Those who seek righteousness become humble, poor in spirit. They reverence the Lord, acknowledging that "all things which are good cometh of God" (Moroni 7:12).

They mourn for their sins—and their "godly sorrow worketh repentance" (2 Cor. 7:10). They also compassionately "mourn with those that mourn; yea, and comfort those that stand in need of comfort" (Mosiah 18:9).

The righteous strive to be meek—kind and long-suffering, generous, sacrificing, patient, filled with love for their enemies, not "puffed up," and "not easily provoked" (1 Cor. 13:4–5).

Hungering and thirsting after righteousness, they continually seek the Lord through sincere PRAYER, FASTING, scripture study, Sabbath WORSHIP, and service in the holy temples.

They seek to be merciful—to forgive as they would be forgiven, to judge as they would be judged, to love as they would be loved, to serve as they would be served (D&C 38:24–25).

They seek to be pure in heart—thinking no evil, envying not, and rejoicing not in iniquity but in the truth (1 Cor. 13:4–6). They are honest in their COVENANTS with God and in their dealings with their fellowmen. They are chaste and also virtuous.

Seekers of righteousness are peacemakers. They avoid contention, anger, and evil-speaking. They promote goodwill, brotherhood, and sisterhood; they seek to establish God's will and his kingdom on earth as it is in heaven.

When persecuted for righteousness' sake or when reviled or maligned for their allegiance to the Lord, they bear all things and endure all things (1 Cor. 13:7).

Such scriptural descriptions of righteousness are not to be reduced to lists that individuals self-righteously check off. They are constant reminders on the journey toward God, who has promised a Comforter—the HOLY GHOST—to give guidance and direction on that path (John 14:26).

The Lord delights "to honor those who serve [him] in righteousness" (D&C 76:5). At the last day, "the righteous, the saints of the Holy One of Israel, they who have believed in the Holy One of Israel, they who have endured the crosses of the world, and despised the shame of it, they shall inherit the kingdom of God, which was prepared for them from the foundation of the world, and their joy shall be full forever" (2 Ne. 9:18).

BIBLIOGRAPHY

Benson, Ezra T. "A Mighty Change of Heart." *Ensign* 19 (Oct. 1989):2–5.
McConkie, Bruce R. "The Dead Who Die in the Lord." *Ensign* 6 (Nov. 1976):106–8.
Scoresby, A. Lynn. "Journey Toward Righteousness." *Ensign* 10 (Jan. 1980):52–57.

MARVIN K. GARDNER

S

SACRIFICE

God requires sacrifice of his people both to make or renew COVENANTS with him and to test their ultimate loyalties (D&C 98:12–15). When the Lord drove Adam and Eve from the Garden of Eden, he gave them the law of sacrifice, whereby they were to offer the firstlings of their flocks to him (Moses 5:5). From the beginning, offerings to the Lord that involved the shedding of blood were in similitude of the future sacrifice of Jesus Christ, who would come to atone for the sins of mankind (Moses 5:6–8). The Book of Mormon includes accounts of Lehi's people making burnt offerings in compliance with the Law of Moses (1 Ne. 5:9; Mosiah 2:3).

With the sacrifice of Jesus, "the performances and ordinances of the Law of Moses" were fulfilled (4 Ne. 1:12), and his death ended the practice of sacrifices on an altar. To his disciples in the western continents, Jesus said that he would no longer accept burnt offerings, but that anyone who believes in him should offer a broken heart and a contrite spirit (3 Ne. 9:19–20; cf. D&C 59:8).

For members of The Church of Jesus Christ of Latter-day Saints, sacrifice is required of those who wish to become the Lord's people (D&C 64:23). All are invited to come to Christ—rather than to a sacrificial altar—with humble, teachable spirits and repentant hearts, willing to sacrifice all things for the Lord and for one another (cf. Mosiah 18:8–9). The Prophet Joseph Smith taught that only a religion that requires total sacrifice has power sufficient to produce the faith necessary for salvation (*Lectures on Faith* 6:5–7). To appreciate the need to sacrifice, one need only recall Jesus' words to the rich young ruler: "Sell all that thou hast, and distribute unto the poor . . . and come, follow me" (Luke 18:22).

Covenants made by Church members embrace the commitment to sacrifice all for the KINGDOM OF GOD. Examples of willingness to sacrifice are legion among early Latter-day Saints who sacrificed homes, comforts, and even their lives for their beliefs. Prior to his martyrdom, Joseph Smith knew that he was going as "a lamb to the slaughter" (D&C 135:4). Sacrifices made by Mormon pioneers to establish the Church in the western United States have become legendary. And sacrifices are still required of Latter-day Saints. For instance, faithful members pay one-tenth of their income as tithing to the Church, contribute financially to mission funds, and give fast offerings for the poor. Missionaries spend one or two years preaching the gospel at their own or their families' expense while delaying education, employment, marriage, or retirement. Members serve their congregations—without pay—in assigned lay positions that make possible the operation of Church programs. It is service to others through formal callings and through personal concern for their welfare that leads Church members to know that "sacrifice brings forth the blessings of heaven" (Hymns, p. 27).

BIBLIOGRAPHY

Benson, Ezra Taft. "This Is a Day of Sacrifice." *Ensign* 9 (May 1979):32–34.

Hymns of The Church of Jesus Christ of Latter-day Saints. Salt Lake City, 1985.

Matthews, Robert J. "The Doctrine of the Atonement—The Revelation of the Gospel to Adam." In *Studies in Scripture*, ed. K. Jackson and R. Millet, Vol. 2, pp. 111–29. Salt Lake City, 1985.

GLORIA JEAN THOMAS

SALVATION

Salvation is the greatest gift of God (D&C 6:13). The root of the word means to be saved, or placed beyond the power of one's enemies (*TPJS*, pp. 297, 301, 305). It is redemption from the bondage of sin and death, through the ATONEMENT OF JESUS CHRIST. Some degree of salvation will come to all of God's children except the sons of perdition. Jesus said, "In my Father's house are many mansions: if it were not so, I would have told you. I go to prepare a place for you" (John 14:2). Paul said, "There is one glory of the sun, and another glory of the moon, and another glory of the stars. . . . So also is the resurrection of the dead" (1 Cor. 15:40–42). Paul also explained that "as in Adam all die, even so in Christ shall all be made alive" (1 Cor. 15:22). The Latter-day Saint concept of salvation derives from the teachings of Jesus Christ and the revelations given to ancient and latter-day prophets. It is evident from such teachings that there are different degrees or levels of salvation in the afterlife (*see* DEGREES OF GLORY).

There are various levels of salvation because there are various levels of belief and works among people (D&C 76:99–101). The Prophet Joseph Smith observed, "If God rewarded every one according to the deeds done in the body the term 'Heaven' as intended for the Saints' eternal home, must include more kingdoms than one" (*TPJS*, pp. 10–11).

The gospel of Jesus Christ comprises fundamental principles and ordinances that must be followed to obtain a fulness of salvation. The first steps are FAITH in the Lord Jesus Christ, REPENTANCE, BAPTISM by immersion for the remission of sins, and the LAYING ON OF HANDS by one who is in authority for the GIFT OF THE HOLY GHOST. Additional ordinances are administered in the temple. And finally, "he only is saved who endureth unto the end" (D&C 53:7).

The most sacred ordinances pertaining to the salvation of both the living and the dead are performed in the temples. These ordinances include the ENDOWMENT, the sealing of husband and wife to form an eternal marriage, and the sealing of children to parents to form an eternal family. All the ordinances that are essential for the salvation of the living are likewise essential for the dead, beginning with proxy baptism for the dead. These can only be performed in a temple. Baptism is for entrance into the CELESTIAL KINGDOM; the endowment and the sealing ordinances are for EXALTATION in the celestial kingdom. In the mercy of God and his love for his children, the PLAN OF SALVATION provides for everyone to hear and respond to the gospel either in this life or in the SPIRIT WORLD so that all who will may be saved by obedience to the laws and ordinances of the gospel (D&C 137:7–9; *see also* SALVATION FOR THE DEAD).

Salvation in a Latter-day Saint context includes activity and service in the kingdom of God for all eternity, unhampered by the effects of sin, death, physical pain, sickness, or other impediments to joy. The highest level of salvation is to become like God and involves a family unit. Lesser degrees of salvation are correspondingly less glorious and have restrictions.

ALMA P. BURTON

SALVATION FOR THE DEAD

A distinctive doctrine of The Church of Jesus Christ of Latter-day Saints is that the dead as well as the living may receive the GOSPEL OF JESUS CHRIST. Every man, woman, and child who has ever lived or who ever will live on this earth will have full opportunity, if not in this life then in the next, to embrace or reject the gospel in its purity and fulness.

When this doctrine was first taught at Nauvoo, Illinois, in 1842 (D&C 127; 128), the Prophet Joseph Smith said it was the "burden of the scriptures" and that it exhibited "the greatness of divine compassion and benevolence in the extent of the plan of human salvation" (*TPJS*, p. 192). It is in harmony with the Jewish idea that the family is the instrument of holiness and redemption and that the dead may need atonement. It is also a Christian concept in the writings of Paul and Peter (*see* BAPTISM FOR THE DEAD). "[It] justifies the ways of God to man, places the human family upon an equal footing, and harmonizes with every principle of righteousness, justice, and truth" (*TPJS*, p. 223).

The Prophet posed the dilemma resolved by the doctrine: "One dies and is buried having never heard the gospel of reconciliation; to the other the message of salvation is sent, he hears and embraces it and is made the heir of eternal life. Shall the one become the partaker of glory and the other be consigned to hopeless perdition? . . . Such an idea is worse than atheism" (*TPJS*, p. 192).

Five fundamental principles underlie LDS understanding of salvation for the dead:

1. Life is eternal. Birth does not begin life nor does death end it. In each stage of existence there are ever-higher levels of divine enlightenment and blessedness.
2. Repentance is possible in the next life as well as this one. "There is never a time when the spirit is too old to approach God. All are within the reach of pardoning mercy, who have not committed the unpardonable sin" (*TPJS*, p. 191).
3. The family bonds extend beyond death. The family bonds that are formed on this earth and consecrated to God by sacred covenants and ordinances are indissoluble and extend into the SPIRIT WORLD. "They without us cannot be made perfect—neither can we without our dead be made perfect" (D&C 128:15; Heb. 11:39–40).
4. Ordinances may be performed for the dead. Through the holy priesthood, held by the prophets in the Church, Jesus Christ has authorized mortals to receive ordinances "of salvation substitutional" [that is, by proxy] and become "instrumental in bringing multitudes of their kindred into the kingdom of God" (*TPJS*, p. 191).
5. Temple ordinances are not "mere signs." They are channels of the Spirit of God that enable one to be BORN OF GOD in the fullest sense and to receive all the COVENANTS and blessings of Jesus Christ. The performing of earthly ordinances by proxy for those who have died is as efficacious and vitalizing as if the deceased person had done them. That person, in turn, is free to accept or reject the ordinances in the spirit world.

In harmony with these principles, Latter-day Saints identify their ancestors through family history research, build temples, and, in behalf of their progenitors, perform the ordinances that pertain to exaltation: BAPTISM; CONFIRMATION; ordination to the priesthood; washing and anointing; ENDOWMENT; and sealing. Thus, "we redeem our dead, and connect ourselves with our fathers which are in heaven, and seal up our dead to come forth in the first resurrection . . . [we] seal those who dwell on earth to those who dwell in heaven" (*TPJS*, pp. 337–38). This is the chain that binds the hearts of fathers and mothers to their children and the hearts of the children to their parents. And this sealing work "fulfills the mission of Elijah" (*TPJS*, p. 330; *see also* ELIJAH, SPIRIT OF).

When the Twelve Apostles chosen in Joseph Smith's day were instructed to initiate these ordinances in Nauvoo in 1842, they soon recognized that it was the beginning of an immense work and that to administer all the ordinances of the gospel to the hosts of the dead was no easy task. They asked if there was some other way. The Prophet Joseph replied, "The laws of the Lord are immutable, we must act in perfect compliance with what is revealed to us. We need not expect to do this vast work for the dead in a short time. I expect it will take at least a thousand years" (*Millennial Star* 37:66). As of 1991 vicarious temple ordinances have been performed for more than 113 million persons. The Prophet Joseph said, "It is no more incredible that God should save the dead, than that he should raise the dead" (*TPJS,* p. 191).

BIBLIOGRAPHY

Widtsoe, John A. "Fundamentals of Temple Doctrine." *Utah Genealogical and Historical Magazine* 13 (June 1922):129–35.

ELMA W. FUGAL

SANCTIFICATION

Sanctification is the process of becoming a saint, holy and spiritually clean and pure, by purging all sin from the SOUL. Latter-day Saint scriptures mention several factors that make sanctification possible.

First is the ATONEMENT OF JESUS CHRIST (D&C 76:41–42; 88:18; Moro. 10:33; Alma 13:11). Christ's blood sanctifies God's repentant children by washing them clean in a way that extends beyond the REMISSION OF SINS at BAPTISM. This cleansing is given through GRACE to all who "love and serve God" (D&C 20:31). "For by the water ye keep the commandment; by the Spirit ye are justified, and by the blood ye are sanctified" (Moses 6:60; cf. 1 John 5:8).

Second is the power of the HOLY GHOST, the agent that purifies the heart and gives an abhorrence of sin (Alma 13:12; 3 Ne. 27:20).

Third is progression through personal RIGHTEOUSNESS (*see also* JUSTIFICATION). Faithful men and women fast; pray; repent of their sins; grow in HUMILITY, FAITH, JOY, and consolation; and yield their hearts to God (Hel. 3:35). They also receive essential ordinances such as baptism (D&C 19:31) and, if necessary, endure CHASTENING (D&C 101:5). Thus, Latter-day Saints are exhorted to "sanctify yourselves" (D&C 43:11) by purging all their iniquity (*MD*, pp. 675–76).

King Benjamin's people in the Book of Mormon illustrate the sanctification process. They humbled themselves and prayed mightily that God would apply the atoning blood of Christ and purify their hearts. The Spirit came upon them and filled them with joy; a mighty change came into their hearts and they had "no more disposition to do evil, but to do good continually" (Mosiah 5:2).

Latter-day Saint scripture often states that no unclean thing can dwell in God's presence (e.g., 3 Ne. 27:19; Moses 6:57). Thus, the sanctification that Latter-day Saints seek is more than a physical or moral state; it is a perpetual spiritual life—an ongoing effort to be worthy and pure to live with God—to overcome the evils of one's life and lose "every desire for sin" (*TPJS*, p. 51).

C. ERIC OTT

SECOND ESTATE

"Second estate" is a Latter-day Saint term that refers to mankind's mortal existence on this earth. In scripture it occurs only in the writings of Abraham (Abr. 3:26), but the pre-earth life of spirits is called "their first estate" in Jude 1:6. Latter-day Saints believe that through the process of BIRTH, the spirit children of God who kept their FIRST ESTATE (premortal) enter into their second estate by receiving a PHYSICAL BODY with additional opportunities for experience and development. MORTALITY is then a probationary period in which individuals "prepare to meet God" (Alma 12:24). In the final JUDGMENT all MANKIND will "be judged of their works . . . which were done by the temporal body in their days of probation" (1 Ne. 15:32; cf. Alma 12:14). All who receive the saving principles and ordinances of the GOSPEL OF JESUS CHRIST (including FAITH, REPENTANCE, BAPTISM, the GIFT OF THE HOLY GHOST, ordination to the priesthood for men, ENDOWMENT, and eternal marriage) and seek to live righteous and useful lives, embracing the FULNESS OF THE GOSPEL, will obtain the complete blessings of the ATONEMENT of Jesus Christ. All who had no opportunity to do so during earth life will have it in the postmortal spirit world (1 Pet.

3:18–19; 4:6; D&C 138:36–37). Every person who has lived on the earth will be resurrected with perfected corporeal bodies, and those who have kept the commandments will enter into ETERNAL LIFE, and "have glory added upon their heads for ever and ever" (Abr. 3:26).

ALEXANDER L. BAUGH

SOUL

In Latter-day Saint terminology "soul" is used in various ways, with diverse connotations found throughout the scriptures and in other Church writings. However, the word also has a precise definition given in latter-day REVELATION: the soul is the united entity of the SPIRIT with the PHYSICAL BODY (D&C 88:15–16). This concept is enhanced by an understanding of (1) the creation of humankind as a uniting of the SPIRIT BODY and the physical body (Gen. 2:7; Moses 3:7; Abr. 5:7); (2) the knowledge that God himself is embodied (D&C 130:22); and (3) the doctrine that all mortals will ultimately undergo a literal resurrection of the physical body (Alma 40:17–23; 41:2; 2 Ne. 9:13). Only in this resurrected and permanently united form can a soul receive a fulness of joy (D&C 93:33–34; cf. D&C 138:17). The glory with which the soul arises in the resurrection is related to the glory, form, and qualities of the resurrected body (1 Cor. 15:40–45; D&C 88:28).

"Soul" in a generic sense, however, means a person. This was common usage in the nineteenth century and earlier (i.e., Gen. 17:14 and Mosiah 18:28) as it is today. "Soul" is sometimes synonymous with "the whole self," or what might be described as one's "being" or "essence." Scriptural passages speak of "enlarging" the soul (Alma 32:28; D&C 121:42) and of imploring others with all the "energy" of one's soul (Alma 5:43). The word occasionally also appears as a metaphor implying "strength" (D&C 30:11; 31:5) or "heart" (2 Ne. 26:7, 10–11). "Soul" often is likewise used to refer to a person's intimate feelings or desires, as when one pours out one's "whole soul" (Enos 1:9; Mosiah 26:14) or when one is commanded to love God with "all thy soul" (Matt. 22:37; Mark 12:30–33; Luke 10:27). Other connotations are suggested by the word when it describes an entire community (Num. 21:4; 1 Sam. 30:6; Acts 4:32).

"Soul" is often used where the term "spirit" might also apply

(1 Ne. 19:7; 2 Ne. 1:22; D&C 101:37). Here the soul is essentially that aspect of all human beings which persists independent of the physical body (Matt. 10:28; 1 Ne. 15:31; Mosiah 2:38; Alma 40:11). In LDS doctrine the soul, in this sense, exists both before and after mortal life, and is truly eternal (Abr. 3:22–23; *see also* INTELLIGENCES).

Consistent with the idea that all spirits (or souls) existed prior to their mortal life, LDS doctrine holds that all vegetable and animal life was created spiritually before the physical creation (Moses 3:5; cf. Gen. 2:5). In this sense, every living thing (plant, animal, human) is spoken of as having a soul (Moses 3:9, 19).

The human soul is innately endowed with an AGENCY that should be honored and guarded as sacred and eternal (D&C 134:4). The soul (spirit), being eternal, cannot be fully destroyed but can suffer a type of destruction or SPIRITUAL DEATH through sins that result in total and ultimate estrangement from God (1 Ne. 14:3; Alma 12:16–18, 36; 30:47; 42:9, 16). Scripture teaches that all human souls are children of God and are of infinite worth (Matt. 16:26; Alma 39:17; D&C 18:10–16). God has great joy in a repentant soul, and there is no more important work than the saving of souls and bringing them to God (D&C 18:10–16; 15:6; 16:6).

RICHARD N. WILLIAMS

SPIRIT

The existence of both good and evil spirit beings is a prominent doctrine in LDS theology. Spirits are intelligent, self-existent, organized matter and are governed by eternal laws. Moreover, all living things had a pre-earthly spirit existence. LDS understanding on this subject is formulated by biblical and latter-day scripture and the teachings of latter-day prophets.

Latter-day revelation declares that "all spirit is matter, but it is more fine or pure" than the physical materials of earth life (D&C 131:7–8). The Prophet Joseph Smith explained:

> A very material difference [exists] between the body and the spirit; the body is supposed to be organized matter, and the spirit, by many, is thought to be immaterial, without substance. With this latter statement

> we should beg leave to differ, and state the spirit is a substance; that it is material, but that it is more pure, elastic and refined matter than the body; that it existed before the body, can exist in the body; and will exist separate from the body, when the body will be mouldering in the dust; and will in the resurrection, be again united with it [*TPJS,* p. 207].

Although the Lord has revealed much in ancient and latter-day scripture about spirit matter and spirit beings, many unknowns remain, especially the full meaning of such terms as "INTELLIGENCE," "light," and "truth," which are used in the revelations in association with the word "spirit." Spirit matter is identified with intelligence or the light of truth (D&C 93:29). Joseph Smith taught that elements were not created or made, but can be organized into a spirit being. This spirit, intelligence, or light has always existed, being coeternal with God. It can act and be acted upon; it can be organized, but it cannot be destroyed. Spirits exist upon a self-existent principle, and "all . . . spirits that God ever sent into the world are susceptible of enlargement" (*TPJS,* pp. 351–54), meaning that they are capable of intellectual growth and maturation and that "there is never a time when the spirit is too old to approach God" (*TPJS,* p. 191).

It is LDS doctrine that human spirits are the literal offspring of perfected, exalted parents, a Father and a MOTHER IN HEAVEN (cf. Num. 16:22; Heb. 12:9). God instituted a PLAN OF SALVATION whereby his spirit children could advance and become like him (*see* COUNCIL IN HEAVEN). Paul said that the human family is God's offspring (Acts 17:29). All men and women lived as personal, individual spirit children with God in a PREMORTAL LIFE before they were born into physical bodies. Likewise, one's personal, individual spirit existence extends beyond the death of the mortal body.

Jesus Christ was the firstborn of all God's spirit children and is thus the elder brother of the rest of mankind (*see* JESUS CHRIST: FIRSTBORN IN THE SPIRIT). Because of the faith of the brother of Jared (c. 2200 B.C.), he was permitted to see the Lord's premortal spirit body. The Lord explained to him, "Seest thou that ye are created after mine own image? Yea, even all men were created in the beginning after mine own image. Behold, this body, which ye now behold, is the body of my spirit; . . . and even as I appear unto thee to be in the spirit will I appear unto my people in the flesh" (Ether 3:15–16). Since spirits are the offspring of Heavenly Parents, they are in that image and likeness, both male and female (Gen. 1:26–27; Moses 3:4–7; Abr. 3:18–23).

Enoch was shown a vision of the spirits of all men and women who had lived or who would yet live on the earth and who were first created as spirits in heaven (Moses 6:28; 7:38–40, 57). Abraham also saw the premortal spirits of mankind and noted that they varied in intelligence and obedience (Abr. 3:18–19). Among these were many noble and great ones whom God said he would make rulers and leaders in his kingdom. Abraham was told that he was one of these and was chosen before he was born (Abr. 3:22–23). Many were foreordained to perform certain tasks when upon the earth (*see* FOREORDINATION). In the premortal state, spirits received their first lessons in the gospel and the work of God that they would do on the earth (D&C 138:55–56; cf. Jer. 1:5; Eph. 1:3–4; Titus 1:2). Many of these spirit beings were called and prepared from the foundation of the world because of their faith and good works, to bear the priesthood and teach the gospel and the commandments of God in mortality (Alma 13:1–6).

Inherent in the makeup of their intelligent nature, spirits have AGENCY and are able to make choices. The scriptures teach that spirits are capable of all the emotions, passions, and intellectual experiences exhibited by mortals, including love, anger, hate, envy, knowledge, obedience, rebellion, jealousy, repentance, loyalty, activity, thought, and comprehension. Using their agency, some of God's children rebelled in the premortal life, and war in heaven ensued. The rebellious spirits followed Lucifer and with him were cast down to the earth and became devils or evil spirits, never to receive physical bodies on earth (Moses 4:1–4; D&C 76:25–27; cf. Rev. 12:4, 7–9; D&C 29:36). Satan and his followers remain spirit beings made in the image of God but are still rebellious and evil. They are desirous of having a mortal body. The Prophet Joseph Smith explained, "The great principle of happiness consists in having a body. The devil has no body, and herein is his punishment. He is pleased when he can obtain the tabernacle of man, and when cast out by the Savior he asked to go into the herd of swine, showing that he would prefer a swine's body to having none" (*TPJS,* p. 181; cf. pp. 297–98).

Latter-day revelation has not identified or clarified the nature of seraphim or cherubim mentioned in the Bible (Gen. 3:24; Isa. 6:2) and whether these are spirit beings or merely symbolic representations. Some spirits are messengers of the Lord and minister to mortals (Heb. 1:14; D&C 129), but spirit ministrants cannot perform all the functions of those angels who have resurrected bodies (*TPJS,* pp. 191, 325).

A spirit being who has never entered mortality is in an "unembodied" state. A spirit with a mortal body is in an "embodied" state and the body and spirit constitute the SOUL (D&C 88:15). Death is the separation of the mortal, physical body from the spirit (James 2:26), after which the spirit lives in a "disembodied" state in the postmortal SPIRIT WORLD, while the mortal, physical body, without life, decays in the grave. In the postmortal world, the spirit awaits being "reembodied" in the RESURRECTION, which is the reuniting of the spirit and the body, never to be separated (Alma 11:44–45). Every person in the mortal world has come from the spirit world, and all will eventually die and then be resurrected.

Latter-day revelation teaches that God the Father and Jesus Christ are resurrected, exalted beings, meaning that they have glorified bodies of flesh and bones (D&C 130:22). Man exists that he "might have joy" (2 Ne. 2:25), and the revelations teach that a fulness of joy can be experienced only in the resurrected state—with the spirit and the body inseparably united (D&C 93:33–34). Therefore, existence as a spirit alone in either the premortal or postmortal spirit world has its limitations. Departed spirits who know the plan of God and the value of a physical body are anxious to be resurrected (D&C 45:17; 138:50). Because they rejected God's plan of salvation, Lucifer and his followers have been denied forever the privilege of having a physical body and thus are limited or curtailed in their progress. The Lord declared, "Where I am they cannot come, for they have no power" (D&C 29:29).

The spirit creation pertains not to the human family alone but to all living things. Latter-day scriptures teach that the human spirit is in the likeness of that which is physical, as was demonstrated in the case of the spirit of Jesus Christ, who appeared to the brother of Jared, noted above. Thus, "the spirit of man [is] in the likeness of his person, as also the spirit of the beast, and every other creature which God has created" (D&C 77:2). Moses wrote that every plant of the field, every herb, indeed every thing, was created "in heaven" before it was naturally upon the face of the earth (Moses 3:5–7).

[*See also* First Estate; Hell; Spirit Body; Spirit Prison.]

BIBLIOGRAPHY

"The Father and the Son: A Doctrinal Exposition by the First Presidency and the Twelve." *AF*, pp. 465–73. Salt Lake City, 1963.

Millet, Robert L., and Joseph F. McConkie. *The Life Beyond.* Salt Lake City, 1986.

"The Origin of Man," An official declaration in *MFP* 4:200–206.

Packer, Boyd K. "The Law and the Light." In *The Book of Mormon: Jacob Through the Words of Mormon, To Learn with Joy,* ed. M. Nyman and C. Tate, pp. 1–31. Provo, Utah, 1990.

Smith, Joseph. *Teachings of the Prophet Joseph Smith,* ed. Joseph Fielding Smith, pp. 202–215. Salt Lake City, 1938.

Top, Brent, L. *The Life Before.* Salt Lake City, 1988.

JAY E. JENSEN

SPIRIT BODY

Latter-day Saints believe that each person was born in PREMORTAL LIFE as a spirit son or daughter of God. The spirit joins with a physical body in the process of birth on the earth. At death the spirit and the body separate until they reunite in the RESURRECTION. SPIRITS are capable of intellectual advancement, love, hate, happiness, sorrow, obedience, disobedience, memory, and other personal characteristics. Latter-day Saints believe that "all spirit is matter," but this matter is so fine that it cannot be discerned by mortal eyes (D&C 131: 7–8).

The Doctrine and Covenants explains that "the spirit of man [is] in the likeness of his person, as also the spirit of the beast; and every other creature which God has created" (D&C 77:2). That spirit bodies resemble physical bodies is demonstrated in the account of the premortal Jesus visiting the brother of Jared many centuries before Jesus' birth (Ether 3:9–16). On this occasion, the Lord revealed his spirit body and said, "this body, which ye now behold, is the body of my spirit; . . . and even as I appear unto thee to be in the spirit will I appear unto my people in the flesh" (3:16).

According to Latter-day Saint doctrine, the spirit (sometimes called the SOUL) does not die (Alma 42:9; cf. James 2:26). However, a spirit, though immortal, cannot have a fulness of joy without being inseparably connected to a resurrected physical body (D&C 93:33–34; 138:50). For additional references see Job 32:8; Hebrews 12:9; 1 Nephi 11:11; Abraham 3:18–23.

WILSON K. ANDERSEN

SPIRIT OF PROPHECY

Spirit of prophecy is equated in Revelation 19:10 with "the testimony of Jesus." For members of The Church of Jesus Christ of Latter-day Saints, having a TESTIMONY OF JESUS CHRIST means receiving personal spiritual assurance through REVELATION by the HOLY GHOST that Jesus is the literal Son of God, the creator of the world, and that through his ATONEMENT all people will be resurrected and live forever.

According to the Prophet Joseph Smith, the spirit of prophecy is vital to the principles of salvation, revelation, and the teaching and ministering of the gospel. Each person must receive a testimony of Christ in order to attain salvation and ETERNAL LIFE with him (*TPJS*, p. 160). Since the gospel is to be taught to everyone, it follows that all people of every race and gender can experience the spirit of prophecy. Moreover, in the words of Joseph Smith, "God in his superior wisdom, has always given his Saints, wherever he had any on the earth, the same spirit, and that spirit, as John says, is the true spirit of prophecy, which is the testimony of Jesus" (*TPJS*, p. 300).

It is through the spirit of prophecy that God's continuing revelations are brought to the people of the earth, not only through his ordained prophets but also through all those who have received a testimony of Christ. The gospel cannot be taught on the earth without the spirit of prophecy or a testimony of Christ, because it is only through testimony received by revelation that Christ's teachings are validated in the heart and mind of the person taught. One who preaches the gospel and denies the spirit of prophecy is, according to Joseph Smith, an "imposter" (*TPJS*, p. 269).

While only one person (the President of the Church) may exercise all the keys of the priesthood of God at one time on the earth and receive revelation for the whole Church, the underlying principle of the spirit of prophecy is that all saints who receive a testimony of

Christ are prophets in the limited sense that they may receive revelation and inspiration for themselves (*TPJS*, p. 119). This same idea is implicit in Moses' response to Joshua: "Would God that all the Lord's people were prophets, and that the Lord would put his spirit upon them!" (Num. 11:29).

LOUISE PLUMMER

SPIRIT PRISON

In Latter-day Saint doctrine the "spirit prison" is both a condition and a place within the postearthly SPIRIT WORLD. One "imprisons" himself or herself through unbelief or through willful disobedience of God. In such circumstances, one's opportunities in the AFTERLIFE will be limited. Those who willfully rebel against the light and truth of the gospel and do not repent remain in this condition of imprisonment and suffer SPIRITUAL DEATH, which is a condition of hell (Alma 12:16–18; D&C 76:36–37). Furthermore, since a fulness of joy is not possible without the resurrected body, the waiting in the spirit world for the RESURRECTION is a type of imprisonment (D&C 45:17; 93:33–34; 138:16, 17, 50). However, through the ATONEMENT of Jesus Christ all have a promise of resurrection, and thus of eventual release from this type of spirit prison, although the unrepentant will still be imprisoned by their unbelief (*see* DAMNATION).

Another more far-reaching definition of "spirit prison" is HELL. In this sense, spirit prison is a temporary abode in the spirit world of those who either were untaught and unrighteous, or were disobedient to the gospel while in mortal life (cf. Alma 40:11–14; D&C 138:32).

As part of his redemptive mission, Jesus Christ visited the spirit world during the interlude between his own death and resurrection, and "from among the righteous, he organized his forces and appointed messengers, clothed with power and authority, and commissioned them to go forth and carry the light of the gospel to them that were in darkness"—in other words, to the spirits in prison (D&C 138:30; cf. 1 Pet. 3:18–20; 4:6). Thus, the gulf between paradise and hell that is spoken of in Jesus' parable of the rich man and Lazarus (Luke 16:19–31) was bridged by the Savior's ministry in the spirit world. This bridging allows interaction among the righteous and wicked spirits to the extent that the faithful present the gospel to "those who had died in their sins, without a knowledge of the truth, or in transgression, having rejected the prophets" (D&C 138:32). Latter-day Saints believe that preaching the gospel in the spirit world continues today and will continue until every soul who wishes to do so and repents properly will be released from such imprisonment.

Repentance of imprisoned spirits opens the doors of the prison, enabling them to loose themselves from the spiritual darkness of unbelief, ignorance, and sin. As they accept the gospel of Jesus Christ and cast off their sins, the repentant are able to break the chains of hell and dwell with the righteous in paradise.

[*See also* Salvation for the Dead.]

BIBLIOGRAPHY

Pratt, Orson. "Deity; The Holy Priesthood." In *Masterful Discourses and Writings of Orson Pratt,* N. B. Lundwall, comp., pp. 260–68. Salt Lake City, 1946.

ROBERT J. PARSONS

SPIRITUAL DEATH

Spiritual death is the condition of one who is spiritually cut off, temporarily or permanently, from the presence of God. LDS scriptures speak of two spiritual deaths, and the concept manifests itself in many ways.

The first type of spiritual death is the actual separation from God that automatically comes upon all born into MORTALITY as a consequence of the FALL OF ADAM. All mortals will be redeemed from this death, as well as from physical death, through Christ's Atonement and RESURRECTION (1 Cor. 15:21–23; 2 Ne. 9:10–15; Hel. 14:15–19; D&C 29:41), to be brought back into God's presence to stand before him.

The second spiritual death will be finalized on the day of JUDGMENT for those who have not repented (Rev. 2:11; 20:6–15; Alma 12:16–36). It is the result of a lifetime of choices. For those who ultimately lose the inclination or ability to repent, or commit unpardonable sin, it becomes perdition (2 Pet. 3:7; Alma 34:35; 40:25–26) or "banishment from the presence of God and from his light and truth forever" (*DS* 2:216–30). This does not extinguish the spirit of man, however, for it is eternal (see Alma 12:18; 42:9). The Savior's atonement gives all mankind the opportunity to avoid the second spiritual death and gain IMMORTALITY and ETERNAL LIFE.

The spiritually "dead" may be grouped into several types and categories. For example, Satan and the spirits who joined him during the war in heaven are eternally spiritually dead (D&C 29:36–39; 76:25–29). They are sons of perdition (see 2 Ne. 9:8–9). Mortals who sin "unto death" (D&C 64:7) by denying the Son after the Father has revealed him will join "the only ones on whom the second death shall have any power" (D&C 76:30–38). In yet another sense, all people on earth over the age of ACCOUNTABILITY are to a certain extent spiritually dead, depending on their present state of REPENTANCE and their degree of sensitivity to the LIGHT OF CHRIST and to the HOLY GHOST.

Buddhism, Islam, Christianity, Judaism, and most other religions believe in some form of life after death, judgment, and ultimate punishment for the unrepentant. For example, the ancient Egyptians believed that the hard-hearted would die a second death by being devoured by the Chaos monster (Keel, pp. 72–73). Major differences between the Mormon concept of spiritual death and those of others center on the ATONEMENT OF JESUS CHRIST. The only permanent spiritual death is that which individuals bring upon themselves by refusing to repent of their sins, having denied the Holy Spirit after having received it, and having denied the Only Begotten Son of the Father, having crucified him unto themselves (D&C 76:35).

BIBLIOGRAPHY

Keel, O. *The Symbolism of the Biblical World*, pp. 72–73. London, 1978.

Lund, Gerald N. "The Fall of Man and His Redemption." In *The Book of Mormon: Second Nephi, The Doctrinal Structure*, ed. M. Nyman, pp. 83–106. Provo, Utah, 1989.

Matthews, Robert J. "The Fall of Man." In *The Man Adam*, ed. J. McConkie, pp. 37–64. Salt Lake City, 1990.

Romney, Marion G. "The Resurrection of Jesus." *Ensign* 12 (May 1982):6–9.

RICHARD M. ROMNEY

SPIRIT WORLD

The spirit world is the habitation of spirits. The earth itself and the living things on the earth have spirit counterparts that existed before the physical creation, and a living SOUL consists of a spirit body united with a physical body. This spirit existence, where living things are composed of organized, refined spirit matter, extends beyond the human family and includes animals and plants. Little is revealed about plant spirits beyond the fact that all living things, including plants, were created as spirits before they were created with physical bodies (Moses 3:5, 9). However, latter-day revelation indicates that human and animal spirits are living, active, intelligent beings and that spirits do not need physical bodies for existence (*see* SPIRIT). Since spirits exist before mortality, as well as afterward, there is both a premortal and a postmortal spirit world.

The premortal spirit existence, for mankind at least, was "in heaven," in the kingdom where God lives. Explaining this phase of the Creation, the Lord said, "I, the Lord God, created all things, of which I have spoken, spiritually, before they were naturally upon the face of the earth, . . . for in heaven created I them" (Moses 3:5).

More detail is known about the place and conditions of departed spirits—the postmortal spirit world—than about the premortal. Concerning the postmortal place of human spirits, $Alma_2$ sought an answer to the question "What becometh of the souls of men from this time of death to the time appointed for the resurrection?" (Alma 40:7). It was revealed to him by an angel that at the death of the body "the spirits of all men, whether they be good or evil, are taken home to that God who gave them life" (Alma 40:11). They are then assigned to a place of PARADISE or a place of HELL and "outer darkness," depending on the manner of their mortal life (Alma 40:12–14).

President Joseph F. Smith discussed this subject further:

> The spirits of all men, as soon as they depart from this mortal body, whether they are good or evil, . . . are taken home to that God who gave them life, where there is a separation, a partial judgment, and the spirits of those who are righteous are received into a state of happiness which is called paradise, a state of rest, a state of peace, where they expand in wisdom, where they have respite from all their troubles, and where care and sorrow do not annoy. The wicked, on the contrary, have

> no part nor portion in the Spirit of the Lord, and they are cast into outer darkness, being led captive, because of their own iniquity, by the evil one. And in this space between death and the resurrection of the body, the two classes of souls remain, in happiness or in misery, until the time which is appointed of God that the dead shall come forth and be reunited both spirit and body, and be brought to stand before God, and be judged according to their works. This is the final judgment [p. 448].

President Brigham Young declared:

> When you lay down this tabernacle, where are you going? Into the spiritual world . . . Where is the spirit world? It is right here. Do the good and evil spirits go together? Yes they do. . . . Do they go beyond the boundaries of the organized earth? No, they do not. . . . Can you see it with your natural eyes? No. Can you see spirits in this room? No. Suppose the Lord should touch your eyes that you might see, could you then see the spirits? Yes, as plainly as you now see bodies [Widtsoe, pp. 376–77].

The postmortal spirit world is an actual place where spirits reside and "where they converse together the same as we do on the earth" (*TPJS*, p. 353). "Life and work and activity all continue in the spirit world. Men have the same talents and intelligence there which they had in this life. They possess the same attitudes, inclinations, and feelings there which they had in this life" (*MD*, p. 762).

The postmortal spirit world is a place of continued preparation and learning. In this sense, it is an extension of mortality. Those who have died without an opportunity to hear the gospel of Jesus Christ will have opportunity to hear and accept it in the spirit world. "The great work in the world of spirits is the preaching of the gospel to those who are imprisoned by sin and false traditions" (*MD*, p. 762). The faithful elders and sisters who depart this life "continue their labors in the preaching of the gospel of repentance and redemption . . . Among those who are in darkness" (D&C 138:57; Smith, p. 461; *see also* SALVATION FOR THE DEAD).

Bruce R. McConkie explained, "Until the death of Christ these two spirit abodes [paradise and hell] were separated by a great gulf, with the intermingling of their respective inhabitants strictly forbidden (Luke 16:19–31). After our Lord bridged the gulf between the two (1 Pet. 3:18–21; Moses 7:37–39), the affairs of his kingdom in the spirit world were so arranged that righteous spirits began teaching the gospel to wicked ones" (*MD*, p. 762).

An important LDS doctrine states that Jesus Christ inaugurated the preaching of the gospel and organized a mission in the spirit world during his ministry there between his death and resurrection. This is the substance of a revelation recorded as Doctrine and Covenants section 138. Since Jesus' visit there, the gospel has been taught vigorously in the spirit world (*see* SPIRIT PRISON).

The relative conditions and state of mind in the two spheres of the postmortal spirit world are described by the Prophet Joseph Smith: "The spirits of the just are exalted to a greater and more glorious work; hence they are blessed in their departure to the world of spirits. Enveloped in flaming fire, they are not far from us, and know and understand our thoughts, feelings, and motions, and are often pained therewith" (*TPJS*, p. 326). On the other hand, "The great misery of departed spirits in the world of spirits, where they go after death, is to know that they come short of the glory that others enjoy and that they might have enjoyed themselves, and they are their own accusers" (*TPJS*, pp. 310–11).

A statement regarding conditions in the spirit world among the righteous was given in 1856 by Jedediah M. Grant, a member of the First Presidency. He had related to President Heber C. Kimball a vision he had had of the spirit world, which President Kimball subsequently discussed at Grant's funeral a few days later on December 4, 1856. Although an unofficial statement, it represents concepts generally held by Latter-day Saints. A summary follows: Jedediah Grant saw the righteous gathered together in the spirit world; there were no wicked spirits among them. There were order, government, and organization. Among the righteous there was no disorder, darkness, or confusion. They were organized into families, and there was "perfect harmony." He saw his wife, with whom he conversed, and many other persons whom he knew. There was "a deficiency in some" families, because some individuals "had not honored their calling" on earth and therefore were not "permitted to . . . dwell together." The buildings were exceptionally attractive, far exceeding in beauty his opinion of Solomon's temple. Gardens were more beautiful than any he had seen on earth, with "flowers of numerous kinds." After experiencing "the beauty and glory of the spirit world" among the righteous spirits, he regretted having to return to his body in mortality (*JD* 4:135–36).

Since all who have possessed a body in mortality will be resurrected, a time will ultimately come when the postmortal spirit world pertaining to this earth will cease to exist as the earth will become the celestial home for resurrected beings (*MD*, p. 762).

BIBLIOGRAPHY

Smith, Joseph F. *GD*, pp. 428–77.

Smith, Joseph Fielding. *DS* 2:132–61.

Young, Brigham. *Discourses of Brigham Young*, ed. John A. Widtsoe, pp. 376–81. Salt Lake City, 1946.

WALTER D. BOWEN

T

TEACHING THE GOSPEL

Among Latter-day Saints, the ultimate purpose of teaching the gospel is the transformation of lives. Neither the process of intensive study nor the knowledge gained is an end in itself. In addition to lecture and conceptual approaches, gospel teaching often follows a skill-learning model, in which a skill to be learned or quality to be developed such as prayer, kindness, or service is modeled or exemplified. Learners are encouraged to apply their new or renewed insight. As soon as possible, they become teachers themselves. Thus, teaching is the art of directing activities. Corrective responses from teacher and learner continue until the skill is incorporated into character. In the Church the gaps between priest and layman, teacher and learner, and leader and follower are all but erased. Teaching is a universal and inclusive mode of participation. Results are most impressive when family, church, and community cooperate and support each other's efforts.

Guidelines for teaching the gospel are often summarized in three imperatives:

1. Teach from the scriptures and teach the content of the scriptures. The standard works are studied systematically in recurring cycles, and this pattern is correlated for all age groups, auxiliaries, and priesthood quorums.
2. Teach by the Spirit, meaning under the influence of the HOLY

GHOST. "If ye receive not the Spirit ye shall not teach" (D&C 42:14). "No man can preach the Gospel without the Holy Ghost" (*TPJS*, p. 112).

3. Teach by likening the scriptures to the lives of the learners (cf. 1 Ne. 19:23–24; 2 Ne. 11:2, 8).

These imperatives are reflected in teacher development manuals and courses, which reach hundreds of thousands of members each year in group efforts to inculcate, refresh, and improve teaching skills. They are implicit also in the teacher manuals that are published with student manuals for all classes and quorums of the Church.

Church leaders and teachers constantly emphasize the scriptures as the basis of personal and Church class study. Familiarity with the scriptures is viewed as basic to understanding the gospel and to the development of faith and testimony. Daily scripture study in the home and during family home evening is recommended for all members of all ages and in all Church callings.

Teaching the gospel is more than sharing knowledge. It also involves creating an atmosphere in which the spirit of the learner is touched and the intimate and ultimate strivings of the soul are related to truth. Latter-day Saints recognize that to teach knowledge and wisdom is a spiritual gift to be sought earnestly (D&C 46:16–18). Only when the Holy Ghost, or "spirit of truth"—enhancing the light of Christ (D&C 93:2)—is present is there genuine communication. Then teacher and learner "understand one another, and both are edified and rejoice together" (D&C 50:21–22).

Because of the multicultural base of the Church and its rapid growth, gospel teachers are asked to teach a wide array of members with radically different backgrounds, needs, and levels of understanding and spiritual preparation. This continues to be a major challenge to the Church.

ADRIAN P. VAN MONDFRANS

TELESTIAL KINGDOM

The telestial kingdom in Latter-day Saint understanding is the lowest of the three degrees of glory to be inhabited by God's children in the

AFTERLIFE following the RESURRECTION. The Doctrine and Covenants is the only known scriptural source for the word "telestial" (see D&C 76:88, 98, 109; 88:21). Paul spoke of the differing glories, comparing them to the differences in light we see from the sun, moon, and stars (1 Cor. 15:40–42), mentioning the celestial and terrestrial by name. Although the term "telestial" does not occur in biblical accounts, latter-day REVELATION cites telestial as the kingdom of glory typified by the lesser light we perceive from the stars (D&C 76:98). The CELESTIAL KINGDOM and TERRESTRIAL KINGDOM are typified by the light we perceive from the sun and moon, respectively.

Within the telestial glory there will be varying degrees of glory even as the stars vary in brightness as we see them. It embraces those who on earth willfully reject the GOSPEL OF JESUS CHRIST, and commit serious sins such as murder, adultery, lying, and loving to make a lie (but yet do not commit the unpardonable sin), and who do not repent in mortality. They will be cleansed in the postmortal SPIRIT WORLD or spirit prison before the resurrection (D&C 76:81–85, 98–106; Rev. 22:15). Telestial inhabitants as innumerable as the stars will come forth in the last resurrection and then be "servants of the Most High; but where God and Christ dwell they cannot come" (D&C 76:112). Although the least of the degrees of glory, yet the telestial kingdom "surpasses all understanding" (D&C 76:89).

[*See also* Degrees of Glory.]

CLYDE J. WILLIAMS

TEMPTATION

"Temptation" and related terms in the Old Testament are translated from the Hebrew *nasah,* meaning "to try" or "to test." Such a test elicits responses demonstrating a person's disposition and will rather than abilities. In this sense God is said to "tempt" human beings. Thus did "God tempt" Abraham by commanding him to sacrifice Isaac (Gen. 22:1). In Abraham's account of creation in the Pearl of Great Price, the Lord indicates that mortal experience constitutes such a test (Abr. 3:25). In other latter-day scriptures, temptation usually refers to the enticement of human beings into attitudes and actions that alienate them from God and jeopardize their salvation. The Lord taught people to shun this kind of temptation: "And lead us not into temptation" (Luke 11:4; cf. JST). Although in this kind of temptation the individual is usually enticed from without (whether by human or nonhuman agents), the scriptures make clear the individual's responsibility and accountability:

> Let no man say when he is tempted, I am tempted of God: for God cannot be tempted with evil, neither tempteth he any man. But every man is tempted, when he is drawn away of his own lust, and enticed. Then when lust hath conceived, it bringeth forth sin: and sin, when it is finished, bringeth forth death [James 1:13–16].

Latter-day Saints believe that though God does not tempt human beings to do evil, he does, for benevolent purposes, allow them to be tempted. If people were not confronted with opposing possibilities and inclinations, they would not be able to exercise their AGENCY, and, thus, their opportunity for moral and spiritual growth would be diminished. The prophet Lehi explained:

> To bring about [God's] eternal purposes in the end of man, after he had created our first parents, . . . it must needs be that there was an opposition; even the forbidden fruit in opposition to the tree of life; the one being sweet and the other bitter. Wherefore, the Lord God gave unto man that he should act for himself. Wherefore, man could not act for himself save it should be that he was enticed by the one or the other [2 Ne. 2:15–16].

Though confronting temptation is an essential and unavoidable element of mortal experience, God mercifully limits the extent to which people can be tempted. For example, he does not allow Satan or his hosts to tempt little children until they begin to be accountable (D&C 29:47), nor anyone beyond his or her capacity to endure (1 Cor. 10:13). During the Millennium, Satan and his angels will be bound so that they cannot tempt humankind (1 Ne. 22:26; 4 Ne. 1:15). Satan will be loosed for "a little season" following the Millennium, and will finally be banished with his angels as part of the final judgment (D&C 88:110–15).

Since God knew that all humans would yield in some degree to temptation and become sinners, he planned from the beginning and carried out through Jesus Christ an ATONEMENT whereby people can be forgiven of their sins and obtain power to resist temptation in the future, when they accept and follow his gospel.

The language of temptation in the scriptures can also refer to the various trials that humans experience in mortality. While these trials may become stumbling blocks, they may also become opportunities for moral and spiritual growth. Regarding such temptations, James counsels,

> My brethren, count it all joy when ye fall into divers temptations; knowing this, that the trying of your faith worketh patience. But let patience have her perfect work, that ye may be perfect and entire, wanting nothing. . . . Blessed is the man that endureth temptation: for when he is tried, he shall receive the crown of life, which the Lord hath promised to them that love him [James 1:2–4, 12].

Sometimes the scriptures speak of people tempting God or of sinful human ways of responding or relating to God. People may "tempt God" by complaining against him or by challenging him in unbelief (cf. Ex. 17:1–7; 1 Cor. 10:9), by defying him in disobedience (Heb. 3:8), or by demanding signs or miracles from him for an unworthy motive, such as to exalt themselves or to satisfy their curiosity (Matt. 12:39). Compare also Satan's temptations of Jesus in the wilderness and the Lord's rebuke: "Thou shalt not tempt the Lord thy God" (Matt. 4:1–11).

BIBLIOGRAPHY

Madsen, Truman G. "The Better Music." *IE* 66 (June 1963):554–55.

McKay, David O. "The Temptations of Life." *IE* 71 (July 1968):2–3.

DAVID L. PAULSEN

TERRESTRIAL KINGDOM

The Church of Jesus Christ of Latter-day Saints teaches of three degrees of glory or kingdoms of HEAVEN in the afterlife: the CELESTIAL KINGDOM, TERRESTRIAL KINGDOM, and TELESTIAL KINGDOM. Paul likened these kingdoms to the realtive radiance of the sun, moon, and stars (1 Cor 15:40–41; cf. D&C 76:50–98). Further evidence of a heaven with multiple kingdoms is found in Jesus' statement, "In my Father's house are many mansions" (John 14:2). On February 16, 1832, the Prophet Joseph Smith and Sidney Rigdon saw in vision the three degrees of glory, identifying the glory of the terrestrial kingdom as typical "of the moon [which] differs from the sun in the firmament" (D&C 76:71).

The terrestrial glory is for those who lived honorable lives on the earth but "were blinded by the craftiness of men" and were "not valiant in the testimony of Jesus." Those who did not receive a TESTIMONY of Jesus while on earth, but who could have done so except for their neglect, are also heirs to the terrestrial kingdom (D&C 76:72–74, 79). They obtain not "the crown over the kingdom of our God" (D&C 76:79) and remain without EXALTATION in their saved condition (D&C 132:17). They "receive of the presence of the Son, but not of the fulness of the Father," and their kingdom differs from the celestial "as the moon differs from the sun" (D&C 76:77–78).

[*See also* Degrees of Glory.]

SUSAN EASTON BLACK

TESTIMONY

[*Testimony is a generic term among Latter-day Saints for the assurance of the reality, truth, and goodness of God, of the teachings and atonement of Jesus Christ, and of the divine calling of latter-day prophets. It is the core of LDS religious experience. It reaches beyond secondhand assent, notional conviction, or strong belief. It is knowledge buttressed by divine personal confirmation by the Holy Ghost and is interrelated with authentic faith and trust in God as demonstrated by dedication and discipleship. Fundamental in the Church is the doctrine that "no man can be a minister of Jesus Christ except he has the testimony of Jesus; and this is the spirit of prophecy. Whenever salvation has been administered, it has been by testimony" (*TPJS, *p. 160).*

Articles that relate to this theme and its connections with other aspects of Latter-day Saint spiritual life include Faith in Jesus Christ; Knowledge; Light of Christ; Revelation; Testimony Bearing; Testimony of Jesus Christ; *and* Truth.]

TESTIMONY OF JESUS CHRIST

For Latter-day Saints, the FIRST PRINCIPLE OF THE GOSPEL is FAITH in Jesus Christ. This faith is intertwined with "the testimony of Jesus," which is received from God, "for the testimony of Jesus is the spirit of prophecy" (Rev. 19:10). Joseph Smith said, "No man can *know* that Jesus is the Lord, but by the Holy Ghost" (*TPJS*, p. 223; 1 Cor. 12:3). The essence of a TESTIMONY is a personal inward assurance of Jesus Christ's divinity, and it provides the fundamental basis for a Christian life. One becomes a disciple of Christ in the fullest spiritual sense only when a personal testimony of Jesus is received.

To have such a testimony is to be conscious that God has borne witness within one's soul by the power of the Holy Ghost that Jesus is the Christ (D&C 46:13). How is this witness obtained? As Paul wrote, "faith cometh by hearing, and hearing by the word of God" (Rom. 10:17). The testimony of Jesus Christ comes to those who hear of him. But to hear the GOSPEL OF JESUS CHRIST preached is not yet to have a testimony of him. Divine confirmation must also be received, usually in answer to sincere prayer. These three elements usually occur in a sequence: hearing, praying, receiving the divine witness by the Spirit. They can also occur simultaneously. Following Peter's earnest declaration, "Thou art the Christ, the Son of the living God," Jesus replied, "Blessed art thou . . . for flesh and blood hath not revealed it unto thee, but my Father which is in heaven" (Matt. 16:16–17). Like Peter, prophets and apostles of all ages have testified of Jesus Christ (see John 20:31).

Praying for a testimony of Jesus Christ or for any other truth of the gospel does not assume the presence of the faith being sought. The common phrase, "acting in good faith," may offer insight here. It suggests a willingness to approach a matter not with suspicion but with trust. The Book of Mormon prophet Alma$_2$ asks his listeners to "awake and arouse your faculties, even to an experiment upon my words . . . even until ye believe in a manner that ye can give place for a portion of my words" (Alma 32:27). To those willing to open their hearts at least this much, a testimony may come, but hardly to those without a fervent desire to obtain it. Most Latter-day Saints treasure the spiritual experiences that awaken and confirm testimony.

The gaining of a testimony is best viewed not as a single event but as a continuing process. Just as spiritual indolence and disobedience to the commandments of Christ constantly weaken a testimony, so close communion with God and selfless Christian service progressively strengthen it. Because Latter-day Saints view religion as an active as well as a contemplative way of life, they stress the unity of these two ends. Drawing close to God and serving others are aspects of a single purpose, following Christ. Only those who seek to do this may come to truly know him. "For how knoweth a man the master whom he has not served, and who is a stranger unto him, and is far from the thoughts and intents of his heart?" (Mosiah 5:13). But to all who follow him, the testimony of Jesus Christ gives an assurance of his presence, his all-enveloping care, and his love.

BIBLIOGRAPHY

Muren, Joseph C., and H. Stephen Stoker, comps. *Testimony.* Salt Lake City, 1980.

DENNIS RASMUSSEN

THANKFULNESS

From time immemorial those who believe in God have expressed their thankfulness to him. Giving humble thanks is also among the most basic religious expressions of members of The Church of Jesus Christ of Latter-day Saints, as with religious people everywhere. It is also a prescribed element of prayer (D&C 46:32).

In ancient times Moses offered sacrifices of thanksgiving (Lev. 7:11–13) and King Hezekiah gave "thank offerings" (2 Chr. 29:30–31). Ascribed to David are the Talmud's One Hundred Daily Benedictions that begin with "Blessed are thou, O Lord, our God, King of the Universe!" and express gratitude for common as well as exceptional activities, enjoyments, natural phenomena, and encounters with remarkable persons. Upon receiving good news or blessings, the Hebrews uttered appreciation for God's munificence; when experiencing trials they thanked God because he is just.

Jesus memorably taught the appropriateness of gratitude after he healed ten lepers on his way to Jerusalem. When only one of the ten, a Samaritan, gave earnest thanks, Christ commented, "Were there not ten cleansed? but where are the nine?" (Luke 17:11–19). Later,

Paul emphasized that the righteous should "in every thing give thanks: for this is the will of God in Christ Jesus concerning you" (1 Thes. 5:18).

In the Book of Mormon the prophet $Alma_2$ admonished Christ's followers to acquire his attributes, among them, "asking for whatsoever things ye stand in need, both spiritual and temporal; always returning thanks unto God for whatsoever things ye do receive" (Alma 7:23). Modern scripture promises that "he who receiveth all things with thankfulness shall be made glorious" (D&C 78:19), and that "in nothing doth man offend God, or against none is his wrath kindled, save those who confess not his hand in all things, and obey not his commandments" (D&C 59:21). Thankfulness is to be offered for "all things" received from the Lord whether or not, from limited human understanding, they initially appear to be blessings.

Although thankfulness is most commonly communicated through prayer, a revelation given to Brigham Young counsels, "If thou art merry, praise the Lord with singing, with music, with dancing, and with a prayer of praise and thanksgiving" (D&C 136:28). Additional appropriate means for expressing thanksgiving include singing hymns (the Latter-day Saints Hymnal lists twenty-seven titles under the topic of "gratitude"); participating in regular Church worship services; commemorating such religious holidays as Easter, Christmas, and Thanksgiving; having a devout personal life characterized by a repentant spirit and righteous works; and showing love toward others.

BIBLIOGRAPHY

Faust, James E. "Gratitude as a Saving Principle." *Ensign* 20 (May 1990):85–87.

GARY L. BROWNING

TIME AND ETERNITY

In Latter-day Saint understanding, time and eternity usually refer to the same reality. Eternity is time with an adjective: It is endless time. Eternity is not, as in Platonic and Neoplatonic thought, supratemporal or nontemporal.

In religions where eternity is radically contrasted with time, time is seen as an illusion, or utterly subjective, or an ephemeral episode. God and the higher realities are held to be "beyond." This is still the premise of much classical mysticism, Christian and non-Christian, as it is of absolutistic metaphysics. It is written into many Christian creeds.

But scriptural passages that ascribe eternity to God do not say or imply that God is independent of, or outside of, or beyond time. Nor do they say, with Augustine, that God created time out of nothing. In context they stress that he is everlasting, that he is trustworthy, that his purposes do not fail.

The view that time and eternity are utterly incompatible, utterly irreconcilable, has taxing consequences for theology. If God is supratemporal, for example, he could not have been directly related to the Creation because being out of time—and also beyond space and not subject to change—he could not enter this or any process. Theories of emanation were thus introduced to maintain God as static Being, and intermediaries were postulated as agents of creation, for example, intelligences, hosts, pleromas, etc.

In LDS understanding, God was and is directly involved in creation. The creative act was a process (the book of Abraham speaks of creation "times" rather than of "days"). His influence on creation, then and now, is not seen as a violation of his transcendence or of his glory and dominion but a participative extension of them.

The dogma of a supratemporal eternity led to another set of contradictions in postbiblical thought, the paradoxes of incarnation. The coming of Jesus Christ was recast within the assumptions of Greek metaphysics: God the universal became particular; God the nontemporal became temporal; God, superior to change, changed; God, who created time, now entered it. Most Christian traditions have embraced these paradoxes, but LDS thought has not. In LDS Christology, Jesus was in time before he entered mortality, is in time now, and will be forever.

Whatever the subtleties of the ultimate nature of time, or of scientific postulates on the relativity of time, and of the modes of measuring time, several assurances are prominent features of LDS understanding:

1. Time is a segment of eternity. One may distinguish eternities, long epochs of time, within eternity. Influenced by passages in the writ-

ings of Abraham and Enoch, some early LDS leaders speculated on the length of an eternity. One (W. W. Phelps) suggested that time "in our system" began two billion five hundred million years ago (*T&S,* Vol. 5, No. 24, p. 758). In any case, time itself had no beginning and will have no end.

2. Time unfolds in one direction. It extends rather than repeats precisely. The view of eternal recurrence common in the Far East that leads, for example, to the pessimism of Schopenhauer, is rejected. Worlds and world systems may come and go, as civilizations may rise and fall, but history does not exactly repeat itself. Individual creative freedom modifies the outcomes.
3. Eternity, as continuing time, is tensed: past, present, and future. God himself, eternal in identity, self-existent, and therefore without beginning or end, is nevertheless related to time. At his own supreme and unsurpassable level, he has a past, a present, and a future. Neither he nor his creations can return to or change the past. He has become what he is through eons of time gone by. He is now in relation to, and responsive to, his creations. Response implies time and change.
4. In a cosmic sense, the reckoning of time is according to the rotations of the spheres. It is presumed that God, angels, men, and prophets reckon time differently (see Abr. 3; D&C 130:4). There is some connection between time and space, for example, "one day to a cubit" (*see* Abraham, Facsimile 2, figure 1).
5. The eternal is sometimes contrasted to time as the permanent is contrasted to the transitory. "Every principle proceeding from God is eternal" (*TPJS,* p. 181). The phrase "for time and eternity" is equivalent to "now and forever." LDS thought is uncommon in the Christian world in its affirmation that intelligence, truth, the "principles of element," priesthood, law, covenants, and ordinances are eternal.
6. Time is occasionally used in scripture as a synonym for mortality. In this sense, the time will come when "time shall be no longer" (D&C 84:100; 88:110). The mortal probation will end. But another segment of measurable existence will follow, namely, the Millennium. Time and eternity also function as place names or situations as in such expressions as "not only here but in eter-

nity," or "the visions of eternity" (heaven). Eternal is also the name of God—"endless and eternal is my name"—hence, eternal life is God's life, as it is also everlasting life (*HC* 1:136; cf. D&C 19:10–12; Moses 1:3; 7:35).

The thesis that God is beyond time has sometimes been introduced to account for God's omniscience or foreknowledge. Only if God is somehow transtemporal, it is argued, can he view past, present, and future as "one eternal now." This position is assumed by much postbiblical theology. But, again, this leads to contradiction: What will happen in the infinite future is now happening to God. But "now" and "happening" are temporal words that imply both duration and change. For Latter-day Saints, as for the Bible, God's omniscience is "in time." God anticipates the future. It is "present" before him, but it is still future. When the future occurs, it will occur for the first time to him as to his creatures. The traditional concept of "out-of-time" omniscience does not derive either from the Old or the New Testament but is borrowed from Greek philosophy.

BIBLIOGRAPHY

Kenney, Anthony. "Divine Foreknowledge and Human Freedom." In *Aquinas*, pp. 255–70. Garden City, N.Y., 1967.

Robson, Kent E. "Omnipotence, Omnipresence, and Omniscience in Mormon Theology." In *Line Upon Line: Essays on Mormon Doctrine*, ed G. J. Bergera. Salt Lake City, 1989.

KENT E. ROBSON

TRIALS

Encountering trials, or testing, is one of the purposes of mortality. A key verse of Latter-day Saint understanding is from the Book of Abraham: "And we will prove them herewith, to see if they will do all things whatsoever the Lord their God shall command them" (Abr. 3:25). Although often painful and difficult, trials are an essential and expected part of life and provide experiences necessary for developing Christlike qualities and spiritual strength (Abr. 3:25; D&C 98:12–14; Mosiah 23:21–22).

Abraham's trials provide a prototype for man's dilemma in the world. Early in life he was placed on an altar amidst idol worshippers and delivered by divine intervention (Abr. 1). Later, God commanded him to offer his son Isaac for a burnt offering. Prophets have said that if Abraham's feelings could have been touched more deeply in any other way than by the instruction to offer up his own son (Gen. 22:1–19), that way would have been followed. Modern scripture says that all must eventually be "chastened and tried even as Abraham" (D&C 101:4; 132:37, 51). For Latter-day Saints, trials are not evidence of an indifferent God who allows his children to suffer, but rather evidence of a loving Father who honors the desire of his children to grow (Zech. 13:9; Heb. 12:6; Prov. 3:11–12).

Adversity may be a test of faithfulness and endurance. These tests allow persons to demonstrate to God and to themselves that they will love and trust him "at all hazards" (*TPJS,* p. 150). Ironically, God's love is often felt more closely and abundantly during times of adversity, when prayers are intensified and thoughts are turned to God, than during times of prosperity, when it seems easy to forget the need for divine help. Thus, the Lord has said: "In the day of their peace they esteem lightly my counsel" (D&C 101:8). Prosperity itself can therefore be viewed as a type of trial. Faith grows as one recognizes that, whether or not divine intervention modifies circumstances, God's power may change persons, enabling them to endure well (Mosiah 24:13–15; John 9:1–3). In a very real sense, whatever one's circumstances, life is a trial, a test of faithfulness (Hel. 12:1–3; D&C 101:4; Rom. 5:3–5). Adversity also may generate and perfect attributes of godliness, such as patience, empathy, sacrifice, and compassion.

Like all persons of faith, Latter-day Saints sometimes struggle to reconcile their acceptance of adversity with another important concept: that God has promised to bless and prosper the righteous. Latter-day Saints believe still in this ancient Deuteronomic covenant, renewed in modern times. During times of adversity, often the greatest anguish comes not from dealing with the difficult circumstances, but from introspectively determining whether they came as a result of personal unworthiness. In these situations, adversity can provide the motivation needed to repent (Deut. 11:26–28; 2 Ne. 1:20).

Even with this understanding, faithful Latter-day Saints often find the vicissitudes of life challenging. Nevertheless, they derive great strength and comfort from the teachings and example of Jesus

Christ, and the promise that God will never test them beyond their ability to withstand (1 Cor. 10:13). Jesus' own mortal life was a perfect example of trials well endured. Latter-day Saints believe that Christ suffered every feeling of temptation, pain, sorrow, and despair that anyone has ever felt in the darkest hours of adversity so that he would be able to give comfort (D&C 122:5–8). In addition, they find hope in his assurance that these difficult times are a small moment in the span of eternity with great blessings to follow for those who, without bitterness or despair, prove worthy and endure to the end (D&C 98:3; 121:7–8; 122:5–9; Alma 7:11–13).

BIBLIOGRAPHY
Holland, Jeffrey R. *However Long and Hard the Road.* Salt Lake City, 1985.
Kimball, Spencer W. *Faith Precedes the Miracle,* pp. 95–110. Salt Lake City, 1972.
Madsen, Truman G. "Power from Abrahamic Tests." In *The Highest In Us,* pp. 49–57. Salt Lake City, 1978.
Maxwell, Neal A. *All These Things Shall Give Thee Experience.* Salt Lake City, 1980.
——. *We Will Prove Them Herewith.* Salt Lake City, 1982.

CHRISTIE H. FRANDSEN

TRUTH

The LDS conception of truth does not fit any of the categories in which it has been discussed in the Western philosophical tradition. For Latter-day Saints, truth is found in living the type of life exemplified by JESUS CHRIST.

In the Western philosophical tradition, truth is the characteristic or quality of an idea or statement that justifies belief in it. What this characteristic might be has been the subject of long-standing philosophical debate; some have said it is the correspondence with reality that true statements possess; some, their "tie-in" or coherence with other statements; some, their consequences or practical usefulness. So devastating have been the attacks upon each of these theories that in recent times many philosophers have abandoned altogether the traditional assumption that a firm or absolute kind of truth is possible. These philosophers say that because our knowledge of the world is heavily conditioned by the peculiarities of the particular language in which it is expressed, it is an interpretation at best;

we have no basis for claiming we can ever know "how things really are," they argue, and therefore, whatever truth exists is relative to the speaker's language, culture, and situation. Absolute truth, thought of as a property of ideas or statements, is a concept that has fallen on hard times.

Commonly it is supposed that for Latter-day Saints truth is absolute in a way that makes it vulnerable to the relativist's arguments. But for Latter-day Saints, as their scriptures and everyday discourse reveal, truth is not primarily a matter of the correctness of ideas or statements, and consequently their view is not to be found among the traditional alternatives or any combination of them. Though they do speak of the truth of statements, they most often use the word "truth" to signify an entire way of life—specifically, the way of life exemplified, prescribed, and guided by Jesus Christ.

This conception of truth preserves senses attached to the word from the earliest times of which we have record. For example, central to the original idea of being true was "steadfast . . . adherence to a commander or friend, to a principle or cause, . . . faithful, loyal, constant, trusty," "honest, honourable, upright, virtuous, . . . free from deceit, sincere" ("True," *Oxford English Dictionary*). And among the main original senses of "truth" was "troth"—a pledge or covenant of faithfulness made uprightly and without deceit ("Truth," *OED*). It is in the spirit of these ancient etymologies that Latter-day Saints believe that to walk in truth is to keep one's commitments to follow Christ's way uprightly.

Because Christ perfectly embodies the virtue of being true and faithful (in his case, to the life his Father required of him), there is a crucial sense in which he himself is the truth. "I am the way," he said, "the truth, and the life" (John 14:6). He "received a fulness of truth" (D&C 93:26). His cosmic influence, called "the light of Christ," is also the light of truth, giving life to everything and enlightening human minds. By means of this light, he is "in all and through all things" (D&C 88:6), a permeating presence. Given this sense of the word "truth," it is not odd, as it otherwise would appear, to say, as does a key doctrinal REVELATION, that "truth shineth" (D&C 88:6–13).

Latter-day Saint scriptures indicate that people can come to "know the truth of all things" by the power of the HOLY GHOST (Moro.

10:5). The relevant contexts suggest this means to enjoy that comprehension of things that comes to the person who receives the light of truth and walks obediently in it. "He that keepeth his commandments receiveth truth and light, until he is glorified in truth and knoweth all things" (D&C 93:28). To the brother of Jared, a Book of Mormon figure of extraordinary FAITH, the Lord showed "all the inhabitants of the earth . . . even unto the ends of the earth. For he had said unto him . . . that if he would believe in him that he could show unto him all things" (Ether 3:25–26). Other prophets have had similar experiences (Moses 1:8, 27–29; 7:21; Abr. 3:12).

A certain scriptural definition of "truth" is especially familiar to Latter-day Saints: "Truth is knowledge of things as they are, and as they were, and as they are to come" (D&C 93:24). Taken out of context (as it often is), this definition sounds like a statement of the correspondence theory of truth; but in context it expresses the morally richer idea of the comprehensive vision of reality that comes to those who walk in truth faithfully.

Understood in this way, disobedience and unfaithfulness are rejections of the light of truth. Satan "was a liar from the beginning" (D&C 93:25) and seeks always to "turn . . . hearts away from the truth" (D&C 78:10), partly by enticing people to become liars and deceivers themselves (D&C 10:25). The reason "men [love] darkness rather than light" is "because their deeds [are] evil. For every one that doeth evil hateth the light, neither cometh to the light, lest his deeds should be reproved" (John 3:19–20). It is not for being mistaken that people are damned, but for their resistance to the truth they could receive if they would.

For Latter-day Saints, salvation is a matter of growing in truth and particularly in KNOWLEDGE of the GOSPEL OF JESUS CHRIST. Joseph Smith taught that "a man is saved no faster than he gets knowledge" (*HC* 4:588) and that "it is impossible for a man to be saved in ignorance" (D&C 131:6). In context these statements mean that one cannot be saved in ignorance of the gospel of Jesus Christ. Latter-day Saints who recognize that truth is not merely a property of language but is central to a life of obedience to the Savior do not interpret these passages to mean that the learned—the scholars and scientists—have a better chance of being saved. Gaining knowledge and becoming more godlike are two aspects of a single process, which helps explain the Latter-day Saint emphasis on education and personal scriptural mastery as well as on righteous living.

The prophets of the present dispensation, from Joseph Smith onward, have championed the idea that the Latter-day Saints have no exclusive access to truth. God enlightens people everywhere, and therefore, as Presidents of the Church have all insisted, insofar as other peoples have any principle of truth (and they do), "whether moral, religious, philosophical, or of any other kind, that is calculated to benefit mankind, . . . [we] will embrace it" (John Taylor, *JD* 1:155). However, these same prophets also claim that the truths of the gospel of Jesus Christ that are necessary for salvation have been revealed in modern times exclusively through them.

BIBLIOGRAPHY

Hinckley, Gordon B. "The Continuing Pursuit of Truth." *Ensign* 16 (Apr. 1986):2–6.

Roberts, B. H. *Excerpts from The Truth, the Way, the Life: An Elementary Treatise on Theology.* Provo, Utah, 1985.

Tanner, N. Eldon. "Ye Shall Know the Truth." *Ensign* 8 (May 1978):14–16.

C. TERRY WARNER

U

UNITY

The LDS concept of unity focuses primarily on three doctrinal issues: the nature of the GODHEAD, relations among members of the Church, and the relation between a person and God, although it differs at some points from the tenets of traditional Christianity.

LDS scriptures usually emphasize the separate identities of the members of the Godhead, but sometimes describe them as one. This unity is understood to mean oneness of purpose and testimony—not identity of being. With respect to the Godhead, this means that although God the Father, his son Jesus Christ, and the Holy Ghost are three distinct beings, they are united in purpose. This precept was one of the first to be given to the Prophet Joseph Smith when, in 1820, he beheld both the Father and Son in his first vision (JS—H 1:14–20). In that vision, the Father appeared and bore witness of the Son. LDS scriptures emphasize that the oneness of the Godhead derives partly from the fact that each member of the Godhead bears witness of the others (3 Ne. 11:35–36; 28:10–11; D&C 20:27–28). To the faithful in the New World, Christ taught the same doctrine that he had taught his disciples in the Old World—namely, that the members of the Godhead were one in purpose, glory, joy, and witness, and that this same oneness could be shared with his faithful followers (3 Ne. 19:29; 28:10; cf. John 17:20–22). This LDS understanding is at variance with the traditional concept of a mystical union of the members of the Godhead.

For the members of the Church, "unity" refers to common aspirations, beliefs, and purposes, not to mystical or substantial union. In the Book of Mormon, for example, the Savior explained that to become "one," members must end disputations and CONTENTION (3 Ne. 11:22–28, 36). Latter-day Saints are taught that they must mitigate any condition that undermines unity among members, including significant economic and social distinctions (3 Ne. 6:10–16; 4 Ne. 1:24–35). Unity among members begins with the family (D&C 38:26–27). The concluding words of the Old Testament (Mal. 4:5–6) describe how the earth must prepare for the second coming of the Savior by binding the hearts of the children to the fathers and the hearts of the fathers to the children. In fulfillment of this prophecy and under divine direction, Latter-day Saints perform ordinances in the temples of God that seal parents and children together, not only for the living but also for all those who have ever lived on this earth. The goal is not limited to family unity but includes the unity of all believing and worthy human beings.

Jesus taught that unity among his followers witnesses to the world that he is the Christ (John 17:20–26). Paul exhorts all to become "fellowcitizens with the saints, and of the household of God" (Eph. 2:19) and to "come in the unity of the faith" (Eph. 4:13). Zion refers to the community of believers who, through their unity in Christ, have become "of one heart and one mind" (Moses 7:18). Such unity of faith is achieved through individual obedience to the laws of God and through common dedication to the promotion of faithfulness among all human beings.

The unity of God and human beings refers to the eventual personal reassociation of worthy men and women with God. Entry into mortal life brings about a separation from God, while compliance with the GOSPEL OF JESUS CHRIST enables persons to overcome this separation and return to God through the at-one-ment mediated by Jesus Christ. Latter-day Saints believe that by progressing in knowledge and righteousness, human beings bring their lives into harmony with Christ's and that upon resurrection the body and soul will be inseparably reunited and the exalted person will dwell with God forever.

BIBLIOGRAPHY

Talmage, James E. *AF*, pp. 40–41. Salt Lake City, 1949.

F. NEIL BRADY

W

WORKS

[*God has made provision through the atonement of Jesus Christ for the salvation of the human family. Those things that God does for mankind are called "grace." Those things that people have to do for themselves are called "works." Both are necessary.*

The Lord requires all persons to do all that they can do for themselves to obtain salvation. For instance, James said, "Faith without works is dead" (James 2:26), and John wrote that the dead are judged "according to their works" (Rev. 20:12). Paul emphasized grace, but did not exclude works: "By grace are ye saved through faith; and that not of yourselves: it is the gift of God: not of works, lest any man should boast. For we are his workmanship, created in Christ Jesus unto good works, which God hath before ordained that we should walk in them" (Eph. 2:8–10). Also, "as ye have always obeyed, . . . work out your own salvation with fear and trembling" (Philip. 2:12). Likewise, Nephi$_1$ *wrote, "We know that it is by grace that we are saved, after all we can do" (2 Ne. 25:23).*

Latter-day Saint doctrine teaches that works alone can never bring salvation, but good works accompany both faith and grace. Articles pertaining to this topic are Atonement; Commandments; Enduring to the End; Grace; Judgment Day, Final; Justification; Obedience; Righteousness; Salvation.]

WORLDS

Latter-day Saint prophets and scripture teach that other worlds similar to this earth have been and will be created and inhabited in fulfillment of God's eternal designs for his children. As explained in REVELATIONS to the Prophet Joseph Smith, God has in operation a vast plan for the eternal progress of his children. In a vision given to Moses, the Lord said, "Worlds without number have I created; and I also created them for mine own purpose, . . . there are many (worlds) that now stand, and innumerable are they unto man" (Moses 1:33, 35). This same many-worlds view is echoed in other scriptures (see Heb. 1:2; D&C 76:24; Moses 7:30; Abr. 3:12).

Joseph Smith's version of pluralism shared some similarities with ideas of his religious contemporaries and of modern science. But the pluralistic cosmology that emerged from his revelations and the interpretations of the early generation of LDS leaders taught by him were distinctive. Unlike other religious pluralists, Joseph Smith evidenced no interest in using pluralism for proselytizing purposes, but only to unfold a fuller understanding of God's purposes for people in this life and in the hereafter. The full and coherent picture painted in these Mormon teachings is not plausibly derived from any contemporary view, but is generally compatible with ancient cosmologies, and particularly with ideas attributed anciently to Enoch (Crowe, pp. 245–46; Paul, pp. 27–32; see also *CWHN* 1:180–88; 2:236–40).

Like contemporary pluralists, Joseph Smith's system implied innumerable stellar systems with inhabited planets. In addition (see Paul, p. 28), Joseph taught that old physical worlds pass away while new ones are being formed (Moses 1:35, 38); worlds are governed hierarchically (Abr. 3:8–9); each system of worlds has its own laws (D&C 88:36–38); Jesus Christ is the creator of all these worlds (D&C 76:24; 93:9–10); people assigned to different levels of glory inhabit different worlds (D&C 76:112); the earth has been the most wicked of all worlds (Moses 7:36); resurrected beings also reside on worlds (D&C 88:36–38); and these other worlds exist in both time and space (Moses 1:35, 38; D&C 88:36–38, 42–47; 93:9–10).

Mormons therefore accept the existence of other worlds created by God for a divine purpose that is the same as the PURPOSE OF EARTH LIFE—"to bring to pass the immortality and eternal life" of God's children (Moses 1:39). The inhabitants of these other planets are understood by Latter-day Saints to be children of God and created in his image, though they might differ from the earth's inhabitants in unspecified ways (Moses 1:33; D&C 76:24). The means of SALVATION through the GOSPEL OF JESUS CHRIST is the same for all of God's creations. Creation is continual and expansive and is directed toward the eternal happiness of all intelligent beings, for the Lord told Moses, "As one earth shall pass away, and the heavens thereof even so shall another come; and there is no end to my works, neither to my words" (Moses 1:38). For Latter-day Saints the gospel of Jesus Christ has universal validity, in both time and space. God's PLAN OF SALVATION operates on a universal scale. Latter-day Saints believe that there are now countless planets whose inhabitants—children of God—are progressing, as are human beings on this earth, according to eternal principles towards a Godlike life.

BIBLIOGRAPHY

Crowe, Michael J. *The Extraterrestrial Life Debate 1750–1900: The Idea of a Plurality of Worlds from Kant to Lowell.* Cambridge, Eng., 1986.

Johnson, H. R. "Civilizations Out in Space." *BYU Studies* 11 (Autumn 1971):3–12.

Paul, Robert. "Joseph Smith and the Plurality of Worlds Idea." *Dialogue* 19 (Summer 1986):13–36.

HOLLIS R. JOHNSON

WORSHIP

Latter-day Saint worship is defined as coming unto the Father in the name of Jesus Christ, in spirit and truth (D&C 93:19; cf. JST John 4:24). All of life may be worshipful, as manifest in prayer and in devotion, in the ordinances of the gospel, including the sacrament, in selfless service to mankind, and in the culmination of all worship in the temples of God.

The Lord spoke to the Prophet Joseph Smith, "I give unto you these sayings that you may understand and know how to worship, and know what you worship, that you may come unto the Father in my name, and in due time receive of his fulness" (D&C 93:19). Worship is idolatry unless it is reverent homage and devotion to the living God.

A modern revelation warns against the worship of false gods: "They seek not the Lord to establish his righteousness, but every man walketh in his own way, and after the image of his own God, whose image is in the likeness of the world, and whose substance is that of an idol" (D&C 1:16). Modern prophets have counseled Latter-day Saints against the worship of idols under new names: success, money, prestige, lavish pleasure, fashion (see Kimball, p. 4).

Much traditional religion assumes that only if God is "utterly other," that is, mysterious and unknowable, can he be properly reverenced. For Latter-day Saints, the foundation of worship is not the radical contrast but the intimate kinship of the Father and his children. Christ was near unto God because he was "the brightness of his glory and the express image of his person" (Heb. 1:2). By keeping his commandments and walking in the way of his ordinances, every person walks in the path of the Master. In inspired worship, "truth embraceth truth; virtue loveth virtue; light cleaveth unto light; mercy hath compassion on mercy" (D&C 88:40). The outcome for Christ was that he could pray, "as thou, Father, art in Me, and I in thee" (John 17:21). Beyond this, worship cannot reach.

The restoration of Christ's Church began with the lament from on high, "They draw near to me with their lips but their hearts are far from me" (JS—H 1:19). Worship involves the heart and the whole of man. Unified worship—which occurs when those assembled are of one heart and one mind and are "agreed as touching all things whatsoever ye ask of me" (D&C 27:18)—prevails with the heavens. "By union of feeling, we obtain power with God" (Relief Society Minutes, June 9, 1842, Church Archives; cf. *TPJS*, P. 91).

Worship also involves the mind. "Love the Lord thy God with all thy . . . mind" (Matt. 22:37). The living God has a "fulness of truth," is "glorified in truth and knoweth all things," and is "more intelligent than they all" (D&C 93; Abr. 2, 3). As Elder B. H. Roberts wrote, worship is the soul's surrender to God: "This submission of the mind to the Most Intelligent, Wisest—wiser than all—is worship" (*TPJS*, p. 353, n). Thus, daily prayer and study, penetrating, pondering study of the gospel and the scriptures, are commended to all Latter-day Saints. "It is not wisdom," said Joseph Smith, "that we should have all knowledge at once presented before us; but that we should have a little at a time; then we can comprehend it" (*TPJS*, p. 297). Jacob

Neusner has compared this linkage of worship with the mind to Jewish study-worship of the Torah (Neusner, p. 55). Such communion with God leads one through and beyond the written and the spoken word to the source of Light.

WORSHIP AND SERVICE. For Latter-day Saints, the life of consecrated labor surpasses the life of withdrawal. Thus, although proper worship may require fasting, self-denial, discipline, and sacrifice, the religious life is in the context of the natural and social life. Daily labor is the fulcrum of religion and the locus of holiness. One may bring the spirit of worship to every aspect of life and community life, of which the dedicated family is the apex and paradigm. Nothing is so menial, so servile, so trivial that it is irreligious, as long as it is the way of duty and as long as it is done "in the name of the Son." "Thou shalt love the Lord thy God with all thy heart, with all thy might, mind, and strength; and in the name of Jesus Christ thou shalt serve him" (D&C 59:5).

WORSHIP AND THE TEMPLE The Hebrew verb *la-avodh,* "to worship," also means "to work" and "to serve" and is associated with the temple. Early in Church history, "the house [Kirtland Temple] was constructed to suit and accommodate the different orders of priesthood and *worship peculiar to the Church*" (John Corrill, *A Brief History of the Church of Christ of Latter Day Saints,* 1839, p. 22, italics added), and it has been so with all LDS temples since. The Spirit of the Lord and the descent of his glory are promised the Saints in the House of the Lord, which is defined as a "house of fasting and a house of prayer" and a "house of worship" (D&C 88:119; *HC* 4:205). Anciently, the temple was the locus of feast and provided the joy of sacred place (Hebrew *simha makom*). An Aramaic link of the Hebrew word for joy (*hdw*) connotes both inner and outer joy and relates to temple service. Today, in LDS spiritual life, the temple is a place of the most "solemn assemblies" and the administration of ordinances on behalf of the living and the dead. Within the precincts of the temple, one experiences this shared joy in its most complete form. In Judaism after the destruction of the temple in Jerusalem in A.D. 70, the home became the surrogate temple, the table an altar, and the study of the Torah, especially on Shabbat, the focus of worship and rejoicing. Worship was centered in prayer and sacrificial service. In Christendom the sacraments and private devotion were thought to replace the temple. In the LDS experience, all these forms of worship are regained, renewed, and confirmed in the temples.

In their modern history, Latter-day Saints have worshiped in sobriety and solemnity as well as with rejoicing and gladness. And they have also worshiped in the midst of affliction. Modern revelation commends worship "with a glad heart and a cheerful countenance," especially in the midst of "fasting and prayer," which is defined as "rejoicing and prayer" (D&C 59:14). Thus, on the Eve of their exile from Nauvoo, the Saints assembled in the Nauvoo Temple and prayed, feasted, sang, and danced in rejoicing. They crossed the river in the dead of winter, but still were admonished, "If thou art merry, praise the Lord with singing, with music, with dancing, and with a prayer of praise and thanksgiving. If thou art sorrowful, call on the Lord thy God with supplication, that your souls may be joyful" (D&C 136:28–29). They were not too exhausted after the day's travel to build a fire and share songs of the heart, testimonies, and spiritual gifts. In the same spirit, a century and a half later, amidst the Teton Dam disaster (1975), the Latter-day Saints were counseled by their leaders to end each day by bringing out the violins and rejoicing, acknowledging the hand of the Lord in all things (*Ensign* 6 [Oct. 1976]:95; cf. D&C 59:21).

"The song of the righteous is a prayer unto me, and it shall be answered with a blessing upon their heads" (D&C 25:12). In the last days, it has been prophesied, "all shall know me who remain, even from the least unto the greatest, and shall be filled with the knowledge of the Lord, and shall see eye to eye, and shall lift up their voice, and with the voice together sing this new song, saying:

> The Lord hath brought again Zion;
> The Lord hath redeemed his people, Israel,
> According to the election of grace,
> Which was brought to pass by the faith
> And covenant of their fathers.
> The Lord hath redeemed his people;
> And Satan is bound and time is no longer.
> The Lord hath gathered all things in one.
> The Lord hath brought down Zion from above.
> The Lord hath brought up Zion from beneath.

The earth hath travailed and brought forth her strength;
And truth is established in her bowels;
And the heavens have smiled upon her;
And she is clothed with the glory of her God;
For he stands in the midst of his people.
Glory, and honor, and power, and might,
Be ascribed to our God; for he is full of mercy,
Justice, grace and truth, and peace,
Forever and ever, Amen [D&C 84:98–102].

When Zion is finally established in the last days, "all who build thereon are to worship the true and living God" (*TPJS,* p. 80). Each year people from many lands will come up to worship at the Feast of Tabernacles in Jerusalem. Eventually, "all nations whom thou hast made shall come and worship before thee, O Lord; and shall glorify thy name" (Ps. 86:9).

BIBLIOGRAPHY

Hatch, Verena U. *Worship in the Church of Jesus Christ of Latter-day Saints.* Provo, Utah, 1968.

Heidenreich, John. "An Analysis of the Theory and Practice of Worship in The Church of Jesus Christ of Latter-day Saints." Master's thesis, Brigham Young University, 1963.

Kimball, Spencer W. "The False Gods We Worship." *Ensign* 6 (June 1976):3–6.

Neusner, Jacob. *The Glory of God Is Intelligence.* Salt Lake City, 1978.

JOHANN A. WONDRA

APPENDIX

Doctrinal Expositions of the First Presidency

From time to time the First Presidency (sometimes accompanied by the Council of the Twelve Apostles) has issued official clarifications and pronouncements on doctrinal themes. Three such documents are included here. The first two are on the same subject: the first was published in 1909 and is titled "The Origin of Man," the second is dated 1925 and is titled "'Mormon' View of Evolution." The third document was published in June 1916 and is titled "The Father and the Son," being a detailed statement of the distinctive roles of God the Father and of his Son Jesus Christ.

THE ORIGIN OF MAN

By The First Presidency of the Church
"God created man in his own image."

Inquiries arise from time to time respecting the attitude of the Church of Jesus Christ of Latter-day Saints upon questions which, though not vital from a doctrinal standpoint, are closely connected with the fundamental principles of salvation. The latest inquiry of this kind that has reached us is in relation to the origin of man. It is believed that a statement of the position held by the Church upon this important subject will be timely and productive of good.

In presenting the statement that follows we are not conscious of putting forth anything essentially new; neither is it our desire so to do. Truth is what we wish to present, and truth—eternal truth—is fundamentally old. A restatement of the original attitude of the Church relative to this matter is all that will be attempted here. To tell the truth as God has revealed it, and commend it to the acceptance of those who need to conform their opinions thereto, is the sole purpose of this presentation.

"God created man in his own image, in the image of God created he him; male and female created he them." In these plain and pointed words the inspired author of the book of Genesis made known to the world the truth concerning the origin of the human family. Moses, the prophet-historian, "learned," as we are told, "in all the wisdom of the Egyptians," when making this important announcement, was not voicing a mere opinion, a theory derived from his researches into the occult lore of that ancient people. He was speaking as the mouthpiece of God, and his solemn declaration was for all time and for all people. No subsequent revelator of the truth has contradicted the great leader and lawgiver of Israel. All who have since spoken by divine authority upon this theme have confirmed his simple and sublime proclamation. Nor could it be otherwise. Truth has but one source, and all revelations from heaven are harmonious with each other. The omnipotent Creator, the maker of heaven and earth—had shown unto Moses everything pertaining to this planet, including the facts relating to man's origin, and the authoritative pronouncement of that mighty prophet and seer to the house of Israel, and through Israel to the whole world, is couched in the simple clause: "God created man in his own image" (Genesis 1:27; Pearl of Great Price—Book of Moses, 1:27–41).

The creation was two-fold—firstly spiritual, secondly temporal. This truth, also, Moses plainly taught—much more plainly than it has come down to us in the imperfect translations of the Bible that are now in use. Therein the fact of a spiritual creation, antedating the temporal creation, is strongly implied, but the proof of it is not so clear and conclusive as in other records held by the Latter-day Saints to be of equal authority with the Jewish scriptures. The partial obscurity of the latter upon the point in question is owing, no doubt, to the loss of those "plain and precious" parts of sacred writ, which, as the Book of Mormon informs us, have been taken away from the Bible during its passage down the centuries (1 Nephi 13:24–29). Some of these missing parts the Prophet Joseph Smith undertook to restore when he revised those scriptures by the spirit of revelation, the result being that more complete account of the creation which is found in the Book of Moses, previously cited. Note the following passages:

And now, behold, I say unto you, that these are the generations of the heaven and of the earth, when they were created, in the day that I, the Lord God, made the heaven and the earth;

And every plant of the field before it was in the earth, and every herb of the field before it grew.

For I, the Lord God, created all things of which I have spoken, spiritually, before they were naturally upon the face of the earth. For I, the Lord God, had not caused it to rain upon the face of the earth.

And I, the Lord God, had created all the children of men, and not yet a man to till the ground; for in heaven created I them, and there was not yet flesh upon the earth, neither in the water, neither in the air.

But, I, the Lord God, spake, and there went up a mist from the earth, and watered the whole face of the ground.

And I, the Lord God, formed man from the dust of the ground, and breathed into his nostrils the breath of life; and man became a living soul, the first flesh upon the earth, the first man also.

Nevertheless, all things were before created, but spiritually were they created and made, according to my word (Pearl of Great Price—Book of Moses, 3:4–7. See also chapters 1 and 2, and compare with Genesis 1 and 2).

These two points being established, namely, the creation of man in the image of God, and the two-fold character of the creation, let us now inquire: What was the form of man, in the spirit and in the body, as originally created? In a general way the answer is given in the words chosen as the text of this treatise. "God created man in his own image." It is more explicitly rendered in the Book of Mormon thus: "All men were created in the beginning after mine own image" (Ether 3:15). It is the Father who is speaking. If, therefore, we can ascertain the form of the "Father of spirits," "The God of the spirits of all flesh," we shall be able to discover the form of the original man.

Jesus Christ, the Son of God, is "the express image" of His Father's person (Hebrews 1:3). He walked the earth as a human being, as a perfect man, and said, in answer to a question put to Him: "He that hath seen me hath seen the Father" (John 14:9). This alone ought to solve the problem to the satisfaction of every thoughtful, reverent mind. The conclusion is irresistible, that if the Son of God be the express image (that is, likeness) of His Father's person, then His Father is in the form of a man; for that was the form of the Son of God, not only during His mortal life, but before His mortal birth, and after

His resurrection. It was in this form that the Father and the Son, as two personages, appeared to Joseph Smith, when, as a boy of fourteen years, he received his first vision. Then if God made man—the first man—in His own image and likeness, he must have made him like unto Christ, and consequently like unto men of Christ's time and of the present day. That man was made in the image of Christ is positively stated in the Book of Moses: "And I, God, said unto mine Only Begotten, which was with me from the beginning, Let us make man in our image, after our likeness; and it was so. . . . And I, God, created man in mine own image, in the image of mine Only Begotten created I him, male and female created I them" (2:26, 27).

The Father of Jesus is our Father also. Jesus Himself taught this truth, when He instructed His disciples how to pray: "Our Father which art in heaven," etc. Jesus, however, is the firstborn among all the sons of God—the first begotten in the spirit, and the only begotten in the flesh. He is our elder brother, and we, like Him, are in the image of God. All men and women are in the similitude of the universal Father and Mother, and are literally the sons and daughters of Deity.

"God created man in His own image." This is just as true of the spirit as it is of the body, which is only the clothing of the spirit, its complement; the two together constituting the soul. The spirit of man is in the form of man, and the spirits of all creatures are in the likeness of their bodies. This was plainly taught by the Prophet Joseph Smith (Doctrine and Covenants 77:2).

Here is further evidence of the fact. More than seven hundred years before Moses was shown the things pertaining to this earth, another great prophet, known to us as the brother of Jared, was similarly favored by the Lord. He was even permitted to behold the spirit-body of the foreordained Savior, prior to His incarnation; and so like the body of a man was gazing upon a being of flesh and blood. He first saw the finger and then the entire body of the Lord—all in the spirit. The Book of Mormon says of this wonderful manifestation:

And it came to pass that when the brother of Jared had said these words, behold the Lord stretched forth His hand and touched the stones one by one with His finger; and the veil was taken from off the eyes of the brother of Jared, and he saw the finger of the Lord; and it was as the finger of a man, like unto flesh and blood; and the brother of Jared fell down before the Lord, for he was struck with fear.

And the Lord saw that the brother of Jared had fallen to the earth; and the Lord said unto him, Arise, why hast thou fallen?

And he saith unto the Lord, I saw the finger of the Lord, and I feared lest he should smite me; for I knew not that the Lord had flesh and blood.

And the Lord said unto him, Because of thy faith thou hast seen that I shall take upon me flesh and blood; and never has man come before me with such exceeding faith as thou hast; for were it not so, ye could not have seen my finger. Sawest thou more than this?

And he answered, Nay, Lord, show thyself unto me.

And the Lord said unto him, Believest thou the words which I shall speak?

And he answered, Yea, Lord, I know that thou speakest the truth, for thou art a God of truth and canst not lie.

And when he had said these words, behold, the Lord showed himself unto him, and said, Because thou knowest these things ye are redeemed from the fall; therefore ye are brought back into my presence; therefore I show myself unto you.

Behold, I am He who was prepared from the foundation of the world to redeem my people. Behold, I am Jesus Christ, I am the Father and the Son. In me shall all mankind have light, and that eternally, even they who shall believe on my name; and they shall become my sons and my daughters.

And never have I shewed myself unto man whom I have created, for never hath man believed in me as thou hast. Seest thou that ye are created after mine own image? Yea, even all men were created in the beginning after mine own image.

Behold, this body, which ye now behold, is the body of my spirit, and man have I created after the body of my spirit; and even as I appear unto thee to be in the spirit, will I appear unto my people in the flesh. (Ether 3:6–16.)

What more is needed to convince us that man, both in spirit and in body, is the image and likeness of God, and that God Himself is in the form of man?

When the divine Being whose spirit-body the brother of Jared beheld, took upon Him flesh and blood, He appeared as a man, having "body, parts and passions," like other men, though vastly superior to all others, because He was God, even the Son of God, the Word made flesh: in Him "dwelt the fulness of the Godhead bodily." And why should He not appear as a man? That was the form of His spirit, and it must needs have an appropriate covering, a suitable tabernacle. He came unto the world as He had promised to come (III Nephi 1:13), taking an infant tabernacle, and developing it gradually to the fulness of His spirit stature. He came as man had been coming for ages, and as man has continued to come ever since. Jesus, however, as shown, was the only begotten of God in the flesh.

Adam, our progenitor, "the first man," was, like Christ, a pre-existent spirit, and like Christ he took upon him an appropriate body, the body of a man, and so became a "living soul." The doctrine of the pre-existence, —revealed so plainly, particularly in latter days, pours a wonderful flood of light upon the otherwise mysterious problem of man's origin. It shows that man, as a spirit, was begotten and born of heavenly parents, and reared to maturity in the eternal mansions of the Father, prior to coming upon the earth in a temporal body to undergo an experience in mortality. It teaches that all men existed in the spirit before any man existed in the flesh, and that all who have inhabited the earth since Adam have taken bodies and become souls in like manner.

It is held by some that Adam was not the first man upon this earth, and that the original human being was a development from lower orders of the animal creation. These, however, are the theories of men. The word of the Lord declares that Adam was "the first man of all men" (Moses 1:34), and we are therefore in duty bound to regard him as the primal parent of our race. It was shown to the brother of Jared that all men were created in the *beginning* after the image of God; and whether we take this to mean the spirit or the body, or both, it commits us to the same conclusion: Man began life as a human being, in the likeness of our heavenly Father.

True it is that the body of man enters upon its career as a tiny germ embryo, which becomes an infant, quickened at a certain stage by the spirit whose tabernacle it is, and the child, after being born, develops into a man. There is nothing in this, however, to indicate that the original man, the first of our race, began life as anything less than a man, or less than the human germ or embryo that becomes a man.

Man, by searching, cannot find out God. Never, unaided, will he discover the truth about the beginning of human life. The Lord must reveal Himself, or remain unrevealed; and the same is true of the facts relating to the origin of Adam's race—God alone can reveal them. Some of these facts, however, are already known, and what has been made known it is our duty to receive and retain.

The Church of Jesus Christ of Latter-day Saints, basing its belief on divine revelation, ancient and modern, proclaims man to be the direct and lineal offspring of Deity. God Himself is an exalted man, perfected, enthroned, and supreme. By His almighty power He organized the earth, and all that it contains, from spirit and element, which exist co-eternally with Himself. He formed every plant that grows, and every animal that breathes, each after its own kind, spiritually and temporally—"that which is spiritual being in the likeness of that which is temporal, and that which is temporal in the likeness of that which is spiritual." He made the tadpole and the ape, the lion and the elephant but He did not make them in His own image, nor endow them with Godlike reason and intelligence. Nevertheless, the whole animal creation will be perfected and perpetuated in the Hereafter, each class in its "distinct order or sphere," and will enjoy "eternal felicity." That fact has been made plain in this dispensation (Doctrine and Covenants 77:3).

Man is the child of God, formed in the divine image and endowed with divine attributes, and even as the infant son of an earthly father and mother is capable in due time of becoming a man, so the undeveloped offspring of celestial parentage is capable, by experience through ages and aeons, of evolving into a God.

JOSEPH F. SMITH,
JOHN R. WINDER,
ANTHON H. LUND,
First Presidency of The Church of Jesus Christ
of Latter-day Saints

"MORMON" VIEW OF EVOLUTION

A Statement by the First Presidency of
The Church of Jesus Christ of Latter-day Saints

"God created man in his own image, in the image of God created he him; male and female created he them."

In these plain and pointed words the inspired author of the book of Genesis made known to the world the truth concerning the origin of the human family. Moses, the prophet-historian, who was "learned" we are told, "in all the wisdom of the Egyptians," when making this important announcement, was not voicing a mere opinion. He was speaking as the mouthpiece of God, and his solemn declaration was for all time and for all people. No subsequent revelator of the truth has contradicted the great leader and law-giver of Israel. All who have since spoken by divine authority upon this theme have confirmed his simple and sublime proclamation. Nor could it be otherwise. Truth has but one source, and all revelations from heaven are harmonious one with the other.

Jesus Christ, the Son of God, is "the express image" of his Father's person (Hebrews 1:3). He walked the earth as a human being, as a perfect man, and said, in answer to a question put to him: "He that hath seen me hath seen the Father" (John 14:9). This alone ought to solve the problem to the satisfaction of every thoughtful, reverent mind. It was in this form that the Father and the Son, as two distinct personages, appeared to Joseph Smith, when, as a boy of fourteen years, he received his first vision.

The Father of Jesus Christ is our Father also. Jesus himself taught this truth, when he instructed his disciples how to pray: "Our Father which art in heaven," etc. Jesus, however, is the first born among all the sons of God—the first begotten in the spirit, and the only begotten in the flesh. He is our elder brother, and we, like him, are in the image of God. All men and women are in the similitude of the universal Father and Mother, and are literally sons and daughters of Deity.

Adam, our great progenitor, "the first man," was, like Christ, a pre-existent spirit, and, like Christ, he took upon him an appropriate body, the body of a man, and so became a "living soul." The doctrine of pre-existence pours a wonderful flood of light upon the otherwise mysterious problem of man's origin. It shows that man, as a spirit, was begotten and born of heavenly parents, and reared to maturity in the eternal mansions of the Father, prior to coming upon the earth in a temporal body to undergo an experience in mortality.

The Church of Jesus Christ of Latter-day Saints, basing its belief on divine revelation, ancient and modern, proclaims man to be the direct and lineal offspring of Deity. By his Almighty power God organized the earth, and all that it contains, from spirit and element, which exist co-eternally with himself.

Man is the child of God, formed in the divine image and endowed with divine attributes, and even as the infant son of an earthly father and mother is capable in due time of becoming a man, so that undeveloped offspring of celestial parentage is capable, by experience through ages and aeons, of evolving into a God.

HEBER J. GRANT
ANTHONY W. IVINS
CHARLES W. NIBLEY
First Presidency

THE FATHER AND THE SON: A DOCTRINAL EXPOSITION BY THE FIRST PRESIDENCY AND THE TWELVE

The scriptures plainly and repeatedly affirm that God is the Creator of the earth and the heavens and all things that in them are. In the sense so expressed the Creator is an Organizer. God created the earth as an organized sphere; but He certainly did not create, in the sense of bringing into primal existence, the ultimate elements of the materials of which the earth consists, for "the elements are eternal" (D&C 93:33).

So also life is eternal, and not created; but life, or the vital force, may be infused into organized matter, though the details of the process have not been revealed unto man. For illustrative instances see Genesis 2:7; Moses 3:7; and Abraham 5:7. Each of these scriptures states that God breathed into the body of man the breath of life. See further Moses 3:19, for the statement that God breathed the breath of life into the bodies of the beasts and birds. God showed unto Abraham "the intelligences that were organized before the world was"; and by "intelligences" we are to understand personal "spirits" (Abraham 3:22, 23); nevertheless, we are expressly told that "Intelligence" that is, "the light of truth was not created or made, neither indeed can be" (D&C 93:29).

The term "Father" as applied to Deity occurs in sacred writ with plainly different meanings. Each of the four significations specified in the following treatment should be carefully segregated.

1. "Father" as Literal Parent

Scriptures embodying the ordinary signification—literally that of Parent—are too numerous and specific to require citation. The purport of these scriptures is to the effect that God the Eternal Father, whom we designate by the exalted name-title "Elohim," is the literal Parent of our Lord and Savior Jesus Christ, and of the spirits of the human race. Elohim is the Father in every sense in which Jesus Christ is so designated, and distinctively He is the Father of spirits. Thus we read in the Epistle to the Hebrews: "Furthermore we have had fathers of our flesh which corrected us, and we gave them reverence; shall we not much rather be in subjection unto the Father of spirits, and live?" (Hebrews 12:9). In view of this fact we are taught by Jesus Christ to pray: "Our Father which art in heaven, Hallowed be thy name."

Jesus Christ applies to Himself both titles, "Son" and "Father." Indeed, he specifically said to the brother of Jared: "Behold, I am Jesus Christ. I am the Father and the Son" (Ether 3:14). Jesus Christ is the Son of Elohim both as spiritual and bodily offspring; that is to say, Elohim is literally the Father of the spirit of Jesus Christ and also of the body in which Jesus Christ performed His mission in the flesh, and which body died on the cross and was afterward taken up by the process of resurrection, and is now the immortalized tabernacle of the eternal spirit of our Lord and Savior. No extended explanation of the title "Son of God" as applied to Jesus Christ appears necessary.

2. "Father" as Creator

A second scriptural meaning of "Father" is that of Creator, e.g., in passages referring to any one of the Godhead as "The Father of the heavens and of the earth and all things that in them are" (Ether 4:7; see also Alma 11:38, 39 and Mosiah 15:4).

God is not the Father of the earth as one of the worlds in space, nor of the heavenly bodies in whole or in part, nor of the inanimate objects and the plants and the animals upon the earth, in the literal sense in which He is the Father of the spirits of mankind. Therefore, scriptures that refer to God in any way as the Father of the heavens and the earth are to be understood as signifying that God is the Maker, the Organizer, the Creator of the heavens and the earth.

With this meaning, as the context shows in every case, Jehovah, who is Jesus Christ the Son of Elohim, is called "the Father," and even "the very eternal Father of heaven and of earth" (see passages before cited, and also Mosiah 16:15). With analogous meaning Jesus Christ is called "The Everlasting Father" (Isaiah 9:6; compare 2 Nephi 19:6). The descriptive titles "Everlasting" and "Eternal" in the foregoing texts are synonymous.

That Jesus Christ, whom we also know as Jehovah, was the executive of the Father, Elohim, in the work of creation is set forth in the book "Jesus the Christ" chapter 4. Jesus Christ, being the Creator, is consistently called the Father of heaven and earth in the sense explained above; and since His creations are of eternal quality He is very properly called the Eternal Father of heaven and earth.

3. Jesus Christ the "Father" of Those Who Abide in His Gospel

A third sense in which Jesus Christ is regarded as the "Father" has reference to the relationship between Him and those who accept His Gospel and thereby become heirs of eternal life. Following are a few of the scriptures illustrating this meaning.

In the fervent prayer offered just prior to His entrance into Gethsemane, Jesus Christ supplicated His Father in behalf of those whom the Father had given unto Him, specifically the apostles, and, more generally, all who would accept and abide in the Gospel through the ministry of the apostles. Read in the Lord's own words the solemn affirmation that those for whom He particularly prayed were His own, and that His Father had given them unto Him: "I have manifested thy name unto the men which thou gavest me out of the world: thine they were, and thou gavest them me; and they have kept thy word. Now they have known that all things whatsoever thou hast given me are of thee. For I have given unto them the words which thou gavest me; and they have received them, and have known surely that I came out from thee, and they have believed that thou didst send me. I pray for them: I pray not for the world, but for them which thou hast given me; for they are thine. And all mine are thine, and thine are mine; and I am glorified in them. And now I am no more in the world, but these are in the world, and I come to thee. Holy Father, keep through thine own name those whom thou hast given me, that they may be one as we are. While I was with them in the world, I kept them in thy name: those that thou gavest me I have kept, and none of them is lost, but the son of perdition; that the scripture might be fulfilled" (John 17:6–12).

And further: "Neither pray I for these alone, but for them also which shall believe on me through their word; That they all may be one; as thou, Father, art in me, and I in thee, that they also may be one in us: that the world may believe that thou hast sent me. And the glory which thou gavest me I have given them; that they may be one, even as we are one: I in them, and thou in me, that they may be made perfect in one; and that the world may know that thou hast sent me, and hast loved them, as thou hast loved me. Father, I will that they also, whom thou hast given me, be with me where I am; that they may behold my glory, which thou hast given me: for thou lovedst me before the foundation of the world" (John 17:20–24).

To His faithful servants in the present dispensation the Lord has said: "Fear not, little children; for you are mine, and I have overcome the world, and you are of them that my Father hath given me" (D&C 50:41).

Salvation is attainable only through compliance with the laws and ordinances of the Gospel; and all who are thus saved become sons and daughters unto God in a distinctive sense. In a revelation given through Joseph the Prophet to Emma Smith the Lord Jesus addressed the woman as "My daughter," and said: "for verily I say unto you, all those who receive my gospel are sons and daughters in my kingdom" (D&C 25:1). In many instances the Lord has addressed men as His sons (e.g. D&C 9:1; 34:3; 121:7).

That by obedience to the Gospel men may become sons of God, both as sons of Jesus Christ, and, through Him, as sons of His Father, is set forth in many revelations given in the current dispensation. Thus we read in an utterance of the Lord Jesus Christ to Hyrum Smith in 1829: "Behold, I am Jesus Christ, the Son of God. I am the life and light of the world. I am the same who came unto mine own and mine own received me not; but verily, verily, I say unto you, that as many as receive me, to them will I give power to become the sons of God, even to them that believe on my name. Amen" (D&C 11:28–30). To Orson Pratt the Lord spoke through Joseph the Seer, in 1830: "My son Orson, hearken and hear and behold what I, the Lord God, shall say unto you, even Jesus Christ your Redeemer; the light and the life of the world; a light which shineth in darkness and the darkness comprehendeth it not; who so loved the world that he gave his own life, that as many as would believe might become the sons of God: wherefore you are my son" (D&C 34:1–3). In 1830 the Lord thus addressed Joseph Smith and Sidney Rigdon: "Listen to the voice of the Lord your God, even Alpha and Omega, the beginning and the end, whose course is one eternal round, the same today as yesterday, and forever. I am Jesus Christ, the Son of God, who was crucified for the sins of the world, even as many as will believe on my name, that they may become the sons of God, even one in me as I am one in the Father, as the Father is one in me, that we may be one" (D&C 35:1–2). Consider also the following given in 1831: "Hearken and listen to the voice of him who is from all eternity to all eternity, the Great I am, even Jesus Christ, the light and the life of the world; a light which shineth in darkness and the darkness comprehendeth it not: the same which came in the meridian of time unto mine own, and mine own received me not; but to as many as received me, gave I power to become my sons, and even so will I give unto as many as will receive me, power to become my sons" (D&C 39:1–4). In a revelation given through Joseph Smith in March, 1831, we read: "For verily I say unto you that I am Alpha and Omega, the beginning and the end, the light and the life of the world—a light that shineth in darkness and the darkness comprehendeth it not. I came unto mine own, and mine own received me not; but unto as many as received me, gave I power to do many miracles, and to become the sons of God, and even unto them that believed on my name gave I power to obtain eternal life" (D&C 45:7–8).

A forceful exposition of this relationship between Jesus Christ as the Father and those who comply with the requirements of the Gospel as His children was given by Abinadi, centuries before our Lord's birth in the flesh: "And now I say unto you. Who shall declare his generation? Behold, I say unto you, that when his soul has been made an offering for sin, he shall see his seed. And now what say ye? And who shall be his seed? Behold I say unto you, that whosoever has heard the words of the prophets, yea, all the holy prophets who have prophesied concerning the coming of the Lord; I say unto you, that all those who have hearkened unto their words, and believed that the Lord would redeem his people, and have looked forward to that day for a remission of their sins; I say unto you, that these are his seed, or they are the heirs of the kingdom of God: for these are they whose sins he has borne; these are they for whom he has died to redeem them from their transgressions. And now, are they not his seed? Yea, and are not the prophets, every one that has opened his mouth to prophesy, that has not fallen into transgression; I mean all the holy prophets ever since the world began? I say unto you that they are his seed" (Mosiah 15:10–13).

In tragic contrast with the blessed state of those who become children of God through obedience to the Gospel of Jesus Christ is that of the unregenerate, who are specifically called the children of the devil. Note the words of Christ, while in the flesh, to certain wicked Jews who boasted of their Abrahamic lineage: "If ye were Abraham's children, ye would do the works of Abraham. . . . Ye do the deeds of your father. . . . If God were your Father, ye would love me. . . . Ye are of your father the devil, and the lusts of your father ye will do" (John 8:39, 41, 42, 44). Thus Satan is designated as the father of the wicked, though we cannot assume any personal relationship of parent and children as existing between him and them. A combined illustration showing that the righteous are the children of God and the wicked the children of the devil appears in the parable of the Tares: "The good seed are the children of the kingdom; but the tares are the children of the wicked one" (Matt. 13:38).

Men may become children of Jesus Christ by being born anew—born of God, as the inspired word states: "He that committeth sin is of the devil; for the devil sinneth from the beginning. For this purpose the Son of God was manifested, that he might destroy the works of the devil. Whosoever is born of God doth not commit sin; for his seed remaineth in him: and he cannot sin, because he is born of God. In this the children of God are manifest, and the children of the devil: whosoever doeth not righteousness is not of God, neither he that loveth not his brother" (1 John 3:8–10).

Those who have been born unto God through obedience to the Gospel may by valiant devotion to righteousness obtain exaltation and even reach the status of godhood. Of such we read: "Wherefore, as it is written, they are gods, even the sons of God" (D&C 76:58; compare 132:20, and contrast paragraph 17 in same section; see also paragraph 37). Yet, though they be gods they are still subject to Jesus Christ as their Father in this exalted relationship; and so we read in the paragraph following the above quotation: "and they are Christ's, and Christ is God's" (76:59).

By the new birth—that of water and the Spirit—mankind may

become children of Jesus Christ, being through the means by Him provided "begotten sons and daughters unto God" (D&C 76:24). This solemn truth is further emphasized in the words of the Lord Jesus Christ given through Joseph Smith in 1833: "And now, verily I say unto you, I was in the beginning with the Father, and am the firstborn; and all those who are begotten through me are partakers of the glory of the same, and are the church of the Firstborn" (D&C 93:21, 22). For such figurative use of the term "begotten" in application to those who are born unto God see Paul's explanation: "for in Christ Jesus I have begotten you through the gospel" (1 Cor. 4:15). An analogous instance of sonship attained by righteous service is found in the revelation relating to the order and functions of Priesthood, given in 1832: "For whoso is faithful unto the obtaining of these two priesthoods of which I have spoken, and the magnifying their calling, are sanctified by the Spirit unto the renewing of their bodies: they become the sons of Moses and of Aaron and the seed of Abraham, and the church and kingdom, and the elect of God" (D&C 84:33, 34).

If it be proper to speak of those who accept and abide in the Gospel as Christ's sons and daughters—and upon this matter the scriptures are explicit and cannot be gainsaid nor denied—it is consistently proper to speak of Jesus Christ as the Father of the righteous, they having become His children and He having been made their Father through the second birth—the baptismal regeneration.

4. Jesus Christ the "Father" By Divine Investiture of Authority

A fourth reason for applying the title "Father" to Jesus Christ is found in the fact that in all His dealings with the human family Jesus the Son has represented and yet represents Elohim His Father in power and authority. This is true of Christ in His preexistent, antemortal, or unembodied state, in the which He was known as Jehovah; also during His embodiment in the flesh; and during His labors as a disembodied spirit in the realm of the dead; and since that period in His resurrected state. To the Jews He said: "I and my Father are one" (John 10:30; see also 17:11, 22); yet He declared "My Father is greater than I" (John 14:28); and further, "I am come in my Father's name" (John 5:43; see also 10:25). The same truth was declared by Christ Himself to the Nephites (see 3 Nephi 20:35 and 28:10), and has been reaffirmed by revelation in the present dispensation (D&C

50:43). Thus the Father placed His name upon the Son; and Jesus Christ spoke and ministered in and through the Father's name; and so far as power, authority, and Godship are concerned His words and acts were and are those of the Father.

We read, by way of analogy, that God placed His name upon or in the Angel who was assigned to special ministry unto the people of Israel during the exodus. Of that Angel the Lord said: "Beware of him, and obey his voice, provoke him not; for he will not pardon your transgressions: for my name is in him" (Exodus. 23:21).

The ancient apostle, John, was visited by an angel who ministered and spoke in the name of Jesus Christ. As we read: "The Revelation of Jesus Christ, which God gave unto him, to shew unto his servants things which must shortly come to pass; and he sent and signified it by his angel unto his servant John" (Revelation 1:1). John was about to worship the angelic being who spoke in the name of the Lord Jesus Christ, but was forbidden: "And I John saw these things, and heard them. And when I had heard and seen, I fell down to worship before the feet of the angel which showed me these things. Then saith he unto me, See thou do it not: for I am thy fellowservant, and of thy brethren the prophets, and of them which keep sayings of this book: worship God" (Revelation 22:8, 9). And then the angel continued to speak as though he were the Lord Himself: "And, behold, I come quickly; and my reward is with me, to give every man according as his work shall be. I am Alpha and Omega, the beginning and the end, the first and the last" (verses 12, 13). The resurrected Lord, Jesus Christ, who had been exalted to the right hand of God His Father, had placed His name upon the angel sent to John, and the angel spoke in the first person, saying "I come quickly," "I am Alpha and Omega," though he meant that Jesus Christ would come, and that Jesus Christ was Alpha and Omega.

None of these considerations, however, can change in the least degree the solemn fact of the literal relationship of Father and Son between Elohim and Jesus Christ. Among the spirit children of Elohim the firstborn was and is Jehovah or Jesus Christ to whom all others are juniors. Following are affirmative scriptures bearing upon this great truth. Paul, writing to the Colossians, says of Jesus Christ: "Who is the image of the invisible God, the firstborn of every creature: for by him were all things created, that are in heaven, and that are in earth, visible and invisible, whether they be thrones, or dominions, or principalities, or powers; all things were created by him, and for him: and he is before all things, and by him all things consist. And he is the head of the body, the church: who is the beginning, the firstborn from the dead; that in all things he might have the preeminence. For it pleased the Father that in him should all fullness dwell" (Colossians 1:15–19). From this scripture we learn that Jesus Christ was "the firstborn of every creature" and it is evident that the seniority here expressed must be with respect to antemortal existence, for Christ was not the senior of all mortals in the flesh. He is further designated as "the firstborn from the dead" this having reference to Him as the first to be resurrected from the dead, or as elsewhere written "the firstfruits of them that slept" (1 Corinthians 15:20, see also verse 23); and "the first begotten of the dead" (Revelation 1:5; compare Acts 26:23). The writer of the Epistle to the Hebrews affirms the status of Jesus Christ as the firstborn of the spirit children of His Father, and extols the preeminence of the Christ when tabernacled in flesh: "And again, when he bringeth in the firstbegotten into the world, he saith, And let all the angels of God worship him" (Hebrews 1:6; read the preceding verses). That the spirits who were juniors to Christ were predestined to be born in the image of their Elder Brother is thus attested by Paul: "And we know that all things work together for good to them that love God, to them who are the called according to his purpose. For whom he did foreknow, he also did predestinate to be conformed to the image of his Son, that he might be the firstborn among many brethren" (Romans 8:28, 29). John the Revelator was commanded to write to the head of the Laodicean church, as the words of the Lord Jesus Christ: "These things saith the Amen, the faithful and true witness, the beginning of the creation of God" (Revelation 3:14). In the course of a revelation given through Joseph Smith in May, 1833, the Lord Jesus Christ said as before cited: "And now, verily I say unto you, I was in the beginning with the Father, and am the Firstborn" (D&C 93:21). A later verse makes plain the fact that human beings generally were similarly existent in spirit state prior to their embodiment in the flesh: "Ye were also in the beginning with the Father; that which is Spirit, even the Spirit of truth" (verse 23).

There is no impropriety, therefore, in speaking of Jesus Christ as the Elder Brother of the rest of human kind. That He is by spiritual birth Brother to the rest of us is indicated in Hebrews: "Wherefore in all things it behoved him to be made like unto his brethren, that he might be a merciful and faithful high priest in things pertaining to God, to make reconciliation for the sins of the people" (Hebrews 2:17). Let it not be forgotten, however, that He is essentially greater than any and all others, by reason (1) of His seniority as the oldest or firstborn; (2) of His unique status in the flesh as the offspring of a mortal mother and of an immortal, or resurrected and glorified, Father; (3) of His selection and foreordination as the one and only Redeemer and Savior of the race; and (4) of His transcendent sinlessness.

Jesus Christ is not the Father of the spirits who have taken or yet shall take bodies upon this earth, for He is one of them. He is The Son, as they are sons and daughters of Elohim. So far as the stages of eternal progression and attainment have been made known through divine revelation, we are to understand that only resurrected and glorified beings can become parents of spirit offspring. Only such exalted souls have reached maturity in the appointed course of eternal life; and the spirits born to them in the eternal worlds will pass in due sequence through the several stages or estates by which the glorified parents have attained exaltation.

The First Presidency and the Council
of the Twelve Apostles of The Church
of Jesus Christ of Latter-day Saints
(June 1916)

INDEX